Economics
of the Firm

Sixth Edition

Economics
of the Firm
THEORY
AND PRACTICE

Arthur A. Thompson, Jr.
John P. Formby
The University of Alabama

Prentice Hall, Englewood Cliffs, New Jersey 07632

Library of Congress Cataloging-in-Publication Data

Thompson, Arthur A.
    Economics of the firm : theory and practice / Arthur A. Thompson, Jr., John P. Formby. — 6th ed.
      p. cm.
    Includes index.
    ISBN 0-13-092867-4
    1. Microeconomics. 2. Managerial economics. I. Formby, John P. II. Title.
  II. Title.
    HB172.T58   1993
    338.5—dc20   92-33351
                                                                          CIP

Editorial/production supervision: Kristin E. Dackow
Design supervisor: Pat Wosczyk
Interior design: Christine Ghering Wolf
Cover design: Jayne Conte
Cover art: WestLight/B-50 © Orion Press*III
Prepress buyer: Trudy Pisciotti
Manufacturing buyer: Patrice Fraccio

Printed in the United States of America
10 9 8 7 6 5 4 3 2 1

ISBN 0-13-092867-4

Prentice-Hall International (UK) Limited, *London*
Prentice-Hall of Australia Pty. Limited, *Sydney*
Prentice-Hall Canada Inc., *Toronto*
Prentice-Hall Hispanoamericana, S.A., *Mexico*
Prentice-Hall of India Private Limited, *New Delhi*
Prentice-Hall of Japan, Inc., *Tokyo*
Prentice-Hall of Southeast Asia Pte. Ltd., *Singapore*
Editora Prentice-Hall do Brasil, Ltda., *Rio de Janeiro*

Contents

Chapter 5 ————————————————

Demand Functions, Revenue Functions, and Elasticity 97

Preface

This sixth edition continues to stress solid coverage of microeconomic theory, complemented with an array of pragmatic applications and full-blown treatment of how a competitive enterprise economy functions. The standout features of the sixth edition are the addition of new theoretical treatments and the strong attention given to the drivers of industry structure and market change, the five-forces model of competition, generic competitive strategies, competitive advantage, and the special character of global markets and global competition.

HOW THE BOOK APPROACHES MICROECONOMICS

Because of the strong focus on the economics of firms, markets, and competitive behavior, this book is eminently suitable for courses where the audience consists mainly of MBA students and undergraduate business majors. Our objective has been to cover what every business student needs to know about microeconomic theory and competitive market economics. While the strong microtheory content makes the book quite suitable for courses populated with economic majors, we have deliberately chosen to stress concepts and applications especially pertinent to analyzing the behavior of firms and competitive markets and to give less attention to topics which either have a "purist" flavor or else relate more directly to non-market sectors of the economy.

The primary unit of analysis is the business firm. Readers are exposed again and again to how the conclusions of microeconomic analysis guide firms into one course of action rather than another. The economics of the firm is looked at from the inside as concerns production, cost, profitability, and competitive strategy considerations, and it is examined from the outside as concerns the influences of consumer demand, competition, market structure, and resource supply.

The result is a microtext (1) that is strong on theory and analysis, (2) that takes as its focal point the economics of the firm in a competitive market environment, and (3) that uses examples and applications to bridge the gap between theory and practice. In the overall scheme of approaches to microeconomics the aim has been to stake out a position roughly mid-way between "pure theory" texts and "managerial economics" texts and, further, to differentiate the content based on thorough coverage of competitive forces, competitive strategy, competitive advantage, and techniques for analyzing globally competitive markets.

TRADITIONAL TOPICS WITH A MENU OF EXTRAS

All major aspects of microeconomic theory are explored. The standard models of utility theory, indifference analysis, basic supply and demand, elasticity, production and cost functions, monopoly and perfect competition, resource pricing, and general equilibrium are given full exposure. But there are differentiating extras which can be covered or not as the instructor sees fit:

- A birdseye look at the methods of economic analysis (including "scientific testing," deductive logic, argument by example, diagrammatic models, and the use of mathematical proofs), what a theory is, the role of assumptions and abstraction, and the relevance of theory to explaining real-world economic phenomena (Chapter 1).
- A refresher chapter on supply, demand, and the functioning of markets (Chapter 2).
- Coverage of the product attribute model of consumer demand (Chapter 4).
- Expanded treatment of learning and experience curve effects in achieving higher levels of efficiency and cost savings (Chapter 6).
- A survey of profit concepts, profit theories, the debate over profit maximization, and nonprofit goals of firms (Chapter 9).
- Full exposure to the many models of oligopolistic competition (Chapter 13).
- A survey of multiple-goal models of business behavior (Chapter 14).
- A chapter on the five competitive forces, built around Michael Porter's now classic model for diagnosing how competition works in a given industry (Chapter 15).
- A chapter on ways to create and defend competitive advantage (Chapter 16).
- Sections dealing with a firm's cost competitiveness vis-a-vis rivals, multiproduct pricing, price signaling through the media, the social costs of monopoly power, taxing excess profits, the competitive effects of advertising and product differentiation, first-mover advantages, switching costs, driving forces, the mapping of competitive groups, the wage-employment effects of unions, the impact of minimum wage legislation, and the economics of productivity changes.

What's New in the Sixth Edition. In preparing this edition, we revisited the issue of what theoretical topics to include and elected to expand coverage in a number of places. The most noteworthy additions and changes include:

- A discussion of Nobel Laureate Ronald Coase's ideas on the nature and role of transactions costs (Chapter 2).
- Explicit consideration of the concept of consumer surplus, the gains from trade and exchange, and the techniques that firms use in extracting the surplus from buyers.
- A new section on real-world demand curves and empirical estimates of demand elasticity, plus a new Mathematical Capsule on constant elasticity demand curves (Chapter 5).
- A much revised discussion of the multiple goals of the firm that treats

the array of principal-agent problems arising in manager-controlled firms (Chapter 9).

- A substantial revision of the oligopoly chapter that features cooperative versus non-cooperative behavior, the cartel model, the stability of collusive behavior, and new game theory material involving situations where oligopolistic firms repeatedly confront the same game situation (Chapter 13).
- More explicit treatment has been given to the conditions for general equilibrium of the firm (Chapter 18).
- Seven new Applications Capsules have been added; they relate to such things as airline pricing and consumers' surplus, monopoly in the market for government bonds, the OPEC cartel, oligopoly warfare in snack foods, collusion and profits in major league baseball, and union activity and economic rents in professional football.

The most visible addition to the chapters is the use of "margin notes" highlighting basic principles, major conclusions, and core truths about microeconomics. Most of the notes endeavor to distill the discussion into concise principles and "facts" that every student should learn from a study of microeconomic analysis. Our pedagogical purposes in developing the margin notes were to bring each topical discussion into sharper focus for readers, point them directly to what is important, and better help them grasp key microtheory concepts and principles.

We have also revised the order of the chapters dealing with imperfect competition so that the chapter on perfect competition is followed immediately by the chapter on its analytic opposite, monopoly. However, as before, the chapters on market models are sufficiently self-contained that instructors can cover them in whatever sequence is preferred.

Other Pedagogical Features. The use of boxed off "application capsules" to highlight actual applications of microtheory continues as one of the text's highlights. As before, these aim at keeping the integration of theory and practice always before the student without disjointing the theoretical discussion. In addition to the applications capsules, empirical findings and brief examples are scattered throughout each chapter. The pedagogical thesis is that unless microeconomic analysis is directed at explaining, predicting, and otherwise illuminating the economic behavior of consumers, firms, and markets, its value doesn't go much beyond an exercise in mental gymnastics and intellectual curiosity.

As has now become customary and proper, the theoretical concepts are presented in a modestly mathematical vein in belief that most students, given that they are required to take introductory calculus, are well-equipped to handle nothing more mathematically complex than first derivatives. All mathematical concepts requiring more than basic algebra are explained fully and in terms which can be grasped by the mathematically unsophisticated. The more advanced mathematical treatments of microeconomics have been placed in self-contained "capsules" at appropriate places in the book and can be omitted without a loss of continuity.

Like any new edition, this one too has undergone all the usual rewriting and updating. We've aimed at giving this sixth edition an even better balance between "bare bones" coverage versus in-depth analysis, theory versus application, classical versus contemporary models, mathematical versus verbal/graphical exposition, and conceptual simplicity versus the need to instill students with some technical proficiency and analytical skill. The intended result is (1) a book which suits the "need-to-know" requirements of business school undergraduates, first-year MBA students, and economics majors and (2) a book which is a coherent and teachable synthesis of the best of all that is old and new in microeconomics. Whether we have succeeded is quite fittingly, for "the market" to decide. Your comments regarding coverage and emphasis will be most welcome, as will your calling our attention to specific errors.

THE COMPETITION GAME OPTION

Version one of *The Competition Game* was well received and provoked renewed interest in PC-based simulations. The second version, a companion supplement to this edition, makes the use of a simulation exercise in a microeconomics course even more appealing. In playing *The Competition Game*, students are organized into teams/companies to form an industry; each company produces and sells a product in worldwide competition with other companies in the industry.

The Value a Simulations Adds. First and foremost, the exercise of running a simulated company over a number of decision periods helps develop students' understanding of competitive dynamics, how markets work, and how to apply microeconomic principles in decision-making situations. In playing the simulation students have to react to changing marketing conditions, study the actions of competitors, and weigh alternative courses of action. They get valuable practice in spotting market opportunities, evaluating competitive threats to their company's well-being, and assessing the long-term consequences of short-term decisions. They see a host of microeconomics concepts come alive. Since a simulation game is, by its very nature, a hands-on exercise, the lessons learned are forcefully planted in students' minds: the impact is far more lasting than what is remembered from lectures. Moreover, students' entrepreneurial instincts blossom as they get caught up in the competitive spirit of the game. The resulting entertainment value helps maintain an unusually high level of student motivation and emotional involvement in the course throughout the term.

We think you will find *The Competition Game* a welcome course option. It will add a dimension to your course that can't be matched by any other teaching-learning tool. Moreover, with the aid of today's high-speed personal computers and the technical advances in software capability, there's minimal gear-up time on the instructor's part. You'll find that the time and effort required to administer *The Competition Game* is well within tolerable limits.

About the Simulation. The product for *The Competition Game* is compact disk players. The industry setting is global; companies can manufacture and sell their brands in the United States, Europe, or Asia. Competition is head-to-head; each team of students must match competitive wits against the other company teams. Companies can focus their efforts on one geographic market or two or all three; they can establish a one-country production base or they can manufacture in all three of the geographic markets. Demand conditions, tariffs, and wage rates vary from area to area.

The company that students run has plants to operate, a work force to employ and compensate, shipping expenses and inventories to control and capital expenditure decisions to make; they have to wrestle with price elasticity considerations economies of scale, substitution of capital for labor, technological change, tariff barriers, marginal and average cost analysis, changing demand-supply conditions, price and nonprice competition, and profit maximization. Students must evaluate whether to pursue a low-cost producer strategy, a differentiation strategy, or a focus strategy. They have to decide whether to produce ''off-shore'' in Asia where wage rates are very low or whether to avoid import tariffs and transocean shipping costs by having a producing base in every primary geographic market.

The Competition Game can be used with any IBM or compatible PC with 640K memory and it is suitable for both intermediate and MBA courses in microeconomics. The game is programmed to accommodate a wide variety of computer setups as concerns disk drives, monitors, and printers.

ACKNOWLEDGEMENTS

Our intellectual debt to both the classical and contemporary economists whose fertile contributions have been weaved into the presentation will be obvious to any reader familiar with the literature of microeconomics; we have been particularly influenced by the works of F. M. Sherer, Michael E. Porter, Oliver Williamson, and Ronald Coase. All of the scholarly sources and materials which we have drawn upon are cited in the footnotes and bibliographical references. We genuinely hope that no violence has been done to anyone's ideas in our effort to synthesize them into the body of microeconomic analysis.

Both this edition and previous editions have benefited greatly from the comments of students, reviewers, and adopters. Special thanks are due to the reviewers of all six editions: Keith Lumsden, Robert Clower, Howard Dye, Lloyd Valentine, Richard Hoffman, Frank Falero, Dwight Anderson, Ralph Gray, Thomas C. Anderson, Jay G. Chambers, Larry G. Beall, Melvin C. Fredlund, Wesley Magat, Donald J. Roberts, Ernest Koenigsbert, Stephen L. Shapiro, Stephen Buckles, John Stevens, William A. Hayes, Sharon G. Levin, Walter Ricke, and John Huttman.

Naturally, however, we alone are responsible for whatever blunders or inadequacies you find—we will be grateful if you will call them to our attention at P.O. Box 870225, Tuscaloosa, Alabama, 35487-0225.

Arthur A. Thompson, Jr.
John P. Formby

Note to the Student

Courses in intermediate microeconomics typically have the reputation of being among the most challenging in any college curriculum. The reputation is well deserved—this might as well be admitted at the outset. But despite the analytical rigor, the road ahead is well worth exploring, and we have tried to clear the way of unnecessary obstacles. Pains have been taken to make the text readable and interesting, to provide step-by-step explanations of each concept, to keep the graphs uncluttered and the mathematics simplified. Examples and applications are consistently indicated in enough detail to make them meaningful. Chapter-end problems and questions have been included as a self-test of your command of the material and to increase your mechanical proficiency with important concepts.

Because students begin the course with widely-varying backgrounds and degrees of preparation, the treatment of each new topic is begun at the lowest level of analysis. No prior knowledge of economics is assumed. Thus, while this course is probably not your first exposure to economics, those of you who remember little from previous courses or who feel poorly prepared in economics will find yourselves at no serious disadvantage.

Assuming no prior knowledge and providing complete explanations has made some chapters a bit long. But longer may still be quicker and easier. The intended effect is a more comprehensible presentation that will help you to grasp the more difficult material in less time and convince you of the value and power of economic analysis. A textbook is, after all, primarily for the student, not the professor and, in the final analysis, you the student are an excellent judge of how well the book performs its job of helping you understand the subject matter. We will be pleased to receive your praises and/or criticisms at P.O. Box 870225, Tuscaloosa, Alabama 35487-0225.

Economics
of the Firm

Chapter 1

Introduction to Microeconomic Analysis

The central task of economic analysis is to figure out what makes the world economy and its many subparts work the way they do. The more that is known about economic relationships and economic behavior, the more able are societies to direct their energies toward producing a stream of goods and services that yield the greatest consumer and societal fulfillment.

But the analytical challenge in economics is both big and complicated. Consider that in countries across the world people are making billions of decisions about how to spend their money for the many different things they need and want. Everywhere enterprises of all sizes and types are deciding and redeciding how much of what goods and services to supply and what technologies and resources to use to supply them. All kinds of government agencies and not-for-profit organizations are collecting taxes and soliciting donations to supply goods and services to the public and to special groups like the underprivileged, the aged, and the unemployed.

Moreover, an untold fraction of these billions of economic decisions are arrived at more or less independently using different values, preferences, and priorities. One person buys a microwave oven, another opts for a compact disc player, and a third invests in 100 shares of IBM. Each business firm acts in light of its own situation and industry conditions to carve out a particular market position and to try to boost its sales and profits. Each governmental entity and nonprofit organization is driven to pursue economic policies that satisfy its constituents. In short, each economic unit behaves on the basis of its own perceptions and employs its own specific criteria about economic actions to take or not take. No reference is made to any grand economic plan for guidance, nor does any such plan even exist. The outcome is an incredibly diverse and tangled web of demand supply interactions and economic patterns. The task of economic analysis is to try to make sense out of all these decisions and resulting conditions.

What Is Microeconomics?

There are two essentially different levels at which economic analysis is conducted. *Microeconomics* concerns the behavior and activities of specific economic units—individuals, households, firms, industries, and resource owners. Microeconomic analysis seeks to explain and predict such things as the

1

Microeconomics concerns the study of individual economic units—the behavior of buyers, sellers, product markets, and resource markets.

Macroeconomics concerns the study of how whole economies function—what causes the overall level of economic activity in a nation or the world to expand or contract.

prices and outputs of particular firms and industries, the choices of consumers in buying goods and services, the drivers of technological change, production efficiency and costs, competitive behavior, and the adjustment of markets to new conditions. The focus is on the trees, not the forest.

In *macroeconomics*, the spotlight is on the national and international economic picture, along with the major economic sectors that influence the direction of economywide change. Macroeconomic analysis views all consumers as a unit (the consumer sector), all business as an aggregate unit (the business sector), and all the various public sector agencies as a unit (the governmental sector) in an effort to explain and predict the structure and functioning of whole economies. Macroeconomic analysis is a big-picture exercise, with the central concerns being the overall level of economic activity, total employment, national income, total consumer spending, aggregate levels of saving and investment, interest rates, money-supply measures, the general level of prices, international trade balances, taxes, and governmental spending.

This text deals with microeconomics, especially with "the theory of the firm" and how a market functions. Our study of small, or microeconomic, units (consumers, firms, markets, and resource owners) is not limited to "small" economic issues, however. Many "big" issues come into clearer view when one understands the underlying microeconomic actions and relationships. The vast majority of economic decisions are made by individuals acting in the capacity of consumers of goods and services, suppliers of labor or other resources, savers of money, or managers of organizations. We shall delve into the factors that shape these microeconomic decisions and look at how they merge into the workings of a competitive, market-driven economy. Some of the questions we will examine include: What determines whether demand for a firm's product will be strong or weak? How much will demand for a product change if consumers' incomes increase or if selling price is lowered? How can a firm tell if its production methods are efficient or inefficient? What factors cause a firm's production costs to go down if it operates on a larger scale and produces more units? Why are competitive forces more intense in some markets than others? How do rival firms compete? Why is profit important in a competitive enterprise economy? What determines the prices firms charge for their products? How are wage rates determined? Do unions cause wages to be higher than they otherwise would be? How does a firm decide how much of a resource input to use? These questions not only convey a sampling of what microeconomics is about but they also suggest its relevance to everyday real-world economic events.

At center stage in the study of microeconomics is how markets function.

THE METHODS OF ECONOMIC ANALYSIS

The economist's approach to making sense out of the mass of everyday economic behavior involves (a) discovering good reasons for why economic events happen as they do, (b) carefully weighing more-or-less sound economic facts to arrive at more-or-less plausible cause-effect economic relationships, (c) developing formal *economic theories*, and (d) building empirically based *economic models*. Economists place great stock in taking a "scientific" approach to economic analysis, believing that theoretically grounded analytic models, often undergirded by mathematical-statistical testing, are essential to understanding economic relationships and to predicting the outcomes of alternative economic policies. As a prelude to beginning our study of microeconomics, let's take a brief look at where theories come from, what theoretical models are, and how economists tackle the task of explaining economic events and predicting economic behavior.

THE "SCIENTIFIC METHOD" APPROACH TO DEVELOPING ECONOMIC THEORIES AND CONSTRUCTING MODELS OF ECONOMIC BEHAVIOR

Although there is no one always-used method of economic analysis, economists (in the tradition of natural scientists) rely on the "scientific research method" in formulating economic theories and building economic models. This method consists of five steps:

1. Defining the scope of the problem and the exact phenomena to be investigated.
2. Formulating a hypothesis about the relationships among the relevant variables.
3. Deducing testable conclusions and/or predictions from the hypothesis.
4. Testing the appropriateness of the conclusions and/or the accuracy of the predictions using real-world data and events.
5. Accepting or revising the theory or model based on the testing outcomes.

Many of the techniques of microeconomic analysis draw upon the scientific method.

Defining the Problem. Defining the problem involves isolating the exact economic phenomena of interest to the analyst and framing the specific questions to be explored. Usually, research inquiry is directed toward the whys and hows underlying the behavior of economic phenomena, the process of economic adjustment to new conditions, and the impacts which these adjustments may produce. Economic analysts may also be concerned with how specific cause-effect relationships tie in with the broader body of economic knowledge.

Formulating the Hypothesis. Hypothesis formulation consists of a search for regularity and order in the economic phenomena under investigation. This, of course, presumes that some sort of economic order in fact exists and that cause-effect economic relationships remain unaltered over time. Such a presumption rests upon the notion of a universal order, with the analyst's job being to discover economic relationships, identify patterns of economic behavior, and shed new light on whatever order exists.

BASIC CONCEPT
A hypothesis is a *tentative* explanation of behavior and cause-effect relationships.

Consequently, once the research questions have been tightly framed, the task of the economic analyst is to sort out which economic variables are important and which are not, to probe how the key variables are related, and to form preliminary judgments about probable cause-effect relationships. In the course of this search, many economic happenings and factual details are—and should be—ignored because they are incidental to the problem at hand. But even after the relevant has been sifted from the irrelevant, economic relationships can still be too complex to explore at once. Then abstraction and generalization are relied upon to bring the inquiry down to manageable proportions.

Abstraction involves distilling and restricting the variables and information considered, endeavoring to condense an otherwise cumbersome number of factors and details into a reduced set that can be handled and fully probed. Abstraction usually entails making some simplifying ***assumptions*** that

Economic studies typically utilize assumptions to simplify and to highlight the essential features of the events and behavior under study.

highlight the essential features of the economic events being analyzed or that define basic behavioral traits about the economic units being investigated. Thus, many economic models of business behavior are based upon the assumption that firms behave as if they seek to maximize profits, the rationale being that of all the factors which motivate business decisions, profit maximization is likely to be the overriding, or governing, consideration. And, frequently, in exploring the relationships among two or three economic variables, it is customary to assume that *all other relevant factors remain constant* so that any influence these other factors may have will not contaminate the study of the variables and relationships of primary concern.

Assumptions need not be in *exact* accord with reality; it is enough that they be *reasonable* representations of real-world conditions. One of the arts of abstraction is to employ assumptions that are (1) easy to handle, (2) sufficiently realistic, and (3) not so restrictive as to impair the scope and value of the research. If the assumptions are too detailed and too numerous, the analysis becomes unmanageable and/or overly narrow. On the other hand, if the assumptions are far removed from reality, the resulting analysis can fail miserably in explaining real-life behavior.

An example of what constitutes a reasonable abstraction is the study of consumer behavior. Here it is customary for economists to assume that consumers behave as if they seek to maximize the satisfaction obtainable from their incomes. In fact, this assumption may not be literally true of all consumers in each and every situation. Nevertheless, if over a reasonably interesting range of circumstances most consumers do behave as if they attempt to maximize satisfaction, then the assumption that consumers seek to maximize the satisfaction obtainable from their incomes is a justifiable and reasonable simplification. To restate the link between assumptions and reality in another way, even though the assumptions of a model may not be literally exact and complete descriptions of real-world behavior, as long as they are sufficiently realistic to allow for valid explanations and predictions about the phenomena being investigated, no harm is done to reality.

After the necessary simplifying assumptions have been made comes the task of formulating hypotheses. A **hypothesis** consists of a *tentative* identification of key variables and a *tentative* specification of how these variables may be related in terms of cause-effect or interaction. Hypotheses may be suggested to the analyst by the existing body of knowledge, by experience and familiarity with the problem, by clues uncovered in preliminary investigation, or even by intuition and hunch. The hypothesized relationships are often summarized in graphical or mathematical form to facilitate further analysis and determination of how changes in some variables will affect others. Deductive reasoning and logical argument are used as well. However, research standards require that a hypothesis be subject to empirical verification or disproof. Without testing, there is no way of judging whether the hypothesis really advances the understanding of real-world behavior or is helpful in predicting future events and guiding the formulation of economic policy.

The Deduction of Predictions.   Hypotheses do more than suggest explanations for behavior and cause-effect relationships. If properly formulated, they serve as the basis for deriving predictions about future economic impacts and changes. These predictions (forecasts) or conclusions stem mainly from logical deductive reasoning. To take a concrete example, we might hypothesize that the quantity purchased of an item tends to increase as the level

The validity of a hypothesis is judged by testing the accuracy of predictions based on the hypothesized behavior and cause-effect relationships.

of advertising expenditures on that item is increased, other factors remaining constant. To test whether a cause-effect relationship actually exists between advertising and sales volume, we might logically predict that if IBM increases promotional expenditures for its personal computers, then the sales of IBM personal computers should rise. An even stronger prediction based on the same hypothesis would entail investigating the extent to which higher levels of advertising are associated with higher levels of unit sales for a broad sample of firms and products. The ability to evaluate predictive accuracy is generally believed to be an essential feature of all "soundly constructed" hypotheses and analytical procedures. The conventional wisdom is that unless hypotheses yield predictions or conclusions which are capable of being rigorously tested with empirical data, there is no appropriate way to judge their validity.

Testing the Accuracy of the Predictions.   Once a hypothesis has been set forth and predictions have been made, a multistage process of testing begins. First, facts and data must be collected for evaluating the accuracy of the predictions derived from the hypothesized relationships. Likely sources include published statistics from either governmental or private institutions, the results of previous research studies, or entirely new information generated from questionnaire surveys, interviews, or original source documents. For example, if the problem concerns identifying and measuring the influence of factors which shape the demand for frozen orange juice concentrate, then we might need statistics on the recorded quantities of frozen orange juice concentrate purchased, the prices at which these quantities were sold, the prices of other substitute beverages, consumer income levels, advertising expenditures, and population. Information about the number of concentrate producers and competitive market conditions might also be useful.

After the necessary data have been organized, graphical or quantitative relationships among the variables must be specified. Where graphs are insufficient, more complex mathematical expressions have to be employed and equations must be constructed. Since most economic variables involve numbers (such factors as prices, costs, wage rates, revenues, profits, incomes, and production rates are all numerical), using graphs and equations is the rule rather than the exception. Even when quantitative methodology is not absolutely necessary, economists use it to make the tests of their hypotheses more precise. Once the quantitative and nonquantitative relationships are specified in testable form, the predictive accuracy of the hypothesis is evaluated against freshly emerging data and real-world events.

Evaluating Test Results.   If the predictions flowing from a hypothesis are confirmed by real-world events, then the hypothesis is *accepted*. However, it is not correct to state that the hypothesis has been *proved*; one can only say that events have failed to *disprove* it. According to one eminent authority, hypotheses can never be proved; they can only be tested by seeing whether predictions made from them are in accord with experimental and observational facts.[1] A favorable finding on the accuracy of predictions derived from a hypothesis does not confirm the truth of the hypothesis because there is room for circumstantial evidence to produce correct predictions from a false or flawed hypothesis.

> **Accurate predictions do not *prove* the validity of a hypothesis; they simply fail to disprove it.**

[1] W. I. B. Beveridge, *The Art of Scientific Investigation* (New York: Random House, The Modern Library, 1957), p. 118.

For instance, the truth of the hypothesis that a corporation's profits arise from putting more experienced managers in charge is not established by correctly predicting a rise in XYZ Corporation's profits within a year after a new, more experienced management team takes over the running of XYZ's operations. Other factors not related to experienced management are perfectly capable of generating higher profits. Strictly speaking, then, *a hypothesis is never proved and remains on probation indefinitely*. But the more it survives attempts at disproof, the more it becomes accepted *theory*, especially when it is compatible with the related body of knowledge.[2] After a hypothesis successfully survives a number of tests, it is accorded status as a theory and becomes part of the knowledge of the discipline until evidence appears that shows it no longer yields an acceptable degree of accuracy in its predictions.

If the observed facts contradict the predictions, the hypothesis is *disproved* or *rejected*. Attempts can then be made to revise the hypothesis in accordance with the new evidence.[3] The modified hypothesis is retested and again modified if the test results are unsatisfactory. Theorizing continues until the investigator is satisfied that the hypothesized cause-effect relationships are believable and accurate.

Figure 1-1 summarizes the scientific approach to economic research, indicating the close interaction between the real world and the theoretical world. Note that the process of economic investigation begins by observing the real world and finishes by observing the real world. This is as it should be since the major purpose of economic research is to improve the ability to understand, explain, and predict real-world economic phenomena.

Must Economic Analysis Always Be "Scientific"?

Thoughtful reflection suggests that the "scientific" approach to economic analysis is grounded in several key beliefs:[4]

The study of economics cannot depend entirely on the scientific method because it is not possible to subject economic hypotheses to repeated testing under "laboratory" conditions where all the variables of economic behavior are carefully controlled.

1. All sure knowledge is achieved via a scientific approach where the dominant theme is that we know only what we cannot doubt.
2. Prediction is the core objective of rigorous research—the ability to predict is all that really counts.
3. The really decisive test of a hypothesis about the hows and whys of economic behavior is its ability to predict.
4. Predictive power is measured by constructing objective, reproducible experiments; if the experimental implications of a hypothesis prove false, the hypothesis is proved false.
5. Reasoned argument, deductive logic, and subjective observation may well figure in the discovery of a hypothesis but they cannot figure in its confirmation—only objective, controlled, and repetitive testing can produce scientific and trustworthy knowledge.

---

[2] *Ibid.*

[3] Academic lore has it that Max Weber once was interrupted during a lecture by a student protesting, "The facts are not in accord with your theory." Weber replied, "So much the worse for the facts," and continued his presentation.

[4] Donald N. McCloskey, "The Rhetoric of Economics," *Journal of Economic Literature*, Vol. 21, No. 2 (June 1983), pp. 484–85. The remainder of this section and much of the next section is based on and inspired by this article.

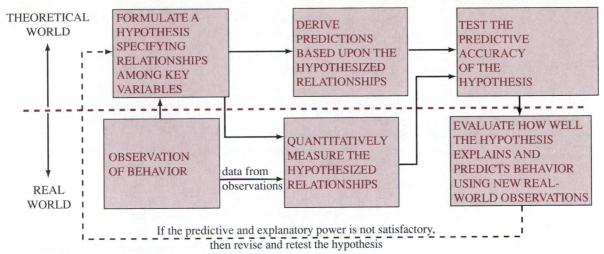

THEORETICAL WORLD

REAL WORLD

FORMULATE A HYPOTHESIS SPECIFYING RELATIONSHIPS AMONG KEY VARIABLES

DERIVE PREDICTIONS BASED UPON THE HYPOTHESIZED RELATIONSHIPS

TEST THE PREDICTIVE ACCURACY OF THE HYPOTHESIS

OBSERVATION OF BEHAVIOR

data from observations

QUANTITATIVELY MEASURE THE HYPOTHESIZED RELATIONSHIPS

EVALUATE HOW WELL THE HYPOTHESIS EXPLAINS AND PREDICTS BEHAVIOR USING NEW REAL-WORLD OBSERVATIONS

If the predictive and explanatory power is not satisfactory, then revise and retest the hypothesis

Figure 1-1
Relationship between theory and the real world

Although such beliefs have inherent appeal, they are not unshakable. In fact, a substantial, respectable, and growing number of philosophers (albeit still a minority) reject the scientific method as being the basis for *all* knowledge. And certainly it is true that the study of economics is not tied as rigorously to the strict scientific approach as many economists like to believe. The official rhetoric of economists is that their methodology is scientific and that there are strong predictive powers in what we know about economic relationships.

Yet, the predictive power of economics is open to doubt—as one noted economist put it, predicting the economic future is "beyond the power of any mortal."[5] The formal arguments for this condition are lengthy and complex, but three intuitively appealing observations illustrate why the predictive powers of economic knowledge are suspect in a rigorously scientific sense: If an economist (or anyone else) has sufficient command of economics to be able to predict the future economic outcomes with confidence, then why don't economics experts enjoy the unlimited wealth that such predictive abilities can surely bring? The second telling point is that books about economics include much information and analyses that are not products of the scientific method. And third, because virtually all economic behavior undergoes more or less constant change and economic conditions are seldom the same from one time period to the next, it is usually not feasible to subject many economic hypotheses to repeated experimental testing under conditions that closely approximate "controlled laboratory observation." Rather, the circumstances surrounding each observation of market conditions and consumer preferences tend to be "one of a kind" and the assumption that all other relevant things have remained constant between observations is seldom met in actual practice. Thus, while it is accurate to say that much economic research draws upon the approach of the scientific method and while the field of economics has some aspects of a science, the study of economics is not a *science* in the way we came to understand that word in high school.[6]

---

[5] Ludwig von Mises, *Human Action* (New Haven, CT: Yale University Press, 1949), p. 867.
[6] McCloskey, "The Rhetoric of Economics," p. 491.

How Economists Explain—Some Alternatives to the Scientific Method

Just because the scientific objectivity of economic research may be a bit overstated, it does not follow that the barbarians are at the gates and that little confidence can be placed in what we think we know about economic behavior. There are sound methodological options to discovering economic principles besides total dependence on the scientific method. People are persuaded of things in more than one way, and certainly most people do not choose to believe something or not depending on whether it comes from supposedly scientific research. This trait is just as characteristic of our beliefs about economics as about our beliefs of anything else.

So what are the methodological options to the scientific method? One is the use of logical argument and deductive reasoning. Economic debate often takes the form of common-sense reasoning, buttressed by examples and points of ''fact.'' Economists, like other dealers in ideas, are active practitioners of the art of mutual persuasion; they spend much of their time probing for good reasons, discovering evidence to support their conclusions, citing bits of empirical data and examples drawn from observable experience, and weighing what evidence can be marshalled in support of their interpretations of what happened and why. They do these things at least as regularly as they engage in repeated testing of already established propositions to see if they can be shown to be false by newly available sets of empirical data. Indeed, many (most?) of the really significant propositions of economics sprung from powerful argument and gained credibility *before* they had been empirically tested repeatedly; comparatively few widely accepted economic propositions owe their standing to having come through rigorous application of the scientific method unscathed.[7]

The second methodological alternative to the scientific method is to construct simplified economic *models* to illustrate and isolate the links among selected economic variables. Economists have a strong affinity for using diagrams and simple mathematical expressions, laced with logical argument, to gain an understanding of how particular economic variables behave and why certain economic phenomena happen as they do. Using diagrammatic models and mathematical formulations of economic relationships constitutes an efficient, effective means of representing how specific segments of the economic puzzle fit together. The advantage of such models is that they reduce the analysis to manageable proportions (it is impossible to consider everything at once!). Simplified models of economic reality serve a pedagogical purpose and an explanatory purpose, as well as offering the potential of predictive power. Models are useful for pedagogical purposes because they permit complex, multifaceted events to be simplified to the point where the analyst can zero in on the links between two or three variables to expose how changes in one affect the others. To the extent that a model allows basic relationships to be under-

Much economic analysis is grounded in rigorous logical argument, deductive reasoning, and powerful examples drawn from observable experience.

---

[7] Why this is so is not hard to explain. If economists or other scientists waited for repeated testing of every proposition before they formed their beliefs, the outcome would be paralysis of research and understanding. In order for propositions about economics to be tested a few times, much less repeatedly, some economists must care enough about the propositions to bother with testing them. They care only when the propositions are believed by enough economic analysts to create a demand for testing. Often, therefore, quantitative studies rely heavily on hypotheses (or theories) that are widely enough accepted to warrant testing. But even this testing may turn out to be fairly limited in scope and frequency (as opposed to being extensive) because the pretesting arguments are so powerfully persuasive as to produce widespread belief with not much room left for doubt. See McCloskey, ''The Rhetoric of Economics,'' pp. 489–90.

stood and interactions among variables to be traced down, it serves to *explain* economic cause and effect and to reveal the reasons why changes in one area spill over to impact another. The "realism" of simple models can often be extended (1) by introducing other relevant variables into the picture and exploring their effects and/or (2) by posing a number of "what if" questions and analyzing how sensitive the results or conclusions of the model are to different magnitudes of change in one or more of the key variables. Both diagrammatic models and mathematically formulated economic models are popular among economists, chiefly because of their versatility and analytical agility.

THE METHODS OF ECONOMIC ANALYSIS—WHERE THINGS NOW STAND

The study of economic behavior, as currently practiced by economists, is a mixture of methodological approaches—the scientific method, rational argument, diagrammatic models, and mathematically formulated models containing anywhere from a few to many economic variables. Most economists endorse the scientific approach as the official methodology for the study of economics. Yet, economic debate and economic analysis often take the form of deductive logic, argument by example, diagrammatic models, and mathematical proofs of economic relationships. The methodological standard of economists often ends up being governed by pragmatic considerations: *Use any of several analytical approaches so long as it has demonstrable capacity to illuminate economic behavior.*

In this book, we shall rely on diagrammatic models and on logical, deductive argument as our primary analytical tools. Numerous examples will be cited as evidence of the capacity of these approaches to illuminate microeconomic relationships.

Contemporary economic analysis uses a mixture of methodological approaches.

WHAT IS A THEORY?

With the preceding as background, we are in position to indicate the precise meanings of the terms hypothesis, theory, principle, and model. It should be noted, however, that authorities are not in strict agreement on the "definitions" of these terms, so how these terms are used varies somewhat from discipline to discipline and writer to writer. Nonetheless, what follows enjoys a consensus among economists and delineates how the terms will be used in this text.

A *hypothesis* is a plausible but largely untested explanation of how phenomena are related. It attempts to pinpoint the key variables in a behavior pattern and to describe how they interact. A hypothesis may be formulated on the basis of informed speculation, ordinary common sense, logical reasoning, or observable example. Supporting evidence for a hypothesis is scanty or inconclusive. It may or may not be widely believed, but it is definitely "unproven" and thus does not stand as part of the formally accepted body of knowledge.

A *theory* is a widely accepted and presumably valid explanation of the behavior of real-world phenomena. For the most part, a theory gains its status from the process of formulating a hypothesis, logically deducing predictions from the hypothesis, and testing and retesting the accuracy of the predictions a sufficient number of times to produce a general confidence in its *predictive power*. However, a hypothesis can cross over the line to become a theory any

BASIC CONCEPT
An economic theory is an accepted, presumably valid, explanation of real-world economic behavior and cause-effect relationships.

A sound economic theory always has good predictive power and good explanatory power.

time the weight of evidence as to its accuracy is deemed preponderant enough to accord it a place in the formally accepted body of knowledge—there is no rigid standard as to the number of tests a hypothesis must survive to become a theory. Moreover, the widespread acceptance of a theory can occur as much because of a theory's perceived ***explanatory power*** as because of its oft-tested predictive power. The explanatory power of a theory arises from its ability to logically account for cause-effect relationships, its capacity to illuminate why the variables are related in the manner which argument suggests, and its compatibility with other generally accepted knowledge. The really significant difference between a hypothesis and a theory thus concerns the confidence that may be placed in it; *a hypothesis is tentative and untested, whereas a theory commands more credibility because of its better-supported predictive and explanatory powers.*

The twin features of explanatory power and predictive power are *equally* important builders of confidence in a theory. Predictive power is essential because it represents the only measure of cause-effect validity using real-world empirical evidence. But even though predictive power is necessary, it is not sufficient to establish theoretical validity. The capacity to make accurate predictions cannot be divorced from whether a theory is logical, believable, and otherwise consistent with what else is "known." More confidence resides in a theory that poses logical cause-effect relationships and that fits in with related theory and evidence. It simply is hard to place confidence in a theory which offers little plausible explanation or common-sense connection with what is being predicted. *Prediction without explanation is sterile.* Only when a theory has adequate explanatory powers does it generally gain widespread standing in the body of economic knowledge.

Economic principles or laws are based on economic theories with unusually strong predictive and explanatory powers.

When a theory has been subjected to scrupulous testing and when its explanatory power is deemed sufficiently profound and universal, it may be termed a ***principle*** or even a ***law***. Designating relationships as principles or laws implies a *very strong* degree of empirical regularity accompanied by a powerful cause-effect rationale. In terms of the predictive and explanatory confidence that can be placed in it, a theory ranks between a hypothesis and a principle.

Sound economic theories are neither impractical nor unrealistic because they have demonstrated predictive and explanatory powers.

Often one hears the complaint that theory is "unrealistic" and "impractical."[8] Such complaints can be valid only in the case of "bad" theory. "Good" theory cannot be unrealistic in an important sense because it both explains and predicts real-world behavior. Nor can good theory be "impractical"; on the contrary, it can serve as a pragmatic guide to what is happening and why, since it has a demonstrated ability to explain relationships and to predict behavior. When a theory truly has appropriate amounts of both explanatory power and predictive power, criticisms of impracticality and lack of realism contain little merit. If legitimate claims of impracticality and lack of realism are levied against a theory, then it must be reexamined in light of current evidence. If its predictive and explanatory powers relative to alternative hypotheses and theories are found lacking, then a theory loses its standing and joins the collection of other out-of-date "theories."

Some users of theory find the constant review of existing theory to be a nuisance. Of course, it would be nice if the need for reverification ceased. But

---

[8] According to one wag, an "ivory tower" economist who had just worked out a particularly esoteric theoretical model is said to have remarked, "And the beauty of this model, which will particularly endear it to the hearts of purists, is that under no conceivable circumstances can it be of any possible practical value."

in economics, it is especially necessary to review the existing body of theory on a regular basis. A moment's reflection is enough to convince one that a 1930s theory of business behavior could easily be lacking in its powers to explain and predict business behavior in the 1990s. Changing consumer needs, the fast-paced international dimensions of competition, and technological change have made the business environment today significantly different from what it was decades earlier. Shifting economic sands force economic theorists to keep a close check on the explanatory and predictive powers of the existing body of economic theory. After all, economic relationships do not stay the same forever; there is ample opportunity for old relationships to change and new ones to emerge.

The term *model* is much harder to describe in unambiguous fashion. In scientific and theoretical investigations there are conceptual models, mathematical models, simulation models, diagrammatic models, experimental models, and theoretical models. Although each of these has its own distinguishing features, there is also a common ground. A model attempts to mirror the essential features of a system in a way that is simple enough to understand and manipulate, yet close enough to reality to yield meaningful results. Usually, it is neither practical nor possible for a model to capture the character of a system in all its original complexity; abstraction must be used, and selecting the appropriate degree of abstraction can greatly enhance the model's value. If the level of abstraction is too low, so that the model has an overabundance of specific detail, the advantages of realism are offset by the unwieldiness of the model and a lack of generalized application. On the other hand, if the model is highly abstract, the advantages gained from its analytic properties may be more than counterbalanced by its dubious connection with the real world.

In the case of *theoretical models*, the goal is to develop a tool that presents simply and accurately the cause-effect relationships among a select group of variables—in which case the terms *theory* and *theoretical model* are, for many intents and purposes, synonymous. Both attempt to specify key variables and establish relationships among them. Both provide a skeletal framework in which the complexities of the real world can be understood with greater insight. Both involve predictions or forecasts about phenomena, and both are judged by their accuracy in predicting and explaining behavior. As long as the cause-effect relationships that a model is attempting to describe are of sufficient scope and importance, a theory and a model stand at the same rank. In the chapters that follow, we will describe a number of theoretical models constructed by economists to demonstrate microeconomic relationships.

THE REALISM OF ASSUMPTIONS

One methodological issue remains to be discussed—can a theory that contains "unrealistic assumptions" still be "valid"? Consider, for example, a theory that is based upon the assumption that business firms behave as if they seek to maximize profits. Suppose further that this theory is judged to predict rather well but that there is a serious question as to whether the firms involved actually are doing all they can to maximize profits. Is the theory then "invalid" because it is based upon an assumption that appears to be false? How does one determine whether the assumption of profit-maximizing behavior is, in fact, an accurate description of reality? Does it even make any difference whether the assumption of profit maximization is descriptively accurate as long as the pre-

One of the biggest debates in judging economic theories concerns whether a theory based on "unrealistic" assumptions can still be valid.

dictive power of the theory is judged to be satisfactory for the purpose at hand? Does a theory that predicts behavior also explain behavior? These are tough questions, and attempts to answer them have generated a heated debate among some prominent economists.[9]

One of the principals in this debate is Milton Friedman, who, in an essay titled "The Methodology of Positive Economics" maintained that whether the assumptions made in the course of formulating a hypothesis were either realistic or unrealistic may not really be significant. Friedman argued that the only relevant way to test a hypothesis is to compare its predictions with experience. He stated that there is no meaningful way to test the validity of a hypothesis by comparing its assumptions directly with reality. In support of his position, Friedman said:[10]

According to one view, unrealistic assumptions do not impair a theory's validity if the theory yields sufficiently accurately predictions.

> In so far as a theory can be said to have "assumptions" at all, and in so far as their "realism" can be judged independently of the validity of predictions, the relations between the significance of a theory and the "realism" of its "assumptions" is almost the opposite of that suggested by the view under criticism. Truly important and significant hypotheses will be found to have "assumptions" that are wildly inaccurate descriptive representations of reality, and, in general, the more significant the theory, the more unrealistic the assumptions (in this sense). The reason is simple. A hypothesis is important if it "explains" much by little, that is, if it abstracts the common and crucial elements from the mass of complex and detailed circumstances surrounding the phenomena to be explained and permits valid predictions on the basis of them alone. To be important, therefore, a hypothesis must be descriptively false in its assumptions; it takes account of, and accounts for, none of the many other attendant circumstances, since its very success shows them to be irrelevant for the phenomena to be explained. To put this point less paradoxically, the relevant question to ask about the "assumptions" of a theory is not whether they are descriptively "realistic" for they never are, but whether they are sufficiently good approximations for the purpose in hand. And this question can be answered only by seeing whether it yields sufficiently accurate predictions.

Here Friedman is saying that the degree of "realism" in the assumptions is often not apparent in the assumptions themselves but becomes apparent only after the theory is constructed and its predictive power evaluated. In other words, if a theory predicts accurately, then the assumptions are realistic enough despite appearances to the contrary.

---

[9] Milton Friedman, "The Methodology of Positive Economics," *Essays in Positive Economics* (Chicago: University of Chicago Press, 1953), pp. 3–43. Friedman's article has provoked a wealth of comment and rebuttal. See, for example, Eugene Rotwein, "On 'The Methodology of Positive Economics,'" *Quarterly Journal of Economics*, Vol. 73, No. 4 (November 1959), pp. 554–75; R. M. Cyert and E. Grunberg, "Assumption, Prediction, and Explanation in Economics," Appendix A in R. M. Cyert and J. G. March, *A Behavioral Theory of the Firm* (Englewood Cliffs, N.J.: Prentice Hall, 1964), pp. 7–11; and the papers published in the *American Economic Review, Papers and Proceedings*, Vol. 52, No. 2 (May 1963), pp. 204–36.

[10] Friedman, "The Methodology of Positive Economics," pp. 14–15.

Other economists take strong issue with Friedman's position. Naturally, an assumption is "unrealistic" if one is applying the standard that it does not exhaustively describe a situation and instead mentions only some of the traits that are present. Yet, no one seriously contends that an assumption is unrealistic, in the sense of being invalid, just because it does not exhaustively set forth every aspect of the situation being analyzed. The purpose of assumptions, say most theoreticians, is to simplify and to set forth essential conditions under which the theory applies. The bone of contention is whether it is always necessary that the assumed conditions be realistic in the sense of being true or accurate.

Most analysts agree that there is one instance in which unrealistic assumptions are tolerable. This concerns those few theories and models that apply to hypothetical or idealized circumstances—for example, the frictionless world often posed in physics and the perfectly competitive market model in economics (the latter model assumes the existence of such "ideal" conditions as perfect knowledge on the part of the buyers and sellers, perfect flexibility and mobility in the use of economic resources, and complete freedom of entry and exit of producers into the market). The situations portrayed in these models are admittedly not met in the real world, but the results and conclusions from studying such artificial situations often make a useful standard of comparison against which the functioning of more realistic situations can be measured. Models of this type are unique in the sense that when real-world events do not conform to the predictions given by the model, it is indicative that the conditions upon which the model is predicated are not being met—not that the model is invalid.

> **Theorists generally agree that assumptions setting certain "ideal" (but admittedly nonexistent) conditions are tolerable in constructing special case theories and models.**

The crux of the argument over unrealistic assumptions concerns the real-world applicability of theories and models that are based on false, highly improbable, or discredited assumptions. Is Friedman correct in his assertion that if a theory containing "unrealistic" assumptions has an impressive degree of predictive power, then the theory automatically is vested with satisfactory explanatory power and its assumptions have an acceptable degree of "realism?" Cohen and Cyert have offered examples where Friedman's position can lead to prediction without explanation.[11] In their view, a theory or model that seems to predict well enough but that explains poorly should arouse suspicion about whether the true variables are correctly represented. In such a case, any predictive power that the model may have could arise from unknown relationship(s) among variables in the model and/or the influence of unknown variables not included in the model. Ernest Nagel, an eminent authority on methodological matters, has observed that a theory which contains an unrealistic assumption in the sense that it is false is "patently unsatisfactory, for such a theory entails consequences that are incompatible with observed fact, so that on pain of rejecting elementary logical canons the theory must also be rejected."[12] The consensus view among economists is that theories and models must provide logical explanation as well as prediction. One can scarcely be confident in the explanatory power of a theory that contains false or empirically discredited assumptions—even if it yields good predictions. Unless the assumptions of a theory or model are agreed upon as having general validity, we have at best a

> **The fundamental problem with a theory containing false, discredited, or unreasonably inaccurate assumptions is that its explanatory power is suspect; there is room to doubt whether such a theory exposes true cause-effect relationships.**

---

[11] K. J. Cohen and R. M. Cyert, *Theory of the Firm: Resource Allocation in a Market Economy*, 2nd ed. (Englewood Cliffs, N.J.: Prentice Hall, 1975), pp. 22–24.
[12] Ernest Nagel, "Assumptions in Economic Theory," *American Economic Review, Papers and Proceedings*, Vol. 52, No. 2 (May 1963), pp. 214–15.

proposed explanation, not an actual explanation; moreover, the accuracy of predictions might well be due to fortuitous circumstances or uncanny chance happenings. Thus, it is imperative that we understand why a theory predicts before we give it credence.

APPLICATIONS CAPSULE

THE WIZARD WHO OVERSIMPLIFIED: A FABLE

In a certain kingdom, there was a school for the education of princes approaching manhood. Since the king and his court spent much of their time playing chess—indeed, chess was called the sport of kings—it was decided that the subject called "games" should be added to the curriculum of this school. A wizard was engaged to develop the course.

Never having played chess himself, the wizard was a little uncertain about what to teach in this course. (Only a *little* uncertain because his ignorance of chess was outweighed by his strong confidence in his general ability.) He sought the advice of a colleague in another kingdom and from him received the following communication:

"Above all else, a course in games should be rigorous and intellectually challenging. We wizards long ago concluded that chess, as actually played, is so complicated that it is impossible to formulate a body of principles and decision rules; these are essential to the rigorous analysis of any subject. We have therefore introduced a few simplifying assumptions. For example, in chess, the pieces move in a bewildering fashion—some forward, some on the diagonal, and some even at a right angle; we have tidied up this confusion by assuming that all pieces move according to the same rule. With such assumptions, we have been able, albeit with great difficulty, to develop a model, a set of principles, and decision rules which are teachable, and intellectually challenging. A 700-page treatise describing these is enclosed."

The wizard was much impressed by the 700-page treatise and used it in his course. He found that it was teachable and that the task of learning this model and solving problems with the decision rules was indeed rigorous and intellectually challenging, as proved by the fact that good students did well on their examinations, while poor students failed them.

The wizard maintained an active correspondence with wizards in other kingdoms about the model and its decision rules. In this correspondence, the game was referred to as "chess" although this was solely for convenience of expression; it was taken for granted that everyone knew that their game was not quite like chess as played in the real world. Eventually, some of this correspondence came to the king's attention. Although he didn't understand the formulas and the jargon, he did notice that the word "chess" was mentioned, so he commanded the wizard to appear before him.

At this audience, the wizard asked, "How can I serve you, O King?"

And the king replied: "I understand that you are teaching the princes how to play chess. I wish to improve my own game. Can you help me?"

"What we call chess may not be exactly like your game, your majesty. So before answering your question, I must analyze the problem. Please describe chess as you play it."

So the king explained the game of chess. As he did so, the wizard noted that it had the same physical layout, the same number of pieces, and apparently the same objective as the game he taught in school. It seemed clear therefore that the solution was simply to apply the decision rules for this game, although he of course did not immediately reveal this fact to the king for he wanted to preserve his reputation for wizardry. Instead, he said thoughtfully: "I will study the problem and return in ninety days."

At the appointed time, the wizard appeared again, carrying a crimson pillow on which lay a spiral-bound report with a Plexiglas cover. It was a paraphrase of the 700-page manuscript. "Follow the rules in this report, your majesty, and you will become the best chess player in the world," he said.

The king avidly studied the report, but soon ran into difficulty. He summoned the wizard again. "I see reference to kings, and men, and squares, which are familiar terms to me; but what is all this about 'jumping,' and 'double jumping,' 'countervailing force,' and 'suboptimization'; and where do you mention queens, rooks, bishops, and knights?"

"But your majesty, as I have clearly explained in the introduction, it was necessary to simplify the environment a trifle. I doubt that these simplifications lessen the practical usefulness of what I have written, however."

"Have you by chance watched some chess players to find out?" asked the king.

"Oh, no, your gracious majesty, but I do carry on an extensive correspondence with other wizards. This is better than observing actual practice because it is generally agreed that wizards are smarter than chess players."

"And your princes. Are they equipped to play chess in the real world because of what they have learned in your course?"

"No offense intended, sir, but we wizards do not believe this to be a proper question. The purpose of our course is to teach princes to think, not to prepare them for a mere vocation."

At this point, the king lost his patience, but since he was a kindly king, he sent the wizard back to his school room rather than to a dungeon.

Source: Harold Peterson, "The Wizard Who Oversimplified," *Quarterly Journal of Economics*, Vol. 79, No. 2 (May 1965), pp. 210–12. Copyright © 1965 by the President and Fellows of Harvard College. Reprinted by permission of John Wiley & Sons, Inc.

It is especially important that a theoretical model possess both predictive power and explanatory power when it is to be used as a guide for designing economic policy. In relying upon a theory to formulate economic policy, a user must be acutely aware of just how the values of one or more variables must be altered to bring about the desired economic changes. This clearly requires predictive power, for the user must be able to forecast accurately the consequences of changing the selected control variables. But were the analyst to rely upon a theory that generated accurate predictions without adequate cause-effect explanation, it would be easy for the prescribed policy to trigger unwanted changes in some other economic variables and/or relationships.

Many of the lessons covered here on the methods of economic analysis come alive in the fable of the wizard who oversimplified—see the Applications Capsule.

KEY POINTS

The methodological approaches of economists in analyzing economic behavior and constructing economic theories are varied enough to preclude making an unequivocal statement about just how we have come to know and not know about what makes an economy function as it does. Some economic knowledge is grounded strongly in the methods of science and is undergirded with sufficient empirical and behavioral evidence to warrant great confidence. But repeated testing of economic relationships, under conditions akin to controlled laboratory testing, is nearly impossible because the forces of economic change are at work continuously—a characteristic that makes it hard to replicate economic experiments under exactly the same conditions each time. As a consequence, to the extent that economics is a science, it is different from the "hard" natural sciences, where controlled experiments can be conducted over and over under the same laboratory conditions. Thus, although the research preference of many economists is to employ the scientific method whenever feasible, many times it is incumbent upon economists to use deductive logic, rational argument, the evidence of examples, and model-building to probe economic cause-effect relationships. In this sense, some economic propositions are "soft," a bit imprecise, and somewhat shy on ironclad empirical evidence. Nonetheless, it would be a mistake to view the study of economics as anything other than a rigorous exercise. Economics is a discipline strongly grounded in theory, in analysis, and in conceptual rigor.

Economic theory is a term that merits careful understanding. It refers to a generally accepted analytical framework whereby the behavior of economic phenomena can be explained and predicted. Economic theory attempts to account for the hows and whys of economic change; it endeavors to explain what happens and why it happens. Good economic theory is very realistic because it has demonstrably high degrees of power to explain economic cause-effect relationships and to predict how changes in one economic variable will affect other economic variables.

Most economic theories contain one or more assumptions describing key aspects of the economic situation being analyzed and specifying certain behavioral conditions. The consensus is that any such assumptions need to keep the theory in close contact with real-world economic behavior. Unless the assumptions upon which a theory is based are reasonable abstractions of reality and do justice to the analysis and conclusions, the theory's explanatory power is suspect and so is its usefulness as a guide for formulating economic policy.

Whatever predictive power a theory containing "unrealistic" assumptions may have could well be due to circumstance or to undetected cause-effect relationships.

Questions for Discussion

1. Characterize each of the steps of economic analysis. How do they compare with "the scientific method"? Which of these steps encompass what might be termed "theorizing"? Explain.
2. What is the difference among the terms *hypothesis, theory,* and *model*?
3. Distinguish carefully between "theory" and a "theoretical model."
4. On what grounds should a theory be evaluated? Which of these are more important and why?
5. What is the role of assumptions in theory construction?
6. Defend Milton Friedman's position regarding the realism of assumptions. How would one go about measuring or assessing the amount of explanatory power inherent in a theory? Does this have anything to do with Friedman's emphasis on predictive power as the main criterion for judging the worth and merit of a theory?
7. On what grounds, if any, is the presence of explanatory power a desirable feature in a theory?
8. When might it be appropriate to build an analysis around assumptions that are extremely simplistic? Could such an analysis still be useful?
9. Can a model intended for explanatory purposes differ from one intended for predictive purposes?
10. **(a)** In an article, a *Wall Street Journal* columnist raised the economic question of why a pack of cigarettes obtained from a cigarette machine costs more than a pack of cigarettes bought over the counter. Feeling that it should be just the opposite, he observed:[13]

    Everyone knows that a machine is a labor-saving device. It does things faster and easier and, one would expect, cheaper than people can. The cigaret machine at my corner luncheonette can stand there all day, every day without getting fallen arches. It never catches flu or has hangovers or sneaks off for an afternoon at the local ballpark. It doesn't require heating or lighting or air-conditioning or five-minute breaks to go the restroom. No one has to worry about the cigaret machine getting shortchanged (quite the opposite), or even slipping a couple of packs into its pocket when no one is looking. No, the cigaret machine would seem to be a classic example of an ideal form of people-replacing automation—wageless, undemanding, highly reliable.

    So, how come a pack of cigarets from the candy store costs 52 cents and a pack of cigarets from the cigaret machine a couple of doors away costs 65 cents?

    Can you identify the variables that might be pertinent in accounting for the puzzlement of the columnist? What hypothesis would you offer as an explanation? How might your hypothesis be tested?

    (b) In the same article, the columnist raised the question of why orange soda costs more than gasoline. His analysis ran as follows.[14]

    Gasoline starts with exploration in some God-forsaken part of the world. If oil is found, it has to be drilled for and then pumped out of the ground by pretty expensive equipment. Then it must be sent through a pipeline (a hefty capital investment), loaded into a tanker (ditto), transported over a vast expanse of water, offloaded to another pipeline, and pumped to a refinery (horrendous capital investment). After a complex refining process, what is now gasoline is loaded into railroad tank cars ($$$) and taken to a distributor's tank farm ($$). Now into tank trucks for delivery to gas stations ($). Finally the stuff is pumped into your automobile for about 60 cents a gallon, of which 12 cents is state and

---

[13] Quoted from John Tracy McGrath, "Ways to Stump an Economist," *The Wall Street Journal*, November 15, 1974, p. 14.
[14] *Ibid.*

federal taxes. Everyone, including the laissez-faire heirs of Adam Smith and John Stuart Mill, agree that this net price of 48 cents a gallon, 12 cents a quart, is a cruel ripoff by greedy oil-producing countries and-or greedy oil companies.

Now, orange soda. Like gasoline, soft drinks are produced largely by automated processes. But the equipment is relatively simple and inexpensive. The bottler puts ordinary tap water (sometimes from his own artesian well) into a can or bottle, adds some sugar syrup which also contains flavoring, coloring and a preservative, carbonates the mixture with a shot of carbon dioxide, seals the containers and delivers them by truck to our friend at the candy store. Friend sells soda for 50 cents a quart, $2 a gallon, no tax.

Yes, I know. The price of sugar has risen sharply. But when sugar (and soda) were cheaper, so was gasoline. In just about the same ratio. And bottlers are now using corn syrup along with sugar to sweeten their soft drinks. But most tantalizing is the fact that quinine water and club soda and artificially sweetened diet drinks, none of which contains any sugar at all, also sell for $2 a gallon.

Identify the economic variables that could help explain why orange soda is more expensive than gasoline. What hypothesis would you offer as a possible explanation to the columnist? How would you test the validity of your hypothesis?

Chapter 2

Buyers, Sellers, Firms, and Markets

The heart and soul of microeconomic analysis revolves around describing, explaining, and predicting the actions and decisions of buyers and sellers "in the marketplace." The word *marketplace* conjures up images of a small geographic site where buyers and sellers meet face-to-face to buy, sell, or trade things of value—as goes on at a farmer's market or an auction or a shopping mall. But the notion of a marketplace or *market* as a place is much too incomplete. Buyers and sellers do not have to meet face-to-face to conduct business; transactions are easily handled using mail-order catalogs, TV shopping channels, telephones, independent brokers, and agents. Moreover, the transactions among the buyers and sellers of blue jeans in a San Francisco shopping mall do not constitute the whole market for blue jeans but only the local area market in that one mall. All the local marketplaces for blue jeans join and interact to make up a national market for blue jeans, and the various national markets for blue jeans interconnect to form a world market for blue jeans. A market, therefore, includes the interplay *among all the relevant buyers and sellers* involved in the exchange of something, whether the something is a good, a service, real estate, stocks or bonds, used equipment, labor, or whatever. The geographic scope of a market can be local, regional, national, international, or worldwide, depending on the item in question.

Markets are important because they represent the economic mechanism most societies use to facilitate production, distribution, and transactions of all kinds. The economies of most modern, industrialized nations are *market-driven* in the sense that people and organizations rely upon the market process to conduct their economic transactions. Every society or nation, no matter how it decides to transact its economic business, has to figure out how to answer four big and very basic economic questions:

1. *What* and *how much* to produce?
2. *How* to undertake production—what technology and how much of which kinds of resource inputs to use in the production process?
3. *Who* is to receive how much of what is produced—how will the fruits of production be distributed to the various members of society?
4. What arrangement will be made for *changing* both *the production mix* and *the distribution mix* whenever the time comes?

BASIC CONCEPT
A market exists whenever individuals and organizations become involved in buying, selling, or trading something of value.

Studying how markets function is fundamental to microeconomics because almost every society in the world uses markets as a mechanism for transacting economic business.

18

In a market-driven economy, the answers to all these questions are generated through the decisions of buyers and sellers to conduct transactions in whatever markets they wish. Among the most important features of a market economy are private ownership of economic resources and the means of production, individual freedom of choice, competition, the profit motive, and prices determined by market demand and market supply conditions. *Buyer wants and needs dominate what and how much to produce*—sellers find no profit in producing something no one wants or is willing to pay too little for! The question of how to achieve the desired levels of production is a function of the technological options, the costs of the various resource inputs which are required for each technological recipe, and what production methods are most cost-effective and/or most profitable. The distribution of the available goods and services is based on the monetary ability of consumers to pay for what they choose to buy—buyers can pretty much depend on getting whatever they are willing to pay the price for. Price is the ruling market force and demand-supply conditions interact to determine price. The mechanism for economic change is also the marketplace; *changes* in what buyers want and will pay for are reflected on the demand side of the marketplace while changes in technology, in the costs and availability of resources, in competitive pressures, and in productive efficiency are reflected on the supply side.

A simplified picture of the market process is presented in Figure 2-1. There are **resource markets** and **product markets**. The principal economic units of society (individuals, firms, governmental units, and nonprofit enterprises), acting as owners of needed economic resources (land, labor, natural resources, investment capital), supply the means of production to business firms through

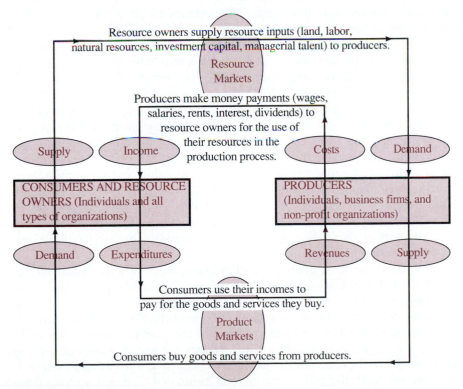

Figure 2-1

A simplified model of a market economy

The two principal types of markets are product markets and resource markets; there is a market for each separate good and service and a market for each type of resource input.

resource markets. Producers constitute the demand side of resource markets and must pay to acquire the necessary resources for production. These payments, which are *costs* from the standpoint of producing firms, become *incomes* to resource providers and take the form of wages, salaries, rents, interest, dividends, and so on. Producers utilize the resource inputs they have purchased to make goods and services. The fruits of production are supplied to consumers through *product markets*, with producers on the supply side and consumers on the demand side. Consumers, using the income they have gotten from supplying resources, pay for the goods and services they buy. These payments, which are **expenditures** from the standpoint of consumers, are **revenues** to producers (revenues provide sellers the wherewithal to cover their production costs—that is, revenues provide the money to pay for the resource inputs used in production). A key feature of the market system is the freedom of consumers and producers to make their own buy-sell decisions and to transact business in whatever markets they choose, the principle being that in encouraging the drive for individual economic self-interest, the outcome more often than not works out to be in the overall best interests of society as well.

But the market mechanism is not the only way a society can manage its economic affairs. In a *traditional economic system* the four basic economic questions are answered by doing things according to custom, habit, and tradition. Prices and markets play second fiddle to long-standing social arrangements, political considerations, and the social culture. Economic change and technological change are slow moving, with production and distribution being done in much the same way year after year. Tradition and the status quo are perpetuated. New ways of doing things are accepted very gradually and become "standard" only over a comparatively long time. Traditional economic systems were dominant until the eighteenth century and they still characterize the economies of many Third World nations.

A *command economic system* relies upon public ownership and centralized control of the basic means of production as a substitute for the market process. Severe limitations are placed on the freedom of consumers and producers to make their own economic decisions because they might conflict with government-determined economic priorities that supposedly are "in society's overall best interests." The questions of what and how much to produce and how to distribute the fruits of production are decided by an economic commander in chief (a head of state, or central planning authority). Heavy use is made of centralized economic control over production and consumption in order to achieve planned economic outcomes. The thesis underlying a centrally planned economy is that the governing authority is in the best position to decide what economic choices and policies are most beneficial for the economy and its component parts. Socialistic and communistic countries typify command-driven economic systems.

Whereas the U.S. economy and the economies of most industrial nations are market-oriented and market-driven, no economy is purely and completely organized on a market basis. It is essential for all nations to have governments that act on behalf of society outside of the market arena; virtually all government actions rely upon the element of command to impose economic outcomes for the benefit of public good. In this sense the economies of the major industrialized nations of the world are properly described as *mixed economic systems*, with the mix of market and command elements varying from case to case.

WHAT IS A MARKET?

In a competitive enterprise system, "the market" or "the market-place" is a factor to be taken into account by all active and would-be participants and by government as well. The market's economic role is akin to that of the sun in the solar system—all really important economic activities for the item in question revolve around it. The market is where buyers and sellers transact their business. The market is, at once, a mechanism for organizing the orderly exchange of a good or service and, through competitive interplay, the master over all voluntary transactions involving that good or service. A market is always two-sided: It reflects both demand and supply conditions—and does so simultaneously. Through a market, buyers make known their decisions to buy or not to buy and on what terms; through a market, sellers make known their willingness and ability to sell or not sell and on what terms. According to an old Russian proverb, "Once you have gone to market you have told the whole world." A market communicates, records, totals, and balances the preferences and freely made decisions of buyers and sellers against one another. Market conditions signal (better than any firm, individual, or governmental agency can) what the current states of supply and demand are. The market is the first to receive and reflect the winds of economic change. So it is that the market's judgment about the balance between supply and demand and its verdict regarding the terms of exchange between buyers and sellers is an impartial and potent economic force to be reckoned with.

WHY DO FIRMS EXIST?

The activities of business firms are such an integral part of the marketplace that there is a tendency to take them for granted and overlook the basic question of why firms come into existence. A firm is simply an economic institution that participates in markets by buying resources and selling goods and services. The firm also organizes the workplace and transforms scarce resources into products or services, which are then sold in markets. But why do firms exist?[1] This question can be addressed by first considering why individuals participate in markets. The answer, of course, is that they expect to gain from trade and exchange. But participating in markets either as a buyer or seller is generally not a costless activity. The decision to buy or sell in a market is often accompanied by certain costs that cannot be avoided if a market transaction is to take place. For example, a potential buyer must have market information, which must be acquired in one way or another. In some transactions the act of acquiring information may involve substantial costs. Another example involves negotiations. Some market transactions involve significant negotiations before an agreement is reached between the buyer and seller. After an agreement is reached, still more costs may have to be incurred to ensure that the other party to the transaction lives up to its side of the bargain. The costs of engaging in trade and exchange in the marketplace are called

"The market" for a good, service, or resource input includes all relevant buyer-seller wants, needs, preferences, and actions; if it matters at all—in the sense that demand or supply conditions are affected—then it is part of "the market."

Firms exist because they are able to provide consumers with goods and services at lower production and transactions costs than consumers could achieve by producing these same things on their own initiative.

---

[1] This question was addressed in a classic paper by Ronald H. Coase, "The Nature of the Firm," *Economica*, Vol. 4 (November 1938), pp. 386–405, reprinted in George J. Stigler and Kenneth E. Boulding, eds. *Readings in Price Theory* (Homewood, Ill.: Richard D. Irwin, 1952). Professor Coase received the 1992 Nobel Prize in Economics, and his contributions to our understanding of the nature of business firms was one of two aspects of his work that the Nobel Committee singled out in making the award.

transactions costs. One basic reason that firms come into existence is that they are able to economize on transactions costs. When trade and exchange in the market entail high transactions costs, performing an economic activity inside the firm may be a more efficient method of accomplishing an objective than by relying solely on exchange and trade between individuals. If firms are more efficient at either production or transactions than individuals, they become economically viable and have social purpose.

An example will clarify why firms come into existence. Consider home building. Each family could attempt to avoid using a home-building contractor and manage all the construction activities themselves. Nails, lumber, wiring, plumbing supplies, architectural services, and carpenters could be acquired in the marketplace. But it is obvious that for most people the transactions costs of building one's own home would be sizable. A home-building contractor can economize on the transactions costs and more efficiently carry out the complex activities associated with building a new home. Some individuals, of course, do decide to serve as their own building contractor, but even they find it advantageous not to be entirely self-sufficient. Thus, they hire subcontractors, who are owners of small firms specializing in particular home-building tasks—plumbing, electrical, roofing, and heating and cooling. As with other business firms, subcontractors in the home-building industry come into existence by economizing on production and transactions costs. Imagine what onerous transactions costs you would incur to obtain a car if there were no firms that made cars!

HOW A MARKET FUNCTIONS: THE MODEL OF DEMAND AND SUPPLY

Markets are composed of buyers and sellers. The actions and decisions of buyers are reflected on the demand side of a market and can be analyzed using *demand curves*. The actions and decisions of sellers are reflected on the supply side of a market and can be analyzed using *supply curves*.

MARKET DEMAND AND DEMAND CURVES

MARKET PRINCIPLE
The lower the price of an item, the greater will be the quantity demanded by buyers, other things being equal.

Market demand reflects the intensity with which buyers want and are willing to pay for an item. The amount of an item that any buyer or group of buyers will purchase at any point in time always depends on many factors (needs, preferences, income, expectations about the future, the prices of related items, the buyer's situation, and so on), but it depends especially on the price of the item. According to the *law of demand*, the lower the price of an item, the more that buyers will be willing to purchase, other things being equal. The condition "other things being equal" is critical because if other things change at the same time the price of the item changes, then the buyer's decision to buy more or less is governed not just by the price change but by whatever influence the "other things" have as well.

Each point on a market demand curve represents the combined quantities that all buyers will purchase at various alternative market prices.

Figure 2-2 shows a hypothetical demand schedule and corresponding demand curve for frozen pizzas. Each point on the curve identifies the total quantity all buyers will purchase at that particular price. For example, at a $6 price, buyers are willing to purchase 500,000 pizzas weekly, while at $5 the quantity demanded will be 700,000 pizzas a week. Note that the *demand* is *not* higher at the lower price; rather, the *quantity demanded* is higher. The term *demand* is reserved for describing the entire relationship along the demand curve; *quantity demanded* refers to one particular quantity on a demand curve.

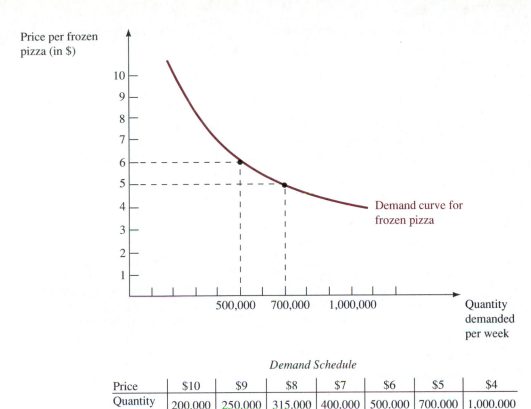

Price per frozen pizza (in $)

Demand curve for frozen pizza

Quantity demanded per week

Demand Schedule

Price	$10	$9	$8	$7	$6	$5	$4
Quantity demanded	200.000	250.000	315.000	400.000	500.000	700.000	1,000.000

Figure 2-2
A hypothetical demand curve for frozen pizzas

The downsloping-to-the-right shape of the demand curve is a graphical reflection of the **law of demand**—lower prices increase the quantity demanded and higher prices lower the quantity demanded. Economists maintain that the demand curve for virtually every thing slopes downward to the right. The downsloping character of the demand curve enjoys the status of a *law* or *principle* because it is probably the most universally valid and broadly supported (by the evidence) proposition in economics—exceptions are so few and far between that no really good or important examples can be cited.

Two other features of demand curves need to be kept in mind. First, a demand curve *always* pertains to a particular point in time. The demand curve in Figure 2-2 might reflect buyer demand for January; in August new conditions may prevail. Second, while the demand curve shows how much buyers will purchase at a given price, it also *shows the top price buyers will pay for a given quantity*. A larger quantity can be sold only at a lower price.

Changes in Demand. As mentioned earlier, considerations other than price affect buyer purchases. A demand curve identifies only price-quantity demanded relationships, the influence of all other factors being held constant. If buyer preferences, buyer incomes, the prices of related items, or any other relevant factors change in any way, then the prevailing price-quantity demanded relationship can change. In other words, *when other things do not remain constant*, the demand curve can shift its position. Figure 2-3(a) illustrates an *increase in demand*—from D_1 to D_2. A rightward shift in the position of the demand curve reflects a situation where *the quantity demanded is*

An increase in demand and an increase in the quantity demanded are not the same; the former concerns an upward-rightward shift in the location of the demand curve while the latter refers to a downward movement along a given demand curve.

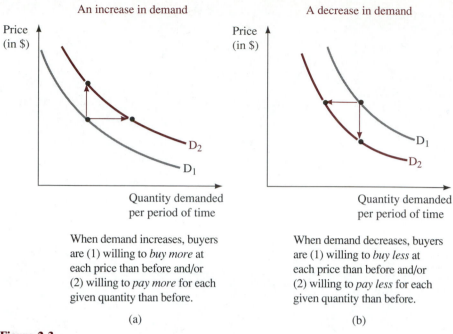

When demand increases, buyers are (1) willing to *buy more* at each price than before and/or (2) willing to *pay more* for each given quantity than before.

(a)

When demand decreases, buyers are (1) willing to *buy less* at each price than before and/or (2) willing to *pay less* for each given quantity than before.

(b)

Figure 2-3
Changes in demand

greater at each alternative price than before or, to put it another way, *buyers are willing to pay a higher price for each given quantity demanded than before.* Conversely, a *decrease in demand,* from D_1 to D_2 in Figure 2-3(b), indicates that for whatever reason (a change in "other things"), buyers are now willing to *purchase less* at each price than before. It can also be said that when demand decreases, buyers are willing to *pay less* for a given quantity than before.

The point here is this: To use demand-curve analysis correctly, it is necessary to distinguish clearly between situations that involve a change in quantity demanded (movement along a given demand curve) and a change in demand (the shift of the whole demand curve to a new position).

MARKET SUPPLY AND SUPPLY CURVES

The supply side of a market concerns the extent to which sellers are willing and able to make supplies of an item available. The amount of an item that any seller or group of sellers decides to offer for sale at any point in time is always conditioned by a host of factors (costs, competitive conditions, technological capabilities, expectations about future market conditions, and so forth), but price is a big and ever-present consideration. In the vase majority of cases, *the higher the price of an item, the more that sellers will be willing to offer for sale, other things being equal.* The reason for this is that sellers typically find it more profitable to intensify their production efforts when price is higher as compared to when price is lower. However, *the "law of supply" is not so absolute as the law of demand;* one can cite instances where the quantity supplied increases even if prices remain constant and, on occasions, the quantity supplied is fixed in the short run and is the same whether price rises or falls. Nonetheless, "normal supply conditions" are such that sellers will make more

MARKET PRINCIPLE
The higher the price of an item, the greater will be the quantity supplied by sellers, other things being equal.

of an item available at higher prices than they will at lower prices—a condition that causes the supply curve to slope upward to the right.

     Figure 2-4(a) shows a hypothetical supply curve and supply schedule for frozen pizzas. Each point on the supply curve identifies the total quantity that all frozen pizza sellers will offer for sale at various alternative prices, other things remaining constant. Because such a curve represents the combined quantities that the separate sellers will offer for sale, the curve is generally called the **market** (or industry) **supply curve**. At a $4 price, 350,000 frozen pizzas will be supplied weekly, while at $7 the quantity supplied is 650,000 pizzas. Again, note that it is the *quantity supplied* which is greater at the higher price, not supply. The word **supply** by itself refers to the whole supply curve, while **quantity supplied** refers to one particular quantity and point on the curve—the terminology parallels that for demand versus quantity demanded.

Each point on a market supply curve represents the combined quantities that all sellers will offer for sale at various alternative market prices.

    Changes in Supply.   As with demand curves, supply curves pertain to conditions at a particular point in time. When conditions change, because supply-determining factors other than price change, the entire supply curve shifts. Figure 2-4(b) shows an *increase in supply*. Such a rightward and downward movement in the supply curve indicates (1) that sellers are willing to

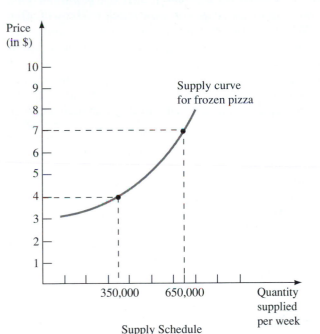

Supply Schedule
for Frozen Pizzas

Price	*Quantity supplied*
$3	100,000
4	350,000
5	480,000
6	575,000
7	650,000
8	700,000

(a)

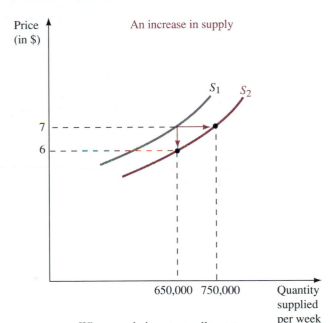

When supply increases sellers are (1) willing to *supply more* at each price than before and/or (2) willing to accept a *lower price* at each given quantity than before.

(b)

Figure 2-4

Supply curves and changes in supply

supply *greater quantities at each alternative price* than before and/or (2) that sellers are willing to supply the *same quantities at lower prices* than before. For example, in Figure 2-4(b), the increase in supply from S_1 to S_2 shows that at a $7 price the quantity supplied of frozen pizzas jumps from 650,000 to 750,000 pizzas per week. At the same time, with curve S_2 sellers are willing to supply the original 650,000 quantity for $6 instead of $7, as was the case when S_1 conditions prevailed. Increases in supply can occur because some key inputs have become much cheaper, because new technological capability allows producers to be more efficient, because sellers have decided to work off excess inventories, or because sellers believe that in a few months demand will weaken, making it more advantageous to sell now rather than later. Decreases in supply can arise when the changes in these kinds of supply-determining factors go in the opposite direction.

DETERMINING THE MARKET PRICE

The interaction of market demand conditions with market supply conditions determines both the going market price and the quantity that changes hands. *The market demand curve portrays how much buyers will purchase at various prices, and the market supply curve depicts how much sellers will offer for sale at various prices.* When the two are put together, there is only one price where the quantity buyers want to buy exactly equals the quantity which sellers are offering for sale. As depicted in Figure 2-5, the market demand and supply curves intersect at a price of P_1 and a quantity of Q_1. Competition causes any other price-quantity combination to be unstable. If sellers try to charge a price above P_1, then surplus conditions will arise and induce some or

MARKET PRINCIPLE
The only price at which the market will be cleared of shortage and surplus conditions is the one where the quantity demanded equals the quantity supplied.

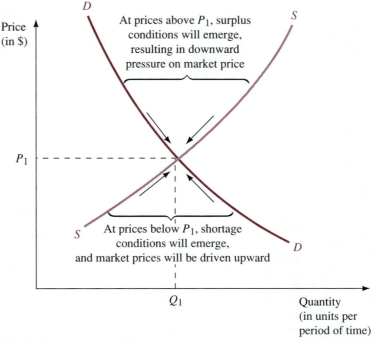

Figure 2-5
Determining market price and quantity sold

all competing sellers to shade their prices to work off the excess inventory buildups. As market price drops, buyers are stimulated to increase their purchases, whereas the quantity supplied (because of reduced profitability) tends to contract, thereby acting to eliminate surplus conditions.

At any price below P_1, the quantity demanded exceeds the quantity supplied such that shortages appear. Those buyers who are most anxious to avoid doing without the product will, when confronted with shortage conditions, either be inclined to bid up their offer prices or else accept a move on the part of sellers to solve shortage conditions by raising prices. What, in effect, happens in periods of shortage is that a competitive scramble among buyers for the available supplies ends to pull the going market price upward—an outcome which automatically acts to eliminate the shortage, owing to the fact that higher prices act to reduce the overall quantity demanded and to increase the overall quantity supplied.

In Figure 2-5, only at price P_1 and quantity Q_1 will the market be cleared. At this price-quantity combination, neither surplus nor shortage conditions exist. A price-quantity *equilibrium* will prevail in the sense that there are no forces currently operating on either the demand side or the supply side of the market to bring about a change in the market result. The tendency of market forces to establish a price at which the quantity demanded will equal the quantity supplied is called the *rationing function* of the price system, and the automatic adjustment of price upward or downward is the vehicle through which market equilibrium is established.

How Big Is a Market?

Markets range in size from tiny to gigantic, from local to worldwide. The market for Rolls Royces is tiny compared to the market for Fords, Chevrolets, or Hondas. The size of the market for toothpicks is well under $100 million, whereas the size of the market for crude oil exceeds $200 billion annually. And, as stated earlier, it is wrong to think of a market as being a small place where buyers and sellers come together to strike a bargain. The markets for most items range beyond a particular locale and assume areawide, regional, national, or worldwide dimensions. A newsprint plant's market typically extends over a multistate region, thereby putting it in direct competition with other newsprint mills where market coverage overlaps. A major international oil company such as Exxon does business in many parts of the world and thus competes head-on with nearly every other oil company in one place or another. The markets for wheat, U.S. Treasury bonds, gold, copper, automobile tires, televisions, crude oil, and diamonds all have a global scope.

Markets vary from tiny to gigantic, from local to global.

According to Alfred Marshall, a distinguished nineteenth-century British economist, the geographical limits of a market are defined by ''an area within which buyers and sellers are in such close communication with each other that price tends to be the same throughout the area.'' However, Marshall's classic definition of a market proves troublesome today. Suppose two supermarkets located across the street from each other are selling a particular brand of toothpaste at different prices—one for 79 cents and the other for 89 cents. Are we then to infer that the two grocery stores are not in the same market? Or, suppose that Avis typically rents cars at prices slightly below Hertz (perhaps because its fleet of cars consists of the less expensive, more economically equipped models). Can we conclude that Avis and Hertz are not

It is hard to put well-defined geographic boundaries around a market and be precise about just how big a geographic territory it covers.

head-on rivals competing in the rent-a-car market? Would it not be more accurate to view Avis and Hertz as operating within the same market but endeavoring to appeal to different market segments via price competition? Consequently, it is fair to say that the size and extent of a market cannot be delimited solely on the criterion of price uniformity. The boundaries of a market have to be determined on a case-by-case basis, looking at both demand-side and supply-side characteristics.

WHAT KINDS OF MARKETS ARE THERE?

There are as many different kinds of markets as there are things being exchanged. There are markets for consumer goods (lettuce, used cars, ski equipment, and newspapers) and there are markets for services (laundry and dry cleaning, quick-copying, housecleaning, and legal advice). There are markets for productive resources (business school graduates, new plant sites, used restaurant equipment, pro football players, bulldozer operators, iron ore, mainframe computers, and rubber plantations). There are stock markets, bond markets, mortgage loan markets, and markets for mutual fund investments.

There are more ways to describe a market than by just size and geographic scope.

It is also possible to describe a market by certain conditions which prevail as well as by the product or service being exchanged. Thus, there are *buyers' markets*, where conditions of oversupply allow buyers to drive especially good bargains with sellers. There are *sellers' markets*, where demand is so strong relative to the available supplies that sellers can command higher and very profitable asking prices. There are *perfectly efficient markets*, where a large number of buyers deal with a large number of sellers, no one of which buys or sells more than an insignificant fraction of the total exchanged, where the goods being offered by sellers are regarded by buyers as essentially identical, where the only criterion for a transaction is that no better bargain is available (that is, no buyers have a loyalty or preference for dealing with a particular seller), and where all traders are aware of all offers and deals available. And there are *inefficient markets*, where some or all of the foregoing conditions are absent. There are intensely *competitive markets* and there are *monopolistic markets*. There are *stable markets* where changes are slow and relatively predictable and *volatile markets* where changes are sudden and unpredictable.

Moreover, there are *vertically connected markets* and *horizontally connected markets*. Markets are linked vertically when items pass through a series of markets on their way to the final user—farmers sell cotton to ginners, who sell baled cotton fiber to cloth manufacturers, who sell yard goods to garment makers, who sell articles of apparel to retailers, who supply consumers in the retail clothing market. Markets are linked horizontally whenever there are substitute or complementary relationships between products. What happens in the market for beef affects the market for pork. Prices in the gasoline market affect the travel and recreation business. Money-market conditions affect residential construction activity.

The nature of the markets in which a firm does business is a matter for its management to study carefully. The firm's sales, profits, and growth potential are a function of both current market conditions and which way the winds of market change are blowing. A firm's success hinges upon its ability to analyze the marketplace accurately and strategically position itself in the right place at the right time with the right goods at the right price.

THE FIRM AND THE MARKETPLACE

Conventional wisdom in economics instructs that business decisions and business behavior are governed by competition and market conditions. The business firm is depicted as reacting and responding to competition and to market demand-supply conditions—forces that are beyond its purview to control or influence. Markets, not firms, therefore assume the analytical spotlight.

Conventional business theory, in sharp contrast, sees markets and competitive forces as *limits* to what a firm can do. Present and future market conditions are looked upon as creating opportunities (and threats) for business action. But market and economic forces are not thought of as *absolute* in determining what a firm can or cannot do and how it should go after the patronage of buyers. A firm's strategy for competing in the marketplace is deemed within its power to determine; moreover, it is thought to be within a firm's power to affect what happens in the marketplace with a well-conceived strategy. In fact, a particularly timely and astute business strategy is viewed as having the potential for generating a major impact on markets, buyers, rival firms, and competition.

One of the big microeconomic issues is whether market forces rule as the master over what firms can and cannot do or whether a firm may be able, because of its own actions, to influence market outcomes.

THE IMPORTANCE OF A FIRM'S COMPETITIVE STRATEGY

The competitive approach that a firm takes is important from several standpoints. To begin with, a host of factors shapes what competitive strategy a firm chooses: consumer buying trends and purchasing habits, technological change, competitive pressures, capital investment requirements, relative profit expectations, the firm's financial condition, an assessment of whether the firm's skills and management know-how qualify it to run a particular business successfully, the personal values and aspirations of management, the firm's obligations to segments of society other than stockholders, and government regulations.

Second, the firm's strategy has a definite bearing on its actions in the market. For instance, some firms are (or try to be) technological leaders, whereas others are content with being technological followers. Some firms are self-acknowledged aggressive risk-takers, whereas others deliberately are more conservative and embrace a strategy of risk avoidance. Some firms emphasize product quality and customer service, whereas others aim at the low-price, budget-conscious end of the market. Some firms position themselves in the forward end of the market, specializing in wholesaling or retailing the mass-produced items of other companies to the final user; examples include automobile dealers, wholesale distributorships, and discount retail chains like Wal-Mart. Other firms station themselves in the backward portion of the production chain and make their business out of supplying one or more enterprises with raw materials, intermediate goods, or component parts (the apparel firm supplying Sears and the local logging operator whose business is furnishing logs to large paper mills serve as good examples). Some firms base their strategy on carving a niche for themselves on the ''competitive fringe'' of markets dominated by well-known, brand-name firms; the producers of the so-called off-brands exemplify this type of firm. Some firms stick to a single line of business, whereas others strive for broad diversification.

Third, a firm's competitive strategy is the foundation for such fundamental market-related decisions as (1) choosing which of several customer

APPLICATIONS CAPSULE

KELLOGG'S STRATEGY IN THE READY-TO-EAT CEREALS BUSINESS

Since 1906, when Will Keith Kellogg formed the company after accidentally discovering a way to make ready-to-eat cereal, Kellogg has aimed its strategy at being the dominant leader in the ready-to-eat cereal business. Kellogg's strategy for competing is based on product differentiation and market segmentation. The company's product line features a diverse number of brands, differentiated according to grain shape, form, flavor, color, and taste—a something for everyone approach. Competing on the basis of low price has been deemphasized in favor of nonprice strategies keyed to extensive product variety, regular product innovation, substantial TV advertising, periodic promotional offers and prizes, and maintaining more space on the grocery shelf than rivals have.

Much of Kellogg's sales efforts are targeted at the under-25 age group (the biggest cereal eaters with an average annual consumption of 11 pounds per capita), and 33% of its cereal sales are in presweetened brands promoted almost totally through TV advertising to children. Kellogg endeavors to sidestep industry maturity and product saturation with introductions of fresh, "new" types of cereals (presweetened cereals in the 1940s, "nutritional" cereals in the 1950s, "natural" and health-conscious cereals in the 1960s and early 1970s, and adult cereals in the late 1970s) and also by advertising a variety of times and places for eating cereals other than at the morning breakfast table. Product-line freshness is additionally enhanced by introduction of brands which differ only slightly from existing brands (flakes vs. shredded, plain vs. sugarfrosted, puffed vs. cocoa flavored).

In 1979, Kellogg introduced five new cereal brands—more than it had ever launched in a single year—as part of a stepped-up and redirected effort to attract consumers in the 25–50 age group (where consumption levels were only half those of the younger age groups). Kellogg also introduced its cereals in four additional countries in South America and the Middle East using campaigns that featured free samples, demonstration booths in food stores, and heavy local advertising so as to promote the use of ready-to-eat cereals as a substitute for traditional breakfast foods (corn meal and bulgur). Both of these moves were aimed at changing the eating habits of adults who had shied away from cereals or who had spurned breakfast altogether. In further support of its attempt to appeal to more customer groups, Kellogg continued to up its research budget (already the industry's most extensive) by 15% annually in an effort to develop more nutritional, health-conscious cereals and breakfast foods for the older consumer segment. The whole of Kellogg's strategy in cereals had three strategic objectives: (1) increasing Kellogg's 42% market share, (2) increasing sales by 5% annually (compared to an industry growth of 2%), and (3) boosting annual cereal consumption from 8.6 pounds per capita to 12 pounds by 1985.

There is no doubt in some cases that market forces are short of being the absolute master over a firm; firms that craft powerful competitive strategies and execute them successfully can become industry leaders, wield *some* influence over market conditions, and achieve competitive advantage over rival firms with weaker competitive strategies.

groups and customer needs to cater to, (2) selecting the most cost-efficient technology and production process, (3) determining the optimum production scale and plant location, (4) trying to gain a competitive edge and win a bigger market share, and (5) responding to new market opportunities and changing demand-supply conditions.

All this is a way of saying that whether a firm is a market success or a market failure is in part a function of the caliber of its strategy and not entirely whether prevailing market conditions happen to be good or bad. A well-managed firm will always seek to impact the markets for its products with a timely, opportunistic strategy aimed at giving it a competitive advantage. Indeed, a major part of crafting a good strategy deals with how to *initiate* and *influence* rather than just *respond* and *react* to the product-customer-technological-competitive changes taking place in the market. The acid test of a good strategy, in fact, is the extent to which the firm's strategy (1) improves the firm's ability to compete successfully in the marketplace, (2) provides a competitive advantage, and (3) allows it to earn above-average profits.

The Applications Capsule on Kellogg's provides an excellent example of what business strategy is, the difference a good strategy can make to a firm's success in the marketplace, and why it is true that a single firm's actions can affect market conditions. As we shall see in later chapters, there is a two-way relationship between firms and markets—*what firms do affects markets and what markets do affects firms*.

THE CONCEPT OF "THE FIRM" REVISITED

Traditionally, microeconomists have spoken of "the firm" as if its every action is directed by an owner-entrepreneur—a risk-taking individual who supplies financial capital, who organizes and supervises the economic resources needed for production, and who is supposedly gifted in the task of running a business. Moreover, the firm is seen as engaging in just a single line of business. The firm's behavior in this single-market, single-industry environment is said to be orchestrated by the owner-entrepreneur, with conformity to the chosen goals being purchased by payments (wages, salaries, prestige, power, security) to employees and by a system of internal controls (authority, budgets), which keeps things on track.

This concept of a business firm or company, while appropriate for small, owner-managed enterprises, is at considerable variance with reality when applied to the modern large corporation. Large corporate enterprises are typically run by a team of professional managers who usually have a comparatively small ownership interest. The majority of the owners of corporations are absentee stockholders whose only critical role is to supply the enterprise with equity capital; the extent of stockholders' involvement seldom goes beyond an emotional concern with how much they are realizing on their financial investment (whether the company's stock price is rising or falling and the size of the dividend). Moreover, the majority of large corporate enterprises are multibusiness, multimarket, transnational firms; the scope of their operations is by no means limited to selling a single, well-defined item in a small, mostly local market.

"The firm" as a comparatively small, owner-managed, single-business proprietorship with a localized market for its products is one thing. "The firm" as a large, diversified portfolio of businesses, managed by a team of professional managers and having thousands of employees and stockholders, is another. The former is the most significant form of enterprise in terms of numbers but the latter also has a major role in modern economies, accounting for 25 to 50% of the sales revenues of all businesses and dominating such important industries as airlines, automobiles, oil, telephone service, beer, cigarettes, soft drinks, mainframe computers, and hotels. At least six distinct types of firms can be found in the population of business enterprises:

1. A single-business enterprise operating in only one stage of an industry's production chain.
2. A partially integrated, single-business enterprise operating in *some* of the stages of an industry's production chain.
3. A fully integrated, single-business enterprise operating in *all* stages of an industry's production chain.
4. A "dominant business" enterprise with sales concentrated in one major core business but with a modestly diversified portfolio of either related or unrelated businesses (amounting to one-third or less of total corporatewide sales).
5. A narrowly diversified enterprise with a "few" (say, 3 to 10) business units operating in either related or unrelated industries.
6. A broadly diversified enterprise with "many" (anywhere from 10 to several hundred) business units operating in a variety of related or unrelated industries.

In practice, *there is great diversity among firms*. They can be privately owned, publicly owned, profit seeking, or not for profit and can be organized as

Business firms are widely diverse in terms of size, the geographic areas over which they operate, the number of stages they span in the industry's production chain, the degree to which they are diversified, and their ownership characteristics.

Because firms are the principal economic unit for producing and distributing goods and services, the study of how firms make economic decisions and how they behave in the marketplace explains much about how markets function.

corporations, partnerships, or proprietorships. But all firms, no matter how diverse their size and scope, share certain fundamental traits and characteristics. First, every business firm must acquire productive resources by participating in resource markets as buyers of labor, investment capital, and natural resources. Second, all firms use scarce resources to produce goods and services. Third, all firms participate in markets as sellers of the products or services that they produce. Fourth, every firm must make crucial economic decisions about how the economic activities of the firm are to be organized. These decisions include what products will be produced, what resources will be used, what techniques of production will be adopted, the relative combinations of capital and labor, and how the firm is internally organized to accomplish its objectives. Finally, in answering the foregoing questions the firm must be concerned with how to compete in *each* line of business it is in. Different businesses have different market demand-supply conditions, different economic characteristics and forces of change, different technology and cost patterns, different competitive pressures, and so on. Thus, even though a firm may have diversified into many businesses, it still needs a specific, custom-tailored strategy for competing in each line of business in which it is engaged and it has to decide how to try to position itself in the marketplace—on a market-by-market and business-by-business basis. We shall take advantage of this business characteristic and use ''the single-business firm'' as the centerpiece for analyzing the economics of the firm. By treating ''the firm'' as if it is in only a single line of business, it is easier to zero in on the economic relationships underlying the demand for a firm's product, efficient production technologies and resource input combinations, the behavior of production costs, pricing and output decisions, and resource pricing and employment. By looking at the whys and wherefores of firm behavior in a variety of market situations, we can expose the circumstances under which competition is strong and the circumstances under which it is weak. Our ultimate goal is to understand thoroughly how a market economy works and to be in a position to judge the contribution of the business firm to the general economic well-being.

KEY POINTS

In a market economy, the business firm is the principal economic agent for the production and distribution of goods and services. Business firms economize on transactions costs and, more than any other economic unit, serve as the hub of economic activity. They build new production facilities, invest in more efficient equipment, implement new technologies, market new and better products, oversee what kinds of economic resources will be engaged in what kinds of productive activities, and serve as the main sources of jobs and income. So crucial is the economic role of business firms that the effectiveness with which they carry out their activities becomes a key determinant of society's economic well-being. Consequently, by focusing analytical attention upon *the economics of the firm*—its internal economic decisions, its behavior in the marketplace, and its responsiveness to consumer demand—it is possible to cut directly into the workings of a market-driven economy.

The demand side of a market reflects the intensity with which buyers want and are willing to pay for the item in question. This intensity, which can be weak or strong or anywhere in between, can be represented graphically as a curve showing the various quantities which buyers are willing to purchase at each of various possible prices, all other things being equal. Since buyers typically are willing to purchase less at higher prices than at lower prices, the relationship between price and quantity demanded is an inverse one (which makes *the demand curve* a downsloping line). Events such as rising incomes, changes in the prices of substitute products, and shifts in preferences and lifestyles can and do shift the shape and position of the demand curve, thereby creating a revised level of demand intensity (either higher or lower).

The supply side of a market depicts the extent to which sellers are willing and able to make supplies of a good or service available. Although many factors can enter into how much suppliers are willing to offer for sale at any given moment of time, supply conditions are usually such that sellers are inclined to produce more of a good or service at higher prices than at lower prices. In other words, the economic relationship between price and quantity supplied tends to produce an upward-sloping supply curve. The reason for this is that, other things being equal, sellers will find it more profitable to intensify their production efforts when price is higher as compared to when price is lower.

The interaction of demand and supply determines the going market price and the quantity that changes hands. Only at the price where the quantity demanded equals the quantity supplied will the market be cleared. At prices above the equilibrium price-quantity combination, surplus conditions will emerge, causing downward price movements. At prices below the equilibrium level, shortage conditions will pull the going price upward.

In the chapters that follow, we shall analyze the microeconomic environment in detail, looking first at the demand side of the marketplace and then at the supply side. By the time you finish Chapter 18, you will have a strong grip on how markets function, how a market-driven economy works, and the economic principles that govern business behavior in the marketplace.

QUESTIONS FOR DISCUSSION

1. What is a market? What is the difference between a market and a market segment?
2. What criteria determine whether a market should be viewed as essentially being local, regional, national, or international?
3. George J. Stigler has remarked [*Memoirs of an Unregulated Economist* (New York: Basic Books, 1988)], "If transactions costs were zero there would be no lawyers." What are transactions costs? How do they relate to many of the activities of lawyers? What do you think Stigler means by his statement?
4. Try to define and identify the market for each of the following products in terms of (1) market scope (local, regional, national, international), (2) the characteristics of the buyers that make up the demand side of the market, (3) whether the demand side is comprised of several distinctive market segments, and (4) any other relevant and identifiable market characteristics:
   (a) Coca-Cola.
   (b) Textbooks in economics.
   (c) Pro football.
   (d) No-return, throwaway glass containers.
   (e) Personal computers.
   (f) Drycleaning services.
5. How would you characterize the strategy of
   (a) McDonald's in the hamburger and fast-food service market?
   (b) *Playboy* in the market for sexy magazines?
   (c) Delta Airlines in the market for airline travel?
6. Why does the concept of a single-product, owner-managed enterprise have questionable validity for large corporations?

7. Explain what is meant by the following terms:
   (a) Strategy.
   (b) A demand curve.
   (c) A supply curve.
   (d) A market economic system.
   (e) An increase in demand.
   (f) A decrease in supply.

8. Explain why price moves toward the level at which the quantity demanded equals the quantity supplied.

9. What is the difference between a change in demand and a change in the quantity demanded? Illustrate graphically.

10. What is the difference between an increase in supply and an increase in the quantity supplied?

Chapter 3

Buyer Demand:
THE CARDINAL UTILITY MODEL

In modern societies the demand for goods and services tends to be characterized by two important features: (1) diversity and (2) insatiability. Consumer wants are diverse in the sense that satisfying the biological, psychological, and cultural desires of millions of people requires an immense volume and variety of goods and services. Individual tastes vary, as do individual circumstances regarding age, marital and family status, social status, income, life-style, and so on—all of which give rise to the need for a diverse, ever-changing mix of goods and services to meet consumer preferences. Consumer wants are insatiable in the sense that scarcely anyone is without a "want list." No sooner are some wants fulfilled than new ones emerge to take their place. Most people find it easy to step up their purchases of more elaborate creature comforts and upgrade their way of life when their income permits. In addition, new wants are regularly created by technological research and entrepreneurial efforts aimed at producing *new* goods and services which consumers will find handy or desirable.

In a market economy how urgently consumers desire various products and services and how able they are to back up their desires with purchasing power governs the process of what and how much to produce. Unless business firms synchronize their production efforts to match the purchasing behavior of consumers (the power of advertising notwithstanding), they face the penalty of unacceptable sales and profits. *No firm, no matter how big or how "powerful," can survive producing something consumers do not want or will not buy.*[1]

It is of the essence, therefore, that a firm understand consumer behavior and the principles of consumer demand. In this chapter we shall explore the hows and whys of consumer purchases, focusing upon the behavior of con-

---

[1] The special genius of a capitalistically oriented economic system is its power to furnish consumers with whatever goods and services they want and in whatever amounts they are willing to buy—subject *only* to the constraint that consumers be willing to pay a price high enough to make furnishing the item profitable. Proof for this assertion is readily obtained from an attempt to compile a list of products which are technologically feasible to produce and which consumers truly want and are willing to pay a profitable price for, but which are not available to those who have the money to buy them. It is a safe wager that you (or anyone else) will come up with a *very* short list of such items, and even the severest critics of the profit-oriented capitalistic system would have to acknowledge the consumer benefit of this accomplishment.

sumers in trying to maximize the satisfaction received from their incomes and upon how the demand side of the marketplace works.

THE CONCEPT OF UTILITY

Economists first began to analyze consumer behavior over a century ago when it was fashionable in psychological circles to assert that much of human behavior could be explained by people's desire to realize as much "pleasure" and to avoid as much "pain" as possible. The pleasure-pain doctrine was quickly borrowed by economists and applied to the sphere of consumer expenditures in what became the first systematic theory of motivated consumer behavior; the basic economic thesis was that rational consumers would manage their purchases of goods and services so as to realize the greatest possible amount of overall total "satisfaction." Economists labeled the want-satisfying power of goods and services as **utility**.

The concept of utility refers to the pleasure or satisfaction associated with having, using, consuming, or benefiting from goods or services. The utility inherent in a good or service derives from whatever qualities it has that gives it want-satisfying capabilities. The sources and causes of utility are legion: better health, esthetic beauty or design, ease of use, flavor and taste, durability, convenience, luxury, comfort, a sense of individuality, pleasure, prestige, status, pride, security, ego gratification, and power—to mention the most obvious. Hence, utility has both objective and subjective features and, most particularly, utility is a matter of individual taste, preference, perception, personality makeup, and state of mind.

As a consequence, the utility that a good possesses or is perceived to possess is in the mind of the beholder, not absolute. In the first place, no two people necessarily will view a good as having the same degree of want-satisfying powers—one person may derive great utility from smoking cigarettes while someone else finds them distasteful; Cadillacs may be important status symbols to some people (and hence have great utility), yet have little or no appeal to other people. Different people buy the same product for quite different uses and motivations. Peanuts, for instance, are bought by some people to serve at cocktail parties, by others to make peanut brittle, and by some to feed to squirrels, with potentially different utilities to each buyer in each case. Moreover, the utility of a good can vary from time to time, or place to place. Higher gasoline prices modify the utility people place on small cars. Wool clothing does not have the same utility or want-satisfying powers for people living in short-winter climates as for those living in long-winter climates. But irrespective of the wide variations that different persons may place on the utility of a good or service, *the utility concept provides a vehicle for comparing the amounts of satisfaction received from different consumption rates of different goods and services.*

It is, of course, doubtful that the intensity of satisfaction one gains from an item can be represented precisely in **cardinal rankings**, whereby numerical values (such as 14, 84.9 or − 115) are assigned to represent utility. One may say that "broiled lobster is my favorite food" or "I enjoy broiled lobster more than any other seafood or meat"; but if asked "how much do you enjoy broiled lobster?" one can scarcely reply "about 17" and expect to convey understanding. The subjective nature of the utility concept is, however, susceptible to **ordinal ranking** measures. In ordinal preference patterns, one only has to be able to rank alternatives—from highest to lowest, best to worst, or

BASIC CONCEPT
A good or service has *utility* if it has want-satisfying capability.

The utility that a good or service possesses is a matter of each individual's tastes and perceptions—the same item has different utility to different consumers.

Although the utility of a good or service cannot be measured in precise numerical terms, we can learn some of the principles of buyer demand by *assuming* that utility is quantifiable.

most satisfying to least satisfying; no attempt is made to quantify the *amount* by which one alternative is better (or worse) than others.

Despite the fact that utility is not subject to precise quantification, it is still analytically useful to *assume* that utility can be represented by cardinal numbers. Doing so makes it easier to illuminate several important aspects of consumer behavior. We shall examine the cardinal utility approach to consumer demand in this chapter and then turn to the ordinal utility approach in Chapter 4.

TOTAL UTILITY FUNCTIONS

For illustrative purposes, assume that we can designate the amount of utility by a unit of measure called a *util*. This mythical unit can be viewed as representing some arbitrary amount of satisfaction, and as such it is simply a fictional device for expressing utility in quantitative or cardinal terms.

The **total utility** which a consumer gains from a good or service may be defined as the *entire* amount of satisfaction obtained from a given amount of the item per period of time. A **total utility function** thus reflects the quantitative relationship between the satisfaction yielded by a product and its rate of consumption.[2] Total utility functions may be described in tabular form, with graphs, or with equations. Consider Table 3-1, which uses hypothetical data to illustrate the various amounts of total utility that an individual might obtain from alternative quantities of good X per period of time. As can be seen from columns 1 and 2, the more of good X consumed by the individual per period of

BASIC CONCEPT
Total utility refers to the total amount of satisfaction associated with consuming a given quantity of a good or service per period of time.

TABLE 3-1   RELATIONSHIPS AMONG TOTAL UTILITY, MARGINAL UTILITY, AND THE RATES OF CONSUMPTION OF GOOD X (HYPOTHETICAL DATA FOR A HYPOTHETICAL PERSON)

Units of Good X Consumed per Period of Time	Total Utility (utils)	Marginal Utility (utils)
0	0	
		15
1	15	
		13
2	28	
		11
3	39	
		9
4	48	
		7
5	55	
		5
6	60	
		3
7	63	
		1
8	64	
		−1
9	63	
		−3
10	60	

---

[2] The word *function* here is nothing more than a shorthand way of referring to the way in which some factors (the independent variables) affect another factor (the dependent variable). In terms of utility functions, this literally means that the total utility obtained from a good or service varies with the amount of it consumed during some specified period of time, in which case total utility is the dependent variable and the quantity consumed is the independent variable.

time, the greater is his or her total utility (or total satisfaction) measured in utils, up to a consumption rate of 8 units of X. At 8 units, total utility is at its maximum value of 64 utils of satisfaction. This point is called the *saturation rate* because the consumer cannot derive any greater satisfaction from consuming more of good X per period of time. Theoretically, at this juncture, if the consumption rate was increased to 9 or 10 units, total utility would decline, perhaps because such a consumption rate would be a nuisance (having TV sets in each room of a nine-room house) or physically debilitating (drinking nine cups of coffee a day). The point here is that while a consumer's wants in general may be unlimited or insatiable, his or her wants for specific goods or services can be totally fulfilled.

Total utility increases as the consumption rate increases up to the saturation point; at the point of saturation, total utility is maximum.

A total utility curve corresponding to the information in Table 3-1 is displayed in Figure 3-1(a). Observe that it rises at a slower and slower rate as the consumption rate approaches 8 units of X, reaching a peak at 8 units (the saturation rate) and then declining. The shape of the *TU* curve implies that the more of a specific product a consumer obtains, the less anxious he will be to acquire even more because the additional units yield progressively smaller amounts of *extra* satisfaction. Eventually, the amounts of extra satisfaction diminish to zero, becoming negative thereafter.

Each such total utility function can also be expressed mathematically by an equation relating total utility to the rate of consumption. It so happens that the total utility function shown in Table 3-1 and in Figure 3-1(a) has the equation

$$TU = 16X - X^2,$$

where *TU* represents total utility in utils and *X* represents the amount of the

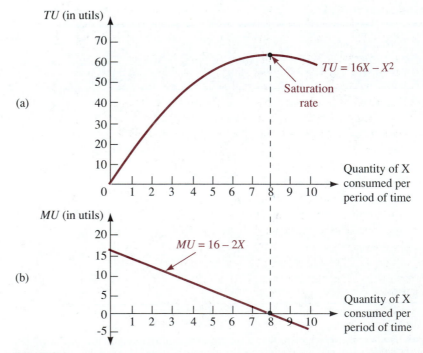

Figure 3-1
Total and marginal utility functions for a good whose total utility increases at a decreasing rate

item consumed per unit of time. Hence, if the consumption rate is 5 units of X, then

$$TU = 16(5) - (5)^2 = 80 - 25 = 55 \text{ utils.}$$

Observe that the value of 55 utils corresponds exactly to the value for total utility in Table 3-1 when the rate of consumption is 5 units and, likewise, to the value of total utility in Figure 3-1(a) at $X = 5$ units. The use of equations to represent total utility functions allows easy calculation of total utility for any consumption rate (X).

THE CONCEPT OF MARGINAL UTILITY

Marginal utility may be defined as the change in total utility resulting from a 1-unit change in the consumption of a good or service per period of time. In the case of an increase in consumption, marginal utility refers to the *extra satisfaction* obtained from the *extra* unit of consumption per period of time. In the case of a decline in consumption, marginal utility refers to the amount of the *decline* in total utility associated with the *decline* in the consumption rate. From Table 3-1 it can be seen that when the consumption rate for good X increases from 1 to 2 units, total utility rises from 15 utils to 28 utils. Thus, the marginal utility of the second unit of X is 13 utils. In like manner the remaining values for marginal utility may be computed.

During any relatively short period of time (wherein all other relevant factors can be assumed not to change), if a consumer increases his or her consumption rate of a good or service beyond some point, the marginal utility (or extra satisfaction) which is obtained from successive units becomes smaller and smaller. This phenomenon is known as the *principle of diminishing marginal utility*, and it is held to apply to virtually all individuals for virtually all goods and services. (Can you think of any exceptions?) The values for marginal utility in Table 3-1 begin to diminish at the outset so that, in the example given, the principle of diminishing marginal utility becomes operative immediately. Each *additional* unit of X consumed per period of time gives less *extra* utility than the previous unit, thereby causing total utility to increase more slowly as the consumption rate rises. The total utility corresponding to any consumption rate can be found from the marginal utility values by calculating the cumulative marginal utility values to that point. Thus, from Table 3-1 the total utility for a consumption rate of 3 units of X equals the marginal utility of the first unit (15 utils) plus the marginal utility of the second unit (13 utils) plus the marginal utility of the third (11 utils) for a total utility of 39 utils.

The marginal utility function corresponding to the previously described total utility function can be illustrated graphically by plotting the marginal utility values given in Table 3-1. The graph of the marginal utility curve is presented in Figure 3-1(b). In plotting the values for marginal utility from Table 3-1, it is important to note that they are plotted halfway between the two values for total utility from which they were derived. This is as it should be because the marginal utility values determined in this fashion should be representative of the *range* of consumption from which they were derived, and this is at the midpoint of that range. For the example given, the marginal utility function decreases throughout and reaches zero at the same consumption rate at which the total utility function is at its maximum height.

Actually, *there is a very precise mathematical relationship between total utility functions and marginal utility functions.* We shall have so frequent

BASIC CONCEPT
Marginal utility refers to the additional amount of satisfaction obtained from an additional amount of consumption per period of time.

PRINCIPLE
At some point, the marginal utility (or extra satisfaction) obtained from consuming progressively larger quantities per period of time will start to decline; this point is called the point of diminishing marginal returns.

Once the point of diminishing marginal returns is reached, each additional unit consumed yields less added utility than the previous unit.

occasion to use these mathematical relationships, not only with reference to utility but also with reference to revenue, production, cost, and other magnitudes, that it is advantageous to master them at this point.

Consider again the total utility function described earlier:

$$TU = 16X - X^2.$$

Using this expression, we can easily obtain the value of TU at any consumption rate of good X by substituting the units consumed of X into the expression and evaluating the right-hand side of the equation.

However, suppose the consumption rate of good X rises from some value X to some value $X + \Delta X$, where ΔX designates an arbitrary increase of any size. We know that total utility must necessarily *change*. Let us symbolize the change that occurs in total utility by ΔTU. Rewriting the total utility function to incorporate the effect of the increase in X to $X + \Delta X$, we have

$$TU + \Delta TU = 16(X + \Delta X) - (X + \Delta X)^2,$$
$$TU + \Delta TU = 16X + 16\,\Delta X - (X^2 + 2X\Delta X + \Delta X^2),$$
$$TU + \Delta TU = 16X + 16\,\Delta X - X^2 - 2X\Delta X - \Delta X^2.$$

The last of the preceding expressions defines the new level of total utility corresponding to a consumption rate of $X + \Delta X$ units. But our major concern is really with the *change* in total utility (ΔTU) associated with the *change* (ΔX) in the consumption rate of good X. We can obtain an expression for determining just the *change* in TU by subtracting TU from the left-hand side of the equation and its equivalent of $(16X - X^2)$ from the right-hand side. This operation yields

$$
\begin{aligned}
TU + \Delta TU &= & 16X + 16\Delta X - X^2 - 2X\Delta X - \Delta X^2 \\
- TU &= & -16X \qquad\qquad + X^2 \\
\hline
\Delta TU &= & 16\Delta X \qquad\qquad - 2X\Delta X - \Delta X^2.
\end{aligned}
$$

We are now in a position to determine the additional utility per additional unit of good X by dividing both sides of the expression for ΔTU by ΔX:

$$\frac{\Delta TU}{\Delta X} = \frac{16\Delta X - 2X\Delta X - \Delta X^2}{\Delta X} = 16 - 2X - \Delta X.$$

The latter equation expresses the change in total utility per unit change in the consumption rate.[3]

Our interest lies yet beyond, however. Up to now all we have done is perform algebraic operations on our original expression of $TU = 16X - X^2$. Something a little different is called for at this point. In particular, we need to know what happens to $\Delta TU/\Delta X$ as the changes in ΔX become smaller and smaller and eventually become very close to zero. The mathematical way of pursuing this question is to determine the "limit" toward which the value of $\Delta TU/\Delta X$ moves as ΔX approaches zero; this limit is symbolized by dTU/dX.[4] Hence, if

$$\frac{\Delta TU}{\Delta X} = 16 - 2X - \Delta X,$$

---

[3] More specifically, this equation defines *average marginal utility* or the average change in total utility per unit change in the consumption rate. For example, if total utility increases by 50 utils when the consumption level rises by 10 units, then $\Delta TU/\Delta X = 50$ utils/10 units = 5 utils per unit of consumption. In other words, the average change in total utility (or average marginal utility) is 5 utils for each of the 10 additional units consumed. The concept of average marginal utility is useful whenever the available data do not permit a unit-by-unit calculation of marginal utility.

[4] This is much like asking what happens to the value of y in the expression $y = (x + 1)/x$ as the value of x approaches infinity.

it follows that as ΔX becomes infinitesimally small (approaches zero):

$$\frac{dTU}{dX} = 16 - 2X.$$

In terms of economics, the expression $dTU/dX = 16 - 2X$ is the equation for the marginal utility function corresponding to the total utility function $TU = 16X - X^2$. The symbol dTU/dX should be read as the *rate of change in total utility as the consumption rate changes*, which, in turn, is a more rigorous and accurate definition of marginal utility. In terms of differential calculus, marginal utility is "the first derivative of the total utility function." Consequently, if total utility is given by the expression

$$TU = 16X - X^2,$$

marginal utility (MU) will be given by the function

$$MU = \frac{dTU}{dX} = 16 - 2X,$$

where $16 - 2X$ is the first derivative of the expression $16X - X^2$. Thus, for each and every total utility function, there is a corresponding marginal utility function. Fortunately, though, as the following examples show, there is a method for determining the marginal utility function that shortcuts the preceding laborious derivation. (The purpose of the lengthy derivation was to illustrate the logic of determining rates of change in variables for those readers not familiar with elementary differential calculus.)

The *general* procedures for finding the marginal function for any variable from the total function for that variable may be illustrated as follows. If the total function is given by

$$T = aX^n,$$

where a and n are arbitrary constants and X is any variable, then the marginal function is

$$M = \frac{dT}{dX} = naX^{n-1}.$$

> **In mathematical terms, the marginal utility function is the first derivative of the total utility function.**

> **The mathematical relationships between total functions and marginal functions are fundamental to microeconomic analysis; we will use these relationships repeatedly in the pages and chapters ahead.**

EXAMPLE 1

If $T = 16X^3$, then

$$M = \frac{dT}{dX} = 3 \cdot 16 \cdot X^{3-1} = 48X^2.$$

EXAMPLE 2

If $T = 160 + 7X + 4X^2 - 2X^3$, then our general rule is applied to *each term* of the expression. Algebraically, the total function may be understood to be $T = 160X^0 + 7X^1 + 4X^2 - 2X^3$. Hence,

$$M = \frac{dT}{dX} = 0 \cdot 160X^{0-1} + 1 \cdot 7X^{1-1} + 2 \cdot 4X^{2-1} - 3 \cdot 2X^{3-1}$$

$$= \frac{dT}{dX} = 0 \cdot 160X^{-1} + 1 \cdot 7X^0 + 2 \cdot 4X^1 - 3 \cdot 2X^2$$

$$= \frac{dT}{dX} = 0 + 7 + 8X - 6X^2.$$

Note that the derivative (or rate of change) of the constant term in the total function turns out to be zero; this is as it should be since the rate of change in a value that is constant is necessarily zero.

EXAMPLE 3

Suppose that the total function is expressed in the form of a general algebraic equation such as $T = a + bX + cX^2$, where a, b, and c are constants. Since the total function T may be rewritten as $T = aX^0 + bX^1 + cX^2$, the corresponding marginal function M is

$$M = \frac{dT}{dX} = 0 \cdot aX^{-1} + 1 \cdot bX^0 + 2 \cdot cX^1,$$

which simplifies to

$$M = b + 2cX.$$

For readers who feel uncomfortable with the mechanics of derivatives, a number of problems and answers are provided at the end of this chapter to strengthen your ability to use this essential aspect of mathematical economics.

To summarize our brief excursion into the mathematical aspects of economic relationships, *the derivative of a function is the rate of change of the dependent variable as the value of the independent variable changes*; the derivative of a total function *defines* the marginal function. As applied to utility functions, *marginal utility* is the rate of change in total utility as the rate of consumption of an item changes and is calculated mathematically by finding the first derivative of the total utility function.

To return to our original example, we have shown that if $TU = 16X - X^2$, then $MU = 16 - 2X$. Knowing the expression for MU allows the value of MU to be calculated easily at any value of X. Moreover, these results may be related to both Table 3-1 and Figure 3-1. For instance, the equation of the MU function is the exact equation which describes the graph of the marginal utility function in Figure 3-1(b). Furthermore, we can see from Table 3-1 that the value for MU between 1 and 2 units of X is 13 units (technically, at $X = 1\frac{1}{2}$, $MU = 13$ utils); if we let X assume a value of 1.5 in the equation $MU = 16 - 2X$, we get a value of 13 utils for MU, which corresponds exactly to the value in Table 3-1.

BASIC CONCEPT
The value of marginal utility at any point along the total utility function is always equal to the *slope* of the total utility function at that point.

The most significant relationship between the TU and MU functions concerns the shape of the total utility function. Defining MU as the rate of change in total utility as the rate of consumption changes is equivalent to saying that *the value for marginal utility at a particular consumption rate equals the slope of the total utility function at that consumption rate*. In other words, viewed geometrically, the derivative of the total utility function is the slope of the total utility function at any X value. When we say that marginal utility is 13 utils at a consumption of 1.5 units of X, we also are saying that at $X = 1.5$ total utility is increasing at a rate of 13 utils per unit of extra consumption, which is, by definition, the slope of the total utility function at the point where $X = 1.5$ units. When total utility is at its highest point, the slope of the TU curve is zero (because the tangent line drawn to the TU function at its highest point is horizontal). Since marginal utility, by definition, has a value equal to the slope of the total utility function, the value of MU corresponding to the peak of the TU function is also zero.

Using these ideas, the total utility function in Figure 3-1(a) may be said to *increase at a decreasing rate*. Why? Because as the consumption rate in-

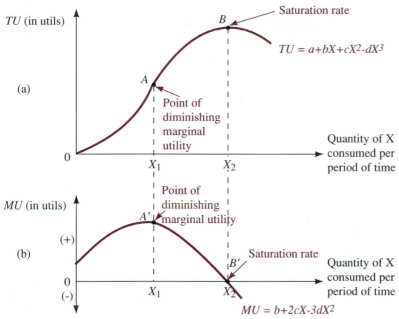

Figure 3-2
Generalized total and marginal utility functions for phases of increasing and decreasing returns as the rate of consumption rises

creases, the *TU* function rises more slowly [i.e., its slope gets flatter (smaller)]. Consequently, the related values for *MU* must be decreasing since these values, by definition, are equal to the slope of the *TU* function. Figure 3-1(b) illustrates just such a pattern of change in the values for marginal utility.

Alternative shapes for the *TU* and *MU* functions are shown in Figure 3-2. In this case, *TU increases at an increasing rate* up to a consumption rate of X_1 units. From X_1 to X_2 units, *TU increases at a decreasing rate*. Point *A* on the *TU* curve is the point of diminishing marginal utility and corresponds to the same consumption rate as point *A'* on the *MU* curve. Point *B* on the *TU* curve defines the saturation rate as does point *B'* on the *MU* graph. Although there are many forms of equations which could represent a total utility function of this shape, the simplest is the general equation for a cubic function:

$$TU = a + bX + cX^2 - dX^3,$$

where *X* represents the units consumed; *a*, *b*, and *c* are positive constants; and *d* is a negative constant. Using the mathematical concepts previously developed, the corresponding general equation for marginal utility is

$$MU = \frac{dTU}{dX} = b + 2cX - 3dX^2.$$

(Can you think of products or situations in which an individual's *TU* and *MU* functions might assume the shapes shown in Figure 3-2?)

While the *TU* functions in Figures 3-1 and 3-2 show total utility as being zero when the consumption rate is zero, this need not be the case; in fact, it may not even be typical. Negative amounts of utility (disutility) may arise from having none of an item, as is witnessed by the dismay of individuals who find themselves without aspirin when a headache appears or who run out of gas on a lonely road. In such cases the total utility function may start below the origin

If the *TU* function is rising at a steeper and steeper rate as consumption increases, then the related values for *MU* are increasing; if the *TU* function is becoming flatter as consumption increases, then the values for *MU* are declining. The peak of the *TU* curve defines the value where *MU* equals 0.

MATHEMATICAL CAPSULE 1

DETERMINING THE POINT OF DIMINISHING MARGINAL UTILITY AND THE SATURATION RATE: AN APPLICATION OF THE MATHEMATICAL CONCEPTS OF MAXIMA AND MINIMA

A maximum point on a curve is a point that is higher than its neighboring point to either side such that the curve is concave downward; a minimum point on a curve is a point that is lower than its neighboring points such that the curve is concave upward.

All maximum and minimum values of a function $y = f(x)$ occur where $dy/dx = 0$, since the first derivative of a function is indicative of its rate of change or slope. This characteristic is frequently termed the *first-order condition*.

If, at the value of x at which $dy/dx = 0$ the second derivative is negative, $d^2y/dx^2 < 0$, that value of x defines a maximum value for y, where $y = f(x)$. If at the value of x at which $dy/dx = 0$ the second derivative is positive, $d^2y/dx^2 > 0$, that value of x defines a minimum value for function $y =$ $f(x)$. This requirement for distinguishing between maximum and minimum values is called the *second-order condition*.

Consider the total utility function $TU = 130X - 2.5X^2$, plotted in the accompanying graph. Suppose that we wish to determine the value of X at which TU is maximum— the saturation rate. The saturation rate corresponds exactly to that quantity consumed at which the slope of the total utility function is zero and where $MU = 0$. If $TU = 130X - 2.5X^2$, then $MU = dTU/dx = 130 - 5X$. Setting the marginal utility function equal to zero, we get

$$130 - 5X = 0.$$

Solving for the value of X which satisfies the equation, we find $X = 26$ units. This, then, is the consumption rate where TU is maximum.

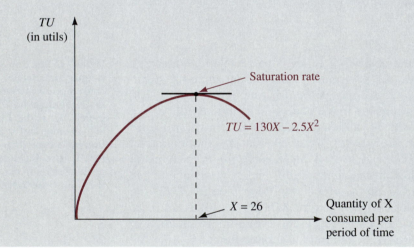

TU (in utils)

Saturation rate

$TU = 130X - 2.5X^2$

$X = 26$

Quantity of X consumed per period of time

and not reach zero utility until the consumption of the item is above the zero rate. Total utility functions for a nuisance or unwanted item may originate at a positive value and *decrease* rapidly as more of the item comes into the possession of the consumer.

UTILITY FUNCTIONS FOR RELATED PRODUCTS

In many instances the utility attached to one product is related to individuals' consumption of another product. The utility derived from eating cornflakes is partially dependent on the availability of milk or cream; the satisfaction from one's VCR is related to the quantity and quality of available video rentals; the enjoyment from one's binoculars is related to the frequency with

Suppose that we wish to find the consumption rate of X at which diminishing MU is encountered for the following total utility function:

$$TU = 18X + 7X^2 - \tfrac{1}{3}X^3.$$

Diminishing MU begins at the point where the MU function is at its maximum value.

The value of X at which the slope of the MU function is zero ($dMU/dx = d^2TU/dX^2 = 0$) can be calculated as follows:

$$MU = \frac{dTU}{dX} = 18 + 14X - X^2$$

$$\frac{dMU}{dX} = \frac{d^2TU}{dX^2} = 14 - 2X.$$

Setting dMU/dX equal to zero and solving for X, we obtain X = 7, the consumption rate at which diminishing MU sets in.

EXERCISE

1. Determine the saturation rate and the point of diminishing marginal utility for each of the following *TU* functions.
   (a) $TU = 36X - X^2$.
   (b) $TU = 10X + 9X^2 - X^3$.

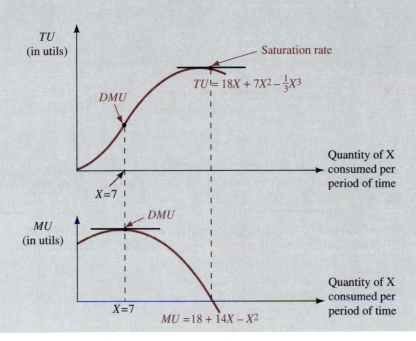

which one goes to spectator events. Thus, while total utility is a function of the quantities of each product consumed per period of time, it need not be simply the sum of the utilities gained separately from each good or service.

When the satisfaction derived from one item hinges in part upon the amounts consumed of other items, the more appropriate concept of utility is that of a ***total utility surface*** relating total utility to the ***joint rates*** of consumption of all goods simultaneously. This notion is illustrated graphically for two products, X and Y, in Figure 3-3. The consumption rates for X and Y define a horizontal plane with total utility measured as a vertical distance above it. The total utility surface is *OIKB*. If Y_1 units of product Y are consumed per unit of time along with X_1 units of product X, total utility is DD'; if the respective onsumption rates are Y_2 and X_1 per period of time, total utility is GG'. The

Often, the utility derived from one item is attached to simultaneous consumption of another item.

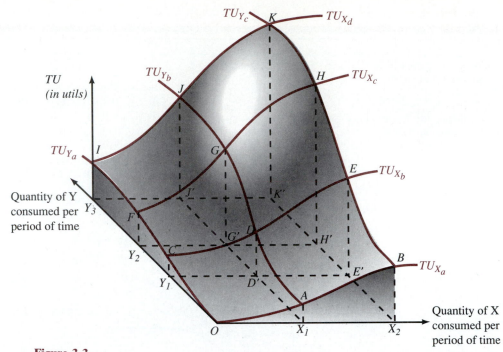

Figure 3-3
Total utility surface for a pair of products characterized by both increasing and decreasing marginal utility

total utility surface pictured in Figure 3-3 thus indicates how total utility changes as the rate of consumption of one product changes, given the rate of consumption of the other. The shape of the total utility surface depends upon the nature of the interrelationship among the products. In Figure 3-3, total utility is shown as increasing at an increasing rate for a few units before diminishing marginal utility sets in, thereby making the total utility surface concave upward for this range of consumption; the surface becomes concave downward as diminishing marginal utility is realized. If diminishing marginal utility occurred from the outset for both X and Y, the total utility surface would be concave downward throughout.

CONSUMER BEHAVIOR IN THE MARKETPLACE

PRINCIPLE
A buyer will elect to purchase whatever combination of goods and services is deemed to maximize total utility, given the amount he or she has available to spend.

Once a consumer's utility functions are known or ascertainable, it is possible to make judgments about which goods and services he or she will buy or not buy in the marketplace. Economists assume that *rational consumers attempt to arrange their purchases so as to maximize the total satisfaction that they can get from their money incomes.* After all, buyers have no reason to try deliberately to get less than the full obtainable satisfaction from the purchasing power they have available. In reality, of course, the assumption of maximizing utility may not be literally true for all consumers in each and every situation. Imperfect information about alternative purchases and about prices tends to hinder consumer attempts at utility maximization, and an exhaustive search for better information may entail greater transaction cost than it is worth. In addition, impulse buying and force of habit work against consumers actually identifying and purchasing the utility-maximizing combination of goods and services.

MATHEMATICAL CAPSULE 2

DETERMINING MARGINAL UTILITY FOR MULTIPRODUCT TOTAL UTILITY FUNCTIONS

When the satisfaction derived from one product is related to the amounts consumed of other products, the consumer's total utility function is of the form

$$TU = f(X_a, X_b, \ldots, X_n),$$

where $X_a, X_b, \ldots, X_n$ represent the array of products available. Given such multiproduct TU functions, the question becomes what is the effect of a change in the consumption rate of one product upon TU, when the consumption rates of other products do not change. The form of the derivative which corresponds to this interest is called the *partial derivative*.

Suppose that the total utility function for two products X and Y is

$$TU = 7X + 4Y - 0.2X^2 - 0.3Y^2 - XY.$$

We find the impact of a change in the rate of consumption of X upon TU when the consumption of Y is kept fixed by *treating Y as a constant* and differentiating the total utility function with respect to X—this gives the partial derivative of TU with respect to X and is denoted by $\partial TU/\partial X$. Accordingly, we get

$$\frac{\partial TU}{\partial X} = 7 - 0.4X - Y,$$

which may be interpreted to represent *the rate of change in TU as the rate of consumption of X changes, the rate of consumption of Y being held constant.* This then is the expression for the marginal utility of product X. Similarly, the partial derivative of TU with respect to Y is

$$\frac{\partial TU}{\partial Y} = 4 - 0.6Y - X,$$

and it represents the expression for the marginal utility of Y.

EXERCISES

1. Determine the relevant marginal utility functions for each of the following total utility functions.
   (a) $TU = 15X^2Y^2 - X^3Y^2$.
   (b) $TU = 20X + 40Y - 3X^2 - Y^2$.
   (c) $TU = 30XY + 10XZ - 3XYZ - 10Z$.
   (d) $TU = 5.4X^{1/2} Y^{1/3}$.

2. Determine the values for MU_x and MU_y at $X = 5$ and $Y = 3$ in each of the following total utility functions.
   (a) $TU = 16X - X^2 + 10Y - XY$.
   (b) $TU = 33X + 2X^2 - X^3 + 4Y - XY^2$.
   (c) $TU = 16X^2 + 15XY + 17Y^2 - 4X^2 Y^2$.

Nonetheless, *the assumption that consumers behave as if they seek to maximize total utility is a justifiable and reasonable abstraction for most consumers most of the time.*

Confronted with a limited number of dollars to spend, the price tags on every item, thousands of items to choose among, and imperfect knowledge as to all alternatives, a consumer's task of trying to get the most for his or her money is indeed daunting. Obviously, consumers cannot buy everything they want because each purchase exhausts a portion of their available money incomes. They are forced to compromise and decide what and how much of each of the many items within their budgetary constraints best suit their needs and tastes. A word about the income constraint facing consumers is in order. *As used here, a consumer's money income refers to the total purchasing power available in a given time period;* this specifically includes (1) current income from whatever source, (2) any savings the consumer has accumulated from past income periods and is willing to spend now, (3) any sums the consumer wishes and is able to borrow, and (4) any other wealth the consumer may wish to allocate to current consumption.

We shall use the term *money income* as shorthand for total funds available for expenditure.

SOME SIMPLIFYING ASSUMPTIONS

To keep the ensuing analysis of consumer behavior manageable, the following assumptions will be made:

1. Each consumer has full knowledge of all information pertinent to his or her expenditure decision—a definitive set of tastes and prefer-

ences, knowledge of the goods and services available, their capacity to satisfy wants, money income, and the prices at which specific products can be bought.

2. The consumer's preference pattern for products is one of diminishing marginal utility for each.[5]

3. The utility function for each product is independent of the rate of consumption of other products.

None of these assumptions does violence to the principles of consumer behavior we wish to derive, and they make the exposition simpler.

THE UTILITY-MAXIMIZING SEARCH

For the time being, suppose that we restrict ourselves to the case of a consumer who is trying to decide what combination of two goods, X and Y, should be purchased with a weekly income of $40. We shall assume that the price of X remains at $3 per unit and the price of Y remains at $5 per unit no matter how much the consumer buys of X and Y. Table 3-2 summarizes the consumer's preference for the two items, along with the consumer's evaluation of the utility obtained from not spending the money, that is, the *marginal utility of saving*.[6]

How should the consumer allocate a $40 weekly income among buying good X, buying good Y, and saving in order to yield maximum satisfaction? To answer this question, let us proceed to ascertain what the consumer should do first. A $40 weekly income allows the consumer to buy some of either X or Y should the consumer decide to do so. If $3 is spent to buy the first unit of X, the consumer receives 54 utils of satisfaction; if $5 is spent to buy the first unit of Y, the consumer receives 75 utils; and if the consumer saves all $40, he or she is well past the saturation rate for money, since the marginal utility for saving a dollar becomes negative when saving exceeds $5. Of these alternatives, the purchase of X is definitely the better bargain, because it gives the consumer 18 utils of satisfaction *per dollar spent,* whereas good Y yields only 15 utils of satisfaction per dollar spent, and saving yields no greater than 9 utils per dollar saved. The proper decision criterion in this instance is neither total nor marginal utility but *marginal utility per dollar of expenditure.* The extra satisfaction received per dollar spent is the best indicator of value received because it combines the factor of satisfaction with the factor of cost, and both factors are requisite for valid comparisons between goods. Since the consumer receives more satisfaction for the money by buying the first unit of X instead of the first unit of Y or instead of saving, the first act should be to exchange $3 for one unit of good X. By the same reasoning, the consumer's second act can be deter-

The correct criterion for deciding to buy or not buy a good or service is the marginal utility received per dollar spent.

---

[5] Actually, this is a more rigorous assumption than need be made. All we need assume is that the marginal utility of one good decreases *relative* to the marginal utilities of other goods as its consumption rate is increased *relative* to the consumption rate of others. Our analysis will be valid in cases where the marginal utility of a good is increasing, as long as it increases by less than proportionally to the marginal utilities of other goods.

[6] The term *saving* is used here to encompass a variety of acts associated with not spending. Consumers may rationally decide not to spend all of their money income during some period of time because (1) they place a high value on saving a portion of their income in order to provide for emergencies, accumulate an estate, or any one of a hundred other reasons; (2) they are unable to find products precisely suited to their tastes and wish to look further before making a purchase; and (3) they wish to postpone spending until some future period so that they may pay cash for the desired items. In any event, the act of not spending (i.e., saving) may bring the consumer satisfaction or utility just as does the act of consuming goods and services.

TABLE 3-2   UTILITY-MAXIMIZING COMBINATION OF GOODS X AND Y OBTAINABLE FROM AN INCOME OF $40

GOOD X (Price = $3)				GOOD Y (Price = $5)				SAVING		
Quantity	TU (utils)	MU (utils)	MU/ Price (utils/$)	Quantity	TU (utils)	MU (utils)	MU/ Price (utils/$)	Number of Dollars Saved	TU (utils)	MU (utils/$1)
0	0			0	0			0	10	
		54	18			75	15			9
1	54			1	75			1	19	
		45	15			60	12			7
2	99			2	135			2	26	
		30	10			40	8			3
3	129			3	175			3	29	
		9	3			25	5			2
4	138			4	200			4	31	
		3	1			15	3			1
5	141			5	215			5	32	
		−3	−1			5	1			0
6	138			6	220			6	32	

mined. The second unit of good X will produce 14 units of satisfaction per dollar spent, as will the first Y; both are superior to saving at this point. Since the consumer has ample funds available for spending ($37 of the original $40), the second and third acts should be to buy the second unit of X and the first unit of Y, leaving the consumer with $29. *At each step the consumer must decide whether the marginal utility of a dollar's worth of spending is greater than the marginal utility of a dollar's worth of saving. If it is, the consumer should buy the good yielding the highest marginal utility per dollar of expenditure. If not, the consumer should save the money.* In the example given, the consumer will maximize total utility by allocating the $40 income so as to purchase 4 units of X and 5 units of Y and to save $3.

No other allocation of the consumer's $40 weekly income will produce as much satisfaction as this one. How do we know? Suppose that our consumer were to buy one less unit of good Y, thereby freeing $5 with which to buy another unit of X and to save an additional $2. This act would reduce total utility. Giving up the fifth unit of Y entails a loss of 15 utils, whereas increasing the purchase rate of X from 4 to 5 units brings 3 utils, and saving two more dollars yields a combined 3 utils, for a total gain of 6 utils from the alternative expenditure of the $5. The consumer would therefore suffer a net loss of 9 utils of satisfaction by transferring dollars out of the purchase of Y and into X and saving. Alternatively, were our consumer to take the $3 saving and apply it to the purchase of the fifth unit of X, he or she would give up 19 utils of satisfaction and acquire only 3 utils of satisfaction, for a net loss in satisfaction of 16 utils. Any act other than buying 4 units of X and 5 units of Y and saving $3 will cause total utility to decline.

Observe carefully the characteristics of the utility-maximizing out-

To maximize utility, a consumer should continue spending as long as the extra satisfaction from a dollar's worth of spending exceeds the extra satisfaction from a dollar's worth of saving; each dollar of additional spending should be allocated to the good or service yielding the greatest extra satisfaction per dollar of cost.

Unless the marginal utilities per dollar spent on the last unit of each and every item purchased are equal, purchases can be rearranged to increase total utility.

come. First, the consumer completely utilizes all available purchasing power—all income is allocated either to the purchase of goods and services or to saving. There are no idle dollars; the dollars that are saved are constructively deployed every bit as much as are the dollars used for purchasing X and Y—since saving money produces utility. Thus, maximization of utility *does not require* that a consumer spend *all* his or her money—saving has utility and serves to further the motives of the consumer. Second, at the utility-maximizing combination the marginal utilities per dollar spent on the last unit of each item purchased are equal. In other words, the consumer has arranged his or her purchases to get an equivalent amount of satisfaction from the last dollar allocated to each item (including saving) bought.

THE CONDITIONS FOR UTILITY MAXIMIZATION

PRINCIPLE
Two conditions are required for a consumer to maximize the total satisfaction received from a given amount of funds available: (1) All funds must be allocated to spending or to saving, and (2) the last dollar spent on each good and service purchased and the last dollar saved must all yield the very same amount of extra satisfaction.

We are now in a position to state the formal conditions for consumer maximization of utility in a multiproduct environment. Two equations suffice:

$$P_a X_a + P_b X_b + P_c X_c + \cdots + P_n X_n + \text{saving} = \text{income,} \qquad (1)$$

$$\frac{MU_{X_a}}{P_a} = \frac{MU_{X_b}}{P_b} = \frac{MU_{X_c}}{P_c} = \cdots = \frac{MU_{X_n}}{P_n} = MU_{\text{saving}}. \qquad (2)$$

Equation (1) says that the sum of the expenditures on each good or service ($X_a, X_b, X_c, \ldots, X_n$) plus saving must be equal to the money income (I) that the consumer has available per period of time. Total expenditures cannot *exceed* the available purchasing power; any income that is not used to buy goods and services necessarily is saved. Thus, all the consumer's money income is accounted for by either spending or saving. Equation (2) says that to maximize total utility the consumer must arrange purchases such that the marginal utilities per dollar of expenditure on the last unit of each item purchased are equal to each other and to the marginal utility of saving an additional dollar.

When the various degrees of satisfaction per dollar of marginal outlays are unequal, total satisfaction may be increased by diminishing expenditures for goods where satisfaction is less and enlarging expenditures for goods where satisfaction is greater. To illustrate, suppose that

$$MU_{X_a} = 42 \text{ utils for the last unit purchased,}$$
$$P_a = \$14 \text{ per unit,}$$
$$MU_{X_b} = 60 \text{ utils for the last unit purchased,}$$
$$P_b = \$12 \text{ per unit, and}$$
$$MU_{\text{saving}} = 4 \text{ utils for each additional dollar saved.}$$

Then,

$$MU_{X_a}/\$ \text{ spent on } X_a = MU_{X_a}/P_a = 42 \text{ utils}/\$14 = 3 \text{ utils}/\$, \quad \text{and}$$
$$MU_{X_b}/\$ \text{ spent on } X_b = MU_{X_b}/P_b = 60 \text{ utils}/\$12 = 5 \text{ utils}/\$.$$

Whenever the last dollars spent on each item purchased do not yield the same amount of added satisfaction, purchases can be reallocated to increase total utility.

The consumer is realizing more satisfaction per dollar spent on X_b than on X_a. Total utility can be increased by transferring dollars out of the purchase of X_a and into the purchase of X_b until $MU_{X_a}/P_a = MU_{X_b}/P_b = MU_{\text{saving}}$. By reducing the expenditure for X_a, the MU of the last unit purchased of X_a would rise (say to 56 utils), thus raising the ratio MU_{X_a}/P_a (to 4 utils per dollar). By increasing the expenditure for X_b, the MU of the last unit purchased would fall (say to 48 utils), thereby lowering the ratio MU_{X_b}/P_b (to 4 utils per dollar). Since X_a costs $14 and X_b costs $12, buying 1 unit less of X_a and 1 unit more of X_b would leave

$2 left over either for the purchase of some other item whose $MU/\$$ of expenditure exceeded 4 utils per dollar or for saving.

Sometimes the indivisibility of units of products can preclude a consumer from *exactly* equating the marginal utilities per dollar spent on the last unit for each and every item. For example, in the preceding case the consumer might find that there are no other goods which could be bought for $2 and receive as much as 4 utils per dollar; saving the entire $2 might reduce the MU of the last dollar saved to 3.8 utils. Then Equation (2) could not be precisely satisfied unless fractional units of X_a and X_b could be bought. Practically speaking, Equation (2) should be interpreted to mean that a consumer seeking maximum utility from a given money income should spend his or her dollars so as to approach *as nearly as possible* the equality of the marginal utilities per dollar spent on the last unit of each good purchased and further to approach as nearly as possible the point at which the marginal utility of spending a dollar equals the marginal utility of saving a dollar.

CARDINAL UTILITY, THE LAW OF DEMAND, AND CONSUMERS' SURPLUS

In addition to providing insight into the concept of rational consumer behavior and the allocation of expenditures among competing goods, the cardinal utility model can be used to verify the law of demand and present the important concept of consumer surplus. It follows from the utility maximizing condition of

$$\frac{MU_{X_a}}{P_{X_a}} = \frac{MU_{X_b}}{P_{X_b}} = \cdots = \frac{MU_{X_n}}{P_{X_n}}$$

that if the price of a product falls, other things being equal, a consumer will be induced to buy more of the product. This is readily demonstrated. Suppose the price of item X_a falls. A decline in the value of P_{X_a} causes the ratio of MU_{X_a}/P_{X_a} to take on a larger value than the other ratios in the utility-maximizing expression ($MU_{X_b}/P_{X_b} \cdots MU_{X_n}/P_{X_n}$).

To restore the utility-maximizing condition, the consumer will find it desirable to increase the quantity purchased of item X_a. Conversely, if the price of an item rises (whether it be P_{X_a} or P_{X_b} or . . . or P_{X_n}), the quantity purchased of that item will tend to fall—all other relevant demand-determining factors remaining equal. This is the basis for the **Law of Demand**, which holds that the price of a product and the quantity purchased of that product vary *inversely* with one another, other things being equal.

It further follows from the utility-maximizing condition of

$$\frac{MU_{X_a}}{P_{X_a}} = \frac{MU_{X_b}}{P_{X_b}} = \cdots = \frac{MU_{X_n}}{P_{X_n}}$$

that there is a common value for all of equilibrium ratios. This common value, often called λ, is referred to as the marginal utility of income.[7]

PRINCIPLE
Whenever the price of an item declines, restoring the utility-maximizing condition entails increasing the quantity purchased of that item.

BASIC CONCEPT
Utility maximization requires that the last dollar spent on each item purchased yield the same amount of extra satisfaction; this common amount of extra satisfaction is designated as the marginal utility of income.

---

[7] The symbol λ (lambda) is mathematical notation for the Lagrangean multiplier, which can be used to formally solve a consumer's utility maximization problem subject to constraints imposed by limited income and fixed market prices. As discussed earlier, utility maximization requires that income be allocated between savings and investment and to the purchase of specific goods so that the last dollar spent on each good and the last dollar saved all yield the same marginal benefit. This common value turns out to be λ, the Lagrangean multiplier. This is further discussed in Mathematical Capsule 3.

A consumer's demand curve for a specific product can be derived explicitly from this utility-maximizing equilibrium condition. The most straight-forward way of demonstrating this is to assume that when the price of one of the goods, say X_a, changes, then the marginal utility of income, λ, remains constant.[8] This permits us to set the first term of the utility-maximizing condition equal to λ as follows:

$$\lambda = \frac{MU_{X_a}}{P_{X_a}}$$

The utility-maximizing condition, combined with the marginal utility of income concept, can be used to derive a consumer's demand curve for a good or service.

Now suppose that the marginal utility function is the same one used earlier in this chapter,

$$MU_X = 16 - 2X_a,$$

and assume that the marginal utility of income is constant at a value of 4, such that

$$\lambda = 4.$$

Substituting the values of MU_X and λ into the expression

$$\lambda = \frac{MU_{X_a}}{P_{X_a}}$$

gives

$$\frac{16 - 2X_a}{P_{X_a}} = 4.$$

Solving for X_a produces the equation

$$X_a = 8 - 2P_{X_a}. \tag{3}$$

This equation represents the consumer's demand function for good X_a and reflects how many units of item X_a the consumer will purchase at alternative prices. For instance, at a price of $3, the consumer will maximize utility by purchasing 2 units; at a price of $2, the utility-maximizing amount is 4 units.

An underlying reason why a consumer's demand curve slopes downward to the right is the consumer's diminishing marginal utility for the item.

Figure 3-4(a) shows the marginal utility curve, and Figure 3-4(b) displays the associated demand curve. It should be clear that *the demand curve slopes downward because of diminishing marginal utility*. The rate at which the demand curve slopes downward depends upon the rate at which MU diminishes and the specific value of the marginal utility of income, λ. Thus, from the perspective of the cardinal utility model, the maximum price buyers are willing to pay declines as more is consumed as long as marginal utility is diminishing.

The Concept of Consumers' Surplus

A point on the demand curve shows the maximum price a buyer will pay for the indicated quantity. For example, at point R in Figure 3-4(b) the buyer will rationally pay at most $3.50 per unit for a quantity of one, receiving marginal utility of 14 utils. Of course, the buyer would be very happy indeed to pay only $.50 for the first unit purchased, but $3.50 is the absolute maximum the buyer is willing and able to pay. Prices are established in markets, and buyers are usually able to purchase whatever quantity they choose at the pre-

---

[8] Alfred Marshall, *Principles of Economics*, 8th ed. (London: MacMillan and Company, 1920).

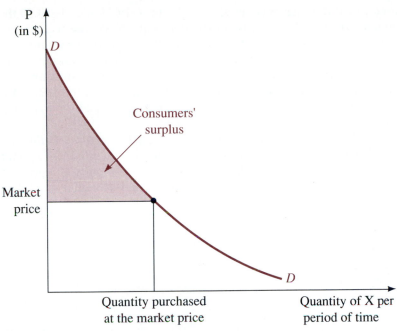

Figure 3-4
Marginal utility, demand, and consumer surplus for linear demand curves

vailing market price. However, since some buyers are typically willing to pay more than the market price for some or all of their purchases, they receive what is called ***consumers' surplus***.

Consumer surplus is defined as the difference between the *actual* dollar amount that buyers end up paying for a specific quantity of a good in a market transaction and the maximum dollar amount that buyers *would have been willing to spend* for that same quantity. If a consumer's demand for item X_a is given by

$$X_a = 8 - 2P_X$$

(which corresponds to Figure 3-4[b]), then the consumer is willing to purchase the following quantities at the indicated prices:

BASIC CONCEPT
Consumers' surplus is the difference between buyers' actual dollar outlays for a specified quantity of a good in a market transaction and the maximum dollar outlays buyers would have been willing to spend for the same quantity.

Market Price	Quantity Demanded
$3.50	1
3.00	2
2.50	3
2.00	4
1.50	5
1.00	6
.50	7

At a market price of $1, the consumer can obtain all 6 units at a total dollar outlay of $6. The buyer benefits from a consumer's surplus of $2.50 on the first

Consumers' surplus represents a potentially sizable monetary gain for buyers and a revenue loss for sellers, who can command no more than the going market price.

unit purchased (the difference between the market price of $1 and the $3.50 the buyer *would have been willing to pay* for the first unit), $2 on the second unit (the difference between the market price of $1 and the $3 the buyer *would have been willing to pay* for the second unit), $1.50 on the third unit, $1 for the fourth unit, and $.50 for the fifth unit—for a total of $7.50. If purchased on a unit-by-unit basis, the buyer would have been willing to spend a total of $13.50 for 6 units; with a market price of $1, the consumer "saves" $7.50 by purchasing all 6 units for $6.

In general, *consumers' surplus is represented by the area below the buyers' demand curve and above the horizontal line designating the market price*. For example, in Figure 3-4(b) buyers would choose 6 units at a price of $1 per unit, and consumers' surplus is the shaded triangle denoted *ABC*. For

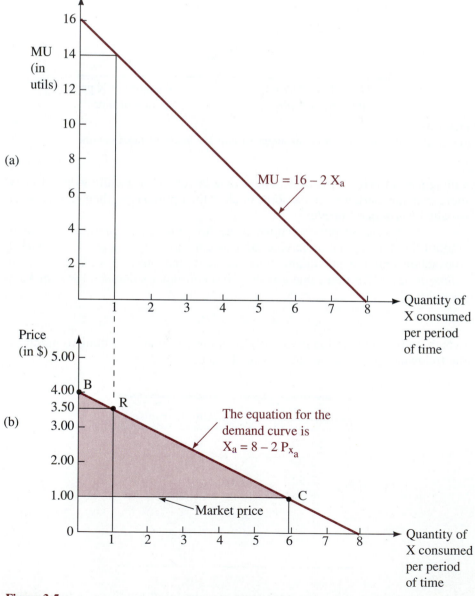

Figure 3-5
Consumer surplus for nonlinear demand curves

simple linear demand curves like the one in Figure 3-4(b), consumers' surplus is always a triangle.

This introduction to the concept of consumers' surplus would be incomplete without pointing out two qualifications. First, for more general demand curves like the one in Figure 3-5, consumers' surplus is not a perfect triangle but continues to be equal to the monetary value of the area below the demand curve and above the horizontal line given by the market price. In Figure 3-5 consumers' surplus resembles a triangle but has curvature on one side and is said to be "roughly triangular" in shape.

MATHEMATICAL CAPSULE 3

DETERMINATION OF THE UTILITY-MAXIMIZING COMBINATION OF PRODUCTS SUBJECT TO AN INCOME CONSTRAINT

Let P_a, P_b, P_c, . . . , P_n be the prices of products X_a, X_b, X_c, . . . , X_n, I be a consumer's money income, and $TU = f(X_a, X_b, X_c, . . . , X_n)$ be the consumer's utility function for n products which the consumer wishes to maximize subject to his or her income constraint

$$I = P_aX_a + P_bX_b + P_cX_c + \cdots + P_nX_n, \quad (1)$$

where saving here is treated as simply one kind of product. To find the utility-maximizing combination of products, a new function is generated which combines the TU function to be maximized and the constraint equation. To keep the solution determinate (as many equations as there are unknowns), an artificial unknown, called a **LaGrange multiplier,** is introduced, giving

$$Z = f(X_a, X_b, X_c, . . . X_n) \\ + \lambda(I - P_aX_a - P_bX_b - P_cX_c - \cdots -P_nX_n), \quad (2)$$

where λ is the LaGrange multiplier. The partial derivatives of Z are found for each variable and equated to zero to establish the first-order conditions:

$$\frac{\partial Z}{\partial X_a} = \frac{\partial TU}{\partial X_a} - \lambda P_a = 0, \quad (3)$$

$$\frac{\partial Z}{\partial X_b} = \frac{\partial TU}{\partial X_b} - \lambda P_b = 0, \quad (4)$$

$$\frac{\partial Z}{\partial X_c} = \frac{\partial TU}{\partial X_c} - \lambda P_c = 0, \quad (5)$$

$$\vdots$$

$$\frac{\partial Z}{\partial X_n} = \frac{\partial TU}{\partial X_n} - \lambda P_n = 0, \quad (6)$$

$$\frac{\partial Z}{\partial \lambda} = I - P_aX_a - P_bX_b - P_cX_c - \cdots - P_nX_n = 0. \quad (7)$$

These equations may be solved simultaneously to determine the utility-maximizing purchase levels for X_a, X_b, X_c, . . . , X_n. From Equations (3) through (6), it is seen that

$$\frac{\partial TU/\partial X_a}{P_a} = \frac{\partial TU/\partial X_b}{P_b} = \frac{\partial TU/\partial X_c}{P_c} = \cdots = \frac{\partial TU/\partial X_n}{P_n} \quad (8)$$

The terms $\partial TU/\partial X_a$, $\partial TU/\partial X_b$, $\partial TU/\partial X_c$, . . . , $\partial TU/\partial X_n$ really are MU_{X_a}, MU_{X_b}, MU_{X_c}, . . . , MU_{X_n}, and the value of λ necessarily is equal to the marginal utility of saving. Thus, Equation (8) translates into

$$MU_{saving} = \frac{MU_{X_a}}{P_a} = \frac{MU_{X_b}}{P_b} = \frac{MU_{X_c}}{P_c} = \cdots = \frac{MU_{X_n}}{P_n}, \quad (9)$$

which we know to be a necessary condition for consumer maximization of total utility. As an example of the foregoing, suppose that we find the utility-maximizing consumption rate for two products X and Y if the total utility function is

$$TU = 10X + 24Y - 0.5X^2 - 0.5Y^2$$

and if $P_X = \$2$, $P_Y = \$6$, and $I = \$44$. Then we have

$$Z = 10X + 24Y - 0.5X^2 - 0.5Y^2 + \lambda(44 - 2X - 6Y),$$

$$\frac{\partial Z}{\partial X} = 10 - X - 2\lambda = 0.$$

$$\frac{\partial Z}{\partial Y} = 24 - Y - 6\lambda = 0.$$

$$\frac{\partial Z}{\partial \lambda} = 44 - 2X - 6Y = 0.$$

Solving $\partial Z/\partial X$, $\partial Z/\partial Y$, and $\partial Z/\partial \lambda$ simultaneously yields $X = 4$, $Y = 6$, and $\lambda = 3$.

EXERCISE

1. Determine the utility-maximizing combination of X and Y when
   (a) $TU = 12XY$,
      $P_X = \$3$,
      $P_Y = \$6$,
      $I = \$60$.
   (b) $TU = 17X + 20Y^2 - 2X^2 - Y^2$,
      $P_X = \$3$,
      $P_Y = \$4$,
      $I = \$22$.

Second, defining and measuring consumers' surplus as triangles below the demand curve and above the horizontal line given by market price is based on the assumption that the marginal utility of income is constant. In the more general case where the marginal utility of income is not constant, as price changes the shaded triangles of Figure 3-4(b) and Figure 3-5 are only approximations of consumers' surplus.[9] Fortunately, the triangles are very good approximations, and much applied analysis of markets rests on these measures of consumers' surplus.[10]

HOW REALISTIC IS THIS MODEL OF BUYER DEMAND?

Since the foregoing discussion may seem rather formal and abstract, it is fair to ask: How realistic is this description of a consumer's disposition of income, especially considering the fact that most consumers have never heard of the conditions for utility maximization? Does the utility model meet the scientific standards of *explaining* and *predicting* real-world consumer behavior? Do real-world demand curves for goods and services actually slope downward to the right? Do buyers actually receive consumers' surplus when they engage in market transactions?

> There are ample reasons to believe that consumers actually make their spending-saving decisions in a manner calculated to maximize total satisfaction or total utility.

We consider each of the preceding questions in turn. The conditions for utility maximization are not as far removed from the purchase decisions of consumers as one might think at first glance. Whenever a consumer goes shopping and considers the purchase of specific item, normally he or she will wonder (consciously or unconsciously) whether the price to be paid is "worth it." If the answer is favorable, he or she can be expected to buy the item, assuming the money is available. If the consumer decides the item is not worth the price, then he or she can be expected not to purchase it and to shop around elsewhere. Translated into the language of utility theory, this mental process is equivalent to deciding whether the $MU/\$$ from consuming the item is greater than the $MU/\$$ of buying some other product. If so, the consumer purchases the item; if $MU/\$$ is less, the consumer elects not to buy the item; and if equality between the two prevails, the consumer is indifferent and may rationally decide to buy or not to buy.

Furthermore, it is quite reasonable to expect consumers to shift their expenditures among competing goods if they believe there is a better allocation (i.e., one which makes them better off). All rational, self-interested consumers can be expected to continue to spend their income as long as they believe the extra satisfaction that they will get from a good or service exceeds the satisfaction of keeping their money. Only when consumers believe that they will obtain more satisfaction from a dollar's worth of saving than they will from a dollar's worth of spending will saving be induced.

Viewed from this perspective, the utility model of consumer behavior becomes persuasive. Consumers are generally careful with their money and attempt to try and allocate it to savings and expenditures and among specific consumption goods in a manner that reflects what they perceive to be their best

---

[9] More exact measures of consumer surplus are available by making use of income and substitution effects, which are discussed in Chapter 4.

[10] The usefulness of the Marshall's measure of consumer surplus in applied studies is stressed by George J. Stigler, *The Theory of Price* (New York: Macmillan, 1988). How well the triangles approximate the true consumer surplus is discussed by Robert D. Willig, "Consumers Surplus Without Apology," *American Economic Review*, Vol. 66, No. 4 (September 1976), pp. 589–97.

interest. This means the model can be used to explain consumer behavior and to predict likely reactions when prices change. The law of demand is quite pervasive and powerful in explaining and predicting consumer behavior and how markets operate.

If demand curves slope downward, as they surely do when all other factors influencing quantity demanded are constant except price, and the market establishes a price, then buyers almost certainly capture some amount of consumers' surplus. Consumers' surplus in a market transaction can be thought of as buyers' gains from trade. This is the case because in a free market buying and selling are voluntary acts and all parties to a transaction must expect to benefit or the exchange simply will not take place. Thus, consumers' surplus tends to exist in all market transactions. However, the exact magnitude of consumers' surplus in a given transaction depends upon how the market works, the nature of the competitive process determining prices, and the specific strategies firms use in pricing their products. Sometimes firms are clever in designing pricing strategies to capture for themselves as much of consumers' surplus as possible—see the discussion of airline pricing in the Applications Capsule.

Difficulties in Maximizing Utility. The cardinal utility model developed in this chapter is useful in explaining consumer behavior and predicting how markets work. But several factors can operate to prevent consumers from realizing the utmost satisfaction from their money incomes. The most important obstacle is a lack of accurate information about the prices charged by various sellers and about product quality.[11] Consumers often pay more for an item at one store than is charged by another store nearby because they are unaware of the price differential. Sometimes they buy products that turn out to be less satisfactory than originally anticipated, perhaps because they mistakenly used price as a surrogate indicator of product quality or because quality was difficult to judge. In these ways they exhaust a larger share of their income than otherwise would have been the case had perfect knowledge existed. On other occasions they buy impulsively, through force of habit, out of brand loyalty, a desire for variety, or just plain curiosity. On still other occasions, they may be unduly influenced by the appeals and nuances of advertising, brand reputation, and emotion.

Even though consumers strive toward utility maximization, they confront several obstacles to actually achieving the maximum utility from their expenditures.

One oft-cited objection to the utility model concerns the postulate that the consumer's behavior consists of a steady flow of rational calculations whereby individuals systematically consider all the various conceivable purchase combinations, evaluate the utility attached to each, and then choose the package with the greatest utility. Many observers contend that this view is both oversimplified and inaccurate. Specifically, habit, loyalty, whim, impulse, inertia, and reluctance to change are held to be normal attributes of consumer behavior which invalidate the view of the consumer as a "rational economic person." Consider, for example, the consumer's purchase of groceries, gasoline, cigarettes, and personal-care items. They do not cost much per item; they are purchased frequently; they are available in many stores and locations; they are bought without great forethought and consultation. There is, therefore,

---

[11] However, it must be recognized that there are costs to consumers from searching out more accurate information. The time and expense involved in comparing the many types and features of products and in shopping around for the best buy may outweigh the associated benefits. Thus, to be completely rational, consumers should balance the costs of acquiring better information against the extra satisfaction they gain from having it.

APPLICATIONS CAPSULE

AIRLINE PRICING STRATEGIES AND CONSUMERS' SURPLUS

In the 1970s and early 1980s, there was a broad movement toward deregulation of markets that were controlled by regulatory commissions empowered with broad discretion to limit competition, control the terms of trade, and determine market prices. Beginning in 1938, the U.S. domestic passenger airline industry was regulated and controlled by the Civil Aeronautics Board (CAB). The industry was also regulated by the Federal Aviation Agency, which focused on safety. But the CAB regulated the economic activities of all the interstate airline carriers by granting virtual monopoly rights on routes between city pairs and limiting entry into the market. A CAB operating certificate required that airlines provide service as common carriers and, in exchange, the CAB established minimum fares, which were set so high that they were in effect maximum prices. Interstate airline firms had virtually no discretion concerning the prices they charged for their services. Considerable evidence indicated that the CAB's regulated prices were excessively high. Due to a provision in the U.S. Constitution relating to interstate commerce, airline firms operating exclusively in intrastate markets were outside the control of CAB regulation. Two states, California and Texas, had several large cities that were located at considerable distance from one another (e.g., Los Angeles and San Francisco in California and Dallas and Houston in Texas), and nonregulated air carriers emerged to serve these markets. The unregulated fares charged by Texas Air and Pacific Southwest Airways in intrastate markets were far below comparable fares on CAB carriers in regulated markets. Under regulation, planes often traveled with large numbers of unfilled seats, and it was the common carrier responsibility of the regulated carriers to provide scheduled service even if it involved economic losses on certain routes and on particular flights. Deregulation was expected to improve airline service and reduce prices, with estimates of savings in terms of reduced air fares running into the billions of dollars.

The Airline Deregulation Act of 1978 ended 40 years of direct control of interstate air fares, and the carriers were faced with devising new strategies for competing in a deregulated environment. Chief among the myriad of new problems facing airline firms under deregulation was how best to price their products. A distinguishing feature of the airline industry is that an unfilled seat on a specific flight, say from Chicago to Miami on November 2, generates zero revenue and the opportunity for selling that particular seat is gone forever. Thus airline firms have considerable incentive to fill up the empty seats. The firms know that demand varies among types of travelers, season of the year, and time of day. In general, some travelers are willing and able to pay much more for a ticket from Chicago to Miami than others. If a single price were established for all tickets—one low enough to fill all or most seats, then buyers would obtain considerable consumers' surplus. By scaling the prices of tickets along a continuum from highest to lowest, airlines can maximize their revenues by extracting some of the consumers' surplus that would otherwise accrue to buyers. They do this by having as many as 15 different prices for a seat on the same flight. Some tickets are sold as first class seats, others as business class, and the bulk are designated coach class. But within coach class there are typically a number of prices that seek to increase the firm's revenue through scaled-down pricing of the product. For example, senior citizens and vacationers (both being sensitive to the fares charged) can get the lowest prices. Travelers who purchase a coach ticket 21 days in advance and stay at least one week might receive the next lowest price, but only a few such tickets may be made available by the airline. Travelers buying seven days in advance and staying over Saturday night receive a lesser discount off the regular fare price. Each step down in price is designed to fill a few more seats by attracting buyers who are willing and able to pay the scaled-down price but who would be unwilling to pay a higher price. The step-downs can be as many and as deep as proves necessary to fill the plane to capacity on each flight. During peak periods and at the most popular departure times, the airlines may decide to offer no discount fares on a particular flight, with all seats allocated to customers willing to pay regular fares. (Economists refer to this type of strategic behavior as "price discrimination," and it is discussed in detail in Chapter 14.) In the airline industry the practice is known as "yield management," and the explicit goal is to generate as much revenue as possible from each flight. By creating an array of prices and adjusting the number of seats available at each price as the flight date approaches, the airlines can effectively extract some of the consumers' surplus of air travelers. Yield management is perfectly legal, but Alfred Kahn, the economist who was the chief architect of airline deregulation, has expressed surprise and dismay at the extent of price discrimination that persists in deregulated airline markets.[1]

---

[1] For further information on developments in the airline industry following deregulation, see Michael E. Levine, "Airline Competition in Deregulated Markets: Theory, Firm Strategy, and Public Policy," *Yale Journal of Regulation*, Vol. 4, No. 2 (Spring 1987), pp. 393–494. For a discussion of Alfred Kahn's views on the persistence of price discrimination under deregulation, see the Preface to the 1989 printing of Kahn's classic work, *The Economics of Regulation: Principles and Institutions* (Cambridge: MIT Press, 1988).

recurring opportunity to repeat the same behavior often and develop buying habits and brand preferences. Moreover, the small expense involved in each purchase may create the feeling that what is bought and when it is bought is of no great consequence, thus dampening the concern that a significant decision problem exists and that alternatives ought to be carefully evaluated.

When different brands of the same item are viewed as essentially identical, there is an even greater tendency to make purchase a function of habit and convenience. Information seeking may go no further than scanning newspaper ads for sales and discounts and adjusting one's shopping plans accordingly. Nonetheless, weighing alternatives to buy again what has proved satisfactory in the past may, indeed, represent the simplest way to overcome the anxiety of "did I buy the right thing?" and "did I pay more than I should have?" Consumers would find it neither practical nor rewarding to repeatedly weigh alternatives; discuss and consult with family, friends, and dealers; shop around; seek out information on competing brands and substitutes; and exhibit concern with price every time they repurchase common household items. Such behavior would increase transactions costs significantly. Hence, reliance upon previous experience with a brand, store loyalty, and advertising may be more "rational" than "irrational," and, as studies have shown, such loyalties and preferences seldom last long when conditions change or dissatisfaction arises.

In addition to the consumers' past experience with particular goods, brands, and stores, such personal factors as the consumers' ego needs, their emotion-colored images of goods, brands, and stores, their desire for conformity and assurance that they are doing the right thing, and their reactions (conscious or subconscious) to on-the-scene factors such as eye appeal, packaging, displays, and store layout all play a role in what they buy and what they do not. Another set of influential factors includes urgent need for an article, the notion that one has a unique opportunity to get an unusually good deal, and satisfaction with other products of the same company.

Granted that these influences exist and that they have a real impact on consumer decision making, does it follow that consumers are often "irrational" and have little interest in or capability for careful, deliberate utility maximization? Or that the consumer's perceptions of utility do not embrace these influences—at least partially? If at the instant of making a purchase decision, the consumer's actions appear to be the best or most satisfying expenditure of his or her income under the circumstances, then the consumer may be said to be rationally endeavoring to maximize utility. Certainly, there is ample reason to presume that if—at the instant of decision—the consumer knew how to spend his or her money to acquire more utility per dollar spent, he or she would do so. This is enough to give the utility model validity, even though the model reveals little about specific factors underlying the consumer's perceptions and motivations.

On the whole, the argument that consumers do not or cannot maximize utility lacks credibility; there is far more reason to believe consumers try to spend their funds in a manner calculated to produce maximum total satisfaction than to believe they do not.

THE IMPACT OF ADVERTISING ON BUYER UTILITY AND BUYER DEMAND

The preceding discussion implies that the worst "enemy" of consumers in attempting to maximize the satisfaction from a limited money income is their own ignorance or irrationality. Even so, consumers are still viewed as possessing the full initiative in buying goods and services. They are assumed to respond only to wants that they originate or needs which are given to them by their environment. They are, above all, independent, and their purchasing behavior in the marketplace instructs producers as to what they want to buy; ultimately, therefore, all power over what and how much is produced is held to lie with consumers—this is what is meant by *consumer sovereignty*.

Sellers can and do use persuasive advertising to bend buyer tastes and preferences to their own advantage; buyers' decisions are not purely a reflection of their independently formed total and marginal utility schedules.

Obviously, this overstates the situation *somewhat*.[12] Much product differentiation, advertising, and marketing strategy is designed expressly to modify individual preferences and to bend consumer demand toward the product offering of individual firms. To deny that these have any effect is untenable, and any model of consumer behavior that fails to acknowledge the role of the marketer, and, in particular, advertising and sales promotion, is sorely lacking in its accounting for real-world purchasing patterns. The attempt to control or manage consumer demand is, in fact, a vast and sophisticated industry in its own right.

Two polar types of advertising and sales promotion strategy may be distinguished: that which is purely informational and that which is purely persuasive. Most advertising strategy incorporates both features and is therefore not pure in either sense. The persuasive type of advertising is of primary concern here.

The significance of persuasive advertising for the study of consumer behavior is that it provides a way for sellers to try to bend consumer tastes and preferences to their own advantage. To the extent that persuasive advertising is successful toward this end, consumer behavior is not purely a response of consumers to their utility schedules. To illustrate: If an individual's satisfaction is less from additional expenditures on soft drinks than on frozen yogurt, this can be just as well "corrected" by a change in the sales strategy of Coca-Cola as by the consumer's increasing his or her expenditures on frozen yogurt. In terms of our utility model, when

$$\frac{MU_{\text{soft drinks}}}{P_{\text{soft drinks}}} < \frac{MU_{\text{frozen yogurt}}}{P_{\text{frozen yogurt}}},$$

either of two acts can restore the equality requisite for consumer equilibrium. The consumer can transfer dollars out of the purchase of soft drinks and into the purchase of frozen yogurt, or the soft-drink manufacturers can attempt to revise upward the consumer's marginal utility for soft drinks by means of a more persuasive advertising and sales strategy. Indeed, *a major purpose of advertising is to shift the consumer's utility function for the item upward such that he or she will have a more intense desire for it*, thereby becoming willing to buy more of it at a given price or else becoming willing to pay a higher price for the same amount currently being purchased.

Consumers, of course, have it well within their powers to reject persuasion. Enough consumers, by their refusal to continue to purchase items they consider unsatisfactory, can force accommodation by producers. *Not even cleverly advertised products can survive when consumers find them seriously deficient.* The notion of the gullible consumer, naked in the jungle of the marketplace and at the mercy of unscrupulous and misleading advertisements, is greatly exaggerated. Still, it is clear that advertising does influence consumer purchases; it can intensify consumer desire to a point where the perceived marginal utility per dollar of expenditure becomes high enough to induce some consumers to buy the item. Consumers are, therefore, well served by the elimination of deceitful or misleading advertising practices.

---

[12] The material in this section draws heavily from the ideas expressed by John Kenneth Galbraith in *The New Industrial State* (Boston: Houghton Mifflin Company, 1967), Chapters 18–20.

APPLICATIONS CAPSULE

HOW ADVERTISING CAN INFLUENCE CONSUMER DEMAND

Angela Wilson is an avid coffee drinker and has always taken pride in the quality of the coffee she brews. When she first began making coffee twenty five years ago Angela compared fresh brewed to powdered, instant coffee and concluded that the quality of drip brewed coffee more than compensated for the convenience of instant coffee. Her husband Mike agreed. Today, however, freeze-dried instant coffee is a staple in the Wilson household. It is instructive to consider how advertising influenced Angela's decision to switch from purchasing ground coffee to freeze-dried coffee and changing her family's demand from one product to another.

Angela was a devotee to ground coffee for years and bought Folger's and the house brand at the supermarket where she shopped. She had a very strong preference for Maxwell House, but she bought Folger's and the supermarket's house brand occasionally when they were on sale or if the store where she shops happened to be out of Maxwell House. Angela's strong preference for Maxwell House was based upon Maxwell House's ability to satisfy her criteria of strength, flavor, aroma, and economy. During the long period of regular purchases of ground coffee Angela was very confident about her preference for Maxwell House because she was quite certain of her evaluations of the other brands she tried.

One day, while watching television, Angela saw a television commercial from Nestlé introducing Taster's Choice freeze-dried coffee. The commercial described what freeze-dried coffee meant and how it combined the flavor of regular coffee with the convenience of instant coffee. Although she usually ignores most commercials, Angela paid attention to this particular one. In fact, she stopped what she was doing and watched the commercial intensely. The commercial exposed Angela to the following bits of information: (1) Taster's Choice is a totally new kind of coffee, (2) made from a freeze-dry process, (3) that has the flavor and taste of regular coffee, (4) but appears and is used like instant coffee. This information led Angela to conclude that Taster's Choice was a new brand of instant coffee, perhaps better in taste than most other instant coffees, because it was manufactured by a new process. Nonetheless, Angela viewed what she heard about the freeze-dry concept with some skepticism and ambiguity. She was still convinced that she preferred regular coffee to instant coffee and decided the information about Taster's Choice was not relevant to her.

A few days later Angela was exposed to the same commercial. This time, she did not pay full attention, but she did listen and watch it. At the end, she concluded with greater firmness that Taster's Choice was a new brand of instant coffee, perhaps with improved taste over other instant coffees because of the new process.

The following week, Angela received a sample jar of Taster's Choice in the mail. While she probably would not have bought it, the free sample generated enough motivation and curiosity for her to try a cup. Angela was surprised to find that Taster's Choice was similar to regular coffee in taste, flavor, and aroma. Her mother-in-law, who happened to be visiting, also praised it as being better than her regular brand of instant coffee. With satisfaction, Angela reevaluated her attitude toward Taster's Choice and concluded that it was the most preferred brand of *instant* coffee.

Angela mentioned Taster's Choice to some of her co-workers at the office, trying to find out how they perceived it and whether they had tried it at all. Then, a few days later, she shared a cup of Taster's Choice with her husband. He, too, liked the taste and praised it. Several of Angela's friends also indicated that they considered it a good product. Angela then began to have such a high opinion of Taster's Choice that she seriously considered it as a replacement for Maxwell House regular coffee. When her sample jar of Taster's Choice was exhausted, she bought another jar to replace it.

QUESTIONS FOR DISCUSSION

1. Do you think Angela was inappropriately influenced by the television commercial to purchase Taster's Choice?
2. How important was advertising in reshaping Angela's preference for Taster's Choice as opposed to Maxwell House coffee?
3. What is there about Taster's Choice that, from Angela's point of view, gave it "utility"? How do you think the utility which Angela associated with Maxwell House compares with the utility she now associates with Taster's Choice?
4. What do you think really caused Angela to think more highly of Taster's Choice?

KEY POINTS

The utility approach to consumer behavior and the formation of individual consumer demand is grounded upon psychological principles. Rational individuals, it is said, will seek to maximize the degree of pleasure and minimize the degree of pain in choosing among alternative courses of action. In furtherance of this proposition, the concept of utility has evolved into the economist's major tool for explaining and predicting the consumer's marketplace behavior.

Utility refers to the want-satisfying power of products—that is, the amount of satisfaction a consumer receives from consuming various quantities of a good or service per period of time. A consumer's total and marginal utility functions for a product can be represented equally well by tables, graphs, and equations. Marginal utility is defined to be the rate of change in total utility as the rate of consumption of a product changes. For each total utility function, there is a corresponding marginal utility function. Every consumer has his or her own unique set of total and marginal utility functions; these vary according to his or her tastes and preferences for different products. Moreover, the satisfaction a consumer obtains from one product hinges in part upon the amounts consumed of other products.

Consumers maximize the satisfaction they can obtain from their limited money income by meeting two conditions. First, they must fully utilize all their income either by purchasing products or by saving. Second, consumers must arrange their purchases so that the marginal utilities per dollar spent on the last unit of each item purchased are equal. In other words, to maximize satisfaction, consumers must get an equivalent amount of satisfaction from the last dollar allocated to each of the items (including saving) that they choose to buy.

The cardinal utility model leads directly to the law of demand. The negatively sloping demand curve shows the maximum prices that buyers are willing and able to pay for particular quantities. When a uniform price is established, and buyers are able to purchase all they want at the prevailing market price, consumer surplus exists and represents the buyers' gains from trade.

Few consumers probably succeed in obtaining the maximum satisfaction from their income. Impulsive buying, habit, imperfect knowledge of product prices and quality, a desire for variety, emotion and personality traits, the pressures of time and circumstances, family roles, and the persuasive powers of advertising, among others, prompt consumers to make purchases with which they may not be fully satisfied.

However, the fact that consumers do not succeed in maximizing utility is not crucial to the validity of utility theory. What is important is whether consumers act consistently on the basis of perceived utility (including both monetary and time considerations) and, accordingly, whether utility theory explains and predicts well.

PROBLEMS AND QUESTIONS FOR DISCUSSION

1. Find the first derivatives of each of the following functions.
    (a) $Y = 124 + 6X$.
    (b) $Y = 15X^2 + 2X^3$.
    (c) $TU_x = 17X - 0.5X^2$.
    (d) $TU_a = 16A + 5A^2 - 0.3A^3$.
    (e) $TU_b = -185 + 7B + 1.9B^2 - 0.05B^3$.
    (f) $TU_c = 0.6C^{1/2}$.
    (g) $TU_y = 1.5Y^{0.75}$.
        Answers: **(a)** $dY/dX = 6$.
                    (b) $dY/dX = 30X + 6X^2$.
                    (c) $dTU_x/dX = 17 - X$.
                    (d) $dTU_a/dA = 16 + 10A - 0.9A^2$.
                    (e) $dTU_b/dB = 7 + 3.8B - 0.15B^2$.
                    (f) $dTU_c/dC = 0.3C^{-1/2}$.
                    (g) $dTU_y/dY = 1.125Y^{-0.25}$.

2. Find the second derivative of each of the following functions (the second derivative is the derivative of the first derivative).
   (a) $Y = 124 + 7X^2$.
   (b) $TU_x = 9 + 14X - 0.2X^2$.
   (c) $TU_a = 130 + 14A + 15A^2 - 0.4A^3$.
   (d) $TU_b = 0.6B^{1.5}$.
   Answers: **(a)** $d^2Y/dX^2 = 14$.
   (b) $d^2TU/dX^2 = -0.4$.
   (c) $d^2TU_a/dA^2 = 30 - 2.4A$.
   (d) $d^2TU_b/dB^2 = 0.45B^{-0.5}$.

3. Explain the nature of the distinguishing features between cardinal and ordinal measures of utility.

4. Adam Smith in *The Wealth of Nations* observed: "Nothing is more useful than water: but it will purchase scarce anything; scarce anything can be had in exchange for it. A diamond, on the contrary, has scarce any value in use; but a very great quantity of other goods may frequently be had in exchange for it."
   (a) How do you account for this?
   (b) Is the term *useful* or *usefulness* synonymous with the concept of utility as we have defined it?

5. An individual's total utility function for product B is as follows: $TU = 18B - 0.5B^2$.
   (a) Graph the *TU* function, and explain the nature of the individual's utility for the product.
   (b) Calculate the equation for marginal utility, and illustrate it graphically.
   (c) How much will total utility be at a consumption rate of 10 units? At 15 units?
   (d) How much will marginal utility be at a consumption rate of 10 units? At 15 units?
   (e) How many units of product B can the individual consume and still gain additional satisfaction?

6. An individual's total utility function for product Q is as follows: $TU = 100Q + 150Q^2 - 2Q^3$.
   (a) Determine the expression for marginal utility.
   (b) Graph the total and marginal utility functions, and explain the nature of the individual's utility for the product.
   (c) How much will total utility be at a consumption rate of 5 units? How much will marginal utility be at 5 units?
   (d) At what approximate consumption rate does diminishing *MU* begin?
   (e) At what approximate consumption rate does the individual reach the saturation rate?

7. The following table shows the marginal utility, measured in utils of satisfaction, which Mr. Johnson would get by purchasing various amounts of products A, B, C, and D and by saving. The prices of A, B, C, and D are $5, $6, $8, and $20, respectively. Mr. Johnson has a money income of $95 to spend in the current period.

Product A		Product B		Product C		Product D		Saving	
Units	MU	Units	MU	Units	MU	Units	MU	Dollars Saved	MU
1	31	1	20	1	39	1	50	1	6
2	27	2	19	2	36	2	55	2	5
3	23	3	18	3	33	3	50	3	4
4	19	4	17	4	30	4	45	4	3
5	15	5	16	5	27	5	40	5	2
6	11	6	15	6	24	6	35	6	1
7	7	7	14	7	21	7	30	7	$\frac{1}{2}$

(a) How many units of A, B, C, and D must Mr. Johnson purchase in order to maximize total utility?

(b) How many dollars will Mr. Johnson elect to save?

(c) State algebraically the two conditions for utility maximization, and show that your answers to parts (a) and (b) satisfy these conditions.

8. Given the two conditions requisite for utility maximization, is it likely that a consumer would ever reach his or her saturation rate for any good or service? Why or why not? Under what circumstances *might* it occur?

9. Dr. Hold has $30 per week available to spend as he wishes on goods A and B. The prices of A and B, the quantities of A nd B he is now buying, and his evaluations of the utility provided by these quantities are as follows:

Product	Price per Unit	Quantity Purchased (units)	Total Utility (utils)	MU of Last Unit Purchased (utils)
A	$0.70	30	500	30
B	0.50	18	1,000	20

Is Dr. Holt maximizing total utility? If so, *explain why*. If not, what might he do to maximize utility? *Explain why*.

10. Suppose that Mr. Pikard has an income of $60 weekly, which he is free to spend or save in any way he sees fit. Mr. Pikard believes that *each* dollar he saves gives him 5 utils of satisfaction. This past week, of the thousands of products available, Mr. Pikard purchased the following list of items and believes he obtained the indicated degrees of utility from them:

Product	Price per Unit	Quantity Purchased (units)	Total Utility (utils)	MU of Last Unit Purchased (utils)
A	$ 2.50	1	15	15.0
B	0.75	2	16	4.5
C	0.50	10	113	3.0
D	4.00	3	248	24.0
E	3.00	6	618	18.0
F	15.00	1	90	90.0

Is it possible, given this information, that Mr. Pikard maximized the total utility he received last week from his $60?

11. The Belmont Company conducted an experiment to see how well its new personal computer would stack up against a personal computer produced by Delta Company, a firm already well established in the market. Belmont utilized three testing conditions: (1) *accurate brand labeling*, whereby both machines were placed in an office use situation with the correct company and brand names indicated; (2) *reverse brand labeling*, whereby both machines were placed in an office use situation with the company and brand names reversed; (3) *blind labeling,* whereby both personal computers were unidentified as to company and brand name. Under test condition (1), Delta's PC was rated moderately superior to the Belmont brand, but under test

condition (2) Belmont's PC was rated far superior to Delta's. In the blind labeling test, the Belmont personal computer was given a slight edge over the Delta machine.

(a) How do you account for these results?

(b) What criteria do you think were being used to rate the two personal computers? (Do you think the users' evaluations were "rational"?)

(c) Are the results consistent with the utility model of buyer behavior?

12. It has been said that "What the customer thinks he is buying, what he considers value is decisive . . . and what the customer buys and considers value is never a product. It is always utility, that is, what a product or service does for him." Do you agree? Why or why not?

Chapter 4

Buyer Demand:
THE INDIFFERENCE CURVE AND ATTRIBUTE MODELS

Although the cardinal utility approach to consumer preference yields insights into consumer behavior, the inability to quantify utility in a satisfactory manner caused economists to seek an alternative mode of individual demand analysis not predicated on numerical measures of satisfaction. The search led to the development of ordinal utility analysis whereby consumer tastes and preferences are indicated by ordering or ranking the utilities of various products.[1] Interestingly enough, this seemingly slight change in approach has produced some versatile analytical tools that stand as an important extension of the cardinal utility model presented in Chapter 3.

THE CONCEPT OF INDIFFERENCE CURVES

The ordinal utility approach to consumer demand is usually called indifference curve analysis because "indifference curves" are its primary analytical tool. To understand the origin and meaning of indifference curves, suppose that we refocus our attention upon the utility interrelationships among goods and services.

Figure 4-1(a) depicts a total utility surface for two desirable goods X and Y. Increasing the rates of consumption of X and Y from zero levels produces the total utility surface $OEFG$. Observe that if the consumption of Y is fixed at Y_1 units, then the consumer's total utility from X and Y increases at a decreasing rate along the path $ECAF$ as the consumption of X per unit of time rises from zero to X_1 units. In like manner, whenever the consumption of X is fixed, total utility increases at a decreasing rate as the consumption of Y is increased per period of time.

---

[1] Although the concepts of cardinal and ordinal utility are distinct notions, it should be pointed out that there is not a wide gulf between the two. Consumers often experience considerable difficulty in deciding which products they actually prefer. For example, a consumer may have no trouble deciding that he prefers item X to item Z and that he prefers item Y to item Z, but he may have quite a hard time deciding whether he prefers item X to item Y, or vice versa. It can then be reliably hypothesized that the cardinal utility difference between the paired comparisons (X, Z) and (Y, Z) is greater than between (X, Y). To put it another way, a consumer may be able to establish an ordinal ranking among three items, X, Y, and Z, ranking X as first, Y as second, and Z as third. Yet it may be quite clear to him that Z is a poor third, while X barely edged out Y for first; this creates a strong inference that the cardinal utility difference between X and Y is much smaller than between either X and Z or Y and Z. Hence, ordinal utility rankings may permit judgments about the numerical amounts of total utility associated with various items.

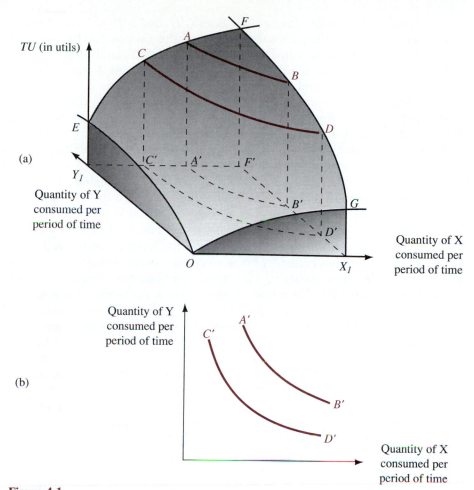

Figure 4-1
Derivation of indifference curves

Suppose that we connect all points on the utility surface *OEFG* which represent a total utility level of *CC'* (where *CC'* = *DD'*), thereby obtaining the contour line *CD*. Thus, all the points along *CD* are associated with a specific amount of total utility *CC'* (or *DD'*). Projecting the curve *CD* vertically downward onto the *XY* plane traces out the dashed contour line *C'D'* and defines all the combinations of products X and Y consumed per unit of time which yield an amount of total utility equal to *CC'* (or *DD'*). Logically, *a consumer would be* **indifferent** *as to which one of the combinations of X and Y along C'D' he had since they all are associated with the same amount of total utility.*

Following the same procedure, suppose that we move up the utility surface to a higher level of total utility *AA'* (= *BB'*). Connecting all points on the utility surface *OEFG* with a total utility of *AA'* (= *BB'*) gives the contour line *AB*. Projecting the image of *AB* perpendicularly onto the *XY* plane gives the dashed contour line *A'B'*. Any point along *AB* represents constant total utility of amount *AA'* = *BB'*, and all combinations of products X and Y lying on *A'B'* yield this amount of total utility. Again, it is reasonable to conclude that a consumer would be indifferent among the combinations of X and Y along *A'B'* because they all are equally satisfying.

BASIC CONCEPT
An indifference curve identifies all the combinations of two products that are equally satisfying to a consumer; thus, each point on an indifference curve represents the same amount of total utility.

A consumer prefers all combinations on higher indifference curves to those on lower indifference curves because higher indifference curves are associated with greater total utility than lower indifference curves.

An indifference map provides a complete description of a consumer's preferences for various combinations of two products.

Predictably enough, the contour lines $C'D'$ and $A'B'$ are called *indifference curves*.[2] An indifference curve shows all the various combinations of two products that yield an equal amount of satisfaction (total utility) to the consumer, or among which the consumer is indifferent. Figure 4-1(b) illustrates indifference curves $C'D'$ and $A'B'$ in a two-dimensional diagram.

Although a consumer is indifferent as to the various combinations along a particular indifference curve, he or she is *not* indifferent as to the various combinations between indifference curves. For example, a consumer would prefer *all* combinations of X and Y on $A'B'$ to those combinations on $C'D'$ because the former are associated with a higher total utility ($AA' > CC'$). Greater degrees of total utility are shown by contour lines higher up on the utility surface, while lower degrees of total utility are shown by lower contour lines. Consequently, in a two-dimensional diagram such as Figure 4-1(b), *indifference curves lying farther from the origin represent higher levels of satisfaction than do those lying closer in.* Therefore, an indifference curve may additionally be thought of as a boundary between combinations of products which a consumer views as less satisfying and those combinations which he or she views as more satisfying. To put it another way, *a consumer is indifferent among any one of the various combinations on a given indifference curve but prefers all combinations on higher indifference curves to those on lower indifference curves.*

There is an indifference curve associated with each distinct degree of total utility on the total utility surface. In this sense, indifference curves are *everywhere dense,* that is, an indifference curve passes through each point in the XY plane. *The family of indifference curves that can be derived from the total utility surface form an* **indifference map**. The indifference map provides a complete description of a consumer's preferences for various combinations of goods and services.

The important point to recognize at this juncture is that *the specific degree of utility associated with an indifference curve is in no way crucial.* In fact, the information provided by an indifference curve does not specify the *amount* of satisfaction produced by the combinations comprising it. In Figure 4-1(b), the total utility attached to $C'D'$ and $A'B'$ could be 10 utils and 14 utils, respectively, or 112 utils and 547 utils. The *amount* by which the combinations on a higher indifference curve are preferred to those on a lower indifference curve is unspecified—it could be a little or a lot. All that is necessary for deriving an indifference curve is for the consumer to know his or her preferences well enough to be able to distinguish whether he or she prefers one combination of goods to another or whether they are viewed as equally satisfying.[3] It is in this sense that *ordinal utility or indifference curve analysis is free of the need to express utility in numerical terms.*

---

[2] The total utility surface in Figure 4-1(a) is mathematically defined by the general expression $TU = f(X, Y)$. The equation for one indifference curve is $TU_1 = f(X, Y)$, where TU_1 is a constant and X and Y represent all the various combinations of two products which yield a utility of TU_1. Other indifference curves on the surface are generated by assigning different values to TU. The family of indifference curves produced by letting TU assume every possible value defines the consumer's indifference map. Significantly, the values for TU need only reflect an ordered preference pattern rather than being expressed as cardinal utility (numerical) values.

[3] The consumer must be able to avoid being thrust into a position similar to that of Buridan's ass. The ass, it may be recalled, stood midway between two equally sized bundles of hay and finally died of hunger because it could not decide which bundle to eat.

THE SHAPES OF INDIFFERENCE CURVES

Although the height of the total utility surface is immaterial, its **shape** is not. In fact, it is the *shape* of the utility surface which determines the shape of the indifference curves, thereby describing a consumer's taste and preference pattern. *Any set of consumer tastes can be portrayed by indifference curves and utility surfaces.* Consider the taste and preference pattern of an individual who enjoys good X immensely (prime ribs) but considers good Y devoid of want-satisfying qualities (parsnips). Figure 4-2(a) depicts a utility surface and indifference map for such a situation. Having more of Y neither raises nor lowers total satisfaction (its marginal utility is zero); only good X has the power to change the level of total utility. The effect is to make each indifference curve in the bottom half of Figure 4-2(a) a vertical line. As the consumption rate of X is increased per unit of time, utility increases; hence, on the indifference map higher levels of satisfaction are shown by moving rightward along the X-axis.

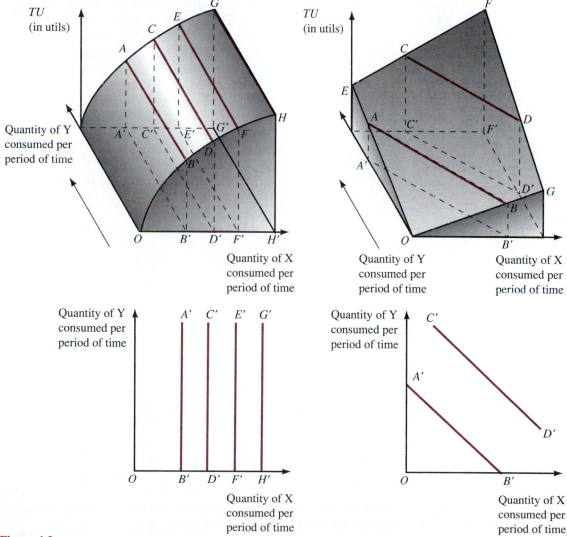

Figure 4-2

Total utility surfaces and indifference maps for special types of products

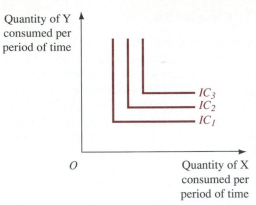

Figure 4-3
Indifference map for items that are perfect complements

Figure 4-2(b) illustrates a total utility surface and corresponding indifference map for a pair of products that are ***perfect substitutes***. Products are said to be perfect substitutes when their qualities are so similar that a consumer would just as soon have more of one as more of the other. Examples could be nickels and dimes (at a constant ratio of 2 : 1), competing brands of pencils, or competing brands of essentially identical food products—milk, eggs, sugar, and black pepper. *The indifference curve for perfect substitutes is a straight line* because the consumer considers them as being absolutely equivalent and is willing, therefore, to substitute one for the other at some *constant* ratio, no matter how much he or she has of either.

The indifference curve for perfect substitutes is a downsloping straight line because the consumer is always willing to substitute one for the other at some constant ratio.

In Figure 4-3 is the indifference map for a pair of products that have a rigid one-to-one complementary relationship in the mind of the consumer (right and left shoes, nuts and bolts). Each indifference curve is a right angle because the consumer is no better off having more of one without the other; this means more units of one complementary item have a marginal utility of zero unless combined with more units of the other complementary item. Therefore, total satisfaction can be increased only by having more of both items. (The shape of the utility surface from which these curves are derived is left as an exercise at the end of this chapter.)

FOUR CHARACTERISTICS OF INDIFFERENCE CURVES

Three assumptions greatly simplify the exposition of indifference curve analysis:

Indifference curves have four properties—they are continuous, "everywhere dense," nonintersecting, and negatively sloped.

1. All products are continuously divisible into subunits so that a consumer is not constrained by the size of the units in which the item is sold.
2. The consumer's tastes and order of preference among combinations of products is well defined and consistent.
3. The consumer views products as being desirable—having more is always preferred to having less; this means that the marginal utility of additional consumption is positive and, further, that useless and nuisance items are disregarded.[4]

---

[4] It is easy enough to redefine a nuisance item to make it a desirable item. Instead of garbage, the item can be called garbage removal; instead of polluted water, the item can be defined as clean water.

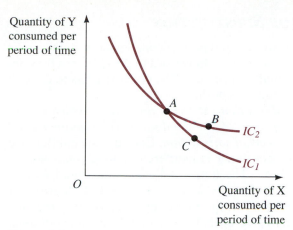

Figure 4-4
Logical inconsistency of intersecting indifference curves

Given these assumptions, indifference curves exhibit four characteristics. From the first assumption it follows that (a) indifference curves are continuous functions rather than collections of discrete points and (b) indifference curves are "everywhere dense"—some indifference curve will pass through every point in the *XY* plane (or *commodity space*, as it is sometimes called), such that every XY combination lies on some one indifference curve.

The second assumption, in conjunction with the third, ensures that indifference curves will be nonintersecting. Consider Figure 4-4, in which two indifference curves, IC_1 and IC_2, are shown intersecting. A moment's reflection should indicate that it is quite illogical for combination *A* to produce simultaneously two levels of satisfaction—as would be the case were it to lie on two different indifference curves. Thus, intersecting indifference curves deny the condition of consistency (or transitivity).[5] But to say that indifference curves are nonintersecting is *not* to say that indifference curves must be equidistant from one another. Two indifference curves may or may not be the same distance apart throughout. The curves for many, even most, pairs of items may become progressively closer (or farther apart) because of differing *MU* functions.

The third assumption causes indifference curves to slope downward to the right (i.e., have a negative slope). Negatively sloped indifference curves reflect the general principle that a consumer is willing to give up units of one product if the loss in satisfaction is compensated for by having more of another product. Stated differently, by having more of one good (say X) and by giving up an appropriate amount of another good (say Y), the consumer can be made to feel just as well off as originally (when he had less of X and more of Y). By *substituting* one item for another in such a way that the gain in satisfaction from consuming more of one is exactly offset by the loss of satisfaction from consuming less of another, the consumer's overall satisfaction level can be held constant.

---

[5] Transitivity is a scale of preference such that if *A* is preferred to *B* and *B* is preferred to *C*, then *A* must be preferred to *C*. Clearly, transitivity cannot be present if (1) *A* and *B* are viewed as equivalent, (2) *A* and *C* are viewed as equivalent, and (3) *B* is preferred to *C* (because combination *B* contains more of both goods X and Y)—this is precisely the illogical condition depicted in Figure 4-4.

THE MARGINAL RATE OF SUBSTITUTION

Except in the case of perfect substitutes and perfect complements, indifference curves for desirable products not only slope downward to the right, but they are also *convex* to the origin of the indifference map. The convexity has to do with the rate of substitution of one good for another.

> The ***marginal rate of substitution*** *(MRS) is the rate at which a consumer is agreeable to trading off some of one good for more of another good yet still achieve the same overall level of satisfaction.* Consider the indifference curve shown in Figure 4-5. The consumer is indifferent among combinations $X_1 Y_1$, $X_2 Y_2$, $X_3 Y_3$, $X_4 Y_4$, and $X_5 Y_5$. The horizontal axis is measured so that distances $OX_1 = X_1 X_2 = X_2 X_3 = X_3 X_4 = X_4 X_5 = 1$ unit of X. Starting at combination $X_1 Y_1$ and proceeding down the indifference curve, observe that initially the consumer is willing to give up $Y_1 Y_2$ units of Y to get an additional unit of X and yet have just as much satisfaction as before. But as he or she acquires more and more of X and has less and less of Y left, the amount of Y he or she is willing to give up to get another unit of X becomes progressively smaller. We can express the ratio at which a consumer is willing to exchange one product for another algebraically as

$$MRS_{xy} = \frac{\Delta Y}{\Delta X},$$

where ΔY represents the number of units of Y the consumer is willing to give up and ΔX represents the number of units of X it will take to compensate the consumer for having less of Y. The expression $\Delta Y / \Delta X$ thus defines the exchange ratio or marginal rate of substitution between Y and X that will precisely maintain the consumer's level of satisfaction. Clearly *the exchange ratio is not constant all along an indifference curve.* The ratio becomes smaller going down the curve, and this is what makes the indifference curve convex. Why does the value of MRS_{xy} diminish going down the curve? One explanation for

BASIC CONCEPT
The marginal rate of substitution is the rate at which a consumer is willing to give up some units of one item for more units of another item and still end up with the same amount of total utility as before.

The exchange ratio that it takes to maintain a consumer's satisfaction at a constant level becomes smaller and smaller as one moves down a given indifference curve—that is, the marginal rate of substitution diminishes going down the curve.

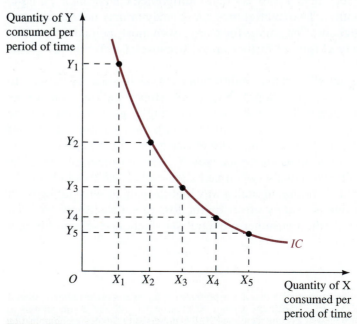

Figure 4-5

Marginal rate of substitution along an indifference curve

diminishing MRS_{xy} is that as a consumer moves to combinations further down an indifference curve, the remaining units of Y become dearer and the additional units of X yield smaller amounts of extra satisfaction; that is, the marginal utility of the remaining units of Y rises, whereas the marginal utility from additional units of X decreases. This argument, although quite plausible since a state of diminishing marginal utility for X and Y is fairly normal, is not always sufficient. When the utility derived from good Y is partially dependent on the amount consumed of X, increasing the consumption of X may decrease the marginal utility from Y and spoil the argument. Fortunately, more powerful evidence for convexity exists. It can, for example, be demonstrated that if the consumer buys some of each of two products, his or her indifference curves must be convex to the origin; otherwise, only one of the products would be bought.

But there is more to be learned about the marginal rate of substitution. We know that in moving from one point to another on the same indifference curve there is no change in total utility. For example, in going from point $X_1 Y_1$ to point $X_2 Y_2$ in Figure 4-5, the amount of utility "lost" from consuming fewer units of Y (Y_1 to Y_2) is exactly compensated for by the "gain" in utility from consuming more units of X (X_1 to X_2). In more formal terms,

$$\underbrace{-\Delta Y \cdot MU_y}_{\substack{\text{"loss" in utility from} \\ \text{consuming } Y_1 Y_2 \text{ (or} \\ \Delta Y \text{) fewer units of} \\ \text{good Y}}} = \underbrace{\Delta X \cdot MU_x.}_{\substack{\text{"gain" in utility from} \\ \text{consuming } X_1 X_2 \text{ (or} \\ \Delta X \text{) units more of} \\ \text{good X}}}$$

Dividing both terms of this equality by $\Delta X \cdot MU_y$ gives

$$\frac{-\Delta Y \cdot MU_y}{\Delta X \cdot MU_y} = \frac{\Delta X \cdot MU_x}{\Delta X \cdot MU_y},$$

which reduces to

$$-\frac{\Delta Y}{\Delta X} = \frac{MU_x}{MU_y} \text{ or } \frac{\Delta Y}{\Delta X} = -\frac{MU_x}{MU_y}.$$

But since $MRS_{xy} = \Delta Y / \Delta X$, we have

$$MRS_{xy} = \frac{\Delta Y}{\Delta X} = -\frac{MU_x}{MU_y},$$

which says that the marginal rate of substitution of X for Y is equal to the ratio of MU_x to MU_y. This expression for MRS_{xy} holds true for any two points on an indifference curve. The negative sign in the expression reflects the fact that having more of one good (X) entails having less of the other good (Y). Additionally, it follows that if any two points on a given indifference curve become so close together that they are really one point, then the marginal rate of substitution of X for Y equals the slope of the indifference curve at that point. One final point: The marginal rate of substitution is meaningful only for movements along an indifference curve—never for movements among curves.

THE CONSUMER'S BUDGET CONSTRAINT

A consumer's indifference map indicates his or her subjective attitudes toward various combinations of products. It shows what combinations are preferred to others and the rates at which he or she is willing to substitute one product for

PRINCIPLE
The marginal rate of substitution of good X for good Y at any point on an indifference curve equals the slope of the curve at that point and also the ratio of MU_X to MU_Y.

Whereas a consumer's indifference map shows which product combinations are preferred to others and the rates at which the consumer is willing to substitute one product for another, the consumer's ability to satisfy these preferences hinges upon the available purchasing power and product prices.

another. However, as was seen in Chapter 3, the extent to which the consumer is *able* to satisfy these tastes and preferences hinges upon (1) the available money income and (2) the respective prices of the products the individual is desirous of having. Taken together, these two factors define the individual's *budget constraint*.

For simplicity, suppose that we continue to restrict our analysis to a situation where there are just two goods X and Y with prices of P_x and P_y. As established previously, the consumer's money income (I) is fixed in the short run; he or she has only so much to spend per period of time. The consumer's expenditures for X will be equal to the selling price (P_x) times the amount purchased (X) or $P_x X$; similarly, the expenditure for good Y is $P_y Y$. The sum of the consumer's expenditures for X and Y must be equal to or less than the available income I. Thus, we may write

$$P_x X + P_y Y \leq I.$$

If the consumer elects to spend all of his or her income on X and Y and save nothing, then,

$$P_x X + P_y Y = I.$$

Otherwise, saving accounts for the margin of difference between the consumer's total expenditures on X and Y and income.

Suppose that the available money income is $50, $P_x = \$5$, and $P_y = \$2$. If the entire $50 is spent on good X, a maximum of 10 units (I/P_x) could be bought; if the entire $50 is spent on Y, as much as 25 units (I/P_y) can be purchased. These combinations are illustrated in Figure 4-6. A straight line joining these two points on the graph shows *all* the other combinations of X and Y that the consumer's income will allow him or her to purchase at these prices. This line is called the *line of attainable combinations* because it represents the locus of combinations of X and Y that can be purchased when the consumer

BASIC CONCEPT
The line of attainable combinations shows all the combinations of two products that a consumer can purchase with his or her available money income, given prevailing prices for the two products.

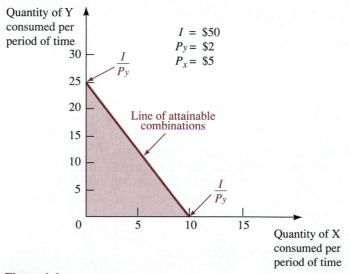

Figure 4-6
Line of attainable combinations

spends the entire amount of money income available.[6] The consumer can also buy any of the combinations of X and Y inside the line (the shaded area); however, if he or she does so, available purchasing power will not be fully utilized and there will be money left over for saving (or for spending on other products). The equation of the line of attainable combinations in Figure 4-6 is $5X + $2Y = 50, where $5 = the price of product X, $2 = the price of Y, and $50 = the consumer's money income. The set of values for X and Y that satisfy this equation are given by the points comprising the line of attainable combinations.

The general equation for the line of attainable combinations in a two-product economy is $P_xX + P_yY = I.$[7] The slope of the line of attainable combinations is negative and is numerically equal to the ratio of the prices of X and Y. This is easily verified by considering the slope of the line in Figure 4-6 between the two extreme points I/P_x and I/P_y:

$$\text{slope of line of attainable combinations} = \frac{\text{change in the quantity of } Y}{\text{change in the quantity of } X} = \frac{-I/P_y}{I/P_x} = -\frac{P_x}{P_y}.$$

The slope of the line of attainable combinations equals the ratio of the prices of the two products.

SHIFTS IN THE CONSUMER'S BUDGET CONSTRAINT

Both changes in money income and changes in product prices have the effect of shifting the position of the line of attainable combinations. Consider first the effect of an increase in money income from I_1 to I_2 when the prices of X and Y remain constant at P_{x_1} and P_{y_1}. The larger money income permits the consumer to purchase more of X, more of Y, or more of both. The maximum amount of X which can be purchsed increases from I_1/P_{x_1} to I_2/P_{x_1} as shown in Figure 4-7(a). The maximum purchase level of Y rises from I_1/P_{y_1} to I_2/P_{y_1}. Since the prices of X and Y are fixed, the slope of the new line of attainable combinations must be identical to the slope at an income of I_1, and it must pass through points I_2/P_{x_1} and I_2/P_{y_1}. Thus, an increase in money income from I_1 to I_2, product prices remaining constant, is shown graphically by a parallel shift in the line of attainable combinations upward and to the right. Similarly, another increase in income (to I_3) will shift the line parallelwise even farther to the right. Conversely, it follows that decreases in money income can be represented by parallel shifts in the line downward and to the left.

Changes in the consumer's purchasing power cause parallel shifts in the line of attainable combinations, whereas changes in product prices cause the slope of the line to change.

---

[6] In the literature of indifference curve analysis, the line of attainable combinations is known variously as the budget line, the price line, the budget restraint, the expenditure line, the price-income line, and the consumption possibility line.

In drawing the line as a continuous function, we continue our assumption of the preceding sections that products X and Y are perfectly divisible into subunits and can be purchased in any quantity.

Normally, an individual consumer's purchases of a product are so small relative to the total amount bought that the price of it can reasonably be anticipated to remain constant irrespective of the amount purchased. Thus, a linear line of attainable combinations may be considered typical. However, if by chance the prices of X and Y depend on the amounts the consumer buys, then the line of attainable combinations becomes curvilinear. When product prices fall as the consumer buys more units, the line of attainable combinations is bowed in toward the origin. When product prices rise with increasing purchase levels, the line is bowed out or concave toward the origin.

[7] For n number of products and where saving is indicated as a separate activity, the general equation of the line of attainable combinations may be written as

$$P_{x_a}X_a + P_{x_b}X_b + P_{x_c}X_c + \cdots + P_{x_n}X_n + \text{saving} = I,$$

where I = money income and $P_{x_a}, P_{x_b}, P_{x_c}, \ldots, P_{x_n}$ are the prices of products $X_a, X_b, X_c, \ldots, X_n$.

MATHEMATICAL CAPSULE 4

THE MARGINAL RATE OF SUBSTITUTION, THE CONVEXITY OF INDIFFERENCE CURVES, AND DIMINISHING MARGINAL UTILITY

Suppose that the total utility function for goods X and Y is

$$TU = f(X, Y);$$

then an indifference curve is defined by

$$TU = f(X, Y) = c,$$

where c is a constant. Finding the total differential of $TU = f(X, Y)$ gives

$$dTU = \frac{\partial TU}{\partial X} dX + \frac{\partial TU}{\partial Y} dY = 0,$$

since $TU = c$. Solving the total differential for dY/dX, we have

$$\frac{\partial TU}{\partial Y} dY = -\frac{\partial TU}{\partial X} dX,$$

$$\frac{dY}{dX} = -\frac{\partial TU/\partial X}{\partial TU/\partial Y} \text{ or } -\frac{MU_x}{MU_y}$$

Hence, dY/dX is the slope of the indifference curve or MRS_{xy}. The negative sign reflects the negative slope of the indifference curve. If the TU function is ordinal rather than cardinal, MU_x and MU_y have no meaningful absolute values—only their ratios are relevant and interpretable.

Diminishing MU for X and Y requires that

$$\frac{\partial^2 TU}{\partial X^2} < 0 \text{ and } \frac{\partial^2 TU}{\partial Y^2} < 0;$$

however, convexity of the indifference curve requires that $d^2Y/dX^2 < 0$, which is not the same. Thus, the convexity of indifference curves does not depend on diminishing MU for X and Y.

Figure 4-7(b) displays the change in the line of attainable combinations when the price of X decreases, the price of Y (P_{y_1}) and money income (I_1) remaining unchanged. Since I_1 and P_{y_1} do not change, the maximum quantity of Y which may be purchased (I_1/P_{y_1}) is unaffected by any change in P_x. As the price of X declines from P_{x_1} to P_{x_2} the maximum quantity of X which can be purchased with I_1 is raised from its original value of I_1/P_{x_1} to I_1/P_{x_2}. Accordingly, the line of attainable combinations becomes flatter and rotates to the right about the point I_1/P_{y_1}. Should the price of X decline to P_{x_3} the line of attainable combinations rotates rightward even more. In contrast, to represent increases

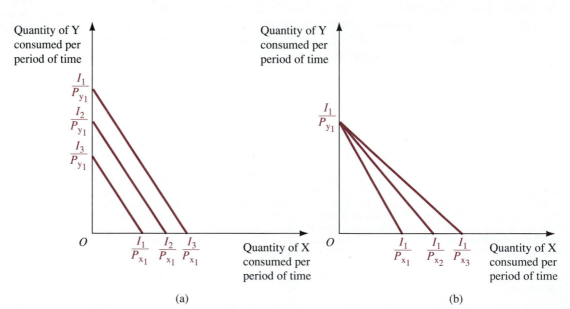

(a)   (b)

Figure 4-7

Shifts in the line of attainable combinations

in the price of X the line of attainable combinations is rotated to the left around the point I_1/P_{y_1}, causing the new line to be more steeply sloped. These changes in the slope of the line follow directly from our finding that the slope of the line of attainable combinations is $-(P_x/P_y)$. Clearly, if P_y is fixed and P_x falls, the slope of the line becomes smaller (or flatter), and when P_x rises, the slope of the line becomes larger (or steeper).

THE MAXIMIZATION OF SATISFACTION

An indifference map provides a diagrammatic representation of a consumer's tastes and intensity of desire for different product combinations. The consumer's purchasing power (and thus ability to satisfy material wants) is reflected by the line of attainable combinations. Putting the two together shows which of all the product combinations on the indifference map is the utility-maximizing combination.

In Figure 4-8, the most satisfying combination among all those which can be purchased is at point C, where the consumer buys X_1 units of X and Y_1 units of Y. Combinations A and B, while attainable, are on a lower indifference curve from C and hence entail lower degrees of satisfaction. Combination D is superior to C, but it costs more than the consumer can afford and therefore is eliminated as an alternative. Indifference curve IC_2 is the highest possible indifference curve that can be reached given the consumer's income constraint, and combination C is the only obtainable combination on that curve. Consequently, C represents the most preferred combination of X and Y and may be said to represent **consumer equilibrium**. In general, the consumer's total utility is maximized *at the point of tangency between the line of attainable combinations and an indifference curve* (provided only that the products are desirable—have positive marginal utilities).

It is relevant at this point to ask: What are the conditions for maximizing satisfaction via indifference curve analysis, and how do these compare with those of cardinal utility analysis? First, we may note that the equilibrium com-

The utility-maximizing combination is identified by the point of tangency between the line of attainable combinations and an indifference curve.

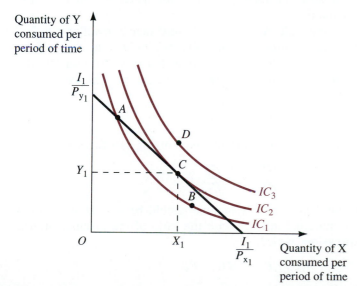

Figure 4-8
Determining the utility-maximizing quantities

bination of X and Y lies *on* the line of attainable combinations, rather than to the inside. This means that *a consumer must fully utilize the available income to maximize satisfaction.* Such a requirement does not preclude saving since saving may appropriately be considered as an item available for "purchase" by the consumer.

Second, at the equilibrium point the slope of the indifference curve is precisely equal to the slope of the line of attainable combinations. This necessarily results from their being tangent at this point. As shown earlier, the respective slopes can be expressed as

$$\text{slope of an indifference curve} = MRS_{xy} = (-) \frac{MU_x}{MU_y},$$

$$\text{slope of the line of attainable combinations} = (-) \frac{P_x}{P_y}.$$

Consequently, *the second condition for maximizing satisfaction requires a consumer to so allocate purchasing power that the marginal rate of substitution of X for Y is equal to the ratio of the price of X to the price of Y.* The interpretation of this condition is straightforward. The MRS_{xy} defines the *rate* at which the consumer is *willing to exchange* X for Y. The price ratio (P_x/P_y) shows the *rate* at which the consumer *can exchange* X for Y. Unless the two rates are equivalent, it is possible for the consumer to alter purchases of X and Y and achieve a greater degree of satisfaction. To illustrate: Suppose that at the current purchase combination, $MRS_{xy} = -4$, meaning that the consumer is willing to exchange 4 units of Y for 1 more unit of X. If $P_x = \$6$ and $P_y = \$2$, then the consumer need only give up 3 units of Y at \$2 each to obtain the \$6 needed to buy another unit of X. Confronted with these circumstances, the consumer will definitely be induced to make the exchange. Why? Because the preference for X and Y at this point is such that one is willing to trade off 4 units of Y for 1 unit of X, yet one has to give up only 3 units of Y to get 1 more unit of X. In general, then, consumer maximization of satisfaction requires equality between the marginal rate of substitution for any pair of products and the ratio of their prices; otherwise some exchange can be made which will increase the consumers' overall satisfaction.

However, the income allocation that will maximize consumer satisfaction can be approached from a more familiar angle. Not only is the slope of the indifference curve equal to the MRS_{xy} at any point, but it is also equal to the ratio of the marginal utilities (ordinally interpreted) of the two goods:

$$MRS_{xy} = -\frac{MU_x}{MU_y}.$$

Thus, we may write the second condition for maximizing satisfaction as

$$-\frac{MU_x}{MU_y} = -\frac{P_x}{P_y}.$$

The utility-maximizing conditions derived from indifference curve analysis are identical to those derived via the cardinal utility model.

This equation states that a consumer's income should be allocated so as to equate the ratio of the marginal utilities with the ratio of the product prices. Rewriting the last expression, we get

$$MU_x \cdot P_y = MU_y \cdot P_x.$$

Dividing each term by $P_x \cdot P_y$ yields

$$\frac{MU_x \cdot P_y}{P_x \cdot P_y} = \frac{MU_y \cdot P_x}{P_x \cdot P_y},$$

which reduces to

$$\frac{MU_x}{P_x} = \frac{MU_y}{P_y}.$$

In an *n*-product economy, the latter expression expands to

$$\frac{MU_{X_a}}{P_a} = \frac{MU_{X_b}}{P_b} = \frac{MU_{X_c}}{P_c} = \cdot\,\cdot\,\cdot = \frac{MU_{X_n}}{P_n} = MU_{\text{saving}},$$

which, combined with the requirement for full utilization of the consumer's income, yields exactly the same conditions imposed upon the maximization of consumer satisfaction via the cardinal utility approach. Yet there is one important distinction: We reached these same conditions *without* the necessity for quantifying utility or satisfaction.

THE IMPACT OF INCOME CHANGES UPON CONSUMER PURCHASES

Changes in a consumer's money income often cause alterations in what is purchased. Suppose that we trace the impact of a change in an individual consumer's money income upon purchases of goods and services, assuming that product prices and the consumer's pattern remain unchanged.

Given the price of X at P_{x_1}, and the price of Y at P_{y_1}, the utility-maximizing purchase combination at an income of I_1 is shown in Figure 4-9(a) as point *A* on indifference curve IC_1, where the consumer buys X_1 units of X and Y_1 units of Y. If the consumer's money income rises to I_2, the prices of X and Y remaining unchanged, the line of attainable combinations shifts in parallel fashion upward and to the right. The right income level allows the consumer to buy more of X, or more of Y, or more of both. According to the preference pattern reflected by the shapes of the indifference curves, an increase in the consumer's money income to I_2 will result in equilibrium purchases of X_2 units of X and Y_2 units of Y at point *B* on indifference curve IC_2. This is a more satisfying combination of X and Y than was permitted formerly by an income of I_1 because it lies on a higher indifference curve. The consumer would realize a further gain in satisfaction should money income rise to I_3, thereby allowing him or her to reach point *C* on indifference curve IC_3 and to purchase X_3 units of X and Y_3 units of Y. The line joining the points of consumer equilibrium as income changes is called the ***income-consumption curve***. The income-consumption curve is the locus of utility-maximizing combinations of products associated with various levels of money income and constant product prices.

When the resulting income-consumption curve is positively sloped, the products are ***normal goods***, meaning that more of the goods are purchased at higher levels of income than at lower levels of income. Such is not always the case. Some items, designated as ***inferior goods***, are purchased in smaller amounts when income rises, in which case the income-consumption curve is negatively sloped. Examples of goods that consumers tend to view as inferior include bologna, dried beans, recapped automobile tires, black-and-white camera film, economy or budget-priced durable goods, and reconditioned shock absorbers.

Derivation of Engel Curves.   The information provided by the income-consumption curve may be used to derive ***Engel curves*** for a product.[8]

BASIC CONCEPT
The income-consumption curve shows all the utility-maximizing combinations of products associated with alternative income levels, other things remaining equal.

An Engel curve shows the effect of income changes on the utility-maximizing quantities of a product which a consumer will purchase, other things being equal.

---

[8] Engel curves are named for Christian Lorenz Ernest Engel, a nineteenth-century German statistician who was a pioneer in the study of consumer budgets.

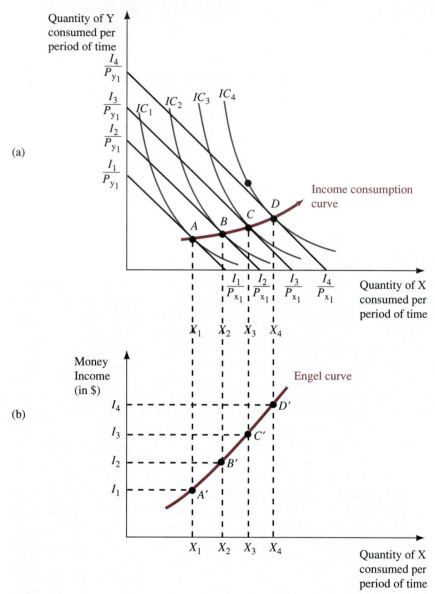

Figure 4-9

The income-consumption curve and derivation of an Engel curve

Engel curves show the equilibrium (utility-maximizing) quantities of a product which a consumer will purchase at various levels of income, other things remaining equal.

    An Engel curve for good X is constructed in Figure 4-9(b). From Figure 4-9(a), we can see that at an income level of I_1 the consumer's equilibrium purchase level is X_1 units of good X. The values of I_1 and X_1 are plotted as point A' in Figure 4-9(b). Again from Figure 4-9(a), we see that when money income is I_2, the consumer will purchase quantity X_2; these values form point B' in Figure 4-9(b). In like manner, point C' corresponds to a money income of I_3 and the resulting equilibrium purchase of X_3 units of X; and point D' is formed from an income of I_4 and the related purchase of X_4 units of X. Connecting points A', B', C', and D' gives the Engel curve relating purchases of X to changes in money income. An Engle curve of this shape indicates that as the consumer's money increases from very low levels, consumption of product X rises in almost equal proportion.

In other cases, as income rises a consumer's purchases of an item tend to increase less than proportionally to income; additional purchases become less and less sensitive to further gains in income, causing the Engel curve to become more steeply sloped at progressively higher incomes. Examples include newspapers, flour, light bulbs, salt, toothpaste, and most types of basic "necessities." For other normal goods, such as restaurant meals, recreation activities, travel, "luxuries," and saving, a consumer's expenditures tend to expand more rapidly than income. This increasing responsiveness of quantities purchased relative to income changes results in an Engel curve that increases at a decreasing rate. (What is the nature of the Engel curve for an inferior good?)

THE IMPACT OF PRICE CHANGES UPON CONSUMER PURCHASES

Not only do consumers typically adapt their consumption patterns to income changes, but they also react to changes in the price of goods and services. Suppose that we examine what happens to the quantity of X when we vary the price of X and hold constant the consumer's income, tastes and preferences (as reflected by the indifference map), and the price of Y.

Given the price of X at P_{x_1}, the price of Y at P_{y_1}, and money income at I_1, the consumer will maximize satisfaction by purchasing X_1 units of X and Y_1 units of Y, as shown in Figure 4-10(a). Now suppose the price of X falls to P_{x_2}; the line of attainable combinations will pivot to the right about point I_1/P_{y_1}, allowing the consumer to purchase as much as I_1/P_{x_2} units of X were all income spent on X. The new line of attainable combinations will necessarily be tangent to a higher indifference curve than previously. Equilibrium will be reestablished by purchasing quantity X_2 of X and quantity Y_2 of Y. In like manner it can be ascertained that a further decline in the price of X to P_{x_3} will permit the consumer to reach an even higher indifference curve, maximizing satisfaction at X_3 and Y_3. The line joining the various points of consumer equilibrium is called the *price-consumption curve*. The price-consumption curve is the locus of the utility-maximizing combinations of products that result from variations in the price of one product, when other product prices, the consumer's tastes and preferences, and money income are held constant.

> **BASIC CONCEPT**
> The price-consumption curve shows all the utility-maximizing product combinations when the price of one product changes and all other things remain equal.
>
> A consumer's demand curve can be derived from the price-consumption curve.

Deriving the Demand Curve. An individual consumer's *demand curve* for product X can be derived directly from the information contained in the price-consumption curve. A consumer's demand curve for a product graphically illustrates the different amounts that the consumer is willing and able to buy at various possible prices during some moment of time wherein all other factors influencing the quantity purchased are held constant. From Figure 4-10(a) it can be seen that when the price of X is P_{x_1} the consumer's equilibrium purchase is quantity X_1 of X. This establishes one point on the demand curve for product X, shown as point A in Figure 4-10(b). At the lower price P_{x_2} the consumer's purchases rise to X_2 units; this becomes a second point on the demand curve for product X—point B in Figure 4-10(b). At the still lower price of P_{x_3} the consumer buys X_3 units of X, which gives a third point on the demand curve—point C in Figure 4-10(b). Other points on the demand curve can be derived in analogous fashion, thereby producing line *dd* in Figure 4-10(b).

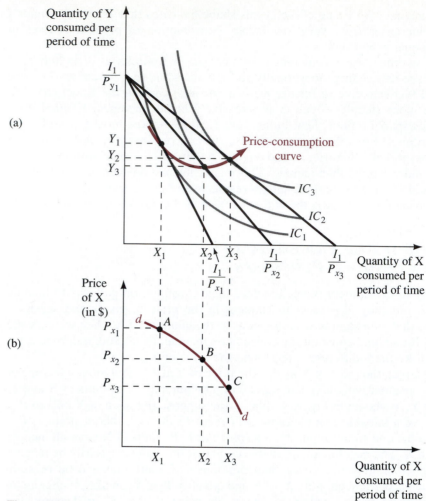

Figure 4-10

The price-consumption curve and the consumer's demand curve

Observe that the demand curve slopes downward to the right. This indicates that the price of X and the quantity purchased of X per period of time vary inversely. As P_x rises, the quantity demanded of X falls; or, as P_x falls, the quantity demanded rises. The fundamental principle between selling price and quantity is pure common sense—*other things remaining equal*, a person will be inclined to buy more of a product per period of time at lower prices than at higher prices. Additionally, this principle is reflected by the negative slope of the demand curve.

INCOME AND SUBSTITUTION EFFECTS

When the price of an item changes (and all other relevant factors remain constant), two forces are activated to cause the consumer to alter the quantity purchased. Take the case of a price decline. First, a decrease in price increases the consumer's real income (purchasing power), thus enhancing to some extent the ability to buy more goods and services. Second, a decrease in the price of a product induces some consumers to substitute it for other now relatively higher-priced items. Indifference curve analysis enables us to readily measure the potency of the income and substitution effects.

Consider Figure 4-11. The consumer's money income is I_1, and the price of Y is P_{y_1}. If the price of X initially is P_{x_1}, then the original equilibrium is at point A on indifference curve IC_1 where the consumer buys X_1 units of X. When the price of X decreases to P_{x_2}, the line of attainable combinations rotates rightward; the consumer moves to a new equilibrium position at B on indifference curve IC_2, purchasing quantity X_2 of X. The overall change in the quantity demanded of X from the first equilibrium point at A to the second equilibrium point at B may be designated as the ***total effect*** of the price change. The total effect can, in turn, be decomposed into the substitution effect and the income effect.

Let us first isolate the substitution effect and determine its magnitude. The decline in the price of X precipitates an increase in the consumer's real income, as evidenced by the movement to a higher indifference curve even though money income remains fixed. Now imagine that we decrease the consumer's income by an amount *just sufficient* to return to the *same* level of satisfaction enjoyed before the price decline. Graphically, this is accomplished by drawing a fictitious line of attainable combinations with a slope corresponding to the *new* ratio of the product prices (P_{x_2}/P_{y_1}) so that it is just tangent to the *original* indifference curve (IC_1). This produces the line in Figure 4-11 with extreme points I/P_{y_1} and I/P_{x_2} tangent to IC_1 at point C.

Combination C is as equally satisfying as combination A because they both lie on the same indifference curve. Yet, given the decline in the price of X from P_{x_1} to P_{x_2} the consumer will prefer combination C to combination A. Why? Because it is cheaper to buy C rather than A now that the price of X has fallen to P_{x_2}. The effect of the lower price thus is to prompt the consumer to increase consumption of X and cut consumption of Y (i.e., to substitute X for Y). This increase in the consumption of X from X_1 to X_3 is the ***substitution effect***;

BASIC CONCEPT
The substitution effect shows the change in the utility-maximizing combination solely attributable to a change in the price of the product.

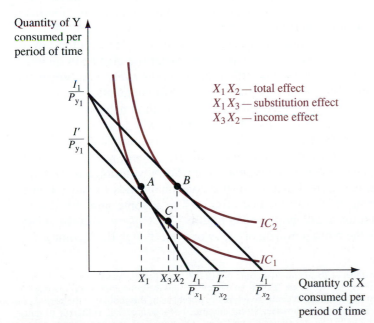

$X_1 X_2$ — total effect
$X_1 X_3$ — substitution effect
$X_3 X_2$ — income effect

Figure 4-11
Income and substitution effects for a normal good in case of a price decline

graphically, it is represented by a movement along the original indifference curve IC_1 from point A to the imaginary intermediate equilibrium at point C. More formally, the substitution effect refers to the *change in the quantity demanded of a product resulting exclusively from a change in its price when the consumer's real income is held constant, thereby restricting the consumer's reaction to the price change to a movement along the original indifference curve.*

The income effect is determined by observing the change in the quantity demanded of a product that is associated solely with the change in the consumer's *real* income. In Figure 4-11 letting the consumer's real income rise from its imaginary level (defined by the line of attainable combinations tangent to point C) back to its true level (defined by the line of attainable combinations tangent to point B) gives the income effect. Thus, the ***income effect*** is indicated by the movement from the imaginary equilibrium at point C at the actual new equilibrium at point B; the increase in the quantity of X purchased from X_3 to X_2 is the income effect. Formally, the *income effect may be defined as the change in the quantity demanded of a product exclusively associated with a change in real income.*

Comparatively speaking, *the magnitude of the substitution effect is ordinarily greater than that of the income effect.* Frequently, the change in the consumer's real income resulting from changes in the price of one commodity is so slight that there is little room for the consumer to alter the quantities of goods he or she purchased.[9] But where items can be readily substituted for one another, price changes are likely to trigger a relatively large substitution effect.

Usually, the income and substitution effects reinforce one another; that is, they operate in the same direction. A *lower* price for a product results in an *increase* in its quantity demanded due to the substitution effect and an *increase* in its quantity demanded due to the income effect. As Figure 4-12 illustrates, when the price of a product *rises*, the substitution effect will bring about a *decrease* in quantity demanded, and the income effect likewise will bring about a *decrease* in quantity demanded. Note that in the event of either a price decrease or a price increase (Figures 4-11 and 4-12, respectively), the quantity demanded of a product varies inversely with its price—the law of demand is operative. Second, note that in either event the change in quantity demanded stemming from the income effect moves in the *same* direction as the change in real income—if real income rises, the quantity demanded rises; if real income falls, the quantity demanded falls. These two relationships characterize the class of goods we earlier delineated as ***normal goods***.

In the case of ***inferior goods***, however, the income and substitution effects work in the *opposite* direction. For an inferior good, a *decrease* in the price of X causes the consumer to buy *more* of it (the substitution effect), but at the same time the higher real income of the consumer tends to cause him to *reduce* consumption of X (the income effect). The income and substitution effects for this situation are diagrammed in Figure 4-13. Observe that the substitution effect still is the more powerful of the two; even though the income effect

---

[9] For instance, if a consumer with an annual income of $10,000 finds that the price of a good he buys once a month has declined in price from 73 cents to 69 cents, then the consumer's real income has increased—but ever so slightly. The 48 cents saved on the purchase of the good over the period of a year does technically increase the consumer's real income, but it scarcely is sufficient to cause even a minor realignment in the consumer's purchases. Of course, if the item is one that is purchased frequently (cigarettes) and/or is purchased in large quantities (gasoline) and/or has a high price (automobiles), then the effect on real income may be quite significant.

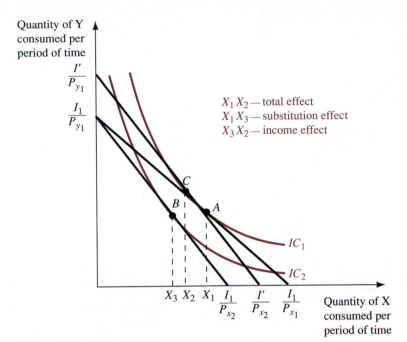

Figure 4-12
Income and substitution effects for a normal good in case of a price increase

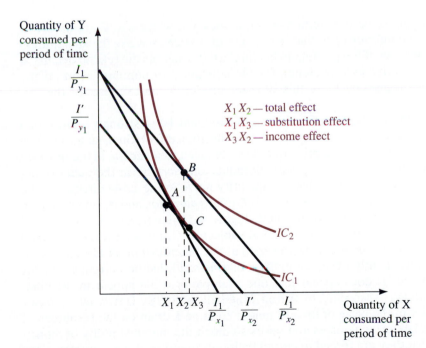

Figure 4-13
Income and substitution effects for an inferior good in case of a price decline

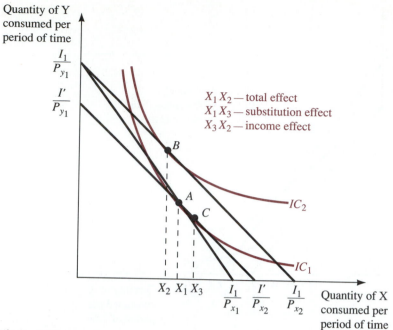

Figure 4-14

Income and substitution effects for an inferior good subject to Giffen's paradox

works counter to the substitution effect, it does not override it. Furthermore, it follows for an inferior good that in the case of a price *increase* the substitution effect causes *less* of the product to be purchased, whereas the related decline in real income activates a tendency for the consumer to purchase *more* of the good. (The diagrammatics of this situation are left as an exercise for the student.)

On the very rarest of occasions, a good may be so strongly inferior that the income effect actually overrides the substitution effect. Such an occurrence means that a decline in the price of a good will lead to a *decline* in the quantity demanded and that a rise in price will induce an *increase* in the quantity demanded—in other words, price and quantity move in the *same* direction. The name given to such a unique situation is ***Giffen's paradox***, and it constitutes the only exception to the law of demand. Figure 4-14 illustrates the income and substitution effects for an inferior good subject to Giffen's paradox. It should be emphasized at this point, however, that the phenomenon of Giffen's paradox is so infrequently observed in the modern world that no current examples can be offered. It does appear that one example of it did appear in the nineteenth century. According to Alfred Marshall, a Sir R. Giffen noted cases where a rise in the price of bread "makes so large a drain on the resources of the poorer labouring families and raises so much the marginal utility of money to them, that they are forced to curtail their consumption of meat and the more expensive farinaceous foods; and, bread being still the cheapest food which they can get and will take, they consume more, and not less of it."[10] But such cases are rare; when they are met with, each must be treated on its own merits.

> **The only possible way that a decline in the price of a good can lead to a decrease in quantity demanded or an increase in price lead to an increase in quantity demanded is when a good is so strongly inferior that the income effect overpowers the substitution effect; such a rarity is called Giffen's paradox.**

[10] Alfred Marshall, *Principles of Economics*, 8th ed. (London: MacMillan, 1920), p. 132.

Even in the case of this outdated example one may surmise that had the price of bread continued to rise, there quickly would have come a point when the purchases of bread began to decline. Thus, Giffen's paradox is likely to hold only for a fairly narrow range of prices. In our type of society Giffen's paradox is likely to be observed in at most a small minority of consuming units (individuals and households) and then only for precious few types of inferior goods.

MARKET DEMAND CURVES

The *market demand curve* for a product represents the various amounts which consumers as a group are willing and able to purchase at various alternative prices at a specific moment of time wherein other factors influencing consumer behavior are held constant. Thus, the market demand curve isolates the relationship between price and the quantity demanded by all consumers. It is found by summing the quantities of a good that each consumer is willing and able to purchase at each and every alternative price.

     Figure 4-15 illustrates this process for a three-person economy with individual demands as indicated. At a price of P_1 dollars, consumer A is willing and able to buy quantity q_{A1} per period of time; consumer B is willing and able to buy quantity q_{B1} per period of time; and consumer C is willing and able to buy quantity q_{C1} per period of time. Together they are willing and able to buy $q_{A1} + q_{B1} + q_{C1} = Q_1$ units at a price of P_1 dollars, as indicated by the market demand curve. Similarly, at price P_2, consumer A is willing and able to purchase q_{A2}; consumer B is willing and able to purchase q_{B2}; and consumer C is willing and able to purchase q_{C2}. Taken together, market demand at price P_2 is Q_2 ($= q_{A2} + q_{B2} + q_{C2}$) units. Additional points on the market demand curve can be similarly determined and the market curve constructed (line *DD* in Figure 4-15). Since the individual demand curves are downsloping to the right, the market demand curve must also slope downward to the right. The law of demand holds not only for individual consumer demand but also for market demand.

     However, adding together the demand curves of individuals to obtain market demand curves is not entirely valid since it implies that one consumer's purchases are completely independent of another consumer's purchase decisions. It has, for example, been noted that (1) some people buy goods not so much to satisfy inner wants as to impress other consumers with their "conspic-

BASIC CONCEPT
A market demand curve shows the quantities demanded by all consumers at various alternative market prices, other things remaining equal; it is derived by summing the quantity demanded by each individual consumer at each alternative price.

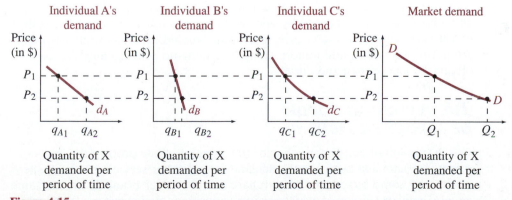

Figure 4-15
Derivation of the market demand curve for a product in a three-person economy

WHICH IS LESS BURDENSOME—AN INCOME TAX OR A SALES TAX?

Suppose that a sales tax is levied on cigarettes and that each week Mr. Tanner buys a carton of cigarettes, paying a fixed sum as sales tax on the cigarettes. The payment of the sales tax effectively raises the price of cigarettes and puts him on a lower difference curve, reducing Mr. Tanner's well-being. The graphics are depicted in the accompanying figure.

Assume that Mr. Tanner has an income of OB_1 dollars and, prior to the imposing of the sales tax, that the line of attainable combinations is B_1A_1. If Mr. Tanner spent all his income on cigarettes, he could buy OA_1 units; hence, the pretax price of cigarettes is OB_1/OA_1. The initial equilibrium purchase of cigarettes is at point R on IC_1, where OQ_1 cigarettes are bought and B_1Y_1 dollars are spent to pay for them. The levying of the sales tax shifts the line of attainable combinations to B_1A_2; Mr. Tanner's new equilibrium point is at S on IC_2, with expenditures for cigarettes of B_1Y_2 dollars and consumption of OQ_2 units. Since before the sales tax was imposed, Mr. Tanner could have purchased OQ_2 units for B_1Y_3 dollars, the amount he pays in sales tax is Y_2Y_3 dollars. (An arithmetic example: Suppose Mr. Tanner formerly bought 52 cartons per year at $4 per carton but after the sales tax was imposed buys 40 cartons per year at $5. With the sales tax he is spending $200 per year for cigarettes. But if there were no sales tax, he would have had to pay only $160 for 40 cartons. Hence, the sales tax costs Mr. Tanner $40 per year.)

But how would Mr. Tanner fare if instead of imposing a sales tax on cigarettes the legislature in his state simply increased his income taxes by an equivalent amount ($40 per year) to raise the desired tax revenue? Would Mr. Tanner be better or worse off? Or would it make any difference one way or the other? Graphically, the effect of higher income taxes is shown by an inward shift of the line of attainable combina-

tions to B_2A_3, with distance B_1B_2 being exactly equal to the dollar amount of the income tax (in our example, $40). B_2A_3 is parallel to B_1A_1 because the income tax need not disturb the price of cigarettes. Mr. Tanner's equilibrium point, given the income tax, is at point T on IC_3 with purchases of OQ_3 units. Since T is on a higher indifference curve than S, it follows that Mr. Tanner would prefer paying an income tax (of $40) rather than a sales tax of the same dollar amount ($40).

The basic reason for this perhaps surprising result is that while both taxes reduce the consumer's real income, the sales tax also triggers a substitution effect because it alters not just real income but relative prices as well. The imposition of a general income tax brings on only an income effect, and the consumer is free to spend the income he has left without any further impact or adjustment. In contrast, imposing a product-specific (or excise) tax involves both an income and a substitution effect: The sales tax reduces consumer purchasing power and also changes the price attractiveness of the taxed good relative to other goods, thereby producing a greater revision in the consumer's expenditure pattern than an income tax alone.

PROBLEMS

1. Suppose that instead of making the dollar amount of the income tax equal to the dollar amount of the sales tax, the size of the income tax is set so as to leave the consumer on the *same* indifference curve as the sales tax. Determine which of the two taxes will raise the most tax revenue.

2. If Congress decided that it was in the pubic interest to conserve gasoline, would it be more effective to impose a sales tax upon gasoline or to increase personal income taxes? Demonstrate graphically. What reasons can you give for this result?

uous consumption," (2) the buying habits of some individuals are influenced by the consumption patterns of persons with whom they associate or come into contact (the "demonstration effect"), and (3) some consumers buy goods because of the social status they connote. Consequently, on occasions the amount of an item purchased by one consumer has a bearing upon how other consumers behave. In such cases, individual demand curves, strictly speaking, are not independent, and a more complex adding-up process must be used to obtain the market demand curve.

THE ATTRIBUTE MODEL OF CONSUMER DEMAND

Our discussion of consumer behavior to this point, while probing the impact of prices, income, and tastes on the demand for a good or service, has been silent about why some buyers opt to purchase brand A over brand B for the same general good or service. A way to analyze consumer choice criteria for competing brands, called *attribute analysis*, emerged in the mid-1960s and early

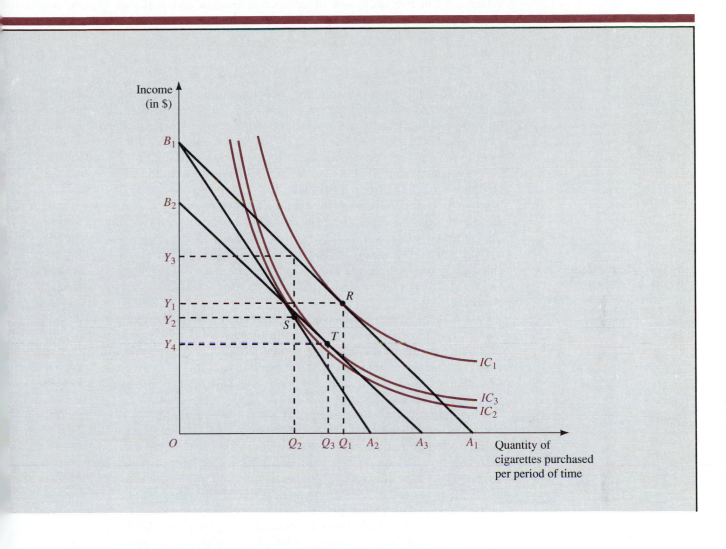

1970s.[11] The attribute model of consumer behavior builds upon the thesis that it is a product's characteristics, performance features, or attributes that which create utility; thus, what causes a buyer to prefer one brand over another has to do with the different attributes of rival brands. For instance, a buyer may choose a Ford Mustang (sticker price of about $19,000) over a comparably equipped Ford Taurus (sticker price about $19,500) because of its more bucket seats, its styling, and its peppier engine, even though the Taurus is given consistently higher ratings for reliability by rating services such as *Consumer Reports.* The thesis of the attribute model is that a consumer's preference for brand A over brand B is rooted in the fact that the consumer attaches more utility or satisfaction to some attributes than to others. The model considers the

[11] Kelvin Lancaster, "A New Approach to Consumer Demand," *Journal of Political Economy*, Vol. 74, No. 2 (April 1966), pp. 132–57, and *Consumer Demand: A New Approach* (New York: Columbia University Press, 1971). The following treatment follows closely the treatment by Evan J. Douglas, who has cogently and systematically illuminated the trail blazed by Lancaster. See his *Managerial Economics: Analysis and Strategy*, 3rd ed. (Englewood Cliffs N.J.: Prentice Hall, 1987. Also see Kelvin Lancaster, *Modern Consumer Theory* (London: Edwin Elgar, 1990) for a more recent treatment.

BASIC CONCEPT

The attribute model of buyer demand holds that a buyer's preference for one firm's brand of a product over another firm's brand is due to the different attributes of competing brands—a consumer attaches more utility to some attributes than to others.

differences in the attributes of competing brands and seeks to explain the decision to buy one brand over another in terms of the preferred brand's differentiating characteristics.

DISPLAYING THE ATTRIBUTES OF RIVAL BRANDS

To explore the rationale for choosing among rival brands, consider the situation of buying a personal computer (PC). Let's assume that a prospective buyer is familiar enough with personal computers to have concluded that the two most important attributes (other than price) are "user friendliness" and "variety of software programs which the computer can handle." Suppose that after evaluating four PC brands, the buyer comes up with the information and attribute ratings shown in Table 4-1.

In Figure 4-16, each PC brand is shown in the "attribute space" as a ray drawn from the origin. Each brand has its own ray, with each ray's position on the graph being defined by the ratio of the user-friendliness rating to the software capability rating, as shown in the last column of Table 4-1. Graphically, this ratio is the *slope of the ray*; the differences in the slopes of the rays mirror the respective ratings' tradeoffs of user friendliness versus software capability.

Differences in the slopes of attribute rays reflect differences in a consumer's preferences for one attribute versus another.

The next analytical issue becomes one of the determining how far out along a given ray a consumer can go. In the case of our PC example, it is very probable that the buyer will want to stop at purchasing just one PC, in which case the relevant distance out each PC ray is one unit. This, of course, implicitly assumes the buyer's budget is large enough to permit the purchase of all four brands despite the price differences. The cost of acquiring each attribute combination one unit out each ray is equal to the price of the respective PC brand. In effect, the buyer's "satisfaction frontier" (analogous to the line of attainable combinations) is bounded by points *A*, *B*, *C*, and *D* in Figure 4-16, assuming that the buyer is *willing* and *able* to pay the price for each brand despite the price differentials. [*Note:* If our example involved a product like beer or going to the movies or dining out, where more than "1 unit" might well be purchased over a short period of time, how far out each ray the consumer can go is found by (1) dividing the consumer's allotted budget for the item by the price of each brand to arrive at how many units can be purchased and (2) calculating the total amounts of each attribute which can thus be obtained. For example, if the consumer's budget allocation is $25 and the price of brand Q is $5, it is possible to buy 5 units; further, if brand Q possesses 2 units of attribute X and 3 units of attribute Y, the consumer's budget provides access to 10 units

TABLE 4-1   ATTRIBUTES AND PRICES OF FOUR BRANDS OF PERSONAL COMPUTERS

PC Brand	PC Price	Attribute Rating[a]		Ratio of User Friendliness to Software Capability
		User Friendliness	Software Capability	
A	$2550	8	3	2.67
B	2700	7	6	1.17
C	3600	6	8	0.75
D	4200	4	9	0.44

[a] On a scale of 1 to 10 where 1 = lowest and 10 = highest.

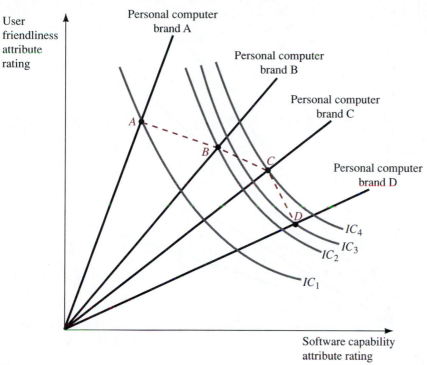

Figure 4-16
Determining the utility-maximizing attribute combination

of attribute X and 15 units of attribute Y insofar as brand Q is concerned. This combination of 10 units of X and 15 units of Y defines how far out the ray for brand Q the consumer can go given the $25 budget constraint and Q's $5 price.]

DETERMINING THE UTILITY-MAXIMIZING ATTRIBUTE COMBINATION

Our personal computer shopper, in comparing the four brands of PCs, will have to evaluate the tradeoff (or marginal rate of substitution) between user friendliness and software options; these evaluations produce a set of indifference curves expressing his or her tastes and preferences at each possible attribute combination. As with "regular" indifference curve analysis, the attribute combinations on higher indifference curves are preferred to those on lower curves, and the curves slope downward to the right, are convex to the origin, and do not intersect.

Since our shopper needs to choose one PC brand or another and is constrained to points A, B, C, or D in Figure 4-16, utility is maximized by choosing the personal computer brand with the attribute combination on the highest indifference curve attainable. This turns out to be brand C on indifference curve IC_4.

PRICE CHANGES AND BRAND SWITCHING

Suppose that the price of one brand of a product declines, while the prices of rival brands remain constant. How might this affect the demands for the lower-priced brand and the other brands against which it competes? Con-

PRINCIPLE
The utility-maximizing brand is the one whose attribute combination allows the consumer to reach the highest possible indifference curve permitted by the consumer's budget constraint.

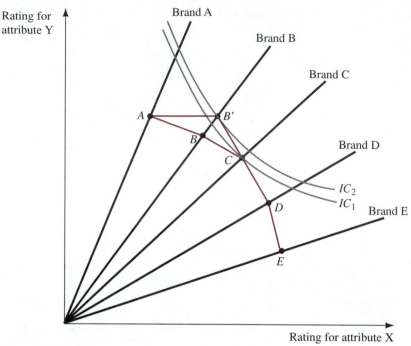

Figure 4-17
The effect of a price cut for one brand upon brand selection

sider Figure 4-17, where five brands are available, the satisfaction frontier is *ABCDE* (given the initial prices of the five brands and the consumer's budget constraint), and the consumer is maximizing the utility from attributes X and Y at point *C*, where indifference curve IC_1 just touches the frontier. Now suppose that the price of brand B is reduced, shifting the satisfaction frontier out along the ray for brand *B* to *B'* and giving a new frontier of *AB'CDE*. The consumer can now reach the higher indifference curve IC_2 by switching to brand B. Not surprisingly, the law of demand prevails here as well: The lower price of brand B induces a greater demand for B by causing some consumers (those with indifference curves like those in Figure 4-17) to switch over from now relatively higher-priced brands. (Can you draw a set of indifference curves on Figure 4-17 to represent a preference pattern such that the lower price for B would not induce brand switching?)

WHEN A BRAND GETS PRICED OUT OF THE MARKET

Not surprisingly, there is always a maximum price a consumer will pay for a brand even though it has the most desired attribute combination. Figure 4-18 shows a satisfaction frontier *ABC* for three brands offering attributes X and Y. The consumer is maximizing utility on indifference curve IC_1 by purchasing brand B. If the price of brand B rises, pulling the satisfaction frontier inward to *AB'D*, the consumer is unable to reach IC_1 and must be content with the utility level on IC_2—still purchasing only brand B but necessarily purchasing less of B because of B's higher price and an unchanged budget allocation.

However, if the price of brand B is raised still further, shifting the satisfaction frontier inward to *AB''C*, the consumer will maximize utility by shifting purchases from brand B to brand C, attaining the level of overall satisfaction associated with IC_3. Thus, brand B has been priced "out of the

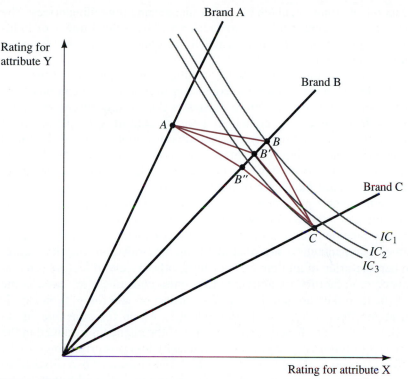

Figure 4-18
How a brand can get priced "out of the market"

market" for this consumer even though its combination of attributes X and Y has otherwise the best fit with the consumer's taste and preference pattern.

The law of demand thus governs the attribute model, too. As the price of one brand of a good or service falls, consumers already purchasing the brand will tend to purchase more units and other consumers will begin to buy their first units of the lower-priced brand (often at the expense of competing brands carrying higher price tags). As a brand's price rises, consumers either buy fewer units or else drop out of the market for the brand altogether and switch their purchases to lower-priced substitute brands.

KEY POINTS

The indifference curve model of consumer demand is both a supplement and an alternative to the cardinal utility model. Indifference analysis has appeal because it does not require the precise quantification of utility and because it does not depend so heavily on the requirement of diminishing marginal utility.

A consumer's taste and preference pattern can be represented by a family of indifference curves. The shapes of the indifference curves are the critical features for displaying a consumer's set of tastes for a pair of products; they can be drawn to represent any set of tastes and preferences.

A consumer's *ability* to satisfy his or her tastes and preferences is represented by the line of attainable combinations. This line incorporates into the consumer's choice pattern the restraints imposed by the consumer's money income and by the prices of the goods the consumer may be desirous of purchasing. The point of tangency between the line of attainable combinations and an indifference curve defines the highest level of satisfaction which the consumer is capable of attaining, given his or her income and prevailing prices. The conditions requisite for maximizing satisfaction via the ordinal utility or indifference curve approach are exactly identical to the conditions derived from the cardinal utility approach.

By allowing income to vary while holding product prices and the consumer's tastes fixed, the consumer's income-consumption curve can be established. The income-consumption curve illustrates the various purchase combinations that will maximize the consumer's satisfaction at different levels of income. From the data provided by the income-consumption curve, an Engel curve showing the relationship between money income and purchases of a good can be derived. Normal goods have positively sloped Engel curves; negatively sloped Engel curves are indicative of inferior goods.

The consumer's price-consumption curve can be found by observing the equilibrium path traced out by changing the price of a product and by holding money income and tastes and preferences constant. Data for plotting the consumer's demand curve are obtained from the price-consumption curve.

When the price of an item rises or falls, other relevant factors remaining unchanged, two factors are activated to prompt consumers to reassess the quantity of the item they are purchasing. The most powerful force, typically, is the substitution effect; it represents the extent to which the consumer is induced to alter what is purchased *solely* because of the change introduced in the relative prices of products. The second, and usually less powerful, force is the income effect; it represents the extent to which the consumer is motivated to buy more or less of a good because of the change in real income brought about by the price change.

In the case of normal goods the income and substitution effects operate in the same direction and reinforce one another. For inferior goods, however, the substitution and income effects work in opposite directions. For most inferior goods, the substitution effect overrides the impact of the income effect and causes the quantity demanded of a good to vary in the opposite direction from the change in the price of the good, thereby validating the law of demand. On the very rarest of occasions, a good may be so strongly inferior that the income effect overpowers the substitution effect and causes the quantity demanded to vary in the *same* direction as the change in price. Such a situation is termed Giffen's paradox and constitutes the only exception to the law of demand.

The market demand curve for a product is obtained by aggregating the quantity demanded by all individual consumers at each alternative market price.

The attribute approach to consumer behavior helps explain why buyers may rationally prefer one brand to another.

PROBLEMS AND QUESTIONS FOR DISCUSSION

1. Illustrate by means of indifference curves the taste and preference pattern suggested by the following statements:
   (a) "There is not enough money to make me eat a raw oyster."
   (b) "What good is a cigarette if you don't have a light?"
   (c) "I would just as soon eat broiled lobster as filet mignon."
   (d) "What good is money if you don't spend it? After all, you can't take it with you."

2. Graphically illustrate in three dimensions the nature of the total utility surface for two goods which are perfect complements.

3. Suppose that a particular consumer has a special dislike for eating turnips but immensely enjoys eating barbecued spareribs. Draw an indifference map for these two items. Indicate the direction of higher degrees of satisfaction.

4. Explain the logical inconsistency involved were two indifference curves to intersect.

5. Suppose that the equation of an indifference curve for a consumer is as follows: $XY = 48$, where X = units of good X, Y = units of good Y, 48 = amount of utility or satisfaction expressed in utils.
   (a) Graphically determine the shape and location of this indifference curve. (Use graph paper.)
   (b) Determine the consumer's MRS_{xy} at $X = 4$ and $Y = 12$.
   (c) Suppose that the price of X is $10 per unit and the price of Y is $4 per unit. Determine the equation for the line of attainable combinations if the consumer's income level is $20. What is the slope of the line of attainable combinations at this income? Determine the equation and slope of the line of attainable combinations at an income of $30. Does the change in income from $20 to $30 influence the slope of the line of attainable combinations? Why or why not?
   (d) Illustrate graphically the point of tangency between the indifference curve $XY = 48$ and a line of attainable combinations where $P_x = 10 and $P_y = 4. How much income will it take for the consumer to attain 48 utils of satisfaction, given these prices?

6. Is a consumer's satisfaction level increased, decreased, or unaffected when the price of a product he or she is purchasing goes down? Illustrate graphically.

7. If indifference curves for perfect substitutes are negatively sloped and linear and if indifference curves for perfect complements are right angles, is it true that the degree of convexity of an indifference curve reflects the degree of substitutability and complementarity among two products? Explain.

8. Graphically illustrate the combination of goods X and Y that will maximize satisfaction in the following set of circumstances:
   (a) Goods X and Y are perfect substitutes.
   (b) $MRS_{xy} = (-)1$.
   (c) $P_x = 2, $P_y = 2.25, and $I = 18.

9. Diagrammatically illustrate the income and substitution effects for an inferior good in the case of a price increase.

10. Diagrammatically illustrate the income and substitution effects for an inferior good subject to Giffen's paradox in the case of a price increase.

11. Suppose that two goods X and Y are judged by consumers to be perfect substitutes for each other. Suppose further that the price of X is higher than the price of Y.
    (a) If consumers behave rationally, what would you predict to happen to sales of the two products?
    (b) Where consumers view products which compete against one another as being close or near perfect substitutes, is it surprising to find that their prices are identical or at least nearly so? Explain your answer.

12. Three frequently encountered Engel curves are as follows:

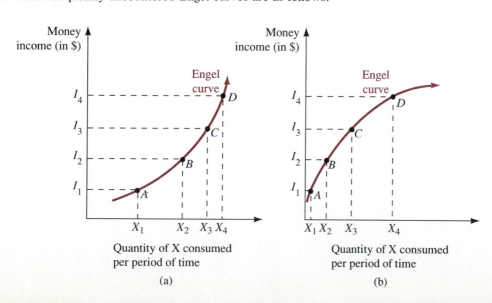

Quantity of X consumed
per period of time

(a)

Quantity of X consumed
per period of time

(b)

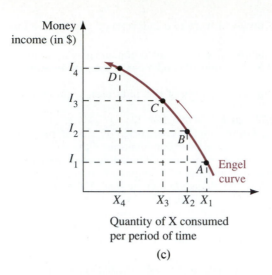

(c)

Describe the nature of the relationship between income and the quantity consumed for each of the three situations. Can you tell from the diagram whether the products in question are normal goods or inferior goods? Why or why not?

13. A cigarette producer is considering introducing a new smokeless brand of cigarette into California to compete directly against the two leading low-tar brands, A and B. Panels of cigarette smokers have rated the two leading brands in two respects— "good taste" and "lightness." Brand A was given a 7 rating (on a 1 to 10 scale) on good taste and a 2 rating on lightness. Brand B received ratings of 5 on good taste and 5 on lightness. Brand A sells for $21 per carton and brand B retails for $23 per carton. In taste tests for the new brand the producer is considering introducing, smokers have given it a 3 rating on good taste and a 7 on lightness. Plans call for the new brand to sell for $25 per carton.
   (a) Draw an indifference map for a representative smoker illustrating the preferences/indifference among combinations of the two attributes.
   (b) Superimpose on your hypothetical indifference map the brand attribute rays for the three brands of cigarettes.
   (c) Which brand will the consumer select if he or she is willing to spend up to $25 per month on cigarettes? (Assume that the consumer agrees with the attribute ratings just cited.)
   (d) What if the price per carton for the new brand is reduced from $25 to $22? Will the smoker switch brands?

Chapter 5

Demand Functions, Revenue Functions, and Elasticity

The role of this chapter is to extend the analysis of consumer demand, first by describing more of the factors that shape market demand for a product, second by looking at the demand for a firm's product, third by deriving the revenue functions that correspond to a firm's demand curve, and, finally, by analyzing the sensitivity of the quantity demanded to changes in price and income.

FACTORS THAT INFLUENCE MARKET DEMAND

Many factors influence the quantity of a good or service that all consumers in the market will purchase at some moment of time. The principal factors influencing the quantity purchased are summarized next.

A Product's Price. The price of a good or service is nearly always an instrumental factor in the demand picture. Other things being equal, the quantity demanded for a product varies inversely with price—buyers are willing and able to purchase more of an item at lower prices than at higher prices. In cases where a product is on sale or discounted from its regular list price or where buyers and sellers habitually haggle and negotiate over price, the appropriate measure of price is the actual amount paid, or *transaction price*, rather than the initial asking price.

A Product's Attributes. Consumers are typically very interested in a product's attributes, especially in comparison to those of competing brands or substitute products. The key attributes are usually quality, performance features, warranties, after-sale service and repair, credit terms, convenience, styling and design, and overall value. In general, the demand for a product is stronger when it possesses the attributes which consumers are seeking. In some industries, the product attributes of different firms are essentially identical, as with wool, natural gas, salt, cast iron pipe, plate glass, eggs, and paper clips; in such cases, the products of sellers are usually viewed as *standard commodities*. But where the products of rival sellers possess distinctly different attributes and are thus *differentiated* (as with soft drinks, automobiles, personal computer software, restaurants, magazines, and ski equipment), the demand for one brand is very much a function of how consumers perceive its attributes in relation to the attributes of competing brands and products. Rival sellers

Price is nearly always the single biggest determining factor underlying the quantity that buyers will purchase at some moment of time.

Demand for a firm's product is affected by buyer perceptions regarding the attributes it possesses or does not possess.

97

typically advertise and promote their product's attributes as a matter of information to potential buyers, the aim being to persuade buyers that their product's attributes are better.

Consumer Tastes and Preferences. The relevance of consumer tastes for determining demand is easily apparent. When consumer preferences for a good or service weaken, market demand for the item weakens. By the same token, an increase in the intensity of consumer desire for an item tends to increase willingness to pay a higher price or to buy more of it or both. Needless to say, consumer tastes and preferences are subject to change, sometimes gradual and sometimes rapid, over time. The emergence of new and better products, changing values and life-styles, new information about health and safety features of products, whether the item is trending in or out of fashion, changing levels of advertising for the product, changes (up or down) in the advertising of competing brands or related items, and the number and convenience of locations in which the product is available, to mention a few, all can account for why consumer tastes and preferences for an item grow stronger or weaker.

Except for inferior goods, rising incomes tend to strengthen demand for a firm's product.

Consumer Income. That income has an impact upon market demand is plain enough. Willingness to buy is in itself insufficient; consumers must be able to pay for the products they want. Typically, the greater is consumer income and purchasing power the greater will be market demand for goods in general and for some items in particular. Only in the case of inferior goods is rising income accompanied by a weakening of demand.

Prices of Related Items. The prices of related items are an important demand variable because of the interrelationships that exist among goods. In the case of substitute goods, how the price of one compares with the price of competing brands can be a pivotal factor in the consumer's selection process. If Stroh's is cheaper than Budweiser, this fact is sure to influence the purchase decision of some buyers. In the case of items that have a complementary relationship and are demanded jointly, it is equally clear that the prices of both are pertinent. If the price of greens fees at golf courses jumps by 50%, the demand for golf balls tends to be weakened; if the price of electricity rises substantially, people will tend to run their air conditioners less in the summer and may, in fact, be inclined to purchase a new energy-saving air conditioner.

Consumer Expectations. Consumers expectations with respect to future price levels, income levels, and product availability tend to influence current purchase behavior. If consumers believe that the prices of goods they expect to buy shortly are going to rise, they will be motivated to buy them now and escape paying the higher prices. Income expectations work much the same way. Some consumers may purchase goods currently with a view toward paying for them later out of expected increases in income; fears of a recession or impending unemployment make consumers more cautious and thrift conscious. Similarly, if consumers for some reason expect a good to be unavailable or in short supply in the near future (because of a strike, crop failures, production or shipping tie-ups, etc.), they will be induced to increase current purchases.

The Number of Consumers and Frequency of Purchase. Since the market demand for an item is the summation of individual consumer demands for the item, it is obvious that the *number of potential* consumers has a direct bearing on market demand, as well as the *frequency* with which they buy the product.

SOME ADDED DEMAND DETERMINANTS

While the preceding factors are generally acknowledged as the "major" demand determinants, other variables can enter the picture. For example, it can make a difference whether consumers perceive a product as a "luxury" or a "necessity." Although perceptions of an item as a luxury or a necessity are a function of individual life-styles and value judgments, the demands for luxuries and necessities tend to be different in their responses to price changes, recessionary conditions, interest rates and credit availability, and frequency of purchase. The necessity-luxury aspect of a purchase explicitly recognizes the multitude of cultural and life-style influences on who buys what and with what degree of urgency; it also brings into play consideration of the ability of buyers to postpone or delay their purchases because of adverse economic circumstances.

The demand for an item may be derived from the demand for other goods, in which case it is referred to as a **derived demand**. For instance, the demand for steel is derived from the demand for products containing steel or requiring steel somewhere in the course of their production. The demand for newsprint is derived from the demand for newspapers. When the demand for a good is derived, as in the case of component parts and goods-producing tools and equipment, considerable information may be gained from examining the buying habits and characteristics of end users of the final product.

The demand for such items as raw materials, parts, and components tends to be *derived* from the demand for the final products they go into.

The degree of market saturation for a product can be a key factor in the sales volume and sales potential of a product, especially for durable goods. The market demand for refrigerators is largely restricted to replacement needs because more than 95% of households today have refrigerators. There is somewhat greater market potential in VCRs; only 78% of American households had a VCR in 1991. In contrast, the market potential of video camcorders is much greater; only 13% of households had one in 1991, which is among the lowest levels of all consumer electronics products. In general, firms have larger sales potential the lower the market saturation for a consumer durable.

The limited demand for items having high saturation levels has prompted some producers of durable goods to adopt a policy of "planned obsolescence," whereby their products are restyled periodically, new features are added, and consumers are in turn induced to increase the frequency with which they replace their "worn-out" and "out-of-date" models.

For those types of consumer goods that are typically purchased with the aid of credit (automobiles, appliances, furniture, houses), the level of consumer debt and prevailing interest rates may be important factors influencing the consumer's buying power and may, in fact, be more closely related to the demand for such items than is current money income. Logic dictates that the higher the ratio of consumer debt to consumer income and the higher the rates of interest on borrowed funds, the less able and less eager consumers will be to make additional commitments toward the purchase of such items.

Additional reflection would, no doubt, suggest still other factors that bear upon the demand variables for certain products. It is to be emphasized, however, that *each good or service has its own set of demand determinants* and that, in turn, these determinants influence demand in ways that may be unique to each specific item.

THE CONCEPT OF THE DEMAND FUNCTION

BASIC CONCEPT
The demand function for a good or service expresses the relationship between quantity demanded and its specific set of demand-influencing variables.

As suggested by the preceding discussion, consumers' demand for an item is the result of a wide variety of forces. In mathematical terms, the demand function for product X can be symbolized as

$$Q_X = f(P_X, P_S, P_C, T, A_X, A_S, A_C, I, E, F, N, O)$$

where

Q_X = total quantity demanded of product X (in units),

P_X = price of product X,

P_S = measure of the prices of the brands and products that are substitutes for product X,

P_C = measure of the prices of products that are complementary to product X.

T = index of consumers' tastes and preferences,

A_X = level of advertising and promotional effort devoted to product X,

A_S = level of advertising and promotional efforts for substitute brands and products,

A_C = level of advertising and promotional efforts for complementary products,

I = measure of consumers' incomes or purchasing power,

E = buyer expectations concerning future prices, incomes, and product availability,

F = features or attributes of the product in relation to other items (whether the product is a standard commodity or a differentiated product),

N = number of potential consumers (the size of the market population), and

O = other demand-related factors specific to product X.

Using the functional notation to symbolize the relationship between the quantity demanded of a particular product and specific demand-influencing variables is a more explicit and conceptually accurate way of representing the demand for a product than is the simple graphic portrayal of price-quantity relationships in the form of demand curves.

Nevertheless, *it is analytically convenient to segregate demand determinants into two groups: (1) the selling price of the product and (2) all other demand determinants.* Using this dichotomization, variations in the purchases of a product associated solely with changes in product price are customarily termed *changes in the quantity demanded* and are represented graphically by movements *along* a given demand curve. In Figure 5-1(a), a decrease in the price of X from P_{X_1} to P_{X_2} increases the quantity demanded from X_1 to X_2—all other factors influencing the purchase volume are assumed to remain unchanged. On the other hand, quantity variations which stem from changes in one or more of demand determinants *other than price* are referred to as *changes in demand* and are represented graphically by shifts in the demand curve.[1] For example, such factors as increases in consumer incomes, a larger advertising budget, a more intensive desire for a good, or an increase in the price of substitutes would tend to shift the position of a given demand curve to the right, say from line D_1D_1 to D_2D_2 in Figure 5-1(b). Such events as a decline in the number of consumers, an increase in the attractiveness of substitute goods, or the expectation of a forthcoming price decrease tend to shift the

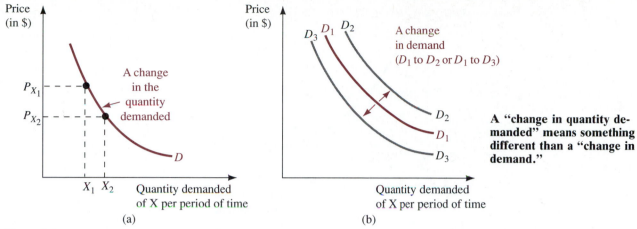

Figure 5-1
Changes in quantity demanded versus changes in demand

demand curve to the left, as illustrated by shifting D_1D_1 to position D_3D_3 in Figure 5-1(b).

The distinction between a "change in quantity demanded" and a "change in demand" correctly suggests that graphically representing the price-quantity relationship in the form of a demand curve does *not* mean that the price of an item is the sole, or even the principal, determinant of the amount purchased at some moment of time. All a demand curve purports to show is the impact that different prices will have upon the amounts purchased *when the remaining factors comprising the demand function are fixed in value.*

AVERAGE, TOTAL, AND MARGINAL REVENUE

Now let's use the demand curve to derive the revenue functions for a particular firm's product. Figure 5-2 depicts a hypothetical demand curve for a firm. The points along this curve represent the *maximum quantities* per unit of time that consumers are willing to buy from this firm at various alternative prices. It is equally accurate to view a firm's demand curve as representing the *maximum prices* that buyers are willing to pay a firm to obtain various quantities of its product. In terms of Figure 5-2, if the firm offered quantity Q_1 for sale, P_1 is the maximum price it would be able to charge and still generate a demand of Q_1 units. (Naturally, consumers would gladly pay less for the item were the opportunity to present itself.) Moreover, it follows that price P_1 represents the *average* amount of revenue the firm will receive *per unit sold*, or simply **average revenue** (*AR*). Accordingly, a firm's demand curve is also its average revenue curve.

A "change in quantity demanded" means something different than a "change in demand."

A firm's demand curve simultaneously shows the maximum quantities that can be sold at each price and the maximum price that each quantity can be sold for.

---

[1] The terms *change in the quantity demanded* and *change in demand* can be explained readily in the language of mathematics. Suppose that the equation of the demand curve is given by

$$P = a - bQ,$$

where P represents the selling price of a product and Q represents the quantity bought. As long as all the demand determinants other than P remain constant, the parameters a and b also remain constant and the equation $P = a - bQ$ defines a unique demand curve. A change in P will result in a movement along this demand curve to the corresponding value of Q—this is what has been termed a "change in the quantity demanded." However, shifts in demand determinants other than P are reflected by changes in the values of a and b. A change in the value of a shifts the level of the curve, and a change in the value of b alters the slope of the curve—either or both of which represent a "change in demand" and define the equation of a new demand curve.

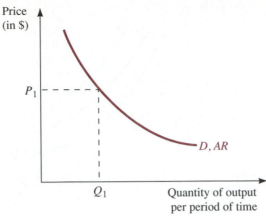

Figure 5-2
Demand or average revenue curve for a firm

As with the demand function, the firm's *AR* function may be expressed as a function of the quantity sold. When a firm sells all its output at the same price, its selling price and its average revenue are the same value, in which case

$$AR = P = f(Q).$$

However, if the firm sells its product at different prices to different customers or stairsteps its price downward to a buyer based on quantity purchased, average revenue is equal to a weighted average of the selling prices, with the weights being the proportions sold at each price. Then the *AR* function becomes

$$AR = \overline{P} = f(Q),$$

where $\overline{P}$ represents the *average* selling price.

Now let us utilize the demand-*AR* concepts to examine properties of a firm's other revenue functions for each of several possible sets of demand conditions.

AVERAGE, TOTAL, AND MARGINAL REVENUE WHEN THE DEMAND CURVE IS HORIZONTAL

Consider first the simple, but rather unusual, case where the firm confronts a horizontal demand curve for its product, as in Figure 5-3(a). A horizontal demand curve means that a firm can sell all the units it wishes at the price given by the intersection of the demand curve with the price axis; in Figure 5-3(a) this is shown as a price of \$10.[2] If the firm raises its price above \$10, no units can be sold. Obviously, if the firm can sell all it wishes at a price of \$10, it

---

[2] Just because a firm's demand curve is horizontal, it does not follow that the law of demand is suspended. Although a firm may be able to sell all it wishes within the limits of its production capacity at a particular price, it still is true that a single consumer will prefer to buy more at lower prices than at higher prices. Similarly, it is still true that consumers as a group will prefer to buy more at lower prices than at higher prices. What may make the demand curve horizontal for a *firm* is the fact that *many* other sellers are offering consumers an *identical* product; thus, all firms may be driven by the market forces of demand and supply to sell at the same price. Because each firm is so small relative to the total market, they are able to sell all they can produce at the prevailing price, and their individual demand curves are, therefore, horizontal.

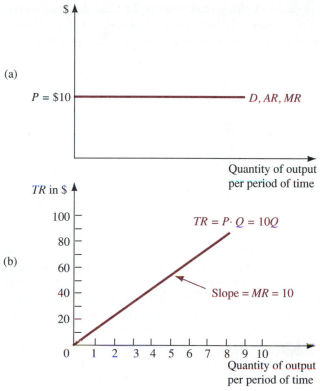

Figure 5-3

Average, total, and marginal revenue functions for a firm whose demand curve is horizontal

BASIC CONCEPT
A price-taking firm's total revenue is always equal to the market price multiplied by the quantity sold; its *TR* curve is always an upward-sloping straight line.

can also sell all it wishes below $10. However, we would logically expect the firm to offer its product for sale at the maximum price of $10, as no advantage can be gained from lowering the price. The equation of the firm's average revenue and demand function in this situation is

$$AR = P = \$10.$$

A firm that is in a situation where its demand and average revenue curve is horizontal, as in Figure 5-3(a), has little choice but to sell its product at the price of $10. Such a firm has no power to control its own price and is referred to as a *price taker*, which means the firm simply accepts the price that has been established by prevailing market forces.

A price-taking firm's *total revenue* is found by multiplying average revenue (*AR*) or selling price (*P*) by the number of units sold (*Q*) as follows:

$$TR = AR \cdot Q = P \cdot Q.$$

When a firm's demand curve is horizontal, its corresponding total revenue curve is always a positively sloped linear function starting from the origin and having a slope equal to the product price [see Figure 5-3(b)]. In this example, the slope of the firm's total revenue function is equal to 10 because every time one more unit is sold, the firm's total revenue rises by $10; the related equation for the price-taking firm's *total revenue function* is

$$TR = P \cdot Q = 10Q.$$

BASIC CONCEPT
A firm is said to be a price-taker when it has no choice other than to sell at the going market price; in such cases, the price-taker's demand-*AR* curve is horizontal at the market-established price.

BASIC CONCEPT
The term *marginal revenue* refers to the change in total revenue associated with a change in quantity sold; mathematically, a firm's marginal revenue function is always the first derivative of its total revenue function, and the value of *MR* at any sales quantity always equals the slope of the *TR* function at that sales quantity.

Marginal revenue is best defined as the rate of change in total revenue as the rate of output changes. This means, in mathematical terms, that the firm's *marginal revenue function* is the first derivative of the total revenue function. Thus, in our example, if

$$TR = 10Q,$$

then

$$MR = \frac{dTR}{dQ} = 10.$$

The constant value of 10 for *MR* means that each 1-unit increase in sales will cause total revenue to rise by $10. Geometrically, the value of marginal revenue is always equal to the slope of the total revenue function; hence, given that the firm's *TR* function is linear whenever the demand curve is horizontal and that linear functions have a constant slope, it follows that *the value of MR for a linear TR function is a constant value no matter what the firm's volume of sales*. In other words, if the firm can sell all it wishes at a price of $10, marginal revenue is fixed at $10 and is exactly equal to the firm's selling price and average revenue. The marginal revenue function corresponding to a horizontal demand-*AR* curve is graphically identical, therefore, to the demand-*AR* curve, as shown in Figure 5-3(a). Thus, *for a price-taking firm AR = MR*.

Sometimes it is helpful to think of marginal revenue as being the change in total revenue associated with a 1-*unit* change in sales ($\Delta TR/\Delta Q$, where $\Delta Q = 1$ unit). This concept of *MR* is appropriate when one has occasion to calculate the change in total revenue associated with a *discrete* change in output; it will be referred to as **discrete marginal revenue**. But where unit volume (Q) can assume any value along continuous demand and revenue functions, it is more mathematically precise to define and calculate *MR* as the derivative of the firm's *TR* function. We shall refer to the latter concept of *MR* as **continuous marginal revenue**. Both concepts of *MR* will have their place in future discussions.

In the preceding example, the nature of the demand function is such that the values for discrete *MR* and continuous *MR* are both $10. This is typical for horizontal demand functions, but it is not true of other types of demand functions, as the next case illustrates.

AVERAGE, TOTAL, AND MARGINAL REVENUE WHEN THE DEMAND CURVE IS LINEAR AND DOWNSLOPING

A somewhat more typical demand circumstance exists when a firm's demand curve is linear and downsloping. The general equation for linear demand-*AR* functions can be expressed as

$$AR = P = a - bQ.$$

The value of *a* in the equation is the price at which the demand curve intersects the price axis and, in economic terms, is the price just high enough so that no consumers will be willing to purchase the firm's product. The value of *b* in the equation is the slope of the demand curve. The minus sign (−) means that the demand curve is negatively sloped and that there exists an inverse relationship between *P* and *Q*, all of which is, of course, the usual case. The graph of a linear downsloping demand-*AR* curve is shown in Figure 5-4(a).

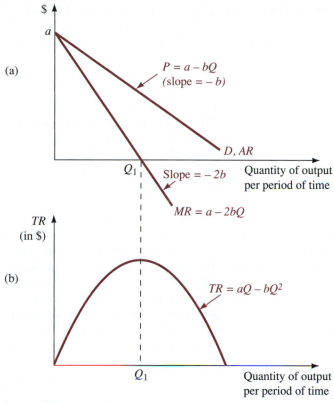

(a)

(b)

When a firm has a linear, downsloping demand curve, its *MR* curve is also linear and slopes downward at twice the rate of the demand curve; the associated *TR* curve is mountain-shaped, reaching its peak at exactly the same sales quantity where *MR* equals zero.

Figure 5-4

Average, total, and marginal revenue functions for a firm faced with a linear downsloping demand curve

Since a firm's total revenue from the sale of a product equals average revenue times the quantity sold (or price times the quantity sold), the expression for *TR* can be obtained by multiplying the demand-*AR* expression by *Q*:

$$TR = P \cdot Q \qquad (\text{or } AR \cdot Q)$$
$$= (a - bQ)Q$$
$$= aQ - bQ^2.$$

A total revenue function of this type is graphically portrayed by a parabola of the shape in Figure 5-4(b).

As before, the corresponding marginal revenue function is the derivative of the total revenue function. Since $TR = aQ - bQ^2$, then

$$MR = \frac{dTR}{dQ} = a - 2bQ.$$

Plotting the *MR* function on the same diagram as the demand and *AR* functions [Figure 5-4(a)] reveals that the *MR* curve lies below the demand curve. Both curves originate at the same value *a*, but the slope of the *MR* function is twice as great as the slope of the demand curve ($-2b$ as compared to $-b$). In geometric terms, the *MR* curve is located by drawing it so as to bisect the horizontal distance between the demand curve and the vertical axis. However, this procedure is accurate only in the case of a linear demand curve.

Marginal revenue is less than price (average revenue) because with a downsloping demand function the firm must lower its selling price to boost the quantity sold. The lower price applies not only to the additional units sold but also to the units of output which otherwise could have been sold at a higher price. For instance, suppose that a firm can sell 50 units at a price of $1 and realize total revenue of $50. To increase sales by 1 unit to 51 units, the firm must lower its price, say to $0.99 on all units sold. The increase in total revenue is *not* the $0.99 gained from the sale of the fifty-first unit, because the firm must give up revenue of $0.01 on each of the previous 50 units formerly selling at $1. The net gain in total revenue is $0.99 − $0.50, or $0.49, as can easily be verified by multiplying 51 units times $0.99, which gives a total revenue of $50.49. Hence, the marginal revenue of the fifty-first unit is $0.49, which is less than its selling price of $0.99.

One further very important relationship remains to be pointed out. This concerns the *MR* and *TR* functions. Observe in Figure 5-4 that the *TR* function increases at a decreasing rate up to a sales volume of Q_1 units; over this same range, *MR* is *positive* but decreasing in value. Earlier it was stated that *MR* at *any sales volume Q equals the slope of the TR function at that value of Q.* Since the *TR* function has a positive slope up to an output of Q_1, *MR* of necessity must be positive; similarly, just as the slope of the *TR* function diminishes as sales volume approaches Q_1 units, so also do the values of *MR* diminish. *Marginal revenue is zero at exactly the same output level (Q_1) at which total revenue is maximum.* Past a sales volume of Q_1, *TR* falls and *MR* is negative. Consequently, when the slope of the *TR* function is zero, *MR* is zero, and when the slope of the *TR* function is negative, *MR* is negative.

A numerical example at this point may serve to clarify and illuminate these relationships among *AR*, *TR*, and *MR*. Suppose that a firm's demand-*AR* function can be represented by the equation

$$P = 12 - Q \quad (or \ AR = 12 - Q).$$

The total revenue and marginal revenue functions can be calculated as follows:

$$TR = AR \cdot Q = P \cdot Q$$
$$= (12 - Q)Q = 12Q - Q^2,$$
$$MR = \frac{dTR}{dQ} = 12 - 2Q.$$

Table 5-1 contains representative values for *P*, *Q*, *AR*, *TR*, continuous *MR*, and discrete *MR* as derived from the preceding equations. Several attributes of the values in Table 5-1 are worth noting. First, when price is $12 or higher, no consumer is willing to purchase any of the firm's product. Second, selling price and *AR* are identical; as stated earlier, this is a necessary result of a single-price policy. Third, *TR* increases rapidly at first, then more slowly, reaches a maximum at 6 units of output, and declines thereafter as sales continue to increase. Fourth, the values of continuous *MR* are positive but steadily declining for the first 5 units of output; *MR* is zero where *TR* is at its maximum value of $36, and *MR* is ever more negative as the sales volume extends beyond 6 units. Fifth, the discrete *MR* values (which are computed by subtracting successive values of *TR* in order to obtain the change in *TR* associated with a 1-unit change in *Q*) do not correspond exactly to the values for continuous *MR*. This is not because the two concepts are inconsistent but because they are really associated with different output or sales levels. For instance, when *TR* rises from $11 to $20 as

TABLE 5-1   DEMAND AND REVENUE DATA FOR A LINEAR DEMAND FUNCTION

Quantity of Output Demanded	Price $(P = 12 - Q)$	Average Revenue $(AR = 12 - Q)$	Total Revenue $(TR = 12Q - Q^2)$	Continuous Marginal Revenue $(MR = 12 - 2Q)$	Discrete Marginal Revenue $(MR = TR_Q - TR_{Q-1})$
0	$12	$12	$ 0	$12	
					$11
1	11	11	11	10	
					9
2	10	10	20	8	
					7
3	9	9	27	6	
					5
4	8	8	32	4	
					3
5	7	7	35	2	
					1
6	6	6	36	0	
					−1
7	5	5	35	−2	
					−3
8	4	4	32	−4	
					−5
9	3	3	27	−6	
					−7
10	2	2	20	−8	

a consequence of a rise in sales from 1 to 2 units, it is fair to say that the $9 gain in revenue is not *MR* when *TR* is $20 and sales are 2 units but is instead *MR* *between* 1 and 2 units of output. The values for discrete *MR* in Table 5-1 are more correctly associated with output rates of $\frac{1}{2}$, $1\frac{1}{2}$, $2\frac{1}{2}$, and so on. This can easily be confined by substituting these values of *Q* into the equation for continuous *MR*; the resulting values for *MR* correspond exactly to the values for discrete *MR* presented in the table. Thus, the discrete and continuous measures of *MR* are perfectly compatible and define the same *MR* function and curve. If the *TR* function is known, it is usually more convenient to use the continuous measure of *MR*. If *MR* must be determined from a table of *TR* values, the discrete measure of *MR* is the simplest to calculate.

Plotting the values in Table 5-1 will yield curves that possess the relationships alluded to in Figure 5-4. The reader should verify this.

AVERAGE, TOTAL, AND MARGINAL REVENUE WHEN THE DEMAND CURVE IS CURVILINEAR

The demand curve for a product can assume a wide variety of curvilinear forms. No attempt is made here to catalog the diverse types of demand curves. In this section, we discuss two basic curvilinear demand curves with relatively simple equations. We first consider a demand curve that is convex with respect to the origin (bows in toward the origin). Then we discuss a demand curve that is concave with respect to the origin (bows away from the origin).

Suppose that the demand curve for a firm's product is given by the general expression

$$P = a - bQ + cQ^2,$$

where *a*, *b*, and *c* are constants. The firm's *AR* function will likewise be

$$AR = a - bQ + cQ^2.$$

Again, the total revenue function is found by multiplying the demand equation (or *AR* equation) by the quantity sold as follows:

$$TR = P \cdot Q = AR \cdot Q$$
$$= (a - bQ + cQ^2)Q$$
$$= aQ - bQ^2 + cQ^3.$$

The marginal revenue function is the first derivative of the total revenue function, giving

$$MR = \frac{dTR}{dQ} = a - 2bQ + 3cQ^2.$$

The shapes of these functions are pictured in Figure 5-5. Observe that the *MR* function lies everywhere below the demand function except at the common beginning value. The values for *MR* are declining but greater than zero for the output range where *TR* is rising; *MR* is zero where *TR* is maximum. When the demand curve is convex to the origin, as in this example, the *MR* curve lies to the left of the line bisecting the horizontal distance between the vertical axis and the demand curve.

Another plausible shape for the firm's demand curve to assume is that shown in Figure 5-6 associated with the general equation

$$P = a + bQ - cQ^2.$$

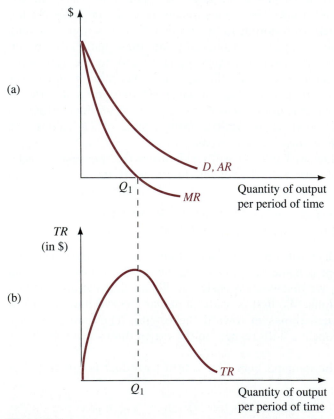

Figure 5-5

Convex demand—average, total, and marginal revenue functions for a firm whose demand equation is of the general form $P = a - bQ + cQ^2$

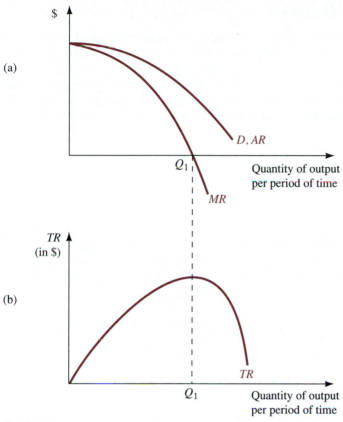

Figure 5-6
Concave demand—average, total, and marginal revenue functions for a firm whose demand equation is of the general form $P = a + bQ - cQ^2$

As before, the *AR* function has the same equation:

$$AR = a + bQ - cQ^2.$$

The *TR* function is again derived by multiplying the demand (or *AR*) equation by Q:

$$TR = P \cdot Q = AR \cdot Q$$
$$= (a + bQ - cQ^2)Q$$
$$= aQ + bQ^2 - cQ^3.$$

Taking the derivative of the *TR* function, we get the *MR* function:

$$MR = \frac{dTR}{dQ} = a + 2bQ - 3cQ^2.$$

Note that the graphs of these functions (shown in Figure 5-6) portray the same basic relations among demand, *AR*, *TR*, and *MR* as stated earlier. Apart from the shapes of the curves, a significant difference between this case and the previous examples is the location of the *MR* function. Although *MR* still lies below the demand function, this time it is located to the right of a line bisecting the horizontal distance between the vertical axis and the demand curve.

BASIC CONCEPT
Elasticity is a measure of how sensitive the quantity demanded is to some change in a specified demand determinant.

ELASTICITY OF DEMAND

The concept of *elasticity* has a most important role in demand analysis. It concerns the *responsiveness* or *sensitivity* of the quantity demanded of a product to a change in some demand determinant. More specifically, elasticity of demand is a measure of the magnitude to which a percentage change in one demand variable causes (or is associated directly with) a percentage change in the quantity demanded. Mathematically, the elasticity of demand ϵ (epsilon) is calculated as

$$\epsilon = \frac{\% \text{ change in quantity demanded}}{\% \text{ change in any demand determinant}}.$$

Elasticity is *always* calculated in relative or percentage terms rather than in absolute or unit terms. This permits comparisons of demand sensitivity for different products, irrespective of the units in which products or product prices are quoted. (A 5% change has the same meaning whether it is measured in tons, dozens, crates, cans, dollars or Japanese yen.) And because elasticity is calculated by dividing a percentage change by a percentage change, the elasticity coefficient (ϵ) is a pure number free of any identification with the units in which the variables are expressed.

There are as many kinds of demand elasticity as there are numbers of demand determinants for a product (price elasticity, income elasticity, and so on). We shall restrict the discussion here to the most important demand elasticity concepts, beginning with price elasticity of demand.

PRICE ELASTICITY OF DEMAND

The relation of product price to sales volume is of major interest to business firms as a basis for pricing policy, sales strategy, and achievement of profit and market share objectives. Consider the case of products X and Y with convex demand curves as shown in Figure 5-7. The negative slopes of both curves indicate that as the prices of X and Y fall, the quantities demanded of X and Y rise. From the diagram, when the prices of X and Y are P_{X_1} and P_{Y_1}

The demand for product X is more responsive to a price change than is the demand for product Y over the indicated price interval.

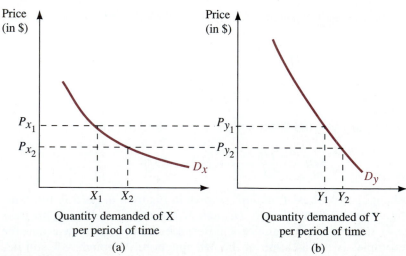

Figure 5-7
Sensitivity of product demand to price changes

(where $P_{X_1} = P_{Y_1}$), the quantities purchased are X_1 units and Y_1 units, respectively. However, if the prices of X and Y decline by an identical amount to P_{X_2} and P_{Y_2}, the change in the quantity demanded of X (X_1 to X_2) is greater than the change in the quantity demanded of Y (Y_1 to Y_2). In other words, the demand for X is more sensitive or responsive to a change in the price of X than the demand for Y is to a change in the price of Y at the indicated prices. Or, in the language of economics, we can say that the price elasticity of demand for X is greater than the price elasticity of demand for Y over the indicated price range.

Price elasticity of demand can be defined more precisely as

$$\epsilon_p = \frac{\% \text{ change in quantity demanded}}{\% \text{ change in price}}.$$

The coefficient of price elasticity is always negative. Why? Because price and quantity demanded are inversely related; when price falls the quantity demanded tends to rise and when price rises the quantity demanded tends to fall. Therefore, with one percentage change being negative and the other being positive, the price elasticity coefficient is necessarily negative.

Two distinct methods for calculating price elasticity exist: the arc elasticity method and the point elasticity method. *Arc elasticity* is a measure of the responsiveness of the quantity demanded between two separate points on a demand curve. *Point elasticity* is a measure of the sensitivity of the quantity demanded at a single point on the curve.

Arc Elasticity. To illustrate the arc technique for computing price elasticity, consider a demand curve having two points *A* and *B* with price-quantity combinations as follows:

	Price	Quantity Demanded
Point A	$12	30 units
Point B	$10	50 units

Now suppose we determine the degree of responsiveness of quantity demanded to a *decrease* in price from $12 to $10—this is equivalent to moving down along the demand curve from point *A* to point *B*. It will be recalled that the usual way of computing percentage change is to find the change in a value relative to its original value (designated by the subscript 1) and multiply by 100 to convert the ratio to a percentage figure. Algebraically, then, our definition of price elasticity is equivalent to

$$\epsilon_p = \frac{\% \text{ change in quantity demanded}}{\% \text{ change in price}} = \frac{[(Q_2 - Q_1)/Q_1] \times 100}{[(P_2 - P_1)/P_1] \times 100},$$

where the pairs (Q_1, P_1) and (Q_2, P_2) represent, respectively, the quantity and price values *before* and *after* their change. Note, however, that the multiplication by 100 of both the numerator and denominator is superfluous and can be omitted, as the terms cancel out in dividing. Substituting the appropriate values into the simplified formula gives

$$\epsilon_p = \frac{(Q_2 - Q_1)/Q_1}{(P_2 - P_1)/P_1} = \frac{(50 - 30)/30}{(10 - 12)/12} = \frac{20/30}{(-2)/12} = \frac{2}{3} \cdot -\frac{6}{1} = -4.0.$$

Yet, if we compute the sensitivity of the quantity demanded to an *increase* in price from $10 to $12 (equivalent to moving up the demand curve from point *B* to point *A*), the coefficient of price elasticity is

$$\epsilon_p = \frac{(Q_2 - Q_1)/Q_1}{(P_2 - P_1)/P_1} = \frac{(30 - 50)/50}{(12 - 10)/10} = \frac{(-20)/50}{2/10} = \frac{-2}{5} \cdot \frac{5}{1} = -2.0.$$

The discrepancy in the two elasticity coefficients arises because the percentage changes going from point *A* to point *B* are not the same as those in moving from *B* to *A*. Indeed, changing the base values for the percentage calculation from P_1, Q_1 to P_2, Q_2 gives two widely diverging measures of price sensitivity for the very same interval along the demand curve.[3] The reason for this discrepancy is that when calculating percentage changes, the base that you begin with is always important.

This is a troublesome matter but not one without a remedy. The ambiguity of arbitrarily using one of the two points (*A* or *B*) as the original or base values for calculating the percentage changes can be partially overcome by using the average of the quantity values as the base for calculating the percentage change in *Q* and the average of the two prices as the base for calculating the percentage change in *P*. Making this adjustment gives the more satisfactory formula

$$\epsilon_p = \frac{\dfrac{Q_2 - Q_1}{\left(\dfrac{Q_1 + Q_2}{2}\right)}}{\dfrac{P_2 - P_1}{\left(\dfrac{P_1 + P_2}{2}\right)}}$$

With the modified formula it makes no difference which of the two points is point 1 and which is point 2; the same elasticity coefficient is obtained either way. For this reason, the modified formula is the accepted way of computing arc elasticity and is the one we shall use henceforth. Still, for the arc elasticity

---

[3] This example demonstrates why arc elasticity calculations are only approximations. This is especially true when the shape of the demand curve is not known and data for only a few prices and quantities are given. For example, it may be observed when the price is $8, that 250 units of the item are purchased, and when the price is $7, that 350 units are purchased. However, as the following figure suggests, an infinite number of demand curves can pass through these two points, and these curves in general have slightly different elasticities in this price-quantity interval.

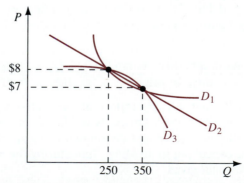

In general, the farther apart the two points between which arc elasticity is computed, the greater is the discrepancy between the price elasticity coefficients obtained from the two-point arc formula.

coefficient to be reliable and susceptible to meaningful interpretation, it should be computed only between points on a demand curve which are reasonably close together. In terms of our previous numerical example, the coefficient of price elasticity for a decline in price from \$12 to \$10 becomes

$$\epsilon_p = \frac{\dfrac{Q_2 - Q_1}{\left(\dfrac{Q_1 + Q_2}{2}\right)}}{\dfrac{P_1 - P_1}{\left(\dfrac{P_1 + P_2}{2}\right)}} = \frac{\dfrac{50 - 30}{\left(\dfrac{30 + 50}{2}\right)}}{\dfrac{10 - 12}{\left(\dfrac{12 + 10}{2}\right)}}$$

$$= \frac{\dfrac{20}{40}}{\dfrac{-2}{11}} = \frac{1}{2} \cdot -\frac{11}{2} = -\frac{11}{4} = -2.75.$$

Returning to our previous numerical example and using the modified formula, -2.75 should be interpreted as meaning that over the indicated range of prices and quantities a 1% change in price will cause approximately a 2.75% change in quantity demanded in the *opposite* direction.[4]

Since the sign of the price elasticity coefficient is always negative (in accordance with the law of demand), it is the *size* of the coefficient itself which is most relevant. By convention, economists say that when the coefficient is a number greater than 1, demand is **elastic**, and that when the coefficient is less than 1, demand is **inelastic**. Should the coefficient turn out, by chance, to be exactly 1, demand is said to be **unitary** or of **unitary elasticity**. The rationale for this classification is straightforward. When the coefficient is greater than 1, the percentage change in quantity demanded must necessarily be *larger* than the percentage change in price. It follows, then, that the quantity demanded is relatively responsive or sensitive to price changes—or, in the language of economists, that demand is elastic. On the other hand, when the coefficient is less than 1, the percentage change in quantity demanded is *smaller* than the percentage change in price, clearly implying that the quantity demanded is relatively unresponsive or less sensitive (or inelastic) with regard to price changes.

Demand is price *elastic* when a given percentage change in price produces a larger percentage change in quantity demanded; demand is price *inelastic* when a given percentage change in price results in a smaller percentage change in quantity demanded.

Point Elasticity. Measuring elasticity at a point eliminates the imprecision of the arc elasticity concept. *Point elasticity*, as the name implies, *refers to the responsiveness of quantity demanded to very small price changes from a given point*. Algebraically, this translates into the following:

$$\epsilon_p = \frac{\Delta Q/Q}{\Delta P/P} = \frac{\Delta Q}{Q} \cdot \frac{P}{\Delta P} = \frac{\Delta Q}{\Delta P} \cdot \frac{P}{Q}.$$

The expression says that price elasticity at a point equals the ratio of the change in quantity demanded to the change in price multiplied by the ratio of price to

---

[4] You should verify at this point that exactly the same coefficient is obtained for an increase in price from \$10 to \$12 as was obtained from a decrease in price from \$12 to \$10 when the modified arc elasticity formula is used. This will confirm that the modification of averaging the prices and quantities eliminates any difference in the size of the coefficient arising from an arbitrary designation of one of the two points on the demand curve as the reference or base point. The effect of the modified formula is to produce an "average" of sorts of the two results obtained with the initial version of the arc formula. To be more exact, the modified arc elasticity formula yields an estimate of the responsiveness or sensitivity of the quantity demanded at the midpoint of the range defined by the two points on the demand curve.

quantity demanded at that point. As the changes in price get smaller and smaller and actually approach zero, the ratio of $\Delta Q / \Delta P$ becomes equivalent to the derivative of the demand function with respect to price, or

$$\lim_{\Delta P \to 0} \frac{\Delta Q}{\Delta P} = \frac{dQ}{dP}.$$

Hence, the formula for point elasticity becomes

$$\epsilon_p = \frac{dQ}{dP} \cdot \frac{P}{Q}.$$

As illustrations of the point elasticity concept, consider the following two examples.

EXAMPLE 1

Suppose that the demand function for an item is defined by the equation

$$Q = 245 - 3.5P.$$

What, then, is the price elasticity of demand at a price of $10? To determine ϵ_p we need to know P, Q, and dQ/dP. At a price of $10,

$$Q = 245 - 3.5(10) = 245 - 35 = 210.$$

The rate of change in Q as P changes, dQ/dP, is found by calculating the first derivative of the demand function:

$$\frac{dQ}{dP} = -3.5.$$

Hence, we can now substitute directly into the point elasticity formula, obtaining

$$\epsilon_p = \frac{dQ}{dP} \cdot \frac{P}{Q} = -3.5 \cdot \frac{10}{210} = -\frac{1}{6} = -0.167$$

The ϵ_p value of -0.167 says that if the price of the commodity changes by a small amount (say 1%) from its value of $10, then the quantity demanded will change by approximately 0.167% in the opposite direction. This relatively small response means demand is quite inelastic at a price of $10.

EXAMPLE 2

Since price is typically put on the vertical axis and quantity demanded is represented on the horizontal axis, the demand equation is normally written so that P is a function of Q rather than Q being expressed as a function of P. Consider the demand function

$$P = 940 - 48Q + Q^2.$$

What is the price elasticity of demand at an output of 10 units?
At $Q = 10$,

$$P = 940 - 48(10) + (10)^2$$
$$P = 940 - 480 + 100 = \$560.$$

Now, it remains to find the value of dQ/dP. However, since the equation is expressed in terms of quantity rather than price, we must find dQ/dP by a slightly more circuitous route. We can determine dP/dQ quite easily as follows:

$$\frac{dP}{dQ} = -48 + 2Q.$$

It so happens (the mathematicians have formally proved it) that

$$\frac{dQ}{dP} = \frac{1}{dP/dQ},$$

thereby giving us

$$\frac{dQ}{dP} = \frac{1}{-48 + 2Q}.$$

At $Q = 10$, this becomes

$$\frac{dQ}{dP} = \frac{1}{-48 + 2(10)} = -\frac{1}{28}.$$

Substituting into the point elasticity formula, we have

$$\epsilon_p = \frac{dQ}{dP} \cdot \frac{P}{Q} = \frac{1}{28} \cdot \frac{560}{10} = -2.$$

Again the proper interpretation of the elasticity coefficient in this case is that for a 1% price change from the current price of $560, the quantity demanded will change by about 2% in the opposite direction. And we would conclude that at a price of $560 demand is elastic.

The examples and the interpretation of the resulting elasticity coefficients illustrate an important point. If the price elasticity of demand is known to have a certain value, such as $\epsilon_p = -3$, then the effects of a price change on quantity demanded can be predicted, assuming, of course, that other factors influencing demand do not change. For example, with $\epsilon_p = -3$, a 1% increase in price will cause quantity demanded to fall by 3%.

When the coefficient of price elasticity is known, the effects of a price change on quantity demanded can be predicted rather accurately.

PRICE ELASTICITY AND THE SLOPE OF THE DEMAND CURVE

The concepts of slope and elasticity are frequently confused. It is sometimes fallaciously assumed that the flatter the demand curve, the greater its elasticity, and the steeper the demand curve, the smaller its elasticity. This assumption is categorically false and is so indicated in the definitions of the terms themselves. The slope of a demand curve depends entirely on the size of an absolute change in price as compared to the size of the associated absolute change in the quantity demanded. At any given point on a demand curve the slope equals dP/dQ. Yet, as we have just seen, elasticity is defined mathematically as

$$\epsilon_p = \frac{dQ}{dP} \cdot \frac{P}{Q}.$$

Elasticity is, therefore, equal to the reciprocal of the slope of the demand curve $[dQ/dP = 1/(dP/dQ)]$ multiplied by the ratio of P to Q and is a measure of the relative or *percentage* changes in P and Q. Clearly, then, since the slope (flatness or steepness) of a demand curve is based upon *absolute* changes in P

Price elasticity is *not* related to the slope of the demand curve.

and Q, whereas price elasticity has to do with *percentage* changes in P and Q, the value of the slope of the demand curve can equal the value of the coefficient of price elasticity only by the rarest of arithmetical coincidences. Moreover, in the case of a linear, downward-sloping demand curve, the slope is constant, whereas the price elasticity varies from point to point along the curve according to the value of P/Q. Thus, any notion that elasticity and slope are the same should be promptly dispelled.

We are now ready to examine some of the practical applications of the price elasticity concept. Of prime interest to business firms is the effect that a price change will have upon sales volume and total revenue. Also, from the viewpoint of consumers it is pertinent to determine the effect of a price change upon the total amount of money consumers are willing and able to spend on a given product.

Consider the demand schedule in Table 5-2 and the corresponding demand curve for a firm shown as line dd' in Figure 5-8(a). At a price of $120 ($P_1$), the firm can sell 100 units (Q_1). If price is lowered to $110 ($P_2$), sales increase to 200 units (Q_2). The *percentage* change in price obviously is small in comparison with the *percentage* change in quantity demanded—the price decline is but a fraction of its original value of P_1, whereas the increase in quantity demanded from Q_1 to Q_2 is double the original volume of 100 units. The information in Table 5-2 verifies that the coefficient of price elasticity over this range is -7.67; thus, demand is *elastic* between points A and B. As shown in Figure 5-8(b), total revenue increases when price is lowered from $120 to $110. That this is so can also be confirmed indirectly from Figure 5-8(a). Since total revenue is price times quantity sold, the size of the area shown by rectangle OP_1AQ_1 in Figure 5-8(a) equals TR at P_1. At price P_2, TR equals the area of rectangle OP_2BQ_2. By inspection, the area of rectangle OP_2BQ_2 exceeds that of rectangle OP_2AQ_1 and, as indicated in Table 5-2, TR at P_2 ($22,000) is larger than TR at P_1 ($12,000). It is larger because the *loss* of revenue due to the lower price per unit (area P_2P_1AD) is *less* than the *gain* in revenue resulting from increased sales (area Q_1DBQ_2). In other words, even though the product is sold at a lower price, the increase in sales volume at the lower price *more* than makes up for the smaller amount of revenue received per unit sold.

This behavior of total revenue over elastic portions of the demand curve is not merely coincidental. In fact, we may state, as a general principle, that *whenever demand is elastic, a decline in price will result in an increase in*

TABLE 5-2   ELASTICITY AND TOTAL REVENUE

Price	Quantity Demanded	Total Revenue	Coefficient of Price Elasticity	Elasticity
$120	100	$12,000		
			-7.67	Elastic
110	200	22,000		
			-3.13	Elastic
100	270	27,000		
			-1.90	Elastic
90	330	29,700		
			-1.03	Elastic
85	350	29.750		
			-0.91	Inelastic
80	370	29,600		
			-0.58	Inelastic
70	400	28,000		
			-0.39	Inelastic
60	425	25,500		

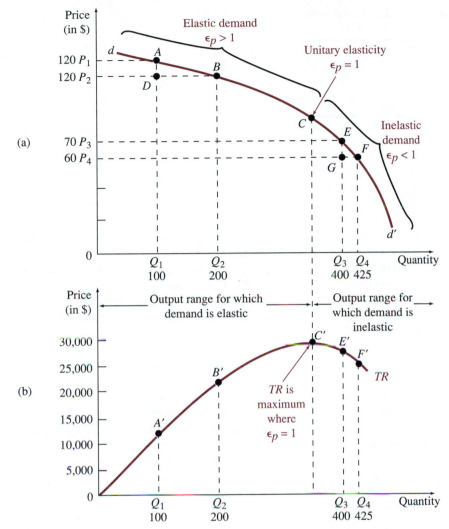

Figure 5-8
Relationships among demand curves, total revenue, and price elasticity

total revenue. The reasoning is reversible: *When demand is elastic, an increase in price will result in a decline in total revenue*, because should price rise (for example, from P_3 to P_2), the gain in total revenue associated with selling the product at a higher price (area P_3P_2BE) is smaller than the loss in revenue stemming from selling fewer units (area Q_2ECQ_3).

    When demand is inelastic with regard to price, a lower price will cause a decline in total revenue. This situation exists for a decrease in price from P_4 ($70) to P_5 ($60), as shown in Figure 5-8(a). Over this price range, the coefficient of price elasticity is −0.39 (Table 5-2). At a price of $70 and sales of 400 units, *TR* is $28,000, whereas at a price of $60 and sales of 425 units, *TR* is $25,500. Graphically, at a price of P_3, *TR* is equal to the area OP_4EQ_4. Total revenue is lower because the modest increase in sales volume precipitated by the price decline (Q_3Q_4) is inadequate to offset the adverse impact of the fall in price; consequently, the *loss* in revenue due to the lower price (area P_4P_3EG) *exceeds* the *gain* in revenue associated with selling more units (area Q_3GFQ_4). Table 5-3 summarizes these relationships.

PRINCIPLE
Whenever demand is elastic, a price cut will produce an increase in total revenue and a price increase will result in a decline in total revenue.

PRINCIPLE
Whenever demand is inelastic, a price cut will lead to lower total revenues and a price increase will produce higher total revenues.

TABLE 5-3   PRICE CHANGES, PRICE
ELASTICITY, AND TOTAL REVENUE

	$\epsilon_p > 1$	$\epsilon_p < 1$
$P \downarrow$	$TR \uparrow$	$TR \downarrow$
$P \uparrow$	$TR \downarrow$	$TR \uparrow$

Most downsloping demand curves tend to be elastic along the upper portion of the curve and inelastic along the lower portion.

It follows that the positively sloped portion of the *TR* function corresponds to the elastic portion of the demand curve, and vice versa (as is illustrated in Figure 5-8). By the same token, the negatively sloped segment of the *TR* function is associated with inelastic demand. Starting from the top of the demand curve and moving down along it, the coefficient of price elasticity is a decreasing value but remains, nevertheless, larger than 1.0; simultaneously *TR* is increasing. Where *TR* is maximum, the elasticity of demand is unitary ($\epsilon_p = 1$). As we move farther down the demand curve past the point of unitary elasticity, the coefficient of price elasticity is less than 1 and decreasing, and *TR* is declining. These relationships are typical of downsloping demand functions.

There is a tendency, therefore, for most demand curves to be elastic at "high" prices and inelastic at "low" prices. As price falls from high levels, the response of consumers produces strong percentage gains in sales and healthy increases in *TR*. Where $\epsilon_p = 1$ corresponds to the price at which consumers are willing to spend the greatest number of dollars on the item; at this price *TR* is maximum. Further price cuts will not induce consumers to buy enough more units to compensate for the price decline. In other words, they are approaching their saturation level for the item, and their marginal utility for additional units is rapidly diminishing; thus, price cuts have less impact upon consumer purchases.

Furthermore, it may be noted that the more elastic demand is, the greater will *TR* rise when price falls. The more inelastic demand is, the greater will *TR* fall when price is lowered. The example in Table 5-2 verifies this.

APPLICATIONS CAPSULE

WHEN A FIRM CAN BE SURE IT'S TIME TO RAISE ITS PRICE

Whenever a firm has good reason to believe that the demand for its product is inelastic at the current selling price, profits can *always* be increased if the firm will raise its price. This outcome stems from the fact that in an inelastic demand situation, a price increase will result in a firm's experiencing (1) rising total revenue and (2) a lower total cost outlay. Whenever the coefficient of price elasticity is less than 1, a price increase will raise total revenues because the revenue gain associated with a higher selling price more than offsets the revenue decline associated with a lower unit sales volume. Also, a firm's total operating costs ought to fall as a result of a higher price, since the higher price (other things remaining equal) will tend to curtail consumer purchases of the product—thereby prompting the firm to produce fewer units, buy

smaller amounts of economic resources, and consequently, spend fewer dollars in the course of its activities. With *TR* rising and total costs falling, the overall profitability of the enterprise will, of necessity, be improved.

Pursuing the same line of reasoning, a firm contemplating a lowering of its price should beware of an inelastic demand situation. A price decrease in face of an inelastic demand will lead not only to a decline in total revenue, but also to an increase in total costs due to a rising sales volume. The firm's profits will be lowered and under such circumstances a lower selling price would seem ill-advised.

It is fair to state, therefore, that *the most profitable price and volume of sales lies somewhere on the elastic portion of a firm's demand curve.*

PRICE ELASTICITY AND LINEAR DEMAND CURVES

Although the law of demand requires only that a demand curve slope downward to the right, it is convenient for illustration and exposition purposes to represent the demand curve in its simplest form—as a straight line. Thus, it is worthwhile to be familiar with the elasticity characteristics of linear demand curves. Figure 5-9 illustrates a typical linear demand function along with its corresponding total revenue and marginal revenue function. It will be recalled that the general equations for these functions are

$$P = a - bQ,$$
$$TR = P \cdot Q = aQ - bQ^2,$$
$$MR = \frac{dTR}{dQ} = a - 2bQ.$$

Additionally, the slope of the *MR* function is twice the slope of the demand curve, and *MR* equals zero where *TR* is maximum. The geometry of the relationships among the three functions is such that the price and quantity at which *MR* = 0 and *TR* is maximum is the midpoint of the demand curve; that is, the length of the segment of the demand curve above this point is equal to the length of the segment below it.

From the discussion in the preceding section it should be evident that demand is elastic on the *upper half* of the linear demand curve and is inelastic along the *lower half* of the curve (see Figure 5-9). The coefficient of price elasticity is one at the *midpoint* of the curve. Moreover, starting at the top of

A linear, downsloping demand curve is elastic along the top half of the curve and is inelastic along the lower half.

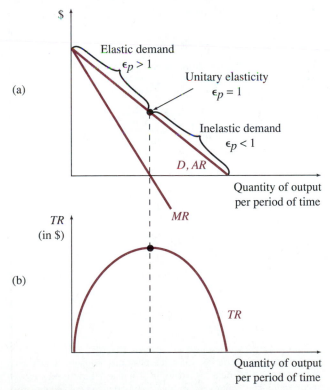

Demand is price elastic where *MR* is positive and is price inelastic where *MR* is negative.

Figure 5-9
Linear demand curves, total revenue, and price elasticity

the demand curve and proceeding down along it, the coefficient of price elasticity declines from very large values to a value of one at the midpoint, becomes less than one upon passing the midpoint, and approaches zero as price declines toward zero. As explained previously, this is because at successively lower prices and progressively larger values of Q, the percentage changes in price get larger, while the percentage changes in quantity demanded get smaller. The coefficient of price elasticity, being equal to the ratio of the percentage change in Q to the percentage change in P, thus necessarily declines as one moves down along the demand curve.

It is not accurate, therefore, to describe linear demand curves as being either elastic or inelastic; rather the upper half of the demand curve is elastic and the lower half is inelastic. It is proper to speak of the price elasticity of demand at a given point or between two given points, but it is inappropriate to speak of the price elasticity of the demand curve as a whole.

MATHEMATICAL CAPSULE 5

THE ELASTICITY OF DEMAND AT THE MIDPOINT OF A LINEAR DEMAND FUNCTION

It is relatively simple to show for a linear downsloping demand function that the price elasticity of demand at the midpoint of the demand curve is -1. All we need do is compute the coefficient of price elasticity at the midpoint utilizing the point elasticity formula.

The general equation for a linear demand curve is

$$P = a - bQ.$$

The general equations for the associated TR and MR functions are

$$TR = P \cdot Q = aQ - bQ^2,$$

$$MR = \frac{dTR}{dQ} = a - 2bQ.$$

To compute point elasticity, we must obtain values for dQ/dP, Q, and P at the midpoint of our generalized demand curve. We can find dQ/dP from the demand equation itself as follows:

$$P = a - bQ.$$

$$\frac{dP}{dQ} = -b.$$

Since

$$\frac{dQ}{dP} = \frac{1}{dP/dQ},$$

we have

$$\frac{dQ}{dP} = \frac{1}{-b} = -\frac{1}{b}.$$

The value of Q at the midpoint of the demand can be derived from the fact that at the midpoint of a linear demand curve $MR = 0$ and TR is maximum. We can find the quantity at

which $MR = 0$ by setting the equation for MR equal to zero and solving for the value of Q that will satisfy this condition:

$$MR = a - 2bQ = 0,$$

$$-2bQ = -a,$$

$$Q = \frac{-a}{-2b} = \frac{a}{2b}.$$

When $Q = a/2b$, the corresponding value for P is

$$P = a - bQ$$

$$= a - b\left(\frac{a}{2b}\right)$$

$$= a - \frac{a}{2}$$

$$= \frac{a}{2}.$$

Substituting the values for dQ/dP, P, and Q into the point elasticity formula, we have

$$\epsilon_p = \frac{dQ}{dP} \cdot \frac{P}{Q}$$

$$= -\frac{1}{b} \cdot \frac{a/2}{a/2b}$$

$$= -\frac{1}{b} \cdot \frac{a}{2} \cdot \frac{2b}{a}$$

$$= -1.$$

Therefore, the coefficient of price elasticity equals -1 at the midpoint of all linear downsloping demand functions, irrespective of the values of a and b in the general equation $P = a - bQ$.

SOME SPECIAL CASES IN PRICE ELASTICITY

Certain kinds of demand curves have unique price elasticity properties. Three special cases will be noted.

When the firm's demand curve is horizontal (meaning that at the going market price the firm can sell all it is able to produce but that its demand is zero at a higher price), demand is said to be **perfectly elastic** and the coefficient of price elasticity is infinity ($\epsilon_p = -\infty$). Such a demand curve is illustrated in Figure 5-10(a). The perfectly elastic feature of the horizontal demand curve arises from the fact that should the firm raise its price above P_1, demand would fall to zero—the largest possible response to a price change. In other words, when the firm's demand curve is horizontal, there exists the highest possible degree of sensitivity to price since even if there is a small price increase above P_1, the firm's customers will reduce their purchases from the prevailing amounts to zero.

A horizontal demand curve is perfectly elastic at the going market price.

In the very improbable event that the demand curve for a product is vertical [Figure 5-10(b)], demand is said to be **perfectly inelastic**. Quantity demanded remains the same despite progressively higher prices. Thus, there is *no response* whatsoever in the quantity demanded to a price change—the least possible degree of price sensitivity. The corresponding coefficient of price elasticity is zero ($\epsilon_p = 0$).

A vertical demand curve is perfectly inelastic.

The third special case arises when consumers spend a fixed amount of dollars for a product irrespective of the price charged and the quantity bought. Every price-quantity combination results in the same amount of expenditure upon the product. The equation for such a demand curve is

$$P \cdot Q = TR = k,$$

where k is a constant and, graphically, it is illustrated by a rectangular hyperbola, shown in Figure 5-10(c). At each and every point on the curve price elasticity is unitary ($\epsilon_p = -1$), and total revenue is constant no matter what the values of P and Q.

THE SENSITIVITY OF MARKET DEMAND TO PRICE CHANGES

Just what causes the market demand for a good or service to be responsive or unresponsive to price changes? If the firms in an industry reduce prices,

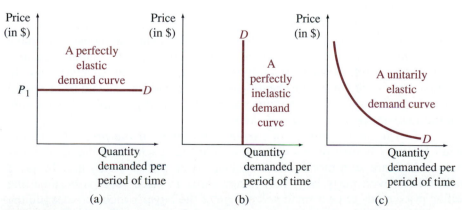

(a) (b) (c)

Figure 5-10
Special cases in price elasticity

will there be a large expansion in the quantity demanded marketwide, a moderate expansion, or very little expansion at all? The answers depend on seven market considerations:

Just how sensitive marketwide sales volumes are to a change in market price depends on seven factors.

1. *The number of good substitutes available at competitive prices.* The availability of substitutes is the single most important determinant of the price elasticity of demand. The market demand for zinc castings for automotive trim may be highly price elastic because of the encroachment of cheaper plastic substitutes as zinc prices climb. On the other hand, there is as yet no good substitute for the use of glass windows and windshields in the manufacture of automobiles, and thus there is little risk of diminished demand through the substitution of other materials, as the price of automotive glass goes up.

2. *The number of uses a product has.* There is a tendency for the demand for a product to be more elastic the wider the range of uses it has. With a larger number of uses, more opportunity exists for variation in the quantity sold when price changes. Increases in price reduce the number of economical uses of a product, whereas price declines expand the range of economically feasible uses. This aspect of demand elasticity is especially pertinent for steel, aluminum, other primary metals, plastics, wool, and paper products.

3. *The time period under consideration.* In general, the market demand for a product tends to be more elastic in the long run than in the short run. This is primarily due to lags in consumer response to price changes and to increased chances that more good substitutes will appear as the time frame lengthens.

4. *The durability of the product.* Price elasticity can be partly a function of product durability because of the possibility of delaying the purchase of replacements. Postponing the purchase of new durable goods by repairing them may be an effective, albeit temporary, substitute for replacing goods whose prices are rising, thus making for a more elastic demand in the short run than would otherwise be the case.

5. *The importance of the product to buyers.* When products are very important to consumers from the standpoint of daily living and life-styles (toothpaste, coffee, haircuts), market demand is often not very sensitive to price; as prices go up, buyers merely dig deeper in their pockets. On the other hand, there are many items that are not viewed as so crucial—going skiing in Colorado, eating fresh fish twice a week, or buying a big-screen TV. Most postponable, less urgent, or ''luxury'' types of products tend to exhibit higher degrees of price elasticity.

6. *The degree of market saturation for the product.* Market saturation has relevance to price elasticity in the sense that if nearly all households have refrigerators, it is unlikely the appliance manufacturers can stimulate the market demand for refrigerators much by cutting their average selling prices. In contrast, the use of solar water heating is far from widespread and price reductions in installed solar-water-heating equipment would probably trigger a substantial percentage gain in market sales.

7. *The income profile of current consumers of the product.* The demand for truly luxury products (such as 100-foot yachts and diamond necklaces) which are sold more or less exclusively to the very rich may be price inelastic for even fairly large percentage shifts in price. This is because the selling price tends to be a small percentage of the buyer's income—despite the size of the price tag. Yet the market demand for 16-foot fiberglass outboard runabouts, sold to the ''mass market,'' may be fairly sensitive to price changes.

When the price of an item is large in relation to income, buyers are more likely to be price-conscious and substitute-conscious; hence a given percentage change in price can be expected to have a significant demand impact, owing to the large difference it makes upon the consumer's pocketbook. From another angle, products such as videotape recorders are often initially priced well above the reach of the mass market, and the first round or so of price cuts may not generate much demand response. But as prices continue to be reduced, successively lower income levels are tapped, and market demand becomes increasingly responsive to lower prices.

Plainly, more than one of these factors can affect the price elasticity of market demand simultaneously. Moreover, it is important to recognize that different classes of customers within the same market frequently have different price elasticities. For instance, industrial demand for electricity may be much more price sensitive than residential demand for electricity, owing to the greater options manufacturers have to use different fuel sources or to convert to more energy-efficient equipment. Under such circumstances, the total revenues of electric utility firms can be increased by charging higher prices to the market segment where demand is less elastic (residential users) and lower prices to price-sensitive buyers (industrial users).

PRICE ELASTICITY AND DEMAND FOR THE PRODUCT OF AN INDIVIDUAL FIRM

The degree to which market demand is price sensitive (elastic) or price insensitive (inelastic) does not completely carry over to the demand for the product of an individual firm. Two factors shape the price elasticity of demand for the products of an individual firm: (1) the elasticity of total *market* demand and the extent to which a firm's *pro rata* market share is affected by a change in the average *market* price, and (2) the ability a firm has to hold onto or increase its market share as it alters its prices above or below the prevailing market level. In other words, price elasticity for a particular firm or brand is affected not only by the factors that govern the price elasticity of total market demand but also by how sensitive the firm's own demand is to the prices being charged by other firms in the marketplace. A couple of illustrations highlight the reasons for this.

Price elasticity for the product of a particular firm depends primarily on how sensitive the firm's own sales are to the prices charged by its competitors.

Consider first the case of an industry where the products of different firms are all essentially alike—as is the case with commodity-type markets (wheat, soybeans, gold, copper, oil). The key pricing feature of commodity products is uniformity of price throughout the market, although there may be minor variations depending upon location (New York or London) or time (futures or spot prices). In such markets, an individual firm has very limited pricing discretion. For example, if one coal supplier raised selling price to $30 per ton while the remaining suppliers stayed at $25, the high-priced seller would have difficulty finding buyers, and demand for the firm's coal would prove quickly to be highly price elastic. Conversely, if the firm decided to undercut the prices of competing coal suppliers by announcing a $2 per ton price, it would be deluged with orders—again a price-elastic condition. But this latter condition may be extremely short-lived if competing firms rapidly implement matching price cuts to prevent losing customers to the low-priced firm. Matching price cuts transform what otherwise would be a highly elastic response to a firm's own price cuts into a response where the firm's price elasticity value is equal to the price elasticity of total market demand.

APPLICATIONS CAPSULE

DO RISING GASOLINE PRICES REDUCE DEMAND?

Economists' estimates of the extent to which gasoline demand will lessen as prices rise show that in the immediate short run, the coefficient of price elasticity is −0.10—in which case the quantity of gasoline used can be expected to decline immediately about 1% for each 10% increase in retail prices at the pump. However, the elasticity picture changes substantially as the period for examining the response of motorists to higher prices is stretched out. This is because the full impact of a price change on demand does not take place immediately; the longer motorists have to make adjustments in gasoline usage, the greater is their ability to do so in terms of making basic changes in the type of car they own, in their driving habits,

and in their dependence on the automobile relative to total miles driven each year. Manufacturers, moreover, have time to design and build cars with greater fuel efficiency.

The price elasticity estimates for periods of 2 to 3 years cluster in the neighborhood of −0.25. Professor Pindyck at MIT projects a 5-year price elasticity figure of −0.49 for the United States. Over a 10-year time frame, his estimate is −0.82 and for 15 years it is −1.03. The sharply increasing degree of price elasticity as the time of response lengthens highlights the fact that the total impact of a change in price may be much more dramatic over the long run than in the short run.

In general, then, when competing firms are selling essentially identical products, any one firm is seldom advised to stray much from the prevailing industry average price. When one firm changes its price *independently* of other sellers, it quickly learns that the demand for its product is highly elastic above the going market price and much less elastic or even inelastic below the ruling price (depending on how the overall market demand will respond to matching price cuts by all producers).

At the other extreme, there are markets where the products of competing firms are sufficiently different so that the demand for a particular firm's product becomes somewhat less sensitive to price. Product differentiation allows competitors the room to charge a range of prices; indeed, there may be no such thing as *the* industry price. In the women's dress market, for instance, there exists a broad range of prices and styles, from the bargain basement to the high-fashion salon, and each merchant is able to establish a differential market image according to the selection of dresses, decor and location of the retail shop, type of sales assistance, credit arrangements, alteration services, advertising, and so forth. Stocking dresses selling at high prices may be congruent with one merchant's approach, and stocking dresses selling at low prices with another. In strongly differentiated product markets, the degree of price elasticity confronting the individual seller is influenced by the extent to which that firm's prices are synchronized with (1) the overall character and image of its total product offering, (2) the importance consumers attach to nonprice product features, and (3) the extent to which higher prices can be obtained through increased promotional efforts.

The more strongly differentiated are the products of rival sellers, the more price inelastic the demand for any one seller's product tends to be.

Therefore, appraising the price elasticity of demand for an individual firm's product entails examining the full dimensions along which buyers assess a product's relative attractiveness—consideration of price alone is insufficient. Particularly one must assess how the attributes of a firm's product stack up against the attributes of competing brands and products. When all rival firms are selling comparable products, price elasticity among brands tends to be high, since consumers are prone to switch to lower-priced brands. But the more strongly differentiated are the products of rival sellers, the less sensitive the demand of any one firm will be to a change in its selling price. Moreover, if a firm successfully increases the degree of product differentiation between its brand and other brands, it often finds buyers tolerant of a modest increase in price—thus resulting in demand being less price elastic than before.

INCOME ELASTICITY OF DEMAND

As stated in earlier chapters, the purchase levels of many items are quite sensitive to variations in consumer incomes. The responsiveness of the quantity demanded to a change in consumer income (other demand determinants being held fixed) is called *income elasticity of demand*.

Just as price elasticity was found by determining the ratio of the percentage change in the quantity demanded to some percentage change in price, so income elasticity is calculated by finding the ratio of the percentage change in quantity demanded to a percentage change in income. Hence, we may write

$$\epsilon_I = \frac{\% \text{ change in quantity demanded}}{\% \text{ change in income}}$$

As with price elasticity, there are also two measures of income elasticity: arc elasticity and point elasticity. The arc formula for computing income elasticity is

$$\epsilon_I = \frac{\dfrac{Q_2 - Q_1}{\left(\dfrac{Q_1 + Q_2}{2}\right)}}{\dfrac{I_2 - I_1}{\left(\dfrac{I_1 + I_2}{2}\right)}},$$

where ϵ_I represents the coefficient of income elasticity and I is income. The point formula for income elasticity is

$$\epsilon_I = \frac{dQ}{dI} \cdot \frac{I}{Q},$$

where dQ/dI symbolizes the rate of change in the quantity demanded as income changes.

For all items except inferior goods, the sign of the coefficient of income elasticity is positive because for normal goods income and quantity purchased vary in the same direction. If the value of the income elasticity coefficient is greater than $+1$, the demand for the item is said to be income elastic; if it is less than $+1$, then demand is said to be income inelastic. The coefficient of income elasticity is negative for inferior goods. The greater the size of the coefficient, the greater the degree of responsiveness of the quantity demanded to a change in income.

Income elasticity varies widely from item to item. Light bulbs, dairy products, aspirin, and cigarettes are examples of products whose income elasticities are typically low. In contrast, jewelry, T-bone steak, Cadillacs, art objects, education, foreign travel, and scotch have high income elasticities. Generally, products that consumers regard as necessities have low income elasticities, while luxuries tend to have high income elasticities. Indeed, one way of designating items as either luxuries or necessities is by the size of their income elasticities.

The results of some actual studies of price and income elasticity of demand are shown in Table 5-4.

BASIC CONCEPT
Income elasticity concerns the responsiveness of quantity demanded to a change in income, other things remaining equal.

Demand is *income elastic* when a given percentage change in income produces a large percentage change in quantity demanded; demand is *income inelastic* when the percentage change in income results in a smaller percentage change in quantity demanded.

TABLE 5-4   RESULTS OF STUDIES OF ELASTICITY OF DEMAND

Product	Elasticity Finding
Air travel	
Short business-oriented routes	Price inelastic
Vacation routes	Highly income elastic
Residential electricity	
Short run (1 year)	−0.06 (price); +0.06 (income)
Long run	−0.52 (price); +0.88 (income)
Cigarettes	−0.3 to −0.4 (price); +0.5 (income)
Coffee	−0.15 (price); +0.29 (income)
China, glassware, tableware, utensils	
Short run	−1.2 (price)
Long run	−1.3 (price)
Kitchen appliances	−0.6 (price)
Tires	
Short run	−0.6 (price)
Long run	−0.4 (price)
Radio and television receivers (short run)	−1.2 (price)
Automobiles (long run)	−0.2 (price)
Legal services	−0.5 (price)
Physicians' services	−0.6 (price)
Housing	−0.40 (price)
Soybean meal	−1.65 (price)
Local residential telephone service	
Short run	−0.10 (price); +0.10 (income)
Long run	−0.14 (price); +0.14 (income)
Local telephone service, business use	
Short run	−0.08 (price); +0.10 (income)
Long run	−0.15 (price); +0.19 (income)

Sources: H. S. Houthakker and Lester D. Taylor, *Consumer Demand in the United States, 1929–1970* (Cambridge, Mass., Harvard University Press, 1966); Philip K. Verleger, Jr., "Models of the Demand for Air Transportation," *Bell Journal of Economics and Management Science*, Vol. 3, No. 2 (Autumn 1972), pp. 437–57; James M. Griffin, "The Effects of Higher Prices on Electricity Consumption," *Bell Journal of Economics and Management Science*, Vol. 5, No. 2 (Autumn 1974), pp. 515–39; S. M. Sackrin, "Factors Affecting the Demand for Cigarettes," *Agricultural Economics Research*, Vol. 14, No. 3 (July 1962), pp. 81–88; John J. Hughes, "Note on the U.S. Demand for Coffee," *American Journal of Agricultural Economics*, Vol. 51, No. 4 (November 1969); R. W. Eberts and T. J. Gronberg, "Wage Gradients, Rent Gradients, and the Price Elasticity of Demand for Housing: An Empirical Investigation," *Journal of Urban Economics*, Vol. 12, No. 2 (September 1982), pp. 168–76; Hendrik C. Knipscheer, Lowell D. Hill, and Bruce L. Dixon, "Demand Elasticities for Soybean Meal in the European Community," *American Journal of Agricultural Economics*, Vol. 64, No. 2 (May 1982), pp. 249–53; John P. Formby, Vincent G. Munley, and Larry D. Taylor, "Electricity Demand in Multi-Family, Renter-Occupied Residences," *Southern Economic Journal*, Vol. 57, No. 1 (July 1990), pp. 178–94; and the New York Telephone Company.

APPLICATIONS CAPSULE

WHY SOME BUYERS ARE LESS PRICE SENSITIVE THAN OTHERS

Buyers of products differ greatly in the degree to which they are sensitive to price changes. The demand curves of some buyers may be very elastic while other buyers may have very inelastic demands. Where buyers are insensitive to price and to price changes, one or more of the following conditions tend to prevail:

1. *The buyer is very concerned about product performance.* Buyer demand tends to be price inelastic whenever a product that "fails" or does not perform up to expectations causes the buyer to incur substantial penalties, costs, or inconvenience. The adverse risks of product failure make it worthwhile for buyers to pay a premium price for high performance characteristics and inclines them to stick with products and brands that have proven reliable in the past. A good example where this happens is in the oil-field-equipment industry. The demand for blowout preventors (a piece of oil field equipment that prevents oil from escaping a well if there is a surge in pressure) tends to be price inelastic; if the blowout preventor fails, the user faces considerable costs in terms of lost oil, lost time of skilled crews, and environmental sanctions, particularly in the case of offshore wells, where the clean up of spills is particularly expensive. As a consequence, buyers of blowout preventors are reluctant to switch from proven brand names even in the face of price increases and even when other companies seeking to penetrate the market offer lower-priced products with allegedly comparable performance features.

2. *The buyer wants a differentiated or custom-designed product and is willing to pay extra for it.* Whenever buyers want a specially designed product to fit their own particular needs, they often become locked into purchasing from a particular supplier who is willing to go to the trouble to satisfy the buyer's special design requests. In such instances, buyers may conclude that

extra effort on the part of the supplier merits the compensation of a higher price. Of course, later, the supplier's willingness to accommodate the buyer's wants may provide the leverage needed to impose a price increase without much risk of losing the buyer's business.

3. *The buyer purchases the product because it is perceived to contribute to the high-quality image the buyer is trying to project on behalf of its own product.* Buyers of items that are components of the buyer's own final product often have price inelastic demands because they perceive that the item's quality will enhance the performance of their product, or because the brand name of the component carries prestige value which reinforces the high-quality image they are trying to project. For example, the manufacturers of expensive pieces of equipment will often use the electric motors of prestige suppliers as a component part because doing so upgrades the image of their machinery and helps enhance its market attractiveness. Manufacturers of the component part, knowing of the benefit their component gives the final product, are then in a position to ask for and get a slightly higher price when other firms cannot.

4. *The buyer obtains major savings from using a particular product or service.* Whenever a product or service can save a buyer time and money because it performs well, the buyer will tend to have an inelastic demand for the product. The same holds true when a buyer can benefit from timely delivery of a product, rapid maintenance and repair in the event of breakdowns, and technical advice. To cite an example, when a firm has high stakes in the outcome of a particular situation (such as an electric utility filing for a $200 million rate increase), the firm will be willing to pay a premium for the very best advice it can get from lawyers, accountants, consultants, and other experts having specialized knowledge and talents to offer. Another example, drawn again from the oil industry, is where a

CROSS ELASTICITY OF DEMAND

Insofar as their demand is concerned, goods can be related in any one of three ways:

1. They may be **competing** products or **substitutes**, in which case an increase in the purchase of one is at the expense of another. So it is with various *brands* of margarine, soap, razor blades, and gasoline; similarly, hamburgers may be a substitute for hot dogs, a trip to Florida may be a substitute for a trip to the Great Smoky Mountains, and a Toyota Celica may be a substitute for a Ford Mustang.

2. They may be **complementary** products, in which case an increase in the purchase of one causes a rise in the purchase of another. Complementary implies that goods are consumed *together*. Examples include electric appliances and electric power, shoes and socks, notebook paper and ballpoint pens, and carpets and vacuum cleaners.

company such as Schlumberger uses sophisticated electronic techniques to detect the likely presence of oil in substrata rock formations; the information obtained from such instruments has the potential for steering oil-drilling companies away from locations where there is greater probability of a dry hole. Understandably, then, oil-drilling companies are willing to pay substantial fees for Schlumberger's services, particularly when they face difficult and costly drilling expenses because of great depth or offshore location.

5. *The cost of the item is small compared to the buyer's purchasing budget.* Many consumers do not bother to shop around for the best price and to undertake time-consuming product comparisons when the cost of the item is low. This is especially true when the buyer's major motive in purchasing the item is convenience, taste, or some other subjective preference criterion. In the case of industrial buyers, the relevant cost of an item is the firm's total expenditure for the item over some time period (a month or a year), not the cost per unit. Low unit cost is not a sufficient consideration because the number of units purchased may make the dollar costs of the item very important. In industrial purchasing, the purchase of component parts or raw materials that entail a high total dollar cost is usually handled by top executives and/or senior specialist purchasing agents who may well be very price conscious—thereby creating an elastic-demand situation.

6. *The buyer is in a position to absorb a price increase and/or can readily pass on higher costs of component parts and raw materials.* As a rule, the more a firm is in position to pass along rising costs, the less tenacious and aggressive it will be in haggling over prices and price increases. The same can hold true when an industrial buyer has a sufficiently high profit margin that it is willing to absorb a price increase rather than go to the trouble of seeking out alternative sources of supply.

(However, in such instances the item is probably a sufficiently low cost item that the basic reason for price insensitivity is that the buyer falls into category 5.)

7. *The buyer is poorly informed and/or does not adhere to a policy of purchasing according to well-defined specifications.* Buyers tend to be less sensitive to prices and price increases when they are poorly informed about prevailing price conditions, demand-supply conditions, the availability and prices of substitutes, and the performance-quality-service features offered by rival brands and suppliers. More-informed buyers tend to be hard bargainers on price and other conditions of purchase. Indeed, many large purchasers make a special effort to learn the business of their suppliers so well that they know when they are getting a good price and when they are not. A poorly informed buyer is easily swayed by persuasive advertising, a good sales pitch, and efforts to downplay the performance differences among competing products.

8. *The cost to a buyer of switching from one seller to another is very high.* In some cases, an industrial user of a component part may tie the specifications of its products to that of a particular supplier, or the firm may make heavy investments in installing and using a particular supplier's equipment (as is often the case with a computer). When buyers' switching costs are high, they may well be insensitive to price changes—especially small price changes that would not make it worthwhile to switch.

Source: Adapted with permission of The Free Press, a Division of Macmillan, Inc. from *Competitive Strategy: Techniques for Analyzing Industries and Competitors,* by Michael E. Porter. Copyright (c) 1980 by The Free Press. pp. 24–26, 114–18.

3. They may be *independent*, such that the purchase of one has no direct bearing upon the demand of another. Independence implies that goods are neither consumed together nor in place of each other. Pairs of items whose purchases are for all intents and purposes independent include shrimp and pillows, football tickets and a spool of thread, and fishing tackle and lingerie.

BASIC CONCEPT
Cross elasticity concerns the responsiveness of the quantity demanded of one item to a change in the price of another item.

Cross elasticity of demand is a measure for interpreting the relationship between products. As between two products X and Y, cross elasticity measures the percentage change in the quantity demanded of product Y in response to a percentage change in the price of product X. In mathematical terms,

$$\epsilon_{yx} = \frac{\% \text{ change in quantity of Y}}{\% \text{ change in price of X}}$$

where ϵ_{yx} symbolizes the coefficient of cross elasticity between X and Y. Again, there are two ways of actually computing cross elasticity. The arc formula for calculating the coefficient of cross elasticity is

$$\epsilon_{yx} = \dfrac{\dfrac{Q_{y_2} - Q_{y_1}}{\left(\dfrac{Q_{y_1} + Q_{y_2}}{2}\right)}}{\dfrac{P_{x_2} - P_{x_1}}{\left(\dfrac{P_{x_1} + P_{x_2}}{2}\right)}}$$

The point elasticity formula is

$$\epsilon_{yx} = \frac{dQ_y}{dP_x} \cdot \frac{P_x}{Q_y}.$$

The cross-elasticity coefficient may be either positive or negative. *When ϵ_{yx} is positive, products X and Y are substitutes for each other*. This is illustrated by a simple example. Other factors remaining constant, if the price of shipping goods by rail increases, the freight traffic via motor carrier should rise. Conversely, if the price of shipping goods by rail declines, the freight traffic via motor carrier should decrease. In either case, the percentage changes in rail rates and the volume of motor freight are in the same direction. Thus, whether the price changes are up or down, the cross-elasticity coefficient is positive.

Complementary goods have negative cross-elasticity coefficients. Automobiles and automobile insurance serve as a case in point. An increase in the price of automobiles tends to reduce purchases of automobiles and cuts back on the sales of automobile insurance. In contrast, lower automobile prices tend to stimulate car sales, thereby boosting sales of auto insurance. Hence, a change in the price of automobiles is followed by a change in sales of auto insurance in the opposite direction. As a consequence, the coefficient of cross elasticity is negative.

The strength of the relationship between substitute and complementary products is reflected by the absolute size of the cross-elasticity coefficient. *The larger the coefficient, the stronger the relationship.* Furthermore, it follows that the closer the coefficient is to zero (approached from either the positive or negative side), the weaker is any substitute or complementary relationship between two products and the more independent the two products are. This is so because as ϵ_{yx} approaches zero, variations in the price of one good induce no appreciable change in the quantity demanded of the other; hence, purchases of the products would seem unrelated or independent.

Measures of the cross elasticity of demand may be indicative of the boundaries of an industry. High cross elasticities indicate close relationships and suggest that the goods are part of the same industry, whereas low cross elasticities imply weak relationships and that the goods may be in different industries. If a good has a low cross elasticity with respect to all other goods, then it may be considered to constitute an industry by itself. Similarly, if several products have high cross elasticities among themselves but low cross elasticities with respect to other goods, then the product group may define an industry. For instance, various brands of TV sets have high cross elasticities among each other but low cross elasticities with other household appliances and fixtures.

However, using the cross-elasticity concept as a means of delimiting an industry is not without difficulty. In the first place, it is arbitrary as to how high

When the cross-elasticity coefficient is positive, the items are substitutes; a negative coefficient signifies that the items are complementary goods.

MATHEMATICAL CAPSULE 6

PARTIAL ELASTICITIES OF DEMAND: A MORE RIGOROUS CONCEPT OF DEMAND ELASTICITY

In its most general form, the demand function for a good can be expressed as

$$Q_1 = f(P_1, P_2, \ldots, P_n, I, E, R, N, T, O),$$

where

Q_1 = quantity demanded of good 1,
P_1 = market price of the good,
$P_2, \ldots, P_n$ = prices of other goods,
I = level of consumer incomes,
E = consumer expectations regarding future prices, incomes, and product availability,
R = range of goods available to buyers,
N = number of potential buyers, and
O = all other factors relevant in influencing Q_1.

The elasticity of demand with respect to any demand determinant refers to the degree of responsiveness of the quantity demanded relative to some percentage change in that demand determinant *when the values of all other demand determinants are held fixed.*

In mathematical terms, this definition translates into the following expressions for point elasticity:

$$\epsilon_p = \frac{\partial Q_1}{\partial P_1} \cdot \frac{P_1}{Q_1}, \qquad (1)$$

which is the partial elasticity of good 1 with respect to its price, P_1, or price elasticity of demand;

$$\epsilon_{12} = \frac{\partial Q_1}{\partial P_2} \cdot \frac{P_2}{Q_1}, \qquad (2)$$

which is the partial elasticity of good 1 with respect to the price of good 2, or cross elasticity of demand between good 1 and good 2;

$$\epsilon_{1n} = \frac{\partial Q_1}{\partial P_n} \cdot \frac{P_n}{Q_1}, \qquad (3)$$

which is the partial elasticity of good 1 with respect to the price of good n, or cross elasticity of demand between good 1 and good n;

$$\epsilon_I = \frac{\partial Q_1}{\partial I} \cdot \frac{I}{Q_1}, \qquad (4)$$

which is the partial elasticity of good 1 with respect to income, or income elasticity of demand; and so on for the other demand determinants. Hence, when given the demand function for a product containing more than one variable, the procedure for determining point elasticity requires using the *partial derivative* of the demand function with respect to that demand determinant rather than the first derivative.

EXERCISES

1. Suppose that the demand function for product X is specified by the equation $Q_x = 34 - 0.8P_x^2 + 0.3P_y + 0.04I$.
   (a) Determine the price elasticity of demand for X when $P_x = \$10$, $P_y = \$20$, and $I = \$5000$.
   (b) Determine the cross elasticity of demand for X with respect to good Y when $P_x = \$10$, $P_y = \$20$, and $I = \$5000$. Are X and Y substitutes or complements?
   (c) Determine the income elasticity of demand for X when $P_x = \$10$, $P_y = \$20$, and $I = \$5000$. Is X a normal or an inferior good?
2. Suppose that the demand function for good Y is specified by the equation $Q_y = 1665 - 0.5P_y^3 - 0.1P_x^2 - 0.05I$.
   (a) Determine the price elasticity of demand when $P_y = \$10$, $P_x = \$20$, and $I = \$2500$.
   (b) Determine the cross elasticity of demand for Y with respect to good X when $P_y = \$10$, $P_x = \$20$, and $I = \$2500$. Are X and Y substitutes or complements?
   (c) Determine the income elasticity of demand for Y when $P_y = \$10$, $P_x = \$20$, and $I = \$2500$. Is Y a normal or an inferior good?

cross elasticities must be to be considered in the same industry. Cross elasticities among canned vegetables may be quite high, yet the cross elasticity between canned vegetables and canned meats is liable to be rather low. Such circumstances render it difficult to define rigorously the boundaries of an industry—should it be canned vegetables or canned meats or canned foods?

A second complication rises from the existence of chains of cross relationships. The cross elasticity between a color TV console and a table model color TV may be high, as might the cross elasticity between portable color TVs and black-and-white portables. But console color TV sets and portable black-and-white sets may have low cross elasticities, thereby raising issues of just how closely related the markets for console color TV sets and portable black-and-white TV sets are to one another.

REAL-WORLD DEMAND CURVES AND ELASTICITIES

It is apparent from the preceding discussion that the price elasticity of demand is an important concept, and having valid and reliable estimates of it could be extremely useful to business firms that must make pricing decisions and to government policy makers who are faced with decisions about changing commodity taxes or responding to oil price shocks, which quickly drive gasoline and other energy prices upward in short periods of time. The first step in figuring out what real-world demand elasticities are for specific goods and services involves specifying what the demand curve looks like. If other factors influencing demand are constant, then by the law of demand we know that the demand curve slopes downward and ϵ_p is negative. But are real-world demand relations best approximated by specifying linear, convex, or concave demand curves? There are sound reasons for ruling out linear and concave demand curves and estimating price elasticities by specifying a general form for the convex demand curve. This is explained with the aid of Figure 5-11, which depicts a linear and constant elasticity (convex) demand curve.

If demand is linear as in Figure 5-11(a) and is given by $Q_x = 100 - P$, then a rise in price from \$1 to \$2 (a doubling of the price) will decrease quantity by 1 unit (quantity will change from $Q_x = 99$ to $Q_x = 98$). But a rise in price from \$98 to \$99 (a rise of 1.02%) will also decrease quantity by 1 unit (changing quantity from $Q_x = 2$ to $Q_x = 1$). It seems unreasonable to expect real-world demand curves to be characterized by such widely differing impacts of percentage change in price on quantity. Rather than assuming a constant slope of the demand curve as in Figure 5-11(a), economists believe that it is almost always more appropriate to think of real-world demand curves as having constant elasticity, as in Figure 5-11(b). All demand curves of the constant elasticity

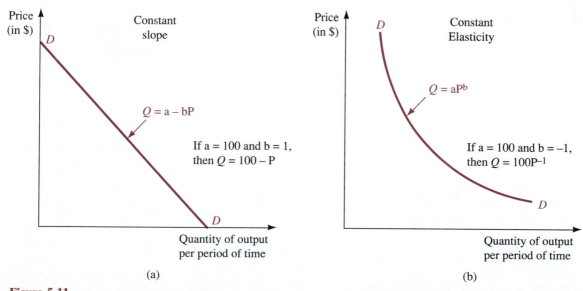

(a)   (b)

Figure 5-11

Two widely discussed specifications of demand—a linear (constant slope) demand curve and a constant elasticity demand curve

class are convex like the one in Figure 5-11(b) and are given by the expression

$$Q = aP^b,$$

where a is a positive constant and b is a negative constant. A characteristic of the constant elasticity demand curve is that they are linear in logarithmic form,

$$\log Q = \log a + b \log P.$$

For example, in Figure 5-11(b) the values of the constants are $a = 100$ and $b = -1$, and we have an example of the unitary elastic demand curve. As demonstrated in Mathematical Capsule 7, in a constant elasticity demand curve the coefficient b is always equal to ϵ_p. In Figure 5-11(b) a rise in price from \$1 to \$2 reduces quantity by 50% (changing quantity from $Q = 100$ to $Q = 50$, and a rise in price from \$98 to \$99 reduces quantity by 1.01% (changing quantity from $Q = 1.0204$ to $Q = 1.0101$). In statistically estimating real-world elasticities of the type summarized in Table 5-4, economists always use constant elasticity demand curves. Therefore, the values of the price elasticities in Table 5-4 are estimated using a demand curve specification that is linear in logarithmic form.

Key Points

The analysis of the demand for a product can be approached from the standpoint of an individual consumer (individual consumer demand), from the standpoint of all consumers taken as a group (market demand), or from the

Mathematical Capsule 7

Constant Elasticity Demand Curves

A constant elasticity demand curve is of the general form

$$Q = aP^b,$$

where $a \geq 0$ and $b < 0$. The constant elasticity demand curve can be written equivalently as

$$\log Q = \log a + b \log P.$$

It is important to note that

$$\epsilon_p = b.$$

This can be demonstrated as follows. Price elasticity of demand is

$$\epsilon_p = \frac{dQ}{dP} \cdot \frac{P}{Q} = abP^{b-1} \cdot \frac{P}{Q} = \frac{abP^b}{P} \cdot \frac{P}{aP^b} = b.$$

Thus, for any constant elasticity demand curve the value of ϵ_p is the same at all points.

As emphasized earlier, the quantity demanded of any good depends not only on its own price but on a number of other variables as well. These other determinants of demand are incorporated into the constant elasticity demand function in a straightforward fashion by using the following general expression

$$Q_x = aP_x^b P_y^c I^d O^e,$$

where, as in Mathematical Capsule 6, P_y is a related good, I is income, and O denotes any other determinant of demand that is important in a particular real-world situation. Writing this general constant elasticity demand function in logarithmic form yields the log linear equation

$$\log Q_1 = \log a + b \log P_x + c \log P_y + d \log I + e \log O.$$

In a manner analogous to the demonstration that $\epsilon_{p_x} = b$, it can be shown that $\epsilon_{p_y} = c$, $\epsilon_I = d$, and $\epsilon_o = e$. By the law of demand $\beta < 0$, but c, d, and e can take on positive or negative values. For example, if goods 1 and 2 are substitutes, then $c > 0$. If goods 1 and 2 are complements, $c < 0$. Similarly, if good 1 is normal, $d > 0$; and if it is inferior, $d < 0$.

The fact that constant elasticity demand curves are linear when expressed in logarithmic form is important for empirical estimates of real-world demand functions. As explained earlier, economists believe that it is more accurate to specify real-world demand as being of the constant elasticity form rather than the general linear form. But converting the constant elasticity demand functions to their logarithmic equivalents makes them linear in log form. This fact makes them relatively easy to estimate using standard econometric methods of demand analysis, which are the source of the elasticity estimates in Table 5-4.

standpoint of a particular business firm (product demand or firm demand). Demand is determined in the main by (1) the selling price of the item; (2) consumer tastes and preferences; (3) the money income of consumers; (4) the prices of related products; (5) consumer expectations with regard to future prices, income levels, and product availability; (6) the product's attributes and what they do for the user; and (7) market size as determined by the number of consumers and the frequency with which they consume the item. Other peripheral considerations include whether the good in question is viewed as a luxury or a necessity, whether its demand is derived from the demand for other goods, the extent of market saturation, the price and availability of consumer credit, and the discretionary purchasing power of consumers. The separate impacts of the major and minor demand determinants vary in intensity from product to product; to a degree each item has its own unique set of demand determinants.

A firm's demand curve provides the basis for deriving its revenue curves. A firm's average revenue (*AR*) curve summarizes the relationship between average revenue (average price) and quantity sold; it is identical to the firm's demand curve. A firm's total revenue (*TR*) equals the total receipts it obtains from the sale of its output. A firm's marginal revenue (*MR*) is the change in total revenue that results from a very small increase or decrease in output sold. Marginal revenue may be thought of as either *continuous* or *discrete*. Continuous marginal revenue is appropriate when output changes by infinitesimally small amounts. Discrete marginal revenue is used in situations where output changes in amounts of 1 unit (or more). A firm's average revenue can be found by dividing total revenue by the number of units sold. The shapes of the various *TR*, *MR*, and *AR* functions depend on the shape of the demand curve.

Elasticity of demand measures the responsiveness or sensitivity of quantity demanded to changes in a demand determinant. Price elasticity of demand is defined specifically as a ratio of the percentage change in quantity demanded resulting from a percentage change in price. Arc elasticity is an approximate measure of demand sensitivity between two points, while point elasticity measures elasticity at a single point on the demand function. When the coefficient of price elasticity is greater than one, demand is elastic and a price decrease will cause *TR* to rise. When the coefficient of price elasticity is less than one, demand is inelastic and a price decrease will cause *TR* to fall. Total revenue is maximized at the output rate where the price elasticity coefficient is 1. The degree of price elasticity for a product varies according to (1) the region of the demand curve within which price changes, (2) the number and availability of substitutes, (3) the price of the item relative to consumer income, (4) whether the item is a luxury or a necessity, (5) the number of uses for the good, (6) the length of the time period being considered, (7) the durability of the item, and (8) market saturation.

In estimating real-world demand elasticities, economists use constant elasticity demand functions, which are always convex and are generally thought to be more reasonable approximations than linear or concave demand curves. In addition to price elasticity of demand, two other elasticity concepts of particular importance are income elasticity and cross elasticity. High, positive income elasticities characterize luxury-type items; low, positive income elasticities are typical for necessities; and negative income elasticities denote inferior goods. Cross elasticity is a measure of the sensitivity of the demand for one product relative to price changes in another product. When the cross-elasticity coefficient is positive, the two goods are substitutes; when the coefficient is negative, a complementary relationship is indicated. The closer the coefficient is to zero, the more independent are the two items.

PROBLEMS AND QUESTIONS FOR DISCUSSION

1. The following table presents hypothetical data for the market demand for a good. Complete the table.

Price	Quantity Demanded	AR	TR	Discrete MR	Coefficient of Price Elasticity
$50	1	___	___	___	___
40	2	___	___	___	___
30	3	___	___	___	___
20	4	___	___	___	___
13	5	___	___	___	___
8	6	___	___	___	___

2. Given: The demand equation is $P = 81 - 9Q$.
   (a) What is the equation for MR?
   (b) At what output is $MR = 0$?
   (c) At what output is TR maximum?
   (d) Determine the price elasticity of demand at the output where TR is maximum.

3. Suppose that the demand equation for a good is $Q = 20 - 3P$. What is the price elasticity of demand at a price of $1? At a price of $4?

4. If the demand equation for an item is $Q = 16 + 9P - 2P^2$, calculate the price elasticity of demand at a price of $4 and at a price of $3.

5. If the demand equation for an item is $P = 1000 + 3Q - 4Q^2$:
   (a) Determine price elasticity of demand at $Q = 10$ units.
   (b) Determine the equations for TR and MR.

6. Given the following hypothetical data for a consumer, compute *all* meaningful elasticity coefficients (price elasticity, income elasticity, and cross elasticity). Remember that prices must be constant when income elasticity is computed and that income and the prices of other products must be constant when price elasticity is computed, and so on. In other words, the computation of elasticities of any kind is valid *only* when *all other* variables are held constant.

Period	Price of X	Quantity of X Purchased	Price of Y	Income
1	$1.00	200	$0.50	$6000
2	1.05	190	0.50	6000
3	1.05	200	0.52	6500
4	1.05	220	0.54	6500
5	1.03	210	0.53	6500
6	1.03	215	0.55	6500
7	1.03	205	0.55	6300
8	1.07	190	0.55	6300

7. Given: The market demand equation for widgets is $Q = 840 - 0.50P$, where $Q =$ quantity demanded per period of time and $P =$ price of widgets in dollars.
   (a) If the price of widgets were lowered from $40 to $38, would you expect consumer expenditures for widgets to rise, fall, or remain unchanged?

(b) If the economy's sole producer of widgets lowered its price from $40 to $38, what predictions, if any, can you make about the effect the price reduction would have upon the firm's *profits*?

8. Given: The relationship between product A and product B is $Q_A = 80P_B - 0.5P_B^2$, where Q_A = units of product A demanded by consumers each day and P_B = selling price of product B.
   (a) Determine the cross-elasticity coefficient for the two products when the price of product B = $10.
   (b) Are products A and B complements, substitutes, or independent, and how "strong" is the relationship?

9. Given the price levels now prevailing for steel products, would you expect that the price elasticity of demand for the output of U.S. Steel Corporation is higher or lower than the price elasticity of demand for the output of the steel industry as a whole? Why?

10. The Tastee Food Company estimates that the demand-income relationships for its line of frozen pies can be represented by the equation $Q = 500 + 0.10I$, where Q = cases of frozen pies and I = average family income.
    (a) Determine the point income elasticity of demand at I = $15,000, I = $20,000, and I = $25,000.
    (b) The calculations in part (a) should show that ϵ_I increases as income increases. Why does this relationship exist? Would the same relationship hold if the demand-income equation were $Q = 0.10I$?
    (c) Would you characterize the demand for Tastee Foods' frozen pie line as susceptible to recessionary influences in the economy? Explain. Would sustained inflation over a period of years tend to alter the demand-income equation because of the effects that inflation has on the purchasing power of the dollar?

11. The Fairfax Apparel Company manufactures sports shirts for men; during 1987 Fairfax sold an average of 23,000 sports shirts for $13 per shirt. In early January 1988, Fairfax's major competitor, Lafayette Manufacturing Co., cut the price of its sports shirts from $15 to $12. The orders Fairfax received for its own sports shirts dropped sharply, from 23,000 per month to 13,000 per month for February and March 1988.
    (a) Calculate the cross elasticity of demand between Fairfax's sports shirts and Lafayette's sports shirts during February and March. Are the two companies' sports shirts good or poor substitutes?
    (b) Suppose that the coefficient of price elasticity of demand for Fairfax's sports shirts is −2.0. Assuming that Lafayette keeps its price at $12, by how much must Fairfax cut its price to build its sales of shirts back up to 23,000 per month? (*Hint*: Use the arc formula for price elasticity and substitute the known values into it and solve for the unknown price.)
    (c) Would you recommend that Fairfax cut its price to the value calculated in part (b)? Why or why not?

12. The George Washington Uniform Co. has received a report from a microeconomics consulting firm that the demand function for its model x revolutionary war uniform is $Q_x = 10P_x^{-2.1}P_y^2P_z^{-1.5}I^{1.8}A^{0.9}$, where Q_x is quantity of uniforms demanded per time period, P_x is the price of model x uniforms per unit, P_y and P_z are prices of related goods, I is income, and A is advertising.
    (a) What type of demand function has the consulting firm estimated? What are its characteristics? Why do economists generally believe that this type of demand function is a better approximation of the actual (real-world) demand than a linear demand function would be?
    (b) Is the price elasticity of demand for model x uniforms elastic, unitary elastic, or inelastic? Why? What factors would likely cause the coefficient of price elasticity of demand to be in the general range that the consulting firm has estimated?
    (c) What exactly does the estimated demand function tell us about the effect of advertising on uniform sales? Explain.
    (d) Is good y a substitute or complement for the George Washington Uniform Company's model x uniform? Why?
    (e) Is good z a substitute or complement for the George Washington Uniform Company's model x uniform? Why?
    (f) Is the George Washington Uniform Company's model x uniform a normal good or an inferior good? Why?

Chapter 6

Production Functions and Technology

With the insights gained about consumer behavior and how the demand side of the marketplace works, it is time to switch over and look at the economics of the supply side. We begin our study of market supply economics by surveying the properties of a firm's production process and exploring why technological change ranks as one of the principal drivers of competition and market change. This chapter is organized around five topic areas: (1) the concept of production and the types of production processes, (2) the properties of production functions, (3) the role of technology in altering productive efficiency, (4) how technological change creates important new competitive forces in the marketplace, and (5) the pros and cons of technological leadership versus technological followership.

THE CONCEPT OF PRODUCTION

It is common to think of "production" as being synonymous with manufacturing. However, quite a large number of activities qualify as production. Collecting taxes, operating a jewelry store, drilling for oil, auditing a company's financial statements, designing a system to measure air pollution, dictating a letter, managing a United Fund drive, discussing with officials of the Federal Trade Commission the factual basis for claims made in a TV commercial, driving a garbage truck, and interviewing applicants for food stamps all represent production of one sort or another. Each involves some aspect of furnishing a good or service to some economic entity that values it.

In general, *any activity that creates value is production*. The term *production* thus covers every economic activity associated with furnishing a good or service to the final user—in the case of bread, the stages of production extend all the way from growing wheat to putting the loaf of bread in the buyer's sack of groceries at the supermarket. Nevertheless, because manufacturing activity illustrates the production process so well, we shall focus our discussion about production and technology on manufacturing-type situations. The principles exposed will apply to virtually any productive endeavor, irrespective of whether it is goods-oriented or service-oriented, profit-oriented or not-for-profit.

BASIC CONCEPT
Production occurs anytime an activity creates value—every activity associated with providing goods and services to the final user is part of the production process.

136

PRODUCTION: THE ACT OF TRANSFORMING INPUTS INTO OUTPUTS

Ask a production engineer how to make a product and you'll likely get a description of the basic technology and how raw materials flow through the various processing stages to end up in final product form. Describing production in terms of a technological process would serve as a beginning, but there's more to it. ***Raw material ingredients*** do not get combined and processed by technological means alone; production operations require human intervention or ***labor*** input. In addition, various tools, machinery, equipment, and physical facilities are normally used in the technological transformation of raw material ingredients into a finished good—such inputs define a general category of economic resources called ***capital***. Furthermore, production activity must occur in some location and so occupies space or ***land*** (this is particularly apparent in the case of agricultural production). Finally, production activity requires supervision, planning, control, coordination, and leadership—in effect, an input of ***entrepreneurial*** or ***managerial talent***.

> **The basic types of productive inputs are land, raw materials, technological know-how, labor, capital, and managerial skills.**

Broadly viewed, ***production*** is a series of activities by which resource inputs (raw materials, labor, technology, capital, land utilization, and managerial talent) are used to generate outputs of goods or services. The time period needed for the transformation of inputs into outputs is variable among products and from technological recipe to technological recipe for a given product. Sometimes a single production process yields several products. In meat packing, for example, the slaughter of beef cattle produces numerous cuts of meat products, hides for leather goods, lard for cooking purposes, and ingredients for pet foods.

> **Production is the act of transforming inputs into outputs.**

Figure 6-1 depicts the generic nature of production activity. Of course, as concerns a specific product or technique, the size of the box and the details of what goes on inside it tend to change over time as a consequence of modifications in technology, changes in the efficiency levels of one or more inputs, and a need to modify the item being produced.

BASIC CATEGORIES OF PRODUCTION ACTIVITY

The various types of production activities can be grouped into four categories: (1) custom-order production, (2) rigid mass production, (3) flexible mass production, and (4) process or flow production.[1] Each type has distinctive features and requirements.

> **There are four basic types of production activity.**

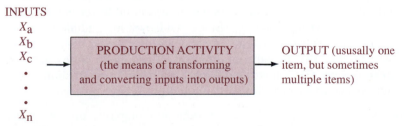

INPUTS
X_a
X_b
X_c
·
·
·
X_n

PRODUCTION ACTIVITY
(the means of transforming
and converting inputs into outputs)

OUTPUT (ususally one
item, but sometimes
multiple items)

Figure 6-1
Production activity

---

[1] This classification scheme and ensuing discussion is drawn from Peter F. Drucker, *Management: Tasks, Responsibilities, Practices* (New York: Harper & Row, 1974), pp. 203–16.

Custom-Order Production. This type of production activity involves made-to-order products. Each item produced is more or less custom-made according to the buyer's specifications—a power plant, a golf course, a bridge, an office building, an aircraft carrier, the services of a law firm or an accounting firm. Custom-order production typically places high demands on skill and craftsmanship. It requires people who are good at unique designs and one-of-a-kind production techniques. Custom-order production can be efficient at low output levels and production volumes can often be scaled way up or way down by changing the size of the work force. The trigger point for production activity to commence is for an order to come in.

Work tends to be organized more around the stage of production than around craft skill. The model is the construction of a single-family home, where production is grouped around the stages of setting the foundation in place; putting up the framing and roofing; installing the plumbing, wiring, and heating and cooling equipment; and doing the interior finishing. Craft skills are much in evidence, but they are grouped according to the production stage of the house.

Rigid Mass Production. In rigid mass production both the end product and the materials, technology, and processing steps tend to be standardized. When Henry Ford said "The customer can have a car in any color as long as it's black," he expressed the essence of rigid mass production—the manufacture of uniform products in large quantity using a well-defined, proven, and usually inflexible technology.[2]

Rigid mass production normally entails a capital-intensive technology that churns out a high and consistent volume of output; minor fluctuations in production levels adversely affect the economies of the technology-driven system. Because the nature of the final product is tightly constrained by inflexible production methods, firms making standard mass-produced items have to condition customers to adapt their tastes and needs to narrow product variety—otherwise the low-cost economy of mass production cannot be realized.

Flexible Mass Production. Here the idea is to take advantage of economical mass production by assembling several product varieties using different combinations of mass-produced, standardized components. The result is a family of similar products, each with features appealing to a segment of the buyer population. The key to making flexible mass production a viable approach is systematic analysis of customers, markets, and products to find the patterns around which diversity can be organized; this pattern then becomes the basis for taking the burden of diversity out of manufacturing and shifting it into assembly. General Motors has skillfully practiced the principle of developing many different models and sizes of cars out of fewer and fewer parts. Many makes of GM cars (Chevrolet, Pontiac, Buick, Oldsmobile, Cadillac) use the same frames, brakes, electrical systems, mechanical parts, and very substantially the same engines. Yet, because of different colors, body styles, fabrics, trim, and interior design, GM cars look different, have different attributes, and appeal to different customer groups and taste and preference patterns.

Process Production. Process production employs an integrated technology to move a continuous flow of raw material inputs through the sys-

---

[2] Ford realized that it would be easy enough to give buyers a color choice; all that was needed was several paint spray guns instead of one. But his argument was that the uniformity of the product would be lost once he made a concession to product diversity. To him, product uniformity was the key to mass production economies.

tem to produce a continuous flow of output. Typically, the system is highly automated and mechanized, thus requiring a large capital investment in facilities and equipment and only small doses of labor inputs. The continuous flow nature of the process makes for high production efficiency as long as it is operated at or near peak capacity 24 hours a day, 7 days a week; the greater the utilization of the facilities, the lower unit costs will be.

The classic example of process production is an oil refinery where crude oil is dispatched through a complex processing system to spawn a variety of refined end products for very different end uses. Process production is also the rule in the chemical industry. Other examples include milk processing, the manufacture of plate glass, and papermaking.

PRODUCTION FUNCTIONS

Economists use the term *production function* to refer to the relationship between a firm's input of productive resources (raw materials, labor, capital, land managerial talents) and its output of goods or services per unit of time. This relationship can be expressed as

$$Q = f(X_a, X_b, X_c, \ldots, X_n),$$

where $X_a, X_b, X_c, \ldots, X_n$ represent quantities of various types of inputs and Q represents the quantity of output obtainable per period of time. Input-output relationships depend partly on the quantities of resources employed and partly on the way in which they are combined (the production technology adopted by the firm). For illustration, suppose that a firm has two technologically feasible ways of combining inputs X_a, X_b, X_c, and X_d:

BASIC CONCEPT
A production function describes the relationship between the quantity of productive inputs and the quantity of output obtainable per period of time.

Production Technology	Resource Inputs	Output
Technology A	50 units each of X_a, X_b, X_c, and X_d	5,000 units
	100 units each of X_a, X_b, X_c, and X_d	10,000 units
	150 units each of X_a, X_b, X_c, and X_d	15,000 units
Technology B	50 units each of X_a, X_b, X_c, and X_d	6,000 units
	100 units each of X_a, X_b, X_c, and X_d	12,000 units
	150 units each of X_a, X_b, X_c, and X_d	18,000 units

By employing technology A the firm can produce 5000 units of output with 50 units each of inputs X_a, X_b, X_c, and X_d. Using 100 units of each input results in 10,000 units of output, and 150 units of each input yield an output of 15,000 units. However, the input-output relationship is quite different for technology B. Technology B generates more output for the same volume of input than does technology A and consequently is more efficient than A.

The example illustrates that *there is a corresponding production function for each production technique or recipe for making a product*. A firm can alter its quantity of output by varying the amounts of input used, by switching from one production technology to another, or by undertaking both actions. The efficiency of a production technique determines the output yield from each combination or inputs, while the state of technological know-how determines the number of available techniques.

Over the long run, competition and profit incentives induce firms to invest in the most efficient production technology available. In the short run, though, a firm is stuck with trying to utilize its current production technology in such a way as to obtain the maximum output from each alternative combination of inputs it might select. In mathematical terms, for a production function of the form

$$Q = f(X_a, X_b, X_c, \ldots, X_n),$$

PRODUCTION PRINCIPLE
Achieving maximum production efficiency with a particular technology or production recipe requires (a) obtaining the maximum output from a given combination of inputs or else (b) minimizing the amount of inputs to produce a designated amount of output.

each numerical value of Q corresponding to specified numerical values of X_a, $X_b, X_c, \ldots, X_n$ is interpreted as being the largest possible value of Q obtainable, given the present production technology employed by the firm. For instance, in studying the production function for a firm producing red fireplugs, the most relevant output value is the *maximum* number of red fireplugs per period of time that can be produced from specific combinations of machine time, hours of skilled labor, floor space, electricity, hours of managerial input, metal casing, red paint, and so on. Anything less than the maximum output represents productive inefficiency, and it is reasonable to presume that most firms in most cases are endeavoring to get the largest possible amount of output for a specified set of inputs.

However, one can also define a firm's production function in terms of the *minimum* input requirements for a designated level of output. To use the fireplug example again, the input-output relationship for a firm producing red fireplugs can be estimated by studying the *minimum* amounts of machine time, hours of skilled labor, floor space, electricity, hours of managerial input, metal casing, red paint, and so on requisite for producing specified quantities of red fireplugs with the facilities and technology presently in place.

Whichever approach is preferred, *the production function for a firm defines the limits of the firm's technical production possibilities*. At any given time, when a firm producing at these limits wishes to increase output, it must use more inputs; similarly, the firm cannot use fewer inputs without decreasing its rate of output. Thus, *as long as a firm is using the most efficient technology available, its output rate is dependent upon (1) the quantities of resource inputs employed in the production process and (2) how efficiently it is using these quantities of resource inputs*. Once the production function is known, a firm can get answers to the following questions:

1. To what extent will total output change if the quantity of one input is increased and the quantity of all other inputs is held constant?
2. To what extent will total output change if the quantity of one input employed is decreased while the quantity of some other input is increased?
3. To what extent will output change if some or all inputs are increased in either equal or unequal proportions?

FIXED AND VARIABLE INPUTS

Once a firm installs a particular production technology, some of its inputs cannot be readily changed whereas the usage of other inputs can be raised or lowered rather easily.

Resource inputs can be classified as being either fixed or variable. A *fixed input* is defined as one whose quantity cannot *readily be changed in the short run* in an effort to alter the rate of output. Although few inputs are absolutely rigidly fixed, even for very short periods of time, practically speaking the costs of varying the use of an input may be prohibitive. Even where they are not, changing the quantity of an input may be severely impeded by the current in-place technology, by the unavailability of additional supplies of certain inputs, and/or by the length of time it takes to make acceptable changes in their usage.[3] Examples of fixed inputs include major pieces of equipment and machinery, the space available for productive activity (buildings, factory size), and the know-how of key managerial personnel.

In contrast, a ***variable input*** is one whose usage rate may be altered quite easily in response to a desire to raise or lower the volume of output. Resource inputs whose quantity can be easily varied within a very short time include electric power, most raw materials, transportation services, and the labor services of production and office employees. With respect to raw materials, however, there are a number of products (aspirin, cake mixes, paint, liquid bleach) where the inputs can be changed only in some fixed proportion to one another and to output; otherwise, the product's character is fundamentally changed.

THE SHORT RUN AND THE LONG RUN

Given that the concepts of fixed and variable inputs are tightly linked to time, we need to be clear about the distinction between the short run and the long run. The ***short run*** is a time period so short that the firm is constrained from varying the quantity of its fixed inputs (major pieces of equipment, key managerial personnel, technology, and space for production activities). Yet the short run is long enough a time period to allow for variation in the firm's variable inputs. Hence, in the short run a firm's output capability must be accomplished exclusively through changes in its usage of variable inputs.

The ***long run*** is defined as a period of time sufficiently long to allow *all* inputs to be varied; no inputs are fixed, including technology. Thus, in the long run a firm's output capability can be increased or decreased by altering technology or resource input usage in whatever way may be most advantageous to the firm. For instance, whereas in the short run a firm may be forced to expand production by operating its facilities at overtime rates, in the long run the firm may find it more economical to construct larger facilities or install capital-intensive machinery and avoid overtime wage rates.

The length of the short run varies from industry to industry. In industries where the quantities of fixed inputs are small or where the character of production permits fixed inputs to be changed readily, the short run may not extend beyond a period of several months. The apparel, mobile home, and food-processing industries are cases in point. For other industries the short run may be 1 to 3 years—automobiles, coal mining, aircraft, aluminum, and paper products. In the electric utility industry it takes as much as 6 to 10 years to design, construct, and start up a new power plant.

The production significance of differentiating between fixed and variable inputs and between the short and long runs should now be more apparent. The quantities of a firm's fixed inputs determine the size of the firm's short-run production capabilities or its ***scale of operations***. The scale of a firm's plant sets an upper limit to the amount of output per period of time that the firm is capable of producing in the short run. Output can, in the short run, be varied up to that

BASIC CONCEPT
The short run is a time period so short that the quantity of fixed inputs cannot be changed.

BASIC CONCEPT
In the long run, there are no fixed inputs; there is enough time to alter the quantity of each and every input.

BASIC CONCEPT
The bigger the quantity of a firm's fixed inputs, the bigger is its scale of operations.

---

[3] Actually, fixed inputs are not always as fixed as it might first appear. While a firm may possess a given amount of fixed input, say 10 machines, the operating pattern for the machines can be "changed" by altering (1) the speed at which the machines are operated, (2) the number of hours per day the machines are used, and (3) the number of days of operation per year. However, a firm may not have full flexibility in choosing among these options due to the constraints imposed by maintenance requirements, union work rules, and wage differentials among work shifts.

limit by increasing or decreasing the usage of variable inputs in conjunction with the amount of fixed input. The limits of output can, in the long run, be raised or lowered by changing the scale of production, the technological character of the production process, and the utilization rate of any and all inputs.

CHARACTERISTICS OF SHORT-RUN PRODUCTION FUNCTIONS

A firm's short-run production function indicates the output obtainable from combining various amounts of variable inputs with the available fixed input. To illustrate exactly what is meant by a short-run production function, consider a firm operating a plant of some given size and technology and having a fixed amount of equipment and managerial capability. Since we shall have occasion to refer to the amount of these fixed inputs, suppose that we arbitrarily designate the amounts of fixed inputs for our fictional firm's plant as constituting 2 "units." Now suppose that we conduct an experiment in which successively larger doses of variable input are combined with the 2 units of fixed input and the resulting output rates are observed and recorded.[4]

A TABULAR ILLUSTRATION

From Table 6-1 we see that when progressively larger doses of variable input are combined with the available fixed inputs, the quantity of output rises more rapidly at first, then more slowly, reaches a maximum, and begins to decline. The exact change in output associated with the use of one more unit of variable input per period is known in economics as the **marginal product of the variable input**.[5] The change in the quantity of output per period of time resulting from a *1-unit change* in the quantity of that input used per period of time is defined as **discrete marginal product**. In our example the values for discrete marginal product are shown in column (4) of Table 6-1; verify for yourself that the numbers in column (4) are derived by subtracting each successive pair of numbers in column (3). Alternatively, marginal product can be calculated from the first derivative of the equation expressing the mathematical relation between the flow of output and the flow of variable input.[6] Hence, if the relation-

BASIC CONCEPT
Marginal product is the amount of change in output associated with employing one additional unit of variable input.

---

[4] Strictly speaking, the different amounts of variable input are best conceived as being applied to different plants of equal size and type, rather than to a progressively larger application of additional units of variable input to a single plant. Practically, however, real-world implementation of this concept of measuring a firm's production function is usually not possible—many identical plants may simply not exist. The sensible alternative, therefore, is to observe the relation between input and output for a single operation at various points in time where the rates of variable input usage are different.

[5] It cannot be inferred from the definition of marginal product that the change in output is due just to the efforts and contribution of variable input. An increase in variable input by itself is not *the cause* of changes in output; output changes as a consequence of having more units of variable input employed in conjunction with the fixed input. An example may serve to clarify this point. Suppose a firm has five pieces of machinery, each requiring one skilled operator. As the firm increases its labor inputs from one to five skilled operators to run the five machines, it is clear that the resulting output gains are not due solely to the productive powers of labor but rather are the joint products of using more labor with the five available machines. Economists, however, customarily refer to the gains in output from using more labor as being the marginal product of labor, despite the fact that gains in output from employing more units of labor reflect the *joint* contributions of labor and the other inputs with which it is combined.

[6] Should more than one variable input be present in the expression defining the short-run production function, the relevant concept of the marginal product of an input is the partial derivative of the production function. See Mathematical Capsule 8.

TABLE 6-1   DATA FOR HYPOTHETICAL SHORT-RUN PRODUCTION FUNCTION

(1) Units of Fixed Input	(2) Units of Variable Input (X)	(3) Quantity of Output $Q = 21X + 9X^2 - X^3$	(4) Discrete Marginal Product of Variable Input	(5) Continuous Marginal Product of Variable Input $MP = 21 + 18X - 3X^2$	(6) Average Product of Variable Input $AP_{vi} = 21 + 9X - X^2$	(7) Average Product of Fixed Input $AP_{fi} = \frac{21X + 9X^2 - X^3}{2}$
2	0	0		—	—	0
2	1	29	29	36	29	14.5
2	2	70	41	45	35	35
2	3	117	47	48	39	58.5
2	4	164	47	45	41	82
2	5	205	41	36	41	102.5
2	6	234	29	21	39	117
2	7	245	11	0	35	122.5
2	8	232	-13	-27	29	116
2	9	189	-43	-60	21	94.5

ship between the quantity of output (Q) and the units of variable input (X) is

$$Q = 21X + 9X^2 - X^3,$$

then the marginal product of the variable input is

$$MP = \frac{dQ}{dX} = 21 + 18X - 3X^2.$$

This concept of marginal product is called ***continuous marginal product*** to distinguish it from discrete marginal product. Continuous marginal product represents the rate of change in total output as the rate of variable input changes per period of time and can be calculated by substituting the numbers 0, 1, 2, . . . , 9 for X in the equation shown in column (5) of Table 6-1.[7] In a mathematical sense, marginal product is meaningful only for inputs whose rate of usage can be changed; thus, there is no such thing as the marginal product of fixed inputs, since fixed inputs by definition do not change in the short run.

The average product of the variable input is shown in column (6) of Table 6-1. It is found by dividing the output rate by the required number of units of variable input:

$$AP_{vi} = \frac{\text{units of output}}{\text{units of variable input}}.$$

Thus, if $Q = 21X + 9X^2 - X^3$, where X represents the units of variable input, the expression for AP_{vi} becomes

$$AP_{vi} = \frac{Q}{X} = \frac{21X + 9X^2 - X^3}{X} = 21 + 9X - X^2.$$

BASIC CONCEPT
The average amount of output produced per unit of variable input is defined as the average product of variable input.

[7] The definitions and concepts of discrete and continuous marginal product are analogous to our earlier definitions of marginal utility and marginal revenue. In treating marginal product as a continuous function, we assume that both variable input and output can be varied by extremely small amounts.

Similarly, the average product of the fixed input [shown in column (7) of Table 6-1] is defined as the quantity of output divided by the available units of fixed input:

BASIC CONCEPT
The average amount of output produced per unit of fixed input is defined as the average product of fixed input.

$$AP_{fi} = \frac{\text{units of output}}{\text{units of fixed input}}.$$

Given that $Q = 21X + 9X^2 - X^3$ and that 2 units of fixed input are present, AP_{fi} can be calculated as follows:

$$AP_{fi} = \frac{Q}{FI} = \frac{21X + 9X^2 - X^3}{2}.$$

Alternatively, AP_{fi} can be computed by dividing the output values in column (3) by the number of units of fixed input given in column (1), yielding the values in column (7) of Table 6-1.

PRODUCTION PRINCIPLE
As more and more variable input is utilized with the available quantity of fixed input, eventually—at the point of diminishing marginal returns—the resulting gains in output start to get smaller and smaller.

In our example, observe that marginal product increases for the first 3 units of variable input to its maximum value of 48 [column (5)]. Beyond 3 units of variable input marginal product diminishes, reaching zero at an input of 7 units per period of time and becoming increasingly negative past 8 units of variable input. The reason for this pattern of change in marginal product has to do with the ***principle of diminishing marginal returns***.

The principle of diminishing marginal returns holds that *as the amount of a variable input is increased by equal increments and combined with a*

MATHEMATICAL CAPSULE 8

DETERMINING MARGINAL PRODUCT WHEN THE PRODUCTION FUNCTION IS COMPOSED OF SEVERAL VARIABLE INPUTS

In most production processes the quantity of output in the short run is a function of several variable inputs such that

$$Q = f(X_a, X_b, X_c, \ldots, X_n).$$

The marginal product of a specific variable input, say X_a, is found by observing the impact upon Q of a change in the usage of X_a, when the quantities of the remaining variable inputs $(X_b, X_c, \ldots, X_n)$ are held constant. Mathematically, this procedure involves determining the *partial derivative* of the production function with respect to X_a.

Suppose that the production function for a commodity is

$$Q = 7X_a^2 + 8X_b^2 - 5X_aX_b.$$

We can find the effect of a change in the rate of usage of resource input X_a when the usage of X_b is held constant by treating X_b as a constant and differentiating the production function with respect to X_a—this gives the partial derivative of Q with respect to X_a and is symbolized as $\partial Q/\partial X_a$. Thus, we obtain

$$\frac{\partial Q}{\partial X_a} = 14X_a - 5X_b,$$

which is the expression for the marginal product of input X_a. In precise economic terms the expression for MP represents

the rate of change in output as the usage of input X_a changes, the usage of input X_b remaining constant. In less formal terms, the expression for the marginal product of X_a tells us how changes in the use of X_a will affect the quantity of output, provided X_b does not change.

Similarly, the marginal product for input X_b is the partial derivative of the production function with respect to X_b, or

$$\frac{\partial Q}{\partial X_b} = 16X_b - 5X_a,$$

It shows the impact of changes in X_b upon Q when X_a is held constant.

EXERCISES

1. Determine the marginal product functions for labor (L) and capital (C) for each of the following production functions.
   (a) $Q = 18L^2 + 14C^3 - L^2C$.
   (b) $Q = 10L^{0.5}C^{0.5}$.
   (c) $Q = 17L + 9C + 0.6L^{0.4}C^{0.5}$.

2. Determine the values for MP_L and MP_C at $L = 10$ and $C = 20$ for each of the following production functions.
   (a) $Q = 36L - L^2 + 20C - LC$.
   (b) $Q = 5L^2 + 4LC + 6C^2 - 8(L/C)$.

specified amount of fixed inputs, a point will be reached (sometimes more quickly and sometimes less quickly) where the resulting increases in the quantity of output will get smaller and smaller. In other words, as more and more variable input is added to a given fixed input, *eventually* the marginal product of variable input will begin to diminish. Furthermore, should the amounts of variable input applied to a given fixed input get large enough, output will reach a maximum and thereafter may *decrease* if still additional amounts of variable input are utilized.

Prior to reaching the inevitable point of diminishing marginal returns, the gains in output from larger applications of variable input may either increase at an increasing rate such that marginal product of variable input increases, or the increases in output may increase at a constant rate such that marginal product is constant. For example, in Table 6-1 the first 3 units of variable input cause the quantity of output to increase at an increasing rate. This may occur because when a small amount of variable input is combined with a relatively large dose of fixed input the fixed-variable input proportions are likely to be out of balance, causing production to be inefficient.[8] Hence, whenever variable input is being used in too sparse a proportion to the available fixed input, adding more units of variable input diminishes the associated inefficiencies and allows output to increase at an increasing rate.

A GRAPHIC ILLUSTRATION

The hypothetical data in Table 6-1 are graphed in Figure 6-2. Since output is a function of variable input, output is the dependent variable and variable input is the independent variable. Accordingly, output per period of time is plotted on the vertical axis, and the units of variable input are plotted on the horizontal axis. Joining the points by a smooth curve yields a graphical illustration of the firm's production function for the good [Figure 6-2(a)].

The production function of Figure 6-2(a) conveys the same input-output relation as does the production schedule in Table 6-1.[9] Note that output increases at an increasing rate up to a level of usage of variable input of 3 units per period of time; accordingly, we may say that *increasing returns to the variable input* exist over this range. By this is meant that the increases in output are *more* than proportional to the increases in variable input. As the possibili-

BASIC CONCEPT
Increasing returns to variable input exist whenever raising the usage of variable input results in progressively bigger gains in the rate of output; increasing returns occur *prior* to reaching the point of diminishing marginal returns.

---

[8] Examples of this condition are commonplace in manufacturing. Suppose that a plant of a given size has been designed to operate with 400 employees. If an attempt is made to operate with 50 employees, the multiplicity of functions to be performed by each employee with the attendant inefficiencies in execution, coupled with the time lost in changing from job to job, will no doubt cause output to be more than proportionately *less* than might be gotten, say, from 100 employees. Thus, up to some point, equal increments in the amount of labor used may well produce successively larger gains in the quantity of output.

[9] In this example the production function is shown as beginning from the origin of the diagram. This is the case only when the variable input under consideration is absolutely essential to the production of the item and when output may be obtained immediately upon applying variable input. Needless to say, these characteristics do not typify all production processes or all kinds of variable inputs. For variable inputs not essential to the production of the item, the production function may begin above the origin (installing carpets in an office building to reduce noise and to enhance the esthetic quality of the working conditions, thereby boosting employee productivity is a case in point). In other situations no output may be forthcoming until substantial amounts of variable input are used with the available fixed inputs. For example, five people in a huge pulp and paper mill can produce nothing. Ten people can do little better. Where a minimum complement of variable input is requisite for any production to take place, the production function or total product curve begins to the right of the origin and at that point on the horizontal axis corresponding to the minimum input requirement.

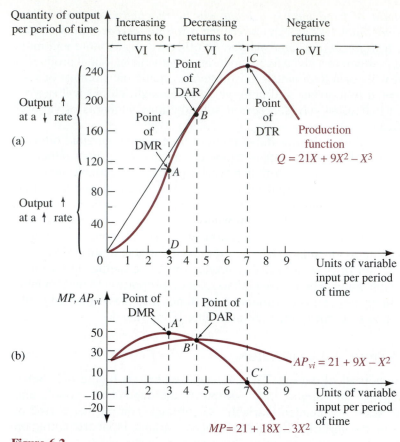

Figure 6-2

A short-run production function and its corresponding marginal and average product functions

BASIC CONCEPT

Decreasing returns to variable input exist whenever increased usage of variable input results in smaller and smaller gains in the rate of output; decreasing returns occur *past* the point of diminishing marginal returns.

ties for increasing returns to variable input are exhausted, the ***point of diminishing marginal returns*** (DMR) is encountered—a point which, mathematically, corresponds to the "inflection point" on the production function. Beyond this point, heavier usage of variable inputs results in a declining marginal product (i.e., extra units of variable input yield successively smaller amounts of extra output). The curvature of the production function becomes such that it rises more slowly (i.e., output increases at a decreasing rate). Thus, between a level of usage of 3 and 7 units of variable input per period of time there exist ***decreasing returns to variable input***, or, to put it another way, the increases in the quantity of output are *less* than proportional to the increases in variable input. Output is maximum when 7 units of variable input per period of time are combined with the fixed input. No further increases in output are possible without employing additional amounts of the fixed inputs in the production process. This is not feasible in the short run. For reference purposes we may label the maximum output rate in the short run as the ***point of diminishing total returns*** (DTR). Should more than 7 units of variable input per period of time be used in conjunction with the fixed inputs, the quantity of output would actually fall. The rationale for this derives from the existence of a limit to which fixed inputs can accommodate additional variable input and still yield additional output. Past 7 units, variable inputs are present in uneconomically large proportions relative to the available fixed input, and growing inefficiencies in resource usage cause total output to fall.

The marginal product curve corresponding to the aforementioned production function is shown in Figure 6-2(b). The data for deriving the shape and position of the marginal product curve come from columns (4) and (5) in Table 6-1. Since by the marginal product of the variable input we mean the rate of change in the quantity of output as the usage rate of variable input changes, the slope of the production function at any variable input rate is the value of marginal product at that quantity of variable input. When the quantity of output is increasing at an increasing rate (as it does up to a level of 3 units of variable input), marginal product is increasing. Marginal product attains its maximum value at the point of diminishing marginal returns (DMR), which in this example is at 3 units of variable input where $MP = 48$ [point A in Figure 6-2(a)]. Between 3 and 7 units of variable input, where the quantity of output increases at a decreasing rate, the values of marginal product are positive but diminishing. At 7 units of variable input, total output is maximum, and marginal product is zero. Beyond 7 units, additional units of variable input cause output to decline, meaning that in this range the marginal product of variable input is negative. The negative values for marginal product in the range beyond 7 units reflect the fact that the production function is declining and therefore has a negative slope.

MATHEMATICAL CAPSULE 9

THE RELATIONSHIP BETWEEN AN INPUT'S MARGINAL AND AVERAGE PRODUCTS

That an input's marginal and average products are necessarily equal at the maximum value of average product is easily proven mathematically. Let the production function be of the general form $Q = f(X)$. Then,

$$AP_{vi} = \frac{Q}{X} = \frac{f(X)}{X},$$

$$MP = \frac{dQ}{dX} = f'(X).$$

From Mathematical Capsule 1 in Chapter 3 we know that the condition which must be satisfied for AP_{vi} to be maximum is that the slope of AP_{vi} be zero. This in turn means that the derivative of the AP_{vi} equation must be zero:

$$\frac{dAP_{vi}}{dX} = 0.$$

Using the rule of calculus for finding the derivative of a quotient, and calculating dAP_{vi}/dX, where $AP_{vi} = f(X)/X$, gives

$$\frac{dAP_{vi}}{dX} = \frac{X \cdot f'(X) - f(X)}{X^2}.$$

For dAP_{vi}/dX to equal zero requires that the numerator of the expression above be equal to zero, or that

$$X \cdot f'(X) - f(X) = 0.$$

Rewriting the condition above yields

$$f'(X) = \frac{f(X)}{X}.$$

Since $f'(X) = MP$ and $f(X)/X = AP_{vi}$, the input rate that makes AP_{vi} maximum is also the value of X at which $MP = AP_{vi}$.

Furthermore, if the expression for dAP_{vi}/dX is rewritten as

$$\frac{dAP_{vi}}{dX} = \frac{f'(X) - [f(X)/X]}{X},$$

it becomes apparent that the slope of the average product function will be positive if $f'(X)$, marginal product, is greater than $f(X)/X$, average product. This reflects the fact that as long as the value for marginal product exceeds the value for average product, the average product curve is rising. Conversely, it is clear that if marginal product is less than average product, the slope of the average product curve is negative and the value of average product is declining.

The average product curve for the variable input originates from the same point as does the marginal product curve (in this instance, both assume a value of 21 when $X = 0$). From this point the average product curve rises until it reaches its maximum value at 4.5 units of variable input. It subsequently declines, conceivably becoming zero should variable input ever be added to such an extent that output falls back to zero. The average product curve has a definite relationship to the marginal product curve. As long as the value for MP is greater than the value for AP_{vi}, the average product curve will rise. The value for MP equals the value of AP_{vi} when AP_{vi} is at its maximum value. When the value for MP is less than the value for AP_{vi}, the average product curve falls. The explanation for this relationship is rooted in simple arithmetic.

Consider a student who after 2 years of college has managed to earn a 2.5 overall grade average in her coursework. If *this term* she earns a 2.8 average in her courses, her new *overall* grade average will rise above the 2.5 level. However, if she earns a 2.0 average *this term,* her overall grade average will *fall* below 2.5. The overall grade average of our hypothetical student is analogous to average product, while the grade average this term is analogous to marginal product. Thus, *for average product to be increasing, marginal product must exceed the average. For average product to be decreasing, marginal product must be less than average product.*

The rate of variable input usage at which the AP_{vi} curve reaches its maximum value can be ascertained directly from the graph of the production function. Suppose that a ray is drawn from the origin to point B on the production function in Figure 6-2(a). Since average product equals the quantity of output divided by the units of variable input employed, AP_{vi} at point B equals distance BD (the quantity of output) divided by distance OD (the number of units of variable input), or, more simply, BD/OD, which in turn is equivalent to the slope of the ray OB. As the number of units of variable input increases from 0 to 4.5 units (point D), the slopes of rays drawn from the origin to points on the production function become progressively greater. Since AP_{vi} is mathematically equivalent to the slope of a ray from the origin to the corresponding point on the production function, AP_{vi} is maximum at that value of variable input where the slope of such a ray is steepest. This occurs when the ray from the origin is just *tangent* to the production function (point B) or at 4.5 units of variable input. We shall designate the peak of the AP_{vi} curve as the **point of diminishing average returns** to variable input (DAR).

ALTERNATIVE TYPES OF SHORT-RUN PRODUCTION FUNCTIONS

A firm's production function need not exhibit the shape illustrated in Figure 6-2. Let's look at three alternative shapes of production functions and their distinctive properties.

Constant Returns to Variable Input. Some production processes have qualities that make the firm's short-run production function linear over the *normal* ranges of output. A linear production function, along with its corresponding marginal and average product curves, is shown in Figure 6-3. The general equation for a linear input-output relationship is

$$Q = a + bX,$$

where Q is the quantity of output, X represents the units of variable input per

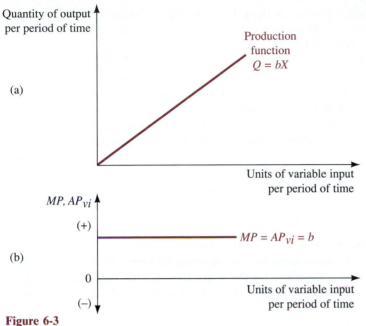

Figure 6-3

A production function characterized by a phase of constant returns to variable input

period of time, and a and b are constants. For the production function shown in Figure 6-3(a) it is assumed that variable input is essential for production to occur and that some output can be obtained as soon as variable input is combined with the available units of fixed input. The effect of this rather reasonable assumption (and we shall continue to use it in the succeeding illustrations) is that the production function begins at the origin and the value of a in the equation for the production function is zero, thereby reducing the equation of the production function to

$$Q = bX.$$

From the preceding definitions of average and marginal product, we can write

$$AP_{vi} = \frac{Q}{X} = \frac{bX}{X} = b$$

and

$$MP = \frac{dQ}{dX} = b.$$

Thus, in the case of a linear production function both marginal and average product are constants and $MP = AP_{vi}$. These relationships are illustrated in Figure 6-3(b).

The key properties of the production function in Figure 6-3(a) and its corresponding MP and AP_{vi} curves are as follows. A linear production function means that as additional units of variable input are combined with the given units of fixed input, the quantity of output increases at a *constant rate*—there exist **constant returns to variable input**. Each unit of variable input contributes just as much to total output as did the previous unit and as will the next unit. Since successive units of variable input are *equally* productive, their marginal products are necessarily equal. This factor makes the production function lin-

BASIC CONCEPT
Constant returns to variable input exist whenever output increases at a constant rate as additional units of variable input are combined with the available fixed input; in such cases, the marginal products of each unit of variable input are all equal.

ear, because marginal product is the rate of change in the quantity of output as variable input changes. When this rate is constant, the production function is linear. Moreover, with additional units of variable input being equally productive, the average product of the units of variable input is itself a constant value equal in size to the value of the marginal product of the variable input.

It does not follow, however, that a linear production function contradicts the principle of diminishing marginal returns. Rather, linearity implies that the point of diminishing marginal returns is yet to be reached. There can be *no doubt* that if *enough* units of variable input are combined with the given amount of fixed input, diminishing returns will set in. But in production processes where a standard worker-machine ratio is employed, this point might not be encountered until the limit of the plant's capacity is approached, say around 90 to 95% of practical capacity. Thus, up to this limit, experiencing constant returns to the variable input is neither inconceivable nor unrealistic.

Decreasing Returns to Variable Input.   Another type of production function displays **decreasing returns to variable input** as soon as the *first* dose of variable input is combined with the fixed input. Although several equations can be used to describe this behavior, the simplest is the quadratic equation:

$$Q = a + bX - cX^2,$$

or, more simply,

$$Q = bX - cX^2$$

if the variable input is essential for production. Here b is a positive constant and c, as indicated, is negative. The corresponding average and marginal product functions are

$$AP_{vi} = \frac{Q}{X} = \frac{bX - cX^2}{X} = b - cX,$$

$$MP = \frac{dQ}{dX} = b - 2cX.$$

These three curves are illustrated in Figure 6-4. Observe that the MP curve lies below the AP_{vi} curve; in fact, it declines at twice the rate of AP_{vi}, as can be verified from the equations of the two functions (the slope of AP_{vi} is $-c$, and the slope of MP is $-2c$).

When a production function exhibits decreasing returns to variable input, each additional unit of variable input is *less* productive than the last.

Here the nature of the production process is such that each additional unit of variable input adds *less* to total output than the preceding unit. Therefore, the quantity of output increases at a decreasing rate up to the maximum output. Diminishing marginal returns to variable input are encountered with the first increment of variable input. Increases in the intensity of use of the fixed input brought about by larger doses of variable input yield progressively less and less in additional output. The marginal product of variable input then is a declining, but positive, value up to X_1 units of variable input, at which point the peak of the production function is reached. Since additional usage of variable input lowers marginal product, the average product of variable input is always falling, being pulled downward by the declining values of MP.

When X_1 units of variable input have been combined with the fixed input, the units of fixed input are being utilized to their fullest extent so that no greater output can be gotten until the fixed inputs are increased. Larger applications of variable input beyond the level of X_1 will cause the quantity of output to

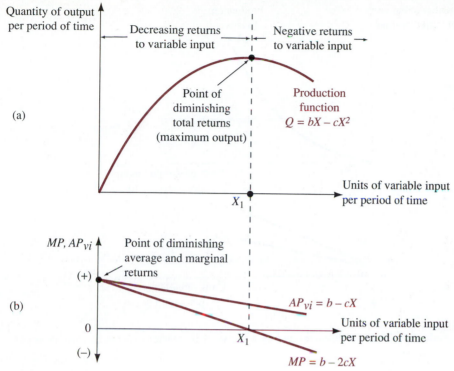

Figure 6-4

A production function characterized by a phase of decreasing returns to variable input

fall and the marginal product of variable input to become negative, since the fixed input is being *overutilized* to such an extent that all inputs become less efficient and less productive.

Increasing Returns to Variable Input. The last and least likely type of production function has the quantity of output increasing at an increasing rate as large amounts of variable input are used with the fixed output. The simplest form of this function is given by the equation

$$Q = a + bX + cX^2.$$

Again, if $a = 0$ and if b and c are positive constants as indicated, the equation for this production function reduces to

$$Q = bX + cX^2.$$

The general equations for the corresponding average and marginal product curve can be derived as follows:

$$AP_{vi} = \frac{Q}{X} = \frac{bX + cX^2}{X} = b + cX$$

and

$$MP = \frac{dQ}{dX} = b + 2cX.$$

The graph of these three functions is shown in Figure 6-5.

For production functions of this type, output increases at an increasing rate. Adding extra units of variable input results in larger and larger gains in

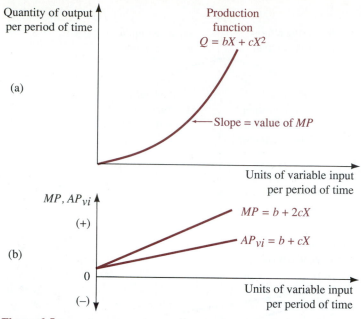

Figure 6-5

A production function characterized by a phase of increasing returns to variable input

---

When a production function exhibits increasing returns to variable input, each additional unit of variable input is *more* productive than the last.

output as reflected by the rising marginal product of variable input. ***Increasing returns to variable input*** are said to prevail, because the gains in the quantity of output are *more* than proportional to the increased usage of variable input. The average product of variable input rises persistently, being pulled up by the increases in marginal product.

It is important to note that a production function of this form is likely to describe the behavior of output *only* for relatively small values of variable input, where the fixed input is being utilized far less than it could be. In other words, increasing returns to variable input are likely to prevail only for low rates of output—and then only in those instances where combining more variable input with the fixed input causes a dramatic increase in the productivity of the inputs such that output can be increased at an increasing rate. Situations of this nature can be anticipated only when the fixed inputs are being so grossly underutilized that additional variable input will permit great reductions in inefficiencies, thereby making for disproportionately greater gains in output.

A More General Type of Production Function.   When one looks at input-output relationships over the *entire* range of output—from producing nothing to operating at capacity—the most general type of production function involves a (short) range of increasing returns to variable input, then a (perhaps long) range of *approximately* constant returns to variable input, and, finally, a range of decreasing returns to variable input as production capacity is approached. A simple form of a production function which captures these basic elements is like that described earlier and shown in Figure 6-2. The general equation for a production function of this shape and character is

Increasing, then constant, and then decreasing returns to variable input tend to dominate the input-output relationship over the relevant range of output.

$$Q = a + bX + cX^2 - dX^3;$$

or, given our assumption that $a = 0$, we have

$$Q = bX + cX^2 - dX^3,$$

where b and c are positive constants and d is a negative constant. The general equations for the corresponding average and marginal product curves are

$$AP_{vi} = \frac{Q}{X} = \frac{bX + cX^2 - dX^3}{X} = b + cX - dX^2$$

and

$$MP = \frac{dQ}{dX} = b + 2cX - 3dX^2.$$

The general applicability of this type of production function is wide. No doubt many production processes contain a stage of increasing returns to variable input at very low output rates, and almost every production process is certain to reflect decreasing returns to variable input as the upper limit to production capacity is approached. Moreover, for many production processes constant returns (or nearly so) to variable input can characterize the range in between. This can be seen from Figure 6-2(a), where the production function assumes an *almost* linear shape along the range from point A to just beyond point B.

Because the cubic type of production function does incorporate the key characteristics of other production functions, we shall in future discussions use it to describe input-output relations over the entire range of a firm's output capacity. However, when there is some special reason to expect increasing, decreasing, or constant returns to the variable input to dominate the input-output relationship over the relevant range of output, we shall depart from use of the cubic form of production function and employ instead the indicated form.

How Technological Advance Impacts Production Functions

It is a matter of historical fact that technological advances have altered how firms produce products. Advances in production technology increase the number of production recipes available and usually alter input-output relationships:

Technological change can impact a firm's production possibilities in any of four ways.

1. A new production technology may permit the same amount of resource inputs to be combined differently so as to yield a greater output than before.
2. A new production technology may require a *smaller* quantity of one or even several inputs and *no more* of the remaining inputs to produce the same quantity of output as before, thus yielding greater efficiency and lower unit costs.
3. A new production technology may make it feasible to use *less* of some inputs and *more* of others, yet with a smaller total cost and rate of input usage, to produce the same quantity of output as before.
4. A new production technology may require inputs, or yield outputs, that are of a kind not heretofore used or available at all.

The first two of these four impacts are illustrated graphically in Figure 6-6.

For several reasons, technological proficiency is often not uniform among firms producing the same product. Age differences among the plants of different firms are certain to exist, with newer plants embodying efficiency-increasing technological improvements unavailable to older plants. Also, there may be locational differences in labor efficiency and raw material quality. Managers, engineers, and technical staffs in some firms may simply have failed to

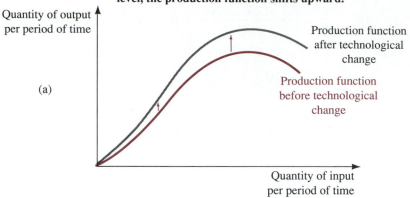

When technological change permits the same amount of resource input to yield a greater output at each input level, the production function shifts upward.

Quantity of output per period of time

(a)

Production function after technological change

Production function before technological change

Quantity of input per period of time

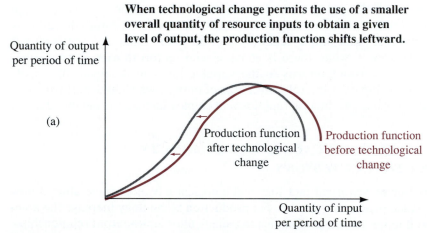

When technological change permits the use of a smaller overall quantity of resource inputs to obtain a given level of output, the production function shifts leftward.

Quantity of output per period of time

(a)

Production function after technological change

Production function before technological change

Quantity of input per period of time

Figure 6-6
How technology can cause shifts in the production function

keep up with current developments and may not know of better processes that other firms are using. As a consequence, rival producers may well have somewhat heterogeneous production functions and output capabilities.

WHERE TECHNOLOGICAL PROGRESS COMES FROM

Technological advance and innovation have their origins with the internal research efforts of business firms and from knowledge transfer among firms, industries, governments, and educational institutions. Some technological breakthroughs originate with basic research—investigations conducted without special concern for the usefulness of the results. But many technological discoveries emerge from purposive investigations where the intent is to obtain results for specific uses. Implicit in a firm's search for new or improved production techniques is the hope that successful research and development activities will increase the productive efficiency of the firm's operations, which in turn will give the firm a cost advantage and ultimately allow for a higher degree of profitability.

The application of *new* production techniques is not, however, the sole means of technological progress. Progress in the form of higher degrees of productive efficiency commonly derives from learning to apply existing techniques more effectively. Obviously enough, as firms obtain more experience with a given process, opportunities will be identified for improving the production technique. Particularly during the early stages of using a new technique is it possible to spot ways for improvement. This facet of technological progress is called *learning by doing* and is often neglected as a feature of progress and as a factor causing gradual, yet persistent shifts in a firm's production function.[10] The importance of learning by doing originated with studies done in the 1930s showing that a doubling of the cumulative production of airframes was accompanied by a 20% reduction in unit labor costs; this phenomenon, called *the learning curve*, was attributed to (1) the ability of workers to get better at doing a repetitive task the more times they did it and (2) the discovery of more efficient labor-related ways to perform the task as time passed and labor experience grew.

> **Technological progress comes from (a) the introduction of new production technologies and (b) improvements in existing production technologies.**

Learning and Experience Curves. Since that first airframe study was done, experience with new technologies has taught us again and again that it can take years to work out the ''bugs'' in a new technology. The separate steps in a new production process do not always function and mesh as neatly together on the production floor as they were envisioned in the design and engineering stage. Parts of the process sometimes have to be torn out and redesigned. There is always a learning curve for labor in working with new equipment and new procedures, such that it takes time for workers to learn how to avoid mistakes and to perform tasks at peak efficiency. Moreover, as firsthand operating experience is gained, managers and workers see ways to make further improvements and enhancements. The gains in technical know-how associated with learning by doing and with experience in operating a particular production technology tend to be significant as ideas bubble up and are gradually incorporated into how things are done. Even with a known technology, the period from initial startup to peak efficiency in a new plant can take 1 to 3 years.

A recent study of technological innovation in farm tractors, locomotives, oceangoing tankers, aircraft, and digital computers concluded that the most important source of technological advance is learning by doing.[11] The gains came in small increments and often occurred in the course of implementing a technological breakthrough.

In the late 1960s Bruce Henderson, president of the Boston Consulting Group (BCG), a premier management consulting firm, noticed a recurring theme running through the cost studies being done for client companies: The declining cost principle underlying the learning curve went beyond just labor costs and seemed to apply to all costs (except purchased materials and components) measured in constant dollars. Further analysis by BCG showed that each time the cumulative number of units manufactured doubled, the deflated value-added cost per unit declined by a given percentage. In integrated circuits and cement, BCG found that a doubling of cumulative production volume entailed about a 30% unit cost reduction. In air conditioners and power tools,

> **The more experience that a firm has with a production technology, the more able it is to boost efficiency and drive costs per unit down.**

[10] Kenneth J. Arrow, ''The Economic Implications of Learning by Doing,'' *Review of Economic Studies,* Vol. 29 (June 1963), pp. 155–73.
[11] Devendra Sahal, *Patterns of Technological Innovation* (London: Addison-Wesley, 1981), Chapter 6.

the deflated unit cost declines ran about 20%. In primary magnesium and industrial trucks, the declines averaged 10%. Deflating the actual historical cost data was necessary to remove the effects of inflation (when the cost data were not expressed in constant dollars, inflationary factors tended to obscure the true size of the cost savings being realized). The declines in unit cost with each doubling of cumulative production experience was attributed to the combined effects of:

- Learning associated with the repetitive performance of labor tasks.
- Cost-effective improvements in product design.
- Incremental gains associated with debugging the production technology.
- The making of bit-by-bit improvements in the whole operating process (better use of materials, more efficient inventory handling, more efficient distribution methods, and computerization and automation of assorted production, sales, and clerical tasks).
- An increased scale of operation that yielded new operating economies.
- Enriched know-how in managing and operating the business.

BCG plotted the declines in unit cost against cumulative production volume on a graph; the resulting graphical relationship was labeled *the experience curve*.

Figure 6-7 shows an 85% experience curve. Unit cost drops from $100 at a production volume of 10 to $85 ($100 × 0.85) when production reaches an accumulated volume of 20 units, and then goes down further to $72.75 (0.85 × $85) at an accumulated volume of 40 units. The significance of the experience curve effect for a given *industry* depends not only on the percentage decline (whether it is 15% as in the case of an 85% curve or 30% as in the case of a 70% curve) but also on the rate at which experience accumulates, reflected by the annual growth rate in market demand. The following table shows the potential

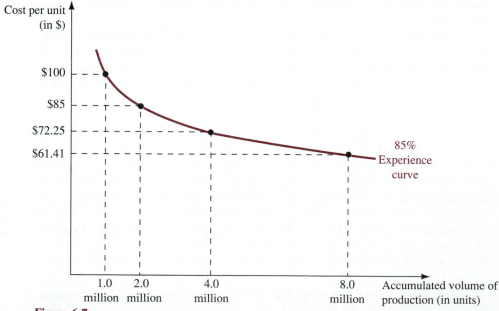

Figure 6-7

An 85% experience curve

for annual cost reductions for different combinations of experience curve effects and growth in demand:

Experience Curve Effect	Annual Cost Reduction Based on a Market Growth Rate of				
	2%	5%	10%	20%	30%
90%	0.3%	0.7%	1.4%	2.7%	4.1%
80	0.6	1.6	3.2	6.4	9.6
70	1.0	2.5	5.0	10.0	15.0
60	1.4	3.5	7.0	14.0	21.0

A *firm* can achieve annual cost reductions via the experience curve that are bigger than the industry average if the demand for its own products is increasing faster than the market as a whole. When a firm's sales volume grows faster than the overall market rate, it accumulates production experience faster than the industry as a whole. The stronger the experience curve effect, the greater the strategic importance of a firm's market share in determining its ability to lower costs and achieve above-average profitability. See the Applications Capsule for a discussion of how a firm can parlay the experience curve effect into a low-cost competitive advantage.

The firm that is farthest down an industry's experience curve has a cost advantage over its rivals; the steeper the experience curve, the bigger its cost advantage.

Technological Progress Is Uneven. An important feature of technological progress is that its impact and rate of advance is uneven from firm to firm and industry to industry. Some firms are more able to finance invention and innovation efforts. A number of enterprises believe that a sounder, longer-lasting competitive edge can be achieved via technological superiority and innovation because technology-based competitive advantages are harder for rivals to overcome; hence, they push research and development activities and allocate a higher percentage of their budget for technological improvement. In some cases, advancing technology seems to allow firms to purchase greater amounts of production capacity per dollar of investment. In other instances the dollar investment in production facilities per unit of output is increased. The trends of modern production technology are toward automation, robotics, computer-aided design techniques, computer-assisted operation of machinery and equipment, "factory of the future" approaches, and flexible mass production—trends that tend to raise the capital intensity of many production processes.

Technological progress is uneven across industries and uneven across firms within the same industry.

At the same time, firms and industries have displayed a wide disparity in the rates with which they have adopted new technologies.[12] Taking into account a period of 15 years after the discovery of a new technology, it has

---

[12] F. Lynn, "An Investigation of the Rate of Development and Diffusion of Technology in Our Modern Industrial Society," in *Studies Prepared for the National Commission on Technology, Automation, and Economic Progress,* Appendix Volume II: *Technology and the American Economy* (Washington, D.C., 1966); E. Mansfield, "The Speed of Response of Firms to New Techniques," *Quarterly Journal of Economics* (May 1963), pp. 290–311; E. Mansfield, "Size of Firm, Market Structure and Innovation," *Journal of Political Economy,* Vol. 71 (December 1963), pp. 556–76; John M. Blair, *Economic Concentration; Structure, Behavior, and Public Policy* (New York: Harcourt Brace Jovanovich, 1972); G. F. Ray, "The Diffusion of New Technology," *National Institute Economic Review* (May 1969), pp. 40–83; A. A. Romeo, "Interindustry and Interfirm Differences in the Rate of Diffusion of an Innovation," *Review of Economics and Statistics,* Vol. 57, No. 3 (August 1975), pp. 311–19; P. Dasgupta and J. E. Stiglitz, "Uncertainty, Industrial Structure and the Speed of R&D," *Bell Journal of Economics,* Vol. 11, No. 1 (Spring 1980), pp. 1–28.

APPLICATIONS CAPSULE

USING LEARNING AND EXPERIENCE CURVE EFFECTS TO GAIN COMPETITIVE ADVANTAGE

One of the Boston Consulting Group's first efforts at applying experience curve theory was with the Norton Company of Worcester, Massachusetts. Norton was having trouble profitably penetrating the market for pressure-sensitive tape—a market dominated by the 3M Company. Norton had successfully cut production costs and lowered prices but still was unable to make a dent in increasing its market share. BCG's experience curve analysis showed that Norton, in effect, was chasing 3M down the experience curve, and that so long as 3M followed pricing and growth strategies that kept its market share (and thus its accumulated production volume) ahead of Norton's, it was a fruitless struggle for Norton. Subsequently, Norton concluded it could not compete successfully against 3M by trying to produce a broad range of products sold in a large number of markets; rather, the company decided it was better off concentrating in selected areas. In BCG's view, the Norton situation illustrated *an important experience curve commandment: If you cannot get enough market share to be efficient and cost competitive, then get out of the business.*

Another instance where the same lesson applied was the effort of Allis-Chalmers Company (A-C) to compete against General Electric and Westinghouse in steam turbine engines. Between 1946 and 1963, Allis-Chalmers's market share was too small for it to be competitive on cost and therefore on price with large-volume manufacturers; thus, A-C's best decision was to withdraw from the industry.

Black & Decker, Texas Instruments, and Weyerhaeuser at one time or another have applied experience curve analysis. In 1973 Texas Instruments described its strategy in semiconductors in strong experience curve language: "Follow an aggressive pricing policy, focus on continuing cost reduction and productivity improvement, build on shared experience gained in making related products, and keep capacity growing ahead of demand."

The lesson in competitive strategy which seemed to emerge from BCG's work with experience curve economics was that the following cause-effect chain existed in many industries and markets where new manufacturing technologies were being put into place:

high   high   low   high
market ⟶ accumulated ⟶ unit ⟶ profitability
share   volume   cost

The implications of this chain can be seen by looking at the following graph, which shows the relative positions of three competing firms on an industry's experience curve. Firm A, with the largest cumulative volume and thus the largest historical market share, has a commanding cost advantage over firms B and C. At the current industry price, firm C is losing money; to become profitable, it has little choice but to move aggressively to increase its market share and thereby move down the experience curve quickly enough to get its costs below the industry price level. Firm B, though able to survive, must live with subpar profitability (in comparison to the leader). Plainly, as long as firm A maintains greater cumulative experience than competitors, it can sustain its cost advantage.

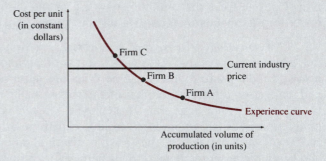

When an industry is characterized by a fairly strong experience curve effect, competitors with less than one-quarter the market share of the largest firm are hard-pressed to survive. A shakeout of the low-share firms is virtually inevitable, barring some unusual external constraint or control on competition. As firms exit, the remaining competitors have to grow faster than the industry at large just to maintain their relative positions; if runner-up firms want to gain on the leader, then they have to use the exit of weak firms as their opportunity to add volume faster than the leader and move

Several factors account for why some new production technologies are put in place more quickly than others.

been observed that some innovations languish in oblivion for as much as 10 years and then are rapidly adopted, that other innovations never mount a serious challenge to displace predecessor processes and facilities, and that still other innovations come quickly into general use and soon are being used to produce 80% or more of the total output of the industry. The differences in the diffusion rates of new production techniques have several root explanations. In the first place, some innovations are slow to be employed because although they are technologically possible, they are risky or are only marginally profit-

down the experience curve closer to the leader's position. If they fail to capture enough volume to approach the leader's experience curve position, very likely their profits will remain subpar or negative; the best long-run choice then may be to cash out their investment in the industry and reinvest elsewhere.

Estimates of the experience curve effect can be used to forecast costs. Such forecasts become the basis for setting realistic cost-reduction goals and for setting prices based on anticipated costs rather than on current or historical costs. Lowering prices at the same rate at which costs decline may well discourage the entry of competing firms into the industry.

Some Added Complexities of Experience Curve Economics

There are some subtleties in diagnosing experience curve economics in an industry:

- Occasionally experience effects are lumpy and uneven, causing the curve to decline not at a smooth, uniform rate but rather at rates that change at somewhat unpredictable intervals—the experience curve becomes flatter, then steeper, then flatter again.
- A new entrant with improved technology and/or smart followership abilities may be able to ride its own experience curve down more quickly and achieve a cost position significantly closer to the low-cost leaders than would be the case if it was forced to operate on the same experience curve as established competitors.
- There can be different experience curve effects in each part of the production chain—research and development, design engineering, manufacturing of parts and components, assembly of the final product, marketing, wholesale distribution, and retailing. While the accumulation of experience may result in cost reductions in all stages, seldom will the sizes of the reductions be the same. In like fashion, if a firm produces a whole line of different models, experience will accrue faster to the best-selling models, and their costs may fall faster than for slower-selling models.

Some Cautions About the Experience Curve

Three warnings about the experience curve are in order. One, experience curve effects do not exist in all industries; the size of the experience curve effect can range from tiny (or inconsequential) to large, making the appraisal of just how important experience is in generating efficiency gains a case-by-case analytical problem. Two, even where a fairly strong experience curve exists, the cost-reduction benefits do not occur automatically—a concerted effort to capture the cost-reduction opportunities has to be made.

Three, an overly strong emphasis on driving costs down the experience curve can produce some unwanted competitive consequences for a firm. Selecting a strategy based on sustained cost reduction associated with growing experience means putting cost-price-efficiency considerations ahead of building in attractive performance features and quality attributes. For an "efficiency," or low-cost, leadership strategy to succeed, there need to be significant numbers of customers who want low price as opposed to quality/service/product innovation/specialized use and other such brand-differentiating attributes. Moreover, once a firm decides to pursue a low-cost leadership strategy, it has to guard against losing its ability to respond to product-technology-customer changes; trying to beat out competitors solely by riding down the experience curve faster frequently results in narrow skills-building, rigid task performance, and relatively inflexible facilities and technologies. As a consequence, zealous pursuit of experience-based efficiency gains can blind a firm to the need to (1) respond to changes in customer needs and product uses, (2) match or better the product innovations of rivals, and (3) shift to an even more innovative production technology.

Sources: "Selling Business a Theory of Economics," *Business Week,* September 8, 1973, pp. 85–90; Derek F. Abell and John S. Hammond, *Strategic Marketing Planning* (Englewood Cliffs, N.J.: Prentice Hall, 1979), pp. 106–11; Arnaldo C. Hay and Nicolas S. Majluf, *Strategic Management: An Integrative Perspective* (Englewood Cliffs, N.J.: Prentice Hall, 1984), Chapter 6; David A. Aaker, *Developing Business Strategies* (New York: John Wiley, 1984), Chapter 10; and Pankaj Ghemawat, "Building Strategy on the Experience Curve," *Harvard Business Review,* Vol. 64, No. 2 (March-April 1985), pp. 143–49.

able. An innovation may require resource inputs which are not readily available or which have prohibitive costs, thereby undercutting the incentive to adopt it. Second, there usually is ample room for the managers of firms to possess different perceptions of the actual degree of technological superiority of an innovation, thus partially accounting for why one firm adopts an innovation and another does not. Unless an innovation has substantial technological and economic superiority over existing methods, firms are likely to switch to the technology only in the normal course of replacing worn-out equipment. Third, an innovation may require capital commitments beyond the reach of small firms; this may explain why larger firms are, on occasion, technologically superior to smaller firms. Fourth, small, aggressive "high-technology" firms may build their whole business around spotting opportunities to be technological pioneers and thereby outcompeting lethargic, bureaucratic enterprises intent upon defending their position with an entrenched technology. What makes production technology unique as a strategic variable is its considerable power to shape the competitive rules of the marketplace.[13] A technological edge that translates either into a cost advantage or a product quality advantage can be a great equalizer, nullifying the reputation of entrenched incumbents and creating opportunities for the technologically proficient. *Technological change is perhaps the single most important source of major market share changes among rival firms and probably the most frequent cause of the demise of long-standing dominant firms.*

How Technology can Drive Competition in the Marketplace

Technological change often intensifies competitive forces. The power of technology to drive competition in the marketplace stems from its ability to (1) affect the rivalry among incumbent competitors, (2) increase or decrease the ease of entry of potential newcomers to the industry, (3) change the bargaining power of customers, (4) change the bargaining power of buyers, and (5) increase or decrease the market threats of substitute products.[14]

Technological change often causes competition to intensify.

When changes in production technology lower production costs, adopters are more able to use the appeal of a lower price to win customers away from rival sellers.

Technological Change and Competitive Rivalry.   To the extent that changes in production technology lower adopters' production costs, the pressure for price cutting grows. Lower-cost producers can use the appeal of a lower price to win customers away from rival sellers. While high-cost firms can try to defend their market shares by matching the lower prices of low-cost firms, they face the penalty of slim profit margins or even losses. Cost-reducing technological changes thus enhance the appeal of a competitive strategy based on *striving to be the low-cost producer* in the industry—especially when the nature of the changes can be kept proprietary (via secrecy or patents) and rival firms are blocked from implementing an imitative technological approach.

When changes in production technology enhance product quality and product performance, adopters can use the appeal of a better product to win customers away from rivals.

On the other hand, when changes in production technology result in enhanced product quality and product performance attributes, adopters may win customers away from rivals by following a ***differentiation strategy*** based on the appeal of "our product is better than theirs." The more that buyers are interested in a product's quality-performance attributes, the more successful that a differentiation strategy is likely to be and the more that early adopters/innovators can benefit from the changes in production technology—unless, of course, competitors find it easy to implement their own matching technological changes very quickly.

Whenever technological change involves a heavy dose of learning by doing and firsthand experience with the technology paves the way for pushing the technological frontiers out still faster, then if a firm can keep its learning proprietary, it stands to gain an important competitive edge from its technological advantage. It may well be possible to translate this technological edge in

---

[13] Michael E. Porter, "The Technological Dimension of Competitive Strategy," Working Paper, Harvard Graduate School of Business Administration, September 1981, p. 3.

[14] The discussion that follows is based on Porter, "The Technological Dimension of Competitive Strategy," pp. 4–8.

production into gains in buyer patronage, thereby increasing sales and market share at the expense of rivals.

Technological Change and the Ease of Potential Entry. There are a number of ways for changes in production technology to make it easier or harder for interested firms to enter an industry:

Some changes in production technologies raise entry barriers; others lower entry barriers.

1. Technological change raises entry barriers when innovative production methods can be kept proprietary by the pioneering firm (or firms). When the requisite technical know-how and expertise are fairly easy to acquire and when the learning curve is not steeply sloped downward, it is easier for a new firm to enter the market insofar as the production part of the business is concerned.

2. Technological changes in production techniques can alter the capital requirements it takes to enter the industry by (a) requiring firms to invest heavily and continuously in research and development to remain abreast of fast-breaking technological developments (a strong commitment to R & D spending characterizes all firms in so-called high-technology businesses), and (b) affecting the capital investment it takes to build and equip a new production facility. The greater the capital requirements induced by changes in production technology, the higher the barriers to the entry of outside firms.

3. Changes in production technologies can (a) increase or decrease the need for after-sale service, (b) make it easier or harder to circumvent conventional distribution channels, (c) make it more or less expensive for buyers to switch their purchases to another seller, (d) make it easier or harder for a low-quality manufacturer to catch up with a high-quality manufacturer, or (e) make the learning curve steeper or flatter. Depending on the direction of these changes, entry barriers become higher or lower. Michelin's technological lead in producing high-quality, long-lasting radial tires proved significant enough in terms of cost-savings and product differentiation to allow it to overcome the otherwise high entry barriers associated with advertising (to acquire name recognition) and retail distribution (to gain access to the lucrative tire replacement market).

For the most part, whether advances in production technology act to make the entry of new firms easier or harder (and for that matter whether they solidify the position of innovating firms) depends on the extent to which those firms which adopt the advances are able to prevent imitation by existing or would-be competitors. Normally, technological change that originates within a firm is easier to defend against imitation because it is proprietary and may even be patentable. But some innovations are extremely easy to copy—the know-how to build automatic drip coffee makers spread quickly and no manufacturer was without an ability to produce such products. Bausch and Lomb, however, was able to defend its low-cost spin-casting techniques for making soft contact lenses for a period of several years before competitors came up with their own techniques for making a soft contact lens of comparable quality.

Plainly, when an innovating firm can protect a cost-saving or quality-enhancing technological innovation from imitation, it has potential for being translated into a competitive edge in the marketplace. However, even if a technological change triggers industrywide imitation, lowers barriers to entry, and stimulates competitive rivalry, it can still boost the profit potential of all industry participants (including the innovating firm) enough to justify the cost of implementing the change.

Sometimes changes in production technology enhance the bargaining leverage that producers have over their customers; at other times such changes give customers more bargaining power.

Technological Change and the Power of Buyers.

Changes in production technology have a way, sometimes, of tilting the bargaining and negotiating scale between producers and their customers. When technological change causes the products of producers to become more standardized, it becomes easier and less costly for customers to switch suppliers; the lower are customers' switching costs, the harder the bargain they can drive with sellers, favoring whichever supplier offers the best overall deal. Technological change can also make it easier or harder for customers to integrate backward; the easier it is for them to integrate backward, the more bargaining leverage they have over their suppliers. In some cases, technological change influences the basis of customer choice for one producer's product over another's. For example, if a producer of small electric motors discovers how to manufacture a motor that runs on less electricity, the energy-saving attribute of its product could help it win contracts to supply the motor as a component to air-conditioner manufacturers. Any time that technological change allows a seller's product to affect favorably the performance of a buyer's product, there emerges a market potential to create strong preferences on the part of the buyer and even to induce the buyer to pay a higher price. (Would you expect the demand for an energy-saving electric motor to be less price elastic in comparison with electric motors that take more electricity to run? Other things being equal, would not at least some buyers be willing to pay a higher price to enjoy the benefits of the energy-saving attribute?)

Changes in production technology can either increase a firm's bargaining power with its suppliers or reduce it.

Technological Change and the Power of Suppliers.

Just as technological change can shift the bargaining leverage between a firm and its customers, so can it affect a firm's competitive relationships with its suppliers. New production technologies can eliminate the need to purchase an otherwise essential component from powerful suppliers having key patents or proprietary technical know-how themselves. Conversely, technology can emerge in ways which, for reasons of either cost savings or product performance or both, force an industry to purchase component inputs from a supplier or group of suppliers. The development of plain-paper copying machines eliminated the need of users to purchase specially coated papers. The approval of aspartame as an artificial sweetener quickly swung the market over from the use of saccharin, which had been linked to causing a higher incidence of cancer. When advances in production technology give a firm more flexibility in sourcing materials and components from different suppliers, it tends to gain bargaining leverage over such suppliers and, as long as switching costs are low, can play off one supplier against another to get more favorable supply terms. On the other hand, technological change can act to raise the costs of switching suppliers, thus putting a firm into a weaker bargaining relationship with its suppliers.

Changes in production technology can either widen a firm's use of substitute inputs or narrow it.

Technological Change and the Use of Substitute Inputs.

The degree to which technological change can induce a firm to substitute one input for another is a function of the relative price and performance of alternative inputs (something we will explore at length in Chapter 7) and the switching costs of changing between them. Production technology in containers has evolved to where soft-drink bottlers have the option of using aluminum cans, plastic bottles, or glass bottles—the options they have give them leverage over suppliers. Changes in materials technology have brought steel, aluminum, and plastic increasingly into competition as components for automobile bodies, engine parts, and interior trim. Aluminum has made inroads as a substitute for copper in the manufacture of electrical wiring products because of its lower price. Technological advances in making synthetic fibers have given polyester fabrics wrinkle-resistant, no-iron attributes and paved the way for them to substitute for cotton and wool in the garment trade.

TECHNOLOGICAL CHANGE AND INDUSTRY BOUNDARIES

The boundary of an industry is often imprecise because of the market interrelationships between incumbent firms and suppliers or buyers who may be partly vertically integrated and between an industry's product and its substitutes. (Given that glass bottles, paper cartons, tin cans, and aluminum cans are in competition with one another, is there such a thing as the glass bottle or tin can industry, or are both a part of the container industry?) Nevertheless, it is useful to understand that however one elects to try to draw an industry's boundaries, technological change can widen or shrink them.[15] Technological change that reduces the costs of manufacturing products tailored to meet market differences among nations can enlarge the geographic scope of an industry, turning a domestic market into a globally competitive industry. In telecommunications and data processing, technological change has caused heretofore separate industries to reform and merge—AT&T, once thought of as a telephone company, was driven by technological advances in long-distance data transmission to become involved in the information and data-processing industry and thus evolved into a competitor of IBM and other data-processing companies. Technological developments in the manufacture of computerized energy management systems are bringing telephone companies, electrical equipment manufacturers, and communications firms into competition with electric power companies as concerns the conservation of electric energy. Technological changes which led to the ability to manufacture microwave ovens expanded the definition of the cooking appliance industry; similarly, the advent of solar water heating technology has expanded the boundaries of the water-heating industry.

Technology can narrow boundaries and subdivide industries as well. The ability of TV manufacturers to make portable miniature TV sets with 1- to 3-inch screens created a product segment quite distinct from the table and console models which traditionally defined the industry. The technology of making personal computers spawned an industry and set of firms quite apart from the industry of making large mainframe computers—only IBM has chosen to compete in both industries. Cray Research, Digital Equipment, and Amdahl, together with IBM, are the big names in large computers, whereas IBM, Apple, Compaq, Zenith, and Dell are the big names in small computers. The computer industry has thus split into two fairly distinct industries because of technological advance.

THE IMPETUS FOR TECHNOLOGICAL INNOVATIONS

Producers, even if they are lucky enough to be sheltered temporarily from the cold winds of competition, are beset with a multitude of motivations and pressures for seeking out better production techniques and implementing

---

[15] Porter, "The Technological Dimension of Competitive Strategy," p. 9.

Many motivations and pressures drive producers to keep their production techniques close to the cutting edge of technology.

promising innovations.[16] The biggest driver to adopt new technologies is to improve profitability and, ultimately, to safeguard the chances for market success. But such an explanation is a bit umbrellalike, for it hides the specific forces that drive investments in new technology and innovation.

First, product-related technological innovation (as distinct from innovations having to do with production technology) offers a major avenue for better meeting the needs and wants of buyers and, in the face of the competition for buyer patronage from rival firms, it becomes a virtual necessity for maintaining one's current market position. Firms consistently attempt to outmaneuver competitors by introducing products with more attractive attributes—a lower price, higher quality, more after-sale service, greater durability, longer warranties, more appealing design, improved convenience, and so on. To defend successfully against such competitive tactics, a firm must be active in developing new and improved products that can win consumer favor, protect against shifts to substitute products, and make the firm's reputation grow. In addition, market pressures for quality improvements, for product standardization in terms of sizes or performance, and for lower prices dictate a progressive and efficient technology.

Adverse developments in the markets for a firm's resource inputs are also a source of pressure for innovation and technological change. A portion of the trend to automate production originates from the desire of firms to escape rising labor costs and higher raw material prices associated with natural resource scarcity.

Sticking with out-of-date production technologies is an invitation to competitive disaster.

Rare is the firm or industry that can insulate itself successfully from the pervasive pressures to remain technologically up to date in the long run. Technical obsolescence spells almost certain competitive disaster for a firm, subject only to the propensity of government to rescue it by the granting of subsidies, protective tariffs, or regulation. On the positive side, technological prowess and virtuosity can be used to win a competitive advantage based on either lower cost or a uniquely differentiated product offering. If a firm can develop production technologies that give its product a lower delivered cost to the customer and can protect the source of this technological advantage from imitation, it can build a defensible competitive position and earn above-average profits. Similarly, if a firm can use technology to achieve unique product attributes, it can also have a defense against competitive forces and perhaps earn above-average profits.

Technological Leadership or Followership?

The conceptual distinction between technological leadership and technological followership is clear enough. The strategic objective of technological leadership is usually to use technological innovation as either the vehicle for becoming the low-cost producer in the industry or the vehicle for introducing unique attributes into one's product offering in order to achieve superiority over rivals' products. The strategic appeal of being a technological follower is to learn from

---

[16] Even firms with a stranglehold on the production of an item cannot long afford to be complacent about technological developments. Given that the threat of potential substitutes looms over every market and that technological frontiers are being pushed out along broad fronts and at accelerating rates, it is not likely that many firms, even monopolies, will choose to risk the fates of technological stagnation and obsolescence.

the leader's experiences, avoid the costs of pioneering, and improve on the new technology to outmaneuver the leader in becoming the low-cost producer or in fine-tuning the product offering to better meet customers' needs.[17] In principle, therefore, *either technological leadership or followership can be routes to securing a competitive advantage.*

Choosing Whether to Lead or Follow

The choice of whether to pursue leadership or followership is not a simple matter. A variety of considerations have to be taken into account. In general, the attractiveness of technological leadership is governed by:[18]

1. *The size of the technological opportunity.* The bigger the technological opportunity, the greater the chance to create a significant cost or differentiation gap vis-à-vis rivals.

2. *The caliber of a firm's technological skills.* Leadership is favored when a firm's superior technical expertise gives it an edge in trying to open up a technological gap; the benefits of leadership are fleeting when competitors have essentially equivalent technical skills and probably can match the leader's technological achievements in timely fashion. Superior technical skills may derive from more proficient R & D capability, and ability to obtain pieces of technological know-how from customers or suppliers, accumulated technical experience, and patent protection.

3. *The fraction of the industry's technology that flows into the industry from suppliers, customers, or other industries sharing the same basic technology.* The risk of leadership increases the more that technological change flows into the industry from outside sources; this is because competitors' access to technology does not depend so heavily on their internal technical skills and investment in R & D.

4. *The nature and size of any first-mover advantages.* **First-mover advantages** are factors which allow a leader to translate a technology edge into other competitive advantages that persist even if the technology gap is later closed. Potential first-mover advantages which can accrue to a technological leader include (a) being able to establish an identity and reputation as the premier producer (prompting repeat purchases by old customers and the attraction of new customers aware of this reputation) and giving the leader a differential image, (b) the existence of switching costs (if the leader makes the sale to the customer, the existence of switching costs gives the firm an advantage in gaining the customer's repeat business even if its product no longer is superior to rivals'), and (c) the existence of a steep learning or experience curve. If first-mover advantages are sizable, the leader may need to open up a one-time technological advantage to reap a substantial long-term competitive advantage. However, if first-mover advantages are slight, it becomes important to maintain technical leadership through continued innovation.

5. *Whether the movement of technology is likely to progress along a continuous path or shift to an entirely new path.* When technological changes involve continuity, a leader stands to retain any first-mover advantages. But should technological changes unexpectedly produce shifts to new paths, the

> **Technological leaders sometimes gain lasting competitive advantages from being a "first-mover."**

---

[17] Excluded from consideration here is the passive-follower type of firm, which knowingly or unknowingly ignores the competitive aspect of technological change.

[18] Porter, "The Technological Dimension of Competitive Strategy," pp. 18–23.

leader's technical skills and investments can be nullified, rendering the payoff for leadership risky and uncertain.

As the foregoing discussion hints, there are times when being a technological follower is more advantageous than being a leader:[19]

Prompt technological followership is sometimes much less expensive than striving to be a trailblazing pioneer.

1. *When investments in a new technology are specialized and inflexible and the pace of change in production technology is fast.* Rapid-fire technological developments, which frequently characterize young industries with immature technologies, allow followers to leapfrog leaders rather easily and quickly.

2. *When customer needs and purchasing behavior change quickly.* A leader's first-mover advantages are often nullified by changes in customer needs or purchasing behavior. In such cases, neither repeat nor first-time buyers are likely to place as much value on a leader's past reputation and their loyalty to the leader's products can prove to be low. In fact, an old leader can actually be disadvantaged if its identity and reputation is linked strongly with the old needs and ways.

3. *When the nature of technological change involves sporadic shifts from one technological path to another technological path rather than moving predictably along a single path.* Here, any advantage the technological leader has is transitory and the competitive edge that the leader earns may cost more than it is worth, given that a new breakthrough on another technological branch can shift future technological and market opportunities in fairly dramatic ways.

Uncertainty over which of several competing technologies will ultimately prove to be "the best way to go" makes technological leadership risky.

4. *When there is great uncertainty about the appropriate technological direction.* In some industries, there can be several competing technologies with no clear indication as to which one will develop into the best approach or the dominant design. There is risk in trying to be a leader and having to bet heavily on one technological approach or another (pursuing them all at once is usually not feasible); a cautious "wait and watch" strategy predicated on following quickly when the uncertainty clears and trying to improve upon the leader's efforts (while avoiding the leader's mistakes and costly experiences) becomes attractive in comparison.

5. *When the leader's technological efforts are readily copied.* Occasions arise when new technology in an industry spreads quickly and imitation costs are low. This can occur because the technology cannot be either patented or kept proprietary and thus readily finds its way into the public domain through the activities of trade associations and trade publications, on-site inspection of new facilities and pieces of equipment, reverse engineering (where rivals tear down a leader's products part by part to learn how it was designed and engineered), and information gained from the leader's suppliers, customers, and ex-employees. In such instances, the lead-time advantage of the technological pioneer is shortened enough that followers are not really at a competitive disadvantage and are in the enviable position of being able to avoid the extra cost of pioneering (as concerns costly mistakes and false starts, redesign and reengineering, testing, and working out the bugs).

6. *When there are major market barriers to be overcome in making the innovation a market success.* The trials and tribulations of exercising technological leadership may entail hurdling such barriers as the need to secure regulatory approval, the difficulty of educating customers to the benefits, and the need to make support investments in repair and service personnel, in sources of

---

[19] *Ibid.*, pp. 21–25.

supply for new components and inputs, and in distribution channels. Overcoming these obstacles can be time-consuming and expensive enough to make technological followership a comfortable, acceptable strategy as compared to leadership.

TECHNOLOGY LICENSING

One other technology strategy deserves mention, and that is licensing. *Technology licensing* is a device for leaders to secure additional profits from their technological investments and for followers to gain access to a leader's technology achievements without investing in imitation. Where a leader can license technology to other firms, charging either a fixed fee or a percentage royalty, it increases the profitability and attractiveness of a leadership strategy. Although licensing a follower reduces or eliminates the technology gap between the leader and the follower, there are times when the leader can derive substantial benefits from having competitors with the same technology. This can occur in situations where (1) there are many competing technologies and the industry as a whole would benefit from a common technological approach, (2) the industry is young and the products of rival firms are so different that consumers are confused and would benefit from a more standardized product offering, and (3) the product is so new that having competitors would help develop the industry and expand the market for the leader's product. From a follower's standpoint, licensing can be attractive when licensing costs are below the cost of imitation; the follower's biggest disadvantage is that the follower is locked into the leader's technology in a way that may impede its own strategy for building a competitive edge.

There are times when a leader, rather than keeping its technological capabilities proprietary, finds it advantageous to license others to use its technology.

KEY POINTS

Production refers to any activity that creates value. Production includes virtually all phases of economic activity except consumption. Four types of production activities are identifiable: custom-order production, rigid mass production, flexible mass production, and process production. A production function indicates, in quantitative terms, the relationship between the input of resources and the output of goods or services per period of time.

In analyzing production processes, resource inputs are generally divided into two categories: fixed and variable. Corresponding to the notion of fixed and variable inputs is the notion of the short run and the long run. In the short run, output can be changed only by altering the amount of variable input used in conjunction with the given fixed input. In the long run, output can be changed by altering the scale of production, the technology of the production process, and the rate of usage of any and all inputs.

The principle of diminishing marginal returns states that as the amount of a variable input is increased by equal increments and combined with a specified amount of fixed input, eventually a point will be reached where the resulting increases in the quantity of output will get smaller and smaller. Should the usage rate of variable input get sufficiently large, the quantity of output will reach a maximum and may then decrease as still larger amounts of variable input are employed.

Technological change has major consequences for a firm's production function. Not only can a new technological "recipe" result in important cost savings but it also can open up opportunities to improve product performance and otherwise allow a firm to succeed in differentiating its product from those of rival firms. As a consequence, changes in technology serve as an important way for firms to build a technology-based competitive advantage. Choosing whether to be a technological leader or a follower thus becomes an integral aspect of a firm's competitive strategy.

The power of technological change is readily visible in the marketplace. Innovative production technologies can alter the competitive rules of the marketplace and also serve as a great equalizer, nullifying the advantages of incumbent firms, opening up competitive opportunities for followers and newcomers, and shifting the bargaining leverage a firm has with suppliers and customers. Analyzing the competitive impact of technological changes is, therefore, an integral part of the economics of the firm.

PROBLEMS AND QUESTIONS FOR DISCUSSION

1. Fill in the values for discrete MP, AP_{vi}, and AP_{fi} based upon the information given in the table.

Units of Fixed Input	Units of Variable Input	Quantity of Output	Discrete MP	AP_{vi}	AP_{fi}
3	0	0		_____	_____
3	1	120	_____	_____	_____
3	2	270	_____	_____	_____
3	3	390	_____	_____	_____
3	4	480	_____	_____	_____
3	5	540	_____	_____	_____
3	6	560	_____	_____	_____
3	7	540	_____	_____	_____

2. Given: The production function $Q = 12X$, where Q = units of output per period of time and X = units of variable input.
   (a) Determine the equations for MP and AP_{vi}.
   (b) Assuming 5 units of fixed input are presently being employed in the production process represented by the preceding production function, determine AP_{fi} when 10 units of variable input are combined with the 5 units of fixed input.
   (c) Graphically illustrate the production function and the corresponding MP and AP_{vi} functions.
   (d) How would you describe the important properties of this production function?

3. Production managers for the Cosmic Paper Corporation estimate that their production process is currently characterized by the following short-run production function: $Q = 72X + 15X^2 - X^3$, where Q = tons of paper products per production period and X = units of variable input employed per production period.
   (a) Determine the equations for MP and AP_{vi}.
   (b) What is the value of MP when 7 units of variable input are employed?
   (c) By how much does output rise when the usage of variable input is increased from 7 to 8 units per production period?
   (d) At what rate of usage of variable input is the point of diminishing marginal returns encountered?
   (e) What is the maximum output capability per production period? What rate of usage of variable input is required to reach the maximum output level?

(f) Graphically illustrate this production function and the corresponding *MP* and AP_{vi} functions. Indicate on your graph the output ranges where output is increasing at an increasing rate and where output is increasing at a decreasing rate. Also indicate the output where the point of diminishing average returns to variable input is encountered.

4. Why is it important for business firms to keep their production techniques close to the frontier of technological know-how?

5. Explain how technology can be a driving force that shapes competition and the way a market functions. Be specific in indicating how technological change can (a) affect the rivalry among incumbent competitors, (b) change barriers to entry into the industry, (c) influence the bargaining power a firm has with its suppliers and its customers, and (d) affect the competitive pressures from substitute products.

6. How can changes in technology affect the boundaries between industries? Cite examples.

7. What incentives do firms have to be technologically progressive?

8. Under what circumstances is technological leadership an attractive strategy?

9. When may being a technological follower be attractive?

10. How can a firm use technology to create a competitive advantage?

Chapter 7

Determining the Conditions for Efficient Production

Having sketched the roles of technology and production functions in shaping supply capability, we now turn to an in-depth examination of the conditions for achieving peak production efficiency, for optimizing the mix of resource inputs in both the short run and the long run, and for achieving economies of scale. Analyzing the conditions for production efficiency provides the foundation for understanding the economics of cost functions and what it takes to achieve low-cost production.

THE STAGES OF PRODUCTION

Production functions of the form

$$Q = a + bX + cX^2 - dX^3$$

and the associated average and marginal product curves can be divided into three stages, as illustrated in Figure 7-1. Stage I extends from zero usage of variable input to the point where the *average* product of variable input is maximum. Stage II extends from maximum AP_{vi} to where the quantity of output is maximum and *MP* is zero. Stage III coincides with the range of variable input where the total output is falling and marginal product is negative. These stages are of special significance for analyzing the efficiency with which resource inputs are used.

    Stage I. Included as stage I is the entire range over which AP_{vi} is increasing. Note that in stage I the point of diminishing marginal returns is reached (point *A*) and passed. Up to the point of DMR, output is increasing at an increasing rate; past this point it increases at a decreasing rate. The marginal product of variable input rises to its peak and begins to fall, yet it remains a greater value than average product throughout the stage. Stage I ends when the point of diminishing *average* returns is reached (point *B*).

    What about the efficiency with which the fixed and variable input are being used in stage I? The **efficiency** of an input is best measured by its *average* product because it indicates the amount of output obtained *per unit* of input. An input's marginal product is a measure of the efficiency of one additional unit of variable input, but it does not reflect the efficiency of *all* the units of variable input taken as a group. Since the average product of variable input is rising

The best measure of input efficiency is the amount of output obtained per unit of input—in other words, the input's average product.

170

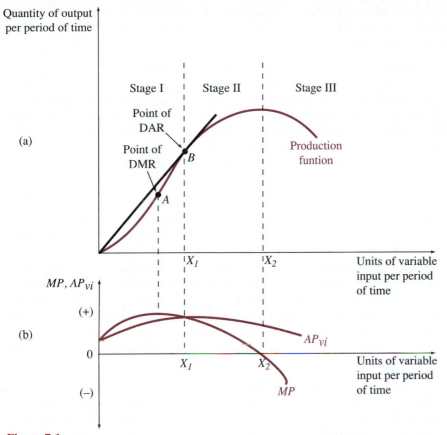

Figure 7-1
The stages of production

throughout stage I, it is evident that variable input is being employed with *increasing* overall efficiency as the end of stage I is approached. Indeed, maximum efficiency of the variable input is attained at the border between stages I and II, where AP_{vi} is maximum. So much for variable input; now what about the efficiency of the fixed inputs in stage I? Although there is no curve representing the average product of fixed input (AP_{fi}) in Figure 7-1, we still know that the quantity of output rises throughout stage I and that the level of fixed input remains unchanged. Thus, because AP_{fi} = units of output/units of fixed input, it follows that the average product of fixed input must also be rising throughout stage I.

   Therefore, in stage I using more variable input with the given quantity of fixed inputs raises the efficiency with which *both* fixed and variable inputs are being utilized. Just *why* the efficiency of both fixed and variable inputs rises in stage I stems from a relative imbalance between the fixed and variable inputs. Throughout stage I the amount of fixed input is excessive compared to the amount of variable input employed. The unduly large proportions of fixed input to variable input in stage I result in fixed inputs being *underutilized* and the variable inputs being *overutilized*. Hence, as more variable input is used, the imbalance is relieved, and the efficiencies of both inputs rise.

   When the efficiencies of fixed and variable inputs are both rising, the *unit* costs of producing more output are declining. Thus, *from the standpoint of*

Maximum efficiency of variable input occurs at the border between stage I and stage II; maximum efficiency of fixed input occurs at the border between stage II and stage III.

improving production efficiency and lowering unit costs, a firm should always move through stage I to at least the border of stage II before ceasing to use more variable input.

Stage II.   In stage II the quantity of output rises at a slower and slower rate; accordingly, the marginal products associated with each additional unit of variable input become progressively smaller, approaching zero. More significantly, the average product of variable input is falling throughout stage II. The average product of fixed input, however, continues to rise in stage II, because the quantity of output continues to rise even though the amount of fixed input is held constant. In stage II, then, additional units of variable input add to the efficiency of fixed input but diminish the efficiency of variable input.

Stage III.   At the boundary between stages II and III, short-run output is maximum, and the fixed input is being utilized to its fullest extent—the efficiency of the fixed input has reached its peak level. The marginal product of variable input at this point is zero. With further doses of variable input, the amount of variable input relative to fixed input becomes so large that total output *falls*. There simply is too little fixed input relative to the amounts of variable input being used. Thus, using larger quantities of variable input per period of time in stage III reduces AP_{vi} still more, and MP becomes increasingly negative. And with total output falling, AP_{fi} is also decreasing. In sum, the efficiency of variable input and the efficiency of fixed input both drop once the stage III border is crossed.

Optimal production efficiency is always attained somewhere in stage II.

The Optimum Stage.   The foregoing description of the three stages should make it apparent that operating in stage II is best from the standpoint of overall production efficiency and low unit costs. In stage I, variable input is used too sparingly with the available fixed input; increases in variable input will so increase the efficiency of all inputs that the *unit costs* of producing more output will decline. Thus, efficiency and cost considerations will induce the firm to employ at least an amount of variable input sufficient to reach stage II.

Stage III is obviously irrational. It makes no sense whatsoever for a firm to incur the added expense of purchasing and using more units of variable input per period of time when the payoff is a decline in total output and a reduction in overall operating efficiency.

Therefore, stage II is optimum from the standpoint of overall production efficiency and cost. Just where in stage II is the best rate of variable input usage depends on the prices of fixed and variable input (we shall pursue this point later on in this chapter). However, *stage II is not the stage in which profit is necessarily maximized.* Demand for a firm's product may in the short run be so low that it is actually more profitable to operate in stage I. Stage III can never be more profitable than stage I or stage II because the decline in total output is accompanied by rising total costs (as more variable input is used) and potentially lower revenues.

FIXED INPUTS AND THE SHORT-RUN PRODUCTION FUNCTION

Given that optimal production efficiency is achieved only in stage II, what can a firm do if demand for its product does not warrant producing enough output to reach stage II? For instance, suppose, as is shown in Figure 7-2(a), that a firm reaches stage II at an output of Q_2 units but that the quantity

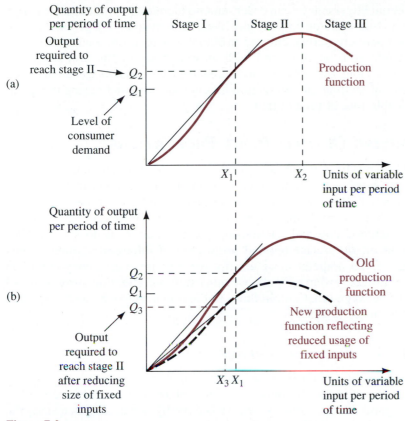

Figure 7-2
How using fewer fixed inputs impacts the production function

demanded at the current selling price is only Q_1 units. Several alternatives are open to the firm. In the short run it can (1) tolerate the production inefficiency of operating in stage I—which may, incidentally, still allow for ample profit to be earned; (2) try to increase product demand by lowering its selling price and/or increasing promotional and selling efforts; or (3) add new products to its product line to take up the slack in production capacity. If these prove unworkable for whatever reasons, in the long run the firm can reduce its scale of production operations by cutting back on the size of fixed inputs. Scaling down fixed input usage has the impact of shifting the production function down and to the left, as shown in Figure 7-2(b).[1] Then the firm can reach stage II at a lower output (Q_3 as compared to Q_2) and with a smaller amount of variable input (X_3 as compared to X_1). Demand for the firm's product can be satisfied by using fewer inputs, thereby cutting production costs and widening the firm's profit margin at the current price.

Similarly, when buyer demand exceeds a firm's total output capability in the short run, the firm can take any of several actions. If strong demand for the item appears temporary, a price increase to ration the available supply

There are several remedies for situations where a firm cannot utilize its inputs efficiently because demand for its product is either too small or too great.

---

[1] In the event that fixed inputs are "lumpy" and can be reduced only by a relatively large proportion, the production function conceivably could shift downward and *to the right*, meaning that the firm can reach stage II at a lower output provided its usage of variable input is increased. Whether the firm would prefer to use less fixed input and more variable input in producing its product would depend on the relative prices of fixed and variable inputs.

among potential buyers may be in order, and no increase in production capacity is warranted. But when demand seems likely to remain above production capacity on a relatively permanent and profitable basis, a price increase in the short run might well be combined with an expansion of the firm's scale of operations in the long run. This means increasing fixed input usage; such action has the effect of shifting the production function upward and raising the maximum obtainable rate of total output.

DETERMINING OPTIMAL INPUT PROPORTIONS

So far, the firm has been pictured as changing its rate of output in the short run by employing more or less units of variable input. In the long run, changes in the usage of fixed inputs may also be undertaken to adjust output capabilities. Although the fixed-variable input approach to output adjustment helps specify certain fundamental physical relationships of production, it does not permit determination of the precise optimal proportion of different resource inputs within stage II. To pinpoint more exactly the maximum efficiency-minimum cost combination of resource inputs, we must shift our attention away from the relationships between input-output flows to the relationships between resource inputs and resource prices.

To determine where in stage II that input usage is most efficient (and production costs per unit of output are lowest), it is necessary to bring input prices into the analysis.

THE PRODUCTION SURFACE

To simplify our analysis of optimal input combinations, capital and labor are assumed to be the only two types of resource inputs required in producing a good. No disservice to reality is done by this assumption since the relevant principles we shall derive for two inputs apply equally to any greater number of inputs. Capital may be thought of as symbolizing those kinds of resource inputs which are fixed in the short run and labor as symbolizing those kinds of inputs which are variable in the short run. (Letting capital be the proxy for fixed inputs in the short run and labor be the proxy for variable inputs serves to identify the optimal combination of fixed and variable inputs in the long run.)

In the three-dimensional diagram of Figure 7-3(a), the coordinates in the horizontal plane show the alternative combinations of capital and labor. The quantity of output associated with each combination of the two types of resource inputs is measured vertically above the plane. Varying the quantities of capital and labor generates the hill-shaped production surface *OCPL*.[2] If *OC* units of capital are used, varying the quantity of labor generates the production function *CDAP*. Similarly, given *OL* units of labor, varying the quantity of capital input gives the production function *LEBP*. Notice that the shapes of the production functions generated by holding the input of one resource constant and letting the other change [lines *CDAP* and *LEBP* in Figure 7-3(a)] correspond to the cubic type of production function, a type of production relationship which often typifies the entire output range for a plant.

Suppose that we connect all points on the production surface *OCPL* associated with an output of *AA'* units (where *AA' = BB'*), obtaining the contour line *AB*. All the points along *AB* are associated with the *same* amount of output (*AA' = BB'*). Projecting line *AB* vertically downward onto the horizontal plane gives the dashed contour line *A'B'*. The line *A'B'* defines all the combinations of capital and labor employed per unit of time that will yield an

---

[2] Observe that the concept of the production surface is analogous to the utility surface discussed in Chapters 3 and 4.

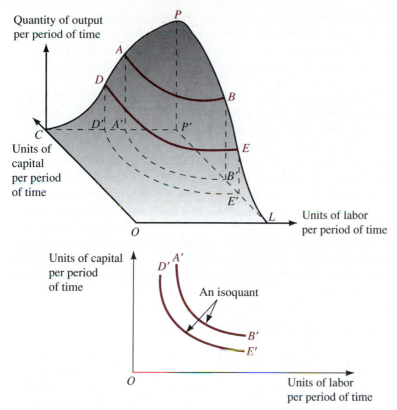

Figure 7-3
Derivation of isoquants from a production surface

output flow of $AA' = BB'$; such a line is called an ***isoquant***.[3] For movements along an isoquant the rate of output remains constant, but the input ratio (in this case the ratio of capital to labor) changes continuously.

Following the same procedure, suppose we move down the production surface to a lower rate of output, say DD', and connect all points on the production surface $OCPL$ representing an output of DD' (where $DD' = EE'$). This gives the contour line DE, which, projected vertically downward onto the horizontal plane, traces out the dashed contour $D'E'$. Any point along DE represents constant total output, and all combinations of capital and labor lying on $D'E'$ are capable of producing this amount of output. Contour line $D'E'$ is also an isoquant.

Figure 7-3(b) illustrates isoquants $A'B'$ and $D'E'$ in a two-dimensional diagram. All input combinations lying on $A'B'$ yield more output than the input combinations on $D'E'$. Higher rates of output are represented by isoquants lying farther from the origin, as indicated by the positions on the production surface of the contour lines from which isoquants are derived. A complete set of isoquants for a production surface is called an ***isoquant map***.[4]

BASIC CONCEPT
An isoquant represents all combinations of resource inputs that are capable of producing a given amount of output.

---

[3] The term *isoquant* is derived from the prefix *iso-*, meaning equal, and the word *quantity*; hence, it literally means equal quantity (of output). In the literature of economics isoquants are sometimes referred to as product indifference curves, equal product curves, or isoproduct curves.
[4] Suppose that a firm's production function is $Q = f(L, C)$; then a particular isoquant is defined by assigning a value to Q and observing all the different technically feasible values of L and C which will yield that value of Q. The firm's isoquant map is derived by repeating this procedure for many values of Q.

Isoquants may be viewed as analogous to the contour lines on a topographic map. Each isoquant connects all points of the same altitude or output rate. From this standpoint, the entire production surface (of which only a section is shown in Figure 7-3) can be considered as a "production mountain" with isoquants as the contour lines encircling it.

Although production function and production surface are shown in Figure 7-3 as being continuous, with the isoquants derived therefrom also being continuous, some resource inputs (especially capital and technology) do not lend themselves to being used in continuously divisible subunits. After all, anything less than a whole machine is less than satisfactory. Rarely are production technologies so flexible that an infinite number of combinations of resources can be used to produce equivalent amounts of output. Consequently, it is probably more accurate to conceive of an isoquant as a series of points, where each point represents a technically feasible combination of resource inputs that yield an equivalent amount of output. However, as long as the limited potential for substituting one resource input for another is recognized, it does little harm to simplify the presentation by drawing isoquants as smooth curves.

THE CHARACTERISTICS OF ISOQUANTS

The properties of isoquants are similar to those of indifference curves: (1) Isoquants are nonintersecting; (2) all *rational* combinations of resource inputs lie on that portion of an isoquant which slopes downward to the right; and (3) the rational segments of isoquants tend to be convex to the origin. Each of these properties warrants brief discussion.

It is illogical for isoquants to intersect.

For two isoquants to intersect is illogical and contrary to our assumption of efficiency. Intersection would mean that two different amounts of output could be produced with the same combination of resource inputs. This could occur only if a firm uses its inputs so inefficiently that the marginal products of some of the resources are zero or negative—something that a firm is not likely to do knowingly. Hence, an isoquant shows only the maximum output obtainable from resource inputs, which precludes intersection.

As indicated earlier, an isoquant map consists of a series of concentric rings around the hill of production. A single such isoquant is reproduced in Figure 7-4. All the points along the isoquant in Figure 7-4 represent input combinations capable of producing the same level of output. Although all the combinations of capital and labor lying on this isoquant represent possible recipes for producing this output, some of the combinations are more rational than others. For example, combination B would never be chosen over combination A. Why? Combination A requires the same amount of capital input as B (C_2 units) but requires considerably less labor input (L_1 units as compared to L_3 units); hence, combination A is *cheaper* than B. Similarly, combination D is always preferable to combination C, since it requires much less capital input (C_1 as compared to C_3 units) while using the same amount of labor input (L_2 units). It follows that the economically practical resource combinations fall within the lower left quadrant of the isoquant—the boldly inscribed portion in Figure 7-4 lying between the vertical and horizontal tangents to the isoquant at points E and F. The remaining points on the isoquant constitute economically foolish resource combinations, even though they represent technically feasible recipes. Thus, for reasons of economy in resource use and in minimizing costs, *the rational segment of an isoquant is the portion sloping downward to the right and bowed in toward the origin.*

The only practical resource combinations on an isoquant lie in the lower left quadrant where the isoquant is downsloping and convex to the origin.

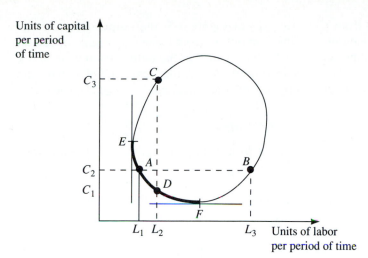

Figure 7-4

The cost-efficient region of an isoquant

The downward slope of the economic region of an isoquant derives from the possibility of substituting one resource input for another in the production process and still maintaining the same production rate. Consider the *rate* at which one input must be substituted for another to keep output constant. From Figure 7-5, we see that a change from input combination C_1L_1 to input combination C_2L_2 involves a substitution of labor for capital. The rate at which labor is substituted for capital over this range is

$$\frac{C_2 - C_1}{L_2 - L_1} = \frac{-\Delta C}{\Delta L}$$

and is called the ***marginal rate of technical substitution*** of labor for capital. The marginal rate of technical substitution (MRTS) measures the reduction in one input (ΔC) per unit increase in the other (ΔL) that is just sufficient to maintain a constant level of output.

BASIC CONCEPT
The rate at which one input must be substituted for another to keep output constant is termed the marginal rate of technical substitution.

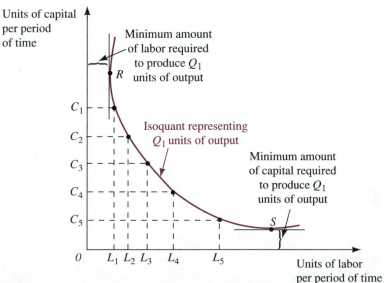

Figure 7-5

Marginal rate of technical substitution

In moving from C_1L_1 to C_2L_2 in Figure 7-5, the output rate remains unchanged; consequently the "loss" in output from using fewer units of capital input is exactly compensated for by the "gain" in the output from using more units of labor input. The loss in output from using less capital equals the reduction in capital usage multiplied by the "average" marginal product of these units, or

$$-\Delta C \cdot MP_C.$$

By the same token the gain in output from using a larger dose of labor equals

$$\Delta L \cdot MP_L.$$

Since the loss and the gain are equivalent in size, we can say that

$$-\Delta C \cdot MP_C = \Delta L \cdot MP_L.$$

Dividing both sides of this equation by $\Delta L \cdot MP_C$ gives

$$-\frac{\Delta C \cdot MP_C}{\Delta L \cdot MP_C} = \frac{\Delta L \cdot MP_L}{\Delta L \cdot MP_C},$$

which reduces to

$$-\frac{\Delta C}{\Delta L} = \frac{MP_L}{MP_C} \quad \text{or} \quad \frac{\Delta C}{\Delta L} = -\frac{MP_L}{MP_C}.$$

Therefore, it is apparent that between combinations C_1L_1 and C_2L_2,

$$MRTS_{LC} = \frac{\Delta C}{\Delta L} = -\frac{MP_L}{MP_C}.$$

That $MRTS_{LC}$ is negative derives from the substitution of one resource for the other and the negative slope of the isoquant; however, for our purposes it is the *size* of the ratio that is important, not its sign.

Now suppose that combination C_1L_1 in Figure 7-5 is moved closer and closer to C_2L_2 so as to merge eventually with it to form a single point. The ratio $\Delta C/\Delta L$ will then approach the value of the slope of the tangent to the isoquant at point C_2L_2. Consequently, we may say that the *marginal rate of technical substitution of one input for another input at any point along an isoquant is equal to the slope of the isoquant at that point.*[5]

The *MRTS* of labor for capital *diminishes* as more and more labor is substituted for capital because the greater the extent to which labor is substituted for capital, the more labor it takes to compensate for a reduction in the use of capital. The other points along the isoquant in Figure 7-5 make this clearer. The vertical axis in Figure 7-5 is measured so that $C_1C_2 = C_2C_3 =$

---

[5] Mathematically, the *MRTS* can be found by taking the first derivative of the equation defining an isoquant. For example, if the expression

$$LC = 100$$

defines an isoquant, then the $MRTS_{LC}$ can be found as follows:

$$C = \frac{100}{L} = 100L^{-1},$$

$$\frac{dC}{dL} = -100L^{-2} = -\frac{100}{L^2}.$$

Since $MRTS_{LC} = dC/dL$, we have

$$MRTS_{LC} = -\frac{100}{L^2}$$

for any value of L in which interest may focus.

$C_3C_4 = C_4C_5 = OC_5 = 1$ unit of capital. Starting at resource combination C_1L_1 and proceeding down the isoquant, we find that it takes a relatively small increase in the use of labor (L_1L_2 units) to compensate for using one less unit of capital and still produce the same quantity of output. But, as we move farther *down* the isoquant and continue to substitute labor for capital, reductions in capital must be offset by progressively larger increases in labor input ($L_1L_2 <$ $L_2L_3 < L_3L_4 < L_4L_5$). Plainly, then, the *MRTS* of labor for capital diminishes as the degree of substitution is increased. Where the isoquant becomes horizontal, the substitution of labor for capital has reached its maximum limit, and the $MRTS_{LC} = 0$. Further reductions in capital will cause output to *fall*; no longer is it possible to reduce the use of capital and maintain output by using more labor. The amount of capital corresponding to point S in Figure 7-5 is the minimum amount of capital which can be used to produce an output of Q_1. By the same rationale, as we move back up the isoquant toward point R, capital is being substituted for labor, and the ratio of ΔC to ΔL is rising. At point R, capital has been substituted for labor to the maximum possible extent; the *MRTS* of capital for labor is infinity, and the slope of the isoquant is vertical. The amount of labor corresponding to point R is the minimum amount of labor which can be used to produce output Q_1.

It is the changing marginal rate of technical substitution that makes the isoquant bowed in toward the origin. Should two inputs be perfect substitutes for each other, the isoquant is linear and downsloping. Such a relationship between inputs is rare, especially regarding inputs as diverse as labor and capital. An example indicates why most isoquants are convex. Consider the tradeoff between labor and capital in making fenders for automobiles. A metal-stamping machine with a single operator can transform a piece of sheet steel into the shape of an automobile fender in a matter of seconds. Within limits, less expensive stamping machines requiring more labor time can be used to make the same fender. But the more labor and the less capital used to shape sheet steel into fenders, the more difficult it becomes to carry the degree of substitution further without jeopardizing the quantity and quality of output. The hammering out of the fender, for example, would require an inordinate amount of labor time and cost, as well as entailing a major reduction in fender quality. The same reasoning applies equally well to other resource inputs; consequently, *a diminishing marginal rate of technical substitution of one resource input for another is a generally encountered phenomenon in production processes.*

PRODUCTION PRINCIPLE
It takes progressively larger increases in one input to compensate for reductions in another input.

THE ISOCOST CURVE

Isoquants delineate the possible ways that firms can combine resource inputs—no restrictions, save those of a technical nature, are brought into play. In deciding which of these resource input combinations is optimal, a firm has to consider the prices it will have to pay for the inputs and the total dollar outlay it can afford to spend for inputs and remain competitive.

An *isocost curve* portrays the various alternative combinations of resource inputs which a firm can purchase, given prevailing prices for resource inputs and some maximum allowable expenditure on resources.[6] Continuing

[6] The concept of isocost curves is analogous to the concept of lines of attainable combinations (Chapter 4). The only difference is that isocost curves deal with the resource combinations which a firm can purchase, whereas lines of attainable combinations relate to a consumer's ability to purchase goods and services.

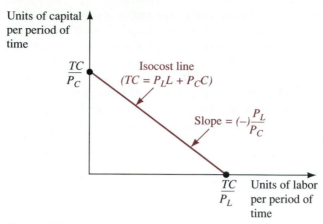

Figure 7-6
Isocost curve

BASIC CONCEPT
An isocost curve represents all combination of resource inputs that can be purchased for a fixed dollar outlay, given prevailing input prices.

our assumption of only two inputs, capital and labor, let the price of labor be P_L, the price of capital be P_C, and the stipulated amount of expenditure on resources be TC (total cost). The firm's expenditure for labor equals the price of a unit of labor (P_L) times the amount of labor purchased (L) or $P_L \cdot L$; similarly, the firm's expenditure for capital is $P_C \cdot C$. With only two resource inputs to choose from, the sum of the firm's expenditures for labor and capital must be equal to or less than the maximum allowable expenditure (TC). Thus, the expression defining the isocost curve may be written as

$$P_L L + P_C C = TC.$$

Provided that P_L and P_C are unaffected by the quantity of labor and capital purchased, if the firm elects to spend all its cost outlay (TC) for labor, a maximum of TC/P_L units can be employed; if the firm elects to spend all its cost outlay for capital, a maximum of TC/P_C can be bought.[7] A straight line joining TC/P_C and TC/P_L shows all the combinations of capital and labor obtainable from an expenditure of TC dollars. Figure 7-6 illustrates such an isocost curve. The slope of the isocost curve can be derived from points TC/P_C and TC/P_L. Between these two points, the

$$\text{slope of isocost curve} = \frac{(-)TC/P_C}{TC/P_L} = -\frac{TC}{P_C} \cdot \frac{P_L}{TC} = (-)\frac{P_L}{P_C}.$$

THE OPTIMUM MIX OF RESOURCE INPUTS

A firm's basic production efficiency objective is to realize the greatest amount of output from the total cost outlay for resource inputs. In terms of isoquant-isocost analysis this means getting to the highest isoquant permitted by the firm's isocost curve. In Figure 7-7, the output rate corresponding to

---

[7] Resource prices need not remain constant irrespective of the amounts purchased of labor and capital. A large employer in a tight labor market may have to raise wage rates to attract and hire more labor. A large purchaser of capital goods may be able to squeeze price concessions from suppliers of capital goods as the firm's usage of capital increases. Likewise, quantity discounts may be received on raw material purchases. When the prices of resource inputs fall as the amounts purchased go up, the isocost curve is bowed in toward the origin. In the event that resource prices rise as their levels of usage are increased, the isocost curve is bowed out from the origin.

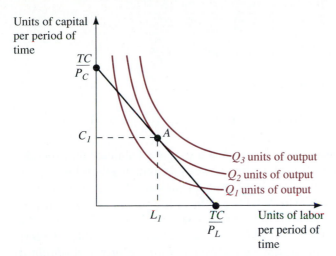

Figure 7-7
Determining the least-cost resource combination

isoquant Q_2 is the highest output which can be attained given an outlay of TC dollars and prices P_L and P_C. Accordingly, the optimum combination of resource inputs for producing output Q_2 is C_1 units of capital and L_1 units of labor. From a slightly different viewpoint, this resource combination may also be designated as the ***least-cost resource combination***, since it represents the minimum cost of producing Q_2 units of output when the prices of capital and labor are P_C and P_L, respectively. In other words, the point of tangency between the isocost and isoquant curves defines the optimum resource combination, whether interest centers upon (1) finding the maximum output for a given total cost outlay and at given resource prices or (2) finding the minimum cost for producing a given output at given resource prices.

> The most cost-efficient resource combination is defined by the point of tangency between the isocost and isoquant curves.

If capital symbolizes fixed input and labor symbolizes variable input, then the mix of capital and labor at the least-cost resource combination in Figure 7-7 defines the most cost-efficient combination of fixed and variable input for producing Q_2 units of output. This proportion is optimum because, given the prices of the two inputs, no other combination of fixed (capital) and variable (labor) input yields Q_2 units as cheaply—hence the term *least-cost resource combination*.

The Conditions for Optimizing the Resource Mix.   There are two conditions associated with the least-cost combination of labor and capital inputs. First, the optimum resource combination of capital and labor lies *on* the isocost line rather than inside it. In effect, a firm must fully utilize its available dollars in purchasing inputs if it is to maximize output. Translated into the language of mathematics, we can say that optimization requires

$$P_L L + P_C C = TC.$$

Second, at the point of tangency between the isocost line and the maximum attainable isoquant, the slope of the isocost line is equal to the slope of the isoquant. From prior discussions the

$$\text{slope of the isoquant} = MRTS_{LC} = (-)\frac{MP_L}{MP_C}$$

PRODUCTION PRINCIPLE

Least-cost production efficiency requires a firm to allocate its expenditures for any pair of resource inputs so that their marginal rate of technical substitution equals the ratio of their prices.

and the

$$\text{slope of the isocost line} = (-)\frac{P_L}{P_C}.$$

Since the slopes are equal, we may write

$$MRTS_{LC} = (-)\frac{P_L}{P_C},$$

which states that to optimize the resource mix a firm must allocate its expenditures so that the marginal rate of technical substitution of labor for capital equals the ratio of the price of labor to the price of capital. The interpretation of this result is straightforward. The $MRTS_{LC}$ defines the *rate* at which a firm is *technically able* to substitute labor for capital. The price ratio P_L/P_C shows the *rate* at which a firm is *economically able* to substitute labor for capital. *Unless the two rates are equivalent, a firm can alter its resource mix and obtain a larger output or else reduce its costs for a given output.* For example, suppose that $MRTS_{LC} = -\frac{1}{2}$, meaning that a firm is technically able to substitute 2 units of labor input for 1 unit of capital input without changing output. If $P_L = \$10$ and $P_C = \$30$, then a firm is economically able to give up 1 unit of capital in return for 3 units of labor. Giving up 1 unit of capital releases $30, of which only $20 is needed for purchasing labor, since 2 units of labor at $10 each will compensate for a 1-unit reduction in capital input. The remaining $10 can be applied to the purchase of additional resources for increasing output or else to reducing the total costs of the current output rate. In either event the firm will be better off. In general terms, therefore, *optimizing the input combination requires equality between the marginal rate of technical substitution for any pair of resource inputs and the ratio of their prices*; in the absence of equality some substitution of one resource for another can be initiated to increase output, or else expenditures on resource inputs can be reduced.

However, we can approach this second condition for optimizing the resource mix from another angle. Now only is the slope of the isoquant equal to MRTS at any point, but it is also equal to the ratio of the marginal products of the resource inputs:

$$MRTS_{LC} = (-)\frac{MP_L}{MP_C}.$$

Thus, we may rewrite the second condition for optimizing the resource combination as

$$(-)\frac{MP_L}{MP_C} = (-)\frac{P_L}{P_C}.$$

This equation states that *the firm's total cost outlay should be allocated among labor and capital so as to equate the ratio of their marginal products with the ratio of their prices.* Transforming the latter equation still further by cross-multiplying, we get

$$P_L \cdot MP_C = P_C \cdot MP_L.$$

Dividing both sides by $P_L \cdot P_C$ gives

$$\frac{P_L \cdot MP_C}{P_L \cdot P_C} = \frac{P_C \cdot MP_L}{P_L \cdot P_C},$$

which reduces to

$$\frac{MP_C}{P_C} = \frac{MP_L}{P_L}.$$

The latter expression says that *a firm should arrange its input purchases so as to obtain an equivalent amount of additional output from the last dollar spent on each input.* When the extra outputs per dollar spent on the last unit of each resource are unequal, the quantity of output can be increased (or total costs reduced) by diminishing expenditures where the marginal product per dollar spent is less and by enlarging expenditures where the marginal product per dollar spent is greater. For example, if

MP_L = 42 units output for the last unit of labor purchased,
P_L = \$7 per unit,
MP_C = 80 units of output for the last unit of capital purchased,
P_C = \$10,

then

$$\frac{MP_L}{P_L} = \frac{42 \text{ units}}{\$7} = 6 \text{ units of output/\$ spent on labor}$$

and

$$\frac{MP_C}{P_C} = \frac{80 \text{ units}}{\$10} = 8 \text{ units of output/\$ spent on capital.}$$

The firm is realizing more extra output per dollar spent on the last unit of capital than on the last unit of labor. This situation calls for (1) reallocating dollars away from the purchase of labor, thereby raising MP_L and increasing the output per dollar spent on labor, and (2) spending more dollars on the purchase of capital, thereby decreasing MP_C and decreasing the output per dollar spent on capital. Substituting capital for labor will tend to equalize the ratios MP_L/P_L and MP_C/P_C.

When There Are More Than Two Resource Inputs. The preceding conclusions are easily expanded for cases where more than two distinct kinds of resource inputs are used in a production process. In the event that a production process requires multiple types of resource inputs $(X_a, X_b, X_c, \ldots, X_n)$ obtainable at prices $(P_{X_a}, P_{X_b}, P_{X_c}, \ldots, P_{X_n})$, the optimal mix of resource inputs is attained by meeting the following two conditions:

$$P_{X_a}X_a + P_{X_b}X_b + P_{X_c}X_c + \cdots + P_{X_n}X_n = TC, \qquad (1)$$

$$\frac{MP_{X_a}}{P_{X_a}} = \frac{MP_{X_b}}{P_{X_b}} = \cdots = \frac{MP_{X_n}}{P_{X_n}}. \qquad (2)$$

THE EXPANSION PATH

It is not likely that a firm will maintain its output at the same rate for long. Market conditions change frequently and cause firms to adjust output rates accordingly. For this reason, the firm has an interest in knowing the least-cost resource combinations for several rates of output. Especially pertinent is the issue of how much more of each input to use should market conditions warrant a long-term expansion or contraction of output.

Consider Figure 7-8, where inputs of C_1 units of capital and L_1 units of labor are being used to produce an output of Q_1 units at a total cost of TC_1

PRODUCTION PRINCIPLE
Least-cost production efficiency requires a firm to allocate its expenditures for resource inputs so as to obtain an equivalent amount of additional output from the last dollar spent on each input.

The expansion path identifies a firm's least-cost resource combination for each possible output rate, assuming input prices remain constant.

MATHEMATICAL CAPSULE 10

DETERMINATION OF THE OPTIMUM RESOURCE COMBINATION

Let P_L and P_C be the prices of units of labor (L) and capital (C); let TC symbolize the budget a firm has available for purchasing the two resource inputs; and let $Q = f(L, C)$ represent the firm's production function for a commodity. The issue is how to best allocate the available dollars (TC) among purchases of labor and capital input so as to maximize the quantity of output (Q) subject to the constraint that the total expenditures on inputs just exhaust TC. More formally, what values of L and C will cause $Q = f(L, C)$ to be maximum, yet just meet the constraint that

$$TC - P_L L - P_C C = 0?$$

The mathematical solution requires using the Lagrangian multiplier method of finding the maximum value of a function. A new function is generated that combines the production function to be maximized with the constraint to be met. To keep the solution determinate (as many equations as there are unknowns), an artificial unknown, called a Lagrange multiplier and symbolized by λ, is introduced into the new function, giving

$$Z = f(L, C) + \lambda(TC - P_L L - P_C C).$$

Note that the constraint has been expressed in such a way that it is satisfied when $TC - P_L L - P_C C = 0$. Next, the partial derivatives of Z are found for each variable and equated to zero to establish the first-order conditions:

$$\frac{\partial Z}{\partial L} = \frac{\partial Q}{\partial L} - \lambda P_L = 0,$$

$$\frac{\partial Z}{\partial C} = \frac{\partial Q}{\partial C} - \lambda P_C = 0,$$

$$\frac{\partial Z}{\partial \lambda} = TC - P_L L - P_C C = 0.$$

These three equations are then solved simultaneously to determine the combination of L and C which will maximize the quantity of output subject to the cost constraint.

As an example of the foregoing, suppose that the production function is

$$Q = 20L + 65C - 0.5L^2 - 0.5C^2$$

and that $TC = \$2200$, $P_L = \$20$ per unit, and $P_C = \$50$ per unit. To find the maximum output obtainable from an expenditure of $2200, we generate the function

$$Z = 20L + 65C - 0.5L^2 - 0.5C^2$$
$$+ \lambda(2200 - 20L - 50C).$$

Finding the partial derivatives of Z and setting them equal to zero, we have

$$\frac{\partial Z}{\partial L} = 20 - L - 20\lambda = 0,$$

$$\frac{\partial Z}{\partial C} = 65 - C - 50\lambda = 0,$$

$$\frac{\partial Z}{\partial \lambda} = 2200 - 20L - 50C = 0.$$

Solving these three equations simultaneously gives $L = 10$, $C = 40$, and a maximum Q of 1950 units.

EXERCISE

1. Determine the optimum resource combination of labor and capital when

   (a) $Q = 140L + 160C - 5L^2 - 2C^2$,
   $P_L = \$12$,
   $P_C = \$24$,
   $TC = \$732$.

   (b) $Q = 6LC$,
   $P_L = \$5$,
   $P_C = \$10$,
   $TC = \$180$.

dollars. Now suppose that the firm wishes to expand output to Q_2 units per period of time. Clearly, a greater total cost outlay is required. Assuming that the prices of capital and labor remain constant at P_{L_1} and P_{C_1}, an increase in the expenditure level for resource inputs will shift the isocost curve outward *parallel* to itself. Thus, an outlay of TC_2 dollars using C_2 units of capital and L_2 units of labor represents the least possible cost of producing output Q_2. Similarly, an outlay of TC_3 dollars with inputs of C_3 units of capital and L_3 units of labor is the least possible cost of producing Q_3 units of output. The line joining these and all other least-cost resource combinations is called the **expansion path** of the firm. *The expansion path shows the locus of optimum input combinations for each possible rate of output when the prices of the resource inputs remain constant.*

The shape of the expansion path for labor and capital has a certain amount of economic significance. It is probable that increasing the output of most commodities over the long run entails a technological and economic bias

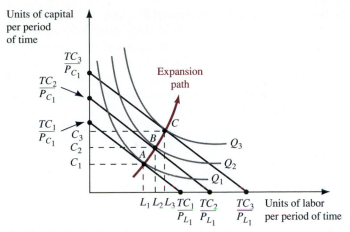

Figure 7-8

Determining the optimum resource combination for various output rates

toward using relatively more capital than labor, meaning the expansion path is as shown in Figure 7-9(a). Support for this stems from the readily observable tendency of large firms to use a more capital-intensive production recipe than do smaller firms producing the same item—presumably because it is almost always more efficient than labor-intensive production techniques. Occasionally, the expansion path may be linear or very nearly so [Figure 7-9(b)]. A linear expansion path for a product implies that the costs of additional output are minimized by using more of both inputs *in the same proportion* as before, perhaps because technological requirements call for a constant ratio between inputs. In rare cases the expansion path could assume the shape of that in Figure 7-9(c), where maximum efficiency-minimum cost requires using relatively more labor than capital to expand total output.

  If we think of capital as the proxy for fixed inputs and labor as the proxy for variable inputs, then the expansion path shows the least-cost combinations of fixed and variable inputs that the firm should use as it expands its *long-run* rate of output. But in the short run the firm has no alternative to

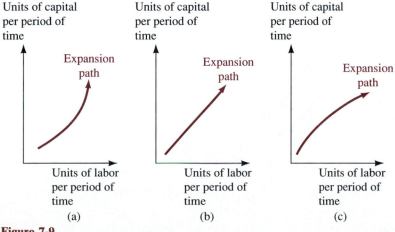

Figure 7-9

Alternative shapes for the expansion path

adjusting output rates by using more or less variable input with the given amount of fixed input. To minimize costs in the short run a firm should alter its usage of variable resources so as to keep the ratios of the marginal products per dollar spent on variable inputs equivalent. In other words, if *in the short run* a firm uses four *variable* inputs (X_a, X_b, X_c, and X_d), even though the fixed inputs cannot be changed, then optimal resource usage entails adjusting *variable* input combinations such that

$$\frac{MP_{X_a}}{P_{X_a}} = \frac{MP_{X_b}}{P_{X_b}} = \frac{MP_{X_c}}{P_{X_c}} = \frac{MP_{X_d}}{P_{X_d}}.$$

THE IMPACT OF CHANGES IN RESOURCE PRICES

The prices of resource inputs, as with the prices of goods and services, are subject to change. When they do change, least-cost production efficiency is achieved with a different input combination. Suppose we examine the effect of an increase in the price of labor upon the optimum mix of capital and labor.

Given the price of labor P_{L_1}, the price of capital P_{C_1}, and the firm's total cost outlay TC_1, the firm will optimize its inputs at an output of Q_1 by combining L_1 units of labor with C_1 units of capital, as shown by point A in Figure 7-10. If the price of labor rises to P_{L_2}, then the isocost curve pivots to the left about point TC_1/P_{C_1} and restricts the maximum usage of labor to TC_1/P_{L_2} units (were the entire total cost outlay used to buy labor). The new isocost curve will necessarily be tangent to a lower isoquant than previously and it will not be possible to produce Q_1 units of output with an expenditure of TC_1 dollars. The optimum input mix becomes L_2 units of labor and C_2 units of capital (point B in Figure 7-10) at an output of Q_0 units. The firm must choose between being content with a lower output (Q_0) or else increasing TC to permit maintenance of output at Q_1. If the latter alternative is chosen and assuming the input of capital

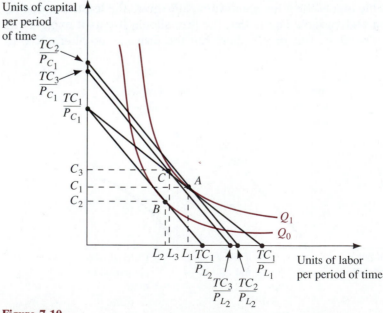

Figure 7-10

Adjusting to changes in resource prices

is fixed *in the short run* at C_1 units (as can be the case in the real world), then the firm will find it most advantageous *in the short run* to continue to produce Q_1 units of output by using C_1 units of capital and L_1 units of labor (point A). Why? Because when the firm's capital input is fixed at C_1 units, the *smallest* amount of labor that can be used to produce an output of Q_1 units is L_1 units of labor. An examination of Figure 7-10 verifies this statement. Consequently, *in the short run* point A represents the least cost of producing Q_1 units when no more than C_1 units of capital are available, despite the fact that the price of labor has risen from P_{L_1} to P_{L_2}. But, since the price of labor has gone up, it is clear that the cost of producing Q_1 units of output must be greater than TC_1. The higher cost can be illustrated graphically by drawing a new isocost line with a slope of P_{L_2}/P_{C_1} (so as to reflect the new ratio of resource prices) through point A. The extreme points of this isocost line are TC_2/P_{C_1} and TC_2/P_{L_2}, where $P_{L_2} > P_{L_1}$ and $TC_2 > TC_1$. *In the short run*, therefore, the fixed aspect of capital input may cause the firm to leave its input combination unchanged in response to an increase in the price of labor, provided it elects to continue to produce Q_1 units and provided it can afford to increase its expenditures on resource inputs from TC_1 to TC_2.

However, *in the long run* the firm has incentive to change its usage of capital and labor in response to the higher price of labor. As soon as time and money permit, the firm will be induced to produce Q_1 units of output by shifting from point A to point C in Figure 7-10. Point C is determined by finding the point of tangency between isoquant Q_1 and an isocost line with a slope of P_{L_2}/P_{C_1}; this isocost line is parallel to the isocost line defined by extreme points TC_2/P_{C_1} and TC_2/P_{L_2}, because both lines reflect the resource inputs obtainable when the price of labor is P_{L_2} and the price of capital is P_{C_1}. The shift in the optimum resource mix from point A to point C will reduce the costs of producing Q_1 units of output from TC_2 to TC_3, an amount which is indicated graphically by the distance between the isocost line defined by extreme points TC_3/P_{C_1} and TC_3/P_{L_2} and the isocost line defined by extreme points TC_2/P_{C_1} and TC_2/P_{L_2}.

Thus, *in the long run an increase in the price of labor relative to the price of capital will induce the firm to substitute capital for labor.* The logic of such action is compelling. Whenever a resource becomes more expensive, it makes sense to use less of it and more of other less expensive inputs. This is precisely what many firms have proceeded to do. In manufacturing, for example, as unions and other wage-increasing forces have combined to drive up the relative price of labor, firms have put forth a concerted effort to substitute capital for labor. High labor costs are, in fact, a major motive for introducing automated production processes. Substitution of capital for labor is most evident in the steel, coal-mining, chemical, petroleum, automobile, aluminum, and pulp and paper industries, as well as in the use of computers to perform tasks formerly handled by white-collar employees.

However, the degree to which firms have substituted capital for labor has been obscured somewhat by growing output rates. Suppose that a firm simultaneously experiences a rise in the price it must pay for labor inputs and an increase in the demand for its product. As just explained, the increase in the price of labor, given the price of capital, will eventually precipitate a substitution of capital for labor. This result is shown in Figure 7-11 as the movement from point A to point C. But should the increase in demand for the firm's product dictate a change in output from Q_1 to Q_2 units, then the firm will find it advantageous to shift from the input mix at point C to the input mix at point D.

PRODUCTION PRINCIPLE
When the price of one or more inputs rises, a firm may be trapped in the short run by the constraint of its fixed inputs into not altering its input mix and simply paying out more dollars to cover the higher input prices.

But in the long run, a firm has cost-saving incentive to substitute inputs that have gone up in price for inputs that are more cost-effective.

Rising demand for a firm's product dampens the incentive to cut back on the usage of inputs that have become relatively more expensive.

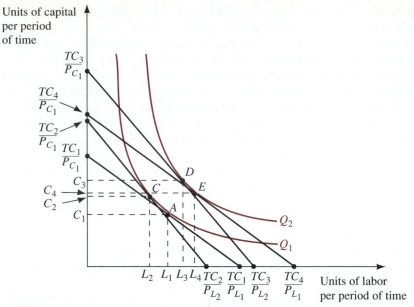

Figure 7-11
Effect of simultaneous changes in resource and output rates upon the optimum resource combination

The movement from point C to point D ultimately calls for using both more capital and more labor than originally. In this case, the labor-increasing effect of raising the firm's output rate more than offsets the labor-decreasing effect of the rise in the price of labor input. But had the price of labor input not risen, the firm would have preferred to use L_4 units of labor instead of L_3 units to produce Q_2 units of output. Thus, the increase in the price of labor input served to restrict the use of labor and caused the firm to select a more capital-intensive production technology (point D) than it otherwise would have selected (point E).

Insofar as an entire economy is concerned, rising consumer demand is essential to keeping unemployment rates from rising to prohibitive levels as business enterprises shift to more capital-intensive production technologies. Nonetheless, *the net effect of increases in labor input prices is still to restrict the growth of employment opportunities to less than what would be realized if rising wages did not further increase the propensity of firms to substitute capital for labor*. Fortunately, in the United States the demand for goods and services has usually grown fast enough to override much of the labor-decreasing effect of automation and technological change.

RETURNS TO SCALE

BASIC CONCEPT
Returns to scale concern whether the productive efficiency of resource inputs rises, falls, or remains unchanged when the usage of all inputs is increased in the same proportion.

Up to now, the principles of production have been examined primarily from a short-run point of view, where a portion of the firm's resource inputs are fixed. The concept of *returns to scale* deals with production relationships over a time span sufficiently long to allow changes in any and all inputs, especially those inputs such as plant space, major pieces of capital equipment, and managerial capability, which are typically fixed in the short run.

Consider a firm using L units of labor in combination with C units of capital to obtain an output of Q units. Then

$$L + C \rightarrow Q.$$

Now suppose that the amounts of both labor and capital are increased by some arbitrary proportion a. Plainly, output will rise; the question is by what proportion. Suppose that we design the proportion by which output increases as b. Then

$$aL + aC \rightarrow bQ.$$

1. When the change in output is *more than proportional* to the change in input ($b > a$), **increasing returns to scale** are said to prevail. For example, if the inputs of capital and labor are increased by 20% per period of time, and output rises by 30%, increasing returns to scale are present.

2. When the change in output is equal to the proportional change in input ($b = a$), **constant returns to scale** are present. In this case a doubling of the inputs of both capital and labor per period of time leads to a doubling of the number of units produced.

3. When the change in output is *less than proportional* to the change in input ($b < a$), the firm experiences **decreasing returns to scale**. An illustration of decreasing returns to scale would be where inputs are increased by 40% but output rises by only 30%.

Factors Contributing to Increasing Returns to Scale.   Five factors combine to produce increasing returns to scale for a firm. The most pervasive of these five factors originates with opportunities for specializing in the use of labor as a firm's scale of operations is increased. The gains in efficiency from specialized use of production-type labor are well chronicled.[8] In overly small-scale operations the typical employee often has to perform several different and perhaps diverse tasks, making it difficult to attain a high degree of proficiency

PRODUCTION PRINCIPLE
As a firm's scale of operation grows bigger, new avenues open up for utilizing labor inputs more efficiently.

---

[8] The productive powers of specialized use of labor are amply illustrated in a famous passage from Adam Smith's *The Wealth of Nations*, written over 200 years ago: "To take an example . . . from a very trifling manufacture; but one in which the division of labor has been very often taken notice of, the trade of the pinmaker; a workman not educated to this business (which the division of labour has rendered a distinct trade), nor acquainted with the use of the machinery employed in it (to the invention of which the same division of labour has probably given occasion), could scarce, perhaps, with utmost industry, make one pin in a day, and certainly could not make twenty. But in the way in which this business is now carried on, not only the whole work is a peculiar trade, but it is divided into a number of branches, of which the greatest part are likewise peculiar trades. One man draws out the wire, another straights it, a third cuts it, a fourth points it, a fifth grinds it at the top for receiving the head; to make the head requires two or three distinct operations; to put it on, is a peculiar business, to whiten the pins is another; it is even a trade by itself to put them into the paper; and the important business of making a pin is, in this manner, divided into about eighteen distinct operations, which in some manufactories, are all performed by distinct hands, though in others the same man will sometimes perform two or three of them. I have seen a small manufactory of this kind where ten men only were employed, and where some of them consequently performed two or three distinct operations. But though they were very poor, and therefore but indifferently accommodated with the necessary machinery, they could, when they exerted themselves, make among them about twelve pounds of pins in a day. There are in a pound upwards of four thousand pins of a middling size. Those ten persons, therefore, could make among them upwards of forty-eight thousand pins in a day. Each person, therefore, making a tenth part of forty-eight thousand pins, might be considered as making four thousand eight hundred pins in a day. But if they had all wrought separately and independently, and without any of them having been educated to this peculiar business, they certainly could not each of them have made twenty, perhaps not one pin in a day; that is, certainly, not the two hundred and fortieth, perhaps not the four thousand eight hundredth part of what they are at present capable of performing, in consequence of a proper division and combination of their different operations."

at each one. Mediocre performance of some tasks, with an attendant loss of efficiency, is almost unavoidable; in addition, time is lost in changing from task to task. As scale increases, however, it becomes feasible to assign workers to tasks for which they are particularly adept. In concentrating upon a single, well-defined task, people tend to develop greater speed and accuracy—plus they are better at identifying shortcuts and ways for improvement. Time lost in switching from task to task is eliminated. Also, the costs of training individual workers may be reduced by increased specialization. However, specialization in the use of labor can be carried so far that the monotony of performing a simpler and simpler task becomes excessively fatiguing and mindless, and efficiency gains are neutralized. Hence, firms must be alert to dividing up work tasks in ways that do not end up undercutting the benefits of labor specialization.

PRODUCTION PRINCIPLE
Larger-scale production operations can be more efficient than smaller-scale operations because of the ability to utilize advanced technologies and high-speed, automated equipment.

Second, the larger the scale of production, the greater the feasibility of utilizing the most advanced technology and high-speed, automated equipment.[9] Frequently, the most efficient recipe from a technological point of view involves capital-intensive mass-production methods. Small enterprises cannot justify using production technologies that require large outputs to be cost effective. Thus, small-scale operations often must rely upon "less-advanced" machinery and equipment lacking the speed of the equipment used in larger-sized production units. Not only can larger-scale enterprises employ efficient mass-production technologies, but they also have more organizational ability to capture efficiencies associated with shipping, distributing, and marketing larger volumes of output.

Purely dimensional factors are a third reason for increasing returns to scale. Doubling the diameter of a natural-gas pipeline can more than double the flow through it. A 100-watt light bulb does not require $2\frac{1}{2}$ times as much labor and materials as a 40-watt light bulb. Doubling the labor and materials in a motor can easily more than double the horsepower of the motor. To build and operate a paper plant capable of producing 5000 tons of paper products per week does not require 5 times as much labor, managerial talent, equipment, and building space as a paper plant capable of producing only 1000 tons per week. In a somewhat related fashion, tripling the rate of output of an assembly line may require only one additional inspector instead of two; a diesel locomotive may have sufficient power to pull 50 freight cars as adequately as 20; and a bookseller may be able to sell books in both economics and business administration subjects as well as just those in economics with less than a proportional increase in time, effort, and cost.

Fourth, *since technologically complex production processes require several major pieces of equipment, the scale of production may have to be large to overcome potential bottlenecks in the process*. Suppose two machines, A and B, are required for packaging a product, machine A being used to fill the package with the proper amount of the product and machine B being used to wrap the package in cellophane. If machine A can fill 15,000 packages per day and machine B can wrap 20,000 packages per day, then at an output of 60,000 units per day, where four type A machines and three type B machines are used, both types of machines can be efficiently utilized. At less than 60,000 units of output full utilization of both machine types is not possible, and some amount of idle capacity will be present.

_____
[9] M. A. Adelman found that employment among the 200 largest firms was about 60% more capital intensive than in the economy as a whole. See M. A. Adelman, "The Measurement of Industrial Concentration," *Review of Economics and Statistics*, Vol. 33, No. 4 (November 1951), p. 278.

APPLICATIONS CAPSULE

HENRY FORD, THE MODEL T, AND THE BENEFITS OF SPECIALIZATION

"The way to make automobiles," Henry Ford once observed, "is to make one automobile like another automobile; just as one pin is like another pin, or one match is like another match when it comes from a match factory." By 1910 Henry Ford was convinced that this vision of car manufacturing was what it would take to make cars both better and cheaper. Toward this end, Henry Ford began to figure out how to break away from garage-shop car-making, where a small team of skilled crafts-people built a whole car, obtaining some components from outside suppliers but making most of the main parts (engine, transmission, frame) themselves and doing all of the assembly.

The approach that Henry Ford and his managers eventually came up with was to introduce techniques that broke each major car-making function down into smaller and smaller pieces, so that the production of each part could be mechanized (using semiskilled workers instead of craftspeople) and speeded up. Next, the production of each unit was organized so that it would mesh directly into the subsequent production phase. What Ford envisioned was a continuous, mechanized process that flowed like a group of tributaries into a main river, with the production of each component merging piece by piece to produce an ever-more-assembled car.

The first area where labor specialization and assembly line production were tried was the magneto coil. In the earliest car factories, one skilled worker made a flywheel magneto from start to finish; a good employee could make 35 to 40 a day. Ford felt that while this was better than the garage-shop approach, it was still too inefficient, and he urged greater use of the principles of labor specialization being advocated by Frederick W. Taylor, the father of time-and-motion studies and scientific industrial management. Ford managers responded by dividing magneto production into 29 different operations performed by 29 different workers, in the process cutting production time for a magneto from 20 minutes to 13 minutes. The same labor specialization rationale was quickly extended to the production and assembly of motors and transmissions.

By the summer of 1913, the company had streamlined everything but the final assembly process, a task then being done by several workers moving as quickly as they could around a stationary chassis, putting on parts and components until the car was complete. Charles Sorensen, who had become one of Ford's top production people, got the idea of pulling a Model T chassis slowly across 250 feet of factory floor while six workers, picking up parts from carefully spaced piles on the floor, fitted them to the chassis. Thus was born the moving assembly line, where the product gradually took shape as it moved down the line through workstation after workstation. Before it had taken some 13 hours to assemble a car; with Sorensen's moving-assembly "innovation," the time was cut to 5 hours 50 minutes. Not satisfied, Ford's managers pushed harder for more productivity, lengthening the line, increasing the number of workstations, and simplifying the tasks done by each worker. Within weeks, the final assembly time was down to 2 hours 38 minutes. Six months later, Ford installed the first automatic conveyor belt (fashioned after an overhead trolley that Chicago meatpackers employed to move beef). Within 2 months of that installation, the company could assemble a car in 93 minutes, a stunning reduction from the 728 hours it took in the days of garage-shop manufacture.

In 1914 the Ford Motor Company produced 268,000 cars with 13,000 employees; the other 299 American auto companies, with 66,350 employees, produced just 287,000 cars. With the benefit of its dramatic productivity gains, Ford was able to reduce the price of its Model T from $780 in 1910–11 to $690 in 1912, then to $600, to $550, and in 1914–15 to $360. With such sharp cuts in prices, sales of the Model T took off, and it became a best-seller, cheap enough for families of modest means and a provider of reliable transportation as well.

Source: Based on information in David Halberstam, *The Reckoning* (New York: Avon Books, 1986), pp. 70–74.

And, finally, *as its size increases a firm can afford to employ management specialists, thereby realizing the benefits to be gained from a specialized use of managerial talents* (just as from a specialized use of labor). The added presence of management specialists can give larger firms an edge in managerial efficiency over smaller firms whose managers, being fewer in number, must spread their time over a wider range of problems. In fact, a large firm may find that one of its strongest competitive weapons is its superior number of people and its potential for specializing its personnel more deeply.[10]

PRODUCTION PRINCIPLE
Large-scale production can be more efficient than small-scale production because of opportunities for greater management specialization.

[10] Alfred D. Chandler, Jr., *Strategy and Structure* (New York: Doubleday, Anchor Books edition, 1966), pp. 126–27, 156–57, 195–96, 230, 256, 321–23, 369, 382–83; Oliver E. Williamson, *Corporate Control and Business Behavior* (Englewood Cliffs, N.J.: Prentice Hall, 1970), Chapters 7 and 8; Jay R. Galbraith, "Matrix Organizational Designs," *Business Horizons*, Vol. 14, No. 1 (February 1971), pp. 29–40; Peter F. Drucker, *Management: Tasks, Responsibilities, Practices* (New York: Harper & Row, 1974); Henry O. Armour and David J. Teece, "Organizational Structure and Economic Performance: A Test of the Multidivisional Hypothesis," *Bell Journal of Economics*, Vol. 9, No. 1 (Spring 1978), pp. 106–22.

In sum, there are good reasons why a firm can experience increasing returns to scale.

Factors Contributing to Constant Returns to Scale.   Increasing returns to scale cannot continue indefinitely; the factors responsible for obtaining output at rates more than proportional to the volumes of resource inputs will sooner or later be exhausted—and usually sooner. This is particularly true for the production unit of a firm—the plant. But constant returns to scale can prevail well beyond the point where the potential for increasing returns is exhausted. It is no secret in business that certain size plants are more efficient than others. Moreover, experts in technology and engineering can peg quite closely the most efficient plant size for producing a given product. It is then a simple matter for large-scale enterprises to build as many of these optimum-sized facilities as may be necessary to satisfy the firm's need for productive capacity for that product. For example, if the most efficient plant size is one capable of producing 100,000 units per year, a large firm selling 1 million units per year can realize constant returns to scale in producing this item by building 10 plants, each capable of producing 100,000 units. Where a firm produces

Even when the potential for increasing returns is exhausted, a firm can increase its size substantially without impairing input efficiency.

APPLICATIONS CAPSULE

FORD'S RIVER ROUGE PLANT: A CASE OF DECREASING RETURNS TO SCALE

One of the most dramatic examples of pushing a plant's scale of operations beyond a point of manageable size occurred in the 1920s when Ford Motor Company built a gigantic new manufacturing and assembly plant at River Rouge, outside Detroit. The River Rouge plant was intended to centralize at one site a broad spectrum of activities relating to automobile production. At this one facility Ford employed 75,000 workers producing coke, pig iron, steel, castings, forgings, and parts and components for cars and tractors, as well as assembly line activities. The plant occupied over 1000 acres and included 93 separate structures, 23 of which were main buildings. The site contained 93 miles of railroad tracks and 27 miles of conveyors. It took a maintenance force of nearly 5000 people to try to keep the plant clean; each year janitorial crews wore out 5000 mops and 3000 brooms and used 86 tons of cleaners on the floors and walls and on the 330 acres of windows.

It soon became evident that the size of the plant was well beyond the optimal point. According to some observers, the plant was so massive and complex that top-level plant managers had little contact with and understanding of what was happening from a plantwide perspective; lower-level managers were lost in the hubub of so many large and complex activities. The constant and unremitting tempo of the huge quantities of materials coming in and automobiles going out took its toll on both workers and management. According to a former Ford official:

Everybody was on edge. They ran around in circles and didn't know what they were doing. Physically everybody

was going like a steam engine but not so much mentally. As long as their feet were on the go they were working hard. The more a man ran around the better he was. . . . Officials had no offices—only desks in the open factory at which they stood. They couldn't keep records, and lower officials could not discuss their problems together.[a]

In the final analysis, sheer bigness was the undoing of the giant plant. The coming and going of a virtual army of workers, the incoming shipment of huge volumes of raw materials, the maze of manufacturing and assembly line activities, and the shipping out of thousands of cars—all going on at one centralized site—not only created enormous problems of congestion but became a nightmare to manage and operate.

Ford soon found that it was cheaper to ship parts and components for final assembly to scattered, decentralized plants than it was to try to centralize the manufacturing and assembling of cars at one site. Within a few years Ford Motor Company began establishing branch assembly plants and by 1928 had 35 in the United States alone. For many years now, most of the mighty industrial complex at River Rouge has been shut down; in recent years only the foundry has been in use.

[a] Allan Nevins and Ernest Hill, *Ford, Expansion and Challenge: 1915–1933* (New York: Charles Scribner's Sons, 1957), p. 296.

several products, it can organize itself into divisions and scale them to the most efficient size. In so doing a large firm may be able to realize constant returns to scale for an almost indefinitely large volume of output. And by centralizing purchasing, selling, and administrative activities under one management, it may even be possible to realize increasing returns from these latter inputs, making the firm's overall operations more efficient than that achievable by a smaller enterprise. Since the ability to decentralize into optimum-sized plants and product line divisions is restricted only by a firm's capacity to manage its operations, the range of output for which a firm can experience constant returns to scale in its production activities is quite large.

Factors Contributing to Decreasing Returns to Scale. The principal factor causing a firm to experience decreasing returns to scale is the limit to which the managerial function can be efficiently performed. As a firm becomes larger, the problems of integrating the many facets of its activities multiply. Decision-making is more complex, and the burdens of administration become disproportionately greater. Conventional wisdom insists that "diminishing returns" to management will be encountered as top management loses touch with the daily routine of operation and finds it increasingly necessary to delegate authority to lower-echelon managers whose level of competence may not be as great. Red tape and paperwork expand with size; bureaucratic procedures emerge, causing the managerial hierarchy of larger firms to be sluggish and unwieldy and allowing growing inefficiencies to creep in.

> **PRODUCTION PRINCIPLE**
> The principal cause of decreasing returns to scale is the limit on efficient performance of the managerial function as the firm's operating scale becomes larger and larger.

KEY POINTS

The relationships between the production function, average product, and marginal product can be used to define three stages of production. Stage I covers the range of variable input where AP_{vi} is rising; stage II includes the range where AP_{vi} is falling *and* where MP is declining yet positive; and stage III encompasses the range where MP is negative and total output is falling.

The optimum resource combination is in stage II at the input rate where (1) the firm is fully utilizing its dollars in purchasing inputs and (2) an equivalent amount of extra output is being obtained from the last dollar spent on each input. Graphically, this condition is achieved at the point of tangency between the isocost curve and an isoquant.

If the firm increases all its inputs by a given proportion and output increases by *more* than this proportion, increasing returns to scale prevail. If the firm increases all its inputs by a given proportion and output rises by the *same* proportion, constant returns to scale characterize the production process. If the firm increases all its inputs by the same proportion and output rises *less* than proportionally, decreasing returns to scale are present. Increasing returns to scale occur because of increased specialization in use of resources, technological considerations, dimensional factors, and indivisibility of inputs. Constant returns to scale arise when the production process embodies standard worker-machine ratios and when it is feasible to assimilate a number of optimum-sized production units under a single management. Decreasing returns to scale occur primarily because of limitations to efficient performance of the managerial function.

MATHEMATICAL CAPSULE 11

DETERMINING RETURNS TO SCALE FROM THE PRODUCTION FUNCTION

Suppose that a large, diversified enterprise carefully examines the input-output relationships for each of its three major products (X, Y, and Z) and concludes that the production functions for these products are

$$Q_X = 1.6L^{0.4}C^{0.4}M^{0.1},$$
$$Q_Y = \sqrt{0.4L^2CM},$$
$$Q_Z = 10L + 7C + M,$$

where Q represents output per period of time, L is units of labor input, C is units of capital input, and M is units of managerial input. The question immediately arises as to what returns to scale are encountered in manufacturing the three products. The answer can be determined by observing what happens to output when the inputs of labor, capital, and management are increased *in equal proportions*. The production function is "tested" by multiplying each input by a constant factor (say a) and ascertaining whether output changes (1) by an amount greater than a, in which case increasing returns to scale are signified; (2) by an amount equal to a, in which case constant returns to scale are signified; or (3) by an amount less than a, in which case decreasing returns to scale are indicated.

The returns to scale indicated by the production function for product X are found in the following manner. Multiplying each of the three inputs by a, where $a > 1$ so as to indicate an increase in the inputs, we obtain

$$1.6(aL)^{0.4}(aC)^{0.4}(aM)^{0.1},$$

which becomes

$$1.6a^{0.4}L^{0.4}a^{0.4}C^{0.4}a^{0.1}M^{0.1}.$$

Factoring a out of the function gives

$$a^{0.4+0.4+0.1}(1.6L^{0.4}C^{0.4}M^{0.1})$$

or

$$a^{0.9}(1.6L^{0.4}C^{0.4}M^{0.1}).$$

The expression in parentheses defines the level of output prior to the change in input, and $a^{0.9}$ represents the proportional change in the output product X when each input is increased by a. Because the exponent for a is less than 1, increasing the inputs by a results in a *less than proportional* increase in the output of X, and the production function for X may be said to exhibit decreasing returns to scale.

In the case of product Y, increasing each input by an arbitrary proportion a, where $a > 1$, yields

$$\sqrt{0.4(aL)^2(aC)(aM)}.$$

Simplifying this expression, we get

$$\sqrt{0.4a^2L^2aCaM} = \sqrt{0.4a^4L^2CM} = a^2\sqrt{0.4L^2CM}.$$

Hence, increasing each input by a causes output to expand by a^2—obviously, increasing returns to scale are present, since output expands at a rate more than proportionally compared to inputs in this hypothetical example. Suppose, originally, that $L = 5$, $C = 5$, and $M = 2$; then

$$Q_Y = \sqrt{0.4L^2CM}$$
$$= \sqrt{0.4(5)^2(5)(2)}$$
$$= \sqrt{100}$$
$$= 10.$$

If all the inputs are doubled ($a = 2$), we have $L = 10$, $C = 10$, $M = 4$, and

$$Q_Y = \sqrt{0.4(10)^2(10)(4)}$$
$$= \sqrt{1600}$$
$$= 40.$$

Consequently, doubling the inputs of labor, capital, and management causes the output of product Y to quadruple (since $a^2 = 4$ when $a = 2$), and increasing returns to scale may be said to characterize the production function for product Y.

PROBLEMS AND QUESTIONS FOR DISCUSSION

1. Graphically illustrate the stages of production for each of the following general types of production functions.

   (a) $Q = bX.$ **(b)** $Q = bX - cX^2.$ **(c)** $Q = bX + cX^2 - dX^3.$

2. The production department of the National Cabinet Corporation employs 20 unskilled laborers, 45 semiskilled workers, and 60 skilled craftspeople. A careful assessment of the productivity of the three types of labor indicates that the marginal product of an unskilled laborer is currently 10 units of output per worker-day, the marginal product of a semiskilled worker is 20 units per worker-day, and the marginal product of a skilled craftsperson is 50 units per worker-day. The wage rates for the three types of labor result in labor costs of $20 per worker-day for unskilled labor, $30 per worker-day for semiskilled workers, and $50 per worker-day for skilled craftspeople. Output is currently at the desired level. Would you suggest a change in the labor mix used by the production department? Why or why not?

Increasing the inputs by a for the production function for product Z gives

$$10(aL) + 7(aC) + aM,$$

or, more simply

$$a(10L + 7C + M).$$

Here output changes by the same proportion as input, so constant returns to scale are present.[a] Again, a simple example verifies existence of constant returns to scale for product Z. If $L = 15$, $C = 10$, and $M = 5$, then

$$\begin{aligned} Q_Z &= 10L + 7C + M \\ &= 10(15) + 7(10) + 5 \\ &= 225. \end{aligned}$$

Doubling the inputs ($a = 2$) so that $L = 30$, $C = 20$, and $M = 10$, we get

$$\begin{aligned} Q_Z &= 10(30) + 7(20) + 10 \\ &= 450. \end{aligned}$$

Therefore, doubling each input causes the output of product Z to double—a constant-returns-to-scale situation.

The character of the production functions for the three products X, Y, and Z provides a guide to management for choosing the products upon which to concentrate its limited resources. *Other things being equal*, cost and efficiency considerations call for steering resources (financial and otherwise) to those products with the most favorable returns to scale. The most favorable, of course, is increasing returns to scale, followed in order by constant returns and decreasing returns. Hence, products Y, Z, and X in that order yield the enterprise the greatest amounts of output for a given amount of input.

However, a word of qualification must be offered. Returns to scale in no way reflect the demand side of the picture. The mere fact that the ouptut of a commodity is characterized by decreasing returns to scale does not mean that it is unprofitable. The price which can be obtained for product X may be so favorable that it is relatively more profitable than either product Y or Z. In fact, the competitive forces prevailing in the markets for Y and Z could make those commodities unprofitable, even though they can be produced under very favorable conditions. Returns to scale indicate only the direction of change in productive efficiency and unit costs which can be anticipated if the size of the firm's production operations is increased or decreased. Also, the nature of the production function for a product can change over a period of time because of scientific and engineering developments, innovation, and advances in managerial technology. Thus, in the long run the production process for an item can be transformed from decreasing to constant or increasing returns to scale.

EXERCISE

1. Determine the returns to scale implied in each of the following production functions.
    (a) $Q = 0.4A^2 + 0.3AB + 2.0B$.
    (b) $Q = 0.7L^{.8}C^{.3}$.
    (c) $Q = 10 + 4A + 9B$.
    (d) $Q = (10/L) + 6C$.

[a] The mathematics of production functions is not always as neat and clear-cut as the three preceding cases might indicate. Consider the production function

$$Q = 16L + 0.5LCM + 1.4L^{0.5}C^{0.3}M^{0.1}.$$

Changing the inputs by a yields

$$16(aL) + 0.5(aL)(aC)(aM) + 1.4(aL)^{0.5}(aC)^{0.3}(aM)^{0.1},$$

which simplifies to

$$16aL + 0.5a^3LCM + 1.4a^{0.9}L^{0.5}C^{0.3}M^{0.1}.$$

Inspecting the foregoing expression term by term, we find that the first term ($16aL$) has the characteristic of constant returns to scale, the second term ($0.5a^3LCM$) has the characteristic of increasing returns to scale, and the third term ($1.4a^{0.9}L^{0.5}C^{0.3}M^{0.1}$) displays decreasing returns to scale. Whether the entire production function exhibits increasing, constant, or decreasing returns to scale on balance depends on the relative strengths of the three terms. In this instance the strong increasing returns influence found in the second term will overpower the mildly decreasing returns shown in the third term, with the result that the entire production function shows increasing returns to scale.

3. The Fashion Dress Corporation is considering the contruction of a new plant. Engineers have submitted the following possible plant designs—all of which are equally capable from a physical standpoint of producing the desired output of 1000 dresses per day:

Plant Design	Units of Capital	Units of Labor
1	50	500
2	75	400
3	150	200
4	250	100
5	350	50

(a) Illustrate the technically feasible production alternatives by means of an iso-quant.

(b) Suppose that the price of capital is $100 per unit and the price of labor is $50 per unit. Which plant design should be selected? Justify your answer with an isocost-isoquant graph.

(c) What will be the required total cost outlay for capital and labor for the selected plant design?

4. Suppose that Apex Manufacturing Corporation has its choice of three production processes for producing its product. With process A, Apex can produce 100 units of output per hour using 5 units of labor and 20 units of capital; by process B, 100 units per hour with 10 units each of labor and capital; by process C, 100 units per hour with 20 units of labor and 5 units of capital. All three processes are characterized by constant returns to scale.

(a) Graphically illustrate isoquants for outputs of 100, 200, and 300 units per hour.

(b) If the price of labor is $5 per unit and capital costs $10 per unit, which process should be selected to produce 200 units? *Illustrate* your answer by means of isoquant and isocost curves.

(c) If the price of labor is $8 per unit and the price of capital is $8 per unit, which process should be selected to produce 100 units per hour? Verify your answer with an isoquant-isocost graph.

(d) If the price of labor is $14 per unit and capital is $7 per unit, which process should be selected to produce 300 units per hour? What will be the necessary total cost outlay?

5. Jupiter Products, Inc., has derived the following production function for its operation: $Q = 0.65L^{0.42}C^{0.38}M^{0.20}Z^{0.08}$, where Q = units of output per period of time, L = hours of labor, C = hours of machine services, M = hours of managerial input, and Z = miscellaneous resource services.

(a) Assuming that Jupiter's operations are sufficiently flexible to vary the usage of L, C, M, and Z, what kind of returns are indicated by this production function? Why?

(b) What inference, if any, can you make about the firm's unit costs for producing additional units of output?

6. A diversification-minded company has employed a team of analysts to advise it on acquiring prospective enterprises. Four small firms, each producing the same commodity but employing radically different production technologies, are currently being carefully scrutinized for possible acquisition. The analytical team has initiated investigations of the production, marketing, and financial aspects of the four firms for the purpose of singling out one of them as the best candidate for acquisition. As part of their investigation they have sought to estimate the production functions for each of the four firms; their estimates are as follows:

Firm A: $Q_A = 0.8L^{0.6}C^{0.2}M^{0.1}$.

Firm B: $Q_B = \frac{7}{3}L + \frac{3}{2}C + M$.

Firm C: $Q_C = \sqrt{0.09L^{0.5}C^{1.0}M^{0.5}}$.

Firm D: $Q_D = 6L^2 + 7C^2 - LC + 0.1M^2$.

On the basis of these estimates alone, which of the four firms appears to offer the acquisitive company the best prospects? Why?

7. What is the difference between "returns to variable input" and "returns to scale"?

Chapter 8

Cost Analysis

The costs of goods and services derive from the technology and the inputs used to produce them. The analysis of cost behavior is therefore grounded in the principles of production. In this chapter we shall convert the relationships among production technology, input efficiency, input prices, and outputs into cost functions. After examining the multidimensional aspects of *cost*, short-run and long-run cost curves will be derived for a variety of possible production functions. The chapter concludes with a look at economies of scale and a new analytical tool called "strategic cost analysis."

DEFINING AND MEASURING COSTS

Mention of the word *cost* immediately conjures up the thought of "money outlays." In the context of business operations, costs are commonly viewed as a firm's actual or historical expenditures for resource inputs. However, the costs that really matter for business decisions are *future* costs; *historical* costs are useful primarily as bench marks for anticipating behavior and should be treated warily since changing input prices, efficiency changes, changing input supply conditions, new technologies, and so on can make past costs an obsolete indicator of the future.

To illustrate the many facets of cost, consider the apparently innocuous statement: "General Electric's cost of producing a refrigerator in 1991 was $450.24." The most obvious interpretation of this statement is that the cost incurred by General Electric (GE) in operating its refrigerator division amounted to an average of $450.24 in 1991. No doubt the basis for such a figure would be the historical expenses for resources bought outright or hired by GE and which were routinely recorded in its accounts according to GE's scheme of accounting practice. These explicitly incurred expenses might consist of production labor costs, payments for component parts purchased from suppliers, managerial salaries, interest costs, payments for electric power, transportation costs, sales force expenses, advertising, depreciation charges, administrative expenses, property taxes, and other miscellaneous payments.

Despite the apparent accuracy and completeness of including all actual operating expenses, the figure of $450.24 per refrigerator will in all probability not prove to be as definitive and all-inclusive as first appears. First, anyone familiar with the techniques of cost accounting is aware that two manufacturers of physically identical products who use different, but acceptable, methods of measuring cost could differ in their reported costs by 20% or more.[1] Historical cost statistics can thus be misleading unless one knows a great deal about the particular cost accounting system from which they are derived.

The reported costs of a product often do not include an allowance for the cost of equity capital supplied by the firm's owners.

Second, it is easy to overlook allowances for equity capital supplied by the firm's stockholders as being a valid cost element.[2] If a company borrows money from banks or other financial institutions, the interest costs are shown as an expense on the profit and loss statement; yet if the same funds are raised by selling new issues of common stock, no cost for capital is entered in the firm's ledger. Nonetheless, if stockholders fail to receive a return on their invested capital equivalent to what could be earned were they to invest their funds in the best alternative investment of equal risk, then they will understandably be reluctant to supply the enterprise with financial capital in the future. Thus, for GE to continue to use equity capital as a source of financing for its activities (including making refrigerators), in the long run GE must not only cover all actual operating expenses but also have enough revenue left over to reward stockholders with a return on their investment at least equivalent to stockholders' *opportunity costs*—the return GE's owners are sacrificing by not having invested in other ventures of comparable risk. GE must cover this opportunity cost of equity capital in order to induce continued stockholder participation and confidence in the firm's activities. These opportunity costs represent a minimum acceptable return to stockholders and are just as legitimate a cost of doing business as recorded operating expenses and interest costs on borrowed capital.

BASIC CONCEPT
One measure of an input's true economic cost is the benefits forgone or the sacrifice incurred by not having used the input in the next best alternative economic activity—such costs are termed opportunity costs.

Third, for some purposes the best measure of the true economic worth (cost) of a resource input may be the resource input's opportunity costs rather than the dollar outlays for the input appearing in historical accounting records. As before, we use the term *opportunity costs* to represent the *benefits* (monetary or otherwise) *forgone* or the *sacrifices incurred* by not having done something else. For example, the cost to GE of making its own compressors for use in GE refrigerators is in some very real way the price at which GE could sell these compressors to other firms were they not to use them in their own refrigerators. In periods of strong demand for GE products, the cost to GE of using available resources for refrigerator production is the profit GE gives up by not devoting these resources to the production of other GE appliances and products. The costs to GE of using valuable executive and managerial talents in refrigerator production are not just the related salaries but also the contribution to profits that these executives and managers could make by devoting their time to other GE activities. The cost of building a new $30 million plant to manufac-

---

[1] Cost differentials can "artificially" be produced by judiciously selecting among the following options for measuring a firm's costs: (1) using an accelerated depreciation schedule instead of the straight-line method; (2) using the first-in, first-out (FIFO) method of inventory valuation instead of the last-in, first-out (LIFO) method; (3) employing a direct costing system rather than a full-cost accounting system; (4) selecting any one of several acceptable rules for determining the time period to which certain kinds of expenses will be charged; and (5) using artificial transfer prices for intermediate goods passing from one operating division to another instead of open market transfer prices.

[2] In the case of entrepreneurial or owner-managed firms the cost of other owner-supplied resources may be overlooked. For example, the proprietor may elect not to pay himself a salary but instead rely upon "profits" as payment for his services. Such a practice clearly understates the operating costs of the enterprise, since the value of the managerial skills furnished by the proprietor is not included. Similarly, if no allowance is made for the costs of land and working capital supplied by the proprietor, total costs will be underestimated.

ture GE refrigerators is not just the interest that GE might have to pay on the borrowed money but rather the profits or cost savings that could be achieved by investing the $30 million in making dishwashers, steam turbines, numeric-controlled process equipment, longer-lasting light bulbs, or any other of GE's many products.[3] Opportunity costs are, therefore, a measure of the sacrifice incurred from a decision not to take advantage of an alternative opportunity; putting a dollar value on opportunity costs involves a comparison between the chosen course of action and the best alternative course of action.

Although calculating either the costs of equity capital or opportunity costs can be subjective, considering these two aspects of cost in conjunction with historical costs improves the accuracy of profit assessments. For instance, unless GE's revenues from the sale of refrigerators exceed both the historical and opportunity costs of refrigerator production, GE cannot be said to be truly earning a profit on refrigerators. Moreover, unless GE's return on its dollar investment in refrigerator production is at least equivalent to what it could earn by putting this investment in another activity, GE should discontinue refrigerator production and shift its resources into the better alternative. Thus, while the size of a firm's opportunity costs is difficult to determine, some estimate of their size is crucial to key decisions. In this regard it is better to have a rough estimate of the right concept of cost than an accurate estimate of the wrong concept.

Fourth, to view the concept of cost in exclusively monetary terms is to leave out a portion of what may rightfully be considered as cost. The *social costs* of noise, congestion, and environmental pollution attributable to a firm's production activities are not easily reduced to dollars and cents. Nor are *psychic costs* readily expressed in monetary terms; these involve the mental anguish and mental dissatisfaction associated with such activities as dismissing employees, moving one's family to accept a transfer to an undesirable location, working on holidays, pressures from one's boss for outstanding performance, and the monotony of repetitious tasks.[4] Plainly, social costs and psychic costs abound in many business situations, yet they never appear in an enterprise's financial accounts.

Social and psychic costs associated with a firm's productive activities are almost never fully reflected in a firm's cost accounts.

A thread common to all the many dimensions of cost can be summed up in the word **sacrifice**. *All costs entail a sacrifice of some type; the form of the sacrifice may be tangible or intangible, objective or subjective, monetary or nonmonetary.* For this reason, it is not always possible in many cases to reduce costs to simple dollars and cents, nor is it possible to arrive at a single, unambiguous, and universally acceptable way to calculate *the cost* of a product. To look further into why this is so, let's take the stated cost of $450.24 for producing a GE refrigerator and consider the following questions:

While every measure of cost entails some type of sacrifice, there is no single, unambiguous, and universally acceptable way to calculate the cost of a product.

---

[3] From a broader social viewpoint, the cost of producing a refrigerator can be thought of as the utility consumers forego from giving up the goods that could have been produced had not some of society's existing pool of economic resources been used to manufacture refrigerators. Resources used to produce refrigerators cannot be used to produce other things—items from which certain segments of society may derive great satisfaction. Thus, the cost to society of a GE refrigerator is not $450.24 but is the sacrifice of utility associated with not having more of some other item which GE or some other firm could have produced instead.

[4] Psychic costs are not unique to business enterprise, nor can they be lightly dismissed as inconsequential. For example, few students would question that they incur significant psychic costs from preparing for and taking final exams; nor would professors deny the existence of psychic costs in preparing and grading exams and in assigning final grades. The examination process is very painful indeed, and to ignore the psychic costs which it entails would probably mean omitting the greatest of the costs of administering examinations.

1. How much of the $450.24 represents costs directly related to the production of refrigerators (direct costs), and how much of the $450.24 represents costs not directly traceable to refrigerators [e.g., the chief executive's salary and other costs common to the production of several of GE's products (common costs)]?

2. How much of the $450.24 represents fixed charges associated with the plant, equipment, and management needed for refrigerator production (fixed costs), and how much is accounted for by direct production labor and raw materials (variable costs)?

3. To what extent would the $450.24 cost be altered by a 10% increase in GE's production of refrigerators (incremental costs)?

4. What portion of the $450.24 represents controllable costs (managerial bonuses), and what portion represents cuttable costs (such as using less advertising)?

5. How would a labor strike affect the costs of producing a refrigerator (shutdown costs and startup costs)?

6. To what extent can the $450.24 cost be expected to change in the long run (long-run versus short-run costs)?

7. How is the $450.24 cost of a refrigerator divided between materials costs, labor costs, maintenance costs, sales and service costs, fixed overhead and administrative costs, and interest costs?

8. How would the introduction of a completely automated assembly line alter the $450.24 cost?

9. What portion of the $450.24 could be postponed in the event of a decision to trim the costs of refrigerator production (postponable costs)?

10. How much of the $450.24 could be avoided if it became necessary to reduce refrigeration production by 20% (escapable versus unavoidable costs)?

These questions suffice to indicate that no one measure of the costs of production is adequate for decision-making purposes. Different decision problems call for different kinds of cost information. Depending on the purpose at hand, one may wish to determine total costs, average costs, marginal costs, fixed costs, variable costs, direct costs, common costs, historical costs, future costs, opportunity costs, controllable costs, shutdown costs, postponable costs, long-run costs, replacement costs, incremental costs, manufacturing costs, selling costs, administrative costs, labor costs, interest costs, shipping and warehousing costs, advertising costs, and pollution control costs, to mention only some of the most frequently used cost measures.[5]

COST-OUTPUT RELATIONSHIPS

The fundamental starting point in cost analysis is that a functional relationship exists between the costs of production and the rate of output per period of time. A cost function indicates what the cost will be at alternative output rates; in

---

[5] More complete discussions of the many aspects of cost are found in J. M. Clark, *Studies in the Economics of Overhead Costs* (Chicago: University of Chicago Press, 1923), Chapters 4–6; Joel Dean, *Managerial Economics* (Englewood Cliffs, N.J.: Prentice Hall, 1951), Chapter 5; and Milton H. Spencer, *Managerial Economics,* 3rd ed. (Homewood, Ill.: Richard D. Irwin, 1968), Chapter 7.

other words,

$$\text{cost} = f(\text{output}).$$

But, as indicated in Chapter 7, the rate of output is, in turn, a function of the rate of usage of the resource inputs:

$$\text{output} = f(\text{inputs}).$$

Since the production function displays the relationship between input and output flows, once the prices of the inputs are known the costs of a specific quantity of output can be calculated. As a consequence, the level and behavior of costs as a firm's rate of output changes depend on two important factors:

1. The character of the underlying production function.
2. The prices the firm must pay for its resource inputs.

The first factor determines the shape of the firm's cost functions, whereas the second factor determines the level of costs. To simplify our examination of cost-output relationships, we shall assume that the prices a firm pays for its resource inputs are not affected by changes in its output rate.

The shape of a firm's cost function is determined by the shape of its production function; the level of a firm's costs is determined by input prices.

SHORT-RUN COSTS VERSUS LONG-RUN COSTS

In exploring the relationships between cost and output, it is necessary to differentiate between cost behavior in the short run and cost behavior in the long run. In the short run a firm lacks ready ability to vary such inputs as the amount of space available for production activity, major pieces of equipment, basic technology, and key managerial personnel (the so-called fixed inputs); output is alterable only by increasing or decreasing the usage of variable inputs (production labor, raw materials, and so on). In the long run, however, there is time and opportunity to modify technology *and* the usage of any and *all* inputs—a condition which makes every input, including technology, variable in the long run. Designating resource inputs as fixed or variable in the short run and as all variable in the long run provides the basis for distinguishing between short-run cost functions and long-run cost functions.

In the short run, all costs a firm incurs can be classified as either fixed costs or variable costs; in the long run, all costs are variable because a firm has the ability to vary all inputs.

COST-OUTPUT RELATIONSHIPS IN THE SHORT RUN

THE FAMILY OF TOTAL COST CONCEPTS

Three concepts of total cost are important for analyzing a firm's short-run cost structure: total fixed cost, total variable cost, and total cost.

The fixed inputs of a firm give rise to fixed costs, the amount of which depends on (1) the quantity of each of the various fixed inputs, and (2) the respective prices paid for them. Salaries of top-management officials, property taxes, interest on borrowed money, depreciation charges, rents on office space, the costs of equity capital, and insurance premiums are examples of fixed costs. A firm's fixed costs represent the dollar value (or market worth) of its fixed inputs. Because the amounts of fixed input do not vary with output in the short run, it follows that fixed costs also do not vary with output. In formal terms, ***total fixed cost*** *(TFC) is defined as the sum total of the costs of all the fixed*

The family of total cost concepts consists of total fixed cost, total variable cost, and total cost.

inputs associated with the firm's operations.[6] Because the firm's fixed input quantities are not subject to change in the short run, *TFC* is constant unless the *prices* of the fixed inputs change (higher property taxes, increases in insurance rates or rents, lower interest rates, and so on). Moreover, total fixed costs continue even if production facilities are idle.

Similarly, those inputs that are variable in the short run give rise to short-run variable costs. Since in the short run a firm modifies its output rate by buying more or less units of variable input, variable costs depend on and vary with (1) the quantity of output and (2) the prices paid for each variable input. *Total variable cost* (*TVC*) *is the sum of the amounts a firm spends for variable inputs employed in the production process.*[7] Examples of variable costs include payroll expenses, raw material outlays, power and fuel charges, and shipping costs.[8] Total variable cost (*TVC*) is zero when output is zero because no variable inputs need be employed to produce nothing. However, as output increases, so does the usage of variable input; thus, *TVC* increases as output increases.

The **total cost** (*TC*) *of a given output rate in the short run is the sum of total fixed cost and total variable cost*:

$$TC = TFC + TVC.$$

At zero output, total variable cost is zero and total cost is equal to total fixed cost. As soon as output rises above zero in the short run, some variable inputs must be used, variable costs are incurred, and total cost is the sum of the fixed and variable expenses.

THE FAMILY OF UNIT COST CONCEPTS

There are four major *unit cost concepts*: average fixed cost (*AFC*), average variable cost (*AVC*), average total cost (*ATC*), and marginal cost (*MC*). All these may be derived from the total cost concepts discussed earlier.

Average fixed cost is defined as total fixed cost divided by the units of output, or

The family of unit cost concepts consists of average fixed cost, average variable cost, average total cost, and marginal cost.

$$AFC = \frac{TFC}{Q}.$$

---

[6] In terms of more formal mathematics, total fixed costs may be defined as

$$TFC = \sum_{i=1}^{n} p_i x_i,$$

where

p_i = price of a specified fixed input,
x_i = quantity of the specified fixed input, and
n = number of various kinds of fixed inputs.

[7] Total variable costs may be defined in mathematical terms as

$$TVC = \sum_{j=1}^{m} p_j x_j,$$

where

p_j = price of a specified variable input,
x_j = quantity of the specified variable input, and
m = number of various kinds of variable inputs.

[8] Some expenses incurred by firms have both fixed and variable aspects. These include telephone service, advertising outlays, research and development costs, office supplies, expense account allowances, payroll taxes, and fringe benefit costs.

Since total fixed cost is a constant amount, *average fixed cost declines continuously as the rate of production increases*. For example, if $TFC = \$1000$, at an output of 10 units $AFC = \$1000/10 = \$100$; at an output of 20 units $AFC = \$1000/20 = \$50$; at an output of 50 units $AFC = \$1000/50 = \$20$; and so on. The reduction of AFC by producing more units of output is commonly called *spreading the overhead*. The calculation of average fixed cost can also be approached from a slightly different direction. Assuming a firm's inputs consist of a number of identical units, then total fixed cost equals the number of units of fixed input (FI) multiplied by the unit price of the fixed input (P_{fi}), or $TFC = (P_{fi})(FI)$. Substituting into the expression for AFC gives

$$AFC = \frac{TFC}{Q} = \frac{(P_{fi})(FI)}{Q} = P_{fi}\left(\frac{FI}{Q}\right).$$

Recalling that in Chapter 6 we defined average product of the fixed input as total output (Q) divided by the number of units of fixed input (FI), it follows that the term FI/Q equals $1/AP_{fi}$ and that

$$AFC = P_{fi}\left(\frac{1}{AP_{fi}}\right).$$

Average variable cost is total variable cost divided by the corresponding number of units of output, or

$$AVC = \frac{TVC}{Q}.$$

As with AFC, the concept of AVC may be related to the underlying production function. Total variable cost equals the units of variable input employed (VI) multiplied by the price per unit of variable input (P_{vi}). Assuming a single type of variable input is used, $TVC = (P_{vi})(VI)$. Hence, we have

$$AVC = \frac{TVC}{Q} = \frac{(P_{vi})(VI)}{Q} = P_{vi}\left(\frac{VI}{Q}\right).$$

Since the average product of variable input is defined as Q/VI, then

$$AVC = P_{vi}\left(\frac{1}{AP_{vi}}\right).$$

Average total cost is defined as total cost divided by the corresponding units of output, or

$$ATC = \frac{TC}{Q}.$$

However, since $TC = TFC + TVC$,

$$ATC = \frac{TC}{Q} = \frac{TFC + TVC}{Q} = \frac{TFC}{Q} + \frac{TVC}{Q}.$$
$$= AFC + AVC.$$

Last, **marginal cost** *is the change in total cost associated with a change in the quantity of output per period of time*. As with previous marginal concepts, we can make a distinction between discrete marginal cost and continuous marginal cost. **Discrete marginal cost** *is the change in total cost attributable to a 1-unit change in the quantity of output*. For example, the marginal cost of the 500th unit of output can be calculated by finding the difference between total cost at 499 units of output and total cost at 500 units of output. Hence, the increase in total cost of producing one additional unit of output equals the marginal cost of that unit. ***Continuous marginal cost*** *is the rate of change in total cost as the quantity of output changes*, and it can be calculated from the first derivative of the total cost function. Thus,

$$MC = \frac{dTC}{dQ}.$$

However, because *in the short run all output-related changes in total cost are attributable solely to changes in total variable cost* (*TFC* is constant), it is equally accurate to measure discrete marginal cost by observing changes in total variable cost—the marginal cost of the 500th unit of output equals the difference between *TVC* at 499 units of output and *TVC* at 500 units of output. And continuous marginal cost can be calculated from the first derivative of the *TVC* function:

$$MC = \frac{dTVC}{dQ}.$$

As with the other unit cost concepts, the value of marginal cost is related to the underlying production function. Marginal costs stem from the changes in variable costs associated with altering the quantity of output. Since in the short run output is altered by increasing or decreasing the usage of variable inputs, changes in total variable cost (ΔTVC) may be calculated by multiplying the price of variable input (P_{vi}) by the associated change in variable input (ΔVI), giving

$$\Delta TVC = P_{vi}(\Delta VI).$$

As indicated earlier, $MC = \Delta TVC$ for a 1-unit change in output, or if output changes by several units, then

$$MC = \frac{\Delta TVC}{\Delta Q}.$$

But since $\Delta TVC = P_{vi}(\Delta VI)$, we have

$$MC = \frac{P_{vi}(\Delta VI)}{\Delta Q} = P_{vi}\left(\frac{\Delta VI}{\Delta Q}\right).$$

In Chapter 6, marginal product (*MP*) was defined as the change in output attributable to a change in variable input, or $MP = \Delta Q/\Delta VI$. It follows, therefore, that

$$MC = P_{vi}\left(\frac{1}{MP}\right).$$

Marginal cost is of central interest because it reflects those costs over which the firm has the most direct control in the short run. More particularly, *MC* indicates the amount of cost which can be "saved" by reducing output by 1 unit or, alternatively, the amount of additional cost which will be incurred by increasing production by 1 unit. Average cost data do not reveal this valuable bit of cost knowledge.

Now let us use these definitions to investigate the behavior of a firm's costs for a variety of production functions. Specifically, we shall examine the total, average, and marginal cost functions for each of the following types of short-run production functions:

1. $Q = a + bX + cX^2$ (increasing returns to variable input).
2. $Q = a + bX$ (constant returns to variable input).
3. $Q = a + bX - cX^2$ (decreasing returns to variable input).
4. $Q = a + bX + cX^2 - dX^3$ (increasing and decreasing returns to variable input).

Here Q is the quantity of output and X designates the units of variable input.

COST BEHAVIOR UNDER INCREASING RETURNS TO VARIABLE INPUT

When a firm's production function exhibits increasing returns to variable input, each additional unit of variable input adds more to total output than does the previous unit. As more units of variable input are utilized, the efficiency of both fixed and variable inputs increases. Graphically, then, the production function increases at an increasing rate and has, in the simplest case, the general equation $Q = a + bX + cX^2$, where $a = 0$, provided that variable input (X) is essential for any output (Q) to be produced. Figure 8-1(a) illustrates

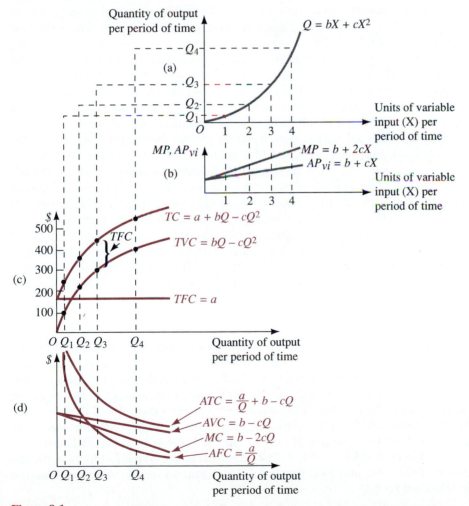

Figure 8-1

Production and cost behavior for an increasing-returns-to-variable-input situation

Note: The coefficients b and c in the equations for the production functions will have different values than the coefficients b and c in the cost function equations.

this type of production function. The corresponding marginal and average product functions are shown in Figure 8-1(b).

As previously indicated, a firm's fixed inputs, not being easily susceptible to change in the short run, give rise to a constant amount of cost. Hence, graphically, the firm's *TFC* function is a horizontal line, reflecting the fact that *TFC* does not vary with the quantity of output—as depicted in Figure 8-1(c). Note that, in drawing the *TFC* curve, costs (in dollars) are plotted on the vertical axis and the quantity of output is on the horizontal axis. Algebraically, the dollar amount of *TFC* can be represented by a constant, say *a*, making the general equation for the total fixed-cost function

$$TFC = a.$$

The total variable cost (*TVC*) function gets its shape directly from the production function. To illustrate the tie between the production function and *TVC*, consider the behavior of *TVC* as successive units of variable input per period of time are added to the given amount of fixed inputs. Suppose that the price of variable input is $100 per unit. From Figure 8-1(a) it can be seen that employing 1 unit of variable input with the given fixed input will yield an output of Q_1 units; this translates into *TVC* of $100 for Q_1 units of output [Figure 8-1(c)]. Similarly, employing 2 units of variable input yields Q_2 units of output and results in *TVC* of $200. Note that in panel (a) the marginal product of the second unit of variable input is larger than the marginal product of the first unit (distance Q_1Q_2 > distance OQ_1) in accordance with increasing returns to the usage of variable input. Adding the third unit of variable input causes the quantity of output to increase even faster to Q_3 units (distance Q_2/Q_3 > distance Q_1Q_2), and *TVC* at Q_3 is $300. When the fourth unit of variable input per period of time is employed, output rises by yet a greater increment to Q_4 units (distance Q_3Q_4 > distance Q_2Q_3), and *TVC* becomes $400. From Figures 8-1(a) and (c) it is apparent that *when the quantity of output increases at an increasing rate, TVC must necessarily increase at a decreasing rate*. With each additional unit of variable input, *TVC* rises by a constant amount equal to the price per unit of variable input, yet the associated increases in output get larger and larger owing to the rising productivity of additional variable input. To put it another way, when increasing returns to variable input characterize the production function, the quantity of output rises faster than does total variable cost. The simplest equation for representing *TVC* which captures the properties of such cost behavior is

$$TVC = bQ - cQ^2.$$

COST PRINCIPLE
When a firm's production function exhibits increasing returns to varible input, such that output increases at an increasing rate as more variable inputs are used, then both *TVC* and *TC* increase at a decreasing rate as output rises.

[It must be emphasized that while the equations for the production function ($Q = bX + cX^2$) and the *TVC* function ($TVC = bQ - cQ^2$) are very similar in form, the values of the constants *b* and *c* in the production function *are not equal* to the values of *b* and *c* in the *TVC* equation—except in the rarest of coincidences.] Notice that *TVC* equals zero at zero output and that the *TVC* function begins at the origin. Also, the greater is the usage of variable input, the greater is both the quantity of output and the level of total variable costs.

Given that *TC* = *TFC* + *TVC*, the total cost curve is found by vertically summing the *TFC* and *TVC* functions. The equation for the total cost function in this case is

$$TC = a + bQ - cQ^2,$$

where *a* represents the *TFC* component of *TC* and $bQ - cQ^2$ represents the

TVC component. From Figure 8-1(c), it can be seen that *the shapes of the TVC and TC curves are identical*. At every rate of output their slopes are equal and the two curves are separated by a constant vertical distance equal to the amount of *TFC*. At zero output, *TVC* = 0 and *TC* = *TFC*.

The AFC curve decreases continually as the quantity of output increases—as indicated in Figure 8-1(d). Its equation is

$$AFC = \frac{TFC}{Q} = \frac{a}{Q}.$$

As explained earlier, the decline in *AFC* derives from the spreading of *TFC* over a greater number of units of output. Geometrically speaking, the *AFC* curve is a rectangular hyperbola, meaning that the curve approaches the vertical and horizontal axes asymptotically. In addition, were we to pick any point on the *AFC* curve, draw lines perpendicular to the two axes, and calculate the area of the resulting rectangle, this area will be the same irrespective of the point chosen. Why? Because this area measures $AFC \times Q$ and because $AFC \times Q = TFC$ = a constant value.

The nature and behavior of average variable cost can be deduced from the total variable cost function. When the production function exhibits increasing returns to variable input and *TVC* is represented by the equation $TVC = bQ - cQ^2$, then

$$AVC = \frac{TVC}{Q} = \frac{bQ - cQ^2}{Q} = b - cQ.$$

The *AVC* curve corresponding to this type of production function is shown in Figure 8-1(d). The significant point here is that *increasing returns to variable input cause unit variable costs to fall as output increases*. That this is so can be verified by means of the relationship between *AVC* and the production function:

$$AVC = P_{vi}\left(\frac{1}{AP_{vi}}\right).$$

Given increasing returns to variable input, the average productivity of variable input rises as more units of variable input are added [see Figure 8-1(b)]. As AP_{vi} goes up (and provided that the price of variable input does not change), then *AVC* must necessarily fall.

The average total cost function can be derived by dividing the equation for total cost by the units of output, obtaining

$$ATC = \frac{TC}{Q} = \frac{a + bQ + cQ^2}{Q} = \frac{a}{Q} + b - cQ.$$

The equation for *ATC* could just as well have been found by adding together the equation for *AFC* (a/Q) and the equation for *AVC* (b − cQ) since *ATC* = *AFC* + *AVC*. The shape of the average total cost curve is obtained by vertically summing the *AFC* and *AVC* curves at every rate of output, as illustrated in Figure 8-1(d). Here, *ATC declines throughout because both AFC and AVC are decreasing*. Observe that the *ATC* curve is asymptotic to the *AVC* curve. Why? The difference between *ATC* and *AVC* is the amount of *AFC*. At low rates of output *AFC* is relatively large, and the values of *ATC* are well in excess of the *AVC* values; however, as output increases, the values of *AFC* decline and the values of *ATC* more closely approach the values of *AVC*. Thus, while *ATC* always exceeds *AVC*, the greater the quantity of output, the smaller the value of *AFC* and the smaller the distance between the *AVC* and *ATC* curves. This asymptotic relationship between *AVC* and *ATC* is not unique to cost behavior in the instance of increasing returns to variable input but rather is a general and necessary trait for all types of production and cost situations.

The marginal cost function is obtained by finding the first derivative of the *TC* function (or *TVC* function—the result is the same in either event). If $TC = a + bQ - cQ^2$ and $TVC = bQ - cQ^2$, then

$$MC = \frac{dTC}{dQ} = \frac{dTVC}{dQ} = b - 2cQ.$$

The *MC* curve is, therefore, both linear and downsloping, as shown in Figure 8-1(d). *The MC curve decreases here because under increasing returns to variable input the marginal product of successive units of variable input rises.* In other words, since

$$MC = P_{vi}\left(\frac{1}{MP}\right),$$

COST PRINCIPLE
When a firm's production exhibits increasing returns to variable input and both fixed and variable input efficiency rise as more variable input is used, then *AFC*, *AVC*, *ATC*, and *MC* all decrease as output rises—the higher the output rate, the lower are costs per unit produced.

it follows that if *MP* is increasing and if P_{vi} remains constant, then *MC* must necessarily be falling. Moreover, note that the slope of the *MC* curve $(-2c)$ is twice as large as the slope of the *AVC* curve $(-c)$; both curves originate at a common point (b). Further, the value of *MC* at a given output is equal to the slopes of the *TVC* curve and the *TC* curve at that output rate.

The salient feature of increasing returns to variable input is that the efficiency with which resource inputs are used rises as the quantity of output increases, with the concomitant result of declining unit costs. In other words, the larger the quantity produced, the lower the costs of each unit—clearly, a most favorable set of circumstances. But unfortunately for the firm, increasing returns to variable input are not likely to be realized except at output rates well below the normal operating range.

Table 8-1 presents hypothetical production and cost data for a production function exhibiting increasing returns to variable input. (Before proceeding, you would do well to examine the numbers in each column to be sure that you fully understand how each one is computed.)

TABLE 8-1   HYPOTHETICAL PRODUCTION AND COST DATA FOR INCREASING RETURNS TO VARIABLE INPUT

Units of Fixed Input	Units of Variable Input	Quantity of Output	TFC[a]	TVC[b]	TC	AFC	AVC	ATC	"Average" MC
2	0	0	$100	$ 0	$100	—	$ 0	—	
2	1	10	100	40	140	$10.00	4.00	$14.00	$4.00
2	2	25	100	80	180	4.00	3.20	7.20	2.67
2	3	45	100	120	220	2.22	2.67	4.89	2.00
2	4	70	100	160	260	1.43	2.29	3.72	1.60
2	5	100	100	200	300	1.00	1.00	3.00	1.33

[a] The price of fixed input is assumed to be $50 per unit.
[b] The price of variable input is assumed to be $40 per unit.

COST BEHAVIOR UNDER CONSTANT RETURNS TO VARIABLE INPUT

When a firm's production process is characterized by constant returns to variable input, each additional unit of variable input used per period of time adds the same amount to total output as the preceding unit. The quantity of output increases at a constant rate, and the production function is linear. The related MP and AP_{vi} functions are horizontal lines, indicating that the values of MP and AP_{vi} are the same for every unit of variable input. As more variable input is added, variable input efficiency is constant and fixed input efficiency rises. The general equation for the production function is

$$Q = a + bX,$$

where $a = 0$. The related equations for marginal and average product are

$$MP = b, AP_{vi} = b,$$

where b is a constant equal to the slope of the production function. Panels (a) and (b) in Figure 8-2 illustrate the family of product curves corresponding to a constant-returns-to-variable-input situation.

The TFC curve for a production process displaying constant returns to variable input is again a horizontal line [see Figure 8-2(c)]. As before, this is because *TFC* is determined by the prices and quantities of fixed input, not by the relationship between variable input and output. The equation for total fixed cost thus remains

$$TFC = a,$$

where a is a given amount of dollars and is determined by the amount and prices of fixed inputs present.

To discuss the shape of the *TVC* curve given constant returns to variable input, consider how *TVC* and output are affected when additional variable input is used. From Figure 8-2(a) it can be seen that combining 1 unit of variable input per period of time with the given amount of fixed inputs will yield an output of Q_1 units; accordingly, the total variable cost of Q_1 units is $100, as shown in Figure 8-2(c). Combining 2 units of variable input with the available fixed input yields an output of Q_2 units [Figure 8-2(a)]; the marginal product of the second unit of variable input equals the marginal product of the first unit $(OQ_1 = Q_1Q_2)$ in accordance with the condition of constant returns to variable input [Figure 8-2(b)]. *TVC* at Q_2 units of output is $200 [Figure 8-2(c)]. Adding the third unit of variable input causes the quantity of output to rise to Q_3 $(OQ_1 = Q_1Q_2 = Q_2Q_3)$, and the total variable cost of Q_3 units is $300. And so it goes. Each additional unit of variable input produces an equivalent rise in output (MP is constant), and *TVC* rises by a constant amount ($100 in this case) with each unit increase in variable input. Plainly then, the *TVC* curve is *linear*, begins from the origin, and has the general equation

$$TVC = bQ.$$

The *TVC* function is illustrated in Figure 8-2(c).

Since $TC = TFC + TVC$, the shape of the total cost curve is derived by vertically adding the *TFC* and *TVC* curves [see Figure 8-2(c)]. It follows that the equation for *TC* may be found by adding together the expressions for *TFC* and *TVC*:

$$TFC = a, TVC = bQ,$$
$$TC = TFC + TVC = a + bQ.$$

COST PRINCIPLE
When a firm's production function exhibits constant returns to variable input, such that output increases at a constant rate as more variable inputs are used, then both *TVC* and *TC* are linear and increase at a constant rate as output rises.

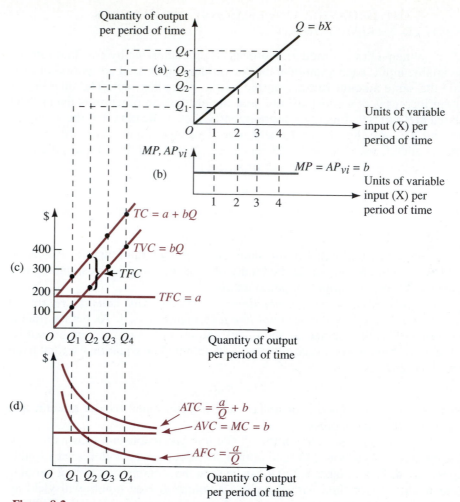

Figure 8-2

Production and cost behavior for a constant-returns-to-variable-input situation

Note: The coefficient *b* in the production function equations will have a different value from the coefficient *b* in the cost function equations.

Since all changes in total cost are solely attributable to changes in variable cost items, the shape of the *TC* curve is identical to the shape of the *TVC* curve. Given constant returns to variable input, the *TC* curve is therefore a linear function with a slope equivalent to the slope of *TVC*; the two curves are separated by a constant vertical distance equal to the amount of *TFC*. At zero output, $TVC = 0$ and $TC = TFC$.

As before, the *AFC* curve decreases continually as the quantity of output increases, and it assumes the shape of a rectangular hyperbola. Its equation is

$$AFC = \frac{TFC}{Q} = \frac{a}{Q}.$$

The reasoning is the same as previously. As a constant value (*TFC*) is divided by an increasing value (*Q*), the resulting values (*AFC*) get smaller and smaller, as depicted in Figure 8-2(d).

The equation for *AVC* can be derived from the expression for total variable cost as follows:

$$AVC = \frac{TVC}{Q} = \frac{bQ}{Q} = b.$$

This means that *with constant returns to variable input AVC is a constant value*. That this is so can be confirmed from the relationship

$$AVC = P_{vi}\left(\frac{1}{AP_{vi}}\right).$$

With constant returns to variable input, AP_{vi} is also a constant, and assuming a given price for variable input, *AVC* must necessarily be a constant. To illustrate, suppose that variable input costs $100 per unit and that AP_{vi} is fixed at 50 units of output. Then,

$$AVC = P_{vi}\left(\frac{1}{AP_{vi}}\right) = \$100\left(\frac{1}{50}\right) = \$2,$$

and it is $2 at each and every output rate. Graphically, the *AVC* curve is a horizontal line with a height of *b* dollars above the horizontal axis [see Figure 8-2(d)].

Since, by definition, average total cost equals total cost divided by the units of output, the equation for *ATC* under conditions of constant returns to variable input becomes

$$ATC = \frac{TC}{Q} = \frac{a + bQ}{Q} = \frac{a}{Q} + b.$$

Observe that since a/Q is *AFC* and *b* is *AVC*, the equation for *ATC* can be found by adding the equation for *AFC* to the equation for *AVC*. Also, *because AVC is a fixed value when there are constant returns to variable input, the associated ATC curve assumes a shape precisely identical to that of the AFC curve and lies above it by the amount of AVC* [see Figure 8-2(d)]. The *ATC* curve is, therefore, asymptotic to the horizontal *AVC* curve and decreases throughout.

With marginal cost being equal to the first derivative of the *TC* function (or the *TVC* function) and the equation for *TC* being $TC = a + bQ$, the equation for *MC* becomes

$$MC = \frac{dTC}{dQ} = \frac{dTVC}{dQ} = b,$$

where *b* is a constant. That *MC is a constant value when constant returns to variable input prevail* follows from its relationship with marginal product:

$$MC = P_{vi}\left(\frac{1}{MP}\right).$$

With constant returns, *MP* is itself a fixed value, and if P_{vi} is also a given, then *MC* becomes the product of a constant times a constant. For example, if $P_{vi} = \$100$ and if the marginal product of every additional unit of variable input equals 50 units of output, then

$$MC = P_{vi}\left(\frac{1}{MP}\right) = \$100\left(\frac{1}{50}\right) = \$2.$$

COST PRINCIPLE
When a firm's production function exhibits constant returns to variable input, such that variable input efficiency is constant and fixed input efficiency rises as more variable input is used, then *AVC* and *MC* are equal and constant and both *AFC* and *ATC* decline as output rises—the greater the output rate, the lower the overall cost per unit produced.

Thus, with constant returns to variable input, $MC = AVC = b$, and the *MC* curve is a horizontal line. The value of *MC* equals the slope of the *TVC* and *TC* curves.

Figure 8-2(d) illustrates how the unit cost curves are related to one another. Table 8-2 presents hypothetical production and cost data for a production function exhibiting constant returns to variable input. Observe that the greater the output rate, the lower is average total cost. This occurs because total fixed costs are being spread over a larger volume of output and *AVC* and *MC* are constant. A number of industry studies show that constant *MC* and *AVC* and slowly declining *ATC* typify many production processes over the "normal" range of output (more about this presently).

COST BEHAVIOR UNDER DECREASING RETURNS TO VARIABLE INPUT

With a production process characterized by decreasing returns to variable input, the marginal product of variable input declines as output rises. Each additional unit of variable input used per period of time with the available fixed input adds less to total output than the previous unit, and the quantity of output increases at a decreasing rate. Both the marginal and average product functions are downsloping. As more variable input is used, the efficiency of variable inputs declines and fixed input efficiency rises. The product curves are illustrated in panels (a) and (b) of Figure 8-3.

As is the case with all types of short-run production functions, the *TFC* curve associated with decreasing returns to variable input is again a horizontal line having the equation

$$TFC = a,$$

where *a* is a constant [see Figure 8-3(c)]. *TFC* is a constant dollar value because neither the amount nor the cost of the available fixed inputs is affected by the nature of the returns to variable input embodied in the production function.

However, the shape of the *TVC* curve is very definitely affected by the nature of the underlying production function. Letting $P = \$100$ per unit, each additional unit of variable input employed will cause *TVC* to rise by $100. From

TABLE 8-2   HYPOTHETICAL PRODUCTION AND COST DATA FOR CONSTANT RETURNS TO VARIABLE INPUT

Units of Fixed Input	Units of Variable Input	Quantity of Output	TFCª	TVCᵇ	TC	AFC	AVC	ATC	"Average" MC
2	0	0	$100	$ 0	$100	—	$ 0	—	
2	1	10	100	40	140	$10.00	4.00	$14.00	$4.00
2	2	20	100	80	180	5.00	4.00	9.00	4.00
2	3	30	100	120	220	3.33	4.00	7.33	4.00
2	4	40	100	160	260	2.50	4.00	6.50	4.00
2	5	50	100	200	300	2.00	4.00	6.00	4.00

ª The price of fixed input is assumed to be $50 per unit.
ᵇ The price of variable input is assumed to be $40 per unit.

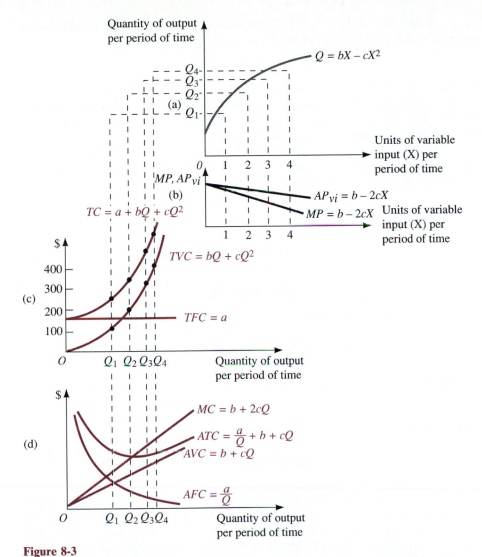

Figure 8-3

Production and cost behavior for a decreasing-returns-to-variable-input situation

Note: The coefficients b and c in the production function equations will have different values from the coefficients b and c in the cost function equations.

Figure 8-3(a) it is evident that combining 1 unit of variable input per period of time with the given fixed input yields an output of Q_1 units. This translates into a *TVC* of \$100 at an output of Q_1 units, as shown in Figure 8-3(c). Combining 2 units of variable input with the fixed input produces a less-than-proportional increase in output to Q_2 units ($OQ_1 > Q_1Q_2$), and *TVC* becomes \$200 at an output of Q_2. Adding the third unit of variable input yields yet a smaller increment in the quantity of output ($Q_1Q_2 > Q_2Q_3$); *TVC* rises to \$300. Successive additions of variable input cause output to rise ever more slowly, while *TVC* increases by a given amount (\$100 in this example) with each unit increase in variable input. *Such behavior produces a TVC curve which increases at an increasing rate with output,* as indicated in Figure 8-3(c). The simplest equation to represent this type of function is

$$TVC = bQ + cQ^2.$$

COST PRINCIPLE

When a firm's production function exhibits decreasing returns to variable input, such that output increases at a slower rate as more variable input is used, then both *TVC* and *TC* increase at an increasing rate as output rises.

Since $TC = TFC + TVC$, the equation for TC under conditions of decreasing returns to variable input becomes

$$TC = a + bQ + cQ^2.$$

The graph of this function, shown in Figure 8-3(c), starts from the point where the TFC curve intersects the vertical axis and thereafter increases at an increasing rate. *The shape of the TC curve is identical to the shape of the TVC and lies above it by a constant amount equal to TFC.*

As is the case irrespective of the character of the production function, the AFC curve is a decreasing function that is asymptotic to the horizontal axis [see Figure 8-3(d)]. Its equation is

$$AFC = \frac{TFC}{Q} = \frac{a}{Q}.$$

The nature and behavior of AVC are easily established. Since the equation for TVC is

$$TVC = bQ + cQ^2,$$

the equation for AVC becomes

$$AVC = \frac{TVC}{Q} = \frac{bQ + cQ^2}{Q} = b + cQ.$$

The graph of the AVC function is linear with a positive slope equal to the value of c. Thus, when the production function exhibits decreasing returns to variable input, AVC rises as output is increased. That AVC rises throughout can be confirmed by examining the expression

$$AVC = P_{vi}\left(\frac{1}{AP_{vi}}\right).$$

With decreasing returns to variable input, AP_{vi} decreases over the entire output range [see Figure 8-3(b)]. Assuming a constant price for variable input, *as output is increased the smaller and smaller values of AP_{vi} result in larger and larger values of AVC.* Aside from the mathematics of the situation, the logic for rising AVC is compelling. When the production function displays decreasing returns to variable input, both the marginal and average productivity of variable inputs decline as output is increased. Hence, the efficiency of variable input falls as more variable input is added and as output rises. *Lower efficiency in the usage of variable input clearly implies higher variable costs per unit of output.*

Since $ATC = TC/Q$, the equation for average total cost is

$$ATC = \frac{TC}{Q} = \frac{a + bQ + cQ^2}{Q} = \frac{a}{Q} + b + cQ.$$

However, the graph of ATC is somewhat less obvious. Whereas the AFC component of ATC (a/Q) decreases as the quantity of output rises, the AVC component of ATC $(b + cQ)$ rises continuously as output rises. Hence, *whether ATC rises or falls hinges upon the decreases in AFC relative to the increases in AVC.* At low output rates the declines in AFC are larger than the increases in AVC, so that the ATC curve declines up to an output of Q_2 units. At Q_2 the decline in AFC is exactly offset by the increase in AVC, and ATC is a minimum. Beyond Q_2, the increases in AVC override the decreases in AFC, with the result that the ATC curve turns upward. But despite the U-shaped behavior of

ATC, the *ATC* curve is still asymptotic to the *AVC* curve for the reason previously given.

A production function displaying decreasing returns to variable input is associated with a rising marginal cost function. Given that $TC = a + bQ + cQ^2$ (and that $TVC = bQ + cQ^2$),

$$MC = \frac{dTC}{dQ} = \frac{dTVC}{dQ} = b + 2cQ.$$

The graph of such an equation is a linear function with a positive slope equal to $2c$ [see Figure 8-3(d)]. The increasing aspect of *MC* stems from its relationship to marginal product:

$$MC = P_{vi}\left(\frac{1}{MP}\right).$$

By definition, decreasing returns to variable input means that the marginal product of additional units of variable input is a declining, yet positive, value—a reflection of the declining efficiency in the use of variable input. *With MP falling as output rises, MC must necessarily rise.* Note that in this instance the slope of the *MC* curve ($2c$) is twice as great as the slope of the *AVC* curve (c). Also, *the MC curve passes through the minimum point of the ATC curve.* The latter property is an inherent feature of the mathematical relationship between average and marginal values. *MC* is the additional cost for 1 unit of output; *ATC* is the average for all the units produced up to that point. As long as *MC* is below *ATC, ATC* is pulled down by the lower cost of the additional output. When the cost of an additional unit is greater than the average cost of previous units, *ATC* is pulled up by the higher cost of the incremental output. At the point of intersection of *MC* and *ATC, ATC* has ceased declining but has not begun to rise; this, then, is the minimum point on the *ATC* curve.

A production-cost structure predicated on decreasing returns to variable input (as in Figure 8-3) is not likely to typify a firm's entire range of output capability. But decreasing returns to variable input are typical of production and cost behavior at near-capacity rates of output since the closer capacity is approached the harder it becomes to increase production without encountering the point of diminishing marginal returns; as this happens *MC, AVC,* and *ATC* will begin to rise.

Table 8-3 illustrates production and cost behavior for a situation characterized by decreasing returns to variable input throughout the indicated output range. Note that the patterns of change in the total and unit cost values parallel exactly the shapes of the cost curves in panels (c) and (d) of Figure 8-3.

Cost Behavior with Increasing and Decreasing Returns to Variable Input

As stated in Chapter 7, the most general and pervasive type of short-run production function is the one illustrated in Figure 8-4(a) having the general equation

$$Q = a + bX + cX^2 - dX^3$$

and having *MP* and AP_{vi} functions as shown in Figure 8-4(b). Up to X_1 units of variable input, output increases at an increasing rate. From X_1 to X_3 units of variable input, output increases at a decreasing rate.

COST PRINCIPLE
When a firm's production function exhibits decreasing returns to variable input (meaning that variable input efficiency declines as more variable input is added), both *AVC* and *MC* rise as output rates are increased; *ATC* declines as long as the declines in *AFC* outweigh the increases in *AVC*; then *ATC* rises as the increases in *AVC* more than offset the declines in *AFC*.

Units of Fixed Input	Units of Variable Input	Quantity of Output	TFC[a]	TVC[b]	TC	AFC	AVC	ATC	"Average" MC
2	0	0	$100	$ 0	$100	—	$ 0	—	
2	1	20	100	40	140	$5.00	2.00	$7.00	$ 2.00
2	2	36	100	80	180	2.78	2.22	5.00	2.50
2	3	48	100	120	220	2.08	2.50	4.58	3.33
2	4	56	100	160	260	1.79	2.86	4.65	5.00
2	5	60	100	200	300	1.67	3.33	5.00	10.00

[a] The price of fixed input is assumed to be $50 per unit.
[b] The price of variable input is assumed to be $40 per unit.

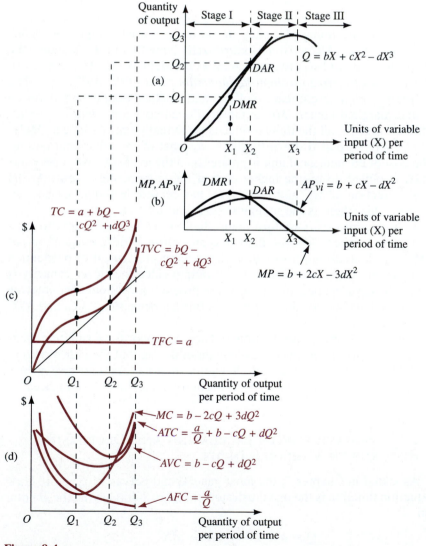

Figure 8-4

Production and cost behavior where both increasing and decreasing returns to variable input are present

Note: The coefficients *b*, *c*, and *d* in the production function equations will have different values than the coefficients *b*, *c*, and *d* in the cost function equations.

Again, the TFC curve is a horizontal line with the equation $TFC = a$ [see Figure 8-4(c)]. The *TVC* curve for this type of production function combines the shapes of the *TVC* curves for both increasing and decreasing returns to variable input. From panels (a) and (c) of Figure 8-4 it can be seen that *over the range of output where increasing returns to variable input prevail (O to Q_1) the TVC curve increases at a decreasing rate*, whereas over the range of output where decreasing returns to variable input are encountered (Q_1 to Q_3) the TVC curve increases at an increasing rate. At the short-run capacity rate of output (Q_3) the slope of the *TVC* curve becomes vertical. The explanation for this behavior of *TVC* rests with the principle of diminishing marginal returns. Where the quantity of output increases at an increasing rate, marginal product is also increasing, and smaller and smaller increases in variable inputs are required to produce successive units of output. This means that *TVC* will increase by progressively smaller amounts as output rises. But when the point of diminishing marginal returns is encountered and marginal product begins to decline, it becomes necessary to use increasingly larger amounts of variable input to obtain the same-sized output gain. Total variable costs therefore increase at an increasing rate over this output range. The general equation for a *TVC* curve with these traits is

$$TVC = bQ - cQ^2 + dQ^3.$$

Total cost equals the sum of *TFC* and *TVC* at each output rate and has the equation

$$TC = a + bQ - cQ^2 + dQ^3,$$

where a equals the amount of *TFC* and the expression $bQ - cQ^2 + dQ^3$ equals the amount of *TVC* at each value of Q. At zero output, $TC = TFC$, and for each successive unit produced *TC* varies in precisely the same fashion and at precisely the same rate as does *TVC*. As indicated in Fig. 8-4(c), *the TC curve is the same shape as the TVC curve but lies above it by the amount of TFC.*

The graph and equation of the *AFC* curve are identical to the preceding cases and are shown in Figure 8-4(d). The behavior of *AVC* can be determined from *TVC*. Since $TVC = bQ - cQ^2 + dQ^3$, the average variable cost equation is

$$AVC = \frac{TVC}{Q} = \frac{bQ - cQ^2 + dQ^3}{Q} = b - cQ + dQ^2.$$

When plotted on a graph, an equation of this type produces a curve which declines initially, reaches a minimum, and then increases. *The AVC curve is therefore U-shaped*, as shown in Figure 8-4(d). The rationale for this behavior of *AVC* can be seen from its relationship with AP_{vi}:

$$AVC = P_{vi}\left(\frac{1}{AP_{vi}}\right).$$

Given a fixed price for units of variable input, *when AP_{vi} is rising* [Figure 8-4(b)] *AVC must be falling; when AP_{vi} is declining AVC must be rising.* Minimum *AVC* (an output on Q_2) corresponds to the output rate where AP_{vi} is maximum (X_2 units of variable input). At Q_2 the point of diminishing average returns is encountered, and the stage II phase of production begins. Thus, *stage I rates of output correspond to the output range where AVC is declining, whereas stage II quantities correspond to the range of output where AVC is rising.*

As previously indicated, *ATC* is calculated by dividing total cost by the quantity of output—or, more simply, by adding *AFC* and *AVC* at each rate of

COST PRINCIPLE
When variable input efficiency is rising, *TVC* increases more slowly; when variable input efficiency is declining, *TVC* increases more rapidly.

COST PRINCIPLE
When variable input efficiency is rising, *AVC* is falling; when variable input efficiency is declining, *AVC* is rising.

output. Here the equation for *ATC* is

$$ATC = \frac{TC}{Q} = \frac{a + bQ - cQ + dQ^3}{Q} = \frac{a}{Q} + b - cQ + dQ^2,$$

where a/Q is the *AFC* component of *ATC* and $b - cQ + dQ^2$ is the *AVC* component of *ATC*. As before, the vertical distance between *ATC* and *AVC* reflects the value of *AFC* at any output. Because *AFC* decreases as output expands, the distance between *ATC* and *AVC* gets progressively smaller. Thus, *the ATC curve is asymptotic to the AVC curve and U-shaped* [see Figure 8-4(d)]. Note that the minimum point on the *ATC* curve corresponds to a quantity of output in stage II. This result is in accord with the rationale for operating in stage II presented in Chapter 7. Also, *the minimum point of the ATC curve is at a larger volume of output than is the minimum point of the AVC curve.* Why? *ATC* continues to fall beyond the output where *AVC* is minimum because the continuing declines in *AFC* more than offset the slight increases in *AVC*. As output expands further, however, the increases in *AVC* begin to override the decreases in *AFC*, and *ATC* turns upward. *The minimum point on the ATC curve defines the most efficient and economical rate of operation in the short run.*

Marginal cost can be determined by calculating the first derivative of the equation for either *TC* or *TVC*:

$$MC = \frac{dTC}{dQ} = \frac{dTVC}{dQ} = b - 2cQ + 3dQ^2.$$

The *MC* function in this instance is a quadratic equation which, when graphed, assumes the U-shape shown in Figure 8-4(d). The curvature of the *MC* function reflects its relationship with marginal product. Since

$$MC = P_{vi}\left(\frac{1}{MP}\right),$$

The least-cost output rate in the short run is where average total cost is lowest.

TABLE 8-4 HYPOTHETICAL PRODUCTION AND COST DATA FOR DECREASING RETURNS TO VARIABLE INPUT

Units of Fixed Input	Units of Variable Input	Quantity of Output	TFC[a]	TVC[b]	TC	AFC	AVC	ATC	"Average" MC
2	0	0	$100	$ 0	$100	—	$ 0	—	
									$4.00
2	1	10	100	40	140	$10.00	4.00	$14.00	
									2.00
2	2	30	100	80	180	3.33	2.67	6.00	
									1.14
2	3	65	100	120	220	1.54	1.85	3.39	
									1.33
2	4	95	100	160	260	1.05	1.68	2.73	
									1.60
2	5	120	100	200	300	.83	1.67	2.50	
									2.00
2	6	140	100	240	340	.71	1.71	2.42	
									2.67
2	7	155	100	280	380	.65	1.81	2.46	
									4.00
2	8	165	100	320	420	.61	1.94	2.55	
									8.00
2	9	170	100	360	460	.59	2.12	2.71	

[a] The price of fixed input is assumed to be $50 per unit.
[b] The price of variable input is assumed to be $40 per unit.

then as long as *MP* is rising, *MC* must be declining. But when diminishing marginal returns set in and *MP* is falling, then the marginal cost of the extra unit of output is rising. Hence, assuming a constant price for variable input, *increasing returns to variable input result in declining marginal costs, and decreasing returns are associated with rising marginal costs*. Marginal cost is minimum at the point of diminishing marginal returns where *MP* is maximum (note that this quantity of output is in stage I). Furthermore, *the MC curve intersects the AVC and ATC curves at their minimum points*—a relationship of mathematical necessity.[9] As long as the cost of producing an additional unit is less than the average total cost of previously produced units, the newly computed values of *ATC* will fall, being pulled down by the lower *MC*. Similarly, when the cost of producing an additional unit is greater than the average total cost of the preceding units, the new value of *ATC* rises, being pulled up by the higher value of *MC*. It follows that *ATC* is minimum at the point of intersection of *MC* and *ATC*. By analogous reasoning the *MC* curve must pass through the minimum point of the *AVC* function.

Table 8-4 illustrates the patterns of change in the total and unit cost values for a production function having phases of both increasing and decreasing returns to variable input.

SHORT-RUN COST FUNCTIONS IN THE REAL WORLD: THE EMPIRICAL EVIDENCE

Economists have conducted a great many studies of the short-run cost functions of particular firms and industries. A wide variety of accounting, engineering, and econometric methods have been used to analyze historical cost and output data. Although both the methods employed and the data used suffer from a number of deficiencies, the results of these studies point consistently to one conclusion: *In the short run a linear TC function with constant marginal cost is the pattern that best seems to describe actual cost behavior over the "normal" operating range of output.* U-shaped marginal and average cost

---

[9] The mathematical proof of this point is relatively simple and follows the procedure presented earlier in Mathematical Capsule 9. Let *TC* be some function of the quantity of output:

$$TC = f(Q).$$

Then, by definition,

$$MC = \frac{dTC}{dQ} = f'(Q) \quad \text{and} \quad ATC = \frac{f(Q)}{Q}.$$

For *ATC* to be a minimum value, it is necessary that the slope of the *ATC* curve be zero, which, in turn, requires that the derivative of the *ATC* equation be equal to zero:

$$\frac{dATC}{dQ} = \frac{Q \cdot f'(Q) - f(Q)}{Q^2} = 0.$$

For *dATC/dQ* to equal zero, the numerator of the above expression must be zero, or

$$Q \cdot f'(Q) - f(Q) = 0.$$

This can be rewritten as

$$f'(Q) = \frac{f(Q)}{Q}.$$

Since $f'(Q) = MC$ and $f(Q)/Q = ATC$, then the output rate that makes *ATC* minimum is also the value of *Q* at which *MC* = *ATC*.

By analogous logic, it can be shown that *MC* = *AVC* at the minimum point of the *AVC* curve when the equation for total variable cost is of the form $TVC = f(Q)$.

APPLICATIONS CAPSULE

USING MARGINAL COST CONCEPTS TO DISPATCH ELECTRIC POWER

Electric utility firms have, for more than two decades, used marginal product-marginal cost concepts to generate and dispatch electric power in a more efficient, lower-cost manner. The Southern Company, the nation's largest electric utility, employs a load-dispatching method that is designed to provide automatic, computerized control of all the company's power production and transmission facilities. The marginal cost of delivering additional kilowatts of electricity to Southern Company customers anywhere in the company's service area is continuously calculated; then, as electricity demand rises or falls at points throughout the system, computers transmit "raise" or "lower" impulses to the company's generating units and route the correct amount of electricity along the most economical transmission path to the end user.

Periodically, Southern Company engineers test the operating efficiency of every piece of power-generating equipment the company has in service. The purpose of the test is to determine how much fuel, labor, and other variable inputs are required to produce electricity with that unit and, subsequently, to calculate a production function for that generating unit. Experience has shown that revised production function equations must be calculated from time to time because normal wear and tear, maintenance problems, and mechanical efficiency vary over time and from generator to generator, depending on who manufactured it, when it was purchased, how long it has been in service, and the reliability with which it has performed. In other words, the production function for a given generating unit shifts by sufficiently large amounts over time to make it worthwhile to update the input-output equation. The equations for the production functions of each generating unit are then fed into the computer and combined with information as to fuel prices, wage rates, and other variable input prices to obtain marginal cost functions; from these, MC values can be calculated for a particular generating unit at whatever rate it is being operated.

In addition, because there is a loss of electricity in the course of "shipping" it through the transmission wires, Southern engineers make studies to determine the transmission loss coefficients from generating units to distribution substations. These, too, have to be updated several times a year since the transmission loss depends not only on the distance factor but also on the varying load characteristics of the system and changes in the transmission grid.

The marginal cost equations, together with the transmission loss coefficients, are the nucleus for computerized control of power generation and transmission. When, during the course of a day, the demand for electricity picks up, the computer system is programmed to compare the marginal costs of generation at each on-line unit and then to send impulses to raise the electricity output of the unit (or units) where MC is lowest. Simultaneously, another computer program analyzes the transmission loss coefficients to calculate how best to allocate the increased load on the transmission grid so as to minimize transmission loss to the many substations and end-user locations. In similar fashion, when electricity demand falls off (as work shifts end and businesses close at the end of the day), the dispatch system automatically sends impulses to reduce electricity generation at those power units where MC is highest and reroutes the remaining load to maintain maximum transmission economy and load-generation balance. At periods of peak demand, when on-line generating units are already operating at or near their minimum cost points, and assuming that water levels in Southern's dammed reservoirs are ample, the computer sends impulses to Southern's hydroelectric facilities to open the gates and generate enough power to get across the peak.

Southern's power-dispatch control center is also equipped to forecast short-term loads for the next hour, day, or week. For example, weather data from all around Southern's four-state service area are fed into the computer network several times a day to help forecast heating and air-conditioning loads. The hourly, daily, and weekly forecasts of upcoming load demands are used to preplan the mix of generating units to put on line and those to put on standby, to schedule maintenance, and to determine whether to exchange blocks of electricity with neighboring utilities. For instance, approximately 15 minutes prior to the beginning of an hour, calculations as to the next hour's generating and transmission costs are made; this information is then compared immediately with similar information obtained from adjoining utilities having interconnections with Southern's transmission network. If it is determined that it would be more economical for Southern to buy a "block" of electricity from an adjacent company than to generate the electricity needed itself (because at the forecasted generating rates the other company will have lower MC than Southern), then an order is placed for that unit at a price set forth in the interchange agreement between the two companies. On the other hand, if Southern's marginal costs are lower than those of its neighbors, then it may agree to sell a block. The exchange of electricity among interconnected companies based upon marginal cost calculations is common throughout the electric utility industry.

QUESTION FOR DISCUSSION

1. Suppose you were the head of a group charged with developing estimates of the production functions and marginal cost functions for power generators. What data would you want, and how would you go about conducting a test of the equipment to obtain the production function?

curves have been found to exist but seem to be less general than commonly thought. Table 8-5 summarizes the findings of a number of these studies.

Despite a lack of strong empirical confirmation for a U-shaped cost structure, there is still ample reason for asserting that the closer a firm approaches its short-run maximum rate of production, the greater becomes the pressure for rising marginal and average costs. As a firm attempts to squeeze more and more output from its production facilities, the chances increase that some wage premium for overtime will be incurred. If second and third shifts are used, the productivity of labor tends to be noticeably lower than on the day shift. Intensive use of equipment induces more breakdowns, leaves less time for maintenance, and induces production bottlenecks. Marginal, and perhaps obsolete, pieces of equipment may have to be brought on stream to achieve rated capacity. Hiring standards may have to be lowered to obtain the needed labor. Hence, in striving to push output toward the limit there is a tendency for a firm to utilize less efficient and/or marginal capital and labor inputs. As this occurs, increases in *MC* and *ATC* can be expected.

Evidence to this effect comes from McGraw-Hill's annual survey of manufacturing firms regarding (1) what percentage of production capacity is currently being used and (2) what percentage of capacity utilization is most preferred. The preferred rates of operation usually range in the neighborhood of 90%, which strongly implies that many firms achieve maximum efficiency-minimum *ATC* at about 90% of the capacity rate of production. Apparently,

Most firms appear to achieve maximum efficiency and minimum unit costs at about 90% of production capacity.

TABLE 8-5   RESULTS OF EMPIRCAL STUDIES OF SHORT-RUN COST FUNCTIONS

Name	Type of Industry	Finding
Lester (1946)	Manufacturing	AVC decreases up to capacity levels of output.
Hall and Hitch (1939)	Manufacturing	Majority have decreasing MC.
Johnston (1960)	Electricity, multiple-product food processing	"Direct" cost is a linear function of output, and MC is constant.
Dean (1936)	Furniture	Constant MC which failed to rise.
Dean (1941)	Leather belts	No significant increases in MC.
Dean (1941)	Hosiery	Constant MC which failed to rise.
Dean (1942)	Department store	Declining or constant MC, depending on the department within the store.
Ezekiel and Wylie (1941)	Steel	Declining MC but large variation.
Yntema (1940)	Steel	Constant MC.
Johnston (1960)	Electricity	ATC falls, then flattens, tending toward constant MC up to capacity.
Mansfield and Wein (1958)	Railways	Constant MC.

Source: A. A. Walters, "Production and Cost Functions," *Econometrica,* Vol. 31, No. 1 (January 1963), pp. 1–66.

producing within the 90 to 100% range would entail, as argued, rising marginal and average costs. It could be, therefore, that the failure of empirical studies to detect rising unit costs is because the cost-output data of the firms and industries examined were, for the most part, below the output range where the pressures on capacity cause unit costs to increase.

If one combines the results of empirical cost studies with the implications of the McGraw-Hill survey, then the cost functions shown in Figure 8-5 may represent a generalized cost structure for a number of firms and production processes. The properties of these cost functions suggest increasing returns to variable input at exceptionally low production rates, constant returns to variable input thereafter up to about 90 or 95% of capacity, and decreasing returns to variable input beyond the 90 to 95% level. Thus, while the marginal cost curve is U-shaped, the bottom of the U has a wide, flat range that encompasses the "normal" and "preferred" rates of output. *AVC* continues to fall over this entire range because *MC* is below *AVC*. This follows from the fact that the slope of *TVC* in the linear portion is a smaller value than the slope of a ray drawn from the origin of the diagram in Figure 8-5(a) to the *TVC* curve; the former slope value equals *MC*, while the latter equals *AVC*.

Cost-Output Relationships in the Long Run

In the long run all resource inputs are variable; a firm can alter its usage of major capital equipment, change top-management personnel, build new plant capacity, close down obsolete facilities, update its use of technology, substitute

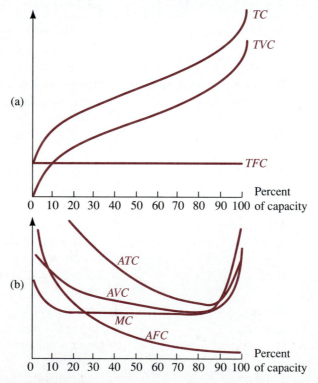

Figure 8-5

Total, average, and marginal cost curves frequently found in business enterprises

cheaper inputs for more expensive ones, or in any other way modify its production process and use of resources per period of time.

Such decisions are important because they determine the character of the short-run cost positions the firm will occupy in the future. For instance, before a firm makes a decision to change its productive potential, the firm is in a long-run position, with several options as to equipment, technology, and capital-labor mix. But once commitments are made and the new production capacity is installed, the firm's situation reverts to the short run, where the types and amounts of certain inputs are, for the time being, frozen.

Generally, *a firm's long-run cost objective is to be in a position to produce the desired output at the lowest possible cost.* This means adjusting its scale of production so as to be "the right size." Sometimes economies can be attained by dividing the production process into smaller production units. On other occasions lower unit costs can be achieved by enlarging the scale of production. In examining how efficiency and costs are affected by the scale of production, it is important to distinguish between *plants* and *firms* because the cost-efficiency advantages and disadvantages of each are different. Moreover, because there are no fixed inputs in the long run, the distinction between fixed and variable costs disappears—there are no *TFC* and *AFC* curves, and, in fact, we need look only at the nature and shape of the long-run average cost curve.

In the long run, a firm has the flexibility to make whatever modification in technology and inputs are needed to produce the desired output volumes at the lowest possible cost.

COST BEHAVIOR AND PLANT SIZE

Suppose that technological constraints allow a firm the choice of constructing any one of three plant sizes: small, medium, and large. The short-run average cost (SRAC) curve for each of these plant sizes is represented by $SRAC_S$, $SRAC_M$, and $SRAC_L$ in Figure 8-6. Whatever size plant the firm has currently, in the long run it can convert to or construct any one of these three plant scales. Obviously, the firm's choice of plant size is conditioned by its estimate of the production capacity needed to meet the demand for its products. For example, if the anticipated demand is OQ_1, the firm should elect to build the small-sized plant, since it can produce OQ_1 units of output per period of time at a cost of AC_1, which is well below either the unit cost of the medium-

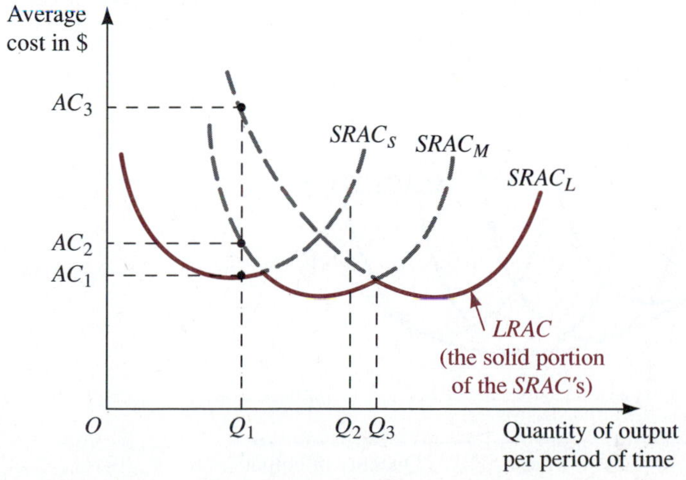

Figure 8-6
Long-run average cost curve when only three plant sizes are available

sized plant (AC_2) or the unit cost of the large-sized plant (AC_3). If the expected demand is OQ_2, the medium-sized plant plainly offers the lowest unit cost. On the other hand, at a demand of OQ_3 the medium- and large-sized plants are equally efficient from a unit cost standpoint. Here the final choice of plants might depend on the forecasted *trend* in consumer demand, with an expectation of strong growth tipping the scales in favor of the large plant. Otherwise, the medium-sized plant is likely to be the more attractive because of its smaller capital investment requirements.

The portions of the three short-run average cost curves which identify the optimum plant size for a given output are indicated by the solid, scalloped line in Figure 8-6. This line is called the **long-run average cost curve** (*LRAC*) and *shows the minimum cost per unit of producing each possible output rate when all resource inputs are variable and any desired scale of plant can be built.* The dashed line segments of the *SRAC* curves all entail higher average costs at each output rate than is capable of being achieved with some other plant scale.

Usually, a firm will have more than just three plant sizes to choose from. When the number of alternative plant sizes approaches infinity, the *LRAC* curve is an "envelope" of the short-run curves that is tangent to each of the short-run average cost curves (see Figure 8-7). *Each point on the LRAC curve represents the least unit cost attainable for a given output rate when the firm has time to change the rate of usage of any and all inputs.* Suppose the firm estimates that an output of OQ_1 is most desirable; then the plant represented by $SRAC_1$ is the most efficient because it can produce OQ_1 units at a lower cost per unit than can a plant of any other size. If consumer demand should expand sufficiently to warrant an output of OQ_2 units, the output of the plant represented by $SRAC_1$ could be increased to meet this demand in the short run. Nevertheless, in the long run the firm would prefer to construct the plant represented by $SRAC_2$ because this slightly larger plant is capable of producing OQ_2 units at a lower cost. Should the level of demand expand even further to OQ_3 although the plant represented by $SRAC_2$ is capable of producing OQ_3 units, the plant represented by $SRAC_3$ is preferable because of its ability to produce OQ_3 units at a lower average cost.

Of all the possible plant sizes, the one which is most efficient of all is the one whose *SRAC* curve is tangent to the *LRAC* curve at the *minimum point*

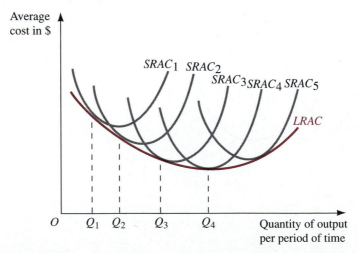

Figure 8-7

Long-run average cost curve for alternative plant sizes

of the *LRAC* curve.[10] The plant capable of producing the product at the lowest unit cost of all the other plants is termed the ***optimum plant size***. In Figure 8-7 the optimum plant size is the one corresponding to $SRAC_4$—no other plant is capable of producing the item at as low an average cost as is the plant associated with $SRAC_4$. It is in this sense that $SRAC_4$ represents the optimum plant size.

Observe that the *LRAC* curve is *not* tangent to the *SRAC* curves at their minimum points except in the one case of the optimum plant size. When the *LRAC* curve is decreasing (up to an output of OQ_4 in Figure 8-7) the *LRAC* curve is tangent to the *SRAC* curves to the left of their minimum cost points. Therefore, for outputs smaller than OQ_4, it is more economical to produce the desired output by "underusing" a slightly larger plant operating at *less* than its minimum cost output than it is to construct a plant that will produce the desired output at the minimum point of its *SRAC* curve. However, when the *LRAC* curve is rising (past an output of OQ_4 in Figure 8-7), the *LRAC* curve is tangent to the *SRAC* curves to the right of their minimum cost points. Hence, at outputs greater than OQ_4 it is more economical to produce the desired output by overusing a slightly smaller plant than it is to build a larger plant to produce the desired output at the minimum point of its *SRAC* curve.

The U-shape of the *LRAC* curve clearly implies that up to a certain output constructing larger-sized plants results in greater efficiency and lower unit cost, but that beyond this output larger plants become progressively less efficient and entail higher unit costs. There are a host of factors that underlie ***economies of scale*** and ***diseconomies of scale***.

Reasons for Economies of Scale at the Plant Level. The biggest reason why larger-scale plants can be more cost efficient than smaller-scale plants has to do with the economies of mass production. Up to a point, larger operations allow greater subdivision of the production process and greater specialization in the use of resource inputs (labor, capital equipment, and supervision). Almost invariably, specialization along functional or task-specific lines maximizes the efficiency gains and cost savings to be had from "the learning curve" (or the "experience curve") and from machine execution of simplified work elements. Moreover, the greater the volume of production and the more intensive the utilization of automated facilities, the lower are fixed costs per unit because the fixed investment costs of capital-intensive techniques are being spread out over a larger number of units of output. This, together with the fact that the cost of purchasing and installing larger machines and equipment is usually *not* proportionately greater than the costs of smaller machines with less capacity, means that large plants have an inherent ability to achieve lower average fixed costs, since they produce more units of output over which to spread proportionately smaller overhead costs.[11]

BASIC CONCEPT
Economies of scale exist whenever larger-scale plants are more cost efficient than smaller-scale plants (as occurs all along the declining portion of the *LRAC* curve); diseconomies of scale exist whenever larger-scale plants are less cost efficient than smaller-scale plants (as occurs all along the rising portion of the *LRAC* curve).

---

[10] In the event that the *LRAC* curve has a horizontal segment, there will be several plant sizes which qualify as the most efficient.

[11] One of the major reasons for lower electric rates during the 1950s and 1960s was the substantial savings in investment costs which electric utility firms realized by increasing generating unit sizes from 40 megawatts to 60, 80, 120, 150, and 250 megawatts. In the mid-70s, a generating plant with two 300-megawatt coal-fired units could be installed for an investment of about $330,000 per megawatt ($198 million total); doubling the size to two 600-megawatt units involved an investment of about $268,000 per megawatt; and doubling again to two 1200-megawatt units entailed an investment of approximately $245,000 per megawatt. However, past sizes of 800 to 900 megawatts, there were offsets against part of the investment savings because of higher transmission and maintenance costs and because of the need to maintain larger reserve margins as a hedge against unexpected breakdowns. Thus, the net savings associated with an increase in size from 880 megawatts to 1000 megawatts was only about $3000 per megawatt.

Also, the larger a plant, the greater the opportunities for taking advantage of and utilizing by-products. Take the case of naphtha; naphtha is a by-product of producing coke from coal and can be commercially marketed by steel plants having a large enough coking facility to make the capture of naphtha worthwhile. Other industries where by-products come into play include petroleum refining, meat packing, chemicals, and paper products. The advantage of building on a scale large enough to capture by-products is that, by gaining salable output which otherwise is waste, firms have added revenues to apply against production costs associated with the primary product.

Large-scale plants are in a position to take advantage of quantity discounts on purchases of raw materials and utility services. Similarly, larger plants can sometimes realize transportation savings by instituting their own shipping.

Eventually, of course, plants can be enlarged to the point where all economies of scale are taken full advantage of; larger plants then bring no additional savings in unit costs. It is here that the minimum level of the *LRAC* curve for plants is reached. Whether the *LRAC* curve begins to rise immediately with further increases in plant size or whether it has a flat portion before turning upward varies from industry to industry, depending on return-to-scale considerations and whether an industry's production technology requires large and indivisible units of capital input for low-cost production. Given the apparent prevalence of constant returns to scale, the *LRAC* curve is likely to have a flat bottom, thereby giving rise to a number of optimum-sized plants, each capable of producing at the lowest achievable unit cost. But there can be little

A number of factors combine to make large-scale plants more cost efficient than small-scale plants.

APPLICATIONS CAPSULE

ECONOMICS OF SCALE IN THE PIPELINE BUSINESS

The operation of oil and natural gas pipelines typically entails substantial economies of scale. According to studies made by Exxon, the relative costs of oil pipelines fall rapidly as the diameter of the pipeline increases—as shown in the diagram.

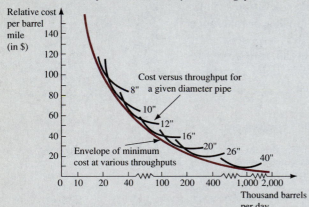

Relative Pipeline Costs versus System Throughput

interstate pipelines in the United States are owned by more than one company and the same pipeline system is often jointly used by many companies, owners, and nonowners. This joint use allows the most efficient-size pipeline to be built and full advantage to be taken of scale economies.

The presence of large economies of scale has dictated a number of operating practices. For example, in the case of oil pipelines, owners may require throughput guarantees or some other provision for the recovery of costs incurred before they will connect a new shipper to the system. The cost of a new connection may include laying a pipeline to the new shipper or installing new metering facilities to account for shipments or building additional working tankage. Throughput guarantees commit the shipper who is requesting the connection to either ship sufficient volumes or pay sufficient tariffs to provide some reasonable assurance that the added investment by the pipeline owner will be paid off.

Pipeline tariffs are regulated by government agencies and have fallen steadily since the early 1950s, mainly because new technology has allowed larger and larger diameter pipelines with their resultant economies of scale and greatly reduced costs. According to statistics, the average cost per barrel moved 1000 miles fell from 65 cents in 1955 to 50 cents in 1971.

The scale economies in the pipeline business are so large that they extend the efficient size beyond the level which a single company may be able to utilize. As a result, most

doubt that, at some juncture, continued increases in plant size will produce diseconomies and cause *LRAC* to rise.

Generally, the production units in aircraft, electric power production, automobiles, oil refining, paper, tires, glassware, aluminum, and inorganic chemicals all involve large-scale, multimillion-dollar plant investments. On the other hand, the manufacture of garments, mobile homes, shoes, furniture, sporting goods, and precision instruments, as well as printing and publishing, coal mining, and farming, can be efficiently conducted in relatively small production units.

Reasons for Diseconomies of Scale at the Plant Level.   The more space over which a plant is spread, the greater the bottlenecks and costs of getting labor, materials, and semifinished goods from one place in the plant to another. Moreover, the larger the plant, the more likely that needed raw materials will have to be shipped from more distant suppliers, thereby driving up the transportation costs of incoming materials. Similarly, the larger the output of a plant, the farther distances outputs may have to be shipped to reach potential buyers, thereby raising the costs of transporting the product from the point of manufacture to the final consumer. To these must be added the growing difficulties of maintaining efficient supervision and coordination. As an extreme example, imagine the incredible problems that would beset General Motors were it to try to produce some 5 million Buicks, Saturns, Cadillacs, Chevrolets, Oldsmobiles, and Pontiacs at a single plant site—the logistics of managing 600,000 employees, millions of component parts, and hundreds of thousands of inventoried cars would entail a colossal logjam and gross inefficiency.

COST BEHAVIOR AND FIRM SIZE

Even after plants have been expanded to their most efficient size and all economies of plant size taken advantage of, there may arise additional cost-efficiency gains from putting a number of plants under common management. The separate units of a multiplant enterprise may perform the same kind of operation and thus be horizontally integrated—a chain of motels or a series of garment plants. Or the plants may be vertically integrated to perform successive phases of the same overall production process. Or they may involve the production of a number of related products, as occurs in diversified enterprises. In all three situations, opportunities for realizing scale economies may exist.

Even after all plant economies of scale have been exhausted, there are still opportunities for a multiplant firm to achieve cost-saving efficiencies not open to a single-plant firm.

Reasons for Economies of Scale at the Firm Level.   To begin with, putting several plants under common management economizes on top-management costs. Spreading the salaries of key executives and administrative staff over 5 million units of output a year instead of 1 million units lowers average cost. Second, multiproduct firms can often achieve cost savings from specializing in serving the full range of needs of a particular customer segment or market, or from using the same distribution channel to market their outputs, or from using a common technology to produce a number of different products.

Third, there are mass-marketing economies associated with nationwide or global distribution systems and sales promotion campaigns that provide a more effective canvassing of markets and consumers per dollar spent.[12] For

[12] This contention is documented in a study by William S. Comanor and Thomas A. Wilson, "Advertising and the Advantages of Size," *American Economic Review, Papers and Proceedings,* Vol. 59, No. 2 (May 1969), pp. 87–98.

example, IBM, in selling 2 million personal computers annually, can well afford to spend $90 million advertising its products (a modest advertising cost of only $36 per PC), but for Tandy to spend $90 million on advertising to sell 300,000 personal computers ($300 apiece) would place it at a distinct price disadvantage. Fourth, a large enterprise is better able to afford expert specialists for research, development, design, and production engineering, thereby sustaining a capability to introduce new and improved products and to embrace new technologies.

Fifth, the debt capacity and capital-raising potential that tends to accompany large size is available for (1) pioneering the development and implementation of cost-saving technological innovations; (2) withstanding the risk of cyclical downturns, sour investments in a new project, or secular decline in demand for some of the firm's products; and (3) investing in specialized management talent proficient in solving problems and developing better managerial technologies. When fully exploited, the outcome is an ***organizational economy of scale*** that can produce sizable cost savings for large enterprises.[13]

The biggest cause of scale diseconomies in large firms is an inability on the part of management to maintain peak efficiency as a firm's scale and scope of operations get larger and larger.

Reasons for Diseconomies of Scale at the Firm Level.   The chief reason why a firm's long-run average cost curve supposedly turns upward relates to the increasing difficulties and costs of managing ever-larger enterprises. Conventional wisdom instructs that beyond some size the larger a firm gets, the more likely it will become burdened down with bureaucratic red tape and unwieldy decision-making procedures; as a result, decisions get bogged down in costly layers of management and the time it takes for the firm to respond to new developments becomes inefficiently long. In addition, large firms may be at a price disadvantage in obtaining the services of blue-collar labor. Unions have had their greatest success in dealing with large enterprises; large firms often pay higher hourly wage rates than do small and medium-sized firms. Thus, to the extent that larger size is accompanied by an increase in the ability of unions to secure higher wage rates, the large enterprise may find itself confronted with diseconomies of scale unless it takes steps to offset them by means of automation or some other productivity-increasing strategy.

The Long-Run Average Cost Curve for Firms.   In some industries economies of scale are negligible and diseconomies assume paramount importance at relatively low outputs. Figure 8-8(a) shows a long-run average cost curve for firms in such situations. The points on the curve show the lowest feasible unit cost of production for various *firm* sizes when the *firm* has sufficient time to adjust its input combinations to optimum levels.[14] Examples where small-scale firms sometimes have cost advantages over large-scale enterprises include steel-making, farming, many of the retail trades, printing, residential construction, baking, automotive repair, concrete products, and dry-cleaning.

An industry's long-run average cost curve determines what size a firm must be in order to be cost efficient.

In other industries economies of scale are extremely important, and the firm's *LRAC* curve declines significantly over a long range of output, as depicted in Figure 8-8(b). Here a firm must be big in an absolute sense if it is to

[13] This point is developed in more detail in Oliver E. Williamson, *Corporate Control and Business Behavior* (Englewood Cliffs, N.J.: Prentice Hall, 1970), especially Chapters 8 and 9.
[14] It is worth noting that cost curves can vary between plants and firms in the same industry because of (1) differences in the firms' products and the impact this can have on costs; (2) age differences in production facilities, with newer facilities incorporating more efficient and cheaper technology-related improvements; and (3) differences in geographic locations—where wage rates, labor productivity, transportation costs, and taxes vary from area to area.

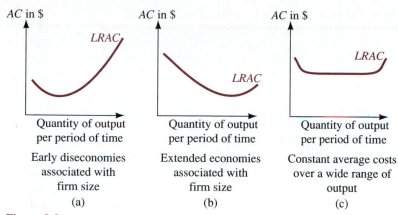

Figure 8-8
Alternate shapes for the long-run average cost curve

stay cost competitive. The automobile, aluminum, railroad, aircraft, paper products, and farm implement industries are cases in point.

In still other industries the *LRAC* curve of firms is virtually horizontal over a wide range of output [see Figure 8-8(c)]. Economies of scale are quickly exhausted, yet diseconomies are not forthcoming until very large outputs are produced. Or, alternatively, economies and diseconomies cancel each other out over an extended range of output. The result is that small, medium-sized, and large firms can operate with roughly an equivalent degree of efficiency. The meat packing, apparel, furniture, oil, household appliance, coal mining, textile, food products, rubber, and chemical industries are representative of this type of long-run cost behavior.

Table 8-6 summarizes the results of several major studies of long-run cost functions. None of these studies present conclusive evidence that large firms actually encounter significant diseconomies of scale in the range of observed data. Rather, the long-run average cost curve has generally been found to decrease and then level off as output rises. However, the failure to find much evidence of diseconomies of large size does not warrant concluding that *LRAC* curves in these industries fail to turn upward at some point. Firms may simply have been wise enough to avoid becoming so large as to incur rising unit costs. Moreover, the lack of truly large firms in several industries indicates that diseconomies do exist, although it does appear that diseconomies do not begin at so small a firm size as some might have imagined.

STRATEGIC COST ANALYSIS

While the nature and behavior of a firm's internal cost curves are important, a full-blown cost analysis must also address a firm's cost competitiveness and ability to compete successfully. *Competitors do not necessarily, or even usually, incur the same costs in supplying their products to end-users.* The disparities in costs among rival producers can stem from:

- Differences in the prices paid for raw materials, component parts, energy, and other items purchased from suppliers.
- Differences in basic technology and the age of plants and equipment. (Because rival companies have usually invested in plants and key pieces of equipment at different points in time, they enter into com-

There are many reasons why competing firms in the same industry do not have identical costs.

TABLE 8-6   RESULTS OF EMPIRICAL STUDIES OF LONG-RUN COST FUNCTIONS

Name	Type of Industry	Finding
Bain (1956)	Manufacturing	Small economies of scale for multiplant firms.
Holton (1956)	Retailing	LRAC is L-shaped.
Alpert (1959)	Metal	Economies of scale up to an output of 80,000 lbs per month; constant returns to scale and horizontal LRAC thereafter.
Moore (1959)	Manufacturing	Economies of scale prevail quite generally.
Lomax (1951) and Gribbin (1953)	Gas (Great Britain)	LRAC of production declines as output rises.
Lomax (1952) and Johnston (1960)	Electricity (Great Britain)	LRAC of production declines as output rises.
Johnston (1960)	Life assurance	LRAC declines.
Johnston (1960)	Road passenger transport (Great Britain)	LRAC either falling or constant.
Nerlove (1961)	Electricity (U.S.)	LRAC (excluding transmission costs) declines and then shows signs of increasing.

Source: A. A. Walters, "Production and Cost Functions," *Econometrica*, Vol. 31, No. 1 (January 1963), pp. 1–66.

petition with facilities having somewhat different technological efficiencies and different fixed costs—older facilities built when technology was less developed are typically less efficient but because they were constructed in times when it took less money to put them in place, they *may* still be reasonably cost competitive with modern facilities costing more to build. Whether older plants having lower fixed investment costs are, overall, cost competitive with newer plants having higher fixed investment costs depends on the tradeoff between the lower depreciation and other fixed costs of older plants and the increased operating efficiency of newer plants.)

• Differences in internal operating costs, owing to the economies of scale associated with different-sized plants, learning and experience curve effects, different wage rates, different energy costs, and the like.

• Differences in rival firms' exposure to rates of inflation and changes in foreign exchange rates (as can occur in global industries where competitors have plants located in different nations).

• Differences in shipping, warehousing, and wholesale distribution costs.

Plainly enough, for a company to be competitively successful, its costs must be "in line with" those of rival producers. The need to be cost competitive is not so stringent as to *require* every firm's costs to be *equal* but, as a rule, the more a firm's costs are above those of the low-cost producers the more vulnerable its market position becomes. Given the numerous opportunities for there to be cost disparities among competing companies, it is incumbent upon firms to be alert to how their costs compare with rivals' costs and how they can remain cost competitive over the long run. This is where **strategic cost analysis** comes in.

Strategic cost analysis focuses on a firm's relative cost position vis-à-vis its rivals. The primary analytical tool of strategic cost analysis is the construction of a *complete production-cost chain* showing the makeup of costs all the way from the inception of production to the end price paid by ultimate customers.[15] The complete production-cost chain thus includes more than just a firm's own internal cost structure; it includes the buildup of cost (and thus the "value" of the product) at each stage in the whole market chain of getting the product in the hands of the final user, as shown in Figure 8-9. Constructing a complete production-cost chain is more revealing than restricting attention to just a firm's own internal costs because a firm's overall ability to furnish end-users with its product at a competitive price can easily depend on cost factors originating either *backward* in the suppliers' portion of the production-cost chain or *forward* in the distribution channel portion of the chain.

The task of constructing a production-cost chain is not an easy task. It requires breaking a firm's own historical cost accounting data out into several principal cost categories and developing cost estimates for the backward and forward channel portions of getting the product to the end-user as well. It also requires estimating the same cost elements for one's rivals—an advanced art in competitive intelligence in itself. But despite the tediousness of the task and the imprecision of some of the estimates, the payoff in exposing the cost competitiveness of one's position and the attendant strategic alternatives makes it a valuable analytical tool. The Applications Capsule on page 234 shows a simplified production-cost chain comparing the cost competitiveness of U.S. and Japanese steel producers over a 20-year period.

The makeup of each firm's total value chain is unique to its own situation and can vary from item to item in the product line, from customer group to customer group (if different distribution channels are used), and from plant to plant (if plants employ different technologies or if plants are located in widely different geographic locations—different countries, for example). Once a firm has constructed production-cost chains for itself and its major competitors, it is in position to diagnose the degree to which it is cost competitive.

Looking again at Figure 8-9, observe that there are three main areas in the complete production-cost chain where important differences in the *relative* costs of competing manufacturers can occur: in the suppliers' part of the cost chain, in their own respective value-added segments, or in the forward channel portion of the chain. To the extent that the reasons for a manufacturer's lack of cost competitiveness lie either in the backward or forward sections of the overall production-cost chain, its job of reestablishing cost competitiveness may well have to extend beyond its own in-house operations. When a firm has a cost disadvantage in the area of purchased inputs, four strategic options

BASIC CONCEPT
Strategic cost analysis concerns how a firm's costs compare against the costs of its competitors.

The key analytical tool in strategic cost analysis is the construction of a production-cost chain showing the item-by-item buildup of cost at each step in the production process—starting at the raw material stage and ending with the distribution activities necessary to get the product to the end-user.

Comparing a firm's production-cost chain with the chains of rivals identifies where cost similarities and cost differences exist.

---

[15] The ins and outs of strategic cost analysis are discussed at greater length in Michael E. Porter, *Competitive Advantage* (New York: The Free Press, 1985), Chapters 2 and 3.

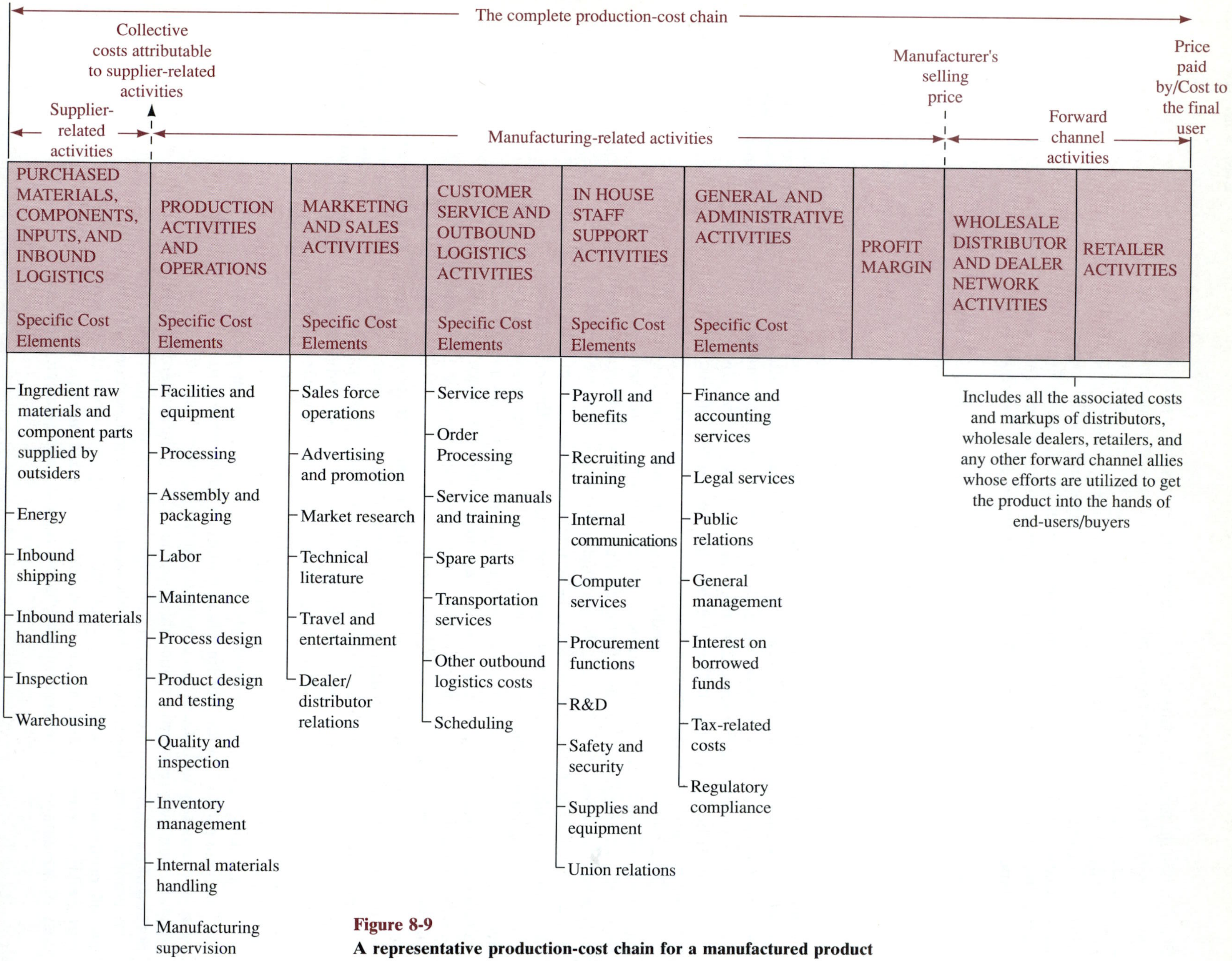

Figure 8-9

A representative production-cost chain for a manufactured product

The complete production-cost chain

Supplier-related activities | Manufacturing-related activities | Forward channel activities

Collective costs attributable to supplier-related activities — Manufacturer's selling price — Price paid by/Cost to the final user

PURCHASED MATERIALS, COMPONENTS, INPUTS, AND INBOUND LOGISTICS	PRODUCTION ACTIVITIES AND OPERATIONS	MARKETING AND SALES ACTIVITIES	CUSTOMER SERVICE AND OUTBOUND LOGISTICS ACTIVITIES	IN HOUSE STAFF SUPPORT ACTIVITIES	GENERAL AND ADMINISTRATIVE ACTIVITIES	PROFIT MARGIN	WHOLESALE DISTRIBUTOR AND DEALER NETWORK ACTIVITIES	RETAILER ACTIVITIES
Specific Cost Elements	Specific Cost Elements	Specific Cost Elements	Specific Cost Elements	Specific Cost Elements	Specific Cost Elements			

Specific Cost Elements

PURCHASED MATERIALS, COMPONENTS, INPUTS, AND INBOUND LOGISTICS:
- Ingredient raw materials and component parts supplied by outsiders
- Energy
- Inbound shipping
- Inbound materials handling
- Inspection
- Warehousing

PRODUCTION ACTIVITIES AND OPERATIONS:
- Facilities and equipment
- Processing
- Assembly and packaging
- Labor
- Maintenance
- Process design
- Product design and testing
- Quality and inspection
- Inventory management
- Internal materials handling
- Manufacturing supervision

MARKETING AND SALES ACTIVITIES:
- Sales force operations
- Advertising and promotion
- Market research
- Technical literature
- Travel and entertainment
- Dealer/distributor relations

CUSTOMER SERVICE AND OUTBOUND LOGISTICS ACTIVITIES:
- Service reps
- Order Processing
- Service manuals and training
- Spare parts
- Transportation services
- Other outbound logistics costs
- Scheduling

IN HOUSE STAFF SUPPORT ACTIVITIES:
- Payroll and benefits
- Recruiting and training
- Internal communications
- Computer services
- Procurement functions
- R&D
- Safety and security
- Supplies and equipment
- Union relations

GENERAL AND ADMINISTRATIVE ACTIVITIES:
- Finance and accounting services
- Legal services
- Public relations
- General management
- Interest on borrowed funds
- Tax-related costs
- Regulatory compliance

WHOLESALE DISTRIBUTOR AND DEALER NETWORK ACTIVITIES / RETAILER ACTIVITIES:
Includes all the associated costs and markups of distributors, wholesale dealers, retailers, and any other forward channel allies whose efforts are utilized to get the product into the hands of end-users/buyers

quickly emerge for consideration:

- Negotiate more favorable prices with suppliers.
- Integrate backward to gain control over material costs.
- Try to use lower-priced substitute inputs.
- Try to make up the difference by initiating cost savings elsewhere in the production-cost chain.

When a firm's cost disadvantage occurs in the forward end of the cost chain, there are three corrective options:

- Push for more favorable terms with distributors.
- Change to a more economical distribution strategy, including the possibility of forward integration
- Try to make up the difference by initiating cost savings earlier in the cost chain.

It is likely, of course, that a substantial portion of any relative cost disadvantage lies within rival firms' own cost structures. Here, five options for restoring cost parity emerge:

- Initiate internal budget-tightening measures aimed at using less input to generate the desired output (cost-cutting retrenchment).
- Invest in cost-saving technological improvements.
- Innovate around the troublesome cost components as new investments are made in plant and equipment.
- Redesign the product to achieve cost reductions.
- Try to make up the internal cost disadvantage by achieving cost savings in the backward and forward portions of the complete production-cost chain.

The analytical contribution of strategic cost analysis is the emphasis it places on a firm looking beyond the inner workings of its own cost structure to see how its costs stack up against the costs of competitors. *Strategic cost analysis is accomplished by examining the cost makeup of one's own complete production-cost chain and comparing it against the production-cost chains of important rival firms. Such comparisons reveal whether a firm has a cost advantage or disadvantage vis-à-vis major competitors and help pinpoint which cost components in the production-cost chain are the source of the cost advantage or disadvantage.* A strategic analysis of a company's cost structure and overall cost competitiveness is integral to the task of appraising how strong a grip a firm has on its market position and assessing a firm's competitive strategy options.

KEY POINTS

Measuring the cost of an activity means assessing the amount of sacrifice associated with conducting that activity. Completeness requires that the nature of the sacrifices considered be both tangible and intangible, objective and subjective, monetary and nonmonetary.

No one measure of cost is adequate for managerial or economic purposes. Depending on the type of problem, one may wish to calculate historical costs, opportunity costs, total costs, average costs, marginal costs, fixed costs, variable costs, direct costs, common costs, long-run costs, short-run costs, labor costs, controllable costs, shutdown costs, escapable costs, replacement

APPLICATIONS CAPSULE

An Illustrative Production-Cost Chain Comparing the Cost Competitiveness of U.S. Steel Producers and Japanese Steel Producers, 1956 and 1976

The following table shows a simplified production-cost chain comparing the cost competitiveness of U.S. steel producers and Japanese steel producers over a 20-year period. The shifts in the several cost components over the period are dramatic. Most resulted from relative shifts in input prices which built up gradually over time, but technological changes in input requirements and labor productivity were also at work.

	1956			
	Per-Ton Cost for Cold-Rolled Sheet Steel			
Cost Chain Elements	Typical U.S. Producer	Typical Japanese Producer	Net Cost Advantage	Production Activities
Coking coal	$ 12.02	$ 19.90	$ 7.88 (U.S.)	Purchased inputs and basic materials
Other energy	9.65	12.35	2.70 (U.S.)	
Scrap steel	17.80	34.75	16.95 (U.S.)	
Iron ore	16.70	26.17	9.47 (U.S.)	
Subtotal	$ 56.17	$ 93.17	$37.00 (U.S.)	
Manufacturing labor	$ 54.07	$ 28.80	$25.27 (Japan)	Manufacturing operations and administrative support
Capital charges for facilities and all other operating costs	9.80	31.17	21.37 (U.S.)	
Profit margin	5.00	4.00	1.00 (Japan)	
Subtotal	$ 68.87	$ 63.97	$ 4.90 (Japan)	
Transocean shipping Import duties	0	$ 35.69	$35.69 (U.S.)	Distribution and forward channel activities
Price paid by U.S. end-user	$125.04	$192.83	$67.79 (U.S.)	

costs, incremental costs, manufacturing costs, selling costs, administrative costs, and so on.

The cost-output relationships for a firm in the short run are governed by the character of the underlying production function. When the production function exhibits increasing returns to variable input, as output rises *TFC* remains constant, *TVC* and *TC* increase at a decreasing rate, and unit costs (*AFC*, *AVC*, *ATC*, and *MC*) decline.

When the underlying production function displays constant returns to variable input, rising output is associated with the following cost behavior: *TFC* is a fixed value, *TVC* and *TC* rise at a constant rate, *MC* and *AVC* are equal and constant, and *AFC* and *ATC* decline.

	1976 Per-Ton Cost for Cold-Rolled Sheet Steel		
Net Cost Advantage	Typical U.S. Producer	Typical Japanese Producer	Cost Chain Elements
$10.70 (Japan)	$ 52.15	$ 41.45	Coking coal
8.76 (Japan)	30.25	21.49	Other energy
.95 (U.S.)	20.80	21.75	Scrap steel
20.30 (Japan)	47.90	27.60	Iron ore
$38.81 (Japan)	$151.10	$112.29	Subtotal
$90.66 (Japan)	$142.93	$ 52.25	Manufacturing labor
7.93 (U.S.)	55.95	63.88	Capital charges for facilities and all other operating costs
1.40 (Japan)	4.90	3.50	Profit margin
$84.15 (Japan)	$203.78	$119.63	Subtotal
$36.36 (U.S.)	0	$ 36.36	Transocean shipping Import duties
$86.60 (Japan)	$354.88	$268.28	Price paid by U.S. end-user

Sources: Compiled by the authors from data in U.S. Federal Trade Commission, *The United States Steel Industry and Its International Rivals: Trends and Factors Determining International Competitiveness* (Washington, D.C.: U.S. Government Printing Office, 1978); and Robert W. Crandall, *The U.S. Steel Industry in Recurrent Crisis* (Washington, D.C.: Brookings Institution, 1981).

When the underlying production function is characterized by decreasing returns to variable input, increases in the output rate generate cost functions such that the *TVC* and *TC* functions increase at an increasing rate, *TFC* remains fixed, *AVC* and *MC* rise, *AFC* decreases, and *ATC* is U-shaped.

When the production function has a range first of increasing returns and then of decreasing returns to variable input, the firm's *TFC* function is again a horizontal line, but the *TVC* and *TC* functions both increase at a decreasing rate over the range of output where increasing returns to variable input prevail, then increase at an increasing rate over the output range where decreasing returns prevail. As usual, *AFC* decreases with increases in output irrespective of the nature of the returns to variable input. And the *AVC*, *ATC*, and *MC* curves are U-shaped functions, with the *MC* curve intersecting the *AVC* and *ATC* curves at their minimum points.

According to the best available empirical evidence, the behavior of total, average, and marginal costs in many firms embraces elements of the four preceding basic types of production-cost-output relationships. At output rates well below normal, increasing returns to variable input are encountered, and unit costs fall as output rises. Beyond these abnormally low output rates, constant returns to variable input prevail up to approximately 85 to 90% of capacity; over this output range total costs rise linearly, *MC* is a constant, and *ATC* declines. Past 90% of capacity, decreasing returns to variable input are encountered, *TVC* and *TC* begin to rise disproportionately to the additional increases in output, and *AVC*, *MC*, and *ATC* rise sharply.

In the long run when there is time to alter the usage of any and all inputs, a firm will seek to become the right size to produce the desired output at the lowest possible cost. The *LRAC* curve for a *plant* shows the minimum average cost of producing a food using various *plant* sizes when all resource inputs are variable and any desired scale of *plant* can be built. The *LRAC* curve for a *firm* shows the minimum average cost of producing a product for various firm sizes when the firm has adequate time to adjust any and all of its inputs to optimal levels. By and large, the *LRAC* curves for both plants and firms are U-shaped.

The behavior of long-run costs is a key force in determining the number and size of firms in a particular industry. Generally speaking, where significant economies are associated with mass production technologies, the structure of the industry will consist of a small number of large-scale producers. When there are few cost advantages to producing in large quantities and many cost disadvantages, production units will be large in number and small in size. In those cases where unit cost is virtually unaffected by the output rate, small, medium, and large firms may be able to compete on fairly equal terms.

Strategic cost analysis is a valuable analytical tool for examining how a firm's costs compare with the costs of its competitors. The core of strategic cost analysis is the construction of complete production-cost chains exposing whether a firm is at a cost advantage or disadvantage and whether it stems from cost differences in (1) the backward portion of the cost chain, (2) its own internal cost structure, or (3) the forward portion of the cost chain. The strategic options for eliminating a net cost disadvantage depend on where the cost disparities lie in the overall chain.

PROBLEMS AND QUESTIONS FOR DISCUSSION

1. Complete the following table:

Units of Output	TFC	TVC	TC	AFC	AVC	ATC	"Average" MC
0	_____	_____	$ 500	_____	_____	_____	
100	_____	_____	750	_____	_____	_____	_____
200	_____	_____	1100	_____	_____	_____	_____
300	_____	_____	1500	_____	_____	_____	_____
400	_____	_____	2000	_____	_____	_____	_____
500	_____	_____	2600	_____	_____	_____	_____

2. Complete the following table. Assume that units of fixed input cost $10 each and that units of variable input cost $20 each.

Units of Fixed Input	Units of Variable Input	Units of Output	"Average" Marginal Product of Variable Input	Average Product of Variable Input	TFC	TVC	TC	AFC	ATC	"Average" MC
100	0	0	___	___	___	___	___	___	___	___
100	20	600	___	___	___	___	___	___	___	___
100	40	1500	___	___	___	___	___	___	___	___
100	60	2000	___	___	___	___	___	___	___	___
100	80	2200	___	___	___	___	___	___	___	___
100	100	2300	___	___	___	___	___	___	___	___

3. Given the total cost function $TC = 10,000 + 9Q$, where Q = units of output:
  (a) Determine the equations for TFC and TVC, and illustrate graphically the relationships among TFC, TVC, and TC.
  (b) Determine the equations for AFC, AVC, ATC, and MC. Graphically illustrate their relationships to one another.
  (c) What, if anything, can you infer about the nature of the underlying production function?
  (d) How much is the marginal cost of the 100th unit of output? How much is AVC at an output of 100 units? Explain why $MC = AVC$ at each rate of output.

4. Given the total cost function $TC = 20,000 + 4Q + 0.5Q^2$, where Q = units of output:
  (a) Determine the equations for TFC and TVC. Graph the TFC, TVC, and TC functions, and graphically show their relationships to one another. How would you describe the behavior of TVC as output increases?
  (b) Determine the equations for AFC, AVC, ATC, and MC. Graph each of these functions, and graphically show their relationships to one another.
  (c) What is the nature of the underlying production function? What will its shape be?

5. Given the following information:
  • $Q = 6X$, where X = units of variable input and Q = units of output.
  • There are 10 units of fixed input.
  • Price of the fixed inputs = $10/unit.
  • Price of the variable inputs = $5/unit.
  Determine the corresponding equations for TFC, TVC, TC, AFC, AVC, ATC, and MC.

6. The total cost function of a shirt manufacturer is $TC = 10 + 26Q - 5Q^2 + 0.5Q^3$, where TC is in hundreds of dollars per month and Q is output in hundreds of shirts per month.
  (a) What is the equation for TVC?
  (b) What is the equation for AVC?
  (c) What is the equation for ATC?
  (d) What is the equation for MC?
  (e) Plot (or sketch) the relationships among TFC, TVC, and TC.
  (f) Plot (or sketch) the relationships among AFC, AVC, ATC, and MC.
  (g) What, if anything, can you infer about the nature of the underlying production function?

7. Given $TC = 2000 + 15Q - 6Q^2 + Q^3$, where Q = units of output:
  (a) How much is TFC at an output of 2000 units? At 5000 units?

(b) How much is *AFC* at an output of 2000 units? At 5000 units?

(c) How much is *AVC* at an output of 20 units?

(d) How much is *MC* at an output of 20 units?

(e) How much is *ATC* at an output of 20 units?

(f) At approximately what output rate is the point of diminishing marginal returns to variable input encountered?

(g) At approximately what output rate does diminishing average returns begin?

(h) At approximately what rate of output does stage II begin?

8. Given the production function $Q = 15X$, where X = units of variable input and Q = units of output. Units of variable input cost $30 each and units of fixed input cost $100 each. Ten units of fixed input are available.

(a) Determine *AFC* at an output of 400 units.

(b) Determine *AVC* when 10 units of variable input are combined with the 10 available units of fixed input.

(c) How much is *MC* at an output of 300 units?

9. Prove that $MC = AVC$ at the minimum point of the *AVC* curve when the equation for *TVC* is of the general form $TVC = bQ - cQ^2 + dQ^3$. (*Hint*: See footnote 9.)

10. What is the relationship, if any, between marginal costs and fixed costs?

11. Given the following cost information:

AFC for 5 units of output is $2000.

AVC for 4 units of output is $850.

TC rises by $1240 when the sixth unit of output is produced.

ATC for 5 units of output is $2880.

It costs $1000 more to produce 1 unit of output than to produce nothing.

TC for 8 units of output is $19,040.

TVC increases by $1535 when the seventh unit of output is produced.

AFC plus *AVC* for 3 units of output is $4185.

ATC falls by $5100 when output rises from 1 to 2 units.

Using this information, complete the following table:

Output	TFC	TVC	TC	AFC	AVC	ATC	MC
0	——	——	——	——	——	——	
1	——	——	——	——	——	——	——
2	——	——	——	——	——	——	——
3	——	——	——	——	——	——	——
4	——	——	——	——	——	——	——
5	——	——	——	——	——	——	——
6	——	——	——	——	——	——	——
7	——	——	——	——	——	——	——
8	——	——	——	——	——	——	——

12. Midwest Foundry Corp. was exploring the construction of one of three types of facilities for manufacturing a new type of cast iron pipe. Estimated costs for each of the three facilities are indicated in the following table:

Cost Component	Plant A	Plant B	Plant C
Cost of materials per unit	$3.00	$3.00	$3.00
Labor costs per unit	$0.25	$0.50	$0.75
Equipment cost (10-year life)	$750,000	$600,000	$250,000
Fixed overhead expenses	$100,000	$60,000	$20,000
Maintenance and variable overhead expense per unit	$0.15	$0.20	$0.40
Annual output capacity (in units)	500,000	375,000	125,000

(a) Determine which plant is capable of achieving the lowest *ATC* at an output of 300,000 units. (For outputs greater than the annual capacity of plant C, assume that Midwest would simply build as many type C plants as necessary to obtain the desired output.)

(b) What is the lowest-cost plant arrangement for an output of 1 million units?

Chapter 9

The Profit Motive and Other Goals of the Firm

A major task of microeconomic theory is to explain and to predict how companies will behave and respond to changes in particular market forces and economic policies. This is not a simple matter in a complex industrialized world where the forms of enterprise range from the freewheeling independent proprietorship to the multiproduct, billion-dollar modern corporation and where competition varies from one industry to the next. Three approaches to studying business behavior have emerged. One explains business behavior through the goals of the firm, the rationale being that decision makers are prone to select the actions and strategies which they perceive best contribute to achieving the firm's goals. A second focuses on the behavior of key decision makers inside the firm and considers how their pursuit of individual self-interest may influence the activities of the firm in a manner not entirely consistent with the announced goals of the firm. The third approach is complementary to the others and rests upon the idea that market conditions and competition drive (or constrain) a firm's behavior. The three approaches are by no means exclusive and we shall find it useful to use each.

In this chapter we examine the factors that motivate and drive firms to behave as they do. The primary focus is on the profit motive, but we consider other objectives of firms as well. Particular emphasis is placed on the character, source, and use of profits, the role and functions of profits in a market economy, and whether firms seek to maximize profits. The last section of the chapter discusses some alternatives to strict profit maximization and considers principal-agent problems that can arise between the managers and owners of firms.

THE MANY WAYS PROFIT CAN BE DEFINED

BASIC CONCEPT
Profit is what is left over after all costs have been paid; it is the margin by which total revenues exceed total costs.

Profit is typically defined as the difference between total revenue and total cost and is conventionally expressed as $\pi = TR - TC$, where π represents profit. This definition of profit, although widely accepted and seemingly straightforward, is nonetheless ambiguous in its application. To the accountant, "profit" usually means total revenue minus actual historical costs; thus *accounting profit* is an *ex post* concept based upon past transactions and historical fact.[1] To the economist "profit" means total revenue minus *all* costs—not just the historical money expenses incurred by the firm but an allowance for a "normal" return on owner's investment as well. The various approaches to what constitutes a cost and how cost should be measured give rise to the concepts of accounting profit, normal profit, and economic profit.

The most significant element of discrepancy between accounting and economic measures of profit relates to the treatment of the stockholders' capital investment in an enterprise. Economists contend that in a capitalistic economy the owners of an enterprise must, over the long run, receive a return on their investment of sufficient magnitude to induce the enterprise to remain in business. Whenever the profitability of a business consistently is below what can generally be earned in other enterprises of equivalent business risk, stockholders can be expected to seek greener pastures for their investment funds. Because additional resources and capital will tend to be withheld from an enterprise if and when realized accounting profits fall below "minimum acceptable levels" for sustained periods, it is appropriate to conceive of this minimum profitability as a "cost." It is a cost in the sense that unless revenues from a firm's operations are adequate to provide acceptable rewards to stockholders, the capital funds needed to sustain operations will dry up and the firm, in time, will wither and die.[2] In other words, *in the long run some minimum amount of profit is a condition of survival.*

How large is this minimum acceptable degree of profitability? A 10% after-tax return on stockholders' investment? Or 15%? Actually, a hard and fast standard does not exist; how much profit is enough varies with such circumstances as the alternatives for profit in other economic activities, the risk involved, the time period, the amount of required capital investment, inflation rates, the health of the economy, the type of industry, the long-run potential of the enterprise, what other firms are earning, and so on. But whatever the size of the minimum, it provides a benchmark for judging whether to remain in business or get out. Firms that cannot earn an acceptable profit doing what they are doing should "get out" and divert capital and resources into activities where *at least* a minimum acceptable profit can be earned. Accordingly, it has become customary in economics to think of the *minimum profit* that is necessary to keep a firm in business in the long run *as being a genuine cost of production* which must be covered if the firm is to remain in existence. We shall refer to this minimum acceptable return on owners' investment as **normal profit**. On the other hand, **economic profit** is defined as any return over and above a normal profit. The following examples illustrate how accounting profit, normal profit, and economic profit are related.

Standard accounting does not include a normal return on owners' investment as a cost; economists contend that accounting definitions of profit overstate true profitability because some minimal payment for the use of owners' capital is a genuine cost that must be covered to keep an enterprise in business.

BASIC CONCEPT
A normal profit is the minimum payment for the use of owners' capital needed to keep the enterprise in business over the long run. Economic profit is any return over and above a normal profit.

---

[1] However, accounting measures of profit are by no means exact just because they are based upon past events with known monetary values. Indeed, several acceptable accounting alternatives exist for determining the "correct" revenues and costs to attribute to a given time period. There are a number of alternative techniques for calculating depreciation, valuing inventories, deciding when to write off overdue accounts receivable as bad-debt losses, and deciding how to adjust the costs of fixed assets for price level changes. In addition, while it is customary to count the costs of advertising, public relations, research and development, and training in the period in which they occur, it is clear that they affect *future* sales, production, and profits. Hence, accounting profit calculations are estimates rather than absolute truth.

[2] The actual or realized return to stockholders takes two forms: (1) dividends and (2) capital gains—increases in the value of a stock in terms of price per share.

EXAMPLE 1

Company A owns production facilities valued at $100 million. Its net earnings after taxes were $12 million—as determined by standard accounting techniques. Assuming that the normal rate of return for firms of comparable position is 8%, the company's normal profit should approximate $8 million (8% of $100 million). Company A's *economic profit* is thus $12 million − $8 million = $4 million. The $4 million represents that portion of the overall return to owners (stockholders) *over and above* what could be earned in comparable alternative ventures.

EXAMPLE 2

Company X has made an equity investment of $50 million in facilities to produce high-speed copying equipment. According to conventional accounting measures, its earnings after taxes were $5 million or 10% on investment. However, an evaluation of the alternatives open to company X indicates that had the firm directed its energies to producing word processors, net earnings after taxes could have been $6 million. Hence, even though company X realized a 10% return on its investment, it lost out on an opportunity to earn 12%, thereby resulting in an *opportunity loss* of 2%.

Business decisions and behavior are based on future profit expectations, not on past profits (or losses); since past experience does not necessarily carry over into the future, the driver of decisions and behavior hinges upon the size of the future stream of expected profits.

In all remaining references to profit, we mean economic profit; a normal return or normal profit is considered as a part of total cost. One final point: Insofar as both decision-making and the analysis of firm behavior are concerned, interest centers more on *expected* profit than upon *realized* profits.[3] Realized profits are relevant as a guide to action and to behavior only to the extent that they influence future profit expectations. Realized profits can also serve as the yardstick for measuring past performance. Nonetheless, expected profit considerations serve as the basis for business decisions and for predicting the behavior of firms.

THEORIES OF PROFIT

The private enterprise type of economic system (i.e., *capitalism*) has provoked a wealth of controversy and discussion about profit—from whence it derives, the economic functions it performs, its ethical and moral qualities, and whether profit is socially justified. The various theories about profit and its economic role can, for convenience, be grouped into three broad categories:

1. Compensatory and functional theories of profit.
2. Friction and monopoly theories of profit.
3. Technology and innovation theories of profit.

This group is indicative of historical patterns of thinking on profit issues and for our purposes offers a logical approach to examining the sources and justification for both normal and economic profit.

---

[3] More precisely, managers are primarily interested in the size of the time-discounted profit flow, or to put it another way, the *present value* of the expected stream of profits. The present value of the stream of profits flowing in from an investment is the amount of money that must be invested *now*, at some rate of return, to produce a cash flow equivalent to the expected profit flow.

COMPENSATORY AND FUNCTIONAL THEORIES OF PROFIT

As applied to owner-managed firms, the compensatory and functional theories of profit hold that *normal profit is a payment to the entrepreneur in return for services performed in coordinating and supervising the many facets of a firm's activities and in bearing the risks of enterprise*. The entrepreneur is the key force in initiating, integrating, and guiding productive activities to a successful conclusion. It is entrepreneurial alertness to unnoticed product-customer-technological opportunities that catalyzes and drives market processes. The entrepreneur is held to be *the* human action element crucial to making the firm a success and to stimulating economic activity in general. Profit, therefore, arises partly as a justifiable compensation and reward to the entrepreneur for fulfilling the various economic and managerial functions successfully. Losses are the penalty for entrepreneurial failure.

Profit can be viewed as justifiable compensation and reward for successfully performing the entrepreneurial function.

From this perspective, the entrepreneur emerges as a laborer of a particular type and talent. Profit becomes the special creation of the gifted entrepreneur, who, by his or her comprehension of the marketplace, capacity for organization, administrative ability, and energy, wisdom, and economy, is most responsible for generating an excess of total revenue over total cost—an excess that may result in the realization of economic profits as well as normal profits. Profit, then, is more than something that just happens to be left over after all costs are covered; rather its existence signals astute entrepreneurship, a vitality of enterprise, and competitive strength.

While this explanation of profit provides a plausible rationale for justifying and explaining why individual proprietorships, partnerships, and small entrepreneurial corporations are entitled to at least a normal profit, it is at considerable variance with the realities of large corporate enterprise. In large corporations, salaried managers perform much of the entrepreneurial function, but the profits accrue to "absentee" stockholders, whose primary function is to supply financial capital to the firm rather than entrepreneurship. Consequently, functional and compensatory reasons other than entrepreneurship must be found for justifying why corporations should earn a normal profit.

One such basis pertains to the risk-taking function which stockholders perform even though they are absentee owners. In furnishing the corporation with venture capital, the stockholder receives no assurance of a return on his or her investment in the form of dividends and/or capital gains. The stockholder can and does lose money when the corporation's activities prove to be unprofitable. Unpredictable changes in the general economic environment combine with sudden changes in consumer tastes, resource supplies, competitive forces, government policy, and technology to produce an abundance of uncertainty that tends to enrich some firms and impoverish others. Investors willing to accept the uncertainties of enterprise are entitled to a reward for the use of their capital—a reward that rightly should be keyed to the degree of uncertainty borne by the investor. The reward for bearing uncertainty and risking one's venture capital is properly considered as normal profit and not economic profit.

Profit can be viewed as justifiable compensation and reward for investors' willingness to risk their venture capital and finance a business endeavor having an uncertain outcome.

At least a portion of corporate profits, then, can be looked upon as a reward to stockholders for confronting uncertainty and supplying venture capital to the enterprise. Naturally, though, a 20% *expected* return will not be valued as highly as a 20% *guaranteed* return. Depending upon the confidence investors place in the estimated profitability of a venture and depending upon their immediate inclinations toward either taking risks or avoiding them, they may evaluate a 20% expected return as equivalent to 10% on a sure thing, or just 8%, or even just 5%. Hence while stockholders are indeed absentee owners, they still perform the essential entrepreneurial functions of bearing the uncertainties of enterprise and of supplying risk capital—both of which contribute to a firm's survival and competitive success. And the element of uncertainty explains why business firms must sometimes earn "high" profits if they are to keep investors willing to supply risk capital—the greater the degree of uncertainty, the greater must be the prospect of reward to justify going ahead with a venture.

Profit can be viewed as justifiable compensation and reward to sellers for having furnished buyers with something they wanted at a price they were willing to pay, thereby rendering a valuable service to buyers.

Another compensatory explanation as to how profit arises attaches to the service that a firm renders to its customers. To some extent, a firm's profit (normal or economic) may derive from the fact that many buyers are willing to pay a price that more than covers the cost of labor, materials, capital, taxes, and other expenses involved in furnishing the good or service because of the time it saves, or its usefulness and convenience, or status and prestige, or any other utility-related reason. *The excess of price over cost thus represents compensation to the supplier for having the skill and foresight to give buyers the kind of value they wanted.* The proponents of this viewpoint observe that when firms are adequately rewarded with profit for fulfilling society's material wants in the face of market uncertainties, they tend to be more efficient, more willing to innovate, more venturesome, and therefore more progressive. Why? Because when the stakes are more attractive, enterprises are more daring and their entrepreneurial spirit more vibrant. Moreover, the earning of economic profit enhances the financial ability of firms to invest in new activities and to make up for the periodic losses of those ventures that turn sour.

FRICTION AND MONOPOLY THEORIES OF PROFIT

A second group of theories maintains that profit can result from luck, good fortune, positions of competitive advantage, various market frictions, and/or a lack of vigorous competition. These have the effect of allowing firms to earn "monopoly" profits. Ideally, competition is always sufficiently strong to preclude firms from "exploiting" consumers; when it is, firms are generally unable to maneuver themselves into the position of being able to influence prices or otherwise "rig the market" to their own advantage.

Friction and monopoly theories attribute the existence of economic profit to luck, market imperfections, weak competition, and the ability of firms to secure positions of monopolistic advantage from which to exploit buyers.

In the real world, of course, competition is not always powerful and responsive enough to foreclose any and all elements of monopolistic advantage. For example, unusually favorable locations for motels, service stations, restaurants, and similar establishments give them distinct locational advantages over less fortunately situated rivals. International trade barriers may give domestic producers a more strategic position in domestic markets. Military and other government installations may bring profit bonanzas to adjacent localities. Windfall profits may be obtained for short periods of time as the result of circumstances (labor strikes, extreme weather conditions, natural disasters) which temporarily create a sellers' market. The granting of patents, trademarks, and copyrights enables the holder to legally exclude competitors. Hence, being in a position of advantage and thereby able to realize "monopoly profits" explains how and why some firms have above-normal degrees of profitability.

However, the ability of firms to extort big profits from their customers is easily exaggerated. Competition is seldom weak enough for great numbers of firms to grab positions of monopoly power. Nor is it valid to conclude that better-than-average profits are always socially undesirable relative to the alternatives. For example, society undoubtedly benefits from the practice of granting patents (a legal monopoly); to do otherwise would surely discourage inventive and innovative activities.

TECHNOLOGY AND INNOVATION THEORIES OF PROFIT

The unifying feature of the third group of profit theories is the potential of technology and innovation for providing the impetus for above-average profitability.[4] New methods of production and distribution enhance profits by lowering costs or else neutralizing cost-increasing factors. New and improved products raise profits by generating favorable changes in demand and/or prices. New managerial, financial, marketing, or accounting practices promote higher profits through operating economies. Taken together, the various forms of innovation constitute perhaps the most powerful and pervasive weapon business firms have for earning sustained economic profits.

That technologically superior production techniques and product innovations are capable of producing attractive economic profits is confirmed by the profit performance of Microsoft, Wal-Mart, Sony, 3M Corp., and pharmaceutical companies—all of which have emphasized innovation-related strategies. However, innovation-related profits are subject to attacks over the long run. As an innovation becomes widely adopted and/or imitated, the innovating firms gradually lose their initial advantage; competitive pressures stiffen, product prices are shaved in response to rising supply capabilities, and profits drift back down to normal levels. Hence, for a firm to continue to profit from innovation it must be able to bring forth new innovations to replace the shrinking profits of previous innovations. In a technologically dynamic environment, the pursuit of innovation profits creates ''a perennial gale of creative destruction'' whereby something new, something better, and something different is constantly being introduced to replace older innovations whose associated profitability has already been undermined.[5]

Technology and innovation theories attribute profits to the power of technologically superior production methods and innovative products to produce revenues well in excess of costs.

PROFIT THEORIES IN PERSPECTIVE

The diversity among the three groups of profit theories suggests that, in practice, profit (both normal and economic) results from a variety of influences, with the mix varying from firm to firm and time to time. In a sense, profit results from any of several elements either within the firm or the environment in which the firm operates; or, to put it another way, *profit arises from differing market positions and competitive advantages among firms*. Since there are many kinds and degrees of market advantages and competitive edges a firm can assemble,

There is no single reason or explanation for profit; the profits a firm earns are nearly always the result of a mixture of influences and causes.

[4] The *innovation theory of profit* is chiefly associated with the late Joseph A. Schumpeter. He made a distinction between invention and innovation; the former he termed as the creation of something new, whereas the latter he viewed as the actual application of an invention in the production process. As originally expounded, Schumpeter used innovation theory to explain business cycles rather than to identify the causes and character of profits. See his *Theory of Economic Development* (Cambridge, Mass.: Harvard University Press, 1934), Chapter 6.
[5] The computer software and pharmaceutical industries offer classic examples of the process of creative destruction. In both these industries the pace of technological progress is rapid and competition is keen. Large profits are earned for short periods of time as new products are introduced, but the forces of competition soon cut severely into earnings as other firms develop similar products or as patents expire. Hence, the maintenance of high earnings is almost entirely dependent upon a firm's ability to sustain a steady flow of new products.

no single theory can adequately justify or explain above-average profit. Furthermore, the various theories themselves are not mutually exclusive. For example, the profit earned by an innovating firm derives in part from the monopoly which the superiority of its innovation provides. At the same time, innovation-related profits may be viewed partly as compensation for successful risk-taking, since, after all, a firm cannot know in advance whether an innovation will be a market success and yield good profits.

THE SOCIAL BENEFITS OF PROFIT

Consumers and society as a whole are the ultimate beneficiaries of a market-driven system where firms are allowed to pursue the earning of a profit.

Traditional theory holds that the owners of enterprise are not the sole beneficiaries of profit—major benefits accrue to society as well. The argument that private self-gain benefits society proceeds as follows. *Profit-seeking enterprises find the rewards greatest for doing what society most wants done simply because it is virtually impossible for a firm to earn profits doing something for which consumer demand is lacking.* The size of the profit flow acts as a feedback mechanism, informing firms clearly and quickly of what is being well received in the market and what is not. Rising profits serve as buyers' signal for an industry to expand. At the same time, rising profits help provide firms with the earning power needed to obtain capital and resource inputs for expansion. When profits are less than satisfactory, a reevaluation of a firm's market offering is warranted and if low profitability is viewed as permanent, a reallocation of the firm's resources to other more profitable ventures is in order. Thus, *profit is the supreme test of a firm's performance.* Profit feedback automatically regulates market processes, signaling how society's resource pool is to be allocated among alternative uses.

With a profit-minded business sector there is an almost ironclad guarantee that production will be in harmony with demand. One can even say that business firms behave responsibly by seeking to earn the largest practicable amount of profit, for by so doing firms will be producing what society is most desirous of having performed.[6] To put it a little differently, socially responsible business behavior requires that firms vigorously pursue the earning of profit, for *it is through the profit mechanism that society signals business firms just which goods and services are most preferred by consumers.* Moreover, the profit-loss discipline is extremely reliable in inducing economic resources to be used in accordance with the tastes and preferences of consumers.

Society is also a prime beneficiary of the profit stemming from innovation. Innovation is a fundamental contributor to the process of economic growth and to advances in the standard of living, and it is, of course, the prospect of profit that stimulates innovative activity. Innovation acts as a spur to expanded production capacity, to higher levels of output, and to growth in employment. These socially beneficial spinoffs from innovative activities are critical to the realization of economical progress and cannot be lightly dismissed.

But perhaps the strongest argument for profit relates to its role in allowing a firm to better serve as a useful social and economic vehicle. *A firm that is not earning at least a normal profit is not a healthy firm.* Firms that are losing money or earning subpar profits are weakly positioned to grow and

---

[6] For a more thorough discussion of this issue, see Milton Friedman, *Capitalism and Freedom* (Chicago: University of Chicago Press, 1962), pp. 133–36.

prosper; the job prospects they offer are dim; they are less able to pay higher wages and salaries; they find it difficult to obtain credit; they are financially unable to commit substantial resources to innovation and technological advance; and they are thrust, sooner or later, into a weak competitive position. Consequently, they have little to contribute in terms of providing new jobs and expanding career opportunities, implementing new technologies, marketing important new products, raising living standards, and meeting societal needs—all of which are crucial to enhancing society's overall economic welfare. The earning of what is generally considered to be at least adequate profits is, therefore, an essential prerequisite for a business to be able to respond to society's needs in a positive and efficient fashion.

THE PROFIT RECORD OF BUSINESS ENTERPRISES

On the whole, the notion that companies earn "high" profits is unwarranted. For instance, after-tax manufacturing profits as a percentage of sales have ranged in the neighborhood of 4 to 6% since 1950 (see Table 9-1)—based on accounting definitions of profit. This means that only 4 to 6 cents out of every sales dollar ends up on the bottom line. After-tax profits as a percentage return on stockholders' ownership have usually ranged from 9 to 15%. The accompanying Applications Capsule discusses how much profit businesspeople think is "reasonable."

TABLE 9-1   PROFITS AS A PERCENTAGE OF SALES AND AS A PERCENTAGE OF STOCKHOLDERS' EQUITY, ALL MANUFACTURING CORPORATIONS, 1950–1975 AND 1985–1991

Year	After-Tax Profits as a Percentage of Sales (or Net Profit Margin)	After-Tax Profits as a Percentage of Stockholders' Equity (or Return on Owners' Investment)
1950	7.1%	15.4%
1955	5.4	12.6
1960	4.4	9.2
1965	5.6	13.0
1970	4.0	9.3
1975	4.6	11.6
1980	4.8	13.9
1985	3.8	10.1
1986	3.7	9.5
1987	4.9	12.8
1988	6.0	16.1
1989	5.0	13.6
1990	4.0	10.7
1991	2.9	7.5

Note: These profit statistics are based upon the accounting definition of profit (revenue minus historical cost) and thus *do not* represent economic profit (a return over and above a normal profit).
Source: The Economic Report of the President, February 1992, p. 401.

DO BUSINESS FIRMS SEEK TO MAXIMIZE PROFITS?

Most theories of business behavior in the marketplace are based on the assumption that firms are driven by the desire to maximize profits.

Because of the strong profit orientation of a competitive enterprise system, it is usually accepted as an article of faith that business firms seek to earn the largest possible profits. Most theories of the firm do not just postulate that profit is *a* goal or the *chief* goal; they state unequivocally that *the* goal is *maximum* profit and that firms can be counted upon to behave *as if* they are profit maximizers. Although it would be an exaggeration to view profit maximization as meaning a firm will point its *every* action and decision in a direction coldly calculated to obtain the largest excess of revenue over cost, it does imply that *a firm faced with several alternatives having different expected profit outcomes can usually be counted upon to select the alternative with the greatest expected profit.*

A wealth of research has focused on profit maximization and the validity of relying upon the assumption of profit maximization in constructing theoretical models to explain and to predict business responses to market forces.[7] One view holds that profit maximization is the dominant motive in business decision-making and, thus, the profit-maximizing assumption is useful in building market models and predicting firm behavior. The contrary view holds that for a variety of reasons business firms do not generally maximize profits, and assuming that they do can be misleading. Both sides have argued from positions of strength, although each appears vulnerable on certain points. Table 9-2 summarizes the main arguments in support of profit maximization. Table 9-3 represents the chief criticisms of the assumption that firms behave as if they seek to maximize profits.

Although a close examination of Tables 9-2 and 9-3 suggests that both the critics and the defenders of the profit maximization assumption have persuasive arguments in their favor, choosing between full acceptance or all-out condemnation of the profit-maximizing assumption is not necessary. There is merit in an intermediate position which recognizes that there are circumstances where the profit maximization assumption will suffice and circumstances where other goals besides profit come into play and need to be incorporated into the analysis.

Profit is sure to be a goal of nearly every business firm—probably the predominant goal. Profit is a universal measure of business performance, and few firms will pursue actions that deliberately lead to lower long-run profits

---

[7] The interested reader may wish to consult the discussions by Lester, Machlup, Oliver, Blum, and Gordon beginning in the *American Economic Review* in 1946. Pertinent literature of more recent vintage includes Joseph W. McGuire, *Theories of Business Behavior* (Englewood Cliffs, N.J.: Prentice Hall, 1964); H. A. Simon, "Theories of Decision Making in Economics and Behavioral Science," *American Economic Review,* Vol. 49, No. 3 (June 1959), pp. 253–83; William Baumol, *Business Behavior, Value and Growth,* 1st ed. rev. (New York: Harcourt Brace Jovanovich, 1967); Edith Penrose, *The Theory of the Growth of the Firm* (New York: John Wiley & Sons, 1959); Robin Marris, "A Model of the 'Managerial' Enterprise," *Quarterly Journal of Economics,* Vol. 77, No. 4 (May 1963), pp. 185–209; R. M. Cyert and J. G. March, *A Behavioral Theory of the Firm* (Englewood Cliffs, N.J.: Prentice Hall, 1963); O. E. Williamson, *The Economics of Discretionary Behavior: Managerial Objectives in a Theory of the Firm* (Englewood Cliffs, N.J.: Prentice Hall, 1964); R. F. Lanzilotti, "Pricing Objectives in Large Companies," *American Economic Review,* Vol. 48, No. 5 (December 1958), pp. 921–40; William L. Baldwin, "The Motives of Managers, Environmental Restraints and the Theory of Managerial Enterprise," *Quarterly Journal of Economics,* Vol. 78, No. 3 (February 1964), pp. 238–56; and Gerald L. Nordquist, "The Breakup of the Maximization Principle," *Quarterly Journal of Economics and Business,* Vol. 5, No. 3 (Fall 1965), pp. 33–46.

TABLE 9-2   SUMMARY OF ARGUMENTS AS TO WHY
FIRMS BEHAVE AS IF THEY SEEK TO MAXIMIZE PROFITS

Arguments for Profit Maximization	*Supporting Rationale*
1. The profit motive is the strongest, the most universal, and the most persistent of the forces governing business behavior.	Although firms may pursue goals other than profit, the impact of such goals upon behavior is quite small. Hence, imputing "more realistic" goals to the firm yields no *significant* improvement in explanation or prediction while greatly increasing the complexity of the analysis.
2. Competition forces firms to adopt a goal of maximum profits.	Where competition is keen, firms must display a behavior pattern very closely akin to profit maximization in order to stand a chance of earning any profit at all. Knowledge that only the fittest will survive is a powerful incentive for all firms to direct their energies in profit-maximizing directions, learning whatever skills are required and emulating firms which are visibly successful in the battle for survival.
3. Assuming that business firms behave as if they seek to maximize profits is an appropriate theoretical approach as long as such an assumption allows accurate predictions to be made about behavior.	The only valid test of a theory is its predictive power. Whether an assumption is realistic enough can be settled only by examining the predictive ability of the theory. Since economists have had considerable success in using the profit-maximizing assumption as a basis for predicting the price and output behavior of business firms, the merit of using this assumption in theoretical models is well established.
4. The profit-maximizing assumption is a useful aid in obtaining a general understanding and explanation of the behavior of groups of firms.	Microeconomic theory is not designed to explain and predict the behavior of *particular* firms; instead it is designed to explain and predict changes in observed prices and outputs as consequences of particular market forces (such as changes in wage rates, resource prices, or taxes). In accomplishing this purpose, the firm serves only as a theoretical link for identifying how one gets from the causes of business behavior to the effects of business behavior. This is altogether different from conceiving of the firm as an object of study in itself and of trying to predict and explain the behavior of Texaco or Holiday Inn.

References: 1. Milton Friedman, "The Methodology of Positive Economics," *Essays in Economics* (Chicago: University of Chicago Press, 1953), pp. 22–23.
2. Fritz Machlup, "Theories of the Firm: Marginalist, Behavioral, Managerial," *American Economic Review*, Vol. 57, No. 1 (March 1967), p. 9.
3. Melvin W. Reder, "A Reconsideration of the Marginal Productivity Theory," *Journal of Political Economy*, Vol. 55, No. 5 (October 1947), pp. 453–54.
4. George J. Stigler, *The Theory of Price* (New York: The Macmillan Company, 1952), pp. 148–49.

than otherwise could be earned. Nonetheless, there is room for some firms to evidence more profit-conscious and profit-oriented behavior than for others.[8]

In general, firms confronted with strong competitive pressures are prone to exhibit short-run profit-maximizing behavior; behavior resembling something other than full profit maximization is most likely to surface in firms

---

[8] Conceivably, there are firms where the profit goal is consistently subordinate to the achievement of other goals. But the list of firms that can afford the luxury of relegating profit to positions of lesser importance in the goal hierarchy is very short and their role in the private sector of the economy is doubtless minimal.

TABLE 9-3   SUMMARY OF ARGUMENTS AS TO WHY
FIRMS DO NOT OR CANNOT MAXIMIZE PROFITS

Arguments Against Profit Maximization	*Supporting Rationale*
1. Uncertainty prevents firms from maximizing profits, even if they wish to do so. Because of imperfect information and uncertainty, it is usually not possible to say unequivocally which of several courses of action appears to be the profit-maximizing alternative. Hence, profit maximization becomes a meaningless goal and prescription for decision-making.	Business decisions are made in a fog of uncertainty; managers are not aware of all the alternative courses of action, much less the possible outcomes associated with each known alternative. Consequently, the path along which profit can be maximized is not easily identified because of imperfect information about demand, costs, competitive responses of firms, and general economic conditions. Moreover, the "best" rule for a firm in one decision situation may not be "best" in another decision situation. Nor is the "best" rule for one firm necessarily identical to the "best" rule for another firm.
2. In the large corporation the separation of control from ownership gives managers the discretion to pursue goals other than maximum profit.	Why should managers assume the onerous task of maximizing the monetary gains of stockholders? What motive is there for them to do so? Managers rarely encounter interference from stockholders as long as earnings remain "acceptable" and show a persistent tendency to increase. Furthermore, competitive pressures are often neither powerful nor quick enough to keep firms on the tightrope of economic survival; this gives corporate managers the discretion to pursue goals other than profit.
3. Many readily observable business practices are inconsistent with profit maximization.	Separation payments to discharged employees, beautification projects around plant facilities, donations to charity, the failure of executives to spend their whole day hard at work, and the failure of cost accounting practices to generate the data required for maximizing profits are all examples of deviations from profit-maximizing behavior. Also, managers may be anxious to maintain such harmonious relations with employees that they tolerate lax work habits and agree to restrictive work practices and cost-increasing union work rules.
4. Firms find it advantageous to avoid making as large a profit as possible.	Some of the most important reasons for not maximizing profits include (1) a fear of attracting competition from firms which have the potential to enter the industry, (2) a fear of provoking antitrust action, and (3) a belief that holding profits down to "satisfactory" levels will restrain union wage demands and will promote stronger public relations.
5. Maximizing profit is too difficult, unrealistic, and immoral.	Strictly speaking, profit maximization requires businesspeople to use every trick in the trade to keep wages and fringe benefits down, to charge as high a price as the consumer can and will pay, to seek as low a quality of merchandise as they can legally hoodwink the consumer into buying, to disclaim any community responsibility, to finagle the lowest prices from suppliers, and so on. Firms seldom pursue these tactics as zealously as is suggested by profit-maximizing behavior.

References: 1. R. N. Anthony. "The Trouble with Profit Maximization," *Harvard Business Review,* Vol. 38, No. 6 (November–December 1960), pp. 126–34.
2. Neil W. Chamberlain, *Enterprise and Environment* (New York McGraw-Hill Book Company, 1968), Chapter 4.
3. John Kenneth Galbraith, *The New Industrial State* (Boston: Houghton Mifflin Company, 1967), p. 117.
4. Melvin W. Reder, "A Reconsideration of the Marginal Productivity Theory," *Journal of Political Economy.* Vol. 55, No. 5 (October 1947), p. 452.

where profits are expected to be ample enough to please stockholders, thereby opening the door for other considerations to influence managerial decisions. There are several reasons why this tends to be so. In highly competitive markets where profit margins are thin, security is shaky, and the ability of firms to absorb losses is weak, there exists (as Darwin's thesis maintains) a fierce struggle in which only the fittest will survive. Market forces allow little room for discretionary action. Under such conditions earning even a normal profit is far from a sure thing and short-run profit considerations dominate the firm's decisions. The elected courses of action are likely to be those *perceived* to have the greatest expected profit because to do otherwise is to endanger the firm's survival. Thus, *strong competitive forces can so constrict a firm's market behavior that it may have little alternative but to pursue a strategy of short-run profit maximization*. A similar condition emerges when recession or inflation weaken consumer demand to such an extent that profits plunge. In methodological terms, the profit-maximizing assumption, although not always an exact representation of reality, is nevertheless a sufficiently good approximation to the actual behavior of most enterprises confronted with these situations. Certainly, it is the best *single* assumption that can be made about the goals of these firms.

On the other hand, *firms that are insulated to a degree from competitive pressures and that are enjoying better-than-ample profits are in the best position to deviate from strict profit-maximizing behavior*. The reason for this is that so long as profits are adequate to satisfy stockholders, management has some leeway to pursue objectives other than higher profits. One cannot stretch this ability too far, though.[9] It would be a gross exaggeration to presume that nonprofit goals govern the market behavior of firms with above-average profits or that management loses sight of the impact that satisfaction of other goals will have on profits. All that is being implied here is that once minimum acceptable profit levels are within reach, then management has some discretion to give more emphasis to nonprofit goals. There is some evidence, for instance, that the pursuit of nonprofit goals is more likely to occur in large, single-product, vertically integrated firms than in larger multiproduct enterprises. The former tend to be organized along functional lines and the heads of functional units appear more prone to disagree over priorities, to resist full organizational coordination, and to bend organizational goals to their own interest.[10] On the other hand, diversified firms with decentralized, quasi-autonomous business divisions seem to have comparatively stronger profit orientations; business units are generally run as profit centers and business-unit managers are rewarded largely on the basis of short-run performance.

To summarize, then, the assumption of profit-maximizing behavior is especially suitable in those situations where (1) large groups of firms are involved and nothing has to be predicted about the behavior of individual firms; (2) competitive forces are relatively intense; (3) the *general effects* of a specified change in conditions upon prices, outputs, and resource inputs are to be explained and predicted rather than the values of these magnitudes before or after the change; and (4) only the directions of change are sought rather than

Profit maximization is the best single assumption about what motivates a firm's decisions and actions.

---

[9] Witness, for instance, the wave of cost-cutting campaigns, reorganizations, and overall belt tightening that transcends the business community when business turns sour and profits fall. Often, it is when profits turn into losses that management discovers how much inefficiency it has overlooked or been tolerating.

[10] See Oliver E. Williamson, *Corporate Control and Business Behavior* (Englewood Cliffs, N.J.: Prentice Hall, 1970).

APPLICATIONS CAPSULE

HOW BUSINESS EXECUTIVES DEFINE WHAT IS A "REASONABLE" PROFIT

Several top-level business executives were recently asked what they considered to be a "reasonable" profit. Excerpts of their answers follow.

Irving S. Shapiro
Chairman of the Board
Dupont Corp.

Asking how much profit is reasonable is like asking how many eggs you should buy for breakfast. It depends on the size of your family and other factors.

By the same token, what is a reasonable profit depends on an industry's needs. Most Americans will agree that a fair profit is essential to a strong economy, but the idea that there are "needs" for earnings may be difficult to accept. It helps to understand the functions of profit.

Profits are not pools of money that sit idle. In all business firms, profits are used—put to work—as soon as they are earned. They are plowed back into the economy through investment in new manufacturing plants and new equipment. They are used to expand production and create jobs. They improve efficiency. In sum, profits are "seed money," the means to insure a healthy, growing economy.

Profits have a second function. A portion is paid out in dividends to the stockholders or owners. These dividends are essentially payment for the use of stockholders' money, which has been invested in the company.

To return to the original question, a reasonable profit is an amount that allows a company to meet its obligation to its stockholders and to acquire the facilities it must have to provide goods, services, and jobs in the future.

These needs will vary among industries. In the chemical industry, stiff competition and new technology mean plants become obsolete quickly. Bigger manufacturing units are required to supply growing markets. These conditions add up to a huge demand for capital investment.

Fletcher L. Byrom
Chairman of the Board
Koppers Company, Inc.

A profit is reasonable when it provides for the survival of an enterprise. Survival is possible only when profits are sufficient to perform their two life-giving functions . . . to pay investors for the use of their savings and to increase the productive base of an enterprise so that it can remain a useful entity. These two functions are essential regardless of whether the enterprise is privately held or state-owned.

Marshall McDonald
President
Florida Light and Power Company

What's a reasonable profit? Let's start the answer with another question.

What does it take to keep a company in business? It takes capital—money to buy the facilities that bring in income. You must pay for the use of this money, and what you pay with is income left over after meeting expenses.

This "left-over" income is what most call "profit"; but since you must pay it to attract capital, business analysts consider it a cost—the "cost of capital." Out of this profit comes capital for reinvestment in the business. Out of profit comes the dividend that attracts shareholder capital. Out of profit comes the ability to borrow

precise numerical results.[11] But when the behavior of specific firms is at issue, where the number of firms is small and the behavior of any one firm affects the behavior of others, where competitive pressures are not profit-threatening, and/or where precise numerical estimates are called for, an explicit identification of a firm's goals is needed before its behavior can be confidently explained and predicted.

THE ALTERNATIVES TO STRICT PROFIT MAXIMIZATION

Dissatisfaction with profit maximization as the sole driver of business decisions in the marketplace has led observers to propose a number of alternative criteria for deciding what is the *best* thing to do.

---

[11] Fritz Machlup, "Theories of the Firm: Marginalist, Behavioral, Managerial," *American Economic Review,* Vol. 57, No. 1 (March 1967), p. 31.

additional capital at reasonable (there's that word again) interest rates.

All this is especially critical for an electric utility because it takes a lot of capital to keep us in business. About four dollars in facilities for each dollar we collect in revenue. Now the key question: How much profit does it take to attract this necessary capital? That depends on the relation between earnings and the risk of their loss, for one thing, and on competition for investors' money, for another.

Homer H. Budge
President
Investors Group of Companies

[A reasonable profit is] one which is somewhat above a rate that will attract investors to a similar enterprise, entailing a similar risk.

Thomas A. Murphy
Chairman of the Board
General Motors Corp.

In my view, many labels have been attached to the word profit, such as reasonable, fair, and equitable, which reflected a misunderstanding of the nature of profit itself. To be specific, I view profit as a resultant of the complex of activities carried on by a business. Profit varies from one year to the next depending upon general economic conditions, the acceptability of the products in the market, and the ability of the enterprise to produce those products efficiently.

I would underscore the fact that our market economy requires that each business must compete for customer favor both in terms of price and product. If it is successful in this competitive effort it earns a profit and if it is successful it can generate the resources for growth. Obviously, no business can maintain itself unless its earnings are adequate to attract investment.

There is one further consideration and this is the risk factor. A company may generate above-average earnings, but when consideration is given to risk its above-average earnings may be no more than is necessary to sustain the investment.

Put in other words, a "high" profit relative to some average of all profits may well be inadequate for growth when risk is considered. If, as I believe, profits are a resultant of the operation of the business, then it follows that descriptive labels such as reasonable, fair, or equitable have little or no meaning.

David Rockefeller
Chairman of the Board
Chase Manhattan Corp.

In a free economy, growing business profits are the key to reaching and sustaining a satisfactory rate of private capital spending. Profits retained by business provide capital for growth. Profits paid out as dividends make it possible for business to raise additional funds for capital investment through the private capital markets. A good profit trend makes it easier for a business to obtain financing through the commercial banking system; this can be especially important for smaller and medium-sized companies.

Source: Downs Matthews, "Just What is a Reasonable Profit?" *Exxon USA,* Vol. 16, No. 3 (Third Quarter 1977), pp. 27–31.

SATISFICING BEHAVIOR

One much discussed alternative to profit maximization is that firms aim for a "satisfactory" rate of profit rather than a "maximum" profit.[12] Stated differently, firms *satisfice* rather than maximize in pursuing profitability. The thesis is that management decision makers are content to go with workable or satisfactory solutions and courses of action rather than undertaking the more burdensome chore of figuring out the very *best* alternative at each and every fork. According to Herbert Simon (winner of the Nobel prize in economics): "Administrative theory is peculiarly the theory of intended and bounded rationality—of the behavior of human beings who *satisfice* because they have not the wits to *maximize*."[13]

One alternative to profit maximization is satisficing—a search for ways to earn a satisfactory profit.

[12] For example, see Herbert A. Simon, *Models of Man* (New York: John Wiley & Sons, 1957); Simon, "Theories of Decision Making in Economics and Behavioral Science"; Cyert and March, *A Behavioral Theory of the Firm*; and Julius Margolis, "The Analysis of the Firm: Rationalism, Conventionalism, and Behaviorism," *Journal of Business,* Vol. 31, No. 3 (July 1958), pp. 187–99.
[13] Herbert A. Simon, *Administrative Behavior,* 2nd ed. (New York: The Macmillan Company, 1957), p. xxiv.

Briefly, the advocates of satisficing view enterprises as aspiring to earn future profits at least as great and probably greater than current profits. When a profit-related decision arises, their thesis is that managers will tend to draw upon their experiences, decision-making conventions, and whatever information is available to select an alternative from among these known to exist that is expected to produce a *satisfactory* stream of profits. But, it is contended, decision makers typically do not exhaustively sort through *every* possibility in search of *the* most profitable alternative because the search process for finding *the* maximizing alternative, given market uncertainty and imperfect information about demand, costs, competitive responses of rival firms, and future economic conditions, will be too time-consuming and cost more than it is worth.[14]

There also exists another rationale for satisficing behavior. Contemporary corporate theory views top management as trustees of the organization, with responsibilities not only to stockholders but to employees, customers, creditors, suppliers, communities, government, and society as well. Corporate executives should, it is said, seek a statesmanlike balance among the interests of stockholders in higher profits, the demands of employees for higher wages and more economic security, the pressures from consumers for lower prices and higher-quality products, the requests of retailers for comfortable profit margins and of suppliers for more stable purchasing arrangements, and the insistence of the public for a cleaner environment—all within a framework that is constructive and acceptable to society. According to the satisficing theorists, these considerations lead management to adopt a posture of trying to resolve organizational conflicts and competing claims and, where feasible, to advance the welfare of *all* groups who have a stake in how the organization conducts its business.

> **One justification for satisficing is the need to balance the interests of all of the firm's different stakeholders rather than singlemindedly pursue profit maximization on behalf of one stakeholder group—the firm's owners.**

Moreover, within the management group itself, there are large numbers of people in middle management as well as in top management who occupy key decision-making and policy-formulating positions. Many of these people share vested interests in pushing for bigger budgets for their own departments, higher wages and salaries, bigger pensions, more staffing for pet projects, nicer offices, more perks, more power and status in decision-making, greater financial liquidity, technological superiority, and so on. Coalitions may form to promote these special-interest causes, with the result that the enterprise is diverted from a path of strict profit maximization.

In effect, then, the large corporation contains many centers of power of varying potency over which top management presides. According to the satisficing theorists, the outcome is to reduce corporate goals and decisions to a matter of politics, tradeoffs, and compromises. In such an environment, *considering only how to maximize the monetary well-being of stockholders is not feasible because the pursuit of profit is constrained by the requirement to satisfy, at least minimally, the demands of other competing interests.* No one center of power, least of all absentee stockholders who may have no more knowledge about the organization than is contained in the annual report, normally has the organizational support needed to impose its goal on all the others

---

[14] Satisficing has been tested in experimental goal-seeking and problem-solving situations and appears to be a verifiable trait of human behavior. See J. G. March and H. A. Simon, *Organizations* (New York: John Wiley & Sons, 1958), pp. 140–141, and R. M. Cyert and J. G. March, "Organization Factors in the Theory of Oligopoly," *Quarterly Journal of Economics*, Vol. 70, No. 1 (February 1956), pp. 44–64.

and thereby *maximize* its attainment. As a consequence, satisficing behavior becomes the rule rather than the exception and is exemplified in such performance standards as seeking to earn a "satisfactory profit," charging "fair prices," obtaining a "satisfactory share of the market," and growing at an "acceptable rate."

REVENUE MAXIMIZATION

A second frequently mentioned alternative to profit maximization is that of constrained revenue maximization.[15] Here it is contended that *once profits reach acceptable levels some firms are inclined to place higher dollar sales ahead of higher profits as the main object of concern.* They are allegedly moved to do so because revenue growth is a key yardstick of business performance. Sales revenue trends reflect consumer acceptance of a firm's products, its competitive position in the marketplace, and growth—all of which are indicative of the firm's vitality. Any position of advantage a firm has in its markets is undermined and its ability to respond effectively to competitive pressures is weakened when sales fall off. At the same time, managerial self-interest underlies an expansive sales strategy to the extent that executive salaries evidence closer correlation with the scale of a firm's operations than with its profitability.

Nonetheless, revenue maximization is pursued with a watchful eye toward profits. Profits must be kept high enough to satisfy stockholders and to help finance new investments. Thus, while decision makers may act to push sales revenues to new peaks, they tend to be constrained from pursuing revenue maximization to such an extent that profits are seriously impaired and the firm is denied the funds it needs for sustained growth and expansion into new markets—profitless growth is not a happy condition!

> **Another alternative to profit maximization is revenue maximization subject to the constraint of earning a satisfactory profit.**

MARKET SHARE GOALS

Many firms, because of the importance of *experience curve* effects, have targets relating to sales volume and market share.[16] Obviously, a big market share can be a valuable asset—not only because being on top or near the top in the market share pecking order is an enviable position to defend but also because it reflects a firm's ability to compete effectively and to benefit from scale economies and being a recognized market leader. However, it is not clear that achieving a big market share necessarily promotes greater profitability and stronger competitive position; by itself, a bigger market share is a hollow victory. For this reason, market share is not likely to be *the* principal goal of the firm. In fact, aggressive pursuit of a higher market share via price cutting and "doing whatever it takes" to win buyer patronage may endanger profitability.[17]

> **Many firms strive to achieve a target percentage of total market sales—indeed, market share objectives can sometimes take precedence over the desire for greater profits.**

[15] This goal was first proposed by William Baumol. Baumol's thesis is fully developed in Chapter 6 of his *Business Behavior, Value and Growth,* previously cited. This section draws heavily from his discussion therein.

[16] Robert F. Lanzilotti, "Pricing Objectives in Large Companies," *American Economic Review,* Vol. 48, No. 5 (December 1958), pp. 921–40; A. D. H. Kaplan, J. B. Dirlam, and R. F. Lanzilotti, *Pricing in Big Business: A Case Approach* (Washington, D.C.: The Brookings Institution, 1958), pp. 181–200; Burnard H. Sord and Glenn A. Welsh, *Business Budgeting* (New York: Controllership Foundation, 1958), p. 149; and Paul N. Bloom and Philip Kotler, "Strategies for High Market Share Companies," *Harvard Business Review,* Vol. 53, No. 6 (November–December 1975), pp. 63–72.

[17] See William E. Fruhan, Jr., "Pyrrhic Victories in Fights for Market Share," *Harvard Business Review,* Vol. 50, No. 5 (September–October 1972), pp. 100–107; and R. D. Buzzell, B. T. Gale, and R. Sultan, "Market Share—A Key to Profitability," *Harvard Business Review,* Vol. 53, No. 1 (January–February 1975), pp. 97–106.

Too successful a pursuit of an ever-larger market share may also produce a market dominance that invites antitrust action.[18]

LONG-RUN SURVIVAL GOALS

Some economists have argued that business firms, like most other organizations and individuals, have a compelling instinct and motivation to survive.[19] The urge to survive is allegedly more fundamental than the profit motive because a firm could maximize profit and still not survive. An inadequate cash flow, shrinking markets, takeovers by acquisition-minded firms, and so on may spell the end, even for profitable firms. Thus, it is contended, survival goals take precedence over other goals, particularly in stress situations.

Survival objectives can take precedence over profit objectives in crisis situations when the firm's long-run existence is at stake.

The importance of long-run survival is apparent. But, as a goal, it is not very helpful in predicting and explaining business behavior. At any one time, there exist many avenues for survival, and thus the choice of one necessarily tends to hinge on other factors. And once survival over the near term seems assured, other goals are sure to motivate managerial decisions. The primary significance of a survival goal is that it is a precondition for achieving other objectives. As an explanation of behavior, its relevance is limited to those occasions where the firm's situation is so grave that every effort must be directed toward getting through the period ahead.

THE GOAL OF SOCIAL RESPONSIBILITY

In recent years much has been said and written about the need for firms, particularly large corporations, to behave in a "socially responsible" manner.[20] Social responsibility has come to mean many things: having a number of diverse interest groups represented in the corporation's governance structure and decision-making process; relating the entire enterprise to the changing needs of society; balancing stockholder interests against the larger interest of society as a whole; revamping corporate policies and practices so as to promote the public welfare in a positive way; and urging firms to help solve the social ills of society while going about their regular business. In essence, the urging of social responsibility upon firms aims at creating a corporate conscience.

Many firms back away from strict profit maximization and spend dollars on activities that are deemed to be in the best interest of society and the communities in which they operate.

The philosophy underlying social responsibility goals is that stockholder interests in the long run are best served by corporate policies that contribute to developing the kind of society in which business firms can grow profitably. In fact, the pursuit of profit and the pursuit of social objectives are held to be mutually reinforcing. Profits can be earned performing functions that entail primary or secondary social benefits. At the same time, social objectives can be achieved more rapidly and more efficiently by enlisting the productive power of business firms through the opportunity for profit and by imposing harsh penalties for business activities that are deemed socially harmful.

---

[18] General Motors is said to exercise care that its share of the automobile market does not go much beyond the 55% level. General Electric officials have stated they do not wish to exceed 50% of any given market; moreover, "the company would rather be pushing to expand a 25% share than defending a 50% share." See Lanzillotti, "Pricing Objectives in Large Companies," p. 933.

[19] Kenneth E. Boulding, *A Reconstruction of Economics* (New York: John Wiley & Sons, 1950), pp. 26–27; Galbraith, *The New Industrial State,* p. 167.

[20] See *Social Responsibilities of Business Corporations,* issued by the Research and Policy Committee of the Committee for Economic Development, New York, June 1971.

Adoption of social responsibility goals probably has the ultimate effect of containing the drive for greater short-run profits. A firm that does more than what the law requires to reduce its pollution emissions probably does so at the expense of profits. A firm that keeps an inefficient plant open in order to try to save jobs in the community probably does so at the expense of profits. Very likely, a firm's efforts to display social responsibility and be a good citizen in the communities where it operates make satisficing an even more viable and more attractive managerial practice. But by no means does social responsibility mean that a firm's profitability is secondary; the earning of adequate profit is a prerequisite for giving a firm the organizational ability and the financial where-withal to respond to social objectives.

Exhorting business firms to be socially responsible has met with resistance from some business managers and several public interest groups. It has been observed, perhaps correctly, that "the business of business is business." Corporate executives, it is said, are neither equipped to be social engineers nor charged to usurp stockholder interests and base decisions on what arguably is or is not in the public interest. The contention is that in many situations the answer to what is in the public interest or what is socially responsible boils down to one's own personal value judgments and not to a clear-cut "this is best for *everybody*" approach. Still, increasing numbers of firms appear to be giving careful consideration to how corporate strategies and policies affect society and they are definitely concerned about avoiding charges that they are "insensitive" and "bad citizens."

GROWTH AND DIVERSIFICATION GOALS

A firm's present activities can lose their sustaining power through changes in consumer tastes, technological change, the appearance of superior products, increased competition from domestic rivals and importers, and growth in the market power of suppliers and customers. A company that does not innovate and grow can eventually find itself managing a tired product line. Not many firms willingly choose "coasting along"—the only thing more damning in the business world than the status quo is getting trapped in a stagnating business that is destined to decline.

Many companies put growth and diversification high on their list of performance objectives.

There are several reasons why firms typically have growth and diversification goals. To begin with, growth is a good defense against adversity. Growth via greater market penetration offers a firm a stronger, more secure market position vis-à-vis competitors, suppliers, and customers. To the extent that a firm can gain on or overtake its rivals, it has greater freedom for maneuver and more influence over important industry decisions. Growth by diversification into a wider range of products frees firms from too much dependence on one or a few products and serves as a hedge against the possible demise of bread-and-butter products. If one product or phase of a firm's operations slows down and becomes unprofitable, the firm still can survive and even grow on the strength of its other activities.

Second, no other measure of business success has such almost unanimous acceptance as long-term growth (i.e., rising sales, rising production, and rising profits). Growth and diversification efforts constitute a recurrent theme in the annual reports of successful companies and receive constant emphasis on financial pages and in journals devoted to business affairs. Investors and financial analysts tend to judge the worth of an enterprise not so much by current sales and profits as by growth potential. In almost all cases, *more attention is given to the rates at which sales and profits have grown than to the absolute size of current sales and profits.* Consequently, firms have a strong motivation to boost their growth rate; they almost always are eager to get into a lively market, and once they are in, many want nothing short of first place.

Finally, growth and diversification provide an effective means of pursuing other corporate goals and objectives. Growth and diversification can be very consistent with earning higher profits, expanding sales, defending and strengthening the firm's competitive position, paying higher dividends to stockholders, achieving higher stock prices, acquiring superior technological capabilities, creating a sound corporate image, and so on. Although growth and diversification just for the sake of growth and diversification are suspect, there is still a pervasive tendency for them to complement and support the achievement of other goals. This alone suffices to put them near the top of the priority list.

MULTIPLE GOALS: CONFLICTS AND TRADEOFFS

When a firm pursues more than one goal simultaneously, it is often the case that increasing performance in one area means accepting lower performance in the other; it is not always feasible to maximize performance in several areas at once.

It is apparent from the preceding discussion that firms may have a number of goals, with profits being only one of them. Statements by chief executives and strategic plans of corporations confirm that firms typically pursue several goals simultaneously, which can lead to conflicts and tradeoffs. For example, at any point in time the firm's options and choices include:

- To emphasize short-run profits or long-run profits.
- To improve profit margins or increase market share.
- To increase penetration of existing markets or to enter new markets.
- To diversify into related products or into unrelated products.
- To compete in low-risk environments or to move into high-risk markets.
- To emphasize profit goals or nonprofit goals.
- To seek out faster growth in new areas of the market or remain content to improve current operations.

Recent developments in the theory of the firm take multiple goals explicitly into account. In this approach the strict profit maximization model of the firm is generalized to recognize the value of other dimensions of the firm's activities, and multiple goals are pursued within a utility-maximizing framework.[21] For example, in addition to profits the firm may also pursue greater market share or faster growth. When one of the objectives of the firm comes into conflict with another, as can easily happen in a multigoal environment, the key decision maker in the firm explicitly addresses the tradeoffs between goals and chooses the best combination of profits, revenues, and growth. The decision maker generally has some discretion, and individual firms will differ in how they emphasize the different goals and make tradeoffs among competing objectives. Firms can also make different decisions about the tradeoffs across time. The choices can be very tough. For example, a firm whose profits are plunging may be tempted to reduce or eliminate expenditures of R & D, adver-

---

[21] The classic paper on the generalization of the strict profit maximization model is Armen Alchian's ''The Basis for Some Recent Advances in the Theory of the Management of the Firm,'' *Journal of Industrial Economics,* Vol. 13, No. 4 (November 1965), pp. 30–41, reprinted in *Readings in Microeconomics,* William Breit and Harold Hochman, eds. (St. Louis: Times Mirror Co., 1986), pp. 124–30.

tising and promotion, investment in new ventures, facilities and equipment, or product innovations—the very things on which long-term profits and growth are built. Evidence also exists to the effect that there is an inverse relationship between profits and profit margins, on the one hand, and growth and market share, on the other hand. The tradeoffs between other alternative goals can be equally serious. On balance, the existence of multiple goals, combined with the changing dynamics of the marketplace, makes it more difficult to predict the behavior of the firm.

PERSONAL GOALS OF CORPORATE MANAGERS

In a multigoal environment, key decision makers in the firm make the tradeoffs and balance the goals when they come into conflict. It is reasonable to expect that where managers have the freedom and discretion to choose among alternatives they will select those that are most favorable to themselves. In fact, even if the owners of corporations (shareholders) favor strict profit maximization, the separation of ownership and management control in some large corporations provides managers with opportunities to pursue personal goals that are not the same as those of the owners, thereby creating a multigoal environment. For example, the chief executive in corporations where there is a separation of ownership and control may pursue such motives as the glory of being the industry leader, personal vanity, the pride of being at the head of a large business empire, the desire for professional recognition in executive circles, an affinity for luxurious offices and executive perks, and the quest for larger compensation packages, all of which may divert managerial decisions down avenues other than *pure* profit maximization on behalf of absentee stockholders. The desires of managers for a quiet, easy life and for more leisure time have also been said to blunt the drive for maximization, since managers with "normal" preferences will exert something less than every ounce of their energy toward maximizing profit.[22]

In the same vein, the urge to create a pervasive interest in technological feats and an ambition to demonstrate professional excellence may lead to managerial actions in conflict with the greatest possible profits. Achieving technological superiority and a leadership position in product engineering in spite of possible adverse effects on profits is said to appeal especially to executives with technical and scientific backgrounds and to firms in high-technology industries. Technological virtuosity meshes well with the needs of those members of the firm (engineers, technical specialists, research scientists) concerned with keeping the firm on the frontiers of technical know-how and product capability because it means opportunities for the technologists to pursue their favorite interests, as well as opportunities for personal advancement in the form of better jobs, higher salaries, and promotions.

As a general rule, when managers have the freedom and discretion to pursue their personal goals within firms, we can expect that they will do so and a multigoal environment is quite likely. An important question concerns whether corporate managers will be able to pursue their personal goals in the long run when they are contrary to the long-term best interests of the firm's owners. This issue turns out to be complex and involves what has come to be

The personal goals and ambitions of a firm's senior managers can conflict with the tireless pursuit of strict profit maximization on behalf of outside shareholders.

---

[22] This point was originally made long ago. See Tibor Scitovsky, "A Note on Profit Maximization and Its Implications," *The Review of Economic Studies,* Vol. 11, No. 4 (Winter 1943), pp. 57–60, and John R. Hicks, "Annual Survey of Economic Theory: The Theory of Monopoly," *Econometrica,* Vol. 3, No. 1 (February 1935), p. 8

called *a principal-agent problem*. It also involves some subtle adjustments in the market for executive talent and some not so subtle workings of the market for corporate control. Each of these is discussed next.

PRINCIPAL-AGENT PROBLEMS AND THE GOALS OF THE FIRM

When the owner-principal of a firm employs a manager-agent and the manager-agent ends up having more information about the situation than the owner-principal, then the manager-agent can use the possession of superior knowledge to pursue activities that enhance his or her own well-being at the expense of the owner-principal.

Individual decision makers, who are called principals, often find it beneficial to contract with an agent, who has specialized skills, talents, and information that are to be used to carry out a designated activity or set of activities that are in the interest of the principal. The intent of the principal is to employ the agent and use the agent's skills and knowledge to bring about an outcome favorable to the principal. The principal-agent problem arises when the agent has more information and knowledge than the principal and uses his or her position to pursue an outcome that benefits himself or herself at the expense of the principal. For example, a star athlete (the principal) often hires an agent to negotiate a contract with a professional sports team. If the agent negotiates a contract for the athlete's services that fails to obtain maximum value for the athlete but results in a deal that rewards the agent (say with a retainer or consulting fee from the sports team), then the principal-agent problem is at work.

Principal-agent conflicts are common in business firms owned by outside shareholders and managed by salaried executives who have little or no ownership stake in the enterprise.

Principal-agent conflicts can occur in a wide variety of business relationships and are common in large corporations characterized by a separation of ownership and control. The absentee stockholders of the corporation are the principals and the chief executive officer and other high-ranking officials and managers are the agents. The agents typically have better information about the firm and its prospects than outside shareholders. This asymmetry in information permits agents to pursue personal goals that can reduce the value of the firm and make the principals worse off than they would have been if the agents had behaved in the principals' best interest. While it is the responsibility of the board of directors of the corporation to oversee the activities of top management, the board cannot second-guess every executive action; the board has less information than management, and most board members have other duties and responsibilities to which they must attend. To avoid the need to monitor and police the behavior of management, the board may create a compensation package for top managers that contains incentives for managers to behave in a manner consistent with the board's stated goals for the firm. For example, this might include compensation in the form of profit-sharing and stock-option plans that have the potential for making the executives wealthy. But the executives receive this wealth if, and only if, the corporation is adequately profitable and other performance targets are met. Such compensation plans have the potential for reducing principal-agent conflicts within firms. Still, boards of directors are likely to be less than completely successful in eliminating the principal-agent problem and ensuring that the goals of the absentee owners are pursued aggressively by management. The primary reason for this is that in corporations where ownership and control are separate, members of the board can also be viewed as agents of the owners, and a principal-agent problem may emerge between the owners and the board. In fact, board members are often not independent of management because company executives typically select and propose board members to the owners. Thus, the actions of the board of direc-

Even though it is the function of a firm's board of directors to represent shareholder interests, board members often do not possess sufficient information to eliminate principal-agent conflicts.

tors do not necessarily eliminate principal-agent problems in large publicly held corporations where most of the shares are owned by outside investors.

The consequences of the principal-agent problem are that the firm's pursuit of profits is impaired, costs may be excessive, and the firm winds up pursuing goals that are not in the best interest of the owners. The bottom line is that managers are in a position to make themselves better off at the expense of owners. By failing to pursue profits as diligently as owners prefer, the value of the firm is reduced below the level that would prevail in the absence of a principal-agent problem within the firm.

THE DISCIPLINE OF THE MARKET

While principal-agent conflicts between owners and managers certainly exist, they may not be as severe as the preceding discussion suggests. There are three important limiting factors that act to reduce principal-agent problems in large corporations and to encourage managers to pursue the goals of owners. All involve discipline imposed by competition in the marketplace. First and foremost, strong competition acts to cause the firm to pursue policies that generate profits. The pursuit of profits tends to maximize the value of the firm, raise share prices, and enhance shareholder wealth. The more competitive the markets in which the firm operates, the less slack there will be in the organization and the more likely the firm is to engage in profit- and wealth-maximizing behavior. In the most competitive markets, the principal-agent problem fades into the background because survival requires that firms engage in cost-minimizing/profit-maximizing behavior. In highly competitive markets only the fittest survive, and firms with serious principal-agent conflicts between the owners and managers are not likely to be among them.

When competition in the markets where the firm operates is not so intense and managers have more discretion about goals, two additional market considerations limit the severity of the principal-agent problem within the firm. There is a well-developed market for executive and managerial talent, and the manager who is concerned about his or her individual well-being is always mindful of what it takes to remain competitive in that market. If executives with a track record for successfully pursuing profits are in high demand in the market for managerial talent, then strong incentives and market discipline encourage all managers to pursue policies that generate profits, maximize share prices, and enhance shareholder wealth. Thus, the market for managerial talent provides incentives that diminish the principal-agent problem within the firm. A final market consideration can also come into play. When the principal-agent problem results in poor management that depresses share values, then the likelihood of a takeover bid increases. The logic of this is straightforward: If principal-agent conflicts severely reduce the value of ownership shares below their potential level, then the firm becomes a likely candidate for takeover. A takeover is one of the principal methods used to oust entrenched and inefficient management. In hostile takeovers the incumbent management is usually dismissed by those who gain control of the corporation. Clearly, there are strong incentives for management to try and avoid such an outcome. One of the most effective weapons against a hostile takeover is for the existing management to run the corporation like the owners want it to be run and to do so in a highly efficient manner.

Competition serves to contain the abuse of principal-agent conflicts in business enterprises.

If principal-agent conflicts erode a firm's value much below potential, the firm becomes a likely candidate for takeover, with the aim being to oust management and restore the firm's ownership value.

KEY POINTS

Few economic concepts are used with a more bewildering variety of well-established meanings than profit. Not only is there accounting profit, normal profit, and economic profit, but each of these may be measured in several ways, depending on the specific accounting conventions employed and depending upon whether the desired profit measure is a dollar amount or a rate of return. Accounting profit is based on a firm's income statement and is conceived as the excess of revenue over historical costs after corporate taxes have been deducted. Normal profit is the minimum amount of profit (or rate of return) sufficient to keep the firm in business in the long run; economists consider normal profit as part of total cost. Economic profit is a return over and above a normal profit. It is economic profit which business firms really seek and which governs much of their behavior.

Profit (both normal and economic) is a mixture resulting from a variety of influences, including business acumen, successful performance of the entrepreneurial function, services rendered to the consumer, a fortuitous coping with uncertainty, the presence of market frictions that inhibit a quick response of competitive forces, monopoly power and positions of advantage, technological superiority, and new product innovation.

Economists' views on profit maximization have changed through time. For some years there was wide disagreement concerning whether business firms, especially large corporations, act as if they seek to *maximize profits*. It is now widely recognized that firms do not necessarily maximize profits, and attention has focused on generalizing the theory of the firm to consider other goals and objectives. Recent developments in the theory of the firm have also focused on identifying factors that tend to cause firms to pursue maximum profits and the conditions under which firms are likely to pursue goals other than strict profit maximization. Diffused ownership, conditions of uncertainty, the principal-agent problem, and insulation from heavy competitive pressures are held to allow firms to pursue goals other than profit maximization. Among the most prominent alternatives to profit-maximizing behavior are satisficing, revenue maximization, and growth via diversification. Lesser and/or corollary goals include a bigger market share, long-run survival, satisfactory and secure profits, a rising dividend rate, financial liquidity, technological leadership, attainment of a good image, behaving in a socially responsible manner, maintaining a strong competitive position, and achievement of personal goals of top management (power, prestige, sense of accomplishment, professional recognition, and big bonuses). Aggressive growth and diversification strategies offer firms an effective means of simultaneously pursuing and achieving many of these goals.

Doubtless, there can be no *single* goal that captures the *whole* truth about business decisions and behavior simply because there are too many subtle shadings of behavior and the decision constraints are far too complex. Furthermore, diversity of goals and variations in motivations are a natural outgrowth of a market economy populated by firms ranging from the small proprietorship to the giant multiproduct corporation. The differences among firms regarding market position, ownership and control, size competition, uncertainty, technological capabilities, personalities of owners and managers, profitability, and diversification opportunities make it highly improbable that all firms pursue the *same* set of goals with the *same* degree of intensity and priority.

Even so, the profit motive is deeply ingrained in the folklore of modern business behavior, and rightly so. Highly competitive product and resource markets and the operation of markets for executive talent and corporate control tend to impose discipline on the behavior of managers and firms and lead them to pursue profits vigorously. As a consequence, the imperatives of earning profits are pervasive and powerful influences. Certainly, profit stands foremost in the goal hierarchy of most firms and *if one were forced to choose a single goal to characterize business behavior, then the choice would have to be long-run profit maximization*. However, in the following chapters we shall find it helpful to use models that incorporate goals other than pure profit maximization in order to predict and to explain the full range of business behavior. In this regard we will make use of recent generalizations of the theory of profit maximization, which treats the firm as though it is managed by utility-maximizing decision makers who value profits as well as other goals and who make the difficult decisions involving tradeoffs among competing goals.

PROBLEMS AND QUESTIONS FOR DISCUSSION

1. **(a)** The Vista corporation has invested $10 million in producing greeting cards. Its after-tax profits according to conventional accounting measures amounted to $800,000. During the same period an average return of 6% would have been obtained by purchasing government securities. Do you think Vista Corporation earned an economic profit? Why or why not? Explain.

   (b) Suppose that the financial vice president of Vista Corporation conducts a thorough study and finds that the prospects are excellent (90% chance of success) that an annual profit of $900,000 could be earned by shifting Vista's $10 million investment into the production of business forms. What implications, if any, does this estimate have for evaluating the profitability of Vista's greeting card operations? for future resource allocation within the firm?

2. How should an enterprise go about estimating normal profit?

3. In which of the following circumstances would an assumption of profit maximization be appropriate and in which would the analysis probably be improved by a consideration of goals other than profit? Justify your answer in each case.
   (a) The effect of steel import quotas on steel prices.
   (b) The effect of the UAW's winning a lucrative wage increase from General Motors upon the prices of GM cars.
   (c) The effect of increased liquor taxes upon the price of liquor.
   (d) The effect of a ban on cigarette advertising upon the sales strategy of the three largest cigarette producers.
   (e) The effect upon coal prices of the major oil firms acquiring producers of coal and thereby gaining control over a large segment of the nation's coal deposits.
   (f) The effect of strong antipollution laws upon the prices of paper products, chemicals, steel, and other products produced by processes with a heavy pollution byproduct.

4. "No single goal of business enterprise is pure in its purpose. Goals tend to be overlapping and interdependent." Discuss the validity of this viewpoint and give examples in support of your answer.

5. Is it possible to determine whether or not a particular firm is maximizing profits? Or, to put it another way, is it possible to ascertain at some moment of time what the maximum potential profit performance of a firm is, thus allowing a comparison with the firm's actual profit performance to see if the firm is maximizing profits? Justify your answer.

6. The Hall-Prentiss Corporation is weighing two alternative projects costing $50 million, one offering a best-guess profit expectation of $10 million with a 10% chance of losing $5 million, the other offering an expected profit of $20 million with a 30% chance of losing $5 million. Which is the profit-maximizing alternative? How does

the decision situation illustrate the problem of trying to maximize profits under conditions of uncertainty?

7. Is there any difference between a firm's having "monopoly power" and having a "position of advantage" in the markets for its products?

8. Henry Ford II, in an address before the Michigan State Chamber of Commerce on October 2, 1962, made the following statements:

> There is no such thing as planning for a minimal return less than the best you can imagine—not if you want to survive in a competitive market. It's like asking a professional football team to win by only one point—a sure formula for losing. There's only one way to compete successfully—all-out. If believing this makes you a greedy capitalist lusting after bloated profits, then I plead guilty. The worst sin I can commit as a businessman is to fail to seek maximum long-term profitability by all decent and lawful means. To do so is to subvert economic reason.

(a) What do you suppose Ford meant when he claimed that to fail to try to maximize long-term profitability is a "sin" and subverts "economic reason"?

(b) Do you agree with Ford's viewpoint? Why or why not?

9. It has been observed by Milton Friedman, one of the nation's most eminent economists, that "few trends could so thoroughly undermine the very foundations of our free society as the acceptance by corporate officials of a social responsibility other than to make as much money for their stockholders as possible."

(a) What is the economic basis for such a statement?

(b) Do you agree with this view? Why or why not?

10. "When managers have the freedom and discretion to pursue their personal goals within firms, we can generally expect that they will do so and the result is not likely to be strict profit-maximizing behavior for the firm." Evaluate this statement from the perspective of the principal-agent problem within large corporations that are characterized by a separation of ownership and control. What factors tend to ameliorate the principal-agent problem in such corporations? Can managers survive who pursue goals that the owners do not support in the long run? Why or why not?

11. According to Peter Drucker, noted professor of management and business consultant, "There is *no* justification and no rationale for profit as long as one talks the nonsense of profit motive and profit maximization." But he goes on to say: "Profit . . . is not the whole of business responsibility; but it is the first responsibility. The business that fails to produce an adequate profit imperils both the integrity of the resources entrusted in its care and the economy's capacity to grow. . . . Business needs a minimum of profit: the profit required to cover its own future risks, the profit required to enable it to stay in business and to maintain intact the wealth-producing capacity of its resources." Is Drucker's view in conflict with how economists view profit? With whom do you agree?

12. Although it is easy to pontificate about the general desirability of business enterprises behaving in "socially responsible" ways and doing what is in "the public interest," it is not so easy to translate such "principles" into concrete prescriptions. For instance:

(a) Is it socially responsible and in the public interest for oil companies to raise their prices for gasoline or to lower them?

(b) Is it in the public interest for electric utilities to invest in and operate nuclear-powered generating plants (given that they are more fuel-cost efficient than other types of generating plants and given that they do not create acid rain or other air pollution problems)?

(c) Is it socially responsible or in the public interest for U.S. companies to build production facilities in foreign countries (where production costs may well be lower) and then ship the goods to the United States to be sold and used domestically? Is "exporting jobs" in the public interest even if it results in lower prices to users of the product?

Chapter 10

How Markets Function:
THE MODEL OF PERFECT COMPETITION

A critical part of examining the market for a product is the structure of competition—whether there are *many* or *few* sellers in the industry. The terms *many* and *few* are delineated not so much by the numbers of firms as by the competitive interaction among firms. There are "many" sellers of a product when no one firm has a big enough volume of business or enjoys high enough standing as a market leader for the remaining firms to be competitively threatened by its actions. Each firm is small enough and insignificant enough in the context of the whole market that it is virtually an anonymous entity, hidden in a crowd of more or less equally capable sellers. In contrast, we say there are "few" sellers of a product whenever the actions of any one firm will be noticed and reacted to by rival sellers. "Few" means few enough so that rival firms find it imperative to watch each other's moves closely. Fewness of sellers also means that each firm is large relative to the size of the market in which it operates; often, when firms are few in number each firm is large in absolute size as well.[1] The single-firm industry, or monopoly, is the limiting case of fewness.

A second key element in market analysis relates to whether the products of sellers are identical or differentiated. The products of sellers may be considered to be identical whenever and wherever customers evidence no particular preference for one firm's brand over that of another firm. This may arise because the item is produced by a process that confers certain measurable qualities that can be graded and which are unrelated to the seller producing it. For instance, choice-grade beef is choice-grade beef, and one cannot tell (nor does it really matter) whether it came from ranch A or ranch B. In such cases, the products of firms in an industry tend to be perfect substitutes; examples include cotton, sulfuric acid, natural gas, coal, cement, and coffee beans.

On the other hand, where the products of firms are branded and each brand has its own distinctive features, they are not perfect substitutes for one another, and buyers may have good reason to prefer one firm's brand over another's. The ultimate test of differentiation is always in the mind of the buyer, and the perceived differences in the products of various firms may be either real or contrived. Real differences involving performance, materials,

Two of the most important determinants of competitive rivalry are whether there are many or few sellers and whether sellers' products are identical or differentiated.

---

[1] Fewness does not always mean bigness. A small community has only a few banks, drycleaners, movies, florists, doctors, lawyers, and hairdressers—none of which is big in an absolute sense. General Motors, however, is big from both an absolute and a relative standpoint.

design, workmanship, and service are obviously important aspects of product differentiation. But contrived differences brought about by brand names, trademarks, packaging, and advertising can also be important to buyers; for example, even though all brands of aspirin are chemically alike, many buyers evidence preferences for one brand over others. In addition, it should be recognized that a firm's product extends beyond the item itself. For example, although a large number of retailers in an area may sell Crest toothpaste, they may not be equally attractive to buyers of Crest—the sales clerks in one store may be more courteous, or its location more convenient, or its checkout system faster, or its delivery service more dependable, or its credit terms more accommodating. Indeed, any number of factors can cause buyers to prefer one seller over another, even though the item purchased is the same. The various brands of shoes, wines, cereal, cosmetics, cars, golf clubs, personal computers, TV sets, and soft drinks are all examples of differentiated products.

Given, then, that the analysis of how markets function hinges on whether there are many or few firms and whether their products are identical or differentiated, there are four main models of market behavior that must be explored:

1. *Perfect competition*—many sellers of a standardized product.
2. *Monopolistic competition*—many sellers of a differentiated product.
3. *Oligopoly*—few sellers of either a standardized or a differentiated product.
4. *Monopoly*—a single seller of a product for which there is no close substitute.

In this chapter we examine the model of perfect competition. Chapters 11 to 13 deal with the market models of monopoly, monopolistic competition, and oligopoly.

THE CHARACTERISTICS OF A PERFECTLY COMPETITIVE MARKET

A perfectly competitive market has four main features. First, the products of firms in the industry are identical or at least so much alike that buyers do not care whether they buy the product of one firm or another. Since the products of the firms are indistinguishable and therefore homogeneous commodities, no buyer is willing to pay one firm a higher price than that charged by rival firms. Buyers are totally indifferent from which firm they purchase as long as price is the same. In fact, differences in price constitute the *only* reason a buyer might prefer one seller to any other.

Second, in perfect competition each and every buyer and seller is without power to affect the going market price of the product. This means that each buyer's purchases must be such a sufficiently small portion of the total bought by all buyers that no one buyer can wrangle a lower price from sellers than can any other buyer. Similarly, the sales made by a particular firm must be such a sufficiently small portion of the total sold by all firms that the price of the product is not materially affected by any one firm's decision to increase or decrease its output rate. Only if many buyers or sellers act in concert can market prices be influenced materially.

Third, in a perfectly competitive market resource inputs of all kinds are completely mobile. In the long run, there are no important restrictions upon the freedom of firms to enter or leave the industry. Resources can be switched from one use to another very readily. Workers are willing and able to move from region to region in response to new job opportunities and changing wage rates. Supplies of raw materials are made freely available to the highest bidders.

Fourth, perfect competition is characterized by a state of perfect knowledge. Decisions are made under conditions of *certainty*. Firms know exactly what their revenue and cost functions are. They also know the prices of all resource inputs and the various alternative technologies which can be used to produce their products. Consumers are aware of the prices charged by all firms. Resource owners are aware of the prices firms are paying for resource inputs and all relevant opportunity costs.

Obviously, these four conditions are so stringent that no market in the real world ever has or ever can meet them. A few markets (those for raw material commodities and certain financial securities like money market funds, certificates of deposit, and government bonds) come close to satisfying the first three requirements but none meet the fourth requirement of perfect knowledge. Nonetheless, the study of perfectly competitive markets is not without value. Recall from the introductory chapter that a model may yield valid conclusions even though its assumptions are "unrealistic." As we shall see, the perfectly competitive model (1) tells us a lot about the functioning of markets where large numbers of relatively small firms sell identical products and (2) illuminates the conditions for maximizing profits. We shall, however, not claim too much for the model of perfect competition, and we shall be especially judicious in deciding whether perfect competition is, as its name implies, really "perfect."

> **The model of perfect competition is predicated upon identical products, powerless buyers and sellers, completely mobile resource inputs, and a state of perfect knowledge.**

SHORT-RUN EQUILIBRIUM OF A FIRM IN A PERFECTLY COMPETITIVE MARKET

In perfect competition the prevailing market price of a product is established by the interaction of market demand and market supply. Given the market demand and supply curves in Figure 10-1(a), a short-run market equilibrium is attained at a price of P_1 dollars and at a total industry output of Q_T units.[2] If price were higher than P_1, then excess supply conditions would drive it downward. By the same token, if price were lower than P_1, then shortage conditions would force it upward.

Under conditions of perfect competition, each firm has a *horizontal* demand-*AR* curve that intersects the vertical axis at the price established by market supply and market demand conditions. This is illustrated in Figure 10-1(b). No firm can sell its output at a price even slightly higher than P_1 dollars because buyers will immediately shift their purchases to other firms selling the same item at the lower market price. And since each firm is so small relative to the total market, it can sell its entire output at the market price of P_1; hence, there is no inducement whatsoever to sell at a price lower than P_1. The result is that *all firms sell at the going price.* At any one time a *single* price prevails throughout the market, as determined by the balance between demand and supply.

When the firm's demand-*AR* curve is horizontal, it can sell additional units of output without reducing price. Thus, marginal revenue (MR) equals price at every output rate since each additional unit sold will cause total reve-

> **Because under conditions of perfect competition a single price prevails throughout the marketplace (as determined by the forces of market demand and market supply), each firm's demand-*AR* curve is horizontal—it can sell whatever volume of output it wishes at the going market price.**

---

[2] The total industry output, Q_T, is the sum of the outputs of all the firms in the industry. It is important to remember that no one firm's output constitutes a significant portion of Q_T.

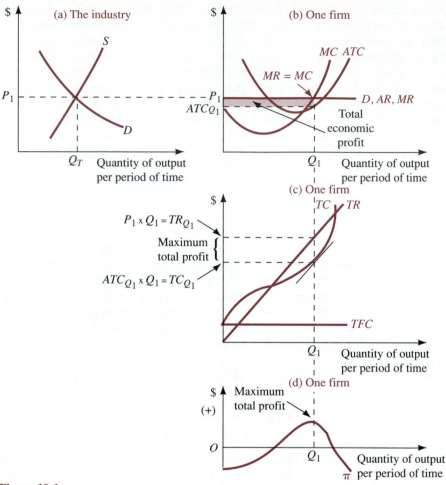

Figure 10-1

The profit-maximizing price and output for a firm operating in a perfectly competitive market

nue to rise by an amount equal to the price of the product. For example, if price is fixed at $10, then the sale of each additional unit causes total revenue to rise by $10; *MR* is therefore constant and equal to $10. The firm's *MR* function corresponds precisely to its demand-*AR* curve, as shown in Figure 10-1(b). *Both marginal and average revenue are equal to the market price of the product at all possible outputs of the firm.*

Since the firm can sell whatever amount it wishes at the going price, its total revenue (*TR*) function will be a linear, upward-sloping curve starting from the origin, as depicted in Figure 10-1(c). *Each and every unit sold will increase TR by an amount equal to the selling price.* Marginal revenue (*MR*) is constant, so *the TR curve rises at a constant rate* (equal to *MR* and price). The general equation for the *TR* function can be written as

$$TR = P \cdot Q.$$

Now suppose that the firm has a cost structure represented by the average total cost (*ATC*) and marginal cost (*MC*) curves in Figure 10-1(b) and by the associated total cost (*TC*) curve in Figure 10-1(c).[3] How much should the firm decide to offer for sale? How will the firm fare at the going price? To answer these questions first requires a consideration of the goal or goals of business enterprises in an environment of perfect competition. As was indicated in Chapter 9, profit is the dominant goal of most firms, so suppose *we assume that the prime objective of perfectly competitive firms is to maximize profits* (or to minimize losses if they cannot make profits). Whether this assumption is valid will be seen shortly.

Since price is established by the market, a perfectly competitive firm has no pricing decision to make. It is a *price-taker*. Each firm must live with whatever price that market demand and supply conditions establish. However, a firm in perfect competition *is* able to exert some measure of control over its destiny by adjusting its output to any rate it is capable of producing. Assuming the firm's goal is profit maximization, the analytical issue is one of determining the profit-maximizing output rate.

PROFIT MAXIMIZATION: THE TOTAL COST-TOTAL REVENUE APPROACH

The easiest and most direct way to determine where profit is maximum is to compare total revenue and total costs. Logic dictates that *total profits are maximized at the output rate where TR exceeds TC by the greatest amount*. In Figure 10-1(c) the firm's profit is maximum at an output of Q_1 units, where the *vertical distance* between *TR* and *TC* is greatest. Geometrically, it so happens that the maximum vertical distance between *TR* and *TC* occurs at the output rate where a tangent to the *TC* curve has the same slope and is parallel to the *TR* curve, as indicated on the diagram.

PROFIT MAXIMIZATION PRINCIPLE
A firm always maximizes its total profits at the output rate where *TR* exceeds *TC* by the greatest amount.

The firm's profit function [Figure 10-1(d)] is derived by subtracting *TC* from *TR* at each rate of output. It indicates how the firm's short-run profits vary with its output rate. The peak of the total profit (π) curve defines the output rate corresponding to maximum short-run profits.

PROFIT MAXIMIZATION: THE UNIT COST-UNIT REVENUE APPROACH

On a unit cost and unit revenue basis, *maximum profits are obtained at the output rate where marginal cost equals marginal revenue*. The validity of this proposition may be established as a matter of common sense. If the production and sale of one more unit of output will add more to a firm's total revenue than to its total costs, the sale of the unit must necessarily add something to the firm's total profits. If, however, the extra cost of producing and selling one more unit is greater than the extra revenues the firm gains, the firm's total profits will be reduced by selling that unit. Marginal revenue is defined as the *addition* to total revenue attributable to the sale of one more unit of output, whereas marginal cost (*MC*) is defined as the addition to total cost resulting

PROFIT MAXIMIZATION PRINCIPLE
A firm always maximizes its total profits at the output rate where *MC* equals *MR*.

[3] It should be recognized that the cost curves portrayed in Figures 10-1(b) and (c) represent just one of the several types of short-run cost functions which firms may possess. As was discussed in Chapter 8, the cubic type of *TC* function is viewed by many economists as representative of the most typical type of cost behavior. However, firms may well possess other types of cost functions depending on the chapter of the technology employed in the production process. The chapter-end exercises incorporate other types of cost functions to illustrate the perfectly competitive firm's output decision under a variety of cost circumstances.

from the production and sale of one more unit of output. Hence, to maximize profits the firm must be cognizant of the marginal revenue and the marginal cost of each successive unit of output.

Thus, in Figure 10-1(b) the most profitable output level is at Q_1 units, where the *MC* curve intersects the *MR* curve. If the firm stops short of selling Q_1 units, then the revenue from selling an additional unit will exceed the cost of selling another unit. Plainly, the firm can increase profits by increasing its rate of output to Q_1. Should the firm produce beyond an output rate of Q_1 units, the marginal costs of all the units in excess of Q_1 will exceed the additional revenue which the firm can obtain from selling them. The firm will lose money on all the incremental units sold past an output of Q_1 units, thereby causing total profits to be smaller than obtainable at a lesser output.

The profit-maximizing output rate in Figure 10-1(b) corresponds exactly to the output rate in Figure 10-1(c), where *TR* exceeds *TC* by the greatest amount. How do we know? Because at an output of Q_1 units in Figure 10-1(c), the slope of the *TR* curve equals the slope of the *TC* curve. *MR*, by definition, equals the slope of *TR*, and *MC*, by definition, equals the slope of the *TC* function. Hence, since the values of the slopes are equal, *MC* must necessarily equal *MR* at the same output where total revenue exceeds total cost by the largest amount. Logical consistency requires further that the profit-maximizing output rate in Figure 10-1(b) coincide with the output rate in Figure 10-1(d), where the total profit function reaches its maximum height.

The profit-maximizing rule may be stated in yet another way: *Total profit is maximum at the output rate where marginal profit equals zero.* Marginal profit is the change in total profit resulting from a 1-unit change in output; this is equivalent to saying that

$$M\pi = MR - MC,$$

where $M\pi$ is marginal profit. More technically, marginal profit equals the rate of change in total profit as the rate of output changes, or

$$M\pi = \frac{d\pi}{dQ}.$$

Marginal profit is, therefore, geometrically equal to the slope of the total profit function. At the peak of the total profit function, its slope equals zero—hence the rationale for saying that total profit is maximized where $M\pi = 0$. *As long as marginal profit is positive, the total profit function is rising, and it pays to increase output.* When the profit earned on the next unit of output has shrunk to zero ($M\pi = 0$), the peak of the total profit function has been reached. *If the firm produces beyond the output rate associated with zero marginal profit, marginal profit becomes negative, and the loss incurred on each of these extra units causes the total profit function to turn downward.* This is evident from inspection of the total profit function in Figure 10-1(d).

PROFIT MAXIMIZATION PRINCIPLE
A firm always maximizes its total profit at the output rate where the marginal profit on the last unit sold equals zero.

CALCULATION OF THE PROFIT-MAXIMIZING OUTPUT

It is useful to examine the mathematics of determining the perfectly competitive firm's optimum output decision. Suppose the going market price for the commodity is $20 and the firm's total cost function is $TC = 75 + 17Q - 4Q^2 + Q^3$. From the preceding discussion we know that profit is maximized at the output where $MR = MC$. Both the *MR* and *MC* functions can be obtained from the information given. At a constant price of $20, *MR* is also $20 at every output rate. The *MC* function is the first derivative of the *TC* function, giving

$$MC = \frac{dTC}{dQ} = 17 - 8Q + 3Q^2.$$

Equating *MR* with *MC*, we have

$$20 = 17 - 8Q + 3Q^2.$$

Solving for Q yields the two roots $Q = -\frac{1}{3}$ and $Q = 3$. Since output can never be negative, the profit-maximizing rate of output is 3 units. Actually, it can be proved that the larger of the two roots is always the profit-maximizing (or loss-minimizing) output rate. It is a simple matter, however, to resolve the issue by calculating total profit at each of the values of Q for which $MR = MC$ and observing firsthand which Q yields the greatest total profit.

The profit-maximizing output can also be determined using the rule that total profit is maximum where marginal profit is zero. Again, let $P = MR = \$20$ and $TC = 75 + 17Q - 4Q^2 + Q^3$. Total profit is defined as

$$\pi = TR - TC.$$

Total revenue, being equal at every output to $P \cdot Q$, can in this case be represented by the expression $20Q$. Substituting into the expression for total profit, we have

$$\pi = 20Q - (75 + 17Q - 4Q^2 + Q^3).$$

Since marginal profit is precisely defined as the rate of change in total profit as the rate of output changes, the expression for marginal profit becomes

$$M\pi = \frac{d\pi}{dQ} = 20 - (17 - 8Q + 3Q^2).$$

Given that total profit is maximum where $M\pi = 0$, the preceding expression is set equal to zero, yielding

$$20 - (17 - 8Q + 3Q^2) = 0,$$
$$20 - 17 + 8Q - 3Q^2 = 0,$$
$$3 + 8Q - 3Q^2 = 0.$$

Solving for Q gives the roots $Q = -\frac{1}{3}$ and $Q = 3$, the same results given by the $MR = MC$ approach.

TOTAL PROFIT OR LOSS

Whether the firm realizes a profit or a loss depends on the relationship between price and average total cost at the output rate where $MR = MC$. If price exceeds *ATC*, the firm will enjoy short-run profits, whereas if price is less than *ATC*, losses will be incurred.

In Figure 10-1(b), selling price is P_1 dollars, and *ATC* at the profit-maximizing output of Q_1 units is ATC_{Q_1} dollars. Profit per unit is therefore $P_1 - ATC_{Q_1}$ dollars at an output of Q_1 units. Total profit is profit per unit multiplied by the number of units sold, or

$$\pi = (P_1 - ATC_{Q_1})Q_1,$$

which is numerically equivalent to the size of the shaded area in Figure 10-1(b).

If market price exceeds *ATC* at the output rate where $MR = MC$, a firm will earn short-run profits; if market price is less than *ATC*, the firm will incur a loss.

This shaded area has a numerical dollar value equal to the vertical distance between *TR* and *TC* at an output of Q_1 units in Figure 10-1(c) and equal to the height of the total profit function in Figure 10-1(d). It should also be clear from Figures 10-1(b) and (c) that multiplying P_1 by Q_1 gives TR_{Q_1} and that ATC_{Q_1} times Q_1 equals TC_{Q_1}.

Observe that at output Q_1, profit *per unit* is *not* maximized; in other words, total profit is not maximum at the same output at which profit per unit is maximum. *Profit per unit is maximized at the output rate where price exceeds ATC by the greatest vertical distance, whereas total profit is maximized where MR = MC.* These two output rates do not coincide, as an examination of Figure 10-1(b) will confirm.

MINIMIZING SHORT-RUN LOSSES

If the prevailing market price does not permit a firm to earn a profit in the short run, it has to decide whether to operate at a loss or temporarily suspend production until the market price increases to a profitable level.

It does not, of course, always work out that perfectly competitive firms can earn positive economic profits in the short run. The equilibrium market price in the short run may fall below the firm's *ATC* curve at every rate of output, thereby making it impossible for the firm to cover all its costs in the short run. What, then, is the firm's optimum output decision? Should it shut down operations and wait for price to return to a more profitable level, or should it produce at a loss? If it continues to operate, at what output will the firm's losses be minimized?

The firm's decision rests on whether or not the market price is high enough to cover the firm's average variable costs (or whether enough total revenue can be obtained to cover total variable costs) at some output rate. Suppose we define ***unit contribution profit*** as the difference between price and average variable cost:

$$\text{unit contribution profit} = P - AVC.$$

The relevance of unit contribution profit is easily demonstrated. If a product sells for \$10 per unit and average variable cost is \$6, the firm is able to cover all the expenses associated with the variable inputs needed to produce the product and has \$4 left over to help pay total fixed costs and to contribute to the earning of profit. Hence, even though price may not be sufficient to cover *ATC, as long as the prevailing price is high enough to permit the firm to obtain a margin over and above AVC, it pays the firm to produce in the short run.* Covering part of *AVC* is better than covering none of *AFC.*

It always pays a firm to continue to produce at a loss in the short run if the prevailing market price exceeds a firm's average variable cost and some contribution profit can be earned toward the payment of its total fixed costs.

A related concept is that of ***total contribution profit***. Total contribution profit is the difference between total revenue and total variable costs:

$$\text{total contribution profit} = TR - TVC.$$

It should be apparent that even if *TR* is not sufficient to cover *TC, as long as TR more than covers TVC, the firm earns some amount of total contribution profit, which can be used to pay at least a portion of the firm's total fixed costs. This is a superior outcome to the situation of shutting down.* When the firm ceases selling in the short run, *TR* falls to zero, and the firm's loss will be equal to its total fixed costs. Furthermore, it stands to reason that the larger the amount of total contribution profit a firm can obtain, the better will be its short-run profit and loss position. The greater the amount by which *TR* exceeds *TVC,* the more dollars the firm will have to pay fixed costs. And when total fixed costs have all been paid, then any remaining total contribution profit represents economic profit.

We are now ready to use the concepts of contribution profit in deter-mining a firm's optimum output decision when price temporarily falls below average total cost. Consider Figure 10-2. Suppose supply and demand condi-tions establish an industrywide price of P_1 dollars. Given the firm's *MC, AVC,* and *ATC* curves, what is the optimum output rate? Clearly, the firm cannot make a profit because the *ATC* curve lies above price P_1 at every output rate; the firm's decision then turns on how to minimize its losses. Observe that between output Q_1 and Q_3 in Figure 10-2(b) price exceeds *AVC*; similarly, between the same outputs in Figure 10-2(c), *TR* exceeds *TVC*. Thus, there are a number of output rates at which both unit and total contribution profits are positive. The significance of this finding is that the firm will minimize its losses by producing somewhere between Q_1 and Q_3, since in this output range *TR* will exceed *TVC*, and the resulting total contribution profit can be applied to the payment of total fixed costs. Common sense tells us that *the firm will want to obtain as much total contribution profit as possible, so as to have the maximum*

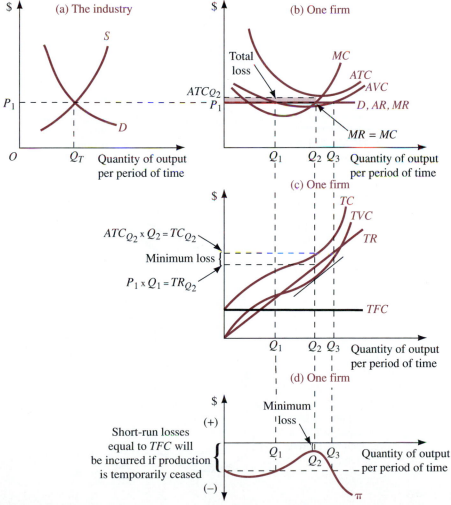

Figure 10-2

The short-run loss-minimizing price and output for a firm in perfect competition

LOSS MINIMIZATION PRINCIPLE
A firm always minimizes its short-run losses at the output rate where *TC* exceeds *TR* by the smallest amount.

LOSS MINIMIZATION PRINCIPLE
A firm always minimizes its short-run losses at the output rate where $MR = MC$ provided that market price covers *AVC* and contribution profit is positive.

number of dollars available for covering total fixed costs and thereby keeping losses to a minimum. Note in Figure 10-2(c) that the output at which *TR* exceeds *TVC* by the greatest vertical distance occurs at output Q_2, where a tangent to the *TVC* curve is parallel to the *TR* curve; this is the output rate associated with maximum total contribution profit. It is also apparent from Figure 10-2(c) that the vertical distance by which *TC* exceeds *TR* is less at Q_2 than at any other output rate, meaning that here the firm's short-run losses are minimized. Thus, from the standpoint of *TC-TR* analysis, *short-run losses are minimized at the output where TC exceeds TR by the smallest vertical distance.* In Figure 10-2(d) the total profit function reaches its highest level at an output of Q_2 units; short-run losses are measured by the vertical distance from the peak of the profit function to the horizontal axis. Insofar as the firm's unit costs and revenues are concerned [Figure 10-2(b)], an output of Q_2 units per period of time corresponds exactly to the output where $MR = MC$ and $M\pi = 0$. Thus, we find that the $MR = MC$ rule and its corollary, $M\pi = 0$, not only identify the

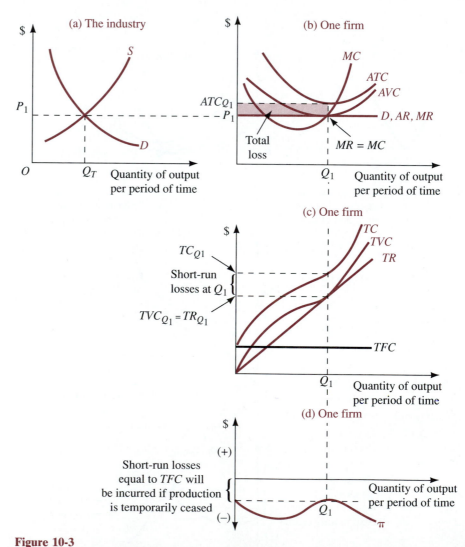

Figure 10-3

The short-run loss-minimizing price and output for a perfectly competitive firm when the demand curve is just tangent to the *AVC* curve

short-run profit-maximizing output but also identify the short-run loss-minimizing output.

Now consider Figure 10-3, where the forces of supply and demand combine to establish a short-run equilibrium price of P_1 dollars such that the firm's demand-AR-MR curve is just tangent to the minimum point of its AVC curve. Again, there exists no opportunity for earning a normal profit, much less an economic profit, and the firm's output decision must be aimed at minimizing short-run losses. If the firm elects to produce where $MR = MC$ and where $M\pi = 0$, then it will produce Q_1 units [Figure 10-3(b)] and will obtain total revenues of TR_1 dollars [Figure 10-3(c)]. Price will be just equal to AVC [Figure 10-3(b)], and total variable costs will be equal to total revenue [Figure 10-3(c)]. Unit contribution profit will be zero, and total contribution profit will be zero. The firm's revenues will just cover variable expenses, and the firm's losses will be equal to total fixed costs. Insofar as minimizing losses is concerned, the firm will be indifferent as to producing and selling Q_1 units or closing down its operations in the short run. In either case, short-run losses will equal total fixed costs, and this is the best the firm can do. At any other output rate revenues will not even be sufficient to cover TVC, contribution profit will be negative, and losses will exceed TFC by the amount of TVC not covered by TR. However, given that short-run losses will be no more by operating at Q_1 than by closing down, the firm will in all probability elect to produce and sell Q_1 units. By so doing, the firm continues to serve its customers and to offer employment to its workers, with no difference in losses from that of the shutdown case.

However, Figure 10-4 shows a situation where the short-run equilibrium market price falls below even minimum AVC. Should the firm again follow the rule of producing at the point where $MR = MC$ [Figure 10-4(b)], then total losses will be equal to the vertical distance between TR and TC in Figure 10-4(c). Observe that TR will not even cover TVC at this output—or any other output for that matter. The vertical spread between TR and TC is always greater at outputs above zero than at zero. Both unit and total contribution profits are negative at every output above zero. Therefore, in this instance the firm will minimize short-run losses by discontinuing production and selling nothing; losses will equal total fixed costs.

The following *principles* summarize the analysis: The relationship between price and AVC tells a firm *whether* to produce; in the short run it is always advantageous from a profit/loss standpoint to continue production if price equals or exceeds AVC at one or more output rates and to cease production if price falls below AVC at every output rate. The relationship between marginal revenue and marginal cost indicates *how much* the firm should produce when price equals or exceeds AVC; profits are maximized or losses are minimized at the output rate where $MR = MC$ and $M\pi = 0$. The relationship between price and ATC indicates the *amount of profit or loss per unit* that results from the decision to produce; total profit or loss equals the difference between price and ATC multiplied by the quantity produced and sold. Thus the firm maximizes short-run profits or minimizes short-run losses by producing and selling the output at which $MR = MC$ and $M\pi = 0$. There is only one exception. When the prevailing market price is below the firm's minimum average variable costs at every output rate, losses will be minimized by stopping short-run operations altogether, holding losses to the amount of total fixed costs. As will be indicated in the next three chapters, these same principles also hold true for firms operating under conditions other than perfect competition.

LOSS MINIMIZATION PRINCIPLE
A firm always minimizes its short-run losses by ceasing to produce and sell whenever market price falls below the firm's average variable costs; in such cases, short-run losses will match the firm's total fixed costs.

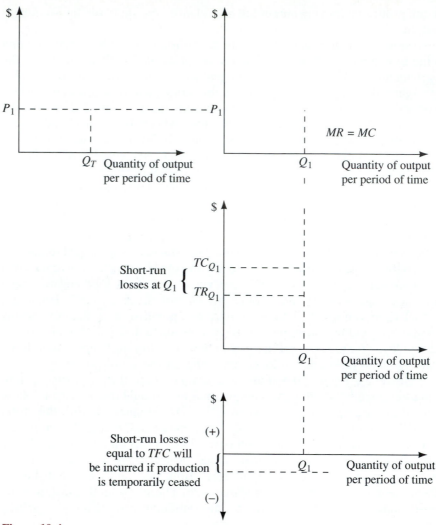

Figure 10-4
The short-run close-down position for a firm in perfect competition

THE PERFECTLY COMPETITIVE FIRM'S SHORT-RUN SUPPLY CURVE

We have just seen in a perfectly competitive market that a firm incurring a loss in the short run will continue to produce in the short run provided it loses no more by producing than by shutting down production entirely. This proposition is useful for deriving the short-run supply curve of an individual firm in a perfectly competitive environment. The procedure is illustrated in Figure 10-5. Suppose that market price is P_0 dollars and the firm's AVC, ATC, and MC curves are as shown in Figure 10-5(a). Since P_0 is below the minimum AVC which the firm can achieve, the firm's short-run equilibrium rate of output is zero. Next, suppose market price is P_1. The corresponding equilibrium rate of output for the firm is Q_1 units, as this is the output at which $MR = MC$ and at which losses are minimum. Thus, the firm is ready, willing, and able to supply Q_1 units at a price of P_1 dollars; the values (P_1, Q_1) define a point (S_1) on the firm's supply curve in panel (b). Now suppose market price is P_2, generating

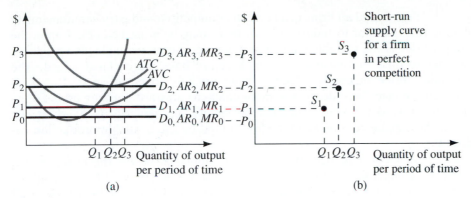

Figure 10-5

Derivation of the short-run supply curve for a firm operating in a perfectly competitive market

D_2, AR_2, and MR_2. In this case, the firm's optimum output decision is to produce Q_2 units and thereby minimize its short-run losses. The values (P_2, Q_2) are associated with point S_2 in Figure 10-5(b). Similarly, a price of P_3 leads to a profit-maximizing output of Q_3 units and point S_3. Other supply points can be derived in like fashion.

Connecting the price-output combinations in Figure 10-5(b) gives the short-run supply curve of the perfectly competitive firm. The supply curve indicates the quantity of output per period of time which a profit-maximizing firm would supply at various alternative prices under conditions of perfect competition. It should by now be apparent that the firm's supply curve is identical in shape and position to that portion of the firm's MC curve lying above its AVC curve. This is illustrated in Figure 10-5(a) as the boldly inscribed portion of the firm's MC curve. In other words, *the short-run supply curve for a perfectly competitive firm coincides with its marginal cost curve for all rates of output equal to or greater than the output at which AVC is minimum.* The firm's supply of output drops to zero at any price below AVC. Herein lies the link between production costs and output rates in the short run for a perfectly competitive enterprise.

The output volumes that a firm operating under perfectly competitive conditions is willing to supply to buyers is indicated by that part of its *MC* curve lying above its *AVC* curve.

THE PERFECTLY COMPETITIVE INDUSTRY'S SHORT-RUN SUPPLY CURVE

In Chapter 4 the market demand curve was derived by horizontally adding together the demand curves of individual consumers. However, factors are present which may preclude a similar determination of the short-run industry supply curve for the commodity in question. The perfectly competitive firm's marginal cost curve is derived from the underlying production function (Chapter 8) on the assumption that the price of variable input is constant, no matter how many or how few units the firm purchases. This is a reasonable assumption in the case of perfectly competitive firms, because any one firm uses such a small amount of the total supply of the variable input that changes in its rate of input usage have no perceptible effect on the market price of the variable input. In other words, a single firm can expand or reduce its output rate, and consequently its variable input usage, without affecting the price it pays for variable input.

Yet, should *all* firms in a perfectly competitive industry simultaneously decide to expand or to reduce output, there may be a marked effect upon the supply price of the variable input. For example, suppose one chicken producer decides to raise more chickens and therefore buys more chicken feed. The prevailing price of chicken feed is quite unlikely to be affected. But if all chicken producers decide to raise more chickens, upward pressure on the price of chicken feed becomes a distinct possibility, particularly in the short run when the supplies of chicken feed are limited by the available production capacity.

As long as the prices of variable input remain fixed, a perfectly competitive industry's short-run supply curve is the horizontal summation of the relevant portions of the marginal cost curves of firms in the industry.

As a consequence, the short-run supply curve for the product of a perfectly competitive industry cannot necessarily be obtained by horizontally summing the relevant portion of the marginal cost curves of each firm. It all depends on what happens to the price of variable input when *all* firms in the industry alter their usage of variable input. In the event that the supplies of variable input to a perfectly competitive industry are perfectly elastic (the input supply curves are horizontal), then it is valid to conceive of the short-run industry supply curve for the product as being the horizontal summation of the relevant portions of the *MC* curves of the individual firms. If the use of more variable input by all firms in the industry precipitates an increase in the price of variable input, then the marginal cost curve of each individual firm will shift upward by the increase in input price, and the short-run industry supply curve will be *more steeply sloped* than had input prices remained constant. If the use of more variable input by all firms in the industry causes the price of variable input to decline (perhaps because it can be supplied more economically in larger quantities), then the marginal cost curve of each individual firm will shift downward by the decrease in input price, and the short-run industry supply curve will be *less steeply sloped* than had input prices remained constant.

If the prices of variable input rise when all perfectly competitive firms use more variable inputs, then the short-run industry supply curve is more steeply sloped than the curve obtained from horizontally summing the relevant portions of firms' *MC* curves.

But regardless of what happens to the price of variable input when all firms use more or less of it, the short-run industry supply curve is upward sloping. How steeply sloped it is depends on the factors determining the shape of the marginal cost curve of each firm and on the effect of changes in industry-wide output on variable input prices. Suffice it to say at this point that to induce greater supplies of output in the short run from a perfectly competitive industry, higher prices will have to be offered. This characteristic gives rise to a short-run industry supply curve that slopes upward to the right—such then is the basis for the industry supply curves drawn in Figures 10-1 through 10-4.

LONG-RUN EQUILIBRIUM CONDITIONS IN A PERFECTLY COMPETITIVE MARKET

Although a perfectly competitive firm finds its short-run output decision constrained by the limitations of the fixed inputs, in the long run the options are more numerous. An established firm can alter its plant size, implement new technologies, or modify the character of its products in line with changing consumer tastes. More importantly, the firm can abandon production entirely and leave the industry if below-normal profits are being earned and the prospects are dim for any improvement. On the other hand, new firms may enter the industry if the profits of established firms are sufficiently attractive. Consider now the transition of a firm from short-run to long-run equilibrium in a perfectly competitive market.

Two assumptions will greatly simplify the analysis without invalidating the important conclusions:

1. We shall assume that all firms in the industry have comparable cost structures. This lets us look at how a *typical* firm is affected by changing market conditions, with confidence that all other firms in the industry will be similarly affected.

2. We shall assume for the moment that the prices of resource inputs are unaffected (a) by changes in the long-run output rates of existing firms, (b) by the entry of firms into industry, or (c) by the exodus of firms from the industry. In other words, the firms in the industry can, singly or as a group, alter their input requirements without affecting the prices they pay for them.

Let the short-run forces of market demand (D_1) and market supply (S_1) result in a market price of P_1 dollars [Figure 10-6(a)]. Further suppose that the typical firm has a short-run cost structure represented by $SRAC_1$ and $SRMC_1$ at the indicated position on the *LRAC* curve [Figure 10-6(b)]. With these revenue and cost functions, short-run equilibrium output for the firm is Q_1 units. At this output rate the firm realizes an economic profit because price exceeds *SRAC* at Q_1 units. Recall from Chapter 9 that an economic profit means the firm is receiving a rate of return on its investment greater than it could earn by diverting its resources into the production of something else. Under these circumstances the earning of an economic profit will have two significant effects. First, it will encourage the firm (if it has not already done so) to expand its production capability and take advantage of any available economies of scale indicated by the firm's *LRAC* curve. Expanding its long-run output potential (to the position defined by $SRAC_3$ and $SRMC_3$) offers the firm the prospect of even greater economic profits. Second, the existence of above-normal profits in this industry will induce new firms to enter with new capacity additions of their own. The process of new entry may be very slow or very rapid, depending on the amount of economic profits being earned by established firms and on the length of time it takes new entrants to begin their production operations.

As time elapses and these two effects take hold, the industry supply curve will shift to the right, say from S_1 to S_3, thereby driving the market price from P_1 down to P_3 and increasing the equilibrium industry output from Q_{T_1} to Q_{T_3}. The larger volume of industry output is a result of both the entry of new firms and the expansion of firms already in the industry.

However, it is also possible that the profit attraction could be strong enough to induce the typical firm to expand its production capacity beyond $SRAC_3$ and $SRMC_3$ to the output range where it has a cost structure repre-

> **COMPETITIVE MARKET PRINCIPLE**
> When firms in a perfectly competitive market environment are earning sizable economic profits, they are motivated to expand their scale of operation (to earn greater profits), and new firms are motivated to enter the industry (to try to capture some of the profit opportunities for themselves).

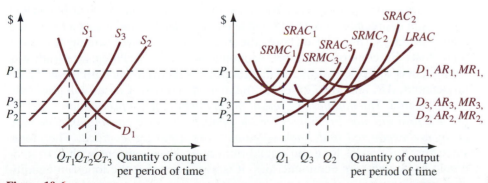

Figure 10-6

Transition to long-run equilibrium for a firm operating in a perfectly competitive market environment

sented by $SRAC_2$ and $SRMC_2$. In such a case, the greater output capabilities of firms would mean a shift of the industry supply to S_2 rather than to just S_3, and the industry price would be at P_2 where D_1 intersects S_2. It is apparent from Figure 10-6(b) that at a price of P_2 dollars the typical firm will sustain losses in the short run, since market price is below $SRAC_2$ at every output rate. Obviously, then, the typical firm and the industry would have both *overexpanded*; no longer would it be possible for firms to earn normal profits. The result will be a readjustment in the industry's production rates. Given that firms can earn higher rates of return in other industries, some firms—most likely the least efficient firms incurring the greatest losses—will elect to cease production of the item in question and shift their energies into the production of products where the profit outlook is brighter. The firms that choose to remain in the industry will find it advantageous over the long term to reduce costs by adjusting their production capabilities to the optimum size—where the $SRAC$ curve is tangent to the minimum point of the $LRAC$ curve. In terms of Figure 10-6(b), the typical firm would be induced to construct production facilities having a cost structure represented by $SRAC_3$ and $SRMC_3$. The outmigration of firms, coupled with the retrenchment of the production capacity of the remaining firms, would then cause the industry supply curve to shift to the left, eventually to S_3. As the industry supply curve moves leftward, market price will rise to P_3 and total industry output will contract to Q_{T_3}. Again, the optimum output rate for the typical firm becomes Q_3 units, where MR_3 intersects $SRMC_3$.

COMPETITIVE MARKET PRINCIPLE
In a perfectly competitive industry, market forces drive price to a level equal to minimum long-run average cost, where each firm earns a normal profit and there is no incentive for firms to enter or exit.

Observe that at this output price is just equal to short-run average total cost and to long-run average cost. The typical firm earns no economic profit but is able to squeeze out a normal profit. Taken together, these conditions define long-run equilibrium for a perfectly competitive market. Given our initial assumptions of (1) perfect mobility of resources into and out of the industry and (2) a goal of profit maximization, the position of long-run equilibrium is necessarily ordained to occur at the point where price equals the minimum value of long-run average cost and where the typical firm earns no more and no less than a normal profit. This is, indeed, the only conceivable point of long-run equilibrium. The reasoning is straightforward. *As long as market price is above the long-run average costs of the typical firm, economic profits can be realized. Established firms will be induced to expand provided it is profitable to do so, and new firms will be attracted into the industry.* Over time the market supply curve will be shifted to the right, thereby driving market price down and lowering the horizontal demand-AR-MR curve confronting each firm. Economic profits will tend to vanish. On the other hand, *whenever price is below the long-run average costs of the typical firm, losses will be incurred.* As their plants and equipment depreciate, some firms will leave the industry, being attracted by the higher profit prospects elsewhere; the remaining firms will attempt to lower their costs by constructing more economically sized facilities. The industry supply curve shifts leftward, and market price is raised along with the horizontal demand, AR, and MR curves for the individual firms. Losses will gradually be eliminated. *The number of firms in the industry and the production capacity of each firm will stabilize only when the opportunities for earning an economic profit are exhausted and when economic losses can be avoided.* Therefore, since the position of long-run equilibrium must be consistent with *zero* economic profit and *zero* economic loss, it is necessary that the long-run equilibrium price be exactly equal to minimum short-run average cost and to minimum long-run average cost. Unless $P = MR = SRAC = LRAC$, a change in firm size or in the number of firms will lead to the appearance of either economic profits or economic losses, in which case the forces of adjustment will spring into motion.[4]

It should now be apparent that we are entirely justified in our assumption made earlier that perfectly competitive firms will seek to maximize profits. Actually, perfectly competitive firms have no choice—they are placed in a position of *forced profit maximization*. Under conditions of long-run equilibrium a firm which operates at any output rate other than minimum *LRAC* will not earn a normal profit. With dismal earnings (or even losses), few firms are likely to pursue alternative goals; they simply cannot afford it. For this reason, it seems justifiable to assume that perfectly competitive firms will behave as if they seek to maximize profits.

In practice, of course, it is not really expected that a perfectly competitive industry will reach and thereafter maintain a state of long-run equilibrium. The market demand curve will certainly undergo frequent shifts as consumer tastes and preferences, incomes, and so on change. Likewise, technological progress, changing input prices, and new product innovation cause periodic shifts in the firm's *SRAC* and *LRAC* curves and the industry supply curve. As a consequence, long-run equilibrium is a moving target that a perfectly competitive industry continually chases but never catches. The process of market adjustment to long-run equilibrium is dynamic and always unfolding, in response to new market circumstances of demand, supply, and prices.

Furthermore, the continual process of adjusting toward a long-run equilibrium position imposes severe constraints on perfectly competitive firms. *The market forces of supply and demand are so powerful that in the long run firms are unable to make a profit any larger than that just sufficient to induce them to remain in business.* The only discretionary action a firm has relates to its output decision. And in the long run even here the firm's option is taken away; it is forced to produce where $P = MR = SRAC = SRMC = LRAC$ if it wants to earn at least a normal profit. Thus, *the firm is truly a captive servant of the market.* All this, according to conventional wisdom, works to the advantage of consumers and society as a whole. *Under long-run equilibrium conditions the consumer pays a price no higher than is required to cover all costs of production, thereby obtaining products at as low a price as is economically feasible. Moreover, all firms produce at the minimum points of their cost curves, thus utilizing in the most efficient manner the pool of resources that society makes available to the industry.*

A CONSTANT-COST INDUSTRY

In the preceding section it was assumed that the expansion or contraction of industry output had no effect on *input* prices. An industry having this characteristic is referred to as a *constant-cost industry*. The existence of such an industry has several implications which merit further exploration.

Figure 10-7 depicts long-run equilibrium under conditions of constant costs. Let D_1 and S_1 be the original short-run market demand and supply

COMPETITIVE MARKET PRINCIPLE
In a perfectly competitive market environment, firms are forced to try to maximize profit; producing at anything other than minimum *LRAC* in the long run risks earning less than a normal profit.

COMPETITIVE MARKET PRINCIPLE
Under long-run equilibrium conditions in a perfectly competitive market, buyers pay the lowest feasible price and resources are utilized in the most efficient manner possible.

---

[4] In practice, however, the profit thermostat regulating the number of firms and the outputs they produce works much better for expansion than contraction. Economic profits and free entry are reliable stimulants for increasing industry output, given sufficient time for firms to construct new facilities and bring new production capacity on stream. But to squeeze firms out of an overexpanded industry where profits are below normal or negative can be a slow and painful process. It takes time for entrepreneurs to accept the harsh fact that profit prospects are bleak, time for production facilities to wear out, and time to shift into other industries or else go out of business entirely. The long death of the small farmer is a case in point.

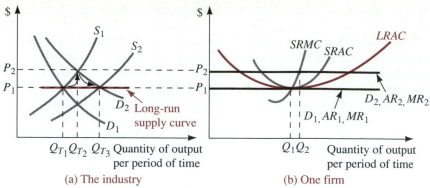

Figure 10-7

Long-run supply curve for a constant-cost industry

curves, with an equilibrium price at P_1 dollars. Assume that each firm in the industry is in long-run equilibrium at Q_1, where the firm's horizontal demand-*AR-MR* curve is just tangent to the minimum points of the firm's *SRAC* and *LRAC* curves, as shown in Figure 10-7(b). Now consider the impact of a shift in the short-run market demand curve to D_2. The market price will rise to P_2 dollars, and the profit-maximizing output for the firm becomes Q_2 units per period of time. However, at a price of P_2 dollars and an output of Q_2 units each firm will earn an economic profit, thereby triggering the entry of new firms into the industry and shifting the industry supply curve rightward, eventually to S_2. *In a constant-cost industry the entry of new firms and the expansion of industry output will not affect the input prices paid by existing firms.* The reason is that the resource inputs employed by this industry are available in such sufficiently large quantities that the appearance of new firms does not bid up the prices of the inputs and raise the costs of the existing firms. As a consequence, the *LRAC* curve of established firms remains fixed, and the new firms can operate with an identical *LRAC* curve.

Long-run equilibrium adjustment to the shift in demand is accomplished when the entry of new firms has caused the market price to fall back to P_1, where $P_1 = MR_1 = SRAC = SRMC = LRAC$, and each firm is producing Q_1 units and earning only a normal profit. The important point here is that the industry has a *constant long-run supply price*, which means industry output can be expanded or contracted in accordance with market demand conditions without altering the *long-run* equilibrium price charged by the firms. To put it another way, *a constant-cost industry operating under conditions of perfect competition has a horizontal long-run supply curve.* Such a curve is illustrated in Figure 10-7(a).

BASIC CONCEPT
In a constant-cost industry, input prices remain fixed when industry output rises or falls; as a consequence, the industry's long-run supply curve is horizontal.

AN INCREASING-COST INDUSTRY

Obviously, a situation can easily arise where changes in the output rate of an industry can cause the prices of resource inputs to change. In this section we examine the case where the expansion of industry output has the effect of *raising* input prices, thereby giving rise to an **increasing-cost industry**.

As illustrated in Figure 10-8, suppose that the industry is in long-run equilibrium. D_1 and S_1 portray the initial market demand and supply conditions, market price is P_1 dollars, and each firm is operating at the output rate where

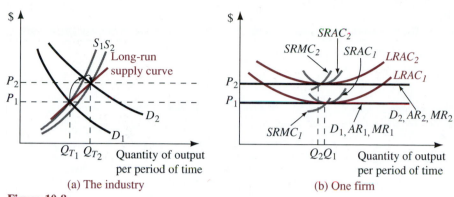

Figure 10-8

Long-run supply curve for an increasing-cost industry

price equals minimum *SRAC* and minimum *LRAC*. Now suppose that market demand increases to D_2, temporarily causing an increase in market price to the level where D_2 intersects S_1. The higher price allows established firms to earn an economic profit, which in turn attracts the entry of new firms. As output expands more resources are needed; at this point resource input prices are bid up by firms competing for the available resource supplies. The effect of rising input price is to increase the operating costs of both established firms and new entrants. As industry output expands and input prices rise, the marginal and average cost curves for the typical firm all gradually shift upward from $SRMC_1$, $SRAC_1$, and $LRAC_1$, say to a position represented by $SRMC_2$, $SRAC_2$, and $LRAC_2$. Moreover, the short-run industry supply curve is shifted to the right by the expansion of industry output. The process of adjustment continues until all economic profits have been eliminated. In Figure 10-8, this is depicted by the intersection of D_2 and S_2 and its associated price of P_2 dollars. Each firm selects the rate of output where $P_2 = MR_2 = SRMC_2 = SRAC_2 = LRAC_2$. The long-run industry supply curve is found by joining the points of long-run equilibrium; in Figure 10-8 these points are represented by the intersection of D_1 and S_1 and the intersection of D_2 and S_2.

> In an increasing-cost industry, input prices rise when industry output rises, resulting in an upward-sloping long-run industry supply curve.

The salient feature of an increasing-cost industry is the presence of a positively sloped long-run supply curve. Whereas in a constant-cost industry the expansion of industry output has no effect on the long-run price of the industry's product, in an increasing-cost industry the effect of greater industry output is a higher product price. The long-run supply curve of an increasing-cost industry slopes upward, because greater rates of output entail rising input prices and hence rising costs. Under these circumstances, higher market prices will be required to give firms the incentive to expand output.

A DECREASING-COST INDUSTRY

Price and output behavior in a *decreasing-cost industry* are depicted in Figure 10-9. The initial long-run equilibrium is given by the market demand curve D_1, the short-run industry supply curve S_1, a market price of P_1 dollars, and each firm producing at the minimum points of $SRAC_1$ and $LRAC_1$. As before, suppose that market demand increases to D_2. Market price rises to the point where D_2 intersects S_1, and established firms find themselves in the position of being able to earn an economic profit. New firms are induced to

APPLICATIONS CAPSULE

AGRICULTURAL MARKETS: AN ILLUSTRATION OF SOME OF THE CHARACTERISTICS OF PERFECT COMPETITION

One sector of the American economy where perfectly competitive conditions are reasonably approximated on the supply side of the marketplace is that of agriculture. This is so for three reasons:

1. The supply side of the markets for many agricultural commodities (wheat, corn, soybeans, tobacco, cattle, hogs, cotton) is composed of literally thousands of firms—each of which tends to be small absolutely and also relative to the market as a whole. True, some farms are much larger than others in terms of acreage, but even the largest farms are seldom as big as a moderately sized manufacturing enterprise. More important, there is virtually no instance in which a single farm produces a large enough fraction of an agricultural product to put it in a position to exert meaningful influence over either price or the total quantity supplied. Indeed, suppliers of most farm commodities are so great in number and so sufficiently equal in size that the chance to act independently and exercise market power is for all practical purposes nil.

2. Agricultural products are essentially identical from farm to farm—at least in terms of each grade and variety. Wheat, for example, is not a branded product at the farm level and carries no identification as to the farm on which it was grown. Meats, dairy products, fruits, and vegetables may carry the brand of a processor or store, but usually not the name of the farmer who raised them (exceptions where the producer's brand name does appear include eggs, bananas, and pineapples). As a result, agricultural products within the same class or grade are *highly* substitutable—so much so that each producer can rightly regard its demand curve as being horizontal at the going market price.

3. Compared to other industries, there are few barriers to the entry of new firms into the production of agricultural products. At the same time, a farmer often finds it easy to shift acreage out of the production of one item (where profit prospects are dim) into the production of another item (where profit opportunities are brighter); in such cases barriers to entry and exit are extremely low since as each new growing season rolls around farmers can readily adjust their production mix in whatever directions market conditions seem to warrant.

A combined effect of these three aspects is to make the markets for agricultural commodities very sensitive to shifts in market conditions. When bad weather produces a smaller than expected crop, market prices rise sharply. If there is an unusually bountiful harvest, the prices that farmers receive can fall drastically. A trade deal with another country can dramatically boost farm export opportunities and thus the prices of the affected products. Prices can and do fluctuate daily on the commodity exchanges, often in response to fleeting demand-supply conditions. Thus, "market" in its role as the governing force is liable to be volatile, causing sometimes sharp swings in farm prices and farm profits. The competitive struggle becomes a contest where each seller, under conditions of considerable uncertainty, must decide whether and how it can profitably survive at the expected market prices.

THE CASE OF SOYBEANS

In 1973–1974, when higher energy costs and economic recession cut into household food budgets, livestock producers began trimming back output as meat sales slacked off and, consequently, reduced their purchases of livestock feeds. Soybean meal prices tumbled from $400 a ton in 1973 to as low as $100 a ton in June 1974 and then recovered slightly to around $125 a ton throughout most of 1975. Soybean oil prices sank to around 20 cents a pound in 1975 from a peak of more than 50 cents in 1974, mainly because cautious processors started switching to competing products such as palm oil.

At planting time in spring of 1975, farmers were confronted with a hard choice of which crop to plant. Prospects for higher prices for corn, cotton, and soybeans were discouraging and the federal government offered no subsidy programs to farmers to take land out of production. Many farmers chose to plant soybeans, saying at the time that soybean prices seemed less vulnerable to a sharp decline. The soybean crop flourished because of good weather, and 1975's crop was 20% greater than 1974's. Brazil's crop, stimulated by planting newly available acreage, exceeded 350 million bushels compared to only 24 million bushels in 1968. Meanwhile the record-high soybean-product prices of previous years spurred production not only of soybeans but also of other oils and meals—from sources like cottonseed, linseed, corn, peanuts, palms, olives, and sunflowers. Particularly, soybean oil was under competitive pressure from palm oil; palm oil imports were up 145% during the first 8 months of 1975.

In addition, soybean growers had another problem with which to contend: because of differing production features, a farmer could grow more bushels of corn than soybeans on an acre of land. Consequently, the price of soybeans had to be higher than corn to get the same financial return per acre (many observers contended that soybeans had to be worth 2.5 to 3 times per bushel more than corn to be equally profitable). Thus the dilemma was whether the market price of soybeans would be low enough to compete with foreign imports and substitute products and yet high enough to justify growing soybeans as opposed to alternative crops.

QUESTIONS FOR DISCUSSION

1. What economic factors are apparent in influencing short-run changes in the equilibrium price of an agricultural commodity (say soybeans)? What about the long-run equilibrium price?

2. Using the soybean market as an example, explain how "the price mechanism" acts to bring market supply and demand into balance. In what ways is competition a factor in this adjustment process?

Source: Adapted in part from *The Dow Jones Commodities Handbook 1976,* pp. 39–46.

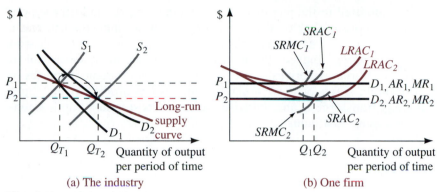

Figure 10-9

Long-run supply curve for a decreasing-cost industry

enter the industry, and the short-run industry supply curve shifts rightward, say to S_2. In a decreasing-cost industry the expansion of output results in *lower* input prices and hence lower costs for the firms in the industry. Thus, as the entry of new firms causes input prices to fall, the short-run and long-run cost curves of the firm shift downward. The adjustment process will continue until a new long-run equilibrium is established. In Figure 10-9 this occurs at the intersection of D_2 and S_2, where the resulting price of P_2 dollars is just equal to the minimum points of $SRAC_2$ and $LRAC_2$. Connecting the two points of long-run equilibrium gives the long-run industry supply curve.

Clearly, a decreasing-cost industry has a negative sloped long-run supply curve, meaning that the equilibrium price of the industry tends to fall as industry output increases. Although it is rare for input prices to fall when industry output expands, it does occur. One example is the case of a young industry which springs up in a relatively underdeveloped area, where resource markets are poorly organized, marketing facilities are primitive, and transportation is inadequate. An increase in the number of firms and in the output of the industry may stimulate the development of marketing and transportation facilities that reduce the costs of individual firms; in addition, supplies of labor and other support services may become more dependable and more efficient. Another example arises in the case of capital goods purchases. The more firms there are in an industry and the larger its output, the more economically suppliers of capital goods may be able to provide these firms with specialized machinery, continuous-process equipment, and higher-quality tools because of their own economies of scale in producing them. By and large, the individual firm has little control over these sorts of decreasing costs; consequently, *cost reductions of this type are often referred to as external economies of increasing production,* or, more simply, just *external economies. They result solely from growth of the industry and from forces outside the control of the individual firm.* External economies should not be confused with internal economies of scale, which are under control of the firm and which can be secured by enlarging the scale of the firm's operations.

In the absence of technological change, most economists regard increasing-cost industries as being the most prevalent of the three types. Decreasing-cost industries are perhaps the least common. Both decreasing- and constant-cost industries are likely to evolve gradually into industries of increasing cost as they grow larger and become more mature. However, if technologi-

In a decreasing-cost industry, input prices fall when industry output rises, resulting in a downward-sloping long-run industry supply curve.

Technological change and external economies usually account for why an industry experiences decreasing costs as its output grows.

cal change is admitted to the picture, a downsloping long-run industry supply curve becomes more probable. Technical progress in an industry can cause costs of production to fall over time, thus giving rise to a downsloping long-run industry supply curve.[5] Indeed, the industries which are most successful in lowering costs and relative prices tend to show the most dramatic increases in output over time. Technological progress can also neutralize rising input prices, thereby transforming an otherwise increasing-cost industry into a constant- or decreasing-cost industry.

KEY POINTS

The behavior of firms and markets under conditions of perfect competition has the following features and results:

1. The standout feature of perfect competition is the pervasive influence of powerful market forces that tend to drive to a level where each firm earns no more and no less than a normal profit and return on investment. Whenever demand and supply conditions allow firms in the industry to earn more than a normal profit, new firms are induced to enter, and where economies of scale permit, existing firms are induced to expand. Subsequently, market price falls toward the point of minimum *SRAC* and minimum *LRAC*, thereby drying up opportunities to earn more than a normal return. Should demand and supply conditions result in a price that inflicts losses upon the firms in the industry, then some firms are induced to exit the industry and redirect resources into the production of other goods and services where the profit prospects are more favorable; the remaining firms seek to adjust their scale of operations in the direction of minimum long-run average cost. As a consequence, market forces move firms toward a "no-profit/no-loss" situation where firms earn only an accounting profit sufficient to induce them to continue in business in the industry.

2. Since every firm is subject to the discipline of the market, it must remain as efficient as the average firm in the industry, or eventually the losses that accompany inefficiency and high unit costs will force it out of business. The processing of adjusting to long-run equilibrium *compels* all firms to try to produce at the lowest possible long-run average cost. A strategy of *striving to be the low-cost producer* thus becomes one of the safest routes to competitive survival.

3. Perfectly competitive firms are *price-takers* and *quantity-adjusters*. They have absolutely zero market power. A single firm exercises no control whatsoever over the going market price, and its only discretionary judgment is how much to produce at the prevailing market price. But even here, as long-run equilibrium adjustment occurs, the discretion over output erodes; firms desirous of earning at least a normal profit find their best chance of doing so at the minimum point of the *LRAC* curve where $P = MR = SRMC = SRAC = LRAC$.

4. Both the output of specific firms and the capacity of the industry are responsive to changes in demand. If market demand increases relative to the supply capabilities of the industry, market price is bid up, entry and expansion are induced, and over time additional output capacity is created. Conversely, if

---

[5] The manufacture of transistors and solid-state components is an excellent example of an industry which has experienced declining costs as a result of new technologies.

market demand falls or if the industry overexpands, then market price falls, expansion is discouraged, and firms may even leave the industry.

5. Perfect competition is a unique form of competition. It does not pit rival against rival; rather, it pits the firm against the market. The firm's competitive struggle is one of responding to changing market conditions and trying to stay cost-efficient enough to earn at least a normal profit at the going market price. Only the most cost-efficient firms survive the struggle in the long run, and the only competitive edge a firm can hope to gain (and this is likely to be very temporary) is that of having lower costs than some or many other firms in the market.

6. With identical products, the competitive focus is on price but most particularly on the ability of firms to compete at lower market prices. In perfect competition, prices are very flexible downward. Prices fall whenever the quantity offered for sale exceeds the quantity purchased and also whenever efficiency gains, technological improvements, or lower input prices (all of which mean lower unit costs) allow firms to earn acceptable profits selling at lower market prices. Those firms that rank as the industry's low-cost producers are in the strongest competitive position in the market.

7. Perfect competition provides consumers maximum protection from exploitation by profit-seeking enterprises. The outcome in the marketplace results from freely made decisions of consumers to buy and freely made decisions of producers to sell. Neither is able to control the other or rig the market to their own advantage. Therefore, there can be no abuse of power and, thus, no need for government intervention or regulation. In short, perfect competition is the epitome of what is meant by a *free market*.

8. The perfectly competitive model takes an overly narrow view of the competitive process because, in a sense, the entire spotlight is on low-cost production, price, and price competition. The model takes no formal cognizance of competition based on product differentiation (because the products of all firms are assumed to be identical) or of technological competition (because all firms are forced to adopt the most efficient production techniques) or of promotional competition (what is there to promote?). In fact, it is fair to say that the model of perfect competition looks upon the only "valid" and "lasting" form of competition as being competition based upon price. Such a view of competition and competitive strategy options, as we shall see in Chapters 11–16, applies only to markets where there are many sellers of an essentially identical good or service.

In conclusion, the major economic significance of the model of perfect competition concerns the benefits to consumers of perfect competition and the efficiency with which it allocates resources. Under conditions of long-run equilibrium, consumers are able to buy the product at the lowest price consistent with covering all costs of production. Since price is barely sufficient to give the firm a normal profit and keep it in business in the long run, consumers obtain the product at as low a price as is economically feasible. In addition, every firm is forced to produce at the most efficient output rate. All scale economies are realized, and all diseconomies of size are avoided. Thus, perfectly competitive firms utilize resources in the most efficient manner possible—full production efficiency is attained. Society obtains the greatest output from the resources used in producing the item. Herein lies the social justification for a free market (or capitalistic) economy. The perfectly competitive model describes how a market economy is supposed to work in theory and provides the theoretical underpinning for free market capitalism. The model is, at least, an excellent starting point for pinpointing the benefits which society gains from a competitive marketplace.

PROBLEMS AND QUESTIONS FOR DISCUSSION

1. (a) A firm's total revenue can be determined by adding the values of *MR* for each unit sold. True or false? Explain.
   (b) A firm's total cost can be determined by adding the values of *MC* for each unit produced. True or false? Explain.
   (c) A firm's total profit can be determined by adding the values of *Mπ* for each unit produced and sold. True or false? Explain.

2. Total profit is maximum at the same output at which total contribution profit is maximum. True or false? Explain.

3. Unit contribution profit ($P - AVC$) is greatest at the same output that total contribution profit ($TR - TVC$) is greatest. True or false? Explain.

4. Why is competition said to be "perfect" in a perfectly competitive market? Just what is so perfect about perfect competition?

5. How do perfectly competitive firms compete? In what form is "competition" present in a perfectly competitive market?

6. Graphically illustrate the short-run curve for a perfectly competitive firm which has a short-run production function characterized by decreasing returns to variable input over the entire range of its output capability.

7. Suppose in a perfectly competitive industry that market supply and demand forces combine to produce a short-run equilibrium price of $70. Suppose further that a firm in this industry has a weekly total cost function expressed by the equation $TC = 200 + 25Q - 6Q^2 + \frac{1}{3}Q^3$. Determine the perfectly competitive firm's profit-maximizing output rate and the amount of its short-run profits or losses.

8. Using the unit cost and unit revenue curves, graphically illustrate the short-run profit-maximizing price and output for a perfectly competitive firm which has a production function that exhibits decreasing returns to variable input over its entire range of output capability. (*Hint:* Determine the shape of the *ATC* and *MC* curves that correspond to a production function characterized by decreasing returns to variable input and then locate the price and output at which $MR = MC$.) Indicate on your graph the area that represents the firm's total profits.

Chapter 11

How Markets Function:
THE CASE OF MONOPOLY

On rare occasions one firm is the sole supplier of a product in a given market area. Such a market situation is called *pure monopoly*. Strictly speaking, *pure monopoly exists only when there are no close substitutes for the product of the single seller*. Not only can there be no rival firms producing the same product, but there can be no firms producing products varying in only minor ways. The pure monopolist's product must be clearly and substantially different. Thus, a monopolist faces no direct competition and, as a consequence, has significant market power. In terms of market structure, monopoly is the extreme opposite of perfect competition.

Real-world examples of pure monopoly are few and far between. Firms that provide electricity, natural gas, local telephone communications, and cable TV service approach the position of pure monopoly. Companies that attained positions of market dominance approaching monopoly in past years include General Motors (with a diesel locomotive market share averaging 77% between 1956 and 1971); IBM (with market shares of 72 to 82% in mainframe computers during the 1960s and early 1970s); AT&T's Western Electric division (with about 85% of the market for telephone equipment in the United States up until the early 1980s); Eastman Kodak (with about 90% of domestic amateur film production and roughly 65% of all film sales); Campbell Soup (with about 85% of canned soup sales); and Xerox (with about 75% of the copier market prior to the expiration of key patents in the 1970s).[1]

One reason for the occurrence of pure monopoly is the presence of pronounced economies of scale. The lowest unit costs and therefore the lowest consumer prices may be achievable only when one firm supplies the entire market demand for the product. When substantially higher units costs at small- or medium-scale outputs effectively bar the entry of new firms, consumers are likely to be better off with just one producer from which to buy the product. Thus, although it may be technologically feasible to have two, three, or more firms, it is nevertheless economically inefficient to have more than one. Industries in which this occurs are called *natural monopolies*. Where market conditions favor natural monopoly, a single firm is usually granted exclusive rights by government to serve a particular market or geographical area; in return the

Pure monopoly can be justified on the basis of superior economic efficiency when economies of scale are so large that a single firm can supply the whole market at lower costs than can two or more firms in open competition.

---

[1] F. M. Scherer, *Industrial Market Structure and Economic Performance*, 2nd ed. (Boston: Houghton Mifflin, 1980), p. 67.

natural monopolist agrees to submit to government regulation to protect consumers against abuses of its monopoly power. Public utility firms typify the natural monopoly type of enterprise.

Monopoly can also stem from situations where a firm has a patent on a product or on a low-cost technological process. Patent-based monopolies are perfectly legal and give the inventor/innovator exclusive rights (for a period of 17 years in the United States). Patents can be very important in preventing the entry of competitors, although it is sometimes possible to "invent around" a patent by developing a closely related product or process.

Pure monopoly can arise in three other situations. One is where a firm obtains a franchise or license to be the exclusive producer/seller for a given geographical area. A second is the rare instance where a firm owns or controls the supply of a key raw material (the most oft-cited instance of this is the pre-World War II control that Aluminum Company of America had over bauxite—a key input in aluminum production). The third is where a firm becomes a monopolist by offering what buyers believe is a superior product and outcompeting its rivals (as approximated by Campbell in canned soups).

Despite the fact that pure monopoly is a limited market phenomenon, it is essential to understand the price and output decisions of a pure monopolist. Doing so illuminates the nature of *market power* and exactly what constitutes monopolistic business behavior, irrespective of whether a firm is a pure monopolist.

MONOPOLY PRICING AND PROFITS IN THE ABSENCE OF REGULATION

We shall assume for the time being that the pure monopolist's market price and output decisions are unconstrained by government regulation. We shall also continue to assume that the principal objective of the firm is to maximize profits.

A key difference between the market situation confronting a pure monopolist and that confronting other enterprises is that the firm's demand-*AR* curve coincides with the industry demand curve. *The firm is the industry.* Being the only seller of an item for which there is no close substitute allows a monopoly firm great discretion in setting its prices. It is in a better position to be a **price-maker** than firms subject to competition. A monopolist, by virtue of its control over market supply, has considerable market power in the sense that it is able to affect the terms of sale. However, the price-setting power of a monopolist is still subject to the law of demand—more units can be sold at lower prices than at higher prices, so the monopolist's demand-*AR* curve is downsloping, as shown in Figure 11-1. Unless demand for the monopolist's product increases, a monopolist cannot raise price without losing sales, and it cannot gain sales without reducing its price.

The downsloping nature of a monopolist's demand-*AR* curve produces a marginal revenue curve that lies below the demand-*AR* curve.[2] For simplicity, suppose that the monopolist's demand curve is not only downsloping but also linear, as shown in Figure 11-1(a); such a demand function has the general equation

$$P = a - bQ.$$

BASIC CONCEPT
A monopolist is a price-maker because its dominant control over market supply gives it considerable price-setting power.

---

[2] To refresh your memory of why this is so, please review the section on "Average, Total, and Marginal Revenue" in Chapter 5.

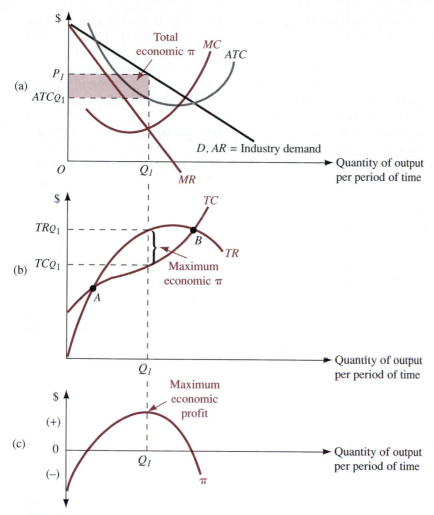

Figure 11-1
Profit-maximizing price and output of a pure monopolist

The corresponding equation for the monopolist's *TR* function is then

$$TR = P \cdot Q = (a - bQ)Q = aQ - bQ^2.$$

Since marginal revenue is, by definition, always equal to the *rate of change in TR as output changes* (which in mathematical terms is the first derivative of the *TR* function), the equation for a monopolist's MR function is

$$MR = \frac{dTR}{dQ} = a - 2\,bQ.$$

Both the demand-*AR* curves start downsloping at a price equal to the value *a*, but the slope of the monopolist's *MR* function ($-2b$) is twice that of its demand-*AR* function ($-b$). Geometrically, a monopolist's *MR* curve bisects the horizontal distance between the monopolist's demand-*AR* curve and the vertical axis—see panel (a) in Figure 11-1. What is important to understand here is that when a monopolist elects to sell more units (for whatever reason), its net revenue gain on the incremental sales volume is *less* than the price it receives

Because a monopolist must lower its selling price to induce buyers to purchase additional units, the marginal revenue gained from each additional unit sold is less than the unit's sales price, and the monopolist's total revenues increase at a slower and slower rate as total sales volume rises, reaching a peak at the point where *MR* = 0.

on these units because of the necessity of lowering its market price to secure additional sales. The total revenue function corresponding to the monopolist's downsloping demand-*AR* and *MR* functions is graphed in Figure 11-1(b). Observe that the monopolist's *TR* rises slower and slower as sales volume increases, reaching a maximum where *MR* equals zero; past this point, the reductions in market price required to gain increased buyer purchases result in *lower* (not higher) total revenues.

Suppose that the cost structure of the monopolist is given by the *ATC* and *MC* curves in Figure 11-1(a) and by the corresponding *TC* curve in Figure 11-1(b). What, then, are the monopolist's optimal price and output levels?

PROFIT-MAXIMIZING PRINCIPLE

A monopolist maximizes profits at the output where *TR* exceeds *TC* by the greatest amount.

PROFIT MAXIMIZATION: THE TOTAL COST–TOTAL REVENUE APPROACH

A monopolist maximizes short-run profits at the output where total revenue exceeds total cost by the greatest amount. Given the *TR* and *TC* functions in Figure 11-1(b), the monopolist will be able to earn an economic profit at any output rate between points *A* and *B*; but short-run profits will be maximum at an output of Q_1 units, where the vertical distance between *TR* and *TC* is the greatest. Geometrically, *TR* exceeds *TC* by the greatest amount at the output rate where a tangent to the *TC* curve has the same slope and is parallel to a tangent to the *TR* function. The total profit function in Figure 11-1(c) is derived by subtracting *TC* from *TR* at each output rate. Logic dictates that the peak of the total profit function correspond to an output rate of Q_1 where *TR* exceeds *TC* by the largest amount.

PROFIT MAXIMIZATION: THE UNIT COST–UNIT REVENUE APPROACH

PROFIT-MAXIMIZING PRINCIPLE

A monopolist's profits are maximized at the price and output where *MC* = *MR* and marginal profit on the last unit sold reaches zero.

On a unit cost and unit revenue basis, *a monopolist's short-run profits are maximized at the output rate where MC = MR and where marginal profit* (*Mπ*) *equals zero.* The reasoning is precisely the same as in the case of firms operating under competitive conditions. As long as an additional unit of output adds more to the monopolist's revenues than it does to the monopolist's costs, profit on that unit will be positive and total profits will be increased (or losses decreased) by producing and selling the unit. Alternatively, when *MR* exceeds *MC* and *Mπ* is positive, total profits can be increased (or losses decreased) by increasing output. In Figure 11-1(a) short-run profits are maximum at an output of Q_1 units—where the marginal cost curve intersects the marginal revenue curve. Observe that this output rate coincides with the value of Q_1 in Figure 11-1(b). At Q_1, the tangents to *TR* and *TC* have identical slopes. Since the slope of *TC* equals *MC* and the slope of *TR* equals *MR*, *MR* must equal *MC* at exactly the output where *TR* exceeds *TC* by the greatest amount.

The highest price that the monopolist can charge and still sell Q_1 units is P_1 dollars. The profit-maximizing price corresponds to the point on the demand-*AR* curve associated with the output at which *MC* = *MR*$_1$ and short-run total profit equals $(P_1 - ATC_{Q1})Q_1$, or the shaded area in Figure 11-1(a). At outputs smaller than Q_1 units, *MR* exceeds *MC* and larger outputs up to Q_1 will add more to total revenue than to total costs; accordingly, total profit will rise. At an output rate beyond Q_1, *MC* exceeds *MR* and additional sales cause total costs to rise faster than total revenue, thereby decreasing total profit.

APPLICATIONS CAPSULE

THE MONOPOLY POWER OF BRAND NAMES AND TRADEMARKS: THE CASE OF THE PHARMACEUTICAL INDUSTRY

The pharmaceutical industry offers a dramatic example of how firms can exploit brand names and trademarks to their fullest. Even though patented drugs occupy center stage in the prescription drug industry (in 1974 no more than 15 to 20 of the 200 most frequently prescribed drugs were available from more than one supplier), trademarks and brand names are very valuable to manufacturers who market a drug that either cannot be patented or, if patented, has been so freely licensed as to allow considerable penetration of the competitive barrier of the patent itself.

Just how valuable brand names and trademarks can be is suggested by the findings of a governmental task force on prescription drugs. The task force reported that Squibb's Noctec brand of chloral hydrate (an unpatentable drug because it had been used medicinally as a sedative for a century) had better than a 50% market share even though the wholesale price of Noctec ran 3 to 4 times the prices of the same generic product offered by reliable small firms. The market for meprobamate (a freely licensed patented drug) was dominated by American Home Products' Equanil brand and Carter-Wallace's Miltown and Meprospan brands; the three brands accounted for nearly 80% of sales at prices to druggists that were more than double the prices charged by generic suppliers. Ciba's brand of reserpine (Serpasil) outsold generic reserpine by a wide margin, at wholesale prices up to 30 times greater than those charged by some of its competitors.

These are impressive price differentials considering that branded and generic versions of the same drug are nearly always chemically and biologically equivalent—in other words, the only real difference between branded and generic versions is that the former is sold under a registered trademark or brand name, whereas the generic version is sold by chemical name derived from the ingredients it contains. There is no other industry in which sellers gain such a wide market advantage from trademarks. Exxon for example, despite being the largest corporation in the world and enjoying worldwide brand recognition of its products for years, is rarely able to command more than a 1- to 3-cent-per-gallon premium over the price of unbranded or off-brand gasoline. Procter & Gamble prices its best-selling Crest toothpaste at a level very comparable to other brands of toothpaste. Miller and Budweiser beers, the two market share leaders, sell at "popular prices."

One major explanation for the monopoly power of brands and trademarks in the prescription drug industry is that the physician makes the buying decision for the patient when the prescription is written. As the late Senator Estes Kefauver observed: "He who orders does not buy; he who buys does not order." Most physicians have little knowledge of the prices of different drugs (although almost all are aware that the branded version will cost the patient more than the generic version). This stems from what probably is a distortion of an excellent medical principle: Prescribe whatever drug is deemed to be the best therapy for the patient. Given that the major drug companies flood doctors with advertising and promotional literature touting their brands of drugs (and seldom is price a featured item in such literature), it is somewhat understandable that doctors are prone to prescribe according to how familiar and knowledgeable they are about particular brand names. The pharmacist is usually obligated to fill the prescription exactly as it is written—thus, if the doctor specifies Achromycin on the prescription, the druggist must supply American Cyanimid's brand of tetracycline and not the chemically identical products of Pfizer, Bristol, Squibb, or Upjohn. When getting a prescription filled, the average patient may not even know what he or she has purchased apart from the fact that it is a small bottle of yellow capsules; moreover, comparatively few people shop around for the lowest price—even though the most prevalent retail markup on prescriptions is 40% of the retail price (a 67% margin above the wholesale cost to the druggist).

All this combines to give the prescription drug firms an excellent position to reap good profits from trademarks and brand names. Interestingly enough, the basis of the value of trademarks and brand names derives more from the marketing aspects than from the manufacturing aspects. From a manufacturing standpoint, entry into the pharmaceutical industry is not overly difficult. The technical expertise and ability to maintain the high quality requisite for drug manufacturing are well within the reach of small firms. Nor are capital requirements a significant entry barrier (in 1968, 95% of the firms in the drug industry reported assets under $5 million). The key to business success lies not, therefore, in becoming an able producer but rather in achieving a high degree of marketing skill, most notably in the form of making physicians sufficiently aware of and knowledgeable about a firm's products that they will confidently prescribe its particular brand for their patients when the need arises.

Source: Based on information in Walter S. Measday, "The Pharmaceutical Industry," in *The Structure of American Industry,* 5th ed., Walter Adams, ed. (New York: Macmillan, 1977), pp. 250–84.

CALCULATING THE PROFIT-MAXIMIZING OUTPUT

The mathematics of determining the profit-maximizing price and output for a monopolist are analogous to the calculations for firms in competitive markets. Suppose that the monopolist's demand function is described by the equation $P = 5000 - 17Q$ and its total cost function by the equation $TC = 75,000 + 200Q - 17Q^2 + Q^3$. From the preceding discussion we know that profit is maximized at the output where $MR = MC$; both MR and MC can be obtained from the information given. If the demand function is $P = 5000 - 17Q$, then

$$TR = P \cdot Q = (5000 - 17Q)Q = 5000Q - 17Q^2$$

and

$$MR = \frac{dTR}{dQ} = 5000 - 34Q.$$

The MC function, being the first derivative of the TC function, is

$$MC = \frac{dTC}{dQ} = 200 - 34Q + 3Q^2.$$

Equating MR with MC gives

$$5000 - 34Q = 200 - 34Q + 3Q^2,$$

which reduces to

$$3Q^2 = 4800.$$

Solving for Q yields the two roots $Q = -40$ and $Q = 40$. Since output can never be negative, the profit-maximizing rate of output is 40 units. (It can be proved that the larger of the two roots is always the profit-maximizing or loss-minimizing output rate.)

The profit-maximizing price is found by substituting the profit-maximizing output rate into the demand function and solving for P. In terms of our example, the profit-maximizing price is

$$P = 5000 - 17Q$$
$$P = 5000 - 17(40)$$
$$P = 5000 - 680$$
$$P = \$4320.$$

MONOPOLY PRINCIPLE
A monopolist's profit-maximizing price is higher and its profit-maximizing output lower than would typically prevail under competitive conditions.

Total profit at this price and output can be calculated by subtracting TC at 40 units of output from TR at 40 units of output; this gives $52,000 per period of time. Since a monopolist is unconstrained by competition from rival sellers, it has the market power to impose its profit-maximizing price and output upon buyers—the monopolist's price-output decisions become the market outcome.

Observe how the price-output outcome in a monopoly market differs from the perfectly competitive market result. In a monopoly market, there are no competitive forces to drive the monopolist's price down to the point where ATC is minimum and the seller is able to earn only a normal profit. As can be seen from Figure 11-1(b), the monopolist's profit-maximizing price is well above minimum ATC. Moreover, the monopolist's profit-maximizing output is smaller than the output where ATC is minimum, a condition which leads to the intuitive conclusion that output levels in a monopoly market are lower than would prevail in a competitive market.

LONG-RUN ADJUSTMENTS IN MONOPOLIZED MARKETS

In the long run a monopoly firm will tend to alter its scale of operations and the characteristics of its product in whatever ways it perceives will enhance profitability. Increases in demand for the monopolist's product will tend to prompt increases in production capacity—as long as there is a good prospect of larger profits. On the other hand, weak or declining market demand may warrant reductions in plant size and/or closing down inefficient production facilities. In general, the relation between the monopolist's market demand and its long-run average cost curve determines whether and to what extent it should alter plant scale and total production capacity. This same relationship also determines whether a monopolistic seller will find it most profitable to build and operate its production facilities just short of, at, or beyond the minimum point on its *LRAC* curve. Thus, whereas in a perfectly competitive market, market forces and competition push firms to construct optimum scale plants and operate at the minimum point of the *LRAC* curve, no such pressures are operative in a monopoly market.

POPULAR MYTHS ABOUT MONOPOLY BEHAVIOR

Thoughtful scrutiny of Figure 11-1 explodes a number of popular fallacies concerning the price and output behavior of monopolists. A monopolist *does not* charge the highest price it can get. There are many prices above P_1 in Figure 11-1(a), but the seller has no incentive to pick them because of the lower profits which they entail. A monopolist's optimum price is high enough to maximize profits but low enough to induce buyers to purchase the profit-maximizing sales volume.

Second, the demand curve for the monopolistic firm's product is not inelastic. As discussed in Chapter 5, most demand curves are elastic at the upper end of the price range and inelastic at the lower end; linear demand curves are half elastic and half inelastic. The output that maximizes a monopolistic firm's profits will *always* fall within the elastic range of the demand curve—not the inelastic range. This proposition is quickly demonstrated. Since marginal cost is positive at all outputs, the output at which $MC = MR$ must necessarily correspond to outputs where MR is also positive and marginal revenue is positive only at output rates where the price elasticity of demand is greater than 1.[3]

A third common misconception about monopolistic firms is that they reap exorbitant profits. Weak demand and high costs are no less injurious to the profitability of a monopolist than they are to firms that face the rigors of direct competition. True, a monopolistic firm faces no competition and in this sense is strategically positioned to earn sizable economic profits, but there is no guarantee that this will prove to be the case. Market demand for the monopolist's product may be so weak that revenues are not high enough to cover operating costs; alternatively, market demand may be just sufficient to allow only a normal profit. Moreover, the lack of competitive pressure removes incentive for efficiency and cost control; inefficiency and high costs can cut deep into a monopolist's profitability.

MONOPOLY VERSUS COMPETITION: THE BIG DIFFERENCES

Despite the myths about monopoly, our analysis of monopoly to this point leads to some powerful conclusions about the market outcomes under monopoly as compared to competition:

MONOPOLY PRINCIPLE
Unlike perfect competition, where market forces drive firms to produce at the output level where *LRAC* is minimum, a monopolist is not subject to the pressure of operating at the output level where *LRAC* is minimum and input efficiency is maximum.

MONOPOLY MYTH
A monopolist charges the highest price it can command; in truth, a monopolist's price, while higher than might prevail under competition, is still low enough to induce buyers to purchase the profit-maximizing sales volume.

MONOPOLY MYTH
Monopolists earn exorbitant profits; in truth, demand for a monopolist's product may be so weak or its inefficiency so great that its profitability is no better than average.

---

[3] The relationship between price elasticity, total revenue, and marginal revenue is described in the section "Elasticity and Total Revenue" in Chapter 5.

1. Market price is typically higher in a monopoly market than in a competitive market.

2. Output levels are typically lower in a monopoly market than in a competitive market.

3. Input efficiency is typically lower in a monopoly market than in a competitive market. Competition causes firms to operate efficiently (at or near minimum *LRAC* where input efficiency is maximum); monopolists face no competitive pressures to be efficient.

4. A monopolist has the market power to impose its price and output preferences on buyers; competition acts as a check on the price-output decisions of firms—in a perfectly competitive market, firms have absolutely no market power. A monopolist is the extreme case of a price-maker. A firm operating under conditions of perfect competition is the extreme case of a price-taker.

BASIC CONCEPT
A firm has monopoly power (or market power) whenever it can impose its price and output preferences on buyers. Pure monopoly is the extreme case of monopoly or market power.

CONSTRAINTS UPON THE MARKET POWER OF A MONOPOLIST

Although being the sole producer of a good or service for which there is no close substitute typically confers a great deal of market power upon a firm, certain restraints are nevertheless imposed upon an unregulated monopolist's behavior. Three such restraints deserve comment.

First, blatant, self-serving exercise of monopoly power is restrained by a fear of government intervention and regulation. A monopolistic firm producing what consumers view as a necessity will undoubtedly draw bitter outcries from buyers if it fully exploits its short-run profit opportunities. Widespread and persistant public criticism increases the risk of some form of government intervention—whether it be antitrust action, government support of new competitors, or direct regulation (as in the case of natural monopolies). Thus, a monopolist may hold back from charging the full amount of "what the traffic will bear" and curtail its pursuit of short-run profits in order to escape consumer resentment and the likelihood of onerous government regulation—and thereby, perhaps, come closer to long-run profit maximization.

Fear of government regulation can restrain a monopolist from fully exercising its market power.

Second, a monopolist may deliberately limit profits so as not to encourage direct competition. When a monopolistic firm exploits its market power fully and earns large economic profits in the short run, it risks attracting the attention of firms having the financial, technological, and organizational resources to crack the monopolist's entry barriers. The monopolist may also trigger efforts on the part of its customers or on the part of other firms to develop acceptable substitutes. In other words, high monopoly profits activate the forces of *potential competition* from both new firms and new products. This threat is very real. The business landscape is littered with ex-monopolists that fell victim to emerging competition—Alcoa, AT&T, American Can, Standard Oil, DuPont, United Shoe Machinery, Ford, International Nickel, Dow Chemical, and Gillette, not to mention the railroads, whose monopoly profits have been reduced by competition from truck carriers and the airlines. Therefore, rather than set price at the level that maximizes short-run profits but invites competition (or regulation), a monopolist may decide to lower price to a level that deters the threat of potential competition and wards off government regulation and antitrust action. Such a pricing practice is called *limit pricing*. The exact level of the limit price depends upon how effectively entry is blocked, the probability of government regulation, and the degree of technological difficulty

A monopolist may deliberately hold its prices and profits down to discourage other firms from trying to enter the market and break its monopoly grip.

in developing substitute products. The obvious purpose of limit pricing is to forgo short-run profit maximization in favor of enhancing the firm's profits over the long term.

The third restraint upon the exercise of monopoly power is the potential for ***countervailing power*** to develop on the buying side of the market.[4] Buyers, especially those heavily dependent on the monopolist's product, have a strong incentive to try to negate a monopolist's market power. This can be done by threatening to seek government regulation, by threatening to curtail use of the monopolist's product and shift partially or wholly to imperfect substitutes, or by trying to invent around the monopolist's product. Technological efforts by buyers to develop suitable substitutes can prompt a monopolist to exercise pricing restraint. In some cases, the countervailing power of buyers is successful in checking the market power of a monopolist and in reducing its price to levels more consistent with competition.

Taken together, these three restraints can dampen the effective market power of monopolists to levels lower than they might otherwise obtain in the short run. True, at a given moment monopolists typically possess substantial power to raise price above competitive levels; they may also earn sizable economic profits. Monopolists that produce necessities and other essential goods—public utility firms, for example—quickly find their rates regulated and their profits reduced to socially acceptable levels. Over time, technological change regularly undermines the market power of unregulated monopolists. And large buyers forced to do business with monopolistic sellers attempt to neutralize their market power through bargaining and threats of vertical integration.

BILATERAL MONOPOLY: THE SINGLE SELLER VERSUS THE SINGLE BUYER

In bilateral monopoly, a single seller must deal with a single buyer. The seller has no other market outlet and the buyer has no other source of supply. Such conditions are approximated in the United States when there is only one defense contractor with the technical capability of producing an advanced weapons system wanted by the U.S. Department of Defense. The question becomes one of analyzing the economics of what happens when monopoly power on the selling side of the market clashes against monopoly power on the buying side of the market.

Suppose that the buyer's demand is described by line D in Figure 11-2; this demand is the same as the demand for the seller's product, given that a single buyer and a single seller constitute the market. Also suppose that the selling firm's marginal revenue curve is MR_S and its marginal cost curve is MC_S. Assuming that the monopolistic seller could exert its will and preference on the buyer, we could logically predict that the seller would produce Q_S units and charge a price of P_S, since these correspond to the profit-maximizing condition of $MR_S = MC_S$.

However, if the buying firm is able to exert its buying power to maximum advantage, the outcome will be different. Ideally, the single buyer would like to view the seller's marginal cost curve (MC_S) as a supply curve— the logic

---

[4] The theory of countervailing power and its application to big businesses with monopoly power were first developed by John Kenneth Galbraith in his book *American Capitalism: The Theory of Countervailing Power* (Boston: Houghton Mifflin, 1952), especially chapter 9.

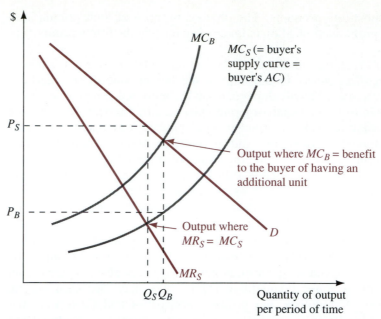

Figure 11-2
The price-output economics of bilateral monopoly

being that if the single buyer can control the market completely, the monopolistic seller can be forced into accepting a perfectly competitive market outcome; in this situation the monopolistic seller's marginal cost curve is also the industry supply curve (as described in Figure 10-5). From the buyer's standpoint, viewing the seller's marginal cost curve (MC_S) as a supply curve indicates the average cost (AC) to the buyer of purchasing various amounts of output. However, when a buyer is confronted with a rising supply curve, the curve marginal to MC_S, labeled as MC_B, represents the marginal cost of *buying* an additional unit.

Optimally, the single buyer would purchase additional units as long as the benefit of doing so (given by the buyer's demand curve) exceeds the marginal cost of purchasing the unit (defined by MC_B). The buyer would like, therefore, to set the purchase level at Q_B—the output at which MC_B intersects the demand curve; the buyer's preferred purchase price would be P_B, which is the lowest price the seller would be willing to accept for Q_B units.

> **When a single buyer must purchase from a single seller, the market outcome is subject to negotiation; neither party has the market power to impose its optimal price-output preference upon the other.**

The problem is that the single buyer can no more control the market completely by forcing the seller into the position of a perfectly competitive industry than the single seller can successfully impose its profit-maximizing price and output preference on a single buyer. What, then, is the outcome? Economic analysis provides no definite answer. It is not possible to predict by logical deduction just what terms the buyer and seller will finally agree to in a bilateral monopoly situation. We can say, though, that the range should be between P_B and P_S and between Q_B and Q_S, since neither party has an incentive to settle outside these limits. Within these limits the outcome is a function of (1) which party has the greatest bargaining strength and negotiating skill, (2) how well informed the buyer and seller are about each other, and (3) who aspires most—for whatever reason—to drive a hard bargain. Generally, speaking, it is easier for the buyer and seller to agree on quantity than on price.

REGULATING MONOPOLY

In situations where pure monopoly and high degrees of monopoly power exist, government frequently elects to undertake some form of regulation so as to "protect the public interest" from undue abuse of market power. Of the various alternatives to regulatory control, two approaches will be discussed here: (1) direct regulation of prices, services rendered, and profitability; and (2) indirect regulation through an "excess profits" tax.

DIRECT REGULATION OF PRICES AND PROFITS

The first serious attempts at regulating monopolies in the United States involved the attempts of city councils to specify the rates and services of electric, gas, and trolley companies. The political nature and makeup of city councils often resulted in franchise awards and terms of services becoming immersed in politics—which made the regulatory process a fertile area for corruption and economic mismanagement. Today, most direct regulation is undertaken by regulatory commissions with civil service staffs to investigate and audit the activities of the regulated firms. Every state has a public service commission, elected in some states and appointed in others, which supervises electric power, natural gas, telephone, and public transportation companies. There is, similarly, another set of regulatory commissions at the federal level to oversee interstate industries where monopoly power may exist—railroads, motor carriers, natural gas pipelines, radio and TV broadcasting, communications satellites, interstate transmission of electricity, and public utility holding companies are all subject to direct federal regulations.

The typical bread-and-butter issue in direct regulation is rate-making—establishing the prices that regulated firms can charge for their products or services. The traditional standard is that regulators should allow monopolists to charge a price just sufficient to cover all allowable operating expenses and yield the firm a fair return on the fair value of the capital investment made by the firm's owners.

In theory, rate regulation is supposed to result in lower prices and greater output than would be the case without regulation. The diagrammatics are shown in Figure 11-3. An unregulated monopolist would prefer a price of P_1 dollars and an output of Q_1 units, thereby maximizing profits where $MR = MC$. However, with regulation, rates are customarily pushed down to a level where price equals ATC, where ATC is defined to include a profit equal to a fair return on the company's capital investment; thus, in Figure 11-3 regulators would aim at establishing a maximum price of P_2, in which case the company's customers would be inclined to purchase Q_2 units.

Regulation of monopoly aims at lower prices and greater output for consumers and a fair profit for the monopolist.

In applying the "fair return on fair value" concept, the regulatory focus is on (1) the **rate base**, which is defined to reflect the fair value of the capital invested by the company in conducting its business, and (2) the **allowed rate of return** on the rate base. Needless to say, controversy swirls around the definition of both what should be included in the rate base and what a fair return is. The search for an appropriate definition of the rate base has narrowed to essentially two measures: (1) the actual historical cost, adjusted for depreciation, of assets in use in the business; and (2) the reproduction value of assets employed (i.e., what it would cost the company to replace its capital assets at current price levels). Each has its pros and cons. Until the 1930s, the reproduction value approach predominated, but since then the original cost less depreci-

APPLICATION CAPSULE

TEMPORARY MONOPOLY IN THE GOVERNMENT BOND MARKET:
HOW TO CORNER THE MARKET AND SQUEEZE YOUR COMPETITORS

In May of 1991 Salomon Brothers Inc., a major brokerage firm and government bond dealer, successfully cornered the market for two-year Treasury notes and a squeeze developed in the bond market. The term "squeeze" is used by bond traders to refer to a situation in which there is a shortage of supply relative to demand for a particular security, as evidenced by a movement in its price to a level that forces the yield on the bond to be out of line with comparable securities. While squeezes can occur for several different reasons, they may be the direct consequence of monopolistic exploitation of the market. In the parlance of Wall Street bond traders, Salomon's market manipulations in May of 1991 were a great "coup" which led to enormous profits by virtue of Salomon being able to squeeze its competitors. A bond market coup occurs when one primary dealer effectively corners the market for a newly issued security that is sold in a Treasury auction. A successful coup allows the dealer to exercise temporary monopoly power in the market for the new issue by forcing higher prices in the secondary market than would ordinarily prevail. But Salomon Brothers' coup was so successful that it to led to an outcry by other market participants, who were the target of the squeeze, and to a joint investigation by three different federal agencies. The joint investigation by the Treasury, Securities and Exchange Commission and Board of Governors of the Federal Reserve System revealed evidence of repeated violations of market rules and led to the dismissal of key Salomon employees and the resignation of the firm's chairman of the board and chief executive officer. It also led to a massive fall in the value of the firm's stock, huge fines, and a prohibition of Salomon Brothers' acting as an agent for other buyers in U.S. Treasury auctions of new debt instruments. Thus, what started out as a great coup came to be known as the Salomon Brothers scandal. To understand the scandal, the market manipulations, and the squeeze it is necessary to know more about the government bond market and how it operates.

The market for U.S. government bonds is the largest and most liquid financial market in the world. In late 1992, the U.S. Government debt was approaching $4 trillion and climbing. The debt is in the form of fixed-income securities called Treasury bills, Treasury notes and Treasury bonds—each with different maturity dates. Treasury bills mature in three months, six months or one year; Treasury notes have maturities between two and 10 years; Treasury bonds have maturities that are in excess of 10 years when they are first issued. Like other markets, the government bond market contains buyers and sellers, but in this market there are also financial intermediaries who play important roles. In fact, there are two distinct markets which are referred to as the primary and secondary securities markets. In the primary market, the Treasury, operating through its agent at the Federal Reserve Bank of New York, sells bonds at auctions to authorized primary market participants. The federal debt is constantly maturing and new debt must be issued to replace the old. Thus, Treasury sales of newly issued bonds in the primary market are the mechanism used to refinance the debt. Prior to the Salomon scandal there were 38 large commercial and investment banks that were authorized as primary dealers. These primary dealers also participate in the secondary or "after" market in which bonds trade after they have been issued by the Treasury and sold in the primary market. Three aspects of the market are particularly important in understanding the monopoly power that a firm receives when it corners the market on a new issue of a security. First, many of the ultimate buyers of government bonds (individuals, pension funds, commercial banks and insurance companies) diversify their holdings and minimize risks by holding a portfolio of different maturities, which are acquired in the secondary market. Second, there is a critical period of about two weeks between the date that the Treasury auction is set and the actual date of the sale. During this window of time, Treasury rules permit the new securities to be bought and sold and the trading is said to take place *when and as if issued.* Dealers take customer orders in advance and make firm sales with promises to deliver securities after they are issued. But the dealers have, in effect, sold the securities short and must purchase them either directly in the primary market or from another dealer when issued. Third, much of the demand in the secondary market for a new issue immediately after an auction is by dealers who are covering their short sales. If a price squeeze develops after a new issue is auctioned then it is sometimes referred to as a "short squeeze," which indicates that dealers selling short are bearing the brunt of the price rise.

ation approach has been used almost exclusively. Even so, there still remains much debate over what a company should be allowed to count as "legitimate" and "necessary" operating expenses (charitable contributions, advertising, and executives' salaries and expense accounts, for example, tend to provoke heated discussions). Quite often, public utility rate-making becomes mired in nit-picking, emotionalism, and headline politics, even though the concept of regulation is a simple one of setting reasonable prices and profits.

What frequently gets lost in the debate is a clear concept of the functions a "fair profit" is intended to perform in a regulated environment. Three

The new issues of securities are auctioned off in sealed bid auctions on dates set by the Treasury. Each sale contains a large block of bonds, notes or bills having the same maturity date. For example, the May 22, 1991 auction, which culminated in the Salomon scandal, involved $12.26 billion in two-year Treasury notes. A detailed set of rules govern the auction, which are codified through an official rule-making procedure provided for in the Government Securities Act of 1986. The "35% rule" is particularly important and is intended to assure that no single buyer controls a new issue by limiting the buyer to no more than 35 percent of the securities sold in an auction. But dealers were allowed to also "roll" customer orders into their own and effectively bid for more than 35%. In the May 22 sale Salomon violated the 35% rule by falsely claiming that it was buying for customers when it was not. On its own account Salomon effectively bid for and received 44%; for customers it bid for another 47%. Government investigators charged that Salomon effectively controlled as much as 85% of the new issue of Treasury notes. In the period immediately following May 22, Salomon used its temporary monopoly position to squeeze other market participants by raising the price and extracting excessive profits.

The joint Treasury-Federal Reserve-Securities and Exchange Commission investigation of Salomon Brothers revealed a number of previous violations of a similar nature. The investigation also demonstrated that Salomon's highest ranking officials knew of the previous illegal activities and had taken no action to stop the market manipulations. Further, there was substantial circumstantial evidence suggesting a continuing pattern of collusion among major players in the primary market for government bonds and that Salomon Brothers and former employees of Salomon played a pivotal role in the anticompetitive practices, which included allegations of information sharing and bid rigging. The government's initial reaction to the scandal was threefold. First, Salomon Brothers was pressured, which led to resignations and employee dismissals. Second, a sweeping investigation was launched and a study of market reforms initiated. Third, Salomon was barred from participating in Treasury auctions for customer accounts but was allowed to continue trading on its own account. More radical changes followed. Perhaps the most important was the change in the entry barriers into the primary market. Rather than limit the market to 38 large firms, beginning in late 1991 the government allowed all bond dealers and brokers registered with the SEC to bid in the primary market. Thus, hundreds of dealers previously restricted to the secondary market were authorized to enter the primary market. Other changes announced at the same time involve tightening the auction rules and spot checks to confirm customer orders.

As for Salomon Brothers, they paid $122 million in fines to the Treasury and put another $100 million into a fund to compensate those who claimed to have been injured by five different "squeezes" that Salomon admittedly imposed on the government bond market. They also paid $27.5-million to settle an antitrust charge that Salomon and unnamed "co-conspirators" restrained trade in the May 22, 1991 sale of two-year Treasury notes by coordinating their actions in the marketplace. As a result of the scandal, the firm also suffered an erosion of its customer base and a mass defection of key employees. The new leadership struggled in its efforts to put the scandal behind the firm and to restore market confidence in what was previously the leading firm in the government securities industry. A temporary monopoly was achieved in an important segment of the government bond market, but Salomon Brothers suffered serious damage as a consequence. In the wake of the scandal, policymakers continue to consider additional changes in the rules for organizing the primary market for government securities. The Antitrust Division of the Department of Justice is also conducting an industry-wide inquiry into collusion in the market that extends back into the mid 1980's.

Source: This application is based on information in the *Joint Report on the Government Securities Market,* U.S. Department of Treasury, U.S. Securities and Exchange Commission and Board of Governors of the Federal Reserve System, (Washington D.C.: U.S. Government Printing Office) January 1992 and periodic reports in *The Wall Street Journal.* In particular, the *Journal* issues of August 19, 1991, May 21, 1992, and June 15, 1992 contain extensive discussion of the Salomon Brothers scandal and the charges of collusion in the primary market for government securities.

functions stand out. First and foremost, profit for a regulated company must be viewed as a payment to investors both for the use of their capital and for assuming the risk that attaches to this use. A regulated firm's profitability must be great enough over the long run that it can attract sufficient new capital to finance whatever new facilities are needed to serve its customers efficiently and reliably. A corollary consideration is that a regulated firm is entitled to a degree of profit that will maintain its financial integrity. By this is meant that the profit a firm is allowed to earn should be sufficient to avoid both an erosion of its stock price and a downgrading of its credit rating. Second, profit performs the

Unless a regulated monopoly is allowed to earn a fair profit over the long run, its ability to serve customers efficiently and reliably is put in jeopardy.

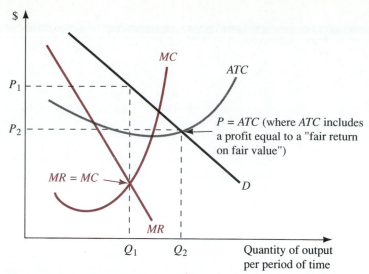

Figure 11-3
Regulating a monopolist's price using the *fair return on fair value* concept

incentive function of rewarding excellent service to customers and punishing the opposite; in this sense *a regulated firm's profit should not be viewed as a "guaranteed" rate of return but rather as an allowed rate of return under honest, economical, and efficient management*. Third, profit serves to redistribute income from the firm's customers to its owners. Here is where standards of fairness enter the picture. How much profit is needed to ensure "fair" compensation of stockholders? How is this counterbalanced by the desirability of ensuring that the rates charged by the regulated firm do not place an "unfair" burden on the ratepayers—particularly when the good or service being supplied is a "necessity" such as electric power, natural gas, or telephone service? Financial theorists take the position that a "fair" rate of return to stockholders is governed by the prevailing rates of return in investments of comparable risk—an amount often judged to be in the range of 10 to 14% after taxes.

CONTROLLING MONOPOLY THROUGH TAXATION

The other general approach to the social control of monopoly power is indirectly through taxation. Although there are several types of monopoly taxation, the one we shall present and discuss here is a profits tax.[5] The logic and rationale underlying a profits tax is very straightforward: Allow the monopolist to set whatever price and output it chooses, then tax away whatever resulting amount of profit is deemed "excessive." This could be done in principle by increasing the percentage of profits paid in taxes from, say, 50% to 75%. The objective would be to set a tax rate on a firm's reported before-tax profit (as measured in accounting terms) that would tax away all (or most) of the monopolist's economic profits and leave only a normal profit.

The effects of an "excess profits" tax on a monopolist's price and output are shown in Figure 11-4. In panel 11-4(a), the profit-maximizing price

---

[5] For a very readable discussion of other types of monopoly taxation, see David R. Kamerschen and Lloyd M. Valentine, *Intermediate Microeconomic Theory* (Cincinnati, Ohio: South-Western Publishing Company, 1977), pp. 371–74.

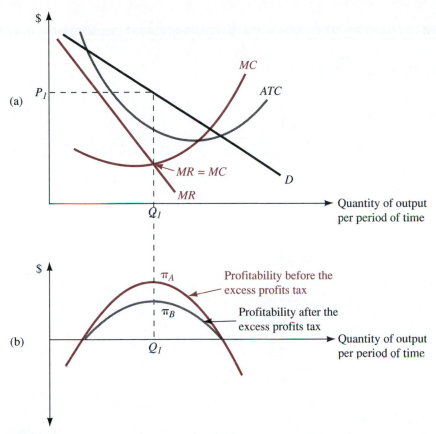

Figure 11-4
Regulating monopoly profits through an "excess profits" tax

and output values are P_1 and Q_1. The monopolist's total profit function is shown as π_A in panel (b) and is derived from calculating the profits at each price and output combination shown in panel (a). Suppose that the maximum profit at P_1 and Q_1 is viewed as "excessive" and that legislation is passed authorizing an excess profits tax on the monopolist's profits, with the form of the tax being one where the marginal *tax rate* on profits is increased sufficiently to bring the firm's after-tax profitability down close to a normal profit. Such a tax has the effect of lowering the firm's total after-tax profit from π_A to π_B.

Observe in this case that the monopolist's profit is still maximized at the same price and output after the excess profits tax is levied as before the tax. This is because a tax based on a certain fixed percentage of profits does not change the output at which $MR = MC$; therefore, it has no effect on the terms of exchange between buyers and sellers. Observe, further, that since the profit-maximizing price does not change, the seller absorbs the full brunt of the tax. None of the tax is passed on to buyers in the form of higher prices. This feature makes it particularly attractive as a policy alternative.[6] What makes an excess

An excess profits tax leaves a monopolist's profit-maximizing price and output undisturbed and transfers the monopolist's excess profits to the government—in contrast to direct regulation, where consumers benefit directly from lower prices and greater output.

---

[6] Such a result is not obtained when a per-unit-sold tax is levied on the monopolist's product. A per-unit tax is a variable cost to the monopolist because the amount of tax paid is a function of the number of units sold. Consequently, a per-unit tax raises both the monopolist's *MC* and *ATC* curves by the amount of the per-unit tax and results in a new intersection of *MR* and *MC*—at a higher price and a lower output. (Examples of per-unit taxes are cigarette, liquor, and gasoline taxes; however, the purpose of these taxes is not to control monopoly.) Because consumers bear part of the burden of a per-unit tax, it is generally not viewed as being appropriate for monopoly control.

Applications Capsule

The Trucking Industry's Experience with Regulation and with Deregulation: Conclusion of the President's Council of Economic Advisors

The Results of Trucking Regulation[a]

Trucking provides a good example of the economic costs of regulations that hold prices above the free-market level. In interstate trucking an antitrust exemption permits motor carriers to agree upon rates through rate bureaus, which are groups of truckers that function like private cartels. Rates tend to be set high enough to cover the costs of less efficient carriers. The result is higher prices to consumers. The Interstate Commerce Commission (ICC) regulates both the entry of new carriers and the expansion of route authority by existing carriers. These restrictions frequently require some trucks to drive extra miles on circuitous routes, prohibit access to intermediate points on routes, limit the commodities that can be handled by some carriers, and prohibit certain kinds of freight on the return trip. The result is excessive truck miles and unproductive consumption of motor fuel, labor time, and other resources.

Where more than one carrier gains a certificate to provide service, competition tends to occur on the basis of service quality—frequency of departure, faster delivery, and so on—rather than through prices. As a consequence trucks are often dispatched with smaller loads than they might otherwise haul. Equipment and labor costs are thus spread over fewer ton-miles and costs and prices are higher than necessary. The regulation of rates precludes price competition, and consequently the range of price-service options available to shippers is restricted. Those shippers who would have chosen less frequent service if it were offered at a lower price pay more for services they do not want. In markets where only one trucker has route authority, this process of rate setting may permit lower costs since the trucker, exercising his monopoly control, may reduce the frequency of scheduling, with the result that a higher proportion of trucks is dispatched fully loaded. However, because such a trucker has no competitors, he is unlikely to lower prices to fully reflect the lower-quality service.

A comparison of the transportation of small parcels with large or bulky shipments illustrates the advantages of multiple price-service options. Shippers of small parcels have several options. The scheduled airlines carry small packages as baggage at substantial prices but with a guarantee of delivery the same day. Some air freight firms collect packages at various cities, fly them first to a central sorting location, then on to their final destination each evening, and provide overnight service at slightly lower prices than those charged by the scheduled airlines. Intercity bus lines and special firms that deliver small packages use surface transportation to furnish delivery service at even cheaper rates. Finally, the U.S. Postal Service offers slower but widely available parcel delivery. The advantage of having multiple options is that shippers of small parcels may choose between various degrees of service at different prices. Although shippers of large or bulky freight have some flexibility, many are chiefly limited to motor carriers, where the range of price-service options is much more limited because of regulation.

The problems of excess capacity, higher prices, and too few price-service options would be reduced if entry into the trucking industry were not restricted. Unlike public utilities, trucking does not exhibit scale economies. Thus price competition is not likely to result in a single survivor—a monopolist. In trucking, fixed costs are low and except for Government restrictions entry is relatively easy. Competition, not monopoly, would be the natural condition in the trucking industry if it were not for Government regulation.

Recent research has demonstrated that common carrier truck regulations cause large losses in production and efficiency. Freight rates in countries that do not regulate motor carriers are significantly lower than rates in countries like West Germany and the United States were regulation is strict. Excessively high motor carrier rates cause some shippers to substi-

---

profits tax different from direct regulation is that an excess profits tax transfers monopoly gains to the government to be used, ultimately, for the benefit of all society members whereas rate regulation benefits consumers of the monopolist's product directly in the form of lower prices and greater consumption.

Monopolistic Practices

It has been astutely observed on numerous occasions that business executives think competition is a good thing—unless and until their firms becomes its victims. It should come as no surprise that firms, large and small, have been ingenious in devising ways to escape the discipline of competition. Despite the illegality of nearly every form of collusive agreement, formal or informal, to fix prices, restrict output, restrain trade, or lessen competition, violations are uncovered each year and unknown numbers of schemes go undetected.

Collusive arrangements may pertain to base or list prices, shipping

The presence of two or more sellers in a market is no guarantee of competition; sellers may enter into collusive arrangements calculated to achieve a monopoly market outcome.

tute alternative modes of transportation, or to provide their own transportation services. These responses to regulation reduce economic efficiency.

AFTER DEREGULATION[b]

The traditional rate and entry regulation of the trucking, freight-forwarder, intercity bus, barge, and maritime industries is now largely out of date. Many studies have demonstrated the absence of significant economies of scale in these industries, weakening the "natural monopoly" rationale for entry restrictions. The high degree of capital mobility in these industries implies that individual city-pair and port-pair markets are highly contestable. The existence of intermodal sources of competition and competitive international output markets for transported commodities further reduces any misallocations resulting from monopoly behavior. Additionally, the high rate of technological development in the transportation sector renders many regulations inapplicable. The experience since the recent deregulation of airlines and the partial deregulation of surface transportation indicates that a competitive industry structure would not reduce the financial viability of firms in these industries.

The effects of the partial deregulation of trucking—initiated by the Interstate Commerce Commission and affirmed by the Motor Carrier Act of 1980—have proven very encouraging. Published trucking rates are now subject to large and widely available discounts. Shippers appear to be overwhelmingly satisfied with the rates, service options, and competition for their business. Service to small communities has not deteriorated, as was originally predicted by the opponents of deregulation, and most shippers in small communities also appear to support deregulation. Both the number of new firms and failing firms have increased substantially, the latter due in part to the recession. Concerns have been expressed over the last year that the Interstate Commerce Commission may be slowing the deregulatory process. For example, the percentage of applications for grants of operating authority approved by the ICC declined slightly in both fiscal years since the passage of the Motor Carrier Act. On net, however, the ICC has facilitated increased competition in the trucking industry. The chaos predicted by the opponents of deregulation has not materialized, even during a sustained recession. The experience to date clearly supports the case for more general deregulation of surface transport.

The experience since the partial deregulation of railroads is similar. Although direct evidence on rail rates is not available, the number of contracts negotiated between rail carriers and shippers (a measure of the operating flexibility granted by the Staggers Rail Act) increased from 580 in fiscal 1980 to 2907 in fiscal 1982. Railroads have increased their share of total freight traffic and have substantially increased their shipments of some commodities, such as fruits and vegetables, that were previously carried almost exclusively by trucks. Railroad profits remained essentially steady despite the sustained recession.

While recent partial deregulation of the surface transportation industries has increased the competitiveness of these industries, the opportunity remains for significant gains from further deregulation. There seems to be little danger that further deregulation would enhance the monopoly power of carriers. The high degree of capital mobility in the trucking, bus, barge, and maritime industries should prevent monopoly pricing over a sustained period, even where there is only one carrier on a route.

---

[a] Taken from the 1977 Annual Report of the Council of Economic Advisors, as published in *The Economic Report of the President*, January 1977, pp. 148–50.

[b] Taken from the 1983 Annual Report of the Council of Economic Advisors, as published in *The Economic Report of the President*, January 1983, pp. 110–11.

allowances, charges for extra features, guarantees, warranties, service policies, output quotas, market shares, or the specific geographic areas or product lines that are to be regarded as each firm's exclusive sphere of interest. In addition, firms may reach understandings regarding product standards, specifications, and the frequency with which products will be restyled and redesigned. Industry trade associations may be formed to promote information sharing among the member firms (these are popular in the lumber and wood products, electrical products, textile, aerospace, alcoholic beverage, utility, transportation, and insurance industries). Among steel, auto, copper, oil, and chemical firms, joint ventures are a popular means of instituting interfirm cooperation and, at times, may have facilitated anticompetitive practices. Some firms have knowingly and willingly, although not necessarily collusively, acceded to price leadership in order to avoid price competition. Other firms have consciously engaged in parallel behavior to sidestep strong rivalries.

Some firms have abused the patent laws by aggressively buying up patents, licences, and copyrights so as to preclude the emergence of competition from rival products.[7] Firms in such fields as plastics, cellophane, shoe machinery, photo supplies, electric lighting, copying equipment, computers, tranquilizers, telephone equipment, television, and synthetic rubber have attempted to insulate themselves from competition by systematically building up an impregnable portfolio of patents. On other occasions, firms patent inventions that they have no real intention of using directly but which they do not want others to have.

A monopolistic approach that is often used because of its effectiveness and compatibility with antitrust and patent laws is for firms holding a key patent to insert competition-reducing provisions into the patent licenses which it may grant (willingly or unwillingly) to potential rival firms.[8] These provisions take several forms. First, firms to which licenses are granted may be constricted to sell only in a specified geographic area. Second, the price of the licensed product may be stipulated as one of the terms of the license. Third, direct or indirect output limitations may be incorporated into the licensing agreements. As a case in point, General Electric in the 1930s granted a license to Westinghouse to produce improved light bulbs that called for a royalty rate of 1 to 2% on the sales made by Westinghouse up to 25.4421% of the two firms' combined sales but the royalty rate jumped to 30% for sales exceeding this quota.[9] Also, Westinghouse had to sell the bulbs at prices and terms set by General Electric.

MONOPOLY PRINCIPLE
The fewer the number of sellers, the easier that monopolistic collusion becomes.

To the extent that monopolistic practices exist, they tend to be more prevalent in markets where there are comparatively few sellers. Monopolistic practices are virtually impossible to institute where markets are comprised of large numbers of firms. The more parties there are to a conspiracy the greater their diversity of situations and own best interests and the harder it is to reach a consensus—the hurdles of reaching an enforceable agreement are so difficult, in fact, that illegal collusion is almost totally absent in markets with numerous competitors. Such is one of the built-in social benefits of competition among the many. This is not to say, however, that small companies do not engage in monopolistic practices. At the local and regional level small firms may compete in small enough numbers that they may well be in a position to exercise monopoly power through collusive activities.

Nevertheless, collusive attempts to monopolize are more an exception than a norm—even in industries where there are only a few rival firms. The frailty of collusive agreements, firms' ambitions for growth and expansion, the general existence of spirited nonprice competition, the forces of technological change and innovation, a fear of potential entry, plus the antitrust laws all combine to make collusive arrangements more an illustration of deviant behavior than normal behavior. Prohibitions against attempts to monopolize, if vigorously enforced, can obviously be an effective deterrent to anticompetitive behavior because of the potential punishment, embarrassment, and loss of public image accompanying discovery of illegal practices. Indeed, the mere likelihood that officials will be diligent in prosecuting the parties to monopolistic agreements, punishing abuses of monopoly power, opposing acquisitions and mergers that tend to consolidate market power and lessen competition, and blocking avenues for creating new kinds of monopolistic arrangements undeniably improves the functioning of markets in constructive ways.

---

[7] Scherer, *Industrial Market Structure and Economic Performance*, pp. 450–51.
[8] *Ibid.*, p. 173.
[9] George W. Stocking and Myron W. Watkins, *Cartels in Action* (New York: Twentieth Century Fund, 1947), p. 309.

TABLE 11-1   BEST-GUESS ESTIMATES OF THE OUTPUT LOSSES ATTRIBUTABLE TO COLLUSION, THE EXERCISE OF MARKET POWER, AND RELATED BREAKDOWNS IN THE COMPETITIVE PROCESS, EXPRESSED AS A PERCENTAGE OF 1966 GNP

Causes of Output Losses	*Estimated Percentage Reduction in 1966 GNP*
Output losses due to monopolistic resource allocation in the unregulated sectors of the U.S. economy	0.9
Output losses due to pricing distortions in the regulated sector of the U.S. economy	0.6
Inefficiencies in production and higher costs associated with enterprises insulated from competition and therefore not compelled to use the lowest-cost production technology	2.0
Inefficiencies due to deficient cost control by defense and space contractors	0.6
Wasteful advertising and sales promotion efforts	1.0
Producing at less than optimal scale for reasons other than product differentiation	0.3
Extra transportation costs stemming from inefficient plant locations	0.2
Idle and inefficient production capacity due to monopolistic practices and collusion	0.6
Total losses	6.2

Source: F. M. Scherer, *Industrial Market Structure and Economic Performance* (Chicago: Rand McNally, 1970), p. 408.

THE COSTS TO SOCIETY OF MONOPOLY POWER

Several statistical studies have been made of the short-run economic impact of collusive practices, the exercise of market power, and resource inefficiency arising from competitive deficiencies and monopoly markets.[10] These studies have found that monopolistic price-output distortions entail societal losses ranging from less than 1% to perhaps as much as 12% of the gross national product; however, most of these studies place the losses at less than 6% and probably less than 3% of GNP.

Scherer's study has produced the most explicit sources of output loss associated with the exercise of market power; his estimates are summarized in

Economic studies show that monopoly is a limited market phenomenon and that the economic losses attributable to the exercise of monopoly power are small.

[10] Arnold Harberger, "Monopoly and Resource Allocation," *American Economic Review*, Vol. 44, No. 2 (May 1954), pp. 77–87; David Schwartzman, "The Burden of Monopoly," *Journal of Political Economy*, Vol. 68, No. 6 (December 1960), pp. 627–30; David R. Kamerschen, "An Estimation of the 'Welfare Losses' from Monopoly in the American Economy," *Western Economic Journal*, Vol. 4, No. 3 (Summer 1966), pp. 221–36; William G. Shepherd, *Market Power and Economic Welfare* (New York: Random House, 1970) pp. 195–98; Scherer, *Industrial Market Structure and Economic Performance* (Chicago: Rand McNally, 1970), pp. 400–9; John J. Siegfried and T. K. Tiemann, "The Welfare Cost of Monopoly: An Interindustry Analysis," *Economic Inquiry*, Vol. 12, No. 2 (June 1974), pp. 190–202; Dean A. Worcester, Jr., "On Monopoly Welfare Losses: Comment," *American Economic Review*, Vol. 65, No. 5 (December 1975), pp. 1015–23; R. A. Posner, "The Social Costs of Monopoly and Regulation," *Journal of Political Economy*, Vol. 83, No. 4 (August 1975), pp. 807–27.

Table 11-1. Although Scherer admits that each of his individual category estimates is subject to a wide margin of error, he concludes that if the "true" output loss could be ascertained, it would probably fall within the 3 to 12% range. This is higher than the estimates of other experts, who have concluded that monopoly losses are "small" and perhaps even "inconsequential."

The wide disparity in the estimates of the social costs of monopoly power correctly suggests that there are major statistical problems in determining how much monopoly power exists, the extent to which monopolistic prices exceed competitive levels, and what the output gains would be if the prices of all monopolized products were driven down to competitive levels—all of which are pertinent to the estimating procedure. Nonetheless, the weight of evidence is heavily on the side of studies indicating that monopoly is not sufficiently prevalent to place an undue burden on the economy.

KEY POINTS CONCERNING MONOPOLY

The major implications and predictions that flow from the market model of pure monopoly are:

1. A monopolistic firm will use its market power to charge a higher price than would tend to prevail under competition.

2. Because a monopolist tends to charge a higher price, output will be less than in a competitive market; this is because customers will buy less of the product at the monopolist's higher price than they would be willing and able to buy at the lower prices that can be expected with competition.

3. An exception to the higher price/lower output predictions of the monopoly model is the case of *natural monopoly*, where economies of scale are so great that monopoly results in a lower price and a greater output than could be expected under competition. In such cases, there is clear conflict between promoting competition, on the one hand, and seeing that the marketplace provides consumers with the greatest possible output at the lowest feasible price, on the other hand.

Generally speaking, any form of unregulated monopoly and/or the exercise of monopoly power works against the best interests of consumers. Only in the case of natural monopoly is a monopolistic market preferable to a competitive market, and then only with some form of effective economic regulation.

The economic case against monopolistic markets and the unregulated exercise of monopoly power is exceedingly strong:

1. Monopoly tends to produce higher prices and restricted outputs as compared to competition.

2. Monopoly has the capability of producing excessive economic profits—an outcome that results in income and purchasing power being redistributed from the buying public to the monopolistic seller.

3. Monopoly can prevent an optimal allocation of economic resources in the sense that monopolistic firms do not necessarily produce at the output rates where unit costs are lowest (the minimum point on the *LRAC* curve), as is the case in perfect competition.

4. Such monopolistic practices as price-fixing, suppression of technological improvements, erecting artificial barriers to entry, tying contracts, exerting reciprocal purchasing leverage, refusing to sell, and attempting to drive rival firms out of business through predatory tactics are all without economic justification.

A monopolist obviously has a great deal of market power, which it almost always will use to its own advantage. This can scarcely be condoned. However, the market power of a monopolist is seldom absolute. It can be weakened and even overcome completely by slack demand conditions, by actual or threatened government intervention and regulation, by potential competition from new firms and new products, by the exercise of countervailing power on the part of buyers, and by technological innovations which create new substitutes for the monopolist's product.

PROBLEMS AND QUESTIONS FOR DISCUSSION

1. Suppose that a pure monopolist's demand schedule and total cost function are as follows:

Selling Price	Quantity Demanded	Total Costs
$20	9,000	$160,000
19	10,000	165,000
18	11,000	171,000
17	12,000	178,000
16	13,000	186,000
15	14,000	195,000

   What price should the monopolist charge in order to maximize profits?

2. The XQT Concessions Company paid $35,000 for exclusive rights to sell beer at the seven home games of the local pro football team. Attendance generally averages 60,000 persons per game. The variable costs of obtaining and selling a 12-ounce cup of draft beer are estimated to be 22 cents. The manager of the XQT company has estimated demand for beer at each home game to be the following:

Selling Price	Quantity Demanded (cups)
$0.75	36,000
1.00	32,000
1.25	26,000
1.50	18,000

   What price should be selected in order to maximize XQT's profits?

3. Is it possible for a pure monopolist to benefit from sales promotion and advertising, given that there are no close substitutes for the monopolist's product? Explain and justify your answer graphically.

4. How can a firm have monopoly power without being a pure monopolist? How could one measure the strength of a firm's monopolistic position?

5. Why might a monopolist charge a price below what would maximize short-run profits? In practice how important are these considerations likely to be?

6. The more profitable a firm, the greater its monopoly power. True or false? Explain.

7. What reasons can you give for why a monopolistic firm's price might be higher under regulation than if it were not regulated? How often and where do you think this might occur?

8. Does a profit-maximizing monopolist typically produce at an output rate which is optimal from a standpoint of cost and efficiency? Why or why not? illustrate graphically.

9. Does a monopolistic firm have less incentive to be efficient than a firm confronted with vigorous price competition? Why or why not?

10. Does monopoly always result in higher prices and lower output than a competitively structured industry? Illustrate graphically. (*Hint*: Consider the result that might occur if the monopolist has access to economies of scale that are not available if there is competitive rivalry among many small firms.)

Chapter 12

How Markets Function:
The Model of Monopolistic Competition

In most real-world markets the products of rival firms are not standardized commodities. Rather the product offering of each firm is in some way *differentiated* from the product offerings of rivals. Indeed, it is common for firms to devote considerable effort to engineering distinctive attributes into their products and to making their products unique through advertising, packaging, brand names, styling, performance features, terms of credit, service, and so on. The particular concern of this chapter is with the economics of the firm in a market environment comprised of *many* firms selling product versions that are very close (but not perfect) substitutes for each other. Such a market structure is labeled by economists as **monopolistic competition**—monopolistic in the sense that each seller has a "monopoly" over its own branded version of the product (McDonald's is the only seller of Bic Mac hamburgers) and competitive in the sense that there are many rivals selling similar versions of the item.

THE CHARACTERISTICS OF A MONOPOLISTICALLY COMPETITIVE MARKET

Four factors combine to set monopolistic competition apart from other types of markets: (1) product differentiation, (2) the presence of large numbers of sellers, (3) competition based on price, and (4) competition based on nonprice considerations.

Introducing the element of product differentiation into the marketplace results in some consumers preferring the products of certain firms over those of other firms. Each firm in creating its own unique version of the product obtains a kind of limited monopoly. There is only one producer of Budweiser beer, only one manufacturer of Hart, Schaffner, and Marx suits, and only one publisher of *Playboy*; even so, each of these firms faces competition from rival firms offering substitute brands—hence, the label *monopolistic competition*. Ultimately, product differentiation has the effect of giving a monopolistically competitive firm limited influence over the price it charges for its product—the firm in a very restricted sense is a "price-maker." It derives this power from the fact that some consumers are willing, within limits, to pay the firm's asking price because they prefer its version of the product. The price differential which a firm is able to charge is a function of the firm's success in differentiating its product in the minds of consumers, thereby creating brand loyalties and com-

The traits that set monopolistic competition apart from other markets are product differentiation, many sellers, price competition, and competition based on such nonprice factors as performance features, quality, and service.

311

pany loyalties. However, the price differential obtainable by any one firm is likely to be slight since close similarity among the products of rival firms makes it quite difficult to create strong brand attachment when price differences are sizable. In more formal terms, we can say that the cross elasticity of demand between the products of monopolistically competitive firms is quite high; so also is the price elasticity of demand for any one firm's product. All this serves to create active price competition among rival sellers.

Like perfect competition, monopolistic competition is characterized by such a sufficiently large number of firms that no one firm has the production capacity to supply a significant share of the industry's output. Monopolistically competitive firms are typically small-sized firms, both absolutely and relatively. Entry into monopolistically competitive industries tends to be comparatively easy, though it is more difficult than in perfect competition because of product differentiation and brand loyalty. A new firm must not only possess the capacity for producing the product but it must also be able to win customers away from established firms. Securing a niche in the market is likely to entail some extra costs by the new firm to incorporate attributes that will distinguish its product from products already on the market. Moreover, unlike perfect competition, advertising and sales promotion may be necessary to inform consumers of the availability of a new brand and to persuade enough customers to switch to the new brand. Therefore, a newcomer into a monopolistically competitive industry faces somewhat greater financial and marketing obstacles than a newcomer into a perfectly competitive market.

Entry into a monopolistically competitive industry is more costly than entry into a perfectly competitive market because of the extra expense of achieving product differentiation and building brand loyalty.

The final feature of monopolistic competition is the presence of vigorous *nonprice competition* among the firms. Competitive rivalry is based partially upon price and partially upon performance features, product quality, service and other conditions of sale, and sales promotion. A firm operating under conditions of monopolistic competition can simultaneously undertake three strategies for influencing its sales volume. First, the firm can change the price it charges—the strategy of *price competition.* Second, the firm can incorporate distinctive attributes into its product offering—*a differentiation strategy based on product performance, quality, service, and similar such attributes which can set a firm's product offering apart from rivals'.* Third, the firm can revise its marketing and sales promotion tactics in ways aimed at capturing greater buyer attention and buyer appeal—*a differentiation strategy based upon promotional forms of competition.* The first strategy of using price as a major competitive weapon represents an attempt to move along the demand curve confronting the firm, whereas the last two strategies involve an attempt to shift the firm's demand curve. From a theoretical standpoint, all three competitive strategies can be pursued in a monopolistically competitive market without explicit regard for the behavior of rival firms and without much concern for retaliation by rival firms. The reason? *With a large number of firms in the industry, the impact of the competitive strategy of a single firm spreads itself over so many of its rivals that the effect felt by any one rival is greatly diluted and does not usually lead to the formulation of a counterstrategy or a readjustment.* Accordingly, each firm may expect its competitive approach to be unimpeded by immediate and pointed retaliation from rivals.[1]

COMPETITIVE PRINCIPLE
A firm with many rivals runs less risk of quick, pointed competitive retaliation from rivals when it launches fresh strategic moves than does a firm with a few, close rivals.

---

[1] Some economists challenge whether a firm can rationally assume its actions will not provoke a response from rival firms. From a behavioral standpoint, a firm can expect that its strategies will in fact invoke retaliation from competitors if its strategies prove successful. One must search long and hard to find a businessperson who does not believe creative or aggressive actions will be noticed by competitors and who, in turn, does not keep close tabs on what rival firms are doing—irrespective

We shall examine each of the foregoing three strategies in the sections immediately following.

SHORT-RUN PROFIT-MAXIMIZING CONDITIONS FOR FIRMS IN MONOPOLISTIC COMPETITION

Under conditions of monopolistic competition, each firm is confronted with a downsloping demand and average revenue curve. Herein lies the biggest fundamental difference between the model of perfect competition and the model of monopolistic competition, and it stems from the presence of differentiated products. Because the particular product of each firm has certain distinguishing features which set it apart from those of other firms, a monopolistically competitive firm has a small measure of discretion in establishing the price of its product. By shaving its price to levels somewhat below the prices of rival firms, a firm can usually induce proportionately more customers to buy its product because it is a good substitute for the products of its competitors. On the other hand, a firm that raises its price can expect a significant decline in sales as many of its customers switch to lower-priced brands. Accordingly, a monopolistically competitive firm has a downsloping demand curve, for it can sell more of its product at lower prices than at higher prices. The firm cannot raise price without losing sales, and it cannot gain sales without charging a lower price (assuming, of course, its demand curve does not shift). Moreover, *the presence of large numbers of good substitutes makes any one firm's own demand curve highly elastic over the relevant range of possible prices.*[2] Graphically, this means that a firm's demand curve tends to be *gently* downsloping, as depicted in Figure 12-1(a); the demand curve is drawn as a straight line merely for simplicity and convenience. Generally speaking, the exact degree of price elasticity reflected in a monopolistically competitive firm's demand curve is a function of the number of rival firms and the degree of product differentiation that prevails among the brands of the competitors. *The larger the number of competitors and the weaker the product differentiation, the greater the price elasticity of demand for any one firm's product or brand over the relevant price range.*

When a firm's demand curve is downsloping, its marginal revenue function does not coincide with the demand-average revenue function; rather, it lies below the demand-*AR* curve.[3] If a firm's demand-*AR* curve is linear and downsloping, its *MR* curve is also linear and downsloping and has a slope twice that of the demand-*AR* curve. Recall from chapter 5 that if the demand function is given by the general linear equation

$$P = a - bQ,$$

Product differentiation has the effect of making a monopolistically competitive firm's demand curve downsloping.

A monopolistically competitive firm's demand curve is usually highly price elastic around the range of prices it and rivals are charging.

---

of how many rivals are in the market. Thus, the ability to act independently is relative, not absolute. But despite this legitimate objection, it still seems fair to conclude that the larger the number of firms in an industry, the more able a firm will be to implement new strategies without provoking direct retaliation from rival firms. The fact that a firm with many rivals can act more independently than a firm with few rivals does indeed lead to differences in firm and market behavior.

[2] The results of one study showed a coefficient of price elasticity of -5.7 for different brands of frozen orange juice, -5.5 for instant coffee, -4.4 for regular coffee, and -3.0 for margarine. Indirect evidence of high elasticity also stems from the fact that rival firms in monopolistic competition act as though they believe that their demand curves are highly price elastic. They usually sell their products at very nearly the same price and display a distinct hesitancy to test consumer loyalty by pricing their products much above the prices charged by rival firms.

[3] To refresh your memory on this point, please review the section "Average, Total, and Marginal Revenue" in chapter 5.

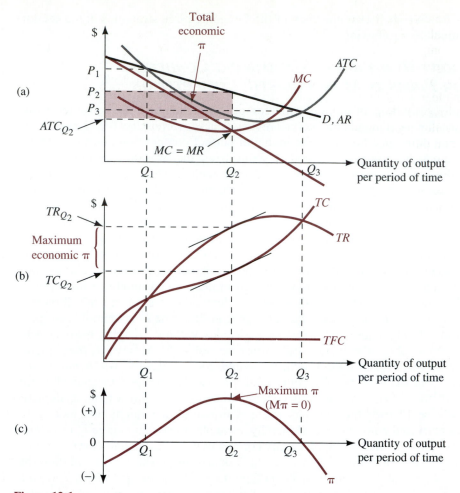

Figure 12-1

Short-run profit maximization for a firm in monopolistic competition

in which case the equation for *TR* becomes

$$TR = P \cdot Q = (a - bQ)Q = aQ - bQ^2.$$

Since the expression for marginal revenue is found by taking the first derivative of the *TR* equation, the general equation for *MR* is

$$MR = \frac{dTR}{dQ} = a - 2bQ.$$

Because a monopolistically competitive firm has a down-sloping demand curve and must lower selling price to induce additional buyer purchases, the marginal revenue it receives from each additional unit sold is less than the unit's selling price; consequently, the firm's total revenues rise at a decreasing rate, reaching a peak at the sales volume where *MR* equals zero.

Both the demand-*AR* curve and the *MR* curve originate at the same value *a*, but the slope of the *MR* function is twice as great as that of the demand-*AR* curve (−2*b* as compared to −*b*). In geometric terms, *the MR curve is located by drawing it so as to bisect the horizontal distance between the demand-AR curve and the vertical axis* [Figure 12-1(a)]. The total revenue function corresponding to the demand-*AR* and the *MR* functions is depicted in Figure 12-1(b). Observe that it increases at a slower and slower rate, reaching its peak at the sales volume and output where *MR* = 0.

Suppose that the cost structure of a typical firm in a monopolistically competitive industry is given by the *ATC* and *MC* curves in Figure 12-1(a) and by the corresponding *TC* curve in Figure 12-1(b). What, then, are the firm's optimal price and output levels? Since monopolistically competitive industries are composed of numerous firms that, in the main, are both small and owner-managed, it is appropriate again to assume that the firm's decisions are motivated by the desire to maximize profits. However, we cannot be completely confident about assuming firms will behave as if they seek to maximize profits, because the element of product differentiation gives each firm somewhat more discretionary decision-making power than was the case in perfectly competitive environments, and market forces operate in ways that give firms modest leeway in deviating from profit-maximizing behavior. Nevertheless, a goal of profit maximization is a reasonable first approximation because of the strong competitive forces which typically inhabit a monopolistically competitive marketplace. Suppose we also assume for the moment that the firm produces an unchanging product and spends a fixed amount on sales promotion activity; this will allow us to pinpoint the principles underlying the price and output behavior of a monopolistically competitive firm. Later, we shall relax this assumption and examine the effect of product variation and promotional expenditures upon price-output behavior.

Profit Maximization: The Total Cost–Total Revenue Approach. A firm in monopolistic competition, like the perfectly competitive firm, will maximize short-run profits at the output where total revenue exceeds total cost by the greatest amount. Given the *TR* and *TC* functions in Figure 12-1(b), the firm will be able to earn an economic profit at any output rate between Q_1 and Q_3 units, but short-run profits will be maximum at an output of Q_2 units, where the vertical distance between *TR* and *TC* is the greatest. Geometrically, *TR* exceeds *TC* by the greatest amount at the output rate where a tangent to the *TC* curve has the same slope and is parallel to a tangent to the *TR* function. The total profit function in Figure 12-1(c) is again derived by subtracting *TC* from *TR* at each output rate. Logic dictates that the peak of the total profit function correspond to an output rate of Q_2, where *TR* exceeds *TC* by the largest amount.

> **PROFIT-MAXIMIZING PRINCIPLE**
> A monopolistically competitive firm maximizes profits at the output where *TR* exceeds *TC* by the greatest amount.

Profit Maximization: The Unit Cost–Unit Revenue Approach. On a unit cost and unit revenue basis, short-run profits are maximized at the output where $MC = MR$ and $M\pi = 0$. The reasoning is precisely the same as in the previous market models. As long as an additional unit of output adds more to the firm's revenues than it does to the firm's costs, profit on that unit will be positive and total profits will be increased (or losses decreased) by producing and selling the unit. Alternatively, when *MC* exceeds *MR* and $M\pi$ is negative, total profits can be increased (or losses decreased) by decreasing the rate of output. In Figure 12-1(a) short-run profits are maximum at an output of Q_2 units per period of time. This is the output rate at which the marginal cost curve intersects the marginal revenue curve. Moreover, it corresponds exactly to the value of Q_2 in Figure 12-1(b). At Q_2, the tangents to *TR* and *TC* have identical slopes. Since the slope of *TC* equals *MC* and the slope of *TR* equals *MR*, *MR* must equal *MC* at exactly the output where *TR* exceeds *TC* by the greatest amount.

> **PROFIT-MAXIMIZING PRINCIPLE**
> A monopolistically competitive firm maximizes its profits at the price and output where $MC = MR$ and marginal profit on the last unit sold reaches zero.

The highest price that the firm can charge and still sell Q_2 units is P_2 dollars. The profit-maximizing price thus corresponds to the point on the demand-*AR* curve associated with the output at which $MC = MR$. Average total cost at Q_2 units of output is ATC_{Q_2}. Total economic profit in the short run equals $(P - ATC_{Q_2})Q_2$, or the shaded area in Figure 12-1(a). At outputs smaller than

Q_2 units, MR exceeds MC, and larger outputs up to Q_2 will add more to total revenue than to total costs; accordingly, total profit will rise as the output rate is raised. At an output rate beyond Q_2, MC exceeds MR, and additional sales cause total costs to rise faster than total revenue, thereby decreasing total profit. Note that the firm can realize at least a normal profit by selling at a price as high as P_1, or as low as P_3, but that a price of P_2 dollars will yield the greatest economic profit. Prices P_1 and P_3 may be thought of as the "break-even" prices and outputs Q_1 and Q_3 may be thought of as the "break-even" output rates.

Calculating the Profit-Maximizing Output.   The mathematical procedure for determining the profit-maximizing price and output for a firm with a downsloping demand function is analogous to the calculations for a firm in perfect competition. Suppose the firm's demand function is given by the equation $P = 11,100 - 30Q$ and the firm's total cost function is given by the equation $TC = 400,000 + 300Q - 30Q^2 + Q^3$. From the preceding discussion we know that profit is maximized at the output where $MR = MC$. Both MR and MC can be obtained from the information given. If the demand function is $P = 11,100 - 30Q$, then

$$TR = P \cdot Q = (11,100 - 30Q)Q = 11,100Q - 30Q^2,$$

and

$$MR = \frac{dTR}{dQ} = 11,100 - 60Q.$$

The MC function, being the first derivative of the TC function, is

$$MC = \frac{dTC}{dQ} = 300 - 60Q + 3Q^2.$$

Equating MR with MC gives

$$11,100 - 60Q = 300 - 60Q + 3Q^2,$$

which reduces to

$$3Q^2 = 10,800.$$

Solving for Q yields the two roots $Q = -60$ and $Q = 60$. Obviously, output can never be negative; hence, the profit-maximizing rate of output is 60 units. As indicated earlier, it can be proved that the larger of the two roots is always the profit-maximizing (or loss-minimizing) output rate. It is a simple matter, however, to calculate total profit at each positive value of Q for which $MR = MC$ and see which root is associated with the greatest profit.

The profit-maximizing price is found by substituting the profit-maximizing output rate into the demand function and solving for P. In terms of our example, the profit-maximizing price is

$$P = 11,100 - 30Q$$
$$= 11,100 - 30(60)$$
$$= 11,100 - 1800$$
$$= \$9300.$$

Total profit at this price and output can be calculated by subtracting TC at 60 units of output from TR at 60 units of output. The reader should verify that total profit at 60 units of output will be $32,000 per period of time.

Total Profit or Loss. If demand is weak, then the monopolistically competitive firm may be unable to make an economic profit or even a normal profit. In such cases the firm must decide whether to shut down its operation in the short run and await more favorable demand conditions or whether to continue operating at a loss. The firm's short-run price and output decision hinges upon whether or not demand is strong enough to allow the firm to cover variable costs at some output rate.

Consider Figure 12-2(a). Between outputs of Q_1 and Q_3 units per period, the firm's demand-AR curve lies above its AVC curve; hence, unit contribution profit $(P - AVC)$ is positive at all outputs greater than Q_1 and less than Q_3. As a consequence, between these outputs the total revenues obtained by the firm are more than sufficient to cover total variable costs, and some total contribution profit can be earned to pay at least a portion of the firm's total fixed costs [see Figure 12-2(b)]. The firm should definitely continue to produce in the short run, since losses will be less than the amount of *TFC*—the amount it will lose if production and sales are temporarily discontinued. The question now is where between Q_1 and Q_3 to operate. Clearly, the firm is motivated to

LOSS-MINIMIZING PRINCIPLE
When weak demand for the firm's product forecloses all profit opportunity, short-run losses will be minimized at the output volume where *TC* exceeds *TR* by the smallest amount.

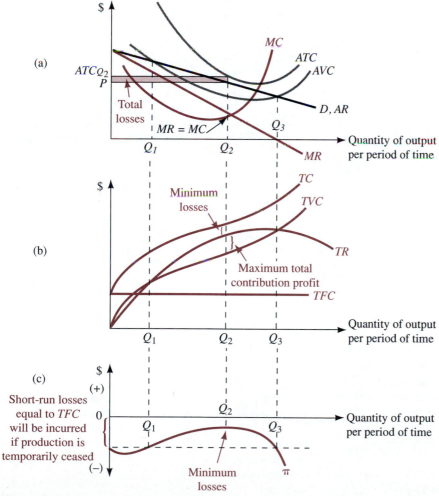

Figure 12-2
Short-run loss-minimizing price and output for a firm in monopolistic competition

obtain as much total contribution profit as possible and thereby cover as large a portion of its total fixed costs as conditions will permit. Total contribution profit is maximum at the output where *TR* exceeds *TVC* by the greatest vertical distance. In Figure 12-2(b) this occurs at an output rate of Q_2 units, where a tangent to the *TR* curve has the same slope as a tangent to the *TVC* curve. By inspection, the vertical distance by which *TC* exceeds *TR* is a minimum at Q_2, meaning that at Q_2 the firm's short-run losses are minimized. Therefore, from the standpoint of *TC-TR* analysis, *short-run losses are minimized at the output rate where total contribution profit is greatest.* This output coincides exactly with the output where the vertical spread between *TC* and *TR* is smallest. The corresponding total profit function reaches its highest level at Q_2, although it still lies entirely in the negative (loss) range. Insofar as units costs and unit revenues are concerned [Figure 12-2(a)], an output of Q_2 units corresponds exactly to the intersection of marginal cost and marginal revenue, where marginal profits equals zero. The loss-minimizing price is *P* dollars. At an output of Q_2 units, average total cost is ATC_{Q_2}; the firm's short-run losses will equal (*P* −

LOSS-MINIMIZING PRINCIPLE

When demand for a monopolistically competitive firm's product is too weak to yield a profit, the firm minimizes short-run losses at the output where $MC = MR$, provided that selling price covers AVC.

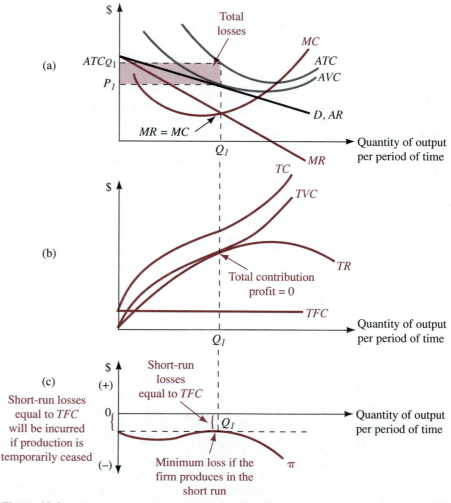

Figure 12-3

Short-run loss-minimizing price and output for a firm in monopolistic competition when the demand curve is just tangent to the AVC curve

ATC_{Q_2}) Q_2—shown as the shaded area in Figure 12-2(a). Thus, provided that at least a portion of the demand-*AR* curve lies above the *AVC* curve (so that $P > AVC$), we see that *the MR = MC rule, along with its corollary, $M\pi = 0$, identifies not only the short-run profit-maximizing output but also the short-run loss-minimizing output.*

Figure 12-3 illustrates a situation where the firm's demand-*AR* curve again lies below the *ATC* curve, foreclosing the opportunity for earning a normal profit in the short run. Note that the demand-*AR* curve is tangent to the *AVC* curve at a single output—Q_1 units. At Q_1, demand is just strong enough to permit the firm to sell at a price that will cover *AVC*. Unit contribution profit equals zero at Q_1; similarly, total contribution profit is zero, since $TR = TVC$ [see Figure 12-3(b)]. From a profit-loss standpoint the firm will be indifferent as to producing and selling Q_1 units or closing down production in the short run. In either event, short-run losses will equal *TFC*, and this is the best the firm can do [see Figure 12-3(b) and (c)]. At any other price and output combination *TR* will be insufficient to cover even *TVC*, both total and unit contribution profit will be negative, and short-run losses will exceed *TFC* by the amount of *TVC* not covered by *TR*. Given that selling Q_1 units at a price of P_1 dollars will have no adverse effects on its profit-loss position (as compared to temporarily closing down operations), the firm will undoubtedly elect to continue production. In doing so, the firm will protect its market share, and, by continuing to place its product before the public, stand a better chance of realizing a favorable shift in demand conditions in the future.

Now consider Figure 12-4, where a firm's demand-*AR* curve lies entirely below the *AVC* curve. At no output rate can sufficient revenues be accumulated to cover the variable costs of production. The vertical spread between *TR* and *TC* is always greater at output rates above zero than at zero. Both unit and total contribution profits are negative at all positive outputs. The total profit function is even more negative at positive output rates than at zero output. Therefore, in this instance the firm will minimize short-run losses by temporarily ceasing production and waiting for a favorable shift of the demand-*AR* curve; short-run losses will equal total fixed costs.

Of course, if the weak demand conditions are perceived as permanent and if over time the firm's costs cannot be lowered sufficiently to allow a normal profit to be earned, then the firm should begin to divert its energies and resources into the production of other more profitable commodities or else dissolve entirely. Short-run losses can be sustained only temporarily. As the time perspective lengthens, some sort of readjustment must be made.

WHY MARKET DEMAND-SUPPLY CONDITIONS CANNOT BE REPRESENTED GRAPHICALLY

Market conditions in a monopolistically competitive industry cannot be satisfactorily represented by industry demand and industry supply curves. Because of product differentiation the product units sold by one firm are not strictly comparable to the product units sold by another. Bottles of hair oil differ from tubes of hair cream. Aerosol cans of hair spray are still different. Thus, there is some difficulty in constructing the quantity axis for industry curves. Furthermore, no single price prevails for the products of firms in the industry. Each firm may charge a slightly different price, according to the costs of producing its particular product and the strength of consumer demand for it. The price and product variations among firms make it difficult to be precise

LOSS-MINIMIZING PRINCIPLE
When demand for a monopolistically competitive firm's product is so weak that there is no price-output combination that yields revenues high enough to cover total variable costs, the firm minimizes short-run losses by halting production and sales and waiting for demand conditions to improve; losses will equal total fixed cost.

In a monopolistically competitive industry, it is not feasible to represent market conditions by means of market demand and market supply curves.

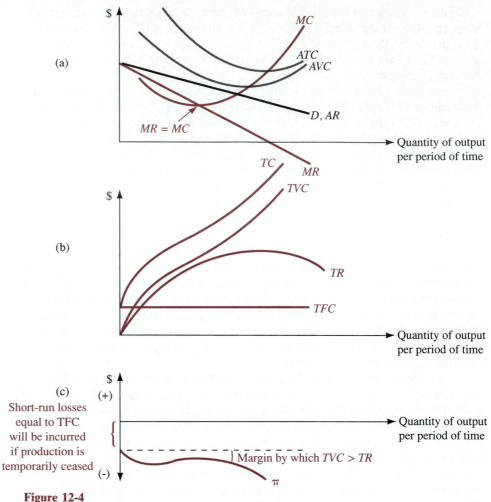

Figure 12-4

Short-run close-down position for a firm in monopolistic competition

about how many ''units'' all sellers will supply or all buyers will demand at a specific price. Moreover, what a firm is willing to produce at a given point in time hinges upon both *MR* and *MC*—the former varies with the demand for the product, and the latter is a function of input prices and the firm's technology. There is no unique price for each alternative output; it all depends on the shape and position of the demand-*AR* curve as to what the profit-maximizing price is for any given output at which *MR* = *MC*. Without a unique price-output combination for each seller in the market, there is no way to construct an industry supply curve. The market as a whole is there, but it has to be described in words rather than graphs.

LONG-RUN PROFIT-MAXIMIZING CONDITIONS FOR MONOPOLISTICALLY COMPETITIVE FIRMS

We saw earlier that in a perfectly competitive industry free entry and exit results in firms being unable to earn more than a normal profit. In monopolistic competition similar forces are present, though they are not quite so powerful as to eliminate completely the earning of economic profit or to guarantee each firm as much as a normal profit. There is, however, *a tendency* for firms to earn a more or less normal rate of return.

The process of long-run adjustment in a monopolistically competitive industry parallels what happens in perfect competition. Entry barriers are low, allowing firms to enter the industry without undue difficulties. When short-run economic profits exist generally throughout the industry, established firms can be expected to pursue additional economies of scale, growth opportunities and other profit-enhancing, cost-reducing options. New firms, attracted by the above-normal rates of return, will be motivated to enter the industry.[4] The entry of new rivals, assuming constant market demand for the products of the industry, will cause the demand curve of each firm to shift to the left. Why? Because each firm will necessarily have a smaller market share, since more firms will be dividing the relatively constant total market among themselves. Moreover, each firm's demand curve will become somewhat more price elastic, owing to the presence of a larger number of close-substitute products. These shifts in demand serve to narrow profit margins. With new firms entering the market and existing firms pursuing their own avenues for increased sales, competitive pressures stiffen and opportunities for earning economic profits start to dry up. Hence, there exists a *tendency* for firms' economic profits to erode and disappear over time.

Figure 12-5 illustrates long-run equilibrium position for a representative firm. In panel (a) the demand-*AR* curve is shown tangent to the *SRAC* curve and the *LRAC* curve at the profit-maximizing output. Output Q_1 is the long-run equilibrium output, and price P_1 is the long-run equilibrium price. Since price equals *SRAC* at Q_1 units of output, the firm is just covering *all* its costs, including a normal profit or a normal rate of return. In panel (b) the *TC* curve is tangent to the *TR* curve at an output of Q_1 units. The total profit function in Figure 12-5(c) climbs just to the zero-economic-profit level at Q_1 units. Plainly, any deviation from an output of Q_1 and a price of P_1 will yield revenues that are insufficient to cover *all* production costs including a normal profit. And since economic profits have dwindled to zero, no incentive exists for additional firms to enter the industry.

Should weak demand conditions preclude established firms from earning a normal profit (as previously illustrated in Figures 12-2, 12-3, and 12-4), the least-efficient, highest-cost firms that are sustaining the largest losses are the most probable candidates for leaving the industry. The remaining firms can be counted upon to seek out ways to increase efficiency, reduce costs, stimulate demand, and thereby trim their losses. The exodus of firms from the industry will tend to shift the demand-*AR* curves of the remaining firms to the right, since the now fewer firms can divide the total market into larger pieces. Also, the reduction in the number of good substitutes will make the demand-*AR* curve a little less price elastic. The net result will tend to be an improvement in the profit-loss position of the representative firm to the point where at least a normal profit can be earned.

Observe that *at the long-run equilibrium position, the representative monopolistically competitive firm is operating short of the minimum point on*

When market demand is strong enough to permit monopolistically competitive firms to earn an economic profit, the entry of new firms and the pursuit of additional sales by existing firms heighten competition and dry up opportunities to earn sustained economic profits.

When market demand is too weak to allow monopolistically competitive firms to earn even a normal profit, some firms exit the industry and those remaining are driven to become more cost efficient and discover ways to stimulate buyer demands; the effect is to improve market conditions enough to allow firms to earn a normal profit.

---

[4] For simplicity, we shall assume that the entry and exit of firms has no effect on input prices and, consequently, upon the *SRAC* and *LRAC* curves of the firms. In other words, the long-run adjustment process is presumed to take place in a constant-cost environment. Shifts in the *SRAC* and *LRAC* curves as firms enter or leave the industry would unduly complicate the discussion without altering the conclusions.

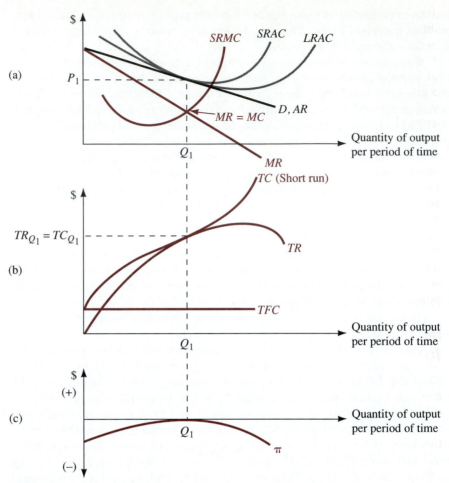

Figure 12-5
Long-run equilibrium for a firm in monopolistic competition

In a monopolistically competitive industry, market forces are not quite powerful enough to *compel* firms to operate at the minimum point of the *LRAC* curve.

the LRAC curve. Each company is too small to achieve the lowest possible unit cost. In one sense there are too many firms in the industry. The same total output could be produced by a smaller number of firms, each operating at minimum *LRAC*. Thus, ***excess production capacity*** may be said to exist in the industry. Also, the long-run equilibrium price is higher than the minimum value of *LRAC*. Both results suggest that a monopolistically competitive market is less efficient than a perfectly competitive market. But there is a need for caution here. The apparently excessive number of firms derives from consumer preferences for one brand over another, as reflected in the downsloping demand-*AR* curve. Consumers evidently believe they *gain* by being able to exercise their preferences for a brand or a store; otherwise, brand and store loyalty would vanish and the demand-*AR* curves of firms would tend to be horizontal (perfectly elastic). Any inefficiency is tolerable if consumer satisfaction is greater because of product differentiation.

However, *the forces of long-run equilibrium adjustment in monopolistic competition are not so powerful as in perfect competition.* The sequence of events leading to long-run equilibrium in monopolistic competition is subject to interruption. In the first place, some firms may be able to develop unique features in their product which are patentable and which give them a significant marketing edge over competitors, even over the long term. Second, some firms may obtain an especially favorable location for their business which allows them to earn sustained economic profits; this arises often in the case of motels, service stations, restaurants, and shopping centers. Third, through ongoing product innovation and the implementing of new technologies, firms may be able to gain advantages over their rivals that are sustainable for long periods. Finally, there are restrictions on both entry and exit. The added financial investment associated with product differentiation and sales promotion activities may pose enough of a barrier to some potential new entrants that modest economic profits can persist in the long run. At the other end of the ladder, below-normal profits may also persist in the long run. The suburban florist may accept a return less than he could earn elsewhere because he likes living near a metropolitan area and because he likes designing floral arrangements. The proprietor of the corner grocery store may reluctantly accept subpar profits because his business is a way of life to him. Consequently, market forces will seldom be powerful enough in monopolistic competition to drive price all the way to equality with short-run and long-run average cost. Nevertheless, there is a *tendency* for market forces to *limit* the profits and to *restrict* the losses of monopolistically competitive firms over the long run.

COMPETITIVE STRATEGIES FOR FIRMS IN MONOPOLISTIC COMPETITION

In a monopolistically competitive marketplace, firms have the option of introducing new and different product attributes as a way to strengthen their position with buyers. Indeed, seeking to differentiate one's product from those of rival firms can be a potent competitive strategy. Setting one's own brand apart from the rest by offering improved quality and performance, new or greater convenience, more selection, extra services, greater durability, better credit terms, or distinctive design normally wins buyer approval. Moreover, successfully differentiating one's products from those of rivals affords a firm breathing space to refrain from trying to win increased buyer patronage solely by meeting or beating the prices of competing items. And from a broader social viewpoint, the pursuit of *product differentiation* often stimulates technological innovation and expands the range of consumer choice.

Given a goal of profit maximization, the representative firm in monopolistic competition can be expected to search among the various possible combinations of product attributes for the one it perceives to be the most profitable. The problem is to select it under conditions of less than perfect knowledge about future market conditions and buyer behavior. One approach is to estimate from available market information the profitability of each of several product differentiation approaches, given the prices and product attributes of rival firms. The firm then maximizes expected profit by choosing the product differentiation theme with the highest expected profit and producing at the price and output where *MC* equals *MR*.

However, from time to time rival firms can be counted upon to incorporate new and different attributes into their own products. When they do, a firm may find further product differentiation necessary to remain competitive. A continuous sequence of product variation moves and countermoves is set in motion, often made feasible by research and development efforts aimed at generating a steady stream of potentially profitable opportunities for modifying product offerings. Rival competitors are prompted to incorporate new product features because they hope to gain a profitable, albeit temporary, competitive

COMPETITIVE PRINCIPLE
Much of the competitive rivalry in a monopolistically competitive market centers around the efforts of rivals to differentiate their products and appeal to the diverse needs and preferences of buyers.

edge. The edge tends to be temporary because if the new attributes catch on in the market, other firms either begin to imitate the variation or to try to go it one better, in hopes of leapfrogging the competitive edge of the leaders.

In the course of this product-differentiating struggle, some firms will perceive it more profitable to adopt product attributes that appeal to price-conscious consumers, with the result that their products are slightly less expensive and of lower quality. Other firms will view it advantageous to cater to those buyers desirous of superior-quality goods, with the result that their products carry above-average prices and are claimed to have more features or special performance capabilities. Still other firms may pursue an intermediate strategy, positioning their products in between the high and low ends of the market. And some rivals may base their differentiation strategy on styling, extra service, bigger selection, easier credit terms, more convenient location, or other such features. These strategy differences reflect the fact that *markets are diverse*—being comprised in part by consumers who are strongly quality-conscious but not especially price-conscious, in part by consumers willing to sacrifice quality to get a lower price, and in part by consumers who are swayed by attributes other than price and quality. Because consumer needs and preferences are not uniform, it is feasible and profitable for firms in the same industry to pursue a *focus* or *specialization strategy* aimed at appealing to *specific* customer needs and *specific* customer groups rather than the whole market. The essence of a focus strategy is to specialize in serving a limited market segment, the premise being that by catering to the needs and preferences of a limited group of buyers a firm can gain a competitive edge in winning the patronage of this buyer group and thereby carve out its own market niche. A focus strategy has merit (1) when there are distinctly different groups of buyers who either have different needs or else utilize the product in different ways, (2) when rival firms have not attempted to specialize, opting instead to try to appeal to all types of buyers, or (3) when a firm's resources do not permit it to go after a wide segment of the total market.

From the standpoint of the consuming public, there is something to be said for a market situation where rival firms pursue different competitive strategies (cost leadership, differentiation, or focus) rather than being constrained to a single, common approach. The different market approaches of competitors provide consumers with a wider range of product qualities, performance features, and prices, thereby permitting each consumer to select the brand which appears best-suited to his or her preferences.[5]

BASIC CONCEPT
In markets where buyer needs and tastes are diverse, firms that do not have the resources to compete broadly may focus their efforts on making specialized products that appeal only to specific buyer needs and specific groups of buyers—such a competitive approach is termed a focus strategy.

---

[5] Product and strategic diversity are not, however, without their drawbacks. Critics warn that proliferation of product varieties and competitive strategies may so confuse the consumer that the exercise of rational choice becomes virtually impossible. Some consumers, confronted with a myriad of similar products, may fall into the "trap" of judging quality by price alone. Critics also point out that many product variations consist of frivolous and superficial attributes which are of dubious value in improving durability, efficiency, or usefulness. In the case of durable and semidurable consumer goods, the process of product change seems to follow a pattern of "planned obsolescence"; firms make gradual but regular changes in their products aimed at increasing the frequency with which consumers become dissatisfied with their present model and trade it in on the new model. As partial remedies for product proliferation, a number of economists propose that information about products be provided to consumers in greater amounts and that laws and penalties regarding infringement on brands and trademarks be relaxed. Increased information and a weakening of trademark protection are held to increase "competition" by promoting a greater degree of product standardization and thereby lessening the powers of producers to vend differentiated products. The end result should be a movement in the direction of perfect competition. For a more thorough argument of this point, see Edward H. Chamberlin, *The Theory of Monopolistic Competition* (Cambridge, Mass.: Harvard University Press, 1933), pp. 271–74, and George J. Stigler, "The Economics of Information," *Journal of Political Economy,* Vol. 69, No. 3 (June 1961), pp. 213–25.

When a firm elects to pursue a particular differentiation or focus strategy, its *SRAC* and *LRAC* curves can shift either up or down, according to the amounts and prices of the resource inputs needed to implement the chosen competitive strategy. In the process, the demand-*AR* curves of each firm can shift both in position and slope as consumers respond to new product variations. One effect of the differences in the products and cost curves of monopolistically competitive firms is to create different long-run equilibrium positions for different firms. Higher-quality firms can exist alongside lower-quality firms. Higher-priced firms can exist alongside lower-priced firms. This condition is readily observed in the sale of foods and cosmetics, where retailers display on the same shelf the high-priced, better known brands and the lesser-known, cut-price varieties. Moreover, at a given moment, some monopolistically competitive firms may be earning sizable economic profits, others may be earning only a normal profit, and others may be sustaining losses.

> **In a monopolistically competitive industry, there is no one single price-cost-profit equilibrium for all firms.**

USING ADVERTISING AND SALES PROMOTION EFFORTS TO GAIN A COMPETITIVE EDGE

The third basic type of competitive approach which monopolistically competitive firms may employ to strengthen their market position concerns advertising and sales promotion. Advertising and promotional campaigns are a strong complement to a firm's pricing and product differentiation strategies. If promotional efforts are well conceived, sales volume and revenues can be increased by drawing new customers away from others brands; at the same time, buyers may be persuaded that the firm's product is worth paying more for. In short, promotional expenditures can shift the firm's demand-*AR* curve to the right and make it slightly *less* price elastic as well. As long as revenues increase by more than enough to compensate both for promotional expenses and for extra production costs associated with greater outputs, the firm will have improved its profits position.

Suppose we look closer at the possible effects of promotional expenses upon a firm's long-run average costs. Initially, for the sake of argument, suppose promotional outlays substantially increase the demand for the firm's product and, consequently, the firm's most profitable long-run output rate. What, then, is the effect on the firm's long-run average costs? As depicted in Figure 12-6, it is obvious that sales promotion outlays will shift the *LRAC* upward.

> **Depending on the shape of the *LRAC* curve and on the responsiveness of sales to advertising, advertising can result in either lower or higher average costs per unit sold.**

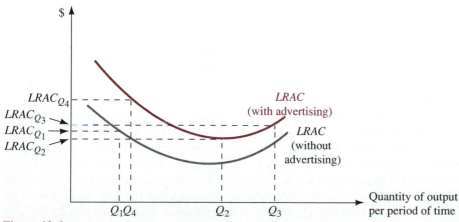

Figure 12-6

Effect of sales promotion expenditures upon unit costs and output rates

APPLICATIONS CAPSULE

ADVERTISING: ITS IMPACT AND ECONOMIC SIGNIFICANCE

A theoretical revolution going by the name of "the economics of information" has begun to affect economists' view of the impact and significance of advertising. The conventional economic wisdom is that advertising tends to act as the handmaiden of market power, of downside price rigidity, and of long-term price inflation. Whereas businesspeople judge advertising primarily in terms of its power to increase sales and attract customers from other firms, economists judge advertising on how it affects the overall performance of markets and the economy at large. The criteria economists generally use to evaluate advertising are its effects on price competition, product prices, the achievement of large-scale economies, and the extent to which it promotes full employment and maximum production efficiency.

By and large, economists view anything but price advertising with hostility, arguing that nonprice advertising is generally aimed at convincing consumers that a firm's products are somehow different from those of rivals. This creates brand loyalty, making the buying public much less sensitive to price and thereby giving the advertiser some degree of price influence. Beyond that, economists maintain that heavy advertising erects financial barriers to the entry of new firms because, to break into a market, companies must be willing and able to spend large sums on advertising to attract buyers' attention. To the extent that advertising barriers keep out new competitors, the market power of those firms already in the industry is enhanced, with the result that prices are higher and output is smaller than would be the case if markets were more oriented toward price competition. This view is supported by statistical studies showing a correlation between the amount an industry spends on advertising and both its profitability and degree of sales concentrated in a few firms.

However, the revolution going on with respect to the economics of information holds that advertising may contain virtue as well as vice. The new view addresses the question of how advertising affects the consumer and, particularly, the kind and scope of information it provides for consumer decision making. Starting with the premise that advertising provides at least some information to consumers that they would not otherwise get, the argument is that information about a variety of products is far more likely to decrease monopoly power than to increase it.

George Stigler, of the University of Chicago, triggered the economics of information revolution in 1961, casti-

gating economists for analyzing the prices in different markets in great depth, while relegating the analysis of consumer information about prices to "a slum dwelling in the town of economics." Whereas the customary economic view of advertising maintained that price differences for the same *type* of product were due to the ability of firms to differentiate their products and were taken as evidence that advertising gave firms too much price-making power, Stigler argued that a good part of the variability of prices, even among homogeneous products, existed because consumers did not know the prices being charged by various firms. It followed, then, that increased information about prices would enable buyers to bargain more effectively with sellers. As a consequence, reasoned Stigler, price advertising that makes search less expensive will reduce the average price consumers pay for a product.

However, Professor Phillip Nelson has carried Stigler's argument a step forward. Nelson claims that getting information on price is relatively easy; the difficult task for the consumer is getting a handle on quality. Nelson's study endeavors to explain how consumers get information about the quality of products from mass-media advertising, given that the information provided is likely to be self-serving and may actually be little more than image-building or boastful puffery. Nelson found that the informational content of advertising differs drastically, depending on the type of product being advertised. For what he called "search goods" (those products whose qualities can be more easily checked before purchase, such as a suit or a dress), the advertising content often consists of direct information on the quality and characteristics of the products; usually, this information is accurate since for advertisers to give misleading information invites legal action.

On the other hand, for "experience goods" (such as soft drinks, soaps, and deodorants, where ascertaining quality requires purchasing the item), advertising generally provides little or no direct quality information. For example, Nelson observes there is no direct information to "join the Pepsi generation." But even here, according to Nelson, the advertiser is saying to the consumer that he believes his product to be of high quality and well worth the consumer's dollar. And to the extent that highly advertised brands have a larger market share than less-advertised brands, there is a strong implication that the heavily advertised brand does have higher quality or yield more value to the consumer.

However, if the demand-*AR* curve shifts such that production is more profitable at Q_2 than at Q_1, units costs will decline from $LRAC_{Q_1}$ to $LRAC_{Q_2}$ because of the economies of scale which the firm can take advantage of. Greater production efficiency more than offsets the increase in unit costs associated with promotional expenses. On the other hand, increased demand realized from sales promotion may force diseconomies of scale upon the firm, as indicated by the movement from Q_1 to Q_3; in this case, unit costs would rise from $LRAC_{Q_1}$ to $LRAC_{Q_3}$. In some cases a great proportion of sales promotion efforts by firms

In support of this proposition, Nelson argues that companies will advertise their winners, not their losers, because heavy advertising of an inferior-quality product risks creating a bad image in the mind of the consumer not only of the brand but of the company as well. In the case of "experience goods" it is especially true that companies live or die from repeat purchases, so it stands to reason that over the long run the higher-quality products will win out over the lower-quality products. This leads Nelson to conclude that *on the average the best buy is the heavily advertised brand*—a proposition which traditionalists find somewhat appalling.

In addition, Nelson maintains that because advertising provides information on many similar products, consumer demand will become more responsive to price for any given product, rather than less responsive, as argued by anti-advertising critics. In other words, advertising increases information about the availability of substitutes, thereby undermining the monopoly power of any one brand—however highly advertised it may be.

Nelson's rule for buying the most advertised brand rests on two key assumptions: one, that sufficient numbers of consumers can judge quality differences between brands after they have used them; two, that quality differences between brands would exist without advertising, given cost-efficiency differences between companies and given that companies have different opinions as to what product features consumers are looking for.

With respect to the overall market efficiency of advertising, Nelson argues that advertising permits the more efficient companies to increase their sales faster and that less efficient companies are weeded out more quickly than if there were no advertising. This yields a net economic benefit to society compared to a situation where companies do not advertise and where marginal firms may be able to hang on for longer periods of time.

The notion that advertising may be more good than bad has come under sharp attack. Perhaps the most fundamental weakness in this approach is the assumption that consumers can validate advertising claims easily and cheaply. If consumers are able to learn from experiences quickly, then it is more likely to be true that the advertised brand is the best buy—for many goods. But there are many products which require extensive testing by consumers, and other products, such as consumer durables, are purchased infrequently; in such cases the experience information which consumers have may be too outdated to be of value. Another view is that advertising shapes and molds consumer tastes and works to the advantage of advertisers, thereby allowing firms to manage demand and to undermine consumer sovereignty. Then, too, there are studies which show that in heavily advertised consumer goods industries (such as nonprescription drugs, soaps, breakfast cereals, razors, and soft drinks) firms consistently are able to earn above-average profits. This finding has been held to confirm the existence of barriers to entry, because otherwise, it is argued, firms would be induced to enter such industries to take advantage of the above-average profit opportunities. To the extent that a new company will have to spend more than a dollar on advertising its product to counteract one dollar's worth of advertising by an entrenched firm, then the new company is at a disadvantage, and a barrier to entry exists. Moreover, it has been observed that investing in advertising is not the same as investing in tangible capital assets because if a firm fails in an industry in which it has invested heavily in capital goods, then those capital goods have a liquidation value. However, if a firm fails in an industry where it has invested heavily in advertising, its investment is water down the drain.

QUESTIONS FOR DISCUSSION

1. In your opinion, how able are consumers to validate the quality of what Nelson calls experience goods? Search goods?

2. Do you agree with Nelson that for most items, the most highly advertised brand is the best buy? Cite examples to support your answer.

3. Can you cite cases where advertising has probably tended to increase the market power of established firms? In what industries is it likely that advertising has reduced market power by facilitating the entry of new firms?

Sources: George J. Stigler, "The Economics of Information," *Journal of Political Economy*, Vol. 69, No. 3 (June 1961), pp. 213–25; Phillip J. Nelson, "Advertising As Information," *Journal of Political Economy*, Vol. 82, No. 4 (July–August 1974), pp. 729–54; William S. Comanor and Thomas A. Wilson, *Advertising and Market Power* (Cambridge, Mass.: Harvard University Press, 1974); "A New View of Advertising's Economic Impact," *Business Week* (December 22, 1975), pp. 49ff.; Phillip J. Nelson, "Information and Consumer Behavior," *Journal of Political Economy*, Vol. 78, No. 2 (March–April 1970); pp. 311–29; and Phillip J. Nelson, "The Economic Consequences of Advertising," *Journal of Business*, Vol. 48, No. 2 (April 1975); pp. 213–41.

are self-cancelling; one seller's stepped-up advertising campaign is matched by rival firms, resulting in only slight gains in sales and output—as suggested by the movement from Q_1 to Q_4.[6] In this instance, unit costs may be driven up substantially by the decision to adopt an aggressive sales promotion strategy.

---

[6] The cigarette, soap, beer, and toiletries industries are good cases in point. Like the Red Queen in *Alice through the Looking Glass*, each firm has to run as fast as it can in its promotional activities just to keep up with where it is. This correctly recognizes that some promotional activity is defensive in nature and is undertaken to protect a firm's position as well as to enhance it.

Plainly, all three outcomes are possible; which one will actually occur in a particular situation varies with the shape of the *LRAC* curve and the size of the effect of sales promotion upon demand and output.

A somewhat more interesting question relates to the effect of sales promotion activity upon a firm's price and profits. Consider Figure 12-7. Panel (a) illustrates a situation where sales promotion outlays have the effect of *lowering* a firm's price and *raising* a firm's profits. In the absence of promotion, the profit-maximizing price and output are P_1 and Q_1, respectively, and total profit equals $(P_1 - SRAC_{Q_1})Q_1$. Initiating promotional activity shifts the demand-*AR* curve rightward from (D_1, AR_1) to (D_2, AR_2) and the *LRAC* curve upward from $LRAC_1$ to $LRAC_2$. The firm will find it advantageous to expand output to Q_2 and to lower price to P_2; total profit will be $(P_2 - SRAC_{Q_2})Q_2$ dollars—an amount that dwarfs the profits earned when no promotional activity is undertaken. Panel (b) shows a situation where promotional activity causes price to rise and profits to fall. Prior to initiating a promotional strategy, profit maximization occurs at P_1 and Q_1 with a resulting total profit of $(P_1 - SRAC_{Q_1})Q_1$ dollars. With promotion activity the profit-maximizing price and output are P_2 and Q_2 and total profit is only $(P_2 - SRAC_{Q_2})Q_2$ dollars. Other possibilities exist: Promotional activity can cause price to rise and profits to rise, price to fall and profits to fall, and so on. *No general answer can be given*

Outlays for advertising and sales promotion can result in higher or lower prices and higher or lower profits, depending upon how such outlays affect the positions and shapes of the *LRAC* and demand-*AR* curves.

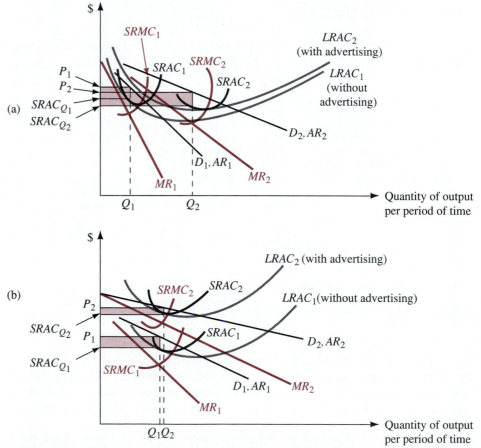

Figure 12-7
Possible effects of sales promotion activity upon prices and profits

MATHEMATICAL CAPSULE 12

DETERMINING THE PROFIT-MAXIMIZING OUTPUT RATE AND LEVEL OF ADVERTISING EXPENDITURE

Advertising and promotional outlays necessarily affect the firm's profitability. Thus, we may say that

$$\pi = f(\text{output, advertising outlays}).$$

Suppose empirical analysis of a firm's operations indicates that the following relationship exists:

$$\pi = 600 - 4Q - Q^2 + 2QA + 116A - 5A^2,$$

where π = total profit per period of time, Q = the firm's output rate, and A = the firm's advertising outlay (in dollars) per period of time.

How can we determine the profit-maximizing output rate and the profit-maximizing amount of advertising expenditure? The answer to this question involves use of partial derivatives (Mathematical Capsule 2) and the principles of profit maximization. In mathematical terms we need to find the specific combination of values of Q and A that will maximize the value of π.

The first-order conditions for maximizing a multivariable function of this type are that

$$\frac{\partial \pi}{\partial Q} = 0 \quad \text{and} \quad \frac{\partial \pi}{\partial A} = 0.$$

Thus, the first step is to find the partial derivatives of π with respect to Q and A and set them equal to zero; this gives

$$\frac{\partial \pi}{\partial Q} = -4 - 2Q + 2A = 0,$$

$$\frac{\partial \pi}{\partial A} = 2Q + 116 - 10A = 0.$$

Solving these two equations simultaneously gives $Q = 12$ and $A = 14$.

To prove that these values represent maximum π rather than minimum π, we must check to see that the second-order conditions are met at $Q = 12$ and $A = 14$. The second-order conditions are that

$$\frac{\partial^2 \pi}{\partial Q^2} < 0, \frac{\partial^2 \pi}{\partial A^2} < 0 \quad \text{and} \quad \left(\frac{\partial^2 \pi}{\partial Q^2}\right)\left(\frac{\partial^2 \pi}{\partial A^2}\right) > \left(\frac{\partial^2 \pi}{\partial Q \partial A}\right)^2.$$

Since

$$\frac{\partial^2 \pi}{\partial Q^2} = -2,$$

$$\frac{\partial^2 \pi}{\partial A^2} = -10,$$

$$\frac{\partial^2 \pi}{\partial Q \partial A} = 2,$$

it is quickly verified that the profit-maximizing output rate is 12 units per period of time and the profit-maximizing advertising outlay is $14 per period of time.

EXERCISE

1. Suppose that the functional relationship among profit, output, and advertising is given by the expression

$$\pi = 1000 - 3Q^2 - 6Q + 6QA + 90A - 10A^2.$$

Determine the profit-maximizing rates of output and advertising expenditure.

---

as to the effect of promotional strategies upon a firm's average costs, price, output, or profits. It all depends on the effect which promotional expenditures have upon the position and shape of the firm's demand-AR curve and its LRAC curve.

KEY POINTS CONCERNING MONOPOLISTIC COMPETITION

The distinguishing features of a monopolistically competitive market are: (1) a fragmented market structure whereby *many* suppliers are selling differentiated, yet similar, products; (2) no one seller has a significant or commanding market share; (3) each firm, because its product tends to be more or less different from what its rivals are offering, has some ability to influence its sales by changing its price; (4) downsloping, but highly elastic, demand-*AR* curves for the relevant output range of the firms; (5) the relative ease with which firms can enter and leave the industry; (6) the small effect the actions of any one firm have upon rival firms; and (7) firms which behave as if they seek to maximize profits.

Monopolistically competitive firms may earn short-run economic profits or incur short-run losses. The relative ease with which firms can enter the industry limits the opportunities for earning large economic profits over the long run. The exodus of firms from the industry tends to eliminate or at least reduce economic losses in the long run.

The firm in monopolistic competition has three basic competitive strategies for pursuing its principal goal of maximum profits: (1) using the appeal of a different (*usually lower*) price to create a clientele of buyers, (2) trying to set one's own product offering apart from those of rival sellers via differentiation and/or focus strategies, and (3) employing advertising and other sales promotion techniques to attract buyer attention and increase sales volume, revenues, and market share. Just what set of specific features and product attributes, selling at what price, and supplemented by what amount of promotional expenses will actually maximize profits is a complex issue. Each possible combination of price, product differentiation themes, and promotional outlay poses a different demand and cost situation for the firm, some one of which will yield the firm maximum profits. A trial-and-error procedure is virtually imperative in arriving at an optimum combination of price, product attributes, and promotional outlays. Some products are so obviously different that sellers feel little pressure or derive little advantage from further promoting and proclaiming differences of which most buyers are already aware. On the other hand, promotional activity can play a big role in those monopolistically competitive markets where buyers are drawn to purchasing the brands whose advertised features they find most to their liking.

Thus, the competitive strategies of firms can assume a variety of forms. Some firms may seek to compete mainly on price, while others aim at quality, and still others use heavier than usual advertising. Product differentiation themes may be aimed at making the item more durable or less durable; various performance features may be made standard or optional; the range of models, colors, and styles may be expanded or contracted; service after the sale may be increased or reduced; credit terms can be tightened or loosened; designs can be made plain or fancy; packaging may be made more or less elaborate and colorful. A stepped-up advertising campaign by one seller may be countered by another seller with improved guarantees to buyers. Lower prices may be met by improved customer services or adding new convenience features.

It is important to observe that formulating a successful competitive strategy is inherently more complex in a monopolistically competitive market environment than it is in perfect competition. In a perfectly competitive market the products of different firms are all alike—the item is a "commodity" in the sense that buyers are purchasing *the industry's product*, not a given firm's product. Buyers do not care which seller they deal with, except if a particular seller's price is higher or lower than the going market price—in which case buyers will switch quickly to a lower-priced seller and away from a higher-priced seller. This commodity feature of a perfectly competitive marketplace creates a competitive environment wherein the most sensible strategy is that of striving to be *the low-cost producer* or at least *a low-cost producer*. Being in a low-cost position is the best single strategic defense against the price-cost style of competitive game that typifies a perfectly competitive market. Moreover, in a commodity market, there is no place for differentiation or focus types of competitive strategies since buyers have no basis for preferring to deal with any one seller and there is no buyer loyalty. Hence, the choice of how to compete is a very simple one insofar as a firm operating in a perfectly competitive environment is concerned. But this is not so in monopolistic competition. The differentiated product environment of a monopolistically competitive market gives a firm plenty of leeway in formulating an answer to the question of "how do we try to compete in this business?" There is space for many different competitive approaches to succeed, thus creating a situation where a firm must analyze carefully which strategic option to pursue. We shall have more to say about the choice of competitive strategy in Chapters 15 and 16.

COMPETITION AMONG THE MANY: THEORY VERSUS PRACTICE

It turns out that the theoretical models of perfect competition and monopolistic competition are reasonably descriptive of firm and market behavior in certain industries. Where large numbers of relatively small firms sell a homogeneous product, market patterns *tend* to conform to the perfectly competitive model. Where large numbers of small firms sell differentiated products, firm behavior regarding prices, outputs, product variation, and promotion parallels the model of monopolistic competition.

Real-world examples of industries where near perfectly competitive conditions prevail include such agricultural markets as corn, wheat, cotton, wool, barley, oats, and livestock; the manufacture of cotton cloth; and some financial markets involving stocks, bonds, and loans to business. Conditions approaching monopolistic competition are found in such industries as machine tools, valves and pipe fittings, wood and upholstered furniture, wine, computer software, sawmills, screw machine products, paperboard boxes, shoes, paints and varnishes, millinery, costume jewelry, lighting fixtures, poultry processing, restaurants, burial caskets, men's and boys' suits and coats, and women's dresses, suits, coats, and skirts; monopolistic competition also typifies the wholesaling and retailing trades in more populated urban centers.

The behavior of prices, outputs, and profits in the just-mentioned industries compares favorably with the conclusions drawn from the two theoretical models of perfect and monopolistic competition. Rates of return on stockholder investment tend to run a bit below average. However, as might be anticipated, profits tend to be somewhat higher in the faster-growing industries and somewhat lower in the slow-growth industries. Supply is generally responsive to changes in consumer demand, rising most dramatically where market demand curves are shifting rapidly to the right. Outputs and prices respond rapidly to cost changes. Industries where technological change has tended to reduce unit costs show a relative decline in prices and a relatively large expansion of output. Consumer demand, output, and cost movements are correlated. Where consumer demand and output are vigorously expanding, technical progress is stimulated, and firms take advantage rather quickly of expansion opportunities. Unless scale economies dictate otherwise, the number of firms in the industry increases with demand. Cost reductions coupled with expanding production capabilities give rise to price cuts, which, in turn, reinforce the expansion process by triggering higher sales and output; this is a familiar cycle during the early and intermediate stages of the life cycle of a product or product group. There is evidence, then, that the models of perfect and monopolistic competition have validity; both are able to predict and explain market behavior in certain circumstances and both have something to say about the pros and cons of different ways a firm can try to compete successfully.

THE BENEFITS OF COMPETITION AMONG THE MANY

The conventional wisdom in economics is that market conditions of perfect competition and monopolistic competition offer consumers the best of all possible worlds. If consumers are willing to accept homogeneous products, a perfectly competitive market structure will give it to them at the lowest possible price consistent with the costs of production. Under conditions of long-run equilibrium each firm operates at the minimum point of its short-run and long-run average cost curve and thus achieves maximum production efficiency. Price is driven to the level of minimum average cost, and investors receive a rate of return just sufficient to induce them to maintain their investment at levels adequate for producing the industry's equilibrium output most efficiently. Firms which fail to attain the lowest possible unit cost incur losses and eventually are driven from the industry. Consequently, resources *tend* to be employed at maximum production efficiency in a perfectly competitive industry.

If consumers exhibit a preference for differentiated products as often they do because of the diversity of preferences and needs of buyers, then monopolistically competitive conditions are held to produce optimum consumer benefits. Competition is strong enough to keep prices down close to costs and profit margins slim. Although monopolistically competitive firms may not quite achieve maximum production efficiency (because at long-run equilibrium the demand-*AR* curve is tangent to the *LRAC* curve just short of the minimum point), unit costs still tend to be as low as can be achieved with differentiated products.

In both perfect and monopolistic competition, the output of goods and services automatically stays in close accord with consumer demand. Prices are no higher than necessary to maintain production. The market power of any one firm is negligible. For these reasons the market structures of perfect and monopolistic competition are commonly thought to yield an overall economic outcome that is most advantageous to consumers. The key benefit of "competition among the many" is having numerous relatively small firms competing under conditions where market forces are so dominant that buyers are well protected from exploitation by sellers and abuses of economic power on the supply side of the market. Firms are, for the most part, price-takers, not price-makers.

SOME DISADVANTAGES OF COMPETITION AMONG THE MANY

However, competition among the many can produce some subtle disadvantages. To see why we have to go beyond industrywide prices, outputs, and profits and look critically at the specific traits that competition among the many can *sometimes* impose upon individual firms. Almost every real-world example of markets that are fragmented with many sellers involves industries where firms are small both relatively *and* absolutely. There is, in other words, a very close correspondence between (1) the existence of near-perfect competition and of monopolistic competition and (2) the presence of small, entrepreneurial enterprises. This is more than mere circumstance. The representative firm operating under conditions of perfect or monopolistic competition *must* be small relatively because both models are predicated on the presence of large numbers of firms, no one of which has a sizable share of the market. In practice, the size of the representative firm is also absolutely small. Firm size is severely limited by the relatively quick appearance of diseconomies of scale. Were significant economies of scale present, firms would tend to be large—not small—relative to the total market because overall market demand is seldom big enough to accommodate the competitive existence of *large* numbers of *large* firms. Moreover, once existing firms take full advantage of scale economies, increased industry output is likely to be achieved *by the entry of new firms rather than by the expansion of existing firms.* In other words, the economic limitations on firm size tend to guarantee an atomistic structure of many small firms. This is not to say that conditions of perfect or monopolistic competition prevail wherever small firms exist, but it does say that perfect and monopolistic competition are found almost exclusively in markets comprised of firms that are small in an absolute sense. Billion-dollar corporations, commonplace in many industries, are the exception not the rule in markets approximating perfect and monopolistic competition.

The small size and entrepreneurial character of firms that operate in an atomistic or fragmented market environment, in conjunction with the nature of competition among the many, are what gives rise to the disadvantages. To begin with, the representative firm in an atomistic or fragmented market is thrust into a position of *reacting* and *responding* to changing market conditions. "The market" calls the shots, with the winds of change just as prone to blow in the direction of lower profits as in the direction of higher profits. Market forces can be harsh and unrelenting. Much like a small boat caught in the midst of a hurricane, the firm's security and survival is extremely tenuous—witness the comparatively precarious condition of many small businesses when market conditions are tough. As a consequence, the actions and strategies of such firms come to be aimed mainly at short-run profit maximization. Profit margins are too slim and too uncertain to allow otherwise. Weak demand may force severe financial retrenchment, bankruptcy, or exit from the industry. Strong demand, on the other hand, may offer limited prospects for above-average profits and growth because of the ease of entry of new firms and because of a lack of financial strength to pursue a large expansion program or gain a position of industry leadership.

In such an environment, profit incentives and financial capacities for risk-taking, for research, and for innovation are definitely impaired—both by the firm's small size and by its susceptibility to stringent treatment by market forces. There is, therefore, an increased likelihood that the pace of technological advance will be slower, not faster, where firms are small as compared to where they are large. A little bit of bigness—sales levels of $100 million to $250 million in most industries—is good for R & D and innovation. Firms of this size and larger find a well-rounded research and development program and the new ideas it generates to be an asset in maintaining their viability and growth. Moreover, they can better afford the talent needed to staff such an effort. Naturally, exceptions exist; some small entrepreneurial firms are known for their technological prowess, being extraordinarily prolific in developing better products and/or cheaper ways of doing things.[7] But in many instances small owner-managed firms are not especially innovation-minded or technologically advanced. This is partially because competition from rivals and low barriers to entry keep profits so slim and uncertain that firms are deprived of the funds to

---

[7] Apple Computer was nothing more than a back-of-the-house garage operation when it pioneered the development and use of small-scale personal computers.

finance technological research and innovation on an ongoing basis. And it is partially because such firms operate on too small a scale to justify spending funds for formal research and development activities; R & D may not pay off from a short-run profit-and-loss viewpoint—the criterion employed by firms in atomistically competitive market environments. Even more significantly, a small firm may not be able to absorb the risk of failure that goes with venture-some R & D efforts.

This argument is supported by the fact that most industries exemplifying the characteristics of competition among the many are low-wage, low-skill industries where the levels of technological sophistication are minimal and capital investment requirements are small. Indeed the *comparatively* slow pace of technological advance in sawmill operations, apparel, and segments of the food products, textile, fabricated metal products, and leather industries suggests that technological progress is more rapid where the rigors of short-run competitive forces are not so relentless as to make firms unwilling and unable to bear the risks and costs of research and innovation.

Thus, upon closer examination competition among the many *can have* some side effects and long-term drawbacks that make the case for perfect competition and monopolistic competition weaker in actual practice than the theory seems to suggest. Basically, this is because it is tough for an industry to be technologically progressive, pay high wages to workers, and otherwise stay on the cutting edge when firms are thrown into a life-or-death competitive struggle, profits are minimal, risks are high, firms have less chance of long-term survival (owing either to competitive failure or death of the owner-entrepreneur), funds for capital investment are hard to come by, and little or no R & D efforts are undertaken.

Still, the two models of competition among the many do convincingly indicate the social value of a competitive market environment. *The case for more competition typically outweighs the case for less competition.*

PROBLEMS AND QUESTIONS FOR DISCUSSION

1. The Morgan Chair Company manufactures rocking chairs and sells them under conditions of monopolistic competition. The owner of the company has estimated its demand function as $P = 1625 - 6Q$, where P is in dollars and Q is in dozens of chairs sold per month. The company believes its monthly expenses vary with output according to the equation $TC = 25,000 + 25Q - 6Q^2 + \frac{1}{3}Q^3$.
   (a) Determine the firm's short-run profit-maximizing price and output rate.
   (b) How much profit will the firm earn at this price and output rate?
   (c) Suppose the Morgan Chair Company's total fixed costs rise by 10%. Calculate the impact upon the firm's price, output, and profits. How do you account for these results?

2. Using the unit cost and revenue curves, graphically illustrate the short-run profit-maximizing price and output for a monopolistically competitive firm which has a production function that exhibits constant returns to variable input over its entire range of output capability. (*Hint:* First determine the shape of the ATC and MC curves which correspond to a production function characterized by constant returns to variable input; then find the price and output at which $MR = MC$.) Indicate on your graph the area which represents the firm's total profits.

3. Using *TR-TC* analysis, graphically illustrate the short-run profit-maximizing output for a monopolistically competitive firm which is faced with a linear, downsloping demand curve and which has a production function displaying decreasing returns to variable input over its entire range of output capability. Then derive the corresponding total profit function for the firm.

4. Suppose that a firm operating under conditions of monopolistic competition is faced with a linear, downward-sloping demand curve and that its production function is of cubic form ($a + bX + cX^2 - dX^3$). Using the unit cost and revenue curves (AR, MR, ATC, AVC, and MC), graphically illustrate the price and output at which short-run profit will be maximized. Indicate on your graph the area which represents the firm's total profits.

5. In Chapter 5 it was shown that a linear, downsloping demand curve is half elastic and half inelastic; that is, the coefficient of price elasticity is greater than one along the top half of the demand curve and less than one along the bottom half. Is it possible for a monopolistically competitive firm which is confronted with a linear, downsloping demand curve to maximize short-run profits at a price and output corresponding to the inelastic portion of the demand curve? Why or why not?

6. Graphically illustrate a situation where the use of sales promotion activity by a monopolistically competitive firm results in a higher price and higher profits. The purpose of sales promotion expenditures is to shift the firm's demand-AR function to the right and, at the same time, to make it more steeply sloped (less elastic over the relevant price range). Assuming that a firm acheives this purpose, graphically illustrate the effect this has upon the shape and position of the firm's total revenue function.

7. **(a)** Under what conditions might a firm in a monopolistically competitive market be attracted to a strategy of striving to be the low-cost producer? What strengths do you see in such a competitive approach? What disadvantages might exist?

   (b) What are the pros and cons of employing a differentiation strategy in a monopolistically competitive market? Cite some of the different ways a firm can try to differentiate its product offering from those of its rivals.

   (c) What are the pros and cons of opting for a focus or specialization type of competitive strategy under conditions of monopolistic competition?

   (d) Explain why there is room for different firms to pursue different types of competitive strategies in a monopolistically competitive market.

Chapter 13

How Markets Function:
THE MANY MODELS OF OLIGOPOLY

In this chapter we shift the spotlight from "competition among the many" to "competition among the few." The distinctive feature of **oligopoly** is that a *few* (say 2 to as many as 10 or 15) highly visible, well-known firms supply the lion's share of demand. Far and away the most prominent examples of competition among the few are found in the corporate sector. A *few* very large corporate enterprises supply most of the market for aircraft, aluminum, automobiles, alcoholic beverages, appliances, cigarettes, computers, copying machines, copper, farm equipment, flat glass, certain food products, gasoline, locomotives and railroad cars, metal cans, network television, sewing machines, steam engines and turbines, steel, synthetic fibers, telephone equipment, tires, and typewriters.

However, competition among the few is not limited to the world of big business. It also arises in markets too small for more than a few firms to exist. For example, the small town with its two or three banks, auto repair shops, drycleaners, doctors, lawyers, accountants, and so on illustrates this situation. In manufacturing, a number of highly specialized tools, component parts, and novelty products have a total market demand (even nationwide) so limited that a few small firms can easily supply the entire output. The zone of demarcation between competition among the many and competition among the few, therefore, does not correspond exactly with the zone between big firms and small firms.

Nonetheless, because of the visibility and importance of "big business," the presentation of oligopoly will be oriented to capture the specific facets of competition among large corporations. Small firm-dominated markets exhibiting the characteristics of competition among the few will be given less attention, but it should be emphasized that many of the conclusions we draw about competition among a few large firms will apply to competition among a few small firms.[1]

---

[1] Recasting the traditional theory of oligopoly to focus on corporate enterprise has much to recommend it. Generalizing oligopoly theory to the point where it applies to both small, single-product firms and large, multiproduct enterprises forces one to exclude the rich industrial detail which supplies powerful understanding of the behavior of large corporations under conditions of corporate capitalism. Such an exclusion is a serious disadvantage when one is trying to explain the functioning of markets dominated by the presence of large corporations. It is very difficult to construct satisfactory models of business behavior which describe equally well the behavior of

We begin our examination of competition among the few with a survey of contemporary models of oligopoly behavior. The assumption that the firm's overriding goal is to maximize profits will be continued (however, we relax this assumption in Chapter 14).

THE CHARACTERISTICS OF OLIGOPOLISTIC MARKETS

Oligopoly is synonymous with competition among the few. Markets are said to be oligopolistic whenever a small number of firms supply the dominant share of an industry's total output. In oligopoly, firms are *large* relative to the size of the total market they serve, and in the case of giant corporations they are large not just relatively but absolutely as well.

The principal effect of fewness of firms is to give each firm such a prominent market position that its decisions and actions have significant repercussions on rival firms. What one firm does affects the others, often prompting them to react in some fashion. If one firm announces a price change, competitors take quick notice. If one firm brings out a new product or changes the attributes of its product offering or steps up its advertising, rival firms must consider whether and how to respond. As a result, competition is highly personalized, with each firm recognizing that its own best course of action depends on the strategies its rivals elect. This *mutual interdependence* among the actions and behavior of oligopolists extends to all facets of competition: price, sales volume, market share, product differentiation, promotional strategies, innovation, customer service, and so on.

Since rival firms may have numerous alternative courses of action, anticipating their actions and reactions introduces a new and exceedingly complex dimension to the firm's decision process. But trying to anticipate the competitive response of rival firms is an exercise no oligopolist can afford to neglect, for the probability is high that a change in one firm's competitive tactics will elicit prompt and ponted reactions from rival firms. The great uncertainty is *how* one's rivals will react. As we shall see shortly, the mutual interdependence and competitive interaction among firms is *the key feature* of oligopoly.

An oligopolistic market has several other characteristics. To begin with, rivalry among the few may involve either standardized or differentiated products. If the firms in an industry produce a standardized product, the industry is called a **pure oligopoly**. The most common examples of virtually uniform products marketed under conditions of oligopoly include steel, aluminum, lead, copper, cement, rayon, fuel oil, plywood, tin cans, newsprint, explosives, and industrial alcohol. If a few firms dominate the market for a differentiated product, the industry is called a **differentiated oligopoly**. The most visible differentiated oligopolies involve the production of automobiles, toothpaste, cereal, cig-

Economists use the term *oligopoly* to refer to competition among a comparatively small number of competitors.

The key feature of oligopolistic markets is that the actions of one firm have a direct impact upon the others.

In a pure oligopoly, the products of rival sellers are essentially identical; in a differentiated oligopoly, the products of rival sellers have distinctly different attributes, such that buyers may prefer one brand over another because of its favored attributes.

---

small proprietorships and the behavior of large managerial firms. After all, the behavior of a hardware store functioning as an oligopolistic firm in a small community differs in several important respects from Coca Cola's behavior in the oligopolistic soft drink market. Thus, while orienting the presentation of oligopoly theory to capture specific facets of competition among market giants may suffer slightly from a lack of generality, this weakness is more than offset by the extra insight into the economics of corporate capitalism. The approach here is also strong pedagogically because it allows for a strong focus on the application of oligopoly theory to readily visible firms and industries.

arettes, TV sets, electric razors, computers, farm implements, refrigerators, air conditioners, soft drinks, soap, and beer.

Entry into an ologiopolistic industry may be formidable, though by no means impossible. In industries where technology is complex, large machine units are used, and sales promotion requirements are substantial, the optimum scale of operation is large; minimum average costs occur at output rates so large that a firm has to be big to be competitive. Moreover, it is a hazardous undertaking for a relatively new or unknown firm to introduce a new product to try and compete directly against the brands of firms whose names are known to everyone. Often, entering such an industry entails so sizable a capital investment that small, newly formed organizations are not likely entrants. The most likely candidates for entry into large oligopolistic markets are well-established enterprises, which have the financial and organizational resources that it takes to become a successful competitor. This is not, however, an especially common occurrence in *mature* or slow-growth markets because the added production of another efficient-sized firm can increase supply enough to drive price below average cost for all firms, thereby making the profit prospects for new entrants rather dim. But in *young* or *rapidly growing* oligopolies the entry of new firms is fairly commonplace because demand is expanding fast enough to accommodate more sellers.

Oligopolists, especially those producing differentiated products, rely upon differences in price, quality, reliability, service, design, product performance, customized features, promotional outlays, and overall image to promote more sales and increase profits. Everything that was said in Chapter 11 about the role of product differentiation and brand promotion applies on an even grander scale among corporate oligopolists. The dimensions of competition under oligopoly are limited only by the imagination of the firms themselves.

> **Entry barriers into an oligopolistic market are typically rather high, though by no means as high as in monopoly.**

WHY THERE ARE MANY MODELS OF OLIGOPOLY BEHAVIOR

> **There are many models of oligopoly behavior, not just one, as was the case for the other three market models.**

In an oligopolistic market structure, there is no nice, neat, clear-cut equilibrium position toward which all firms tend to move—such as we found in perfect competition and monopolistic competition. Two reasons account for this. One, in oligopoly a wide variety of materially different competitive circumstances can and do exist, no one of which is demonstrably more typical than others. Two, even in a given competitive situation, several different and entirely reasonable courses of action may be open to firms in selecting a competitive strategy. Just what firms will decide to do and how their rivals will react may vary from case to case. As a consequence, oligopoly theory consists of many models, each depicting certain facets of oligopolistic conduct and performance but none telling a complete story of competition among the few. Our survey of oligopoly will thus consist of a series of models, each portraying a different set of behavior patterns, traits of firms, and competitive conditions. Taken together, they convey a reasonably accurate picture of oligopolistic competition.

THE KINKED DEMAND CURVE MODEL

One of the key questions which an oligopolistic firm must consider is how will rival firms respond if we decide to alter our selling price? One answer to this

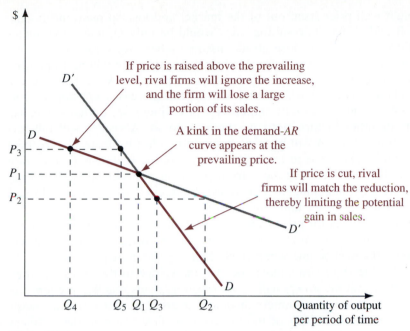

Figure 13-1
The kinked demand curve

question is contained in the **kinked demand curve model** of oligopoly behavior.[2]

    Suppose that three large firms, A, B, and C, are selling their own versions of an essentially identical product, with each firm having about one-third of the total market. Suppose, too, that the firms are selling at a common price of P_1 dollars and that at this price Corporation A's sales volume is Q_1 units, as shown in Figure 13-1. What will happen now if A independently lowers its selling price to P_2 dollars? One possibility is for B and C to ignore A's lower price, in which case A can expect sharply increasing sales, say to Q_2 units, because by underselling firms B and C it will attract many customers away from its higher-priced rivals. A second possibility is for the two rival firms to match A's price cut to prevent A from gaining sales, market share, and profits at their expense. Such a retaliatory move will tend to have the effect of limiting A's gain in sales to its customary share of the increased business which all three firms will tend to realize because of selling at a lower price. In terms of Figure 13-1, matching price cuts by B and C will hold A's sales down to Q_3 units instead of Q_2 units. Thus, A's demand-*AR* curve for lower prices assumes a position along the path of the solid line extending down from point P_1Q_1 when rivals match the price cut but is positioned along the path of the dashed line when rivals ignore the price cut.

    Now, what if A should decide to raise its selling price above P_1 dollars, say to P_3 dollars? Assuming B and C again elect to ignore A's price change, then A would find itself in the lonely position of being the high-priced seller.

In an oligopolistic market a firm's demand curve is kinked at the prevailing price if rivals are strongly inclined to match price cuts and ignore price increases.

[2] The kinked demand curve model was first advanced by Paul Sweezy in 1939. For a more extensive discussion of this model, see his article "Demand under Conditions of Oligopoly," *Journal of Political Economy,* Vol. 47 (August 1939), pp. 568–738. For an evaluation of the model, see George J. Stigler, "The Kinky Oligopoly Demand Curve and Rigid Prices," *Journal of Political Economy,* Vol. 55 (October 1947), pp. 432–49.

Firm A might well price itself out of the market and lose so many of its customers to B and C that its resulting sales would be only Q_4 units; the higher price would not cause A to lose all its customers because some buyers may have strong enough preferences for A's brand that they are willing to pay the higher price. Since B and C stand to gain sales and profits at A's expense, there is a strong chance that they will not follow A's price increase to P_3 dollars. But if they should decide to exactly match A's price increase, perhaps because rising costs or other factors motivate them to do so, A's sales will fall less drastically. Why? Firm A will be at no competitive disadvantage with respect to price, and its sales loss is restricted to its share of the decline in marketwide sales which all three firms will incur from selling at a higher price. Referring again to Figure 13-1, matching price increases by B and C will result in a loss of sales for A from Q_1 to Q_5 units instead of from Q_1 to Q_4 units. Thus, A's expected sales volumes for prices above P_1 will tend to follow the path of the solid line extending up from P_1Q_1 when rivals ignore price increases and will tend to follow the dashed line when rivals follow price increases.

Unless the three firms have specific knowledge to the contrary, they can each expect that *price cuts will be matched* as rivals react to prevent the price-cutter from gaining customers at their expense but that *price increases will be ignored*, because rivals of the price-raising firm will gain the business lost by the price booster. This means that each firm will have a kinked demand curve for its product like the solid line (*DD*) in Figure 13-1, with the kink occurring at the prevailing price. The competitive situation among the firms is therefore such that an *independent* price increase will cause a drastic decline in a firm's sales volume, while a price cut will result in only modest sales gains. In more technical language, the demand curve for each oligopolist tends to be highly elastic above the ruling price and much less elastic or even inelastic below the going price.

Three important predictions about the price and output strategies of oligopolists can be made when competing firms believe they are confronted with a kinked demand curve:

If competing firms believe price cuts will be matched and price increases will be ignored, they will refrain from *independently* raising or lowering their prices; moreover, they will be driven by competition to charge the same or nearly the same prices for their products.

1. Oligopolistic firms will refrain from *independently* raising price above the going rate for fear that charging a price higher than rivals will cause a substantial decline in sales, profits, and market share.

2. Competing oligopolists will generally refrain from *independently* cutting price below the going level since rivals can be expected to match the price cut promptly, thus wiping out most of the potential the price-cutter would otherwise have for increasing sales, profits, and market share. There are two exceptions to the general rule of no price cutting under conditions of a kinked demand curve. First, when rival firms have unequal costs, the low-cost producer may seek to cut price to exploit the cost advantage that it enjoys. Second, if market demand is depressed below normal levels, as it often is in recessions, firms may secretly cut prices to try and attract buyers who are trading with rival firms. To stave off retaliatory price reductions by competitors, the price cutting will be both secret and selective. Such price cutting generally takes the form of secret departures from list or announced price schedules.

3. Competition forces rival oligopolists to charge the same or nearly the same prices for their products since the ease with which consumers can switch from one brand to another results in patronage flocking to the low-priced sellers. Firms simply cannot expect to survive by selling essentially the same product at significantly higher prices than rivals. The chief exception to this fundamental principle of competition is where firms have been so successful in differentiating their products and creating strong brand loyalties that their customers are willing to pay higher prices to obtain a "quality" product.

All three predictions are generally consistent with observed behavior in both pure and differentiated oligopolies. Studies have shown that the prices charged by rival sellers tend to be *identical* whenever products are standardized or else weakly differentiated—as in steel, aluminum, cement, newsprint, explosives, cast iron pipe, plywood, bread, and cigarettes.[3] Where products are strongly differentiated, oligopolists tend to charge prices which are *comparable* (tires, automobiles, household appliances, computers, TV sets). Moreover, executives report a strong conviction that price cuts *will* be matched.

Nevertheless, the model has some serious faults. An important limitation of the kinked demand curve model is its inability to explain how oligopolists initially arrive at the prevailing prices. The model is much better at explaining why price persists at the kink than how it reached that level or why and how it might change.

Second, the assumptions that price cuts will be matched and price increases ignored do not always hold. When a firm lowers its price, competitors need not interpret this to mean that the price-cutter is trying to steal the market. Rivals may take a price reduction to mean that the item has some fault and is not selling well, the item is about to be superseded by a later model, the company is in financial trouble and is trying to improve its sales, or that the company is hoping the whole industry will reduce its prices in the interests of stimulating total demand. Competitors may react differently depending on whether they view the price cut as temporary or permanent. Each rival firm's reaction will be based upon what it *thinks* is motivating the company's price cut, and there is ample room for different firms to react differently.

Finally, when rival firms experience similar shifts in cost or demand conditions, the incentive to change price may be generally recognized and mutually advantageous to all concenred. Indeed, when the incentives for a price hike appear generally throughout the industry, the main problem becomes who will be bold enough to raise price first and wise enough to figure out what size price increase will be competitively acceptable. The tendency to ignore price increases also falls by the wayside in inflationary times when, after prices have been rising along a wide front for some time, consumers become resigned (however, grudgingly) to higher prices, and firms, both independently and as a group, find it easier to initiate price hikes.

MODELS OF MARKET SHARE RIVALRY

Another approach to price-output determination in oligopoly is based upon the competitive patterns emerging from variations in the market shares and costs of rival firms.

---

[3] Actual examples may be found in Harold M. Fleming, *Gasoline Prices and Competition* (New York: Appleton-Century-Crofts, 1966), Chapter 5; R. B. Tennant, "The Cigarette Industry," in *The Structure of American Industry,* 3rd ed., Walter Adams, ed. (New York: Macmillan, 1961), pp. 370–72; the records of the Salk vaccine case (*U.S.* v. *Eli Lilly et al.*) and the tetracycline case (*F.T.C.* v. *American Cyanamid et al.*); and A. D. H. Kaplan, J. B. Dirlam, and R. F. Lanzilotti, *Pricing in Big Business* (Washington, D.C.: The Brookings Institution, 1958), p. 174.

EQUAL MARKET SHARES AND EQUAL COSTS

Consider an industry comprised of only two firms, A and B, selling identical products, having exactly the same production costs, and dividing the market on a 50–50 basis. These conditions mean that the two firms will have identical demand-*AR, MR, ATC,* and *MC* curves, as shown in Figure 13-2. With each firm having one-half the industry demand, the demand-*AR* curves of the two firms are located on top of one another, halfway between the vertical axis and the industrywide demand curve at each price. Since profits are maximum at the price and output rate where *MR = MC,* both A and B will be motivated to charge the same price ($P_{A,B}$) and to produce at the same output rate ($Q_{A,B}$). Each firm will earn a short-run economic profit equal to the shaded area in Figure 13-3. The significant point here is that no pricing conflict exists between the two firms because they maximize profits at the same price.

Each firm can be confident that its preferred price-output strategy will be "satisfactory" to its rival rather than provoking some sort of aggressive competitive activity. Why? Because if one firm initiates a price cut to try to gain increased sales, profits, and market share at the expense of the other, then it is merely inviting a costly price war. The other firm will have little option but to retaliate with price cuts of its own to keep from losing customers and absorbing the high costs of idle production capacity. Price cutting will mean both firms receive less for their product. And, if industry demand is price inelastic, then lower prices mean lower revenues will accompany the increased sales, and, clearly, the profits of both firms will drop. This accounts for why oligopolistic firms selling identical or weakly differentiated products are not usually excited by the prospect of price competition and, indeed, shy away from using price cuts as a competitive weapon.

EQUAL MARKET SHARES AND DIFFERENT COSTS

Suppose, however, that we introduce a cost differential between the two firms, other factors remaining unchanged. Specifically, suppose firm B has a higher *MC* curve, as indicated in Figure 13-3. Firm B's higher costs might

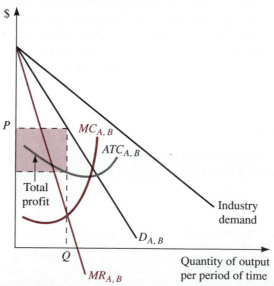

Figure 13-2

Competitive outcome for two firms with equal market shares and equal costs

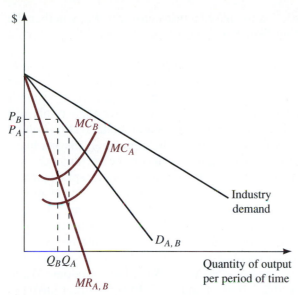

Figure 13-3
Competitive outcome for two firms with equal market shares and different costs

reflect older, technologically inferior production facilities, higher raw material costs, higher labor costs, higher shipping costs due to an unfavorable geographic location, or managerial inefficiency. Examination of Figure 13-3 indicates that firm A's profit-maximizing price and output are P_A and Q_A, whereas firm B will prefer P_B and Q_B.

A pricing conflict is immediately apparent. Each firm is worse off, profitwise, at its rival's favored price than at its own, and therefore each will prefer to see its own profit-maximizing established on an industrywide basis. As long as the two firms continue to sell identical products, buyers are not likely to be as willing to buy from B, the higher-priced firm; patronage will flow quickly to the lower-priced seller. Competitive forces thus will soon drive the two firms to sell at the same price. But what price?

One obvious method by which the two firms may resolve their pricing difference is collusion. Collusive behavior is subject to some serious limitations, not the least of which is that it is generally illegal under U.S. antitrust laws. But collusion can occur and is discussed in detail in a later section of this chapter. For present purposes it is sufficient to point out that collusive agreements among firms are subject to severe risks and for a variety reasons tend to be unstable.

A second alternative is for firm A, which prefers the lower price, to try to force its preferred price upon B. Firm A is in a strong position to impose its price preference on B because of its cost advantage and because buyers flock to the low-priced seller. However, firm B is not entirely powerless. Should B's profits be unacceptable if it is forced to sell at A's lower price, then B may seek to intimidate A into a more "reasonable" price by slashing price below P_A and deliberately provoking a mutually unprofitable price war. This may indeed be a very viable option if firm B is a large diversified corporation, since any losses sustained by B from temporarily selling this product at a low price can be offset by profits from the sale of its other products. On the other hand, if firm A is also large or diversified or has ample financial resources, then it may be in as good or better position to weather a price war. So we cannot say for sure whether

PRINCIPLE
When competing oligopolists have equal market shares and different costs, their respective profit-maximizing prices do not coincide and a pricing conflict exists.

How the pricing conflict will be resolved varies with the circumstances.

firm B will be able to "persuade" A to charge a price closer to P_B, whether the reverse will be true, or whether firm B will be forced to meet A's preferred price.

Only one thing is certain: *Whenever rival firms are selling essentially identical products, competitive forces will sooner or later drive them to sell at the same price.* Until this occurs, even a temporary "price equilibrium" cannot exist, simply because firms attempting to sell at prices above their rivals will face erosion of their sales, profits, and market shares and, conceivably, will be driven out of the market entirely over the long term. In general, then, a high-cost firm has the following options for bringing about a price accommodation: (1) initiating some form of collusive action to raise price to an acceptable level, (2) threatening or actually initiating a price war so as to coerce lower-priced firms into adopting a compromise price somewhere in between the high and low end of the range, (3) revamping its production techniques to bring costs into line with (or even lower than) those of rival firms, (4) shifting into the production of other related items where expected profits are higher, and (5) doing the best it can at the price chosen by the low-cost firms.[4] Very likely options (3) and (5) will prove to be the most viable, short of shifting into some other business (option 4).

Analogous pricing conflicts arise where firms selling differentiated products have cost differences and thus different profit-maximizing prices. However, *the competitive imperative to sell at the same price is not so intense if the products are sufficiently differentiated that buyers can be persuaded to accept modest price differences.* Higher-cost firms preferring to sell at higher prices may be able to compete by successfully using the "ours is better than theirs" theme in promoting their products or by designing more "quality" into their products. To the extent such efforts win over enough buyers, firms are not so strongly compelled by competition to charge a uniform price and may be able to sell at their respective profit-maximizing prices. But if product differentiation results in sizable cost differences between firms and thereby drives a large wedge between their profit-maximizing prices, then a pricing conflict emerges, and competition will prod firms into reaching a more uniform price structure.

DIFFERENT MARKET SHARES AND EQUAL COSTS

Next, consider the case where firms have identical costs but different market shares. All three panels of Figure 13-4 illustrate demand situations where firm A has 60% of the total market at each price and firm B has the remaining 40% of the market. Here, the nature of the pricing conflict varies with the shape of the marginal cost function confronting the two firms. In Figure 13-4(a) the products of the firms are produced under conditions of identically rising marginal costs. Firm A maximizes its profits by producing where $MC_{A,B} = MR_A$; accordingly, A's preferred price is P_A, and its preferred output

---

[4] Going out of business and dissolving the firm, while possible, is not a probable alternative—unless it is driven into bankruptcy by its inability to compete. The closing down of a large corporation is a rare event—much more so than in the case of small owner-managed companies. A large corporation normally responds to market adversity and unprofitable products by either withdrawing from the unprofitable market and redeploying its energies and resources into endeavors with higher expected profits or else undertaking a major overhaul of its production and marketing organization, which it believes will increase efficiency, reduce costs, and improve its long-term ability to compete successfully.

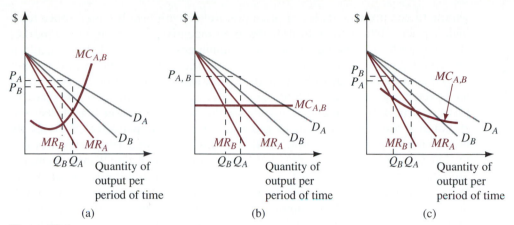

Figure 13-4

Competitive outcome for two firms with different market shares and equal costs

rate is Q_A units. Firm B's profit-maximizing price and output are P_B and Q_B, respectively. A clash of pricing preferences is apparent, with the firm with the *larger* market share preferring the *higher* price. Other things being equal, this result holds not just for a 60–40 market split but also for any uneven market share split—65–35, 80–20, 55–45, or whatever. It turns out that the more divergent the market shares of the two firms, the greater is the gap between their respective profit-maximizing prices. In this situation, whether the large-share firm will accede to the price preference of the small-share firm, whether the reverse will be true, or whether some compromise price will evolve is open to question. It all depends. The firm with the larger market share may try to intimidate the firm with the smaller share and coerce it into accepting a price close to the higher of the profit-maximizing prices. On the other hand, if the small-share firm is in a position to withstand pressure from the large-share firm, then it holds the upper hand, and price equilibrium is likely to be attained near the lower of the two profit-maximizing prices.

In Figure 13-4(b) both firms produce under conditions of identical and constant marginal costs over the relevant output range. In this instance, firm A will maximize profits by producing Q_A units, and firm B will maximize profits by producing Q_B units. However, the profit-maximizing prices of the firms coincide at $P_{A,B}$. Such a result is not circumstantial but rather is an inherent geometrical trait of linear demand curves with a common vertical intercept. And it holds for a market share split of any combination. Therefore, when oligopolists have identical and constant marginal costs, no conflict over price arises, irrespective of the firms' market shares. Given that (1) cost studies of manufacturing enterprises have shown a fairly widespread tendency for *MC* to be constant up to 85 to 90% of capacity [refer back to Figure 8-5(b)], (2) constant returns to scale may prevail as output expands over the long run [see Figure 8-8(c)], and (3) competition forces rival firms to remain cost-competitive, the lack of a sizable differential among the respective profit-maximizing prices of rival firms as shown in Figure 13-4(b) may not be uncommon.

Figure 13-4(c) shows declining marginal cost prevailing for both firms over the relevant output range. Here, firm A prefers a lower price (P_A) than firm B prefers (P_B). The firm with the larger market share prefers the lower price because of the lower marginal costs associated with higher outputs. The production economies stemming from larger outputs will likely make firm A less

PRINCIPLE
When rival oligopolists have different market shares and identically rising marginal costs, the firm with the biggest market share prefers the highest price.

PRINCIPLE
When rival oligopolists have different market shares and produce under conditions of identical and constant marginal costs, their profit-maximizing prices coincide and no pricing conflict exists.

PRINCIPLE
When rival oligopolists have different market shares and identically declining marginal costs, the firm with the biggest market share prefers the lowest price.

willing to compromise its lower price preference with firm B's preference for a higher price. However, both firms have an incentive to capture larger market shares in order to take advantage of declining costs. This is likely to result in persistent downward pressure on price, and the firm with the largest market share has the advantage of being in the best position to lower prices because of its lower marginal costs. While the antitrust laws will undoubtedly serve to restrain firm A from being so aggressive that antitrust action is invoked, the situation is ripe for one firm to grow larger at the expense of its rivals by initiating bold price cuts. Confronted with this threat, underdog firms may opt to defend or improve their position by making major product improvements (quality, service, convenience, etc.) in an attempt to divert buyers' attention away from price. Their major hope lies not in imitation but in achieving a differential advantage based upon a better product (Zenith's "the quality goes in before the name goes on"), or unconventional distribution outlets (Timex), or stronger appeal to special classes of buyers (Volkswagen), or a superior promotional campaign (Avis's "We're No. 2, We Try Harder"), or personal selling (Avon), or the like.

DIFFERENT MARKET SHARES AND DIFFERENT COSTS

Normally, product differentiation and varying degrees of product acceptance combine to give firms different market shares. At the same time, production technologies of differing vintage and efficiency and slight variations in wage rates, transportation costs, and raw material prices owing to geographic factors make it likely that corporate rivals will not have *identical* cost structures—though competition will force costs to be *comparable* from firm to firm. When both market shares and unit production costs are variable among rival firms, a wide range of outcomes exist. The small-share firms may have a lower profit-maximizing price, or it may be the large-share firms that have the lower profit-maximizing price. The variation in the preferred prices of rival firms may be wide or narrow. Conceivably, differences in market shares and costs will cancel out, and no material pricing conflict will emerge.

PRINCIPLE
When rival oligopolists have different market shares and different costs, their profit-maximizing prices diverge—perhaps a little or a lot; nonetheless, market forces compel them to charge a "competitive price."

Yet, if price preferences do differ, some means will have to be found to decide what the going price (or band of prices) will be.[5] The ease with which buyers can switch to the lower-priced brands guarantees that this will be so. The existence of a pricing conflict occasionally surfaces in the form of short-term price wars, the uncovering of price-fixing arrangements, and competitive behavior with a cutthroat or predatory intent. More usually, pricing conflicts remain latent and are gradually resolved via intermediate- and long-term adjustments on the part of firms, including cost reduction schemes, plant relocations, technological innovation, increased attempts to achieve product differentiation, improved product design and performance, aggressive advertising and sales promotion tactics, and other forms of nonprice competition. Experience has shown that such adjustments are safer and more reliable forms of conflict

---

[5] An experiment conducted by J. W. Friedman revealed a tendency for price equilibrium to be reached more than 75% of the time. Despite the opportunity to cheat once equilibrium agreements were reached, the agreed-to price was honored in nine out of ten cases. However, Freidman found that a price equilibrium was reached somewhat less often under conditions of different market shares and production costs as opposed to equal market shares and costs. For further details, see "An Experimental Study of Cooperative Duopoly," *Econometrica*, Vol. 35, No. 3–4 (July–October 1967), pp. 379–97.

resolution than mutually unprofitable price wars and collusive arrangements. In the meantime, firms that are at a competitive price disadvantage will suffer lower profits or even incur losses.

The major conclusion to be drawn from the market share models of competitive behavior is that, despite the difficulties involved, some attempt at reaching a mutually acceptable price structure *must* and *will* be made by firms in oligopolistic competition. In either the short or the long run, *oligopolists have no realistic alternative to charging identical or comparable prices for their products, irrespective of market share and cost differences. Mutual interdependence and personalized rivalry quickly teach oligopolists that no firm can price blindly without regard for the prices charged by its rivals.* Thus, while competing firms may well decide to experiment with charging different prices, the responses of buyers to the prevailing price pattern will exert a natural and powerful force for a uniform price structure to emerge. Daily experience in the marketplace gives each firm a "feel" for what price it can charge and still compete, thereby making either formal or tacit agreements among firms quite superfluous as a mechanism for reaching an accommodation on the going price structure. Consequently, it is hard to tell from simple observation whether uniform pricing among rival corporations is indicative of competition or conspiracy.

Attempts at resolving differences in the preferred prices of oligopolistic rivals can entail any of several forms and results.[6] From an industrywide standpoint, the most attractive price compromise is ***joint profit maximization***, whereby firms cooperate (explicitly or implicitly) to arrive at a price (or range of prices) that is perceived to yield the largest possible *collective* profit. But while joint profit maximization may mean that all firms as a group are better off, some firms may feel they are giving up more than they are gaining; in fact, some firms may not fare well at all at the joint profit-maximizing price (because of cost or market share differences). In this case, attempts at joint profit maximization tend to break down because disadvantaged firms have a strong incentive to act independently on their own behalf.

Another basic approach is ***independent profit maximization***, where one firm (or a small group of firms) is sufficiently powerful and influential to impose its own profit-maximizing price upon rival firms. There are, of course, any number of forms of intermediate or ***hybrid profit maximization***, wherein via the market process a trial-and-error compromise is reached between pricing together for maximum joint profits and pricing independently for maximum individual profits. Although more disorganized and less purposeful than the previous two forms of price coordination, hybrid profit maximization may involve ***conscious parallelism***, where competing firms, without any communication back and forth whatsoever, come to the realization that aggressive actions (such as price cutting) invite retaliation and, in the end, leave all firms worse off; thus, they adopt common prices and policies implicitly and in concert, with the conviction that their mutual independence makes it beneficial for like businesses to be run in like fashion.

The competitive imperative for oligopolists to reach some kind of price compromise can lead to any of several outcomes— joint profit maximization, independent profit maximization, hybrid profit maximization, conscious parallelism, or formula pricing.

---

[6] For one fascinating version of how uniform prices can be attained without collusion or communication between the firms, see Thomas C. Schelling, *The Strategy of Conflict* (Cambridge, Mass.: Harvard University Press, 1960), Chapters 2 and 3. Schelling develops a theory of focal points in which it is contended that a tendency exists for choices among alternatives to converge on some prominent value intuitively perceived by those concerned. The focal point owes its prominence to precedent, analogy, an obvious split-the-difference situation, habit, institutional idiosyncrasies, educated guess, or the like.

Finally, price coordination efforts may lead to **formula pricing**, whereby firms, by custom or agreement, adhere to the same rule-of-thumb procedure of adding a "fair" profit margin to "normal" average total costs to reach a common price. All these price-coordinating procedures are observable in actual situations, but none seems to stand out as *the* predominant form of reconciling price differences among competing oligopolists.

COOPERATIVE VERSUS NONCOOPERATIVE COMPETITIVE STRATEGIES

A further insight into the nature of oligopoly can be gained by more formally considering cooperative and noncooperative (or competitive) oligopoly behavior. It is clear from the preceding discussion of market share rivalry that, to some extent, the fortunes of firms in oligopoly markets are tied together. Decision makers in oligopolistic firms face two basic choices: They can choose to coordinate their actions by imitating each other's prices and competitive approaches (engaging in conscious parallelism for mutual benefit) or pursue a completely independent strategy that seeks to maximize the position of their own firm. If cooperation and conscious parallelism are chosen, then the firms will seek to avoid direct conflict with rivals, particularly with respect to price and output. But if the independent maximizing strategy is selected, the firms are more likely to find themselves in an aggressive competitive environment in which sellers are in direct conflict over price and market shares. Models of oligopoly can thus be based upon cooperation among competing firms or noncooperation, and it makes considerable difference which type of behavior emerges in the marketplace. The choices that lead to a particular type of competitive environment are not permanent, and real-world oligopoly markets can change, sometimes very quickly, from a situation in which firms ostensibly cooperate by avoiding aggressive competition to independent maximizing behavior that results in direct price competition. The choice between cooperation and noncooperation can result in a range of possible outcomes. Two extreme possibilities include overt collusion and oligopoly warfare. It is possible for a group of cooperating oligopoly firms to mimic each other's prices, product promotion policies, and other dimensions of business rivalry so that together they approximate the monopoly solution described in Chapter 11. When two or more firms consciously engage in parallel behavior, the resulting set of prices and outputs leads to a joint monopoly solution. In contrast, a noncooperative oligopoly market results in an independent maximizing solution, which at the extreme can involve oligopoly price wars. In the long run, oligopoly markets which use price as an aggressive element of market strategy can approximate the competitive solution described in Chapter 10. But by the nature of an oligopoly market, intermediate solutions that are in between the extremes given by the perfectly competitive and pure monopoly models are also possible.

This section considers several models concerning cooperative and non-cooperative behavior among rival oligopolists. The most extreme form of oligopoly cooperation is illustrated by the cartel model, in which firms formally agree to restrict competition. The cartel model highlights two conflicting incentives in oligopoly markets. Firms can gain from restricting competition and sharing the market, but all cartels contain powerful incentives that cause firms to pursue independent maximizing strategies that can lead to a breakdown of the cartel. We also consider a less formal method of cooperating in which firms

Over time, the competitive outcome in oligopoly markets often swings either toward intense competition (noncooperative strategic behavior) or conscious parallelism (cooperative strategic behavior).

stop short of a formal cartel but abide by an implicit agreement not to compete. The final model considered in this section is game theory, which involves strategic choices concerning cooperation and noncooperation in an oligopoly market.

THE CARTEL MODEL

A *cartel* is a formal organization of sellers (or buyers) that seeks to restrict competition on a continuing basis. A cartel involves explicit collusion among sellers, and the agreement can take the form of price fixing, schemes to divide up the market, output quotas, or similar acts that have the effect of minimizing competition among the firms. Each member of a cartel expects to benefit from the market restrictions by earning profits in excess of the level that would prevail in the absence of a cartel agreement. The maximum possible profits that can accrue as a result of a cartel is the amount that would prevail under pure monopoly conditions, as discussed in Chapter 11. But unlike a monopoly, a cartel contains two or more firms, and they must reach agreement on how the cartel will operate.

The nature and consequences of a cartel can be explained most easily by adopting several simplifying assumptions that highlight the consequences of

> **The purpose of forming a cartel is to restrict competition and create market conditions where members of the cartel can earn monopoly profits.**

APPLICATIONS CAPSULE

OLIGOPOLY WARFARE IN THE SNACK FOOD INDUSTRY

American consumers spend a lot of money on snack foods including such products as potato chips, corn chips, salted nuts and popcorn. The single largest seller in this robustly growing market is Frito-Lay, an operating unit of PepsiCo Inc., which has a 40 percent market share. For a number of years there were minor outbreaks of oligopoly warfare between national distributors such as Frito-Lay and Bordens (maker of Wise potato chips and other snacks) and their smaller regional rivals with no presence in all geographical markets. But in the 1990s major warfare erupted involving highly aggressive pricing and promotion activities. Prices have been discounted, advertising has been increased, and a new practice of paying supermarkets for shelf space has emerged. In some extremely competitive regional markets retailers are demanding and receiving yearly payments of up to $1000 per foot for shelf and display space. The new competition is intense and has taken a toll on most firms in the industry that is reflected in lower profits and higher selling costs. Some of the smaller, regional firms have responded by pulling out of certain supermarkets and local market areas.

In the market niche involving popcorn, the competition has involved an important new product, microwave popcorn, which can be quickly and easily prepared with minimum clean-up. In the first few years after the product appeared, five firms emerged to vigorously and aggressively compete for customer allegiance and the dominant position in the market. In the interim 10 years popcorn has become a $2 billion industry and microwave popcorn is the growth segment of the market. The popcorn wars, like the oligopoly warfare in the more general snack food market, have been characterized

by aggressive pricing and product promotion policies. But no single firm has emerged as the dominant market leader.

Highly aggressive oligopoly pricing might be expected when a successful new product is developed; and, in essence, the new market is up for grabs. But what accounts for the outbreak of oligopoly warfare in the snack food industry as a whole? Two factors seem to be at work. First, a new entrant, Eagle Brand Snacks, a division of Anheuser-Busch Cos., became a national competitor in the early 1980s and has aggressively expanded its product line and market share through cutrate pricing tactics. Eagle's success led to retaliation by established firms including the industry leader Frito-Lay. Second, the recession of 1991-92 has led to vigorous pricing and product promotion tactics in the industry. The two effects combined led to a recognition that all firms could be made better-off *if prices were not discounted so heavily*. But as one industry observer commented, "They let out the genie to capture market share, then say, 'Thank you,' now get back in the bottle."[1] But once oligopoly warfare breaks out, it tends to take on a life of its own—it is difficult to put the genie back in the bottle.

[1] Quoted in Laurie M. Grossman's article in *The Wall Street Journal,* "Price Wars Bring Flavor to Once-Quiet Snack Food Market," *The Wall Street Journal,* May 23, 1991.

Source: This application is based in part on stories appearing in the *The Wall Street Journal* and *New York Times.* See Laurie M. Grossman, "Price Wars Bring Flavor to Once-Quiet Snack Food Market," *The Wall Street Journal,* May 23, 1991, p. B1 and "Microwave Key to Popcorn War," *New York Times,* June 22, 1987, pp. D1 and D5.

a successful cartel and identify some of the problems inherent in all collusive restrictions on competitive behavior. As in the foregoing discussion of oligopoly rivalry, assume there are only two firms in the market, A and B, that market demand is steady and easy to predict from one time period to the next, and that the market demand curve is linear. Next, assume that firms A and B produce identical products, in which case the market demand for the product is also the cartel's joint or combined demand. Two assumptions need to be made concerning production functions and costs. First, each firm has the same production function and faces the same input costs, with the result that both their short- and long-run cost curves are identical. Finally, the production function is characterized by constant returns to scale. This assumption further simplifies the model by making the long-run average and long-run marginal cost functions constant.

Figure 13-5 shows a two-firm cartel and its potential profits under the aforementioned simplifying assumptions. Each firm's long-run costs are given by $LRAC_A$ and $LRAC_B$, and total market demand is denoted as D_T. If the firms compete vigorously on the basis of price, then the lowest possible equilibrium price that could prevail in the long run is P_c, which is the competitive price discussed in Chapter 10. Total output of the two firms would be OQ_c. Like competitive firms in long-run equilibrium, at a price of P_c and output of OQ_c firms A and B earn zero economic profits. On the other hand, if firms A and B form a cartel and restrict output so as to maximize joint profits, then total output would only be OQ_m, since this is the output where the firms' marginal revenue (MR_T) equals their marginal costs ($LRMC_A = LRMC_B$). The optimal cartel price (or monopoly price) is thus P_m—which is the highest price the two-

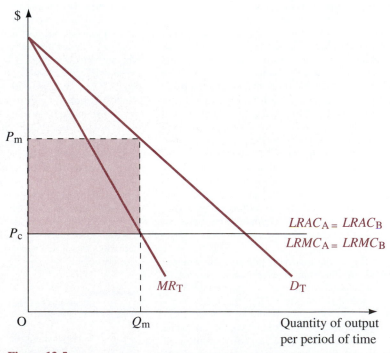

Figure 13-5

Potential cartel profits when two firms, A and B, have equal long-run average and marginal costs

firm cartel can charge for output OQ_m. The cartel's monopoly profit is equal to the shaded rectangle. To obtain the maximum profits, the firms must successfully coordinate their behavior so that jointly they produce the monopoly output. If for some reason the sellers produce a combined output that exceeds the monopoly output, then the monopoly price cannot be sustained and profits will necessarily be less than the maximum possible joint profits. Thus, if the combined output is greater than OQ_m, the price must be below P_m and the resulting profit will fall short of the maximum, represented by the shaded rectangle in Figure 13-5.

Regardless of whether the firms operate under the aforementioned simplified conditions, all cartels face two general classes of problems, which must be solved if the cartel is to be successful. One set of problems is internal and involves several distinct but related difficulties. These include negotiating and reaching agreement on the division of the market among the members of the cartel, monitoring the agreement, and enforcing compliance. The second set of problems are external and relate to competition from firms and products outside the cartel. Both classes of problems are important and warrant further attention.

In organizing a cartel, firms necessarily incur transaction costs in negotiating an agreement and ensuring that all parties adhere to its terms. Reaching market-sharing and price-fixing agreements may be particularly difficult in market environments where cartels are illegal. For example, in the United States, formal market-sharing agreements are generally held to be conspiracies in restraint of trade, which are illegal under the Sherman Antitrust Act of 1890. But in many real-world market situations the potential profits flowing from a successful cartel provide sufficient incentive for sellers to join a collusion even when such behavior is illegal on its face.[7] In Figure 13-5 a mutually beneficial division of the monopoly profits is clearly possible; by participating in a successful cartel each firm can be made better off. Thus, the internal cartel problem of arriving at an agreement to restrict competition and share the market is solvable in many market situations even though such market conduct is illegal.[8]

Oligopoly firms may not find it overly difficult to reach a market-sharing agreement that has the potential for benefitting all firms. But enforcing the restrictive agreement is likely to be much more difficult. Incentives to renege and cheat are inherent in all cartel agreements. For a cartel to succeed, the member firms must be able to detect and deter cheating. Figure 13-6 can be used to illustrate the nature of the cheating problem. Suppose the agreement calls for firms A and B to share equally the output and profits. An equal shares

---

[7] An example may be helpful in explaining how unlawful behavior can be rational. Maximum vehicle speed on highways is established by federal law. Nevertheless, speed limits are routinely violated. Some of the violations are unintentional, but much of the speeding is deliberate and designed to economize on the time it takes to travel from one place to another. Of course, people rationally slow down if the cost of speeding is perceived to be high. Dangerous road conditions and the presence of law enforcement officers who are busily issuing traffic violations both raise the expected costs of speeding and lead to fewer violations of the law. But as soon as driving conditions and the presence of law enforcement officers return to normal, the number of speeders immediately increases. The logic of this behavior is that even though it is illegal, there are expected benefits from exceeding the speed limit. For a discussion of violating versus obeying the speed limit law and how fines can be used to deter speeding, see P. E. Graves, D. R. Lee, and R. L. Sexton, "Statutes versus Enforcement: The Case of the Optimal Speed Limit," *American Economic Review,* Vol. 79, No. 4, pp. 932–36.

[8] D. K. Osborn emphasizes the importance of this point. See his article "Cartel Problems," *American Economic Review,* 66, No. 5 (December 1976), pp. 834–35. In Osborn's model of cartels, the major problem is not the difficulty of reaching agreement. Rather it is in inducing the firms to comply with the agreement once it has been reached.

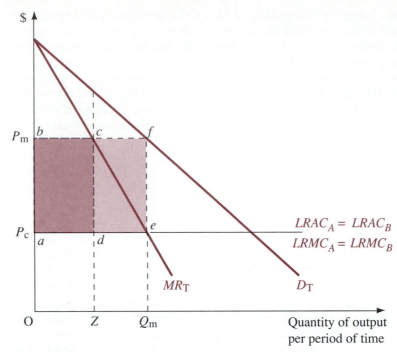

Figure 13-6
The incentive to cheat in cartels

solution does not seem unreasonable under the simplifying assumptions of homogeneous products and identical costs characterizing our cartel model. In an equal shares solution, firms A and B would agree to an output quota equal to one-half of the monopoly profit, $\frac{1}{2} OQ_m$, and if there is no cheating each will receive one-half of the monopoly profits. This is shown in Figure 13-6. Firm A produces $OZ = \frac{1}{2} OQ_m$ and its share of the profit is represented by the area *abcd*. Firm B produces $ZQ_m = \frac{1}{2} OQ_m$ and earns a profit equal to *dcfe*, where the profit rectangles, *abcd* and *dcfe*, are equal. But consider firm A's situation. *If B abides by the agreement and produces $ZQ_m = \frac{1}{2} OQ_m$, then the segment of the demand curve below and to the right of point r is available for exploitation by firm A and the segment of the marginal revenue curve below and to the right of point c is relevant to A's decision concerning output.* Firm A's marginal cost is given by $LRMC_A$, an amount clearly less than its marginal revenue at output OZ, the quota established by the cartel agreement. It is clear from Figure 13-6 that at Firm A's output quota its marginal revenue exceeds its marginal cost. The excess of A's marginal revenue over marginal cost creates the incentive to cheat on the cartel, since it can earn greater profits by selling more than its quota. Firm A has the option of pursuing a strategy that increases its profits by *producing more* than the cartel quota. If this strategy is adopted, it almost certainly will be done in secret to avoid retaliation by firm B. But it deserves emphasis that firm B is in precisely the same position as firm A; both firms have an incentive to renege on the agreement by exceeding their output quota. If one firm cheats and the other sticks to the agreement, then price necessarily falls, profits of the cheating firm rise, and profits of the loyal cartel member fall. But once cheating is detected, there are incentives to retaliate against the firm that broke the agreement. When the discipline of a cartel breaks down, it is no longer in the interest of any single firm to comply with the agreement. As the

One of the biggest problems with making a cartel work successfully over the long run is dealing with the incentive for one or more cartel members to cheat on the agreement and try to enhance their own profits; the conditions which make cheating profitable are fairly normal and widespread.

discipline of the cartel breaks down, independent maximizing behavior tends to replace the cartel's agreed upon joint maximizing behavior and the onset of competition drives price down toward P_c. This creates profit incentives for the firms to try and reorganize it.

To be successful, a cartel must solve the internal problems of detecting and deterring cheating. Even if these problems are solved, as they may well be in some oligopoly markets, then the external problems of competition from other firms and other products must still be confronted. First, consider competition from already established firms that produce the same product and do not join the cartel. For example, the Organization of Petroleum Exporting Countries (OPEC) includes most but not all of the leading crude oil exporters. Several relatively small but significant producers, including Norway and Mexico, chose to remain outside the cartel. For a small firm (or oil-producing country), the decision not to join and participate in the cartel is similar to cheating. The cartel sets a high price, and the small firm outside the cartel produces without the constraint imposed by the quota and is free to engage in independent maximizing behavior.

If all established firms join the cartel and none cheat, there is still the threat of competition from potential new entrants into the market. The capacity of new firms to enter depends, of course, on the barriers to entry into the market. To foreclose the possibility of new entry, it may be necessary for the cartel to produce a larger output and set a lower price than those that would maximize joint profits.

The final external problem confronting cartels may be the most serious. The existence of cartel profits is certain to attract competition from new products that are developed and designed to appeal to the cartel's customers. The continuing presence of cartel profits and the nature of competition as a dynamic process will lead entrepreneurs to develop new products and new methods of doing business that attract the profits away from the cartel. Viewed from the perspective of the dynamics of competition, all cartels must eventually fail. The only question is how long they can survive. On this point, see the Applications Capsule on the English coal cartel and the OPEC cartel.

> **Even if cartel members succeed in deterring cheating, the cartel must still be able to insulate its monopoly profits against the effects of competition from firms outside the cartel and from sellers of substitute products.**

FACTORS INHIBITING THE FORMATION OF CARTELS

We are now in a position to outline the conditions that tend to facilitate the organization of cartels and their successful operation. In an analogous fashion, we can identify the factors that tend to destabilize cartels and cause them to collapse. The first problem confronting oligopoly firms who wish to cooperate with one another and rig the market to their advantage is reaching a mutually beneficial agreement that divides the market. The following factors facilitate or tend to make it more difficult to reach agreement.

The Legality of Cartels. The legal treatment of cartels makes considerable difference. If cartels are illegal, as they generally are in the United States, then a restrictive agreement among firms becomes more difficult. In a legal environment in which cartels are unlawful *per se*, firms are forced into secret negotiations and the cartel must go underground. Under these conditions, the risk of joining a cartel increases and the likelihood that one or more firms will not join rises. On the other hand, if cartels are legal and firms can openly meet to discuss their mutual problems and interests, the risks are lower and nonjoiners are likely to be less of a problem.

> **There are a number of factors in real-world oligopoly markets that act to undermine the success of a cartel and promote its collapse.**

The Number of Sellers.   The smaller the number of firms, the easier it is to reach a cartel agreement. As the number of firms increases, the transactions costs of organizing a cartel rise. The probability of one or more firms not joining also increases with the number of sellers. The refusal of some firms to join reduces the incentives for organizing a restrictive agreement and makes it less likely that firms will incur the cost of trying to create a cartel.

Entry Barriers.   In the absence of entry barriers, there is little incentive to try and organize a cartel. If new firms can enter the market easily, then any short-run benefits of a cartel are soon erased by new competition. With easy entry, established firms are not likely to incur the costs associated with trying to organize a cartel.

The Similarity of Products and Costs.   Identical products and costs greatly facilitate oligopoly coordination and contribute to reaching a cartel agreement. In contrast, differences in products and costs make it more difficult to reach agreement. If products are the same but costs differ, then the firms will not agree on the best output for the cartel. The low-cost producer always prefers a larger output, while the high-cost producer prefers a smaller output. Differences in products raise the potentially serious problem of negotiating price differentials between the products of the various firms. In the absence of collusion, independent behavior and the forces of competition interact to establish price differentials among products, but in a cartel they must be determined by agreement. The more complex the product, the greater is the difficulty of reaching a cartel agreement. In some cases, the rate of technological change in products is such that agreement on prices is infeasible due to the continuing necessity to revise prices, adjust price differentials, and clear technologically outdated products from inventory. In other cases where products are built to individual customer specifications, cartel agreements are virtually impossible.

The Stability and Predictability of Demand.   If demand is generally stable and relatively easy to predict from one period to the next, then firms will find it easier to reach a cartel agreement. Unstable and difficult to predict demand conditions complicate the problem of reaching agreement. Variations in the size of customer orders can also be destabilizing and can cause firms to have greater difficulty in negotiating market-sharing agreements.

Social Relations Among Industry Leaders and the Maverick Factor.   Agreement among firms becomes easier if the chief executive officers and top management of the leading firms are friends and socialize together. Belonging to the same club or interacting socially facilitates oligopoly coordination and contributes to reaching cartel agreements. If one of the industry leaders is a social maverick, agreement is made more difficult. For example, Henry Ford was no socializer and was widely regarded as eccentric. The presence of such a decisive and independent personality among industry leaders makes it less likely that a cartel agreement can be negotiated.

DETECTING AND DETERRING CHEATING AMONG CARTEL MEMBERS

The internal problem of negotiating a cartel agreement is solvable in many real-world market situations. But once organized, a cartel will not last very long if it cannot detect and deter cheating among member firms. Cheating on a cartel takes the form of secret departures from the agreement, and detection requires information. Breaches in the agreement are easier to detect the greater the information each firm has concerning other firms' output and sales. Knowledge of rivals' business activities depends on a number of factors, including the following.

Factors That Disperse Market Information.

These factors include the number of sellers, the number of shipping points, and the number of buyers. A small number of firms does not ensure that detection will be easy even if the firms agree to share detailed records of their business activities. A cheater can also lie, and some firms are known to have kept two sets of books. Detection is facilitated by knowledge of actual shipments that can be verified. A single shipping point greatly facilitates detection. A small number of buyers also contributes to the ability to detect violations of the agreement. But since buyers benefit from secret price cutting and violations of cartel agreements, they are not likely to be anxious to cooperate in efforts to detect cheating.

Factors That Speed or Retard the Flow of Market Information.

If cheating occurs, it can be easy or hard to detect. The longer the detection lag, the more likely cheating is to occur. On the other hand, instantaneous detection is likely to act as an important deterrent. A single shipping point contributes to quick detection. A small number of large buyers also shortens the detection lag. In search of lower prices, buyers are likely to rush to the seller who is cheating on the cartel. Noncheaters are tipped off when their customers desert them for a rival who is supposedly selling at the same price.

Factors That Affect the Quality of Market Information.

If products are made to customer order and each product is to some extent unique, then information about other cartel members' activities becomes difficult to evaluate. Similarly, favorable credit terms, large-order discounts, and freight absorption all make detection more formidable.

A successful cartel must deter as well as detect violations of the restrictive agreement. To deter cheating, the costs of breaching the agreement must exceed the benefits. Violators must be punished or else the deterrence will fail and the cartel will collapse. Some cartel agreements anticipate cheating by individual firms and establish policies designed to punish or prevent it. Deterrence of cheating usually takes one of three forms.

Fines and Reductions in Output Quotas.

The cartel agreement may establish an agency to monitor the behavior of firms and empower it to impose fines and reduce output quotas. But the cartel must take care in imposing this type of punishment. Optimal punishment requires a fine that is high enough to deter cheating and low enough to attract members.

Pooling.

In anticipation of cheating by individual firms, the cartel agreement may require pooling of all revenues and distribution to members on the basis of a predetermined formula. In a pooling cartel there is little incentive to cheat, because exceeding quota means that you incur all of the costs of the output but receive only the agreed-upon share of the revenue. In some cases, pooling is also extended to costs and profits.

Retaliation in Kind.

The ultimate weapon against cheating is retaliation in kind. If all firms announce that they will respond to cheating by immediately increasing output and lowering their prices to at least the level of the violating firm, then the potential cheater may be deterred by prospects of the breakdown in the cartel. Retaliation in kind is not costless; the retaliating firm as well as the cheater may be adversely impacted. It deserves emphasis that retaliation in kind is an effective deterrent only if the detection lag is short. With a long detection lag, the cheater can enjoy substantial profits before incurring the costs of the retaliation.

A review of the experiences of actual cartels suggests that the number of shipping points is a crucial determinant of detection. The concentration of

APPLICATIONS CAPSULE

THE OPEC OIL CARTEL AND THE ENGLISH COAL CARTEL

The importance of the number of shipping points and successful deterrence illustrates the factors that influenced the stability and longevity of two highly successful energy cartels. The Organization of Petroleum Exporting Countries (OPEC) cartel successfully monopolized the world petroleum market in the 1970s, and the English coal cartel had similar power over the energy market in England for approximately two hundred years (roughly 1650 to 1850). OPEC was created in 1960 by the governments of Saudi Arabia, Iran, Iraq, Kuwait, and Venezuela. A number of petroleum-exporting countries joined later, and today there are 13 members that produce over half of the world's output and have more than two-thirds of the proven crude oil reserves. Until the early 1970s, OPEC exerted little influence on the world crude oil market. But following an Arab oil embargo of 1973, which was imposed as a political reaction to Israel's successful war against Syria and Egypt, the cartel learned of its power to control oil prices. In October 1973, the cartel raised prices by 70%. This was followed by a 125% increase three months later. Prices were raised several times in the mid-1970s, with the result that crude oil sold for $20 a barrel in 1977 compared to less than $4 per barrel in 1974. By 1980, OPEC had moved the price to $30 per barrel. Peak prices of $34 occurred in late 1982 and early 1983, at which point the cartel effectively collapsed. By 1987 the spot market price had fallen to $10 per barrel. Other prices had also risen during this time, so the real price of crude oil in 1987 was at approximately the same level as in 1973. But OPEC is not without power to influence the market. Since the lowest prices of 1987, OPEC has managed to raise prices substantially. In 1992 the price gravitated around $20 per barrel, which in real terms is above the 1973 level but far below the level of the late 1970s and early 1980s.

What accounts for the collapse of the OPEC cartel in the early 1980? OPEC has a serious problem in detecting and deterring cheating. There are multiple shipping points for crude oil, and OPEC has been unable to effectively monitor breaches in the agreed-upon quotas. Detection lags have proved to be long, and the only deterrent that the members of OPEC have available is retaliation in kind. Further, given sufficient time, non-OPEC producers demonstrated their capacity to explore for, drill, and bring new oil into production. As a result, OPEC was successful for only a relatively short time.

In contrast to OPEC's short period of success, the English coal cartel lasted almost two hundred years. The ex-

planation for the unusual longevity lies in the fact that the cartel was successful in solving the internal problems of detecting and deterring cheating. Coal is bulky and relative to its value is quite expensive to transport. During the heyday of the coal cartel, shipments were made by sea to London and other industrial cities. This so-called sea coal was the most economically viable energy source in England. Because of the location of coal deposits and energy buyers, all sea coal had to be transported through a single shipping point, the port of Newcastle. To monitor compliance with the restrictive agreement, the cartel simply stationed an inspector at the port and observed the loading of coal onto ships. Coal shipped through Newcastle had a locational advantage over other coal, particularly inland coal, and the cartel priced it to maintain its monopoly position. Output was controlled by a cartel committee that established quotas which varied with demand conditions. The committee was also empowered to levy fines and to reduce quotas. Detection of violations of the agreement was almost instantaneous, and the fines combined with the control of quotas proved sufficient to deter cheating.

The coal cartel was periodically faced with competition from new entry by mines located adjacent to the sea. Eventually, the new mines were incorporated into the cartel and the cartel used three shipping points. The cartel finally came to an end when canals and railroads were built, which opened up previously noncompetitive inland supplies of coal. As these new modes of transport became available, the number of shipping points expanded and the cartel collapsed.

The operation of airline cartels is useful in illustrating the effectiveness of fines and of pooling revenues in deterring cheating. The International Air Transport Association (IATA) uses fines to deter cheating on the cartel agreement that limits competition in the lucrative North Atlantic air transport business. But the fines have not served as an effective deterrent, and cheating has been endemic in this market. In contrast, British Airways and Air France, two firms that are members of IATA, have combined to form a successful cartel in the London-to-Paris market by pooling. They pool both revenues and costs, and the cartel in this market has worked effectively for a number of years.

Source: This application is based in part on D. K. Osborn's article, "Prospects for the OPEC Cartel," *Review* (Federal Reserve Bank of Dallas), January 1977, pp. 1–7.

shipping points reduces the costs of effectively monitoring compliance with the agreement. The history of cartels also suggests that pooling is a more effective deterrent than fines. Each of these points is discussed in the accompanying Applications Capsule on cartels.

PRICE LEADERSHIP AND CONSCIOUS PARALLELISM

The cartel model reveals that firms have an incentive to restrict competition and share the market without competing, while at the same time they have an opposing incentive to depart secretly from the agreement and pursue an independent maximizing strategy. The same motivations are present when the firms do not form an explicit cartel but simply cooperate with one another. Such cooperation is often referred to as implicit collusion or *conscious parallelism* and may be a substitute for an outright cartel when such agreements are illegal. Conscious parallelism occurs when each firm consciously decides, without formal negotiation and agreement, that cooperation with its rivals rather than competition is in its individual best interest.

Suppose all of the factors that contribute to an effective cartel are satisfied except that cartel agreements are illegal *per se*. Firms that wish to avoid violating the law may still be able to coordinate their behavior by acting *as if* an agreement exists. This requires that firms avoid aggressive competitive behavior, particularly with respect to price and output. But parallel behavior among firms is subject to some severe limitations. In addition to all of the aforementioned problems confronting formal cartels, there is the further difficulty of coordinating price changes that are made necessary by changing market conditions. In a cartel the firms can meet, discuss, and agree on how to respond to new market conditions. But where cartels are unlawful and a more informal collusive arrangement is used, firms cannot meet, discuss, or agree on a coordinated response. One alternative method which firms can use to coordinate their behavior is through price leadership. This involves firms implicitly agreeing that one firm will lead with respect to price changes and the others will follow. The leader endeavors to set prices that are beneficial to sellers in general, and follower firms are expected to match the prices.

There are recognizable patterns of price leadership in a number of oligopolistic industries, including cigarettes and cans. But it is a serious mistake to conclude that because price leadership exists it necessarily signifies collusive behavior. Price leadership can occur for other reasons, and there are additional price leadership models of oligopoly which do not involve collusion. Two of these price leadership models are discussed in some detail later in this chapter.

GAME THEORY MODELS

Economists use **game theory** techniques to help analyze oligopolistic markets where competition pits each seller head-on against its rivals.[9] Game theory is a formal method for analyzing choices when what happens to one decision maker (player) depends on the behavior of other decision makers (players). Strategic choices in game situations take into account the expected behavior of rivals and are based upon a recognition of mutual interdepen-

Because oligopolistic competition is very much a game of move and countermove, where the actions of one firm directly affect its competitors, game theory models can be used to determine a firm's best course of action.

[9] The classic work is by John von Neumann and Oscar Morganstern, *The Theory of Games and Economic Behavior* (Princeton N.J.: Princeton University Press, 1944).

APPLICATIONS CAPSULE

COLLUSION AND PROFITS IN MAJOR LEAGUE BASEBALL

For more than a century organized baseball has been regarded as both a sport and the national pastime. But it is also a business in which hundreds of people earn their livelihood. From its inception as a commercial enterprise in the 1870s professional baseball has used a variety of restrictions that explicitly limit competition in the economic sense, while promoting competition among sporting teams. The limitations on economic competition include control of entry by new competitors, exclusive geographical territories, pooling of revenues from broadcast rights and for many years the notorious *reserve clause,* which was a standard condition in every baseball player's contract. Each of these restrictions and others have been defended as being necessary to establish and maintain balance among teams and enhance competition in the sporting sense. Indeed, major league baseball is an anomaly among American businesses and sports industries in that it possesses a unique exemption under the U.S. antitrust laws. Under repeated challenge and for more than half a century the U.S. Supreme Court consistently ruled that baseball was not a business and, therefore, not subject to the Sherman Antitrust Act. This position was reversed in 1972 and the Court held, as they should have all along, that baseball was indeed a business. But, the Court also ruled that baseball was entitled to an exemption from the Sherman Act under the common law doctrine of *stare decisis* (a legal principle that bases decisions on consistent interpretations in previous cases that contain similar legal questions and issues).

The reserve clause was a fixture in baseball contracts until the mid 1970s. The clause gave the owner of the contract the exclusive rights to the services of the player in U.S. professional baseball in perpetuity. The owner's rights were relinquished only if the player was "sold" or "traded" to another team or the player was given an outright release from the contract. The standard baseball contract also contained a provision that provided for arbitration in the event of a contract dispute. In 1975 a pitcher for the Los Angeles Dodgers, Andy Messersmith, insisted on a "no trade" clause in his contract, but the Dodgers refused. A key paragraph of the standard contract specified the terms under which contracts could be renewed and it was this paragraph that was at the heart of the reserve clause. Messersmith played the entire season without a contract and in the fall of 1975 argued that the Dodger's failure to renew his contract made him a free agent. The Baseball Players Association joined Messersmith in filing a grievance and petitioning the arbitrator to settle the contract renewal dispute. The Dodgers claimed the dispute centered on Messersmith's insistence on a no trade clause and had nothing to do with the question of contract renewal or the reverse clause. Their interpretation was that Messersmith was bound in perpetuity to the Dodgers whether he signed the 1975 contract or not. The arbitrator ruled against the Dodgers and effectively brought the reserve clause in major league baseball to an end. The issue was appealed to the courts but the arbitrator's decision was upheld. Thus, following the Messersmith decision, a player could complete one year without signing a contract and effectively become a free agent. But this arrangement proved not to be in the interest of either Major League Baseball or the Baseball Players' Association.

Beginning in 1976 the owners and the players negotiated periodic agreements that defined the terms under which a player could become a free agent. These agreements consistently contained a provision that prohibits collusion among both players and owners. Since the end of the reserve clause, the baseball business has gone through several periods of intense bidding for free agents and other periods where it appeared the owners were in collusion, which resulted in a systematic boycott of free agents. From the perspective of the baseball owners, the problem with bidding for free agents is that it drives the total cost of baseball operations up, but has relatively little effect on joint revenues. Baseball profits inevitably suffer which leads to a recognition among owners of the mutual benefit that accrues from restricting competition for players.

The most recent "collusion era" was engineered by former Baseball Commissioner Peter Ueberroth, who assumed office in 1984. Prior to Ueberroth's appointment, baseball

dence.[10] The appeal of game theory is that it provides a means for identifying a firm's best choice when all firms are engaging in a strategic process of move and countermove.

In an oligopoly game, the firms can be thought of as players, while the key elements of the game are the strategy choices that the players make and their resulting payoffs. The strategic choices can involve all relevant decision

---

[10] For a recent treatment, see Arthur J. Robson's article "Stackelberg and Marshall," *American Economic Review,* Vol. 80, No. 1 (March 1990), pp. 69–82. For surveys and citations to the literature, see Jean Tirole, *The Theory of Industrial Organization* (Cambridge: MIT Press), Chapter 11, and Martin Shubik, *A Game Theoretic Approach to Political Economy* (Cambridge: MIT Press, 1984), Chapters 3–7. For a critical appraisal of the game theory approach to analyzing oligopoly, see Franklin M. Fisher's "Games Economists Play: A Non-cooperative View," *Rand Journal of Economics,* Vol. 20, No 1 (Spring 1991), pp. 113–24.

owners had substantially bid player salaries up and 80 percent of the teams were suffering economic losses. Ueberroth set about to change this using a variety of tactics to create a coordinated approach to common problems. The key problem facing owners was competition for free agents. To bring the problem under control Ueberroth repeatedly berated the owners calling them "stupid" for allowing cooperation and coordination among baseball teams to break down and for competition among players to break out. At one point shortly after becoming Commissioner, he is reported to have said at an owners meeting that he had finally figured out what was wrong with the economics of baseball:

> "Let's say I sat each of you down in front of a red button and a black button. . . . Push the red button and you will win the world series and lose $10 million. Push the black button and you will make $4 million and finish somewhere in the middle. The trouble is most of you would push the red one."[1]

Ueberroth had lawyers present in these meetings to advise him and the owners whenever the conversations began to approach what was regarded as explicit collusion, and the lawyers also gave advice concerning how far the owners could go without crossing the line that was thought to involve a possible violation. Finally, Ueberroth used his powers as Commissioner to discipline recalcitrant owners. He reportedly levied discretionary fines and used his authority to distribute pooled revenues to keep owners in line.

The results of Ueberroth's continuing pressure on and harangue of owners was stunning. The bidding for free agents came to a virtual halt and the market for free agents went into deep freeze. Between the end of the 1985 season and the beginning of the 1986 season 33 players were free agents and 29 received no offer from other clubs. The four free agents that did get another offer were marginal players whose teams had signalled that they did not want them. More telling, the free agents received only an average raise of five percent and

most got one year contracts and none received a coveted three year contract. Under the baseball agreement that governed the relations between owners and players, the only recourse open to the players was to charge the owners with collusion and take the matter before an arbitrator, which involved a long administrative review process. Eventually, the players won in arbitration, but the process of review took so long that the era of collusion lasted another two years, with additional charges of wrongful behavior levied by the player's union after each season. The players won on each count of collusion and the arbitrator levied fines that averaged $10.8 million per team. Ueberroth's reaction was one of surprise, commenting that he knew of "no smoking gun,"[2] meaning that the evidence of collusion was only circumstantial.

The collusion was successful for three years but it began to unravel at the end of the 1988 season. Over the next three years player salaries doubled and a number of teams returned to the red ink that characterized most teams before the era of collusion began. All teams were profitable in 1998, but 10 were losing money by 1991. The message is clear, collusion is clearly profitable to baseball owners; but in the absence of the reserve clause, it cannot be effectively maintained in the marketplace.

---

[1] This statement is taken from John Helyar's article, "How Peter Ueberroth Led the Major Leagues in the 'Collusion Era,'" *The Wall Street Journal*, May 21, 1991, p. A12.

[2] John Helyar, "How Peter Ueberroth Led the Major Leagues in the 'Collusion Era,'" p. A1.

Source: This application is based in part on Simon Rottenberg's article, "The Baseball Player's Labor Market," *Journal of Political Economy*, June 1956, pp. 242–258, reprinted in *Readings in Price Theory*, ed. by William Breit and Harold Hochman, 2nd edition (New York: Holt, Rinehart and Winston, 1972), pp. 427–443; Gerald W. Scully's book, *The Business of Major League Baseball* (Chicago: University of Chicago Press, 1989); and John Helyar's article, "How Peter Ueberroth Led the Major Leagues in the 'Collusion Era,'" *The Wall Street Journal*, May 21, 1991, pp. A1 and A12.

---

variables and include prices, output, advertising, product modifications, research and development, and similar areas of business policy in which the sellers are mutually interdependent. The payoffs are the rewards firms receive as a result of playing the game and are usually expressed in the form of profits. To analyze alternative strategic choices and their associated payoffs, game theory utilizes a convenient device known as a *payoff matrix*. A firm's payoff matrix tabulates the alternative strategies open to the firm and its rivals and shows the payoff from each possible combination of strategies.

Prisoner's dilemma games are one particularly important class of oligopolistically relevant games because they go to the heart of a firm's decision to cooperate or not cooperate with rivals. Consider a very simple situation in which two persons, A and B, have been arrested for criminal behavior and are in fact guilty, but the police are not certain about their guilt nor do they know

BASIC CONCEPT
A payoff matrix tabulates the relevant courses of action competitors can pursue and the estimated outcomes (or payoffs) associated with each strategic option.

the details concerning each prisoner's role in the crime. After reading them their rights, the prisoners, which we designate A and B, are interrogated separately and each develops a very clear expectation concerning possible choices and outcomes. Both prisoners face the dilemma of whether to confess and turn state's evidence by testifying for the prosecution or to tough it out by denying everything. For simplicity, assume A and B have identical expectations of what will happen as a result of each combination of independent strategic choices. If A and B cooperate by consistently denying all knowledge of the crime, they expect to be convicted of a lesser offense and receive three-year jail sentences. However, if one prisoner confesses and testifies against the other who holds out, the expectation is that the squealer gets a light sentence of one year and the judge throws the book at the prisoner who holds out. If both confess, each receives a five-year sentence. The alternative choices and their outcomes can be conveniently represented in the following payoff matrices:

		Prisoner A's Payoff Matrix		
			A's Strategy	
			Confess	Do Not Confess
B's Strategy	Confess		5 years	10 years
	Do Not Confess		1 year	3 years

		Prisoner B's Payoff Matrix		
			A's Strategy	
			Confess	Do not Confess
B's Strategy	Confess		5 years	1 year
	Do Not Confess		10 years	3 years

Consider A's payoff matrix first. The entries in each cell show the specific payoff to A from a combination of choices made by A and B, who are the players in the game. In this game the payoffs are in the form of years of incarceration, and the smaller the jail sentence the better off is the player. If A confesses and B does not, A gets a one-year sentence. But if A confesses and B also confesses, A serves five years in prison. Clearly, what happens to A depends on B's behavior. But A cannot control B's action and can only make the best choice for A. The other strategy for A is not to confess and deny everything. But again what happens to A depends on B's behavior. Now consider B's payoff matrix, which is very similar to A's. In fact, A and B are symmetrical and their payoff matrices are simply mirror images of one another.

What strategy will A choose and what strategy will B choose? Stated differently, what will be the solution to the game? If A chooses the best possible strategy *given B's behavior* and B chooses the best possible strategy *given A's behavior,* the resulting set of payoffs is called a **Nash equilibrium**, which is named after the person who first formally solved for the solution to a game theory model.[11] In a Nash equilibrium each player is doing the best that he or she can *given the behavior of the other players.* In a prisoner's dilemma game there is a special type of Nash equilibrium in which players pursue a **dominant**

---

[11] John von Neumann and Oscar Morganstern's *The Theory of Games and Economic Behavior* developed the basic insights that led to game theory, but two classic articles by John F. Nash, Jr. developed the equilibrium concept and applied it to game theory. See his ''Non-cooperative Games,'' *Annals of Mathematics,* Vol. 54 (September 1951), pp. 286–95, and ''Two Person Cooperative Games,'' *Econometrica,* Vol. 21, No. 1 (January 1953), pp. 128–40.

strategy that makes each player *worse off* than if the players jointly selected an alternative strategy. In general, a dominant strategy for a player is one which is superior to any alternative strategy irrespective of the strategy selected by the other player. A's dominant strategy can be identified by considering B's options and considering what is A's best choice if B confesses. It is apparent from prisoner A's payoff matrix, *when B confesses* A is made better off by also confessing. This follows from the fact that A rationally prefers five years in jail to ten. On the other hand, *if B does not confess,* A is again made better off by confessing. From A's perspective, one year in jail is preferred to three years. Thus, A's dominant strategy is to confess. But, in this game A and B are identical and B's dominant strategy, like A's, is to confess. When each player has a dominant strategy, then the game has a dominant strategy equilibrium. If A and B both choose their dominant strategy, then in equilibrium their choices will result in each receiving a five-year sentence. But notice that both A and B would agree that three years in prison are better than five and that the dominant strategy equilibrium is inferior to an alternative combination of strategies in which neither player confesses. The dilemma is that despite the existence of a superior alternative, powerful incentives are tugging at each prisoner and encouraging them to choose the dominant strategy. Thus, in a prisoner's dilemma game a dominant strategy equilibrium makes each player worse off than they could be if they adopted a cooperative strategy.

Three aspects of prisoner's dilemma games deserve emphasis. First, many economic games involving oligopoly markets turn out to be prisoner's dilemma games. Second, the dominant strategy equilibrium is not inevitable in prisoner's dilemma games, but if the players cannot communicate with one another it is a more likely outcome. In the example, if A and B are interrogated together and can privately discuss their options and gauge each other's resolve, they are more likely to deny the charge and receive sentences of three years rather than both confessing and going to jail for five years. Thus, the ability to communicate and discuss the joint implications of strategic choices can be an important determinant of a prisoner's dilemma game. Third, if the players are involved in a one-shot game (that is, a game that is played only once and never repeated), then they are likely to play their dominant strategy.

It is important to emphasize that *in oligopoly markets the strategy game is played over and over and the firms have the opportunity to learn from past experience.* The importance of repeated games in analyzing the behavior of firms in oligopoly markets can be more clearly conveyed and understood by considering a specific example. Suppose two firms, Able and Baker, have agreed to share the market but face the choice of whether to comply with the terms of the restrictive agreement or cheat by producing an output in excess of their quota. These strategic choices can be represented by the following payoff matrices, where the payoffs are in total profits (in millions of dollars) for each firm.

Able's Payoff Matrix

		Able's Strategy	
		Cheat	Comply
Baker's	Cheat	$355 m	$300 m
Strategy	Comply	$450 m	$400 m

Baker's Payoff Matrix

		Able's Strategy	
		Cheat	Comply
Baker's	Cheat	$355 m	$450 m
Strategy	Comply	$300 m	$400 m

If Able and Baker both comply with the agreement, the outcome of the game is a joint monopoly solution in which they share the monopoly profit. In the payoff matrices each firm receives $400 million in profits if both firms comply with the agreement. Thus, the joint monopoly profit is $800 million. However, if both firms cheat the profits are a smaller amount, $355 million each, for a total of $710 million for the industry as a whole. If Able cheats and Baker complies, Able's profit is $450 million and Baker's is $300 million for combined total of $750 million. The firms are symmetrical, so if Baker cheats and Able complies the payoffs are $450 million for Baker and $300 million for Able. Inspection of the strategic choices and payoffs reveals that this is the prisoner's dilemma game in which each firm's dominant strategy is to cheat on the agreement. To see this, look at the game from Able's perspective. If Baker cheats, Able's highest profits are attained by cheating ($450 million > $300 million). But if Baker complies, Able's highest profits are also attained by cheating ($450 million > $300 million). Thus, regardless of what Baker does, Able is better off by cheating on the agreement, which means that Able's dominant strategy is to cheat. Baker is similarly situated and, like Able, has an incentive to play its dominant strategy by cheating on the agreement.

Now consider a second example that does not involve compliance and cheating on a collusive agreement, but the firms must choose a price that is either cooperative or noncooperative. In this example, we let the firms be named Victor (V) and Zebra (Z) and assume that they are choosing between two price strategies. If the low-price strategy is chosen, the firm sets its price at $10 per unit, while the high-price strategy results in a price of $15. The annual expected profits (in millions of dollars) for each firm appear in matrix form as follows:

Competitors can find themselves in a prisoner's dilemma, selling at lower prices and earning lower profits than would be the case if they all elected to charge a higher price; the way out of the prisoner's dilemma is for rivals to recognize the mutual benefits of raising prices to a higher level and competing more on such nonprice factors as quality, service, and performance.

	Victor's Payoff Matrix		
		Firm Z's Price Strategies	
		$10	$15
Firm V's Price Strategies	$10	$100 m	$180 m
	$15	$ 50 m	$150 m

	Zebra's Payoff Matrix		
		Firm Z's Price Strategies	
		$10	$15
Firm V's Price Strategies	$10	$ 80 m	$ 30 m
	$15	$170 m	$120 m

Examination of firm V's payoff matrix indicates that firm V will prefer the $10 price strategy to the $15 price strategy. And if firm V selects the $10 price, firm Z's best act is to choose the $10 price also. The dominant strategy for each firm is to adopt the low-price strategy. But the paradox of this apparently rational choice is that it pushes each firms profits below the level that could be attained if they cooperated and jointly adopted the high-price strategy. Thus, the price strategy game that Victor and Zebra are involved in is a prisoner's dilemma game that is very similar to the Comply or Cheat game that Able and Baker are involved in.

So far, the oligopoly games we have considered are essentially no different from the Confess or Deny game faced by the two prisoners accused of criminal activity. If Able and Baker act independently and choose their dominant strategies, each earns $355 million, which is less than the $400 million they could have earned if they cooperated by complying with the joint maximizing agreement. If Victor and Zebra cooperated by adopting the high-price strategy, they could increase joint profits by $90 million, of which $50 million would go to Victor and $40 million to Zebra. Thus, playing the dominant strategy causes the oligopoly firms to earn less profits than they could, while it causes prisoners to spend more time in jail. But there are fundamental differences between accused criminals who must select a strategy in a prisoner's dilemma game and oligopoly firms that face similar game theoretic choices. The prisoners are not allowed to communicate with one another and are usually in a one-shot game that will not be repeated. In contrast, the oligopoly firms can communicate and can be viewed as participating in repeated games.

A ***repeated game*** is one in which the players confront essentially the same strategies and the same opponents over and over. The repetition of games introduces a new element into strategic decision-making. Each firm must now weigh the consequences of its current choices in influencing future strategic behavior of rivals when the game is repeated. One of the most important aspects of repeated games is that they allow for firms to learn from their experiences in oligopoly markets. Repeated games open up more strategic alternatives and make it possible for one firm to inflict punishment on another. A firm that cheats on the agreement may be punished by aggressive price cutting that lowers the cheater's profits. Of course, it also lowers every firm's profits, but in a dynamic sense it teaches a lesson: Cheating today will result in retaliation and a loss of profits tomorrow. One approach to behavior in dynamic games is to create an environment in which firms know that while cheating may have benefits in the short run, compliance has a higher payoff in the long run. One strategy for trying to create such an environment is referred to as ***tit-for-tat strategy***; if Able cheats today, Baker retaliates tomorrow. If Able complies today, Baker complies tomorrow. If Baker's behavior in the current period inflicts heavy damage to Able, then Able responds by inflicting heavy damage to Baker in the next period.

What looks like a prisoner's dilemma game when only one time period is analyzed may not have a dominant strategy equilibrium when additional periods and dynamic strategies are considered. This is the case because additional strategies for imposing punishment and creating a learning environment come into play. What happens in repeated oligopoly games? In general, there is no unique outcome. Game theory establishes that a ***cooperative equilibrium*** is possible but so is a ***noncooperative equilibrium***. In a cooperative equilibrium, both firms learn that it pays to cooperate and that behaving in a noncooperative manner results in less profits in the long run. Each firm chooses to cooperate because of the credible threat that their rival can and will inflict punishment on them if they do not cooperate. In contrast, a noncooperative equilibrium emerges if the firms learn that more profits can be earned by abandoning efforts to coordinate oligopoly behavior. It is possible that oligopoly markets can gravitate between cooperation and noncooperation, with neither being a permanent equilibrium condition. Thus, a period in which firms play cooperative strategies could break down and the firms then pursue noncooperative strategies for a while. But at some point they may well find it mutually advantageous to cooperate again. For example, in the preceding energy market Application Capsule, it was pointed out that after 1983 the OPEC cartel collapsed and by 1987 real crude oil prices had tumbled to their 1973 level. But OPEC is alive and well, and since the free fall in crude oil prices bottomed out, the cartel has succeeded in raising prices on several occasions. Of course, the power of OPEC is nothing like it was in the heyday of the cartel between 1973 and 1983.

Most oligopolistic markets involve repeated games of competitive strategy, thus allowing rival firms to learn from their competitive experiences; in such cases firms may soon learn that cooperative behavior is more profitable in the long run than is noncooperative behavior, thereby providing a means of escape from the prisoner's dilemma type of situation.

But if the energy market cycles between cooperation and noncooperation, then it is possible that a new restrictive arrangement involving OPEC and other crude oil exporting countries could again send oil price shock waves through the world economy. But if and when this happens, the cooperation is not likely to be permanent.

USING PUBLIC ANNOUNCEMENTS TO ACCOMPLISH PRICE COORDINATION

A firm's public announcements of its future pricing intentions can be a very effective way of communicating indirectly with rival firms and thereby achieving a coordinated pricing move. For example, firm A, believing that a price increase is warranted, may decide to issue a press release announcing a 10% price increase to take effect in 60 days. By timing its announcement well in advance of when it will take effect and by making its announcement public (so that it will likely be reported in *The Wall Street Journal,* leading trade publications, and similar media), a firm is able to test the sentiments of competitors. If other firms respond favorably to this new pricing development by shortly announcing an equal price increase, A can follow through with the price change as planned and be reasonably confident that its competitors will do the same. However, if the rival firms send signals of disagreement by making no announcement or by announcing a lesser increase, A can opt to withdraw its announced price rise or revise it downward to match those of its competitors. Whichever the case, using the media to communicate pricing desires and decisions can be a useful tactic for learning to what extent a price increase will be matched or ignored by firms in the industry.

One way that rival oligopolists can achieve price coordination is by making public announcements of their intent to raise or lower prices at some future date; sending price signals to competitors through the media allows a firm to learn whether rivals intend to match or ignore the price change.

An alternative way of signaling pleasure or displeasure with an initiating firm's price announcement is by offering one's opinion of the move in interviews with reporters, speeches to securities analysts, and the like. When B disagrees with A's price announcement, it can use speeches and interviews to offer reasons and views about market conditions aimed at persuading A to alter its decision ("if firm A's objective is to make higher profits, its scheduled pricing move is ill-conceived and ill-timed because . . ."). If B's arguments are unsuccessful and if B thinks it is better to go along with A rather than provoke conflict, B can in the due course of events announce it will follow A's lead on price. Using speeches and interviews to communicate reactions and opinions have the advantage of being a less binding commitment to a given course of action because they do not involve making a formal public announcement to actually change or not change one's own price. Doing something later that is inconsistent with opinions expressed earlier does not entail the same loss of credibility that goes with reneging on a prior price commitment.

Publicly announced price changes can also serve as threats. Suppose that firm A announces intentions to lower its prices on certain selected items in its product line. Firm B might elect to retaliate by announcing it is considering lowering its prices significantly below A's. This may suffice to deter A from going through with its intended price cuts because A now has ample indication that B is displeased with the price cuts and is willing to enter into a price war if need be,

On the other hand, a firm can employ public announcements in an effort to minimize the provocation that a price change can have. For instance, firm A may believe that the industry needs to adjust price levels downward. By

APPLICATIONS CAPSULE

OLIGOPOLISTIC COMPETITION AND MILITARY STRATEGY

It is not uncommon for oligopolistic firms to describe their competitive environment in military terms. The analogies are, in fact, very close. In both oligopoly and war there are two or more "sides." Each side seeks to increase its welfare, almost always at the expense of the other. Each side can employ various strategies and tactics to expose or injure the other. Each side has an incentive to resort to decoys, surprises, traps, and other maneuvers to gain an advantage.

Military terms are a standard part of competitive rhetoric. Executives speak of "invading" markets, of competitive "attacks," of developing new sales "weapons," of marketing research as "intelligence," of salesmen as "troops in the field," and of using "secret code names" for special projects. Price "wars" break out in a number of industries from time to time; firms have been known to engage in industrial "espionage" and "spying" with respect to one another's plant facilities, trade secrets, patents, and R & D efforts; advertising is referred to as a "propaganda campaign." Business magazines have talked about "border clashes" and "skirmishes" among computer manufacturers, the "escalating arms budgets" of soap and detergent companies, "guerilla warfare" by Purex against the soap firms, the "battle" over the market share in countless industries, and of "takeovers" by acquisition-minded enterprises.

Often lying behind this talk is a conscious application of military principles to gain a competitive edge. Six well-known military maxims have particular relevance:

1. *Principle of the objective.* Every military operation must be directed toward a clearly defined, decisive, and attainable objective.
2. *Principle of mass.* Superior combat power must be concentrated at the critical time and place for a decisive purpose.
3. *Principle of flexibility of maneuver.* Flexibility must be a major consideration in the selection of plans, although the costs and dangers of flexibility must be weighed against its advantages.
4. *Principle of security.* Security is essential and is achieved by measures taken to prevent surprise, preserve freedom of action, and deny the enemy information.
5. *Principle of the offensive.* The commander must exercise initiative, set the pace, and exploit enemy weaknesses.
6. *Principle of surprise.* Surprise results from striking an enemy at a time, place, and in a manner for which he is not prepared.

Out of these principles emerge a number of strategic and competitive considerations. Should a firm concentrate its competitive resources on rivals' weaknesses or their strengths? Is it more strategically advantageous to defend a position of market strength or to attack a position of market weakness? Does a narrow, concentrated *focus* strategy offer a better chance of success than a broad "hit 'em on all fronts" approach? Does success breed success with respect to winning future competitive struggles? How rapidly should a "victory" be followed up on and the gains consolidated?

However, two major differences between military strategy and business competition should be noted. Whereas wars are fought for "total victory" in which the enemy is either to surrender or be destroyed, competition among firms must be conducted so that no one firm emerges a winner. Winning in oligopolistic competition means becoming a monopolist, and that is a violation of the antitrust laws. In fact, the antitrust apparatus is aimed at *preserving* competition, the philosophy being that competition is properly vigorous and spirited but no one firm is supposed to be so good at competing that it wins the struggle or gains a clear upper hand. Second, whereas "all is fair in love and war," in business competition there are important constraints on the weapon or tactics a firm can use. The antitrust statutes prescribe the rules of "fair competition" and specifically prohibit discriminatory pricing, restraints of trade, predatory tactics to drive another firm out of business, exclusive or tying arrangements, reciprocal dealing, misrepresentations, fraud, deception, and other such attempts to monopolize and/or weaken competitive forces.

Sources: Taken in part from Robert H. Caplan, "Appendix B: Relationships between Principles of Military Strategy and Principles of Business Planning," in *Planning and Control: A Framework for Analysis,* Robert N. Anthony, ed. (Boston: Division of Research, Graduate School of Business Administration, Harvard University, 1965), pp. 148–56, and Philip Kotler, *Marketing Management: Analysis, Planning and Control,* 2nd ed. (Englewood Cliffs, N.J.: Prentice Hall, 1972), pp. 250–54.

announcing its intentions ahead of time and taking care to explain its move in terms of evolving market and cost conditions, it can avoid having other firms interpret the price-cutting move as an aggressive bid for increased market share. At the same time, these explanations serve as an attempt to get rival firms to see the logic and benefits of a lower price structure and to follow the move downward.

Quite often, firms comment publicly on their perceptions of current market conditions, what they believe the trend of demand and prices will be in the months and years ahead, how changes in raw material prices and wage rates

APPLICATIONS CAPSULE

USING THE MEDIA TO SEND "PRICE SIGNALS" TO COMPETITORS— LEGAL OR ILLEGAL?

In 1979 the Federal Trade Commission charged the four major companies selling lead additives for gasoline with using the media to fix prices. The FTC complaint alleged that by publicly announcing their prices and pricing policies the four companies—Ethyl Corporation, DuPont, PPG Industries, and Nalco Chemical—were guilty of "price signaling." The idea behind the FTC complaint was that oligopolistic firms desirous of coordinating any price adjustments do not have to meet secretly in obscure locations to negotiate a common course of action; rather, all one firm has to do is just tell the whole market—buyers and sellers alike—what it plans to do; other sellers will get the message and via a series of press releases back and forth—all duly reported in one place or another— eventually coordinate their actions with just as effective an outcome as if they had formally met face to face and hammered out a collusive scheme.

In addition, the FTC complaint against the four producers alleged other related anticompetitive activities— namely that they sold their additives only at a transportation- cost-included price; that some of the four promised their customers as low a price as anyone got; that all four used a 30- day-advance-notice-of-price-change clause in the contracts with customers; and that they often told the press and *potential* customers of coming price changes. According to the director of the FTC's Bureau of Competition, "the practices amount, under the circumstances in this industry, to a modern form of price-fixing. . . . Sophisticated price signaling usually coupled with other practices, achieves similar results while avoiding traditional agreements." In support of its case, the FTC claimed that there were 18 lockstep price increases in the industry in 4 years (DuPont claimed that this was untrue, saying that there were 18 price changes, including 6 price cuts, and that 9 changes were connected to changes in the price of lead).

The FTC's proposed remedies for the allegedly illegal and collusive price signaling were (1) to forbid firms from making advance announcements on price available to anyone but customers, (2) to forbid the four firms from selling at delivered prices, and (3) to forbid them from promising any customer as low a price as they give to any other customer. In 1978 an assistant attorney general for antitrust in the Justice Department indicated support for the conspiracy theory of price signaling, suggesting that it would be sufficient for a firm to just report its pricing plans to the government; *Forbes* quoted the official as saying "As to whether it's [a public price announcement] a fit subject for general public consideration, I'm not sure."

The FTC case against the sellers of lead additives was not the first of its kind; in 1972 the Justice Department brought a Sherman antitrust case against General Motors and Ford Motor Company for their "coordinated" action to eliminate price discounts on fleet sales of cars; the alleged mechanism for the price-fixing scheme, according to the Justice Department complaint, was that the two companies signaled each other about their positions and coming actions through speeches and press reports. However, both the criminal and civil cases against these two companies were later dismissed by the federal judge and jury because the government failed to prove any conspiracy. Under FTC rules, though, no proof of conspiracy is necessary; it need only be shown that the practice is sufficiently anticompetitive that it is in the public interest to ban sellers from making announcements of pending price changes public.

QUESTIONS FOR DISCUSSION

1. Should firms be allowed to inform their present customers about pending price changes? What about *potential* customers? If firms are restrained from using the media to announce future price adjustments to *potential* customers, then what avenues should they be able to use?

2. Do you see a potential conflict between the FTC's proposed ban on public price announcements and the freedom of speech guarantees provided by the First Amendment to the Constitution?

3. If the FTC were to implement a ban on advance announcements of price increases, then do you think the effect will be procompetitive or anticompetitive? How important is knowledge about firms' prices and pricng policies to an efficient functioning of the market—especially from the standpoint of buyers and from the standpoint of sellers being alert to a need to match the price cuts of rival firms?

4. Suppose that the FTC bans public announcements but permits sellers to inform their customers (by letter or personal contact with salespersons) and then certain customers turn around and "leak" notice of the pending changes either to the press or to rival sellers or to both. What then? Should such leaks also be banned?

Source: Adapted from information reported in "No Body Language, Please," *Forbes,* June 25, 1979, p. 37.

will affect costs, and so on. Such commentaries can act as a coordinating tactic because they reveal a firm's assumptions and beliefs about key market factors. As other competitors speak out and make their views known, it can be determined whether firms in the industry are operating under common assumptions and market perceptions. By trading views and opinions back and forth by means of the media and the customer-distributor grapevine, a consensus can be developed about what actions and changes are appropriate.

PRICE LEADERSHIP MODELS

One of the methods that firms can use to arrive at a cooperative policy is for the firms to collude implicitly and allow one firm to act as a price leader and the other firms to behave as followers. In discussing the collusive price leadership model, we stressed that there are other types of price leadership and that the existence of leader-follower relations in oligopoly markets is not necessarily indicative of collusion. Two major forms of noncollusive price leadership stand out: *dominant firm leadership* and *barometric firm leadership*.[12]

Oligopolists that have a commanding market share lead may have sufficient market power to impose their preferred price on lesser-sized firms, thereby becoming the industry price leader.

DOMINANT FIRM PRICE LEADERSHIP

Dominant firm price leadership arises when one firm accounts for a much larger market share than any of its rivals. Typically, the dominant firm is a large, vertically integrated corporation whose only rivals consist of numerous "competitive fringe" firms, none of which is able to exert a material influence on the market through its own price-output decisions. On rarer occasions, dominant firm industries are composed of one large firm, several medium-sized firms, and a host of small firms that operate on the competitive fringe of the market.

The assumption underlying the dominant-firm model is that the dominant firm establishes its own preferred price as the going market price and allows the competitive fringe firms to sell all they wish at that price; the dominant firm then produces an amount sufficient to meet the remaining demand at the chosen price. In essence, the competitive fringe firms behave just like perfectly competitive firms. They can sell all they want at the price set by the dominant firm and therefore face a horizontal demand curve at the established price. Each of the fringe firms pegs its output at the rate where $MC = MR$; MR is equal to the price set by the dominant firm since the latter lets the fringe firms sell all they please.

The determination of the dominant firm's optimum price is illustrated in Figure 13-7. Suppose that the dominant firm believes the total market demand curve to be D_m. Suppose further that it estimates the amount of output which will be supplied by the competitive fringe firms at various alternative prices to be S_{cf}—found by summing together the portions of the marginal cost

---

[12] There is another form of oligopoly leadership as well. Stackelberg leadership involves one firm figuring out what strategy other firms are pursuing and the leader imposing its own strategy so as to "lead" the followers to a position that maximizes the leader's position in the market. In some ways Stackelberg leadership is similar to dominant firm leadership, but there are important differences. In Stackelberg leadership, there need not be differences in costs and one firm is not dominant. For an analysis of Stackelberg's leadership and a discussion of its relation to an equal shares solution and the Cournot model of oligopoly, see John P. Formby and W. James Smith, "The Chamberlin and Stackelberg Duopoly Relation," *Economic Record,* Vol. 55, No. 4 (December 1979), pp. 368–71.

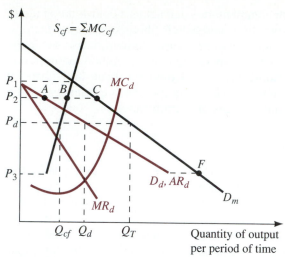

Figure 13-7
Outcome for a situation of dominant firm price leadership

curves lying above average varible cost for each fringe producer. Once the dominant firm estimates how much of the total market demand will be served by the competitive fringe, it can calculate how much will be left over for itself. For example, at prices of P_1 and higher, the competitive fringe is willing to supply all the output the market will absorb, leaving no sales potential for the dominant firm. At price P_2 total market demand is P_2C units; of this, the fringe producers would produce P_2B units, leaving BC units for the dominant firm. To locate the dominant firm's demand curve at price P_2 we set point A such that BC units equals P_2A units of output. This procedure can be repeated for other assumed prices. In each case the dominant firm's demand is found by subtracting the fringe firms' output at a given price from the total industry demand at that price. The result is a series of points which, when connected, give the curve D_d, AR_d. Observe that at prices below P_3 the dominant firm has the entire market to itself; no output will be supplied by the fringe firms when price is less than the minimum average variable cost of every fringe firm. Thus, the dominant firm's demand curve below price P_3 coincides with the segment of the industry demand curve labeled FD_m. The dominant firm's entire demand curve is D_d, AR_d plus the segment FD_m.

> **In the dominant-firm model, the firm with the biggest market share acts as a price leader and a quantity follower.**

The dominant firm determines its profit-maximizing price and output in the customary fashion of equating marginal revenue and marginal cost. The marginal revenue curve corresponding to D_d, AR_d is MR_d, and the dominant firm's marginal cost curve is shown as MC_d. Its profit-maximizing output rate is therefore Q_d units, and its profit-maximizing price is P_d dollars. Total market demand at price P_d is Q_T units. Of this, the dominant firm supplies Q_d units, and its smaller rivals supply the remainder ($Q_T - Q_d$), which equals Q_{cf} units in Figure 13-7.

One of the better current examples of dominant firm price leadership arises in retailing where a nationally known seller (such as K mart, Kraft, Frito-Lay, Pizza Hut, or Sears) competes with numerous small, locally owned retail firms carrying comparable products. The local firms must at least meet the prices of the dominant marketer or risk loss of a major portion of their customers. And they must be wary of trying to undercut the dominant firm's prices because if they get far out of line and begin to cut heavily into the leader's business, they can be certain of retaliatory action. The leader may well decide to discipline small maverick competitors by discreetly cutting its prices in those areas where its most aggressive rivals are strongest. A large firm serving many geographically distinct markets can afford to cut prices to the bone in one or a few areas and still make out with the profits it earns elsewhere.[13] The local firm has no such option. Here, the followership of small firms stems from the dominant firm's market power and not from genuine popularity of the leader's price.

However, it need not at all be the case that the dominant firm prefers a price higher than its smaller rivals and must throw its weight around to keep potential price-cutters in line. The price leader may well have secured its dominant position because of cost economies derived from large-scale production and because its cost advantage produces a profit-maximizing price *below* that of its smaller rivals. In other words, the dominant firm's market position may be due to its greater ability to attract customers by underselling everybody else. In this case, minor firms must match the leader's price or face the prospects of an even smaller market share.

In times past, dominant firm price leaders have included International Harvester in farm implements, U.S. Steel in steel, Firestone in tires, Exxon in petroleum, Alcoa in aluminum, General Motors in autos, Western Electric in telephone equipment, Birdseye in frozen foods, R. J. Reynolds in cigarettes, IBM in computers, Coca-Cola in soft drinks, American Can in tin cans, and International Paper in paper products. However, the position of these dominant firms has gradually been eroded by growth and expansion of once-lesser rivals and stronger competitive forces now prevail.

The number of occasions where dominant firms have lost their dominance suggests that a dominant firm market structure may be short-lived and will eventually distintegrate into highly competitive oligopoly. The reasons are straightforward. When the dominant firm's price allows fringe firms to realize positive economic profits, then, over time, they are encouraged to take advantage of scale economies and expand their outputs.[14] Since the dominant firm is a "quantity-follower" and in effect makes room for fringe firm expansion by curbing its own output, the most aggressive smaller firms, via steady expansion, will begin to increase their market shares at the expense of the dominant firm. Sooner or later, the dominant firm will find itself confronted with several emerging rivals of growing influence and power, and its dominant position will be effectively undermined.

The major point here is that a *dominant firm, if it wishes to retain its position of advantage in the market, must deviate from the pattern of letting smaller firms produce as much as they please. It is "suicide" for it to buy price leadership at the cost of quantity followership.* Instead, to preserve its position

To preserve its leadership position over the long run, a dominant firm must be as aggressive in protecting its market share as it is in establishing the going price for rivals to observe.

---

[13] This is not to say, however, that large firms will readily resort to local price warfare. The profit sacrifices of the dominant firm are likely to be quite large relative to the harm it inflicts upon small rivals. Price wars to discipline minor firms and to teach them the value of cooperation are worthwhile only if the aftermath produces an environment much more conducive to the earning of profits. Otherwise, it may take an inordinately long time to recoup the sacrifices of profit which a price war entails.

[14] The steel industry provides a classic example. In 1901 U.S. Steel controlled 65% of the industry's ingot capacity. As the dominant firm and price leader, it established a high-price policy which stimulated the entry and expansion of smaller steel firms. By 1915 U.S. Steel's share of ingot capacity was down to 52%; its share has since eroded to 28% in 1960 and to under 20% during the 1980s. A new technology, continuous casting, has almost compltely replaced ingot steel production and U.S. Steel has completely phased out the old method. In terms of total capacity, U.S. Steel's share slipped to 11% in the early 1990s.

a dominant firm must abandon the short-run profit-maximizing behavior portrayed in the dominant firm model in favor of long-run profit maximization. Among other things, this means adjusting its short-run profit-maximizing price downward so as to deter small-firm expansion and the entry of new rivals. The dominant firm must be wary of creating short-run market conditions conducive to the growth of the competitive fringe. Of course, it may be that it has no choice in this regard. The antimonopoly laws and the shape of the long-run average cost curve may preclude the establishment of a price that will perpetuate the dominant firm's position.[15] But even should this happen (as obviously it has), all is not lost. The dominant firm can continue to outperform its lesser rivals by being the source of new product ideas, cost-saving discoveries, customer service improvements, and new distribution techniques. By maintaining a leadership posture on nonprice variables as well as price, it may succeed in discouraging upstart competitors. The principle that the best defense is a good offense applies well in this situation.

Another competitive approach the dominant firm can use is the multibrand strategy, whereby it introduces a number of new product variations with different brand names. Although its own brands may be similar and compete with one another, the effect may still be to lock out room for other firms to bring out their brands. Procter & Gamble has used this technique to good advantage. It has several major brands of soaps (Ivory, Zest, Safeguard, Camay, and Lava) and household cleaners (Top Job, Mr. Clean, Comet, and Spic'n Span); this gives P&G a sizable overall market share and reduces the amount of shelf space available to competitors.

Occasionally, when a dominant firm has grown sluggish, inefficient, and complacent and then is challenged by smaller upstarts, it will try to protect its position by throwing its weight around with suppliers, distributors, or legislators and by initiating maneuvers to discipline firms that have "gotten out of line." For instance, it may threaten major suppliers with backward integration unless they give it more favorable prices than smaller competitors; it may pressure distributors to give less attention to competitor's products; its salespeople may gossip with buyers about how the fringe firms' products are "really inferior"; it may lobby with legislators for the passage of bills that will make it harder for small firms to compete. Alternatively, it may give special under-the-table price discounts to competitors' best customers or launch a massive promotional campaign which small firms cannot hope to match.

Thus, a dominant firm has several options for maintaining its dominance: (1) keeping the industry price low enough to deter entry and to make expansion of fringe firms unattractive, (2) an innovational offensive on nonprice competitive variables, and (3) a defensive strategy involving confrontation, disciplinary action, and persecution of maverick aggressors.

The smaller "underdog" firm's best hope in successfully competing with a dominant firm usually lies not in mounting a head-on attack but rather in striking suddenly and with a concentrated effort to catch the dominant firm by surprise. Innovation and product differentiation are an underdog's best strategies. The innovation may involve developing a superior product, cutting costs, finding new ways to distribute goods that offer substantial economies or reach particular buyer segments more effetively, or instituting unique customer services. When one or several of these are coupled with clever advertising, the

---

[15] A penetrating analysis of dominant firm pricing is found in Dean A. Worcester, "Why 'Dominant Firms' Decline," *Journal of Political Economy,* Vol. 65, No. 4 (August 1957), pp. 338–47.

result will usually suffice to give underdog firms a viable and perhaps increasing market share.

BAROMETRIC PRICE LEADERSHIP

Barometric price leadership exists when there are *several* principle firms (surrounded or not, as the case may be, by a competitive fringe of small firms) and when one of the large firms is not powerful enough to impose its will upon the other consistently. Sometimes one, sometimes another of the principal firms will take the lead in initiating price changes. For instance, in rayon yarn, American Viscose (the largest seller) and DuPont (the second largest seller) have in recent years shared the role of leader. In copper, price leadership has been exercised by all of the Big Three—Anaconda, Kennecott, and Phelps Dodge, Anheuser-Busch and Miller Brewing have shared the lead in beer. American Airlines in recent years has been the price leader in commercial air travel.

By and large, the barometric price leader appears to do little more than become the first firm to announce new prices consistent with current market conditions. Seldom does the barometric firm possess power to coerce the rest of the industry into accepting its lead, despite the fact that it may aspire to wield such control. In the usual case, the barometric firm acquires its status as leader because of its experience and respect throughout the industry, because other firms may be unable or unwilling to accept the responsibility of continuously appraising industry demand and supply conditions, or because other firms are hesitant to stick their necks out and formally recognize what is already being acknowledged in private. Thus, *the barometric firm commands adherence of rivals to its price announcements only to the extent that it has accurately perceived the winds of change in industry demand and supply conditions*. But even then, industrywide assent to the price change may not be forthcoming immediately; rival firms often temporize with a wait-and-see strategy for days or weeks or months.

> **Barometric price leaders do not have sufficient market power to impose their price preferences on rivals; their role as price leader entails being first to announce new prices (either higher or lower) that they perceive reflect newly emerging market conditions.**

THE SIGNIFICANCE OF PRICE LEADERSHIP

Successful price leadership has the important effect of eliminating any perceived kink in the demand curves of oligopolists. The firm whose leadership role is widely and consistently accepted can count upon rivals to follow price increases as well as price cuts. However, for barometric firms whose lead is sometimes undermined by failure to follow, the inhibitions of a perceived kink still lurk close by. The evidence is not clear whether price leadership results in the establishment of a price structure higher than it would otherwise be. On some occasions, price leadership undoubtedly facilitates the raising of prices. Yet, when the price leader is the lowest-cost producer, it may hold price below levels preferred by rival firms.

> **What makes price leadership particularly attractive is its potential for eliminating any perceived kink in the demand curve.**

ARE PRICES IN OLIGOPOLISTIC MARKETS "COMPETITIVE"?

The foregoing discussion of oligopoly pricing suggests that the selling prices of rivals will gravitate toward a uniform level. No firm can price its product blindly without regard for what competitors are charging. Although competing firms may well have different profit-maximizing prices (owing to variations in

All the models of oligopoly pricing suggest that rival oligopolists have no long-term option other than to charge prices that either are identical in the case of commodity products or comparable in the case of differentiated products.

There are several avenues that oligopolists can use to arrive at a coordinated price structure.

It is difficult for oligopolists to coordinate their prices at monopolistically high levels for very long because of the active presence of so many destabilizing factors.

demand or costs), they still have no realistic alternative to selling their products at equivalent prices in the case of identical products or at comparable prices in the case of differentiated products. Only when a firm is successful in differentiating its product to a point where its customers are willing to pay a higher price is it feasible for differences in selling price to persist. Otherwise, patronage flocks to the low-priced sellers—an outcome which prompts either the establishment of a more uniform price structure or efforts to achieve more successful product differentiation.

Competitive pressures notwithstanding, collusion is obviously one avenue for deciding upon a mutually acceptable price structure. Price leadership is another. Conscious parallelism is still another. And price signaling through media channels is yet another. Of these, collusion is the riskiest and most fragile because it is outlawed by the antimonopoly statutes and because of the temptations to cheat. In addition, the presence of "maverick" firms, periodic adoptions of new corporate strategies (such as a move to accelerate growth of sales or to asume a leadership position in product innovation), the entry or potential entry of strong competition, and frequently changing demand-supply conditions all tend to make successful price collusion tenuous and often unworkable.

At the same time, a number of factors act to impede anticompetitive price coordination among oligopolistic rivals: (1) the entry into the industry of new firms which ignore current customs and practices or which otherwise disturb established buyer-seller relationships, (2) volatile industry demand conditions, (3) the frequency with which producers' cost functions are modified by technological change and the extent to which these changes make for unequal costs among firms in the industry, (4) different market shares among the firms, (5) extreme product differentiation, (6) frequent product variations, and (7) the emergence of a new industry in which firms have not had time to size up rivals' behavior. Even so, given that one or more of these price-destabilizing factors appear often in almost every oligopolistic market, the fact that rivals still price uniformly is powerful testimony to the imperatives of pricing together—whether for reasons of competition or mutual cooperation.

NONPRICE COMPETITION IN OLIGOPOLISTIC MARKETS

Because of the competitive imperative for the prices of rival oligopolists to be identical or very comparable, there are strong reasons for firms to direct their energies to competing on nonprice considerations.

Although in some markets much of the competitive focus is on *price*, in many markets (and in oligopoly generally) the main force of competition relates to *nonprice* variables. Except when they have an important cost advantage, rival oligopolists are not prone to build their competitive strategy around successfully undercutting the prices of competitors so as to gain a market advantage. Why? For two reasons. One, a firm which uses price cuts to attract business away from rival firms accomplishes little more than to compel competitors in self-defense to match the lower price—a move which neutralizes the price cut, creates lower prices for all firms in the industry, and limits each firm's sales gain to its customary share of the increased business which flows from a lower industrywide price. Two, a price-cutting strategy is quickly and easily imitated by other firms; as a consequence, it is extremely hard for a firm to gain more than a fleeting competitive edge via price cutting. Mostly, what happens when firms try to use price as a primary competitive weapon is that they expose profit margins and total profits to a good possibility of sharp erosion. Consider a simple example which illustrates why this is so. Suppose a firm is selling an item for $1.00 and that *ATC* is 90 cents. If the firm tries to gain more business by cutting price, say to 95 cents, then its profit margin ($P - ATC$) is only 5 cents compared to 10 cents before the price cut. For the firm to make as much profit at the 95-cent price as at the $1 price, it will have to sell *twice* as many units as before. In other words it will have to *double* sales just to recoup the loss of profit associated with earning only 5 cents per unit sold instead of 10 cents. True, unit costs are sometimes lowered by the increase in volume, but even if rising volume lowers unit costs to, say, 87 cents, the firm will still have to sell 20% *more* than before in order to earn as much as it was earning at the $1 price. Very likely demand will not be this price elastic (ϵ_p = % change in unit sales volume ÷ % change in price = 20% ÷ −5% = −4)— especially since rival firms will be sorely tempted to match the price cut in order to avoid losing market share to the price-cutter.

Consequently, unless a firm uses cost-saving technological innovations as the basis for its price-cutting strategy (so as not to impair profit margins with its price cuts) or unless it can realize major cost reductions from an increase in sales volume, using lower prices as a major competitive weapon tends to be an unprofitable strategy. The most attractive strategies for gaining sales, profits, and market share are thus grounded in market variables other than price. Successful nonprice strategies are harder to duplicate and tend to have a longer-lasting effect on strengthening a firm's market position. Hence, there exists a rational tendency among rival oligopolists to channel the main thrust of their head-to-head competitive efforts into forms of product differentiation: product innovation, customer service, quality, performance, convenience of use, terms of credit, styling and design, durability, advertising, and sales promotion.

To strengthen its competitive market position, an oligopolist may also expand its product line. For instance, Procter & Gamble took its successful Ivory Soap brand and followed it with Ivory Flakes and Ivory Snow. General Mills spent millions of dollars promoting Betty Crocker cake mixes and then used this brand identification to introduce Betty Crocker pie crusts, rolls, and dehydrated potatoes. Building a position of competitive strength frequently requires sellers to have a full line of products and thereby offer the customer a "total package." Specializing in the production of only one or two items can sometimes entail serious competitive disadvantages, as well as less than full utilization of organizational resources and expertise.

KEY POINTS

Competition among the few has marked differences from competition among the many. The fundamental economic reason for this is the high degree of mutual interdependence among competing oligopolists. In oligopoly each firm must try to anticipate the actions and reactions of rival firms in formulating and implementing its own competitive strategy. Nowhere is the effect of oligopolistic interdependence more apparent than in pricing. *Where oligopolists produce standardized products, a uniform price is imperative,* since firms which attempt to charge higher prices will be squeezed out of the market. *Where rival oligopolists produce either weakly or strongly differentiated products, prices must be comparable,* though not necessarily identical, since customers will tolerate price differentials they believe are justified.

Moreover, differences among rival firms regarding market shares and production costs give rise to divergent price preferences which somehow must be resolved. Whether firms with higher price preferences will win out over firms with lower price preferences or whether the reverse will occur varies with competitive and market circumstances. Collusion to maximize industry profits certainly is one possibility; however, collusive arrangements are fragile and run the risk of discovery and antitrust action. Price leadership is another possibility if follower firms are prone to cooperate with the leader's price judgment. Conscious parallelism, publicly announced prices, and formula pricing are still other collusive possibilities.

The ability of oligopolists to cooperate in the establishment of a collusive price structure is less likely to be successful the more firms there are in the industry, the larger is the output of competitive fringe firms, the more strongly differentiated and rapidly changing are the products of the firms, the more opportunities there are for secret price concessions, the more unstable are industrywide demand conditions, the more rapid is the rate of technical progress, and the greater is the degree of suspicion and mistrust among company executives. Also, those firms which perceive profits to be greater at lower prices than at higher prices are frequently in a much stronger position to impose their preferences than are the firms which prefer higher prices. Long-run product substitution and the threat of entry by new firms also place a ceiling—and sometimes a low one—upon the ability of oligopolistic producers to peg price at a monopolistic level. As a consequence, oligopolistic markets may turn out to be vigorously price competitive.

PROBLEMS AND QUESTIONS FOR DISCUSSION

1. **(a)** Graphically illustrate the profit-maximizing price and output for an oligopolistic firm confronted with a kinked demand curve and whose production function reflects constant returns to variable input throughout the firm's range of output capability. Indicate on your graph the area that represents total profit.
   (b) Illustrate the effect upon the firm's optimum price and output of a decrease in the demand for its product.

2. Is it possible for an oligopolistic firm confronted with a kinked demand curve situation to increase its short-run profits by increasing its short-run expenditures on sales promotion? Justify your answer by means of a graph.

3. Titanic Corporation and Mammoth Enterprises are only two firms selling robots to perform selected domestic services. The Titanic Corporation believes that the annual demand for its particular style of robot is given by the equation $P_T = 2400 - 0.1Q_T$. Mammoth Enterprises estimates that the annual demand for its robots is given by $P_M = 2400 - 0.1Q_M$. Because their robots have different performance features, the cost of producing Titanic's robot differs from the cost of producing Mammoth's. The estimated total cost function for Titanic's robots is $TC_T = 400,000 + 600Q_T + 0.1 Q_T^2$, where TC is in dollars per year and Q_T is Titanic's annual output of robots. The estimated total cost function for Mammoth's robots is $TC_M = 600,000 + 300Q_M + 0.2Q_M^2$, where TC is in dollars per year and Q_M is Mammoth's annual output of robots.
   (a) Determine the profit-maximizing price and output for both Titanic Corporation and Mammoth Enterprises.
   (b) Does a pricing conflict exist between the two firms?
   (c) If you were the president of Titanic Corporation, what price would you pick? Why?
   (d) If you were the president of Mammoth Enterprises, what price would you pick? Why?
   (e) Would a collusive arrangement between the firms be advantageous? Why or why not?

4. Explain the unusual conditions under which a formal cartel is likely to be successful for a long period of time. What factors make it difficult to organize a cartel? Once a cartel comes into existence, what factors are most likely to cause it to fail?

5. Reston Enterprises and Super-Technical Corporation are the only two firms producing pollution-free turbine engines for use in automobiles. Reston engines account for one-third of the total turbine engine sales, while Super-Technical engines account for two-thirds. Except for several minor features, both engines compare favorably in terms of quality, performance, and economy of operation.

    (a) Suppose that both firms produce their engines under conditions of identically rising marginal costs. Will there arise a conflict of price preferences between the two firms, assuming a goal of profit maximization? Illustrate graphically. Venture a judgment as to how the pricing conflict might be resolved in this particular situation. Is some form of collusion a distinct possibility here? Why or why not? Justify your reasoning.

    (b) Suppose that both firms produce their engines under conditions of identical and constant marginal costs. Will there then be a divergence of pricing preferences? Is it unreasonable to expect marginal costs to be constant?

    (c) Suppose that both firms produce their engines under conditions of identically declining marginal costs. Describe and graphically illustrate the nature of the pricing conflict, if any. If you were the president of Super-Technical Corporation, would you be willing to compromise your firm's preferred price with that of Reston Enerprises? Explain. Is some form of collusive arrangement likely to be reached under these circumstances? Why or why not?

6. Waxy Products, Inc., has discovered a new way to produce a "plastic wax" which, when once applied to hardwood floors, creates a permanent, waterproof, scuff-proof, shiny surface absolutely guaranteed under any conditions to last for 12 months. Waxy Products, realizing the vast market potential for its plastic wax, has employed a market research team to estimate the demand function for plastic wax in both national and international markets. The market research team reports that its estimate of plastic wax demand in the domestic market is $P_D = 100 - 5Q_D$ and that its estimate of demand in the international market is $P_F = 60 - 5Q_F$, where P is in dollars and Q is daily sales in cases. Waxy Products estimates that the short-run production function for plastic wax is $Q = 10X$, where X = units of variable input; units of variable input cost \$220 each. The president of Waxy Products, not knowing very much about price policy, asks you to assist him in *maximizing* the firm's profits. Calculate for him the *specific* price and output levels that will maximize profits from the sale of plastic wax.

7. **(a)** Do you think competition among oligopolists is more strenuous, less strenuous, or about equally strenuous as compared to competition among perfectly competitive firms? Explain your reasoning.

    (b) Do you think competition among oligopolists is more strenuous or less strenuous as compared to competition among monopolistically competitive firms? Explain your reasoning.

8. Barrett Industries is considering reducing the price of its best-selling grease remover from \$20 per gallon to \$17. Barrett estimates its production costs of grease remover are \$14 per gallon; the per-gallon cost is not thought to vary appreciably with volume, owing to constant returns. Currently, sales are running at an average of 20,000 gallons per month, and Barrett's volume, as well as the industry's as a whole, has remained stable for the past two years. Barrett has two major competitors in the grease remover market: Acme Chemical, which has an estimated market share of 40%, and Montana Products, which has approximately 25% of the market. Barrett's market share is thought to be 30%, and the remaining firms have about 5%. The going market price for grease remover is now \$19 to \$21 per gallon.

    (a) If Barrett cuts the price to \$17, how many more gallons will it have to sell to earn just as much total profit after the price cut as before the price cut? What percentage gain in sales volume does this represent?

    (b) What would the value of the short-run price elasticity of demand have to be for the proposed price cut to be profitable for Barrett?

    (c) Would you recommend that Barrett go ahead with the proposed price cut? Why or why not?

    (d) Would your answer be different if the market for grease remover were expanding rapidly? If demand were viewed as being highly elastic and major cost reductions could be achieved if volume could be increased? Explain.

9. **(a)** What conditions would strongly attract an oligopolist to use price cutting as a weapon to gain sales and market share at the expense of rival firms?

   (b) What conditions argue for oligopolists to employ a differentiation type of competitive strategy?

   (c) Would an oligopolist be inclined to pursue a focus or specialist type of competitive strategy? Under what circumstances?

10. Explain the nature of a prisoner's dilemma game. What is the dilemma? Explain why many types of oligopoly games are similar to a prisoner's dilemma game. Does the equilibrium of an oligopoly game depend on whether it is played only once? Does repeating the game matter? Why?

Chapter 14

The Economics of Firms with Multiple Prices, Plants, Products, or Objectives

Up to this point, our analysis of the firm has concentrated upon situations where the firm produces a single product sold at a single price in a single market, with the overriding objective being to maximize profits. In this chapter we relax these conditions, looking specifically at situations where an item is sold at two or more prices, where firms have two or more plants, where firms produce two or more products, and where firms set their prices based on considerations other than strict short-run profit maximization.

WHEN IT MAKES SENSE TO SELL AT DIFFERENT PRICES: THE MODELS OF PRICE DISCRIMINATION

While selling a given product at a uniform price to all buyers is a tolerable first approximation, many exceptions exist. Firms often sell their products in a variety of geographically separate markets (local, regional, national, and international) and to diverse classes of customers (industrial users, commercial users, household users, large-quantity buyers, small-quantity buyers, regular customers, occasional customers, one-time customers, and so on). They sometimes find it more profitable to sell the same item to different customers at different prices depending on the market they are in and/or to sell to a single customer at different prices depending on the quantity purchased. They may also sell products with different costs at the same price (i.e., airlines serve full-course dinners on some flights but only snacks on others, yet ticket prices are the same; some manufacturers may charge all customers the same delivered price even though the freight costs are less for nearby customers than for distant customers).[1]

---

[1] Such practices are not restricted to business enterprises. Universities, for example, charge the same tuition for a large freshmen class taught by a graduate teaching assistant as they do for a small senior seminar taught by a premier professor.

BASIC CONCEPT
Economists use the term *price discrimination* to refer to situations where a firm sells essentially the same item at different prices; the price differences may be based on the type of buyer, the place of sale, the quantity purchased, or the time of sale.

These types of pricing practices are labeled by economists as ***price discrimination***. Price discrimination occurs whenever a firm sells its product at two or more prices; it can take several forms, depending on whether the basis for the different price is the class of customer, the place where it is sold, the quantity purchased, or the time at which it is sold.

For a firm to employ price discrimination tactics in a profitable fashion, three conditions must be satisfied. First, *the firm must face a downsloping demand curve* and thus have some discretion in the price or prices it charges buyers of the product. With a horizontal demand curve, the firm has no motive for selling at different prices; in fact, selling at less than the full market price involves a sacrifice of profits. Second, *the firm must have easily identifiable groups of customers with different types of demand for the product in question.* Put another way, the shape of the demand curve for one class of customers must differ from the shape of the demand curve for another class of customers. Third, *the firm must be able to segregate its sales to each group of customers* in such a way that customers paying the lower price cannot resell the item to customers paying a higher price; the different groups of customers must, in other words, be sealed off from one another so that resale of the product by one group to another is severely constrained or unprofitable.

Two distinct types of price discrimination serve to highlight the attractiveness of charging different prices for the same product. Consider first the case where the price the customer pays depends on the quantity purchased. Suppose that the individual customer has a demand curve DD', shown in Figure 14-1. The firm charges a price of P_1 dollars per unit if the customer buys Q_1 or fewer units per period. The firm reduces its price to P_2 dollars per unit on those units purchased in excess of Q_1 but no greater than Q_2 units. For all units purchased in excess of Q_2, the firm charges a price of P_3 dollars. If a customer elects to purchase a total of Q_3 units in a given time period, the firm's total revenue (the customer's bill) is calculated as follows:

$$TR = P_1(Q_1) + P_2(Q_2 - Q_1) + P_3(Q_3 - Q_2).$$

This amount is equivalent to the gray-shaded area in Figure 14-1. The benefits to the firm of systematically reducing price as purchases increase should now

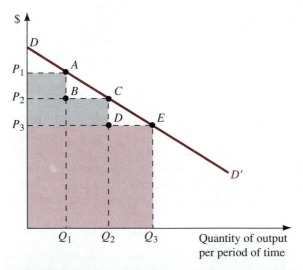

Figure 14-1
Revenue effect of pricing according to volume purchased

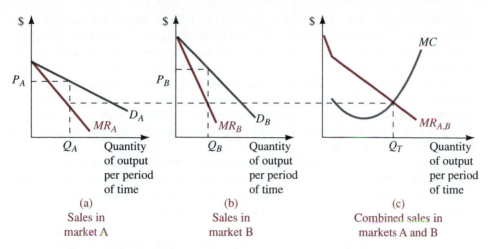

Figure 14-2

Two-market price discrimination

be apparent. Under a single-price policy, sales of Q_3 units would call for charging a maximum of P_3 dollars per unit. Total revenue would amount to only ($P_3 \cdot Q_3$) dollars, a figure P_1ABCDP_3 dollars (the area with diagonal lines in Figure 14-1) less than obtained with a multiple-price policy. From the selling firm's standpoint, such a pricing strategy is attractive because it permits the seller to capture a large portion of consumers' surplus (recall from our earlier discussion in Chapter 3 that consumers' surplus equals the triangle under the demand curve above the going price P_3.

Figure 14-2 illustrates a situation where a firm charges different prices to customers in two different markets, A and B. The respective demand and marginal revenue curves of the two classes of buyers are given in panels (a) and (b).[2] The firm must decide upon its most profitable combined sales volume, how much should be sold to buyers in each of the two markets, and the price to charge in each market. As usual, the most profitable output rate is where *MR* equals *MC*—however, the appropriate marginal revenue concept in this instance is not *MR* in *each* market *separately* but rather *MR* in both markets *combined*. The marginal revenue curves in markets A and B are summed *horizontally* to obtain combined *MR*, shown as $MR_{A,B}$ in Figure 14-2(c). The intersection of $MR_{A,B}$ with *MC* in panel (c) defines the most profitable output rate (Q_T) for the firm. Next, a decision must be made as to how much of the total output of Q_T units to sell in market A and how much to sell in market B. The rule for profit maximization in multimarket situations calls for allocating total sales between the markets in such a way that marginal cost at the optimal output equals marginal revenue *in each market*. In terms of our example, the rule requires that

$$MC = MR_{A,B} = MR_A = MR_B.$$

To locate the equalizing value of marginal revenue in the two markets at the profit-maximizing output, a horizontal line is projected from the point in panel

PRINCIPLE

To maximize profits selling the same item in two or more markets, a firm must allocate its total sales volume among the markets so that *MC* equals *MR* in each market.

---

[2] Two-market price discrimination is quite common. Many firms sell their products at one price in international markets and at another price (sometimes higher, sometimes lower) in domestic markets. In the case of products sold nationwide, prices are often higher west than east of the Rocky Mountains. The rates for telephone service are quite different for business use as compared to residential use.

(c) where $MC = MR_{A,B}$ to panels (a) and (b) to find where $MC = MR_{A,B} = MR_A = MR_B$. This gives an optimal sales level of Q_A units in market A and Q_B units in market B ($Q_A + Q_B = Q_T$). The profit-maximizing prices, P_A and P_B, are found from the respective demand curves in each market. *The firm will necessarily earn higher total profits by engaging in price discrimination than it could earn by following a single-price policy of charging the same price to all buyers.* Furthermore, it can be proven mathematically (see Mathematical Capsule 13) that *the firm's selling price is always higher in the market where demand is less elastic.*

The case of two-market price discrimination is easily expanded to allow for any number of markets. Whenever the firm sells a product in a variety of markets for which demand is different, four steps are required for determining the profit-maximizing prices and outputs in each market. Step 1 is to ascertain the firm's combined marginal revenue curve in each market. Step 2 is to pinpoint the firm's most profitable combined output rate for all markets by locating the output rate where marginal cost equals combined marginal revenue. Step 3 is to allocate the profit-maximizing output among the various markets in such a way that marginal cost at the optimal output rate is equal to the marginal revenues from the last units sold in each market. In mathematical terms, this means the firm must divide its output such that

$$MC = MR = MR_1 = MR_2 = \cdots = MR_n,$$

where MC is marginal cost, MR is the combined marginal revenue, and MR_1, $MR_2, \ldots, MR_n$ are the marginal revenues for the respective markets in which the product is sold. Step 4 is to determine the prices in each market from the respective market demand curves.

Whether price discrimination is good or bad hinges upon subjective evaluations over which reasonable people may disagree. Value judgments inevitably creep into the picture. Most academic economists are suspicious of some forms of price discrimination because, if systematically practiced, they can facilitate adherence to a collusive price structure. In addition, since firms choose freely whether to use a single- or a multiple-price policy, the implication is clear that profits are higher with discrimination than without, thereby causing a redistribution of income from customers to the firm. On the positive side, charging different prices in different markets affects the total output of the product little if at all.[3] And since customers with more elastic demands (and for whom price is lower) are likely to have incomes lower than the customers comprising the less elastic markets, price discrimination may work to the advantage of the economically weak and therefore produce "socially beneficial" effects. Moreover, situations may exist in which the costs of production cannot be covered unless revenues are enhanced by multiple pricing. Hence, where profits can be increased with multiple pricing, the added profits may be the margin between supplying a good or service and not doing so.[4] Finally, price discrimination can enhance competition by encouraging more price experimentation. Where producers are reluctant to engage in across-the-board price changes, they may be much more willing to test the consequences of a price change in one market or for one class of customers. On balance, the complex

Price discrimination, despite its connotations, is not necessarily bad—indeed, it is a commonly used pricing strategy that is well within permissible legal bounds.

---

[3] For a treatment of the output effects of price discrimination, see E. O. Edwards, "The Analysis of Output under Discrimination," *Econometrica*, Vol. 18, No. 2 (April 1950), pp. 163–72, and Joan Robinson, *The Economics of Competition* (London: Macmillan, 1933), pp. 188–95.
[4] George J. Stigler, *The Theory of Price*, 3rd ed. (New York: Macmillan, 1966), pp. 213–14.

APPLICATIONS CAPSULE

THE MANY WAYS THAT BUSINESS ENTERPRISES PRACTICE PRICE DISCRIMINATION

A tremendous variety of price discrimination practices can be found in the real world. Below is a summary of the principal types, along with examples of each. The listing provides a useful description of pricing tactics often used in the business world.

INDIVIDUAL CUSTOMER DISCRIMINATION

1. *Bargain-every-time.* Each sale is an individually negotiated deal. The classic case is the purchase of new and used cars; other examples include made-to-order sales and objects of art.
2. *Size-up-their-income.* Wealthier customers are charged more than less affluent customers; price is partially a function of income. Standard examples are the pricing of medical, legal, accounting, and management consulting services.
3. *Cut-price-if-you-must.* Departures from list price are made when buyers shop diligently for the best price; sellers grant secret concessions as a last resort. Examples include the transactions between steel firms and auto makers for hot and cold rolled sheet steel and virtually any industrial product sold to skilled purchasing agents, who are always on the lookout for a lower price.
4. *Count-the-use.* Price is based upon the level of use, even though unit costs do not vary appreciably with volume. For example, the rental fees on Xerox copying machines are based upon the number of copies made.

GROUP DISCRIMINATION

1. *Promote-new-customers.* New customers are offered "special introductory prices" lower than those paid by established customers in the hopes of enlarging the firm's regular clientele. Record and book clubs and magazine publishers are avid practitioners of this pricing policy.
2. *Forget-the-freight.* All customers are charged the same delivered price, even though transportation costs vary from customer to customer according to the distance located from the production site. Nearby customers are discriminated against in favor of faraway customers. Examples include cement and steel pricing and, additionally, any commodity which is sold at "nationally advertised prices" irrespective of transportation cost differentials.
3. *Get-the-most-from-each-market.* Prices are persistently held higher in markets where competition is weak than where it is strong. Import quotas and tariff barriers allow some firms to charge higher prices in domestic markets than in international markets (sugar, oil, and domestic wool).

4. *Favor-the-big-buyer.* Large purchasers of a commodity are given price cuts perhaps geared to the cost savings derived from large-scale transactions. The large chain discount retailers buy many of their goods at prices below those of the small retailer; firms which purchase in "carload lots" obtain discounts not allowed to purchasers of just a few units.
5. *Skim-the-market.* A product is introduced at a high price within reach mainly of only high-income buyers. Periodically, price is then reduced step by step (and in conjunction with the availability of new production capacity) to allow steady, but gradual, penetration of broader markets. The pricing of TV sets and Polaroid cameras has followed this pattern.

PRODUCT DISCRIMINATION

1. *Make-them-pay-for-the-label.* Manufacturers sell a relatively homogeneous commodity under different brand names, charging higher prices for the better-known, more prestigious brand names. Automobile tires, paints, articles of clothing, and food products are examples.
2. *Appeal-to-quality.* Products are offered in packages ranging from the budget variety to the super deluxe. Differences in price are *more* than proportional to the differences in cost. Household appliances are an obvious example. Traveling first class as compared to tourist class is another example.
3. *Get-rid-of-the-dogs.* Price concessions in the form of "special" sales are made periodically, or continuously in the bargain department of the retail store, in order to reduce stocks of poorly selling items and to make room for new merchandise. The seemingly perpetual end-of-the-model-year sales, close-out specials, anniversary sales, and inventory reduction sales serve as good examples.
4. *Switch-them-to-off-peak-periods.* Lower prices are charged for services identical except for time of consumption in order to encourage fuller and more balanced use of capacity. Off-season rates at resorts, the lower rates for long-distance calls made at night and on Sundays, and the discount fares of airlines are examples.

Sources: Compiled from the observations of several writers, including Fritz Machlup, "Characteristics and Types of Price Discrimination," contained in the National Bureau of Economic Research conference report, *Business Concentration and Price Policy* (Princeton, N.J.: Princeton University Press, 1955), pp. 397–435; Joel Dean, *Managerial Economics* (Englewood Cliffs, N.J.: Prentice Hall, 1951), pp. 419–24, 503–48; and Ralph Cassady, Jr., "Techniques and Purposes of Price Discrimination," *Journal of Marketing*, Vol. 11, No. 2 (October 1946), pp. 135–50.

crosscurrents at work make it prudent to judge each particular instance of price discrimination on its merits.

PRICING STRATEGIES WHERE STRICT PROFIT MAXIMIZATION IS NOT THE DOMINANT CONSIDERATION

The managers of business enterprises, although very profit-conscious, are not always inclined to base their decisions solely upon what will maximize profit. As we saw in Chapter 9, other objectives can influence what a firm does, especially when profits reach acceptable levels and a firm's long-term profit outlook is good. Although economists traditionally view price as *the* dominant competitive variable, in practice many firms view pricing as a major strategic issue in essentially only four types of situations: (1) when a firm must set a price for the first time, as occurs when it introduces a new product, moves into a new market, or regularly enters competitive sealed bids on contract work; (2) when market or competitive circumstances prompt a firm to consider initiating a price change; (3) when one or more rival firms initiate a price change and some response is required; and (4) when the firm produces two or more products having interrelated demands and/or costs, thus posing problems of optimal price coordination. These situations are, of course, not rare, but neither are they so pervasive as to take up the bulk of management's time.

Firms have developed a wide variety of strategic approaches for addressing pricing. Interestingly enough, while profit is unquestionably a major concern in the pricing decision, the evidence is not strong that managerial estimates of the relationship between *MR* and *MC* actually form the basis for price selection.[5]

> *In practice, firms do not view price setting as a pervasive, top-priority consideration, although it is a major strategic issue in certain situations.*

PRICING TO EARN A TARGET RATE OF RETURN

Studies of business pricing practices indicate a widespread use of target return pricing methods. A **target return price** is a price designed to yield the firm a predetermined profit from the sale of specific products or product groups. The desired profit is typically based upon dollar sales (total revenue) or upon some measure of invested capital and may be expressed either as a percentage rate or as a dollar amount. For example, the desired profit target may be stated as a profit on sales of 5%, a profit return equal to 10% of total assets, a profit return equal to 15% of net worth (stockholders' equity), a profit equal to X dollars per share of common stock, or as simply a specific dollar figure. The size of the profit target tends to hinge upon such considerations as (1) industry custom, (2) competitive pressures, (3) what managers believe to be a fair, or reasonable, return given the associated business risk, (4) a desire to equal or better the firm's recent profit performance, (5) a desire to stabilize industry prices, (6) whether the firm's product is new or a unique specialty

> **BASIC CONCEPT**
> A target return price is a price calculated to produce a specified target rate of profitability.

---

[5] The literature on the subject is immense. Among the more definite studies are R. L. Hall and Charles J. Hitch, ''Price Theory and Business Behavior,'' *Oxford Economic Papers*, Vol. 2 (May 1939), pp. 12–45; A. D. H. Kaplan, J. B. Dirlam, and R. F. Lanzilotti, *Pricing in Big Business* (Washington, D.C.: The Brookings Institution, 1958), Chapter 2; Burnard H. Sord and Glenn A. Welsch, *Business Budgeting* (New York: Controllership Foundation, 1958), pp. 88–89 and 148; James H. Miller, ''A Glimpse at Practice in Calculating and Using Return on Investment,'' *NAA Bulletin* (June 1969), p. 73; W. W. Haynes, ''Pricing Practices in Small Firms,'' *Southern Economic Journal*, Vol. 30, No. 4 (April 1964), pp. 315–24.

MATHEMATICAL CAPSULE 13

THE MATHEMATICS OF PRICE DISCRIMINATION

When a firm sells its product in markets that are economically isolated and when the respective market demand curves confronting the firm are different, the firm maximizes total profit by charging different prices in each market. The conditions for maximizing profits may be derived very simply. For illustrative convenience we shall restrict the analysis to a two-market situation.

Suppose that the firm's total revenue from sales of output in market A is represented as

$$TR_A = f(Q_A),$$

the firm's total revenue from sales of output in market B is represented as

$$TR_B = g(Q_B),$$

and the firm's total costs from combined sales in both markets are represented by

$$TC = h(Q_A + Q_B) = h(Q),$$

where Q is total output no matter in which market specific units are sold. In other words, TC depends on the output rate and not on where the output is sold.

As usual, total profit (π) is equal to total revenue minus total cost:

$$\pi = TR - TC.$$

Substituting into this expression gives

$$\pi = TR_A + TR_B - TC,$$

which can be rewritten as

$$\pi = f(Q_A) + g(Q_B) - h(Q).$$

The profit-maximizing conditions are

$$\frac{\partial \pi}{\partial Q_A} = \frac{\partial f}{\partial Q_A} - \frac{\partial h}{\partial Q} = \frac{df}{dQ_A} - \frac{dh}{dQ} = 0,$$

$$\frac{\partial \pi}{\partial Q_B} = \frac{\partial g}{\partial Q_B} - \frac{\partial h}{\partial Q} = \frac{dg}{dQ_B} - \frac{dh}{dQ} = 0,$$

But, by definition, $df/dQ_A = MR_A$, $dg/dQ_B = MR_B$, and $dh/dQ = MC$. Thus, profit maximization requires that

$$MR_A - MC = 0 \text{ and } MR_B - MC = 0,$$

which in turn is equivalent to

$$MR_A = MR_B = MC.$$

Now let us prove that the higher of the two profit-maximizing prices is found in the market with the less elastic demand. Let $P = f(Q)$ represent any demand curve, where P is price and Q is the quantity demanded. The total revenue is

$$TR = PQ,$$

and marginal revenue, according to the rule of differential calculus for the derivative of a product of two variables, is

$$MR = \frac{dTR}{dQ} = P + Q\frac{dP}{dQ}.$$

Multiplying this expression by P/P gives

$$MR = P\left(1 + \frac{Q}{P} \cdot \frac{dP}{dQ}\right).$$

Recalling from our definition of point elasticity that $\epsilon_p = (dQ/dP) \times (P/Q)$ and substituting this into the expression, we get

$$MR = P\left(1 + \frac{1}{\epsilon_p}\right).$$

The latter expression can now be used to demonstrate our proof that price is higher in the market where demand is less elastic. From the preceding expression, it follows that

$$MR_A = P_A\left(1 + \frac{1}{\epsilon_A}\right).$$

$$MR_B = P_B\left(1 + \frac{1}{\epsilon_B}\right).$$

Since at the optimal output $MR_A = MR_B$, then

$$P_A\left(1 + \frac{1}{\epsilon_A}\right) = P_B\left(1 + \frac{1}{\epsilon_B}\right),$$

which can be rewritten as

$$\frac{P_A}{P_B} = \frac{1 + (1/\epsilon_B)}{1 + (1/\epsilon_A)}.$$

Suppose that $\epsilon_A = -4$ and $\epsilon_B = -2$ at the respective profit-maximizing prices of P_A and P_B; then demand is more elastic in market A than in market B. By substituting these values into the last expression, it is clear that $P_A/P_B < 1$ and that $P_B > P_A$. This result is obtained for any values of ϵ_A and ϵ_B such that $|\epsilon_A| > |\epsilon_B|$. Accordingly, two-market price discrimination always leads to a higher price in the market where demand is less elastic with regard to price.

item, and (7) the firm's related goals of sales, market share, and growth. Specific profit targets tend to differ among industries and firms, reflecting differing degrees of competition and differing priorities among alternative goals. Normally, however, *after-tax* profit targets tend to fall within a range of 3 to 7% of sales and 10 to 20% of invested capital.

The mechanics of target return pricing may be set forth briefly in terms of two examples—the first illustrating *pricing to achieve a target return on investment* and the second illustrating what is commonly referred to as *cost-plus pricing*.

To earn a target rate of return on investment, a firm selects a price that, based on sales volume, should yield a big enough profit margin on each unit sold to end up with sufficient total profit to produce the desired return on investment.

1. Assume that a firm has $100 million invested in the production of a particular product and desires to earn a long-run average annual return of 20% before taxes on its investment. This, of course, translates into an annual profit target of $20 million. The initial step is to determine average total cost at some "normal" output rate (often referred to as the *standard volume*). Usually, the normal output rate is arbitrarily pegged somewhere between two-thirds and four-fifths of the capacity rate, instead of being related to the firm's actual operating rate. Many users of this approach base their normal output rate upon what they believe to be their long-run rate of plant utilization. Suppose ATC is estimated to be $50 at the normal output rate of 2 million units. Since the firm wishes a total profit of $20 million on sales of 2 million units, profit per unit must average $10. The target price is then calculated by adding the necessary profit margin of $10 to the projected average total cost of $50 at the normal output rate, giving a price of $60. The target price serves as the initial basis for the firm's price decision; it may be adjusted upward or downward according to prevailing business conditions, actual or potential competition, long-run strategic objectives, and other relevant factors of the moment. Once the target price is chosen, the firm sells whatever amount is then demanded at the target price.

With cost-plus pricing, a firm arrives at its selling price by adding a percentage markup to the average cost of the product.

2. *Cost-plus pricing is a widely used procedure whereby price is calculated by adding a predetermined percentage markup to the estimated unit cost of the product.* To determine unit cost, the firm first computes the costs of labor, raw materials, and other variable inputs to get an estimate of AVC; to this is added the projected AFC at the normal operating rate (or standard volume). To illustrate, suppose that the firm is producing a product under conditions of constant returns to variable input such that $MC = AVC = \$30$. Further suppose that 75% of capacity is viewed as the normal operating rate, and at this output rate AFC is estimated to be $15. Average total cost is therefore $45 at the normal output rate. To this figure is added a markup of 5, 10, 20, 50, or whatever percent is required to achieve the firm's target profit. The size of the markup frequently reflects what managers believe is an equitable relation to cost. If the firm desires a 10% return on sales, it should add a margin of $5 to its unit cost estimate of $45 to give a selling price of $50, which in percentage terms is equivalent to a markup slightly in excess of 11% over cost. If the firm desires a 25% return on sales, it should add a margin of $15 to its $45 unit cost to give a price of $60—a percentage markup of $33\frac{1}{3}\%$ over cost. As with pricing to achieve a target return on investment, cost-plus prices are subject to modification by competitive conditions and other pertinent considerations.

There are numerous variations of these two approaches to pricing. Cost estimates may be based upon normal operating rates, forecasted costs, or costs for the most recent accounting period. The amount of the "plus" or the target profit may be based upon either short-run or long-run considerations; it may be fixed for all products of the firm or variable among products; it may be computed as a percentage of costs, invested capital, or dollar sales. Normally, the specific formula is keyed to long-standing industry practices, competitive conditions, price-cost-volume relationships, capital investment requirements, and the like. It is not uncommon for diversified firms to have different profit targets and to use different target returns for different types of products, depending on price elasticity considerations, competitive pressures, whether the item carries a name brand or a private label, the intricacy and originality of the product and its design, and the estimate of the product's economic worth and utility to the customer. For example, in the retail goods industry where *variable markup pricing* (a cost-plus hybrid) is common, the markups *over cost* have been reported as 67% for cosmetics, 30 to 35% for household appliances, 38% for cameras, 50% for books (though the markup is usually 25% for college textbooks), 85% for costume jewelry, 25% for tobacco products, 80 to 125% for furniture, from 15 to 87% for frozen foods, and 100% for light fixtures and cabinet hardware.[6]

Another common use of target return pricing is found in corporate strategies for new product development and product innovation.[7] In contemplating the introduction of a new product or the revamping of an existing product, a typical procedure is for the firm first to identify a target selling price using such criteria as the prices of similar products, competitors' prices, and the estimated performance value to the customer. Product design and planning then proceed toward producing at a cost that fits within the target market price and at the same time allows a margin of profit sufficient to yield the firm's target rate of return. Engineering and production personnel are assigned the task of designing a product which will conform as closely as possible to the targeted unit cost, price, and profit margin. *Hence, the firm, in developing and pricing new products, starts from established or preconceived prices and works backward to see whether it can profitably offer the product at or below the target.* Failing this, the firm may pursue the question of whether higher costs can be justified by a product that on comparative performance can command a somewhat higher price than the ruling price average and still yield the desired target return. The attempt to design a product within the target cost-price-profit figures is sometimes successful and sometimes unsuccessful. In the unsuccessful instances whether the go-ahead is given depends on management's estimate of the nature of the product in its overall product line. If the product is one which strongly complements or creates a substantial demand for other of the firm's products, the firm may well decide to produce the item regardless of the estimated profits.

Attributes of Target Return Pricing.

In practice, both pricing to achieve a target return on investment and cost-plus offer relatively simple and expedient methods of price determination as well as a demonstrated ability to yield adequate, fair, or reasonable profits. The profitability of the two methods is evidenced by the avowed use of some sort of target return pricing by such firms as Alcoa, DuPont, Exxon, General Electric, General Foods, General Motors, International Harvester, Johns-Manville, Union Carbide, and U.S. Steel.[8]

Once the target price is chosen, the usual procedure is for the firm to stick by its price (barring major changes in market conditions) and sell whatever amounts of output that customers are willing to buy at the target price. The target return price is therefore a fairly stable price—an attribute that highly

---

[6] See, for instance, Lee E. Preston, *Profits, Competition and Rules of Thumb in Retail Food Pricing* (Berkeley: University of California Institute of Business and Economic Research, 1963), p. 31, and *Departmental Merchandising and Operating Results of 1966* (New York: National Retail Merchants Association, 1963), pp. 16, 28.

[7] An excellently documented example of International Harvester's use of this strategy is found in Kaplan, Dirlam, and Lanzilotti, *Pricing in Big Business*, pp. 69–79.

[8] R. F. Lanzilotti, "Pricing Objectives in Large Companies," *American Economic Review*, Vol. 48, No. 5 (December 1958), pp. 921–40.

If a firm employs a target rate of return pricing technique and its sales volume deviates substantially from expected or normal amounts, its profits may miss the targeted level by a wide margin.

recommends itself to oligopoly situations where infrequent price changes are competitively helpful. This may partly explain the popularity of target return pricing among corporate oligopolists. However, *target return pricing does have the effect of causing wide swings in profits when economic conditions turn up or down*; on a year-to-year basis, actual profits may thus turn out to be either higher or lower than the target profit rate. Suppose, for example, that a firm has a short-run average total cost curve as illustrated in Figure 14-3; the target price is P dollars, the normal operating rate is 70% of capacity, the target profit margin is $P - ATC_{70\%}$, and the target amount of total profit is equal to the shaded area. If in a particular year demand is especially strong and actual output corresponds to 90% of capacity, then total profits will be pushed up well above the targeted level. Two reasons can account for this. First, the firm's actual sales of output will exceed the rate required to achieve the profit target. Second, unit costs at 90% of capacity may be lower than at 70% of capacity because of the lower average fixed costs associated with higher production rates. The realized profit margin on each unit sold of $P - ATC_{90\%}$ may therefore be larger than the margin of $P - ATC_{70\%}$ needed to reach the target. The combined effect of wider profit margins and above-normal sales is a realized profit which may be considerably in excess of the target rate of return, as shown in Figure 14-3. On the other hand, if demand for the firm's product is weak and actual sales of output amount to only 50% of capacity instead of the normal 70%, then the profit target will in all probability not be achieved. At production rates below the normal 70% figure, average fixed costs are sure to be higher, and average variable costs may be higher if the production process cannot be operated efficiently at less than normal rates. With average total cost at 50% of capacity exceeding that at 70%, the realized profit margin of

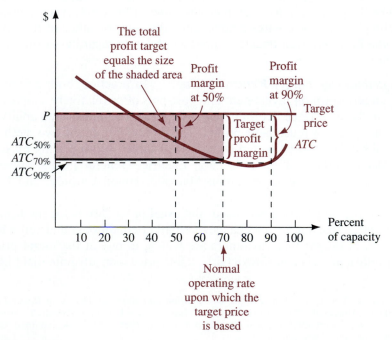

Figure 14-3
The effects of demand fluctuations upon achieving the target rate of return

$P - ATC_{50\%}$ will be narrower than the targeted margin of $P - ATC_{70\%}$. This, together with lower sales, produces total profits well below the target rate of return (see Figure 14-3).

A firm using target pricing is well aware that profits in any given year may not correspond to the profit target because actual sales will almost certainly deviate to some extent from the output rate on which the target price is based. The target profit rate is something the firm hopes to achieve as a long-run average rather than in any particular year. This is apparent from the fact that the target price is predicated upon a normal rate of production instead of the forecasted sales volume for the upcoming period.

It follows from the preceding discussion that *target return pricing is not a strategy for maximizing profits.*[9] This is easily demonstrated. Since the target return price is keyed to the firm's normal operating rate (or standard volume), the target return price and the profit-maximizing price will coincide if and only if the normal operating rate just happens to correspond to the output rate where marginal cost equals marginal revenue. Certainly, there is no reason to expect this to occur—except by mere circumstance and coincidence.

Target return pricing cannot be used to determine price if the firm's objective is to maximize profits.

Actually, the concept of target return pricing exemplifies a behavior pattern closely approximating satisficing. The target rate of return, according to the evidence available, tends to be based upon managerial concepts of what is an "equitable" or "reasonable" or "satisfactory" rate of return, given the degrees of risk and uncertainty involved. Few managers believe or, more accurately perhaps, admit that their profit targets are indicative of the "maximum" obtainable rate of return. Managers exhibit a propensity to use target return pricing techniques because information is often too sketchy or too expensive to obtain for a full analysis of the relevant factors to be conducted. In essence, target return pricing is an imperfect expedient designed to facilitate, in a rough but ready manner, the handling of a thorny decision problem under conditions of uncertainty. Parenthetically, it should be added that executives use similar "rules of thumb" in other decision situations. Advertising expenditures are frequently determined by setting aside some fixed percentage of total revenue; inventory levels may be pegged to some preset turnover norm. By translating complicated problems into simple routines, rule-of-thumb procedures economize on executive time and may even contribute to overall operating efficiency. In any event, they serve as classic examples of precisely what is meant by satisficing—the seeking of satisfactory workable solutions to complex decision problems.

Target return pricing is consistent with a satisficing objective.

---

[9] Some economists have argued that if the firm's target rate of return is based upon some concept of the *largest* rate of return the firm perceives it can get, then the firm's behavior reflects a goal of profit maximization. This is misleading if not erroneous. To illustrate why, suppose a firm believes the maximum rate of return market conditions will allow is 20%. The critical question now becomes whether the perceived maximum rate of 20% can be obtained just as well via target return pricing as by marginal cost–marginal revenue pricing. The answer is only by rare circumstance. If 20% is truly the maximum profit rate, then the only way it can be attained is for the firm to elect the price and output corresponding to the intersection of MC and MR. Since the target return price and the profit-maximizing price will coincide only if the normal operating rate just happens to be the output rate where $MR = MC$. This is a little too much to expect. Thus, while a firm's managers may believe the target return price will yield the maximum rate of profit, the facts of the matter are to the contrary. In a sense, the fallacy in their thinking is akin to the fallacy that maximum profit is achieved at the output where profit per unit $(P - ATC)$ is greatest. As was demonstrated in Chapter 10, the output rate at which price exceeds ATC by the greatest amount *does not* correspond to the output rate where $MR = MC$.

APPLICATIONS CAPSULE

PRAGMATIC PRICING STRATEGIES

Over the years companies have come up with a number of pricing strategies to deal with the situations they face. In practice, quite a large number of enterprises orient their pricing toward cost (as in target return and cost-plus pricing) or toward demand (as in price skimming) or toward market share and sales growth (as in penetration pricing) or toward competition (as in going-rate pricing and sealed bids). Although marginal cost–marginal revenue considerations enter to some extent into these alternatives, they are not decisive in choosing the actual price. Let's look at such pricing strategies as penetration pricing, price skimming, loss-leader pricing, quick-payback pricing, price followership, sealed-bid pricing, and odd-number pricing.

PENETRATION PRICING

In introducing new products and/or in moving into new geographic markets, firms sometimes deliberately set a relatively low price in order to develop the market for the item and to capture a large market share. Any of several conditions favor the use of penetration pricing: (1) when demand is very price elastic and many new customers can be attracted by a lower price (and then later induced to pay higher prices), (2) when major economies of scale and/or strong experience curve effects exist and large sales volumes are needed to achieve maximum efficiency-minimum unit cost, (3) when a low price will discourage the actual or potential entry of new firms as well as the development of substitute products, (4) when it is important for competitive and psychological reasons to get a lead on rival firms and capture as large a market share as quickly as possible, and (5) when a firm is trying to enter an industry and needs to have some basis for attracting buyers' attention and building up a clientele for its product.

Once the firm's market penetration objective is achieved, it can then turn attention to ways to increase profitability, including a planned gradual raising of price over a period of time. A penetration price thus deliberately sacrifices short-run profitability for long-run objectives (long-run profitability, growth in sales, market share, etc.).

PRICE SKIMMING

On occasions, firms try to take advantage of the fact that some buyers are always willing and able to pay a premium price because the product, for any of several reasons, has a high immediate value to them. The objective of price skimming is initially to charge as much as these buyers will pay and then gradually to reduce price to gain access to lower-price market segments. In essence, price skimming is a form of price discrimination *over time*; starting with the price-inelastic buyer segments, the firm proceeds over time to draw in the more price-elastic market segments with progressively lower prices (often, the lower prices are keyed to the introduction of lower-quality models so as not to interfere with continuing to realize substantially higher margins on top-of-the-line models). Price skimming can be attractive to sellers whenever (1) different classes of buyers have materially different price elasticities of demand and the firm has ample time to "ride" down the demand curve, charging each buyer segment as much as the traffic will bear; (2) the innovating firm has a lead time long enough that the initial high price will neither stimulate entry of rival firms nor the development of substitute products; (3) the diseconomies of producing at smaller volumes do not cancel out the advantage of premium prices; (4) high initial prices support the impression that the product is superior and of exceptional quality; and (5) there is substantial risk to setting an initial price that is too low (because demand is uncertain and may not materialize or because unit costs may exceed expectations).

LOSS-LEADER PRICING

Some firms, particularly food retailers and discount stores, price one or a few items at bargain levels (even below

---

REVENUE MAXIMIZATION WITH A PROFIT CONSTRAINT

One of the best known of the multiple-goal models of business behavior is the model of sales revenue maximization with a profit constraint.[10] This model, first proposed by William Baumol, is founded upon the premise that once profits reach acceptable levels, the firm's profit goal becomes subordinate to its goal of increasing its sales revenue (the rationale underlying this goal hierarchy was presented in Chapter 9). According to Baumol, the drive to increase sales revenues assumes such strong proportions that the firm's managers are willing to forgo higher profits to obtain greater sales revenues.

---

[10] Baumol's model, with all of its price-output and strategy ramifications, is presented in his book *Business Behavior, Value and Growth,* rev. ed. (New York: Harcourt Brace Jovanovich, 1967), Chapters 6–8.

wholesale cost) in order to (1) increase future sales of the item or (2) attract customers to their stores and boost sales on other items. The objective, of course, is not to produce losses but rather to increase total profits. A successful loss-leader therefore is really a profit-leader. Loss-leader pricing can be defined as pricing an item at a level which generates a subpar or even negative unit contribution profit (i.e., $P - AVC$ will be less than the customary margin) but which is nonetheless expected to result in higher total profits through either increased future sales of the item or greater sales on the firm's entire line of items. Loss-leader pricing works well in situations where (1) it is desirable for buyers to become familiar with the product (or with the store), (2) it is apparent to buyers that the price represents a good value, (3) the price cut is sizable enough to cause buyers to respond, and (4) the lower price does not signify a reduction in quality.

QUICK PAYBACK PRICING

Some firms aim for a price that offers the quickest payback of sunk investment costs. This could mean pricing either high or low, depending on such factors as buyers' sensitivity to price, whether the market is developed, the competitive threat from substitute products, barriers to entry, and so on. Firms may lean toward such a pricing strategy if they are cash-poor or if market change is too rapid to justify patiently cultivating demand.

PRICE FOLLOWERSHIP

Firms that trail the market leaders may have a pricing strategy that consists of no more than simply charging the going price. This is referred to as going-rate pricing, imitative pricing, or price followership. In oligopolistic markets such a pricing strategy has obvious appeal for firms not in a position to exert price leadership or for firms whose products are not differ-

entiated strongly enough to give them some price freedom. But the strategy is also used by firms unaffected by oligopolistic interdependence. Why? Because it is easy. The price imitator can sit back and let other firms worry about demand elasticities, changing market conditions, and what to do next; managers then have more time to devote to other decisions. This is a tenable position as long as acceptable profits can be earned being a price follower.

SEALED BID PRICING

In construction, defense contract work, and capital goods manufacture, firms compete for jobs on the basis of bid prices. Here, pricing strategy is necessarily keyed to expectations of how competitors will price. While overall market conditions and costs are relevant in deciding how hard to try to get a particular job, the firm's success is predicted upon being low bidder on a sufficient number of jobs to build a viable business. The firm thus confronts something of a dilemma: The higher its bid price is above variable costs, the higher are potential profits but the lower is the chance of getting the contract. On the other hand, if the firm consistently bids too close to variable costs, it may not earn enough contribution profit to cover total fixed costs.

ODD-NUMBER PRICING

Some sellers believe that odd-number prices are more attractive to buyers than round-number prices. A $5.99 price may, for psychological or subconscious reasons, be more stimulating to sales than a $6.00 price. A 33-cent price may have more buyer appeal than a 32-cent or even a 30-cent price. Items may sell more rapidly at 3 for 88 cents than for 29 cents each. The problem here is to determine which numbers have more appeal and to what products this appeal applies.

Figure 14-4 illustrates the revenue maximization model. The firm's *TR, TC,* and π curves are shown in their conventional shapes. Total profit is maximum at an output rate of Q_1 units, and *TR* is maximum at an output rate of Q_3 units. Thus, it is evident that the firm cannot simultaneously maximize short-run profits *and* sales revenue. Profit is always maximum where $MR = MC$, whereas *TR* (or sales revenue) is maximum where $MR = 0$. *The price and the output rate which maximize profits definitely do not correspond to the price and the output rate which maximize sales revenue.* Suppose the firm has a profit target of π_1 dollars [Figure 14-4(b)]. If profits of π_1 dollars are required before other objectives such as sales revenue maximization are pursued, then the firm is in no position to increase the sales of output beyond Q_1 units, since even at the profit-maximizing output the profit target is still out of reach. The firm must produce at Q_1 units just to come as close as possible to satisfying its profit constraint. However, if profits of π_2 dollars will fulfill its profit requirements,

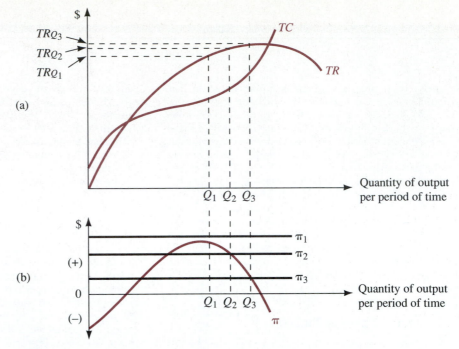

A revenue-maximizer produces and sells a larger quantity of output than a profit-maximizer.

Figure 14-4
Revenue maximization model

A revenue-maximizer charges a lower price than a profit-maximizer.

the firm is in a position to pursue a sales revenue goal as well as a profit goal. By lowering its price, the output rate can be expanded to Q_2 units and sales revenues pushed up to TR_{Q_2} dollars. Profits will still be the desired amount of π_2 dollars, though they will be below their potential maximum. Nonetheless, the firm is able to meet its profit objective, and it enjoys a higher level of sales revenues than it would at the profit-maximizing output of Q_1 units. This is what is meant by sales revenue maximization with a profit constraint. Finally, suppose the profit constraint is only π_3 dollars. Then price can be lowered yet further, the sales of output pushed to Q_3 units, and revenue pushed to the maximum value of TR_{Q_3} dollars. The firm has no motive to expand its output rate past Q_3, even though its profit goal of π_3 dollars is overfulfilled. The reason? Additional output can be absorbed in the market only at prices reduced so much that total revenue will fall. Hence, revenues are smaller at output rates greater than Q_3 than they are at Q_3, effectively undermining the firm's revenue incentive to push sales past Q_3 units.

Observe that at outputs below Q_1 a strategy of lowering price and increasing output enhances both profits and sales revenues. Up to an output of Q_1 units, the two goals are complementary in the sense that success in achieving higher sales is concomitant with success in achieving higher profits. On the other hand, between outputs of Q_1 and Q_3 units, lower prices and greater outputs cause profits to fall but sales revenues to rise. Therefore, between Q_1 and Q_3, greater sales revenues are achieved at the expense of profits—the two goals compete with one another. Beyond an output of Q_3 units, a lower price (and consequently larger sales of output) results in lower profits and in lower sales revenues.

A chief conclusion to be derived from the sales revenue maximization model is this: *If a firm has a goal of maximizing its sales revenue subject to a profit constraint and if the firm's profit constraint (or profit target) is below the maximum attainable profit, then the firm will charge lower prices for its products and will produce greater outputs than it would with a goal of profit maximization.*

Advertising Expenditures and the Goals of the Firm.

The decision as to how much to spend on advertising and sales promotion is also influenced by the firm's choice of goals. *A revenue-maximizer tends to spend more money promoting its products than does a profit-maximizer.* This proposition is illustrated in Figure 14-5. The horizontal axis in panels (a) and (b) represents the dollar magnitude of advertising outlays; the vertical axis measures dollar costs, revenues, and profits. For simplicity, total cost is shown to increase linearly with advertising expenditures, starting from a value of TC_0 dollars where advertising is zero. The *TC* curve includes all production and selling costs, including advertising outlays. The total revenue curve is drawn on the reasonable assumption that increased advertising tends to increase sales of output and revenue, but by progressively lesser amounts. In other words, diminishing returns to promotion exist, and additional advertising expenditures result in ever more slowly increasing revenues. The total profit (π) curve in panel (b) is found by subtracting total costs from total revenues at each level of advertising outlay; it indicates the profitability of various-sized advertising outlays.

Figure 14-5 indicates that the profit-maximizing amount of advertising outlay is A_1 dollars. In contrast, a revenue-maximizing firm with a profit constraint of π_1 dollars has an optimal advertising outlay of A_2 dollars. The additional advertising pushes sales revenues from TR_{A_1} dollars to TR_{A_2} dollars with-

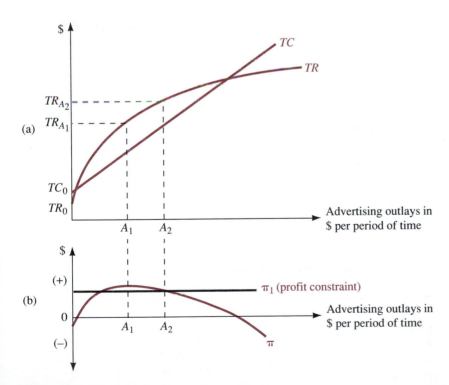

A goal of maximizing revenues subject to a profit constraint leads to greater use of advertising than does a goal of profit maximization.

Figure 14-5
Advertising expenditures and the goals of the firm

out causing total profits to fall below the targeted level of π_1 dollars. As long as the revenue-maximizer's profit target is *less* than the maximum profit level, the revenue-maximizer will find it advantageous to spend more heavily on advertising than will a profit-maximizer. The revenue-maximizer's output rate will, accordingly, be greater than the profit-maximizer's output rate. However, the revenue-maximizing firm's selling price may be higher, lower, or equal to the profit-maximizing firm's, depending on the effect advertising has upon unit costs and upon customer demand for the firm's products. On occasions, the extra advertising undertaken by the sales-maximizer may shift the firm's demand-*AR* curve so as to make it advantageous to charge a price slightly above that of rival firms. On other occasions, the additional advertising may simply result in selling more units at the prevailing price level. And on still other occasions, the extra advertising may entail a lower price as well as expanded sales.

The Effect of Fixed Cost Changes.

One of the most surprising and interesting aspects of the economics of the firm is the effect of fixed cost changes upon price and output decisions. Consider Figure 14-6, where the firm's initial cost-revenue-profit functions are given by TFC_1, TC_1, TR_1, and π_1. Note that if the firm's primary goal is profit maximization, then its optimum output rate is Q_1 units, but if its primary goal is sales revenue maximization with a profit constraint of π dollars, then its optimum output is Q_2 units. Now suppose the firm experiences a rise in the prices of its fixed inputs such that total fixed costs rise to a level indicated by TFC_2. This will cause the firm's total cost function to shift upward by the amount of the rise in fixed costs to TC_2. The rise in fixed costs will further cause the firm's profit function to shift

A rise in fixed costs does not change the profit-maximizing price and output.

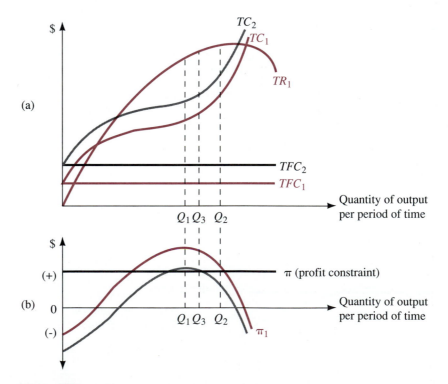

Figure 14-6

Effect of fixed cost changes upon a firm's optimum price and output

downward from π_1 to π_2, with the amount of the downward shift being equal to the increase in fixed costs.

What effect does this sort of cost increase have upon the firm's optimum price and output rate if the firm's principal goal is profit maximization? The answer, surprisingly enough, is *none*. The rise in fixed costs *lowers* the peak of the total profit curve, but it moves the peak neither to the right nor to the left. Moreover, *changes in fixed costs have no effect whatsoever upon MC or upon MR, thus leaving the point at which MC = MR completely undisturbed*. Hence, total profit is maximized at precisely the same price and output as before the rise in total fixed costs. And we have the inescapable conclusion that *changes in fixed costs do not influence the short-run price and output decisions of profit-maximizing firms so long as it is possible to earn positive contribution profits*.

But what of the effect upon a revenue-maximizing firm? From Figure 14-6 it is apparent that given the downward shift in the total profit curve an output of Q_2 units will result in profits below the minimum acceptable level. The revenue-maximizing firm will therefore be compelled to reduce output to Q_3 units to meet its profit constraint; concomitantly, it will raise price as the vehicle for effecting the reduction in unit sales. Thus, the goal of the firm is the pivotal factor in analyzing its response to a rise in fixed costs. *Firms which seek to maximize profits will leave their price and output rates unchanged when fixed costs change, whereas firms which seek to maximize sales revenue subject to a profit constraint will tend to reduce their outputs and raise their selling prices in response to an increase in fixed costs*.

Insofar as actual business practice is concerned, there is little question which of the two responses to fixed cost increases is the more commonly observed. An increase in fixed costs is usually an occasion for serious consideration of a price increase.

If a revenue-maximizing firm experiences a rise in fixed cost, it must raise price and reduce output in order to meet its profit constraint.

The Extent of Revenue-Maximizing Behavior.
The evidence is inconclusive whether or not a significant number of business firms actually base their price and output decisions upon a goal of maximizing sales revenue subject to a profit constraint. The major obstacle is that the decision process of large corporations is exceedingly complex. Many factors influence and constrain corporate pricing decisions; it is quite difficult to know just what set of motivations and priorities are reflected in managerial decisions. In addition, the behavioral differences between profit maximization and revenue maximization are difficult to detect with the available empirical data because so many economic forces must be untangled. The few available studies of business behavior, the public pronouncements of business executives, and the consulting experiences which several academicians have had with major firms do, however, combine to give credence to the revenue maximization model.[11] The numerous examples of target return pricing are also quite consistent with a revenue-

[11] See, for example, the instances cited by Baumol, *Business Behavior, Value and Growth*, Chapter 6; Marshall Hall, "Sales Revenue Maximization: An Empirical Examination," *Journal of Industrial Economics*, Vol. 15 (April 1967), pp. 143–54; J. W. McGuire, J. S. Y. Chiu, and A. D. Elbins, "Executive Income, Sales, and Profits," *American Economic Review*, Vol. 52, No. 4 (September 1962), pp. 753–61; B. D. Mabry and D. L. Siders, "An Empirical Test of the Sales Maximization Hypothesis," *Southern Economic Journal*, Vol. 33, No. 3 (January 1967), pp. 267–77; and Y. Amihud and J. Kamin, "Revenue vs. Profit Maximization Differences in Behavior by the Type of Control and by Market Power," *Southern Economic Journal*, Vol. 45, No. 3 (January 1979), pp. 838–46.

APPLICATIONS CAPSULE

THE EFFECTS OF TAX CHANGES ON PRICES AND OUTPUT RATES

Whether a firm is a profit-maximizer or a revenue-maximizer has significant public policy implications. An outstanding illustration concerns the use of federal taxation policies to control inflationary tendencies. Increases in corporate tax rates have on occasions been used to help contain inflationary forces and tax cuts have been used to stimulate growth. The logic for raising business taxes to dampen inflationary demand conditions seems plain enough: With steeper corporate profits taxes, the business sector has fewer after-tax dollars to spend for new capital investment and less of a profit incentive to invest these dollars, so that investment spending is curtailed and the investment component of economywide spending is reduced. In

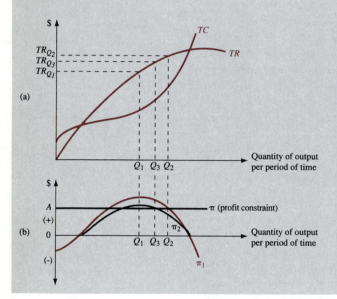

turn, the pressure of total spending upon production capacity is relieved somewhat, and the motive of sellers to raise product prices is dampened. The logic for business tax cuts to boost the economy is, of course, just the reverse of these effects.

However, the successful use of corporate profits taxes as a weapon for fighting inflation or stimulating a sluggish economy depends implicitly on the principal goal of business enterprises. This can be seen from the cost-revenue-profit curves shown in the accompanying figure. Given a total revenue curve of TR, a total cost curve of TC, a net-profit-after-taxes curve of π_1, and a profit target of OA dollars, the profit-maximizing and revenue-maximizing outputs are Q_1 units and Q_2 units, respectively. Now suppose an additional tax of 10% of all profits is imposed upon the firm. The effect of the tax is to shift the firm's after-tax profit curve downward at each level of *profitable output* by the amount of the additional tax, as shown by π_2. Observe that the peak of π_2 corresponds to the same output as does the peak of π_1. Hence, we may correctly conclude that the profit-maximizing output rate is the same after the additional tax is paid as it was before. The profit-maximizing firm therefore has no incentive to change either its output rate or its price. But the same cannot be said if the firm's goal is to maximize sales revenue subject to a profit constraint. Imposing additional corporate profits taxes upon a revenue-maximizing firm induces the firm to restrict its sales of output to Q_3 units and to raise its price as the means of reducing sales of output from Q_2 to Q_3 units. Raising price and restricting output allows the firm to cover the costs of higher taxes and still meet its after-tax profit constraint.

The preceding analysis highlights the effects of different goals upon the optimal price and output decisions of the firm. It indicates how seriously wrong predictions of business price and output behavior can be unless care is exercised first in determining the actual goals of business enterprises.

maximizing goal. Nevertheless, *the final verdict is still out on the extent of revenue-maximizing behavior among business enterprises.*

MULTIPLANT PRODUCTION AND THE CONDITIONS FOR MAXIMIZING PROFIT

The market demand for such items as tin cans, storage batteries, biscuits and crackers, cement, building materials, dairy products, tires, beer, disposable diapers, apparel, computers, floor coverings, and steel, among others, is far larger than the existing number of firms can accommodate by operating one plant.[12] As a result, firms operate several plants to manufacture the same product. American Can and Continental Can, for instance, manufacture containers

---

[12] In contrast, in producing typewriters, soup, sewing machines, photographic equipment, steam turbines, transformers, and locomotives, plants are quite large relative to the size of the total market, and multiplant operations are much less in evidence.

in over 100 domestic locations, often at sites very close to major customers. Boise Cascade in a recent year operated 14 pulp and paper mills, 20 lumber mills, 24 plywood plants, 20 composite can plants, 6 envelope plants, 20 corrugated container plants, 2 particle board plants, 6 kitchen cabinet plants, 2 door plants, and 13 manufactured-housing plants. One decision peculiar to the multiplant firm concerns how to allocate the optimum total output of a product among its several plants in order to minimize costs and maximize profits.

The chances are that the various plants of a particular firm are not only located in different regions but also incorporate different technologies, obtain raw materials and labor inputs at varying prices, and therefore have different cost structures. An illustrative case is indicated in Table 14-1. The firm operates two plants with marginal costs as shown in columns (2) and (3). Inspection of the marginal cost functions of the two plants shows that if the firm wishes to produce three or less units of output it should use plant 1 exclusively, since it has the lowest marginal cost ($3, $5, and $7 compared to $8 for plant 2). However, the fourth through ninth units should definitely be produced in plant 2. Continuing in this fashion, the combined marginal cost curve for the firm can be derived [column (4)]. As usual, profit maximization requires that the firm select the output rate at which the marginal revenue from the last unit sold equals the marginal cost of the last unit produced. This occurs at an output of 11 units and a price of $19; here, the marginal cost of the eleventh unit is $9, and the marginal revenue from selling the eleventh unit is $9.

Given that the optimum total output of the firm is 11 units, how should production of the 11 units be divided between the two plants? The answer is as follows: Produce 4 units at plant 1 and 7 units at plant 2. *Production must be*

TABLE 14-1   ALLOCATION OF OUTPUT AMONG PLANTS

(1) Total Output of the Firm	(2) Marginal Cost, Plant 1	(3) Marginal Cost, Plant 2	(4) Marginal Cost for the Firm	(5) Price	(6) Total Revenue	(7) Marginal Revenue
0				$30	$ 0	
1	$ 3	$8	3	29	29	$29
2	5	8	5	28	56	27
3	7	8	7	27	81	25
4	9	8	8	26	104	23
5	10	8	8	25	125	21
6	11	8	8	24	144	19
7	12	9	8	23	161	17
8	Capacity	Capacity	8	22	176	15
9			8	21	189	13
10			9	20	200	11
11			9	19	209	9
12			10	18	216	7
13			11	17	221	5
14			12	16	224	3

allocated among the various plants such that the marginal costs of the last units produced at each plant are equal both to each other and to the value at which the firm's overall marginal cost equals the marginal revenue of the last unit sold. Unless the marginal costs of the last units produced at each plant are equal, the firm can lower its total production costs for a given output by shifting units of production from the plant where marginal cost is higher to the plant where marginal cost is lower.

In general, then, whenever a firm operates a number of plants to produce a given item, proper application of the profit-maximizing rule involves three sequential steps. Step 1 is to determine the firm's overall marginal cost curve from the marginal cost curves of the various plants. Step 2 is to pinpoint the firm's most profitable output by finding the output rate where overall marginal cost equals marginal revenue. Step 3 is to allocate the profit-maximizing output among the various plants so that the marginal costs of the last units produced at each plant are equal. In mathematical terms, the firm should arrange its production activities so that

$$MR = MC = MC_{P_1} = MC_{P_2} = \cdots = MC_{P_n},$$

where MR is marginal revenue from all sales of the product, MC is the combined marginal cost, and $MC_{P_1}, MC_{P_2}, \cdots, MC_{P_n}$ are the marginal costs of the respective plants which the firm has for producing the item.

The effect of this rule in actual practice is that production activity is concentrated in the most efficient plants and that older, technologically inferior production facilities are used as sparingly as conditions will permit. The newest, most modern plants employing the latest technologies are nearly always operated at or near capacity levels, while older, less efficient plants are relied upon primarily to fill out the balance of the firm's total output and to help fill the firm's need for production capacity in periods of peak demand. In fact, it is partially because a firm's less efficient production facilities are used more intensively at higher output rates that marginal and average costs tend to rise at combined outputs beyond 90% of *total* capacity.

MULTIPRODUCT PRICING MODELS

Many companies sell related products, often producing them in the same plants. Such products may be substitutes, as with GM's Buicks and Oldsmobiles, or they may be complements, as with Betty Crocker cake mixes and cake frostings. These demand interrelationships need to be taken into account in the firm's pricing decision, since a change in the price of one has a bearing on the sales of the other. Determining the optimal prices of complementary and substitute products entails a careful assessment of the cross-elasticity relationships and how various price combinations affect the combined revenues and profitability of the products in question.

A firm's products can also be interrelated from a production standpoint. For instance, products may be jointly produced in a *fixed ratio* (as with leather hides and beef in a slaughterhouse operation) or in a *variable ratio* (as with gasoline and fuel oil in a crude oil refinery). Products may compete with one another in the sense of being alternatives—a butcher shop has to decide whether to cut beef quarters into roasts or grind it for hamburger; a paper producer must allocate paper pulp between making paperboard boxes and brown paper bags. Still another type of interrelationship arises when products are complementary in production, as when one product incorporates wastes generated by the production of another (using wood chips left over from lumber production to make particle board).

THE PRICING OF JOINT PRODUCTS PRODUCED IN FIXED PROPORTIONS

The simplest case of multiproduct pricing concerns that of joint products produced in fixed proportions. Since joint products are produced as a package, their costs can likewise be considered as a package, and one set of cost curves suffices for both—in fact, it may not even be feasible to separate out their individual costs. Figure 14-7 illustrates the demand, marginal revenue, and marginal cost functions for two joint products, X and Y. Not surprisingly, the key to optimal pricing of joint products is still the *MR-MC* relationship. The *MC* curve in Figure 14-7 represents the marginal cost of a 1-unit change in the joint output package of X and Y; MR_x and MR_y have the usual meaning. However, a *vertical summation* of the two *MR* curves is required in order to determine the combined marginal revenue change associated with output changes; the combined-*MR* curve appears as the dashed line MR_{x+y} for outputs up to Q_1 and coincides with MR_y for outputs greater than Q_1, since $MR_x < 0$. The intersection of *MC* and MR_{x+y} defines the short-run profit-maximizing joint output of X and Y; P_x and P_y are the respective profit-maximizing prices and are derived from the respective demand curves for X and Y.

But what if *MC* should happen to intersect MR_{x+y} at a joint output past Q_1 where MR_x is negative? This possibility is shown in Figure 14-8. When *MC* intersects the combined *MR* at a joint output where the marginal revenue of one of the products (X in this case) is negative, profit maximization requires that the firm still produce where *MC* equals combined-*MR*—at Q_2 in Figure 14-8. But whereas the price for *Y* should be set to correspond with the $MC = MR_{x+y}$ intersection (at P_y), the price for X should be pegged at the demand where $MR_x = 0$, at P_x. Why? Because this is where TR_x is maximum; there is no point in setting a price below P_x in Figure 14-8 so as to boost sales to Q_2 because TR_x

PRINCIPLE
To maximize profits from joint products produced in fixed proportions, a firm must produce the output quantity where *MC* equals the combined *MR* from the sale of the two items and sell at the maximum prices allowed by the demand curves for each product.

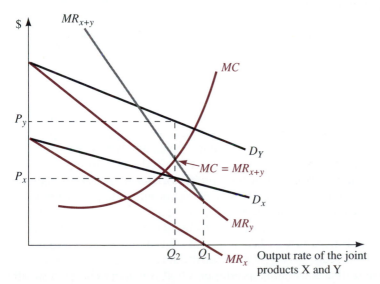

Figure 14-7
Pricing of joint products produced in fixed proportions (case 1)

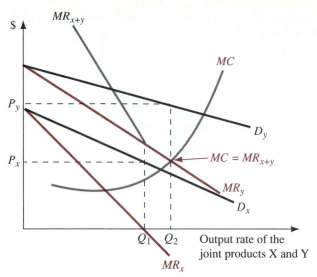

Figure 14-8
Pricing of joint products produced in fixed proportions (case 2)

is lower at Q_2 than at Q_1. In other words, to maximize the excess of joint revenues over joint costs, the firm should offer Q_2 units of Y for sale but should restrict sales of product X to Q_1 so as not to drive MR_x into the negative range. This will, of course, mean that the firm will have an excess of X on its hands, $Q_2 - Q_1$ units to be specific. Naturally, some kind of revenue-producing outlet for the excess amount of X should be sought rather than having the surplus of X go to waste. The criterion here should be to dispose of the excess in ways which will not detract from the firm's primary market objective of selling Q_1 units of X at price P_x. However, in the long run, the firm might react to the excess supply of X by (1) advertising or otherwise promoting increased sales of X so as to shift D_x to the right or (2) seeking out technical means of altering the proportions of joint output in ways to increase Y and decrease X—for example, redesign papermaking processes to permit reductions in the output of cheaper grades of paper and increases in the output of finer grades.

THE PRICING OF JOINT PRODUCTS PRODUCED IN VARIABLE PROPORTIONS

Generally, multiproduct firms are not hemmed in by the constraints imposed by joint products produced under conditions of rigidly fixed proportions. Some flexibility in proportions is usually possible. When the firm can vary the proportions in which the joint output is produced, optimal pricing quickly becomes complex because of the number of alternative combinations which must be examined. Conceptually, what is required is the construction of a series of *isocost curves* showing the locus of all production combinations which can be produced for a given total cost outlay. Such a series of isocost curves is depicted in Figure 14-9 as IC_1, IC_2, and IC_3, with total cost outlays of $400, $550, and $800, respectively. The isocost curves are drawn concave to the origin because of the reasonable assumption that it is increasingly difficult to produce successively more units of one product and fewer units of the other,

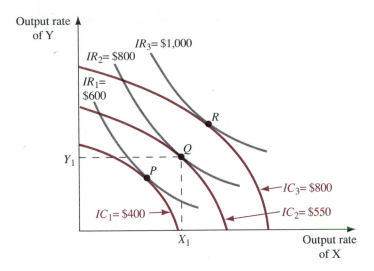

Figure 14-9
Price-output determination for joint products produced in variable proportions

given the inherent limitations on varying the proportions. Next, a set of *isorevenue curves* (IR_1 = $600, IR_2 = $800, IR_3 = $1000) must be derived to show all combinations of the two products which, when sold, result in equivalent total revenues. The isorevenue lines are shown as being convex to the origin, reflecting the typical short-run market necessity of lowering price to sell a larger quantity.

Putting the isocost and isorevenue curves on the same graph defines a set of tangency points (each isocost curve will necessarily be tangent to some isorevenue curve). The tangency points (points *P*, *Q*, and *R* in Figure 14-9) identify the relevant revenue-cost-output combinations since each point represents the lowest cost of reaching the associated total revenue combination. Which of the tangency points represents profit maximization is determined from a comparison of the revenue-cost-profit results at each point. In Figure 14-9 profit maximization is at point *Q*, where total revenue from the sales of X and Y exceeds joint total cost by the greatest amount ($800 − $550 = $250); the profit-maximizing outputs of X and Y are X_1 units and Y_1 units. It can be shown that at point *Q* the marginal cost of producing each product equals the marginal revenue it generates.

MULTIPRODUCT PROFIT MAXIMIZATION WHEN PRODUCTION CAPABILITY IS LIMITED

The odds are excellent that a multiproduct firm sells in markets of varying competitive intensity, has stronger positions of market advantage for some of its products than for others, and enjoys larger profit margins on some of its products than on others. However, since such a firm's production capacity is limited in the short run and since from time to time combined demand may exceed supply capability, the question arises as to how a multiproduct enterprise should best allocate scarce organizational resources so as to maximize the combined profits from all its products. Consider first the simplified case of a two-product firm operating at capacity and unable to increase the output of both items to their respective profit-maximizing rates.

For a two-product firm to maximize total profits from both products, it must divide its limited resource inputs between them in such a way that it receives an equivalent amount of extra profit from the last unit of input allocated to the production of each one. If the condition is violated, the firm can increase total profits by shifting units of input out of the production of the good where profit is less and into the production of the good where profit is greater. As a numerical illustration, consider a firm which has a total of 300 hours of skilled labor available for producing products A and B. The estimated profits from alternative uses of this labor are as follows:

PRINCIPLE
For a multiproduct firm to maximize profits from its current products, it should allocate its resource inputs so as to yield equal marginal profits from the last unit of input allocated to the production of each.

PRODUCT A

Hours of Skilled Labor	Total Profit from A	Added Profit
0	0	
		$500
100	$ 500	
		600
200	1100	
		400
300	1500	

PRODUCT B

Hours of Skilled Labor	Total Profit from B	Added Profit
0	0	
		$600
100	$ 600	
		500
200	1100	
		400
300	1500	

Suppose that the firm is now using 100 hours of labor to produce A and 200 hours of labor to produce B, with resulting joint profits of $1600 ($500 from A and $1100 from B). Is the firm obtaining maximum total profit from both products? The answer is no. Combined profits can be increased by shifting 100 hours of skilled labor time out of producing B and into producing A. In doing so, the firm gives up $500 of profit from the production and sale of B but gains $600 profit from A—for a net gain of $100 and a joint profit total of $1700. By using 200 of the 300 hours of skilled labor to produce A and only 100 hours to produce B, the firm receives $600 profit from the last hundred units of skilled labor used to produce A and also $600 profit from the last hundred units of skilled labor used to produce B. It has equalized the added profit yields of the last batch of input allocated to each product.

The two-product situation is easily expanded to *n* number of items and restated as follows: *Limited resource inputs should be allocated among the production of goods G_1, G_2, G_3, . . . , G_n in such a way as to yield an equivalent amount of profit from the last unit of input allocated to the production of each good.* The significance of the profit-maximizing rule for multiproduct enterprises is that the limited availability of resource inputs often makes it more profitable to diversify into new products and to move into new markets *before* attempting to squeeze the last dollar's worth of profit from existing products and product markets. The most efficient and most profitable use of the firm's limited productive capabilities requires that the available resources be channeled into the production of items with high incremental profit prospects and out of items where incremental profits are low. Thus, short-run profit maximization for a multiproduct enterprise does not require that marginal

It may be more profitable for a firm to diversify into new products before squeezing the last margin of profits from existing products because the profit potential from using its resources in making new products may well exceed the profits such resources can generate from existing products.

revenue be equated to marginal cost for each and every product the firm produces *unless* the firm has adequate resources and sufficient production capacity in the short run to carry the production of *every* current and potential product to the rate where $MR = MC$. From a total organization viewpoint, price and output decisions require a careful balancing of adjustments among specific product markets to obtain the optimal divisional and companywide profits.[13]

KEY POINTS

We have seen that the firm's goals have a definite effect upon its price and output decisions. A profit goal based on target rates of return will not lead to the same price and output decisions as will one based upon marginal revenue and marginal cost concepts. A firm whose primary goal is revenue maximization subject to a profit constraint tends to produce at a greater output rate and to sell at a lower price than does a firm whose goal is profit maximization—other things being equal. Whereas a profit-maximizing firm has no incentive to alter its price and output in the face of increases in either fixed costs or taxes, a revenue-maximizing firm tends to respond by curtailing output and raising selling prices. A revenue-maximizer also tends to spend greater amounts on advertising and sales promotion, which, if effective, will tend to push its output rate beyond that of a comparable profit-maximizing firm.

Companies find it profitable to engage in price discrimination when (1) they have downsloping demand curves and thus have some discretion over the prices they can charge, (2) they have several classes of customers, each with a different demand curve, and (3) they can wall off the classes such that customers paying lower prices have great difficulty reselling the item to customers being charged higher prices.

When a firm produces its product at multiple plant locations, profit maximization requires that production be allocated among the various plants such that the marginal costs of the last unit produced at each plant are all equal to each other and are also equal to the value at which the firm's overall marginal cost equals the marginal revenue of the last unit sold. The effect of this rule in practice is to concentrate production in the most efficient plants.

When a multiproduct firm has limited production capability in the short run and is unable to increase the output of all items to their respective profit-maximizing rates, overall company profitability will be maximized by allocating limited resource inputs across the products of goods $G_1, G_2, G_3, \ldots, G_n$ in such a way as to yield an equivalent amount of profit from the last unit of input allocated to the production of each good.

---

[13] A study of the pricing of steel products by U.S. Steel provides a good illustration. In the production of steel rails and steel cables, where demand was less elastic and also where competition was less intense, U.S. Steel charged proportionately higher prices and maintained wider profit margins. In the markets for stainless steel, galvanized sheets, and tin plate, where U.S. Steel was in strenuous direct and potential competition with aluminum and lumber as well as other steel producers, prices were more than proportionately lower and profit margins were much narrower. Thus, product market elasticities and profit margin differences were major decision variables in U.S. Steel's divisional price and output strategies. For greater detail, see Kaplan, Dirlam, and Lanzilotti, *Pricing in Big Business*, pp. 172–73.

PROBLEMS AND QUESTIONS FOR DISCUSSION

1. If a firm selects its selling price via some sort of "cost-plus" technique, is it possible for the firm to ever lose money? Why or why not?

2. Minnick Corporation has invested $50 million in facilities and equipment to produce miniature portable color TV sets with a 4-inch screen. Minnick's annual production capacity is 2 million sets. Over the last 5 years, Minnick's sales of these miniature TV sets have averaged 1.6 million per year. The company's fixed costs have remained relatively stable at $10 million per year. The firm estimates its annual total variable cost function to be $TVC = 120Q + 10Q^2$, where Q is *millions* of units of TV sets sold per year.
   (a) If Minnick desires to earn a target rate of return on its investment of 30% (before taxes), what target return price should Minnick select?
   (b) If Minnick's pricing policy is to add 15% to its normal production costs to determine selling price, what price should it charge, based upon the preceding information?

3. In the college textbook business, it is standard practice for the author's royalty to be some percentage of the total revenue which the publisher receives from sales of the book. The publisher, of course, incurs all costs of manufacturing, promoting, and distributing the book. Would the price and the sales volume (the number of books sold) that maximize the publisher's profits on the book also maximize the author's royalty payments? Why or why not? Demonstrate your answer graphically.

4. Suppose that in the short run a firm produces under conditions of constant returns to variable input over the entire output range for which it has production capability. Suppose further that the firm selects its selling price in order to earn a target rate of return on its investment and follows the practice of selling at the target return price no matter what short-run demand conditions happen to be.
   (a) Graphically illustrate the firm's short-run *AVC, MC,* and *ATC* curves.
   (b) On the same graph, illustrate a target return price.
   (c) Under these circumstances what is the value of *MR*?
   (d) At what output rate would the firm maximize short-run profits?
   (e) At what output rate would the firm maximize sales revenues?

5. Suppose that a firm's short-run production function is characterized by constant returns to variable input. Suppose further that the firm faces a linear, downsloping demand curve for its product.
   (a) Graphically illustrate the firm's *TR, TC,* and π functions.
   (b) Indicate on your graph the profit-maximizing output.
   (c) Indicate on your graph a profit constraint which is smaller than the maximum amount of profit.
   (d) Indicate the revenue-maximizing output, given the profit constraint.

6. The Harco Instrument Corporation has estimated its monthly demand function to be $P = 416 - 7Q$ and its monthly total cost function to be $TC = 1700 + 16Q + Q^2$.
   (a) If Harco's goal is to maximize sales revenue subject to the constraint that profits equal no less than $3200 per month, what is Harco's optimum price and output rate? (*Hint:* Recalling that $\pi = TR - TC$, substitute the appropriate expressions into this equation and solve for Q.)
   (b) If Harco's goal is to maximize profits, then what is its optimum price and output rate? How does the profit-maximizing price and output compare with the revenue-maximizing price and output?
   (c) Suppose Harco's total fixed costs rise from $1700 to $1750. Determine the impact upon Harco's profit-maximizing price and output rate.
   (d) Determine the impact of the increase in total fixed costs from $1700 to $1750 upon Harco's revenue-maximizing price and output rate, given the profit constraint of $3200.

7. The American Cracker Corporation has three plants for producing soda crackers. The marginal cost functions of the three plants and the firm's estimated demand-*AR* schedule are as follows:

Daily Output in Cartons	Marginal Cost of Plant 1	Marginal Cost of Plant 2	Marginal Cost of Plant 3	Price of Cartons of Soda Crackers
0				$0.50
1	$0.14	$0.13	$0.10	0.48
2	0.16	0.14	0.13	0.46
3	0.18	0.15	0.16	0.44
4	0.20	0.16	0.16	0.42
5	Capacity	Capacity	Capacity	0.40
6				0.38
7				0.36
8				0.34
9				0.32
10				0.30
11				0.28
12				0.26

Determine the most profitable price and output for the American Cracker Corporation. Then determine the optimal allocation of output among the firm's three plants.

Chapter 15

The Five Competitive Forces

It is easy to get the impression from the preceding five chapters about markets and competition that almost "everything" depends on the number of sellers comprising the supply side of the market. Indeed, a principal conclusion of the theory of how markets function is that the strength of competitive forces increases directly with the number of firms. But this conclusion is only part of the story. There is more to analyzing market structure and competitive forces than just counting how many sellers make up the supply side of the market.

The task of this chapter is to expand the picture of market and competitive analysis. The emphasis will be on identifying the competitively relevant features of industry structure, examining where competitive forces come from, and indicating the kinds of factors that cause competitive forces to be strong or weak. Then, in Chapter 16, we look at the ways a firm can win a competitive advantage.

THE FIVE-FORCES MODEL OF COMPETITION: A KEY ANALYTICAL TOOL

Even though every market has a somewhat unique competitive character and makeup, there are enough similarities in how competition works from market to market to use a common analytical framework in gauging the nature and intensity of competition. Generally speaking, competition in the marketplace is the combined result of five competitive forces:

Competition in the market-place is composed of five types of competitive forces.

1. The rivalry among competing sellers in the industry.
2. The market attempts of companies in other industries to win customers over to their own *substitute* products.
3. The potential entry of new competitors.
4. The market power and bargaining leverage that can be exercised by suppliers of inputs.
5. The market power and bargaining leverage that can be exercised by buyers of the product.

The *five-forces model* of competition, as shown in Figure 15-1, is a valuable conceptual tool for diagnosing the principal competitive pressures in a market and assessing how strong and important each one is. Indeed, use of the five-forces model is the best single way to understand how competition works.

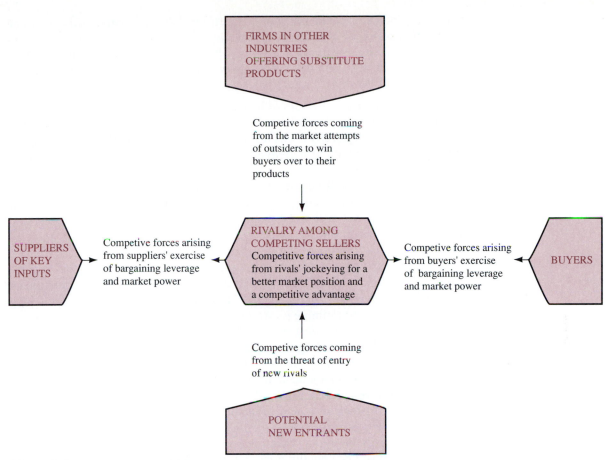

Figure 15-1

The "five-forces" model of competition

Source: Adapted from Michael E. Porter, "How Competitive Forces Shape Strategy," *Harvard Business Review*, Vol. 57, No. 2 (March–April 1979), pp. 137–45.

Five-forces analysis was developed by Professor Michael E. Porter of the Harvard Business School (which explains why Figure 15-1 is often referred to as "the Porter model").[1] Since its appearance in 1980, the five-forces model has become the most widely used technique of competition analysis, and it is easy to work with.

THE COMPETITIVE FORCE OF INTERFIRM RIVALRY

The center ring of the competitive arena, where most of the action takes place, involves the maneuvering of rival firms selling competing versions of the same good or service. In fact, the vigor with which sellers in an industry jockey for a stronger market position and a competitive edge over their rivals is perhaps the

BASIC CONCEPT
A firm's competitive strategy consists of its efforts to achieve market success, its offensive moves to secure a competitive advantage, and its defensive moves to protect its competitive position.

[1] For a thoroughgoing treatment of the five-forces model by its originator, see Michael E. Porter, *Competitive Strategy: Techniques for Analyzing Industries and Competitors* (New York: The Free Press, 1980), Chapter 1.

best single indicator of the pulse of competition.[2] A firm's **competitive strategy** is its *action plans for achieving market success and, whenever possible, gaining a competitive edge over rival firms*. The profit incentive of competitors to develop a "winning" competitive strategy tends to create a competitive interplay with the following characteristics:

1. Rival firms are more or less constantly jockeying for improved market position. The struggle for better position manifests in an *independent striving for patronage*, whereby rivals formulate and reformulate their own competitive strategies aimed at outmaneuvering one another and securing a more profitable market share.

2. The competitive strategies that rival firms may devise and the ways they may seek out new openings to compete are diverse, limited mainly by their imagination, by what will work in the marketplace (i.e., the constraints and reactions of buyers), and by what is legally permissible (based on antitrust legislation and definitions of fair competitive practices).

3. Fresh competitive pressures can be activated any time one or more competitors initiates a new offensive strategic move to improve its position or launches a new defensive move to protect the position it already has. How long a firm goes without fine-tuning its strategy or subjecting it to major overhaul is a function of its market successes (or failures) and the durability of its competitive approach in withstanding strategic challenges from rival firms. When a firm realizes that its competitive strategy has been stymied or defeated by rivals' strategies, then it is challenged to seek out a better strategy not as easily thwarted or else remain content with the position it has been put in.

4. In considering which of several optional moves to make, *there is good reason for a firm to choose a competitive strategy that is neither easily imitated nor easily thwarted*. Offering buyers something that competitors cannot duplicate easily or cheaply gives a firm not only a market edge but also a unique competitive capability—outcomes that can be translated into above-average profitability.

5. Rivalry among direct competitors produces both strategic successes and strategic failures; the strategic successes may, if they are sufficiently dramatic, influence or even "control" the direction of market forces and competitive pressures. Strategic failure, on the other hand, reflects a competitive approach that, in comparison with rival firms, was either poorly conceived, poorly executed, or both, and may lead to a firm revising its strategy, losing market position, or even exiting the industry.

6. The moves and countermoves of competing sellers result in firms both *creating* and *responding to* new market demand–market supply conditions. In other words, the competitive strategies of rivals are to a degree both controlling and controlled by market events and by the sequence of moves and

Competitive rivalry is a game of strategy, of move and countermove, played under "warlike" conditions according to the rules of competition; in a very real sense, competitive markets are economic battlefields.

---

[2] Elements of the strategic aspects of competition go as far back in the economics literature as Adam Smith's *The Wealth of Nations* published in 1776. Cournot, Bertrand, and Edgeworth, all well-known classical economists, incorporated competitive strategy aspects in their writings, but their models were based on assumptions so foreign to contemporary strategic behavior as to render them void of much explanatory power. More modern treatments can be found in Edward H. Chamberlin, *The Theory of Monopolistic Competition* (Cambridge, Mass.: Harvard University Press, 1933), p. 6; Fritz Machlup, *The Economics of Sellers' Competition* (Baltimore: The Johns Hopkins Press, 1952); J. M. Schumpeter, *Capitalism, Socialism, and Democracy*, 3rd ed. (New York: Harper & Brothers, 1950); and J. M. Clark, *Competition as a Dynamic Process* (Washington, D.C.: The Brookings Institution, 1961), pp. 471–76. Numerous other writers have recognized the strategic rivalry aspects of competition in the form of game theory models of oligopoly.

countermoves—*the strategies of rival firms affect the market and the market affects what strategies rival firms can employ with any hope of success.*

These characteristics of interfirm rivalry produce the following picture of how firms "play the game" of competition in the market arena.[3] Each rival tries to formulate a winning competitive strategy—one that will gain it some sort of attractive competitive edge over its rivals. The big complication here is that *the success of any one firm's strategy hinges in large part on what strategies its rivals employ*—what is the best strategy for firm A in its search for competitive advantage depends partly (or mostly) on rivals' choices of strategy; and rivals, in turn, may elect to adjust their strategies when A makes its strategic move.

The efforts of rival firms to win a competitive advantage, in conjunction with the interdependence of their approaches to the market, produces an ongoing series of competitive strategies and maneuvering, some offensive and some defensive, on the part of each seller in the market.[4] In many cases, the choice of competitive strategy incorporates both price and nonprice features, with the exact mix being a function of management perceptions as to what combination will have the most desirable market impact, given market conditions and the prevailing strategies (and anticipated counterstrategies) of rival firms. How long a firm goes without changing its strategy is a function of the firm's market successes (or failures), the durability of its competitive approach in withstanding strategic challenges from rival firms, and how well the existing strategy remains matched to market conditions.

COMPETITIVE PRINCIPLE
The deployment of a powerful competitive strategy by one firm intensifies the competitive pressures felt by rival firms.

But the key point here is that *the launching of new competitive strategies triggers a new, sometimes powerful, round of competitive pressures in the marketplace.* When a firm makes a successful strategic move, it can expect increased rewards, largely at the expense of rivals' market shares and rates of sales growth. The speed and extent of the initiator's competitive encroachment varies with whether the industry's product is standardized or differentiated, the initiator's competence and resources to capitalize on any advantage the strategy has produced, how difficult it is for sellers to convince buyers to switch over to their brands, and the ease with which the new strategy initiative can be copied or blunted. The pressures on rivals to respond are a function of whether the initiator is (1) a major firm with considerable market visibility, (2) a fringe firm whose efforts can be ignored for some time, or (3) a firm in financial distress and thus whose strategy is predicated on desperation. For instance, if a firm's strategic offensive is keyed to a low price and quick market penetration but also carries with it a substantial risk that full costs will not be recovered, rivals may judge that the strategy will be short-lived; they may choose to respond or not, depending on their estimates of whether it will be better to meet the low price on a temporary basis or to ride out whatever buyer resistance may be encountered. If the initiating firm finds its move neutralized by rivals' coun-

---

[3] The portrayal of interfirm rivalry that follows is based on the discussion in Arthur A. Thompson, "Competition as a Strategic Process," *Antitrust Bulletin*, Vol. 25, No. 4 (Winter 1980), pp. 777–803.

[4] The early treatments of competitive strategy by economists simplified the crucial matter of rivals' responses to a new strategic move to two extreme cases: the firm acting as if rivals will not respond or as if they will respond so promptly as to neutralize any gain the initiating firm might make. Such oversimplification misses the really characteristic cases, which lie between the extremes and cannot readily be represented by a curve on a diagram. See Clark, *Competition as a Dynamic Process*, p. 472.

APPLICATIONS CAPSULE

THE MOVES AND COUNTERMOVES OF COMPETITIVE RIVALRY: COCA-COLA VERSUS PEPSI-COLA

Historically, Coca-Cola has dominated the American soft-drink industry. Sales and profits have grown rapidly ever since Coke was first introduced. Until the 1950s there was really no second-place firm worth mentioning. Pepsi-Cola, Coca-Cola's nearest competitor, was a relatively new drink that cost less to manufacture, but its taste was generally thought to be less unique and satisfying than Coke's. Pepsi came in a 12-ounce bottle that sold for approximately the same price as Coke's famous 6½-ounce bottle. Pepsi exploited this difference by advertising "twice as much for a nickel, too." Nonetheless, with its plain bottle and paper label (that often got dirty in transit), Pepsi was generally looked upon as second-class. To many it was "the poor man's drink."

When Alfred N. Steele came to the presidency of Pepsi-Cola, he recognized that the company's main hope for competitive vitality lay in transforming Pepsi into a first-class soft drink and in not being a cheap imitator of Coke. Steele assembled a two-phase grand offensive for improving Pepsi's position relative to Coke. In the first phase, which lasted from 1950 to 1955, a determined effort was made to improve Pepsi's taste. The formula was desweetened. Greater quality control was established over local bottlers, who previously added varying amounts of carbonation to the syrup, with the result that Pepsi's taste varied from locale to locale. Pepsi's bottle and other corporate symbols were redesigned and unified. Following up on the product improvements, Pepsi launched an advertising campaign aimed at upgrading Pepsi's image. The ads featured attractive, well-dressed women and debonair men drinking Pepsi, against a background of high-income surroundings. Along with this went the advertising theme "the light refreshment," suggesting indirectly that Coke was "heavy." At the same time, Pepsi made the decision to take dead aim on the "take-home" segment of the soft-drink market in the first

phase of its grand offensive. Coca-Cola was particularly strong in the *on-premises* segment (soda fountain sales, vending machines, and refrigerated sales). Pepsi felt that the rifle-shot approach, aimed where Coca-Cola was weakest, gave it the best chance for success. Thus, Pepsi massed its efforts at penetrating the market for grocery retail sales of soft drinks—where it already had a small foothold. The final aspect of Pepsi's phase-one offensive involved singling out 25 cities for special promotional efforts. In these "push" markets Pepsi added company funds to those of the local bottlers for advertising and promotion. The concentrated effort to win market share in these 25 cities was successful in increasing Pepsi's market share.

By 1955, Pepsi's phase-one programs had made enough headway to warrant beginning phase two of the grand offensive. It consisted of attempts to increase Pepsi's share of the "on-premises" market, where Coke was so solidly entrenched. However, Pepsi limited its efforts to the vending machine and cold-bottle sales segments because the soda fountain segment showed signs of maturity and perhaps even decline. Pepsi introduced some new bottle sizes to go along with its standard 12-ounce bottle in an attempt to offer more convenience to customers in the take-home and cold-bottle market segments. Additionally, Pepsi offered financing to those bottlers who were willing to buy and install Pepsi vending machines and to begin to push this part of their business.

As Pepsi's phase two began to strike chords of success, Coke decided it was time to initiate some kind of response. Until the latter stages of Pepsi's grand offensive, Coke's attitude had been mostly "ho-hum." For the most part, Coke refused to acknowledge that Pepsi was a threat. Many of Coke's local bottlers had become well-to-do and complacent, owing to Coke's previous success, and were not accus-

termoves, it is challenged to seek out a better strategy or else remain content with the stalemate it has encountered.

It may be that only a few firms (large or small) will tend to initiate fresh strategic moves, and they may not do it often. But to the extent that these few are able to impact the market with their strategic initiatives, the give-and-take of strategic move and competitive response spreads and continues.[5] A fresh move may come from a firm with ambitious growth objectives, from a firm with excess capacity, or from a firm under pressure to gain added business. More generally, though, the classic offensive strategies are made by firms that see market opportunities and a chance to improve their profit performance. Such firms, whether they be actual leaders, would-be leaders, or mavericks, tend to be aware of the risks of undertaking a bold strategic move but they usually exhibit confidence (1) that they are shrewd enough to keep ahead of the game and (2) that they will be better off making a bold move than they would be by

[5] Clark, *Competition as a Dynamic Process*, pp. 473–74.

tomed to tough competition. Initially, Coke's response consisted of launching new advertising campaigns, using such themes as "the really refreshed" and "no wonder Coke refreshes best." Coke also introduced new bottle sizes. Both steps perked up Coke's sales.

In the early 1960s, Pepsi's rate of growth slowed, and Pepsi responded with two new advertising campaigns—"be sociable" and "think young." The latter was quite successful in tying Pepsi to the youth market, a segment which accounted for the highest per capita consumption of soft drinks. But the youth theme, by implication, also tended to mark Coke as an old-fashioned drink. Coke responded with its new advertising theme of "things go better with Coke."

Then competition, which in the past had revolved largely around taste, bottling, and advertising, moved to new arenas. The first concerned the no-deposit bottle and the use of aluminum and steel cans. Both companies found that it was critical to design their containers carefully and time their introduction astutely. For instance, it was discovered that the metal can affected the taste; it was also discovered by one soft-drink company that the aluminum can it was about to introduce was eaten through by its product within a few days.

The second competitive development concerned product innovation. Using the principle of surprise, Royal Crown Cola introduced what proved to be a major new product—the diet soft drink. RC's Diet Cola was formulated without real sugar and was intended to appeal to the calorie-conscious segment of the market. Originally, this class of buyers was thought to constitute a small part of the soft-drink market, but it turned out that diet drinks had very broad appeal. Royal Crown's major success quickly forced both Coke and Pepsi to formulate their own dietetic soft drinks.

The third new competitive arena emerged when the soft-drink companies realized that a whole set of other good-tasting drinks could be formulated besides colas. Seven-Up's "un-cola" theme was so successful that Coke brought out its version of the un-cola—Sprite. Attempting to capitalize upon this development, Dr. Pepper sharply increased its advertising budget and market penetration efforts.

Although Coke continued to retain its number one position in the industry, Pepsi emerged with a much stronger second-place market share and the smaller firms—Royal Crown, Seven-Up, and Dr. Pepper—also made inroads, mostly at Coke's expense.

Still, a fourth competitive arena emerged in the 1980s when Philip Morris, a leader in the cigarette industry and also the parent of Miller Brewing Company, acquired the Seven-Up Company and began an aggressive marketing campaign to expand the market shares of 7-Up and Diet 7-Up. PM's strategy was to exploit the growing awareness and concerns among consumers about health and nutrition by calling attention to the fact that 7-Up and Diet 7-Up were caffeine-free. Seven-Up's "never had it, never will" ads about the caffeine-free attribute of its drinks struck hard at both Coke and Pepsi, since all brands of colas then contained substantial amounts of caffeine. So threatening were the Seven-Up ads that within a period of months both Coke and Pepsi introduced caffeine-free versions of their regular and diet cola drinks.

Sources: Alvin Toffler, "The Competition that Refreshes," *Fortune*, May 1961; "Things Go Better with Coke," *Sales Management*, March 5, 1965, pp. 28ff.; and Phillip Kotler, *Marketing Management: Analysis, Planning, and Control*, 2nd ed. (Englewood Cliffs, N.J.: Prentice Hall, 1972), pp. 254–57.

holding back and letting others take the lead. The defensive responses that follow aggressive moves not only reflect time lags and uncertainties but their character differs according to whether the new offensive consists of a new promotional campaign, introduction of a new product or product variation, opening a new channel of distribution, a move toward vertical integration, or merger with another competitor. Most of the time, any lulls in the competitive storm tend to be temporary, owing to the stream of new possibilities for product differentiation, cost-related technological changes, new buyer needs and preferences, changing demographics and life-styles, shifts in buying power, the availability of new substitutes, and general economic change.

Typically, the strategies of the participant firms cause the spotlight of competition to swing first to one combination of product attributes and then to another—in no set pattern or time interval. At any given time, the central focus of competition might be on one or several of the following: price, new and improved products, a broader product offering, technical sophistication, the adoption of new cost-saving methods of manufacture, customer service, pro-

COMPETITIVE PRINCIPLE
The manner in which rival firms use the various weapons of competition to try to out-maneuver one another shapes the rules of competition in an industry and determines the requirements for market success.

motion, guarantees, styling, function, economy of use, convenience, and so on—and the focus shifts as new demand patterns and competitive responses appear.

It follows from this characterization that *interfirm rivalry can assume many forms and shades of intensity.* The present strategies of firms in a given industry are just snapshots of an ongoing process whereby markets and competitive rivalry affect firms' strategies and firms' strategies affect markets and competitive rivalry. New competitive pressures are regularly created by the never-ending sequence of strategic moves and countermoves of participant firms. Changes in the form and intensity of competitive rivalry are thus the norm, not the exception.

BASIC CONCEPT
Rival firms are said to be in the same strategic group when they employ similar competitive strategies and occupy similar positions in the market.

THE CONCEPT OF STRATEGIC GROUPS

One of the newest and best techniques for revealing the competitive positions of rival companies is ***strategic group mapping***.[6] This analytical tool is useful whenever an industry is populated with several distinct *groups* of competitors, each occupying a distinguishably different position in the overall market and having a distinguishably different appeal to buyers. A *strategic group* consists of those rival firms with similar competitive approaches and positions in the market.[7] Companies in the same strategic group can resemble one another in several ways: they may have comparable product line breadth; emphasize the same kinds of distribution channels; be vertically integrated to much the same degree; offer buyers similar services and technical assistance; use essentially the same product attributes to appeal to similar types of buyers, trying to satisfy buyer needs with the same product attributes; rely upon mass media advertising; depend on identical technological approaches; and/or sell in the same price/quality range.

An industry contains only one strategic group when all sellers approach the market with essentially identical strategies. At the other extreme, there are as many strategic groups as there are competitors when each rival pursues a distinctively different competitive approach and occupies a substantially different competitive position in the marketplace. The major home appliance industry, for example, contains three identifiable strategic groups. One cluster (composed of General Electric and Whirlpool) produces a full line of home appliances (refrigerators, freezers, clothes washers and dryers, dishwashers, cooking appliances, garbage disposals, and microwaves), employs heavy national advertising, is vertically integrated, and has established a national network of distributors and dealers. Another cluster consists of premium-quality, specialist firms (like Amana in refrigerators and freezers, Maytag in washers and dryers, KitchenAid in dishwashers, and Jenn-Air in cooking tops) that focus on high-price market segments and have selective distribution. A third cluster, consisting of firms like Roper, Design and Manufacturing, and Hardwick, concentrates on supplying private-label retailers and budget-priced, basic models for the low end of the market.

A *strategic group map* is constructed by plotting the market positions of the industry's strategic groups on a two-dimensional map using two strategic variables as axes; see the retail jewelry industry example in Figure 15-2. *The map serves as a convenient bridge between looking at the industry as a whole*

---

[6] Porter, *Competitive Strategy*, Chapter 7.
[7] *Ibid.*, pp. 129–30.

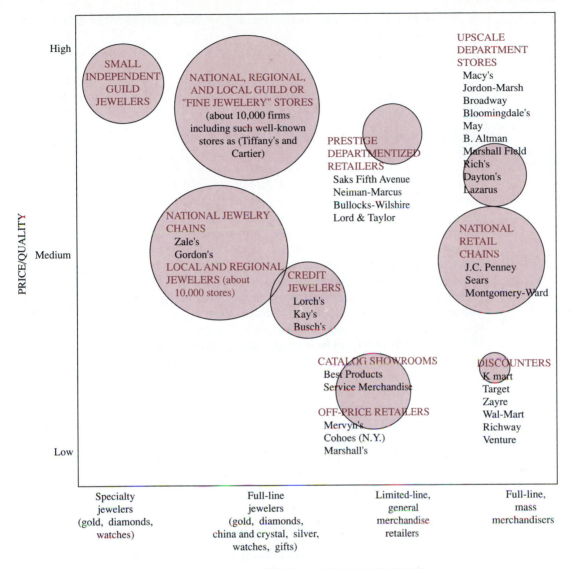

NOTE: The sizes of the circles are roughly proportional to the market shares of each group of competitors

Figure 15-2

Illustrative strategic group map of competitors in the retail jewelry business

and considering the standing of each firm separately. It is an especially useful device when the industry is populated with so many competitors that it is not practical to scrutinize each rival separately.

The procedure for constructing a strategic group map and deciding which firms belong in which strategic group is straightforward:

- Identify the competitive characteristics that differentiate firms in the industry—typical variables are price/quality range (high, medium, low), geographic coverage (local, regional, national, global), degree of vertical integration (none, partial, full), product line breadth (wide, narrow), use of distribution channels (one, some, all), and degree of service offered (no frills, limited, full service).

- Plot the firms on a two-variable map using pairs of these differentiating characteristics.
- Assign firms that fall in about the same strategy space to the same strategic group.
- Draw circles around each strategic group, making the circles proportional to the size of the group's respective share of total industry sales revenues.

BASIC CONCEPT
A strategic group map displays the different market positions that rival firms occupy.

This produces a two-dimensional strategic group map such as the one portrayed in Figure 15-2.

To map the positions of strategic groups accurately in the industry's overall "strategy space," several guidelines need to be observed.[8] First, the two variables selected as axes for the map should *not* be highly correlated; if they are, the circles on the map will fall along a diagonal and the map will tell nothing more about the relative positions of competitors than would considering one of the variables by itself. For instance, if companies with broad product lines use multiple distribution channels while companies with narrow lines use a single distribution channel, then one of the variables is redundant. Looking at broad versus narrow product lines reveals just as much about who is positioned where as is learned by adding in consideration of single versus multiple distribution channels. Second, the variables chosen as axes for the map should expose big differences in how rivals have positioned themselves to compete in the marketplace. This, of course, requires identifying the characteristics that differentiate rival firms and then using these differences as variables for the axes and as the basis for deciding which firm belongs in which strategic group. Third, the variables used as axes do not have to be either quantitative or continuous; rather, they can be discrete variables or defined in terms of distinct classes and combinations. Fourth, drawing the sizes of the circles on the map proportional to the combined sales of the firms in each strategic group allows the map to reflect the relative sizes of each strategic group. Fifth, if more than two good competitive variables can be used as axes for the map, then several maps can be drawn to give different exposures to the competitive positioning relationships present in the industry's structure. Because there need not be one best map for portraying how competing firms are positioned in the market, it is advisable to experiment with different pairs of competitive variables.

Strategic group analysis adds to the picture of interfirm rivalry in an industry. There are five important things to recognize about strategic groups:[9]

1. Changing market conditions often have different implications for different strategic groups. Sometimes the direction of market change closes off the viability of one or more strategic groups, prompting competitors in the affected groups to shift to a more favorably situated group. Sometimes changes act to raise (lower) the entry barriers into a group, causing competitive pressures in the group to increase (decrease).

2. The profit potential of different strategic groups often varies because of strengths and weaknesses in each group's market position.

Firms in the same strategic group tend to be close rivals; firms in strategic groups that are far apart on the map hardly compete.

3. Entry barriers vary according to the particular strategic group that an entrant seeks to join—entry into some strategic groups is easier than into others.

4. Firms in different strategic groups often enjoy differing degrees of

---

[8] *Ibid.*, pp. 152–54.
[9] *Ibid.*, pp. 130, 132–38, and 154–55.

bargaining leverage with suppliers and/or with customers, and they may also face differing degrees of exposure to competition from substitute products outside the industry.

5. Greater numbers of strategic groups generally intensify industry rivalry because firms have to compete both within their group and across groups. However, firms in the same strategic group tend to be close rivals, whereas firms in strategic groups that are *far apart* on the map may compete hardly at all. For instance, Tiffany and K mart both sell jewelry, but they are not competitors to any real degree; in the same way, Timex is not much of a competitive threat to Rolex, and Chevrolet is not a close competitor to Lincoln or Mercedes-Benz.

FACTORS AFFECTING THE STRENGTH OF INTERFIRM RIVALRY

Although many factors influence the strength of interfirm rivalry, certain ones seem to crop up again and again.[10] Let's look at nine of the most important factors.

1. *Rivalry tends to intensify as the number of competitors increases and as they become more equal in size and capability.* The number of firms is important because, up to some point, more firms increase the probability for fresh, creative strategic initiatives and because greater numbers reduce the effects of any one firm's actions upon the others, thereby reducing somewhat the probability of direct retaliation. Also, economists have a strong bias toward more firms because this gives buyers more choice among sellers and thus reduces the likelihood of any one firm being able to rig the market to its own advantage. When rival firms are more equal in size and capability, the chances are better that the firms can compete on a fairly even footing, a feature that makes it harder for one or two firms to win the competitive battle and emerge as dominant firms in a position to exercise leadership and some degree of market control.

2. *Rivalry is usually stronger when demand for the product is growing slowly.* In a rapidly expanding market, rivalry is weakened by the fact that there is enough business for everybody. Indeed, it may take all of a firm's financial and managerial resources just to keep abreast of market growth, much less devoting efforts to steal away the customers of its rivals.[11] But when growth slows, expansion-minded firms and/or firms with excess capacity often cut prices and use other sales-increasing tactics, thereby igniting a battle for market share that can result in a shakeout of the weak and less-efficient firms. The industry then "consolidates" into a smaller, but individually stronger, group of sellers.

3. *Rivalry is more intense when industry conditions tempt competitors to use price cuts or other competitive weapons to boost unit volume.* Whenever fixed costs account for a large fraction of total cost, unit costs tend to be lowest

> There are many factors that explain why the rivalry among competing sellers is strong or weak.

---

[10] These indicators of the intensity of interfirm rivalry are based upon Porter, "How Competitive Forces Shape Strategy," pp. 142–43, and Porter, *Competitive Strategy*, pp. 17–19.

[11] In average growth markets, aggressive firms may move to build new plant capacity *ahead* of the time it will be needed so as to discourage others from expansion and thereby capture a greater market share. Should rivals catch on to this tactic and decide to retaliate with capacity additions of their own, the outcome can be a vigorous competitive struggle in which overall industry profitability is reduced. Such situations usually occur in oligopolistic markets where increased market share is a key to increased profits.

at or near full capacity since the greater the production volume the more units over which fixed costs can be spread. Unused capacity imposes a significant cost-increasing penalty because there are fewer units carrying the fixed-cost burden. In such cases, if market demand weakens and capacity utilization begins to fall off, the pressure of rising unit costs pushes rival firms into secret price concessions, special discounts, rebates, and other sales-increasing tactics, thus heightening competition. Likewise, when a product is perishable, seasonal, or costly to hold in inventory, competitive pressures build quickly anytime one or more competitors decide to dump their excess supplies on the market.

4. *Rivalry is stronger when the costs incurred by customers in switching from one brand to another are low.* The lower the costs of switching, the easier it is for rival sellers to raid one another's customers. On the other hand, high switching costs give a seller some protection from such raids.

5. *Rivalry is stronger when one or more competitors are dissatisfied with their market position and initiate moves to bolster their standing at the expense of rivals.* Firms that are losing ground or find themselves in financial trouble are often driven into taking aggressive action. Such moves as acquisition of smaller rivals, the introduction of new products, a boost in advertising, special price promotions, and the like can all trigger a new round of competitive maneuvering and a heightened battle for market share.

6. *Rivalry increases in proportion to the size of the payoff from a successful strategic move.* The greater the potential reward, the more likely some firm will give in to the temptation of a particular strategic move. How big the strategic payoff is varies partly with the speed of retaliation. When competitors can be expected to respond slowly (or maybe even not at all), the initiator of a fresh competitive strategy can reap the benefits in the intervening period and perhaps gain a lead time advantage which is not easily surmounted; the greater the chance this will occur, the greater will the potential benefits justify the risk of eventual retaliation. Firms that have shrewdly assessed the ''personality'' of each rival firm and that have probed the economics of their rivals' businesses are in the best position to predict correctly how and when rivals may respond to a given strategic move; such knowledge is advantageous in assessing the potential payoffs of strategic alternatives.[12]

7. *Rivalry tends to be more vigorous when it costs more to get out of a business than to stay in and compete.* The higher the exit barriers (and thus the more costly it is to abandon a market), the stronger the incentive for firms to remain and compete as best they can, even though they may be earning low profits or even incurring a loss.

8. *Rivalry becomes more volatile and unpredictable the more diverse competitors are in terms of their strategies, personalities, corporate priorities, resources, and countries of origin.* A diverse group of sellers is more likely to spawn one or more mavericks willing to rock the boat with unconventional moves and approaches, thus generating a more lively and uncertain competitive environment. The added presence of new, lower-cost, foreign-based com-

---

[12] It is worth noting here that it is important for a firm to understand the reasons underlying any shifts in the competitive strategies of rival firms. Unless a firm correctly perceives what the intentions of its competitors are, it is less able to develop appropriate moves and countermoves of its own. When rival firms change their competitive strategy, management is thus obliged to ask: What are they up to, why are they doing this, and what do they expect to accomplish? Is this an aggressive move or is it something we should all be doing? The answers are almost certain to be relevant in figuring out the firm's own strategic response.

petitors intent on gaining market share is a surefire factor in boosting the intensity of rivalry.

9. *Rivalry increases when strong companies outside the industry acquire weak firms in the industry and launch aggressive, well-funded moves to transform their newly acquired competitors into major market contenders.* A classic example of this occurred when Philip Morris, a leading cigarette firm with excellent marketing know-how, shook up the whole beer industry's approach to marketing by acquiring the stodgy Miller Brewing Company in the late 1960s. In short order, Philip Morris revamped the marketing of Miller High Life and pushed it to the number-two best-selling brand. Philip Morris also pioneered low-calorie beers with the introduction of Miller Lite—a move that made light beer the fastest-growing segment in the beer industry.

The jockeying for position among competitors unfolds in round after round of moves and countermoves. Competitive rivalry is "intense" when the actions of competitors are driving down industry profits; rivalry is "moderate" when most companies can earn acceptable profits; and rivalry is "weak" when most companies in the industry can earn above-average returns on investment. Chronic outbreaks of cut-throat competition among rival sellers make an industry brutally competitive.

THE COMPETITIVE FORCE OF SUBSTITUTE PRODUCTS

Firms in one industry are, quite often, in close competition with firms in another industry because their respective products are good substitutes. Soft-drink producers are in competition with the sellers of fruit juices, milk, coffee, tea, powdered-mix drinks, and perhaps some alcoholic beverages (wine and beer). The producers of wood stoves are in competition with the producers of kerosene heaters and portable electric heaters. Sugar producers are in competition with the firms that produce artificial sweeteners. The producers of plastic containers are in competition with the makers of glass bottles and jars, the manufacturers of paperboard cartons, and the producers of tin cans and aluminum cans. The producers of rival brands of aspirin are in competition with the makers of other pain relievers and headache remedies. The producers of eyeglasses compete with the producers of contact lenses.

The competitive force of closely related substitute products comes into play in several ways. First, the presence of readily available and competitively priced substitutes places a ceiling on the prices an industry can afford to charge for its own product without giving customers an incentive to switch to substitutes and then suffering market erosion.[13] This price ceiling, at the same time, puts a lid on the profits that industry members can earn unless they find ways to cut costs. When substitutes are cheaper than the industry's product, industry members come under heavy competitive pressure to reduce their prices and to find ways to absorb the price cuts with cost reductions. Second, the availability of substitutes inevitably invites customers to make quality and performance comparisons as well as price comparisons. For example, firms that buy glass bottles and jars from glassware manufacturers monitor whether they can just as effectively package their products in plastic containers, paper cartons, or tin

COMPETITIVE PRINCIPLE
The competitive threat posed by substitute products is strong when the prices of substitutes are attractive, buyers' switching costs are low, and many buyers believe that the substitutes have equal or better features.

---

[13] Porter, "How Competitive Forces Shape Strategy," p. 142, and Porter, *Competitive Strategy*, pp. 23–24.

cans. The competitive pressure from substitute products thus pushes industry rivals to hunt for ways to convince customers that their product is more advantageous than substitutes. Usually this means devising a competitive strategy that differentiates the industry's product from substitute products via some combination of lower cost, better quality, better service, and more desirable performance features.

Another determinant of whether substitutes are a strong or weak competitive force is whether it is difficult or costly for the industry's customers to switch to substitute products.[14] Typical switching costs include employee retraining costs, the purchase costs of any additional equipment, payments for technical help in making the changeover, the time and cost in testing the quality and reliability of the substitute, and the psychic costs of severing old supplier relationships and establishing new ones. If switching costs are high, sellers of substitutes must offer a major cost or performance benefit in order to steal the industry's customers away. When switching costs are low, it is easier for sellers of substitutes to convince buyers to change over to their product.

As a rule, then, the lower the price of substitutes, the higher their quality and performance, and the lower the user's switching costs, the more intense are the competitive pressures posed by substitute products. The best indicators of the competitive strength of substitute products are the rate at which their sales are growing, the market inroads they are making, the plans of substitute producers for expanding production capacity, and the size of their profits.

THE COMPETITIVE FORCE OF POTENTIAL ENTRY

New entrants to a market bring new production capacity, the desire to establish a secure place in the market and a satisfactory market share, and often substantial resources with which to compete.[15] Just how serious the competitive threat of entry is into a particular market depends on two classes of factors: *barriers to entry* and the *expected reaction of existing firms to new entry*. A barrier to entry exists whenever it is hard for a newcomer to break into the market and/or economic factors put a potential entrant at a price/cost disadvantage relative to its competitors. There are several major sources of entry barriers:[16]

- *Economies of scale*: Scale economies deter entry because they force potential entrants either to enter on a large-scale basis (a costly and perhaps risky move) or accept a cost disadvantage (and consequently lower profitability). The difficulty with large-scale entry is that it can cause overcapacity problems in the industry and it can so threaten the market shares of existing firms that they are pushed into aggressive retaliation (in the form of price cuts, increased advertising and sales promotion, and similar steps) to maintain their position. Either way, the entrant's outlook is for lower profits. Entrants may encounter scale-related barriers not just in production, but in advertising, marketing and distribution, financing, after-sale customer service, raw materials purchasing, and R & D as well.

---

[14] Porter, *Competitive Strategy*, p. 10.
[15] Porter, "How Competitive Forces Shape Strategy," p. 138.
[16] Porter, *Competitive Strategy*, pp. 7–17.

- *Inability to gain access to technology and specialized know-how*: Many industries require technological capability and skills not readily available to a new entrant. Key patents can effectively bar entry, as can lack of technically skilled personnel and an inability to execute complicated manufacturing techniques. Existing firms often carefully guard know-how that gives them an edge in technology and manufacturing capability. Unless new entrants can gain access to such proprietary knowledge, they will lack the technical capability to compete on an equal footing.
- *The existence of learning and experience curve effects*: When achieving lower unit costs is partly or mostly a function of experience in producing the product and other learning curve benefits, a new entrant is disadvantaged in competing with existing firms having more accumulated know-how.
- *Brand preferences and customer loyalty*: Buyers usually have some attachment to existing brands. European consumers, for example, are fiercely loyal to European brands of major household appliances. High brand loyalty means that a potential entrant must be prepared to spend enough money on advertising and sales promotion to overcome customer loyalties and build its own clientele. Substantial time and money can be involved. In addition, in some circumstances it is difficult or costly for a customer to switch to a new brand, in which case a new entrant must persuade buyers that its brand is worth the switching costs. To overcome the switching cost barrier, new entrants may have to offer buyers a bigger price cut or an extra margin of quality or service. All this can mean lower expected profit margins for new entrants—something that increases the risk to startup companies dependent on sizable, early profits to support their new investment.
- *Capital requirements*: The larger the total dollar investment needed to enter the market successfully, the more limited the pool of potential entrants. The most obvious capital requirements are associated with manufacturing plant and equipment, working capital to finance inventories and customer credit, introductory advertising and sales promotion to establish a clientele, and covering startup losses.
- *Cost disadvantages independent of size*: Existing firms may have cost advantages not available to potential entrants regardless of the entrant's size. These advantages can include access to the best and cheapest raw materials, possession of patents and proprietary technological know-how, the benefits of any learning and experience curve effects, having built and equipped plants years earlier at lower costs, favorable locations, and lower borrowing costs.
- *Access to distribution channels*: In the case of consumer goods, a potential entrant may face the barrier of gaining adequate distribution access. Wholesale distributors may be reluctant to take on a product that lacks buyer recognition. A network of retail dealers may have to be set up from scratch. Retailers have to be convinced to give a new brand ample display space and an adequate trial period. The more existing producers have the present distribution channels tied up, the tougher entry will be. Potential entrants, to overcome this barrier, may have to "buy" distribution access by offering better margins to dealers and distributors or by giving advertising allowances and other promotional incentives. As a consequence, a potential entrant's profits may be squeezed unless and until its product gains such good market acceptance that distributors and retailers want to carry it because of its popularity.

- *Regulatory policies*: Government agencies can limit or even bar entry by requiring licenses and permits. Regulated industries like banking, insurance, radio and television stations, liquor retailing, and railroads all feature government-controlled entry. In international markets, host governments commonly limit foreign entry and must approve all foreign investment applications. Stringent government-mandated safety regulations and environmental pollution standards are entry barriers because they raise entry costs.
- *Tariffs and international trade restrictions*: National governments commonly use tariffs and trade restrictions (antidumping rules, local content requirements, and quotas) to raise entry barriers for foreign firms. In 1988, due to tariffs imposed by the South Korean government, a Ford Taurus cost South Korean car buyers over $40,000. European governments require that certain Asian products, from electronic typewriters to copying machines, contain European-made parts and labor equal to 40% of selling price. And to protect European chipmakers from low-cost Asian competition, European governments instituted a rigid formula for calculating floor prices for computer memory chips.

Even if a potential entrant is willing to tackle the problems of entry barriers, there is still the issue of how existing firms will react to new entry.[17] Will incumbent firms offer only passive resistance or will they aggressively defend their market positions using price cuts, increased advertising, new product improvements, and whatever else is calculated to give a new entrant (as well as other rivals) a hard time? A potential entrant is likely to have second thoughts about entry:

COMPETITIVE PRINCIPLE
The competitive threat that outsiders will attempt entry is stronger when incumbents are not expected to fight vigorously to prevent a newcomer from gaining a market foothold and when a newcomer expects to earn attractive profits.

- When incumbent firms have previously been aggressive in defending their market positions against entry.
- When incumbent firms possess substantial financial resources with which to defend against new entry.
- When incumbent firms are in a position to use leverage with distributors and customers to keep their business.
- When incumbent firms are able and willing to cut prices to preserve their market shares.
- When product demand is expanding slowly, thus limiting the market's ability to absorb and accommodate the new entrant without adversely affecting the profit performance of all the participant firms.
- When it is more costly for existing firms to leave the market than to fight to the death (because the costs of exit are very high, owing to heavy investment in specialized technology and equipment, union agreements which contain high severance costs, or important shared relationships with other products).

Naturally, a potential entrant can only guess about how incumbent firms will react to entry. Reactions to past entry are one obvious indication. So is how existing firms behave competitively toward each other. Sometimes the "personality" of rival firms can provide clues to their probable reaction to entry; relevant personality indicators include (1) the propensity a firm may exhibit to be aggressive or conservative, a leader or a follower; (2) the backgrounds and experiences of their executives; (3) the priority that rival firms have historically given to research and development, advertising, technology, and similar key

---

[17] Porter, "How Competitive Forces Shape Strategy," p. 140.

competitive variables; and (4) the assumptions and perceptions which the managements of rival firms seem to have about themselves and their business, as revealed by speeches and interviews, the kinds of people they recruit, and how they tend to reward their executives.

The best test of whether potential entry is a strong or weak competitive force is to ask if the industry's growth and profit prospects are attractive enough to induce additional entry. When the answer is no, potential entry is not a source of competitive pressure. When the answer is yes (as in industries where lower-cost foreign competitors are seeking new markets), then potential entry is a strong force. The stronger the threat of entry, the greater the motivation of incumbent firms to fortify their positions against newcomers, endeavoring to make entry more costly or difficult.

One additional point needs to be made about the threat of entry as a competitive force: *The threat of entry changes as industry prospects grow brighter or dimmer and as entry barriers rise or fall*. For example, the expiration of a key patent can greatly increase the threat of entry. A technological discovery can create an economy of scale advantage where none existed before. New actions by incumbent firms to increase advertising, strengthen distributor-dealer relations, step up R & D, or improve product quality can erect higher roadblocks to entry. In international markets, entry barriers for foreign-based firms fall as tariffs are lowered, as domestic wholesalers and dealers seek out lower-cost foreign-made goods, and as domestic buyers become more willing to purchase foreign brands.

THE MARKET POWER OF SUPPLIERS

Whether the suppliers to an industry are a weak or strong competitive force depends on market conditions in the supplier industry and the significance of the item they supply.[18] The market power of suppliers is minimal to nonexistent whenever the item they provide is a standard commodity available on the open market from a large number of suppliers with ample capability to fill orders. Then it is relatively simple to multiple-source whatever is needed, choosing to buy from whichever suppliers offer the best deal. In such cases, suppliers can win concessions only when supplies become tight and users are so anxious to secure what they need that they agree to terms more favorable to suppliers. Suppliers are likewise in a weak bargaining position whenever there are good substitute inputs and switching is neither costly nor difficult. For example, the power of the suppliers of aluminum cans to soft-drink bottlers is checked by the latter's ability to use plastic containers and glass bottles. Suppliers also have less leverage when the industry they are supplying is a *major* customer. Here the well-being of suppliers becomes closely tied to the well-being of their major customers. This usually means that suppliers have a big incentive to protect the customer industry via reasonable prices, improved quality, and the development of new products and services that might enhance their customers' competitive positions, sales, and profits. Indeed, when industry members form a close working relationship with major suppliers, they may be able to realize substantial benefits in the form of better-quality components, just-in-time deliveries, and reduced inventory costs.

On the other hand, powerful suppliers can put an industry in a profit squeeze via price increases that cannot fully be passed on to the industry's own

COMPETITIVE PRINCIPLE
The suppliers to an industry are a weak competitive force when the item supplied is a commodity available from many sources, when there are good substitute inputs and switching to them is easy, and when the well-being of the customer industry is important to the well-being of suppliers.

---

[18] Porter, *Competitive Strategy*, pp. 27–28.

customers. Suppliers become a potentially strong competitive force in this regard when the item they provide makes up a sizable fraction of the costs of an industry's product, is crucial to the industry's production process, and/or significantly affects the quality of the industry's product. Likewise, a supplier (or group of suppliers) gains bargaining leverage the more difficult or costly it is for users to switch from one supplier to another. Big suppliers with good reputations and growing demand for their output are harder to wring concessions from than struggling suppliers striving to broaden their customer base and more fully utilize their production capacity.

Suppliers are also more powerful when they can supply a component cheaper than industry members can make it themselves. For instance, the producers of outdoor power equipment (lawnmowers, rotary tillers, snowblowers, and so on) find it cheaper to source the small engines they need from outside specialists in small engine manufacture rather than to manufacture their own engines in-house because the quantity needed is too little to justify the investment and master the process. Small engine specialists, by supplying many kinds of engines to the whole power equipment industry, obtain a big enough sales volume to capture scale economies, become proficient in all the techniques, and keep costs well below what power equipment firms could realize on their own. Small engine suppliers then are in a position to price the item below what it would cost the user to self-manufacture but far enough above their own costs to generate an attractive profit margin. In such situations, the bargaining position of suppliers is strong *until* the volume of parts a customer needs becomes large enough for the customer to justify backward integration. Then the balance of power shifts away from the supplier. The more credible the threat of backward integration into the suppliers' business becomes, the more that companies gain an upper hand over suppliers in negotiating favorable supply terms.

A final instance in which an industry's suppliers play an important competitive role is when suppliers, for one reason or another, do not have the capability or the incentive to provide items of adequate quality. For example, if auto parts suppliers provide lower-quality components to the U.S. automobile manufacturers, they can so increase the warranty and defective goods costs of the U.S. auto firms that the latter's profits, reputation, and competitive position in the world automobile market are seriously impaired.

THE MARKET POWER OF BUYERS

Just as with suppliers, the competitive strength of buyers can range from strong to weak. Buyers have substantial bargaining leverage and market power in a number of situations.[19] The most obvious is when buyers are large and purchase a sizable percentage of the industry's output. The bigger buyers are and the larger quantities they purchase, the more clout they have in negotiating with sellers. Often, large buyers are successful in using the leverage of their size and their volume purchases to obtain price concessions and other favorable terms. Buyers also gain power when their costs of switching to competing brands or to competing substitutes are relatively low. Anytime buyers have the flexibility to fill their needs by sourcing from several sellers rather than having to use just one brand, they have added room to negotiate with sellers. When sellers' products are virtually identical from seller to seller, it is relatively easy

---

[19] Porter, *Competitive Strategy,* pp. 24–27.

for buyers to switch sellers at little or no cost. The more strongly differentiated sellers' products are, however, the less able buyers are to switch without incurring sizable switching costs.

One last point: All buyers do not have equivalent degrees of bargaining power with sellers, and some may be less sensitive than others to price, quality, or service. For example, in the apparel industry, major manufacturers on the one hand confront significant customer power in selling direct to retail chains like Sears or K mart. On the other hand, they can command much better prices selling to small owner-managed apparel boutiques.

WHY MARKET AND COMPETITIVE CONDITIONS CHANGE—THE CONCEPT OF DRIVING FORCES

Although it is valuable to analyze an industry's *current* competitive forces, it is essential to recognize that any such picture is only a static snapshot. Competitive situations evolve and sometimes they undergo dramatic shifts in direction. Every market is in a constant state of flux—forces of change are either presently at work or building up steam just offstage.

Hence, it is always fruitful to identify what forces are at work to cause important changes in the industry and competitive landscape. *Market and competitive conditions change because forces are in motion that create incentives or pressures for change.*[20] The most dominant of these forces are called *driving forces* because they have the biggest influences on what kinds of changes will take place in the competitive structure of the marketplace.

BASIC CONCEPT
Market and competitive conditions change because important forces are driving industry participants (competitors, customers, suppliers) to alter their actions.

THE KINDS OF DRIVING FORCES AND HOW THEY WORK

Many events can affect market and competitive conditions powerfully enough to qualify as driving forces. Some of these are one-of-a-kind, but most fall into one of several basic categories. The most common driving forces are:[21]

1. *Changes in the long-term industry growth rate:* Shifts in industry growth up or down are a force for market change because they affect the balance between market supply and market demand, entry and exit, and how hard it will be for a firm to capture additional sales. A strong upsurge in long-term demand frequently attracts new firms to the market and encourages established firms to invest in additional capacity. A shrinking market can cause some firms to exit the industry and induce the remaining firms to postpone further capacity investments.

2. *Changes in who buys the product and how they use it:* Shifts in buyer composition and the emergence of new ways to use the product can force adjustments in customer service offerings (credit, technical assistance, maintenance and repair), open the way to market the industry's product through a different mix of dealers and retail outlets, prompt producers to broaden or narrow their product lines, increase or decrease capital requirements, and change sales and promotion approaches. The computer industry has been transformed by the surge of buyers for personal and mid-size computers. Consumer interest in cordless telephones and mobile telephones has opened a major new buyer segment for telephone equipment manufacturers.

There are a variety of factors which can affect market and competitive conditions sufficiently to justify the label of driving force.

---

[20] Porter, *Competitive Strategy*, p. 162.
[21] What follows draws on the discussion in Porter, *Competitive Strategy*, pp. 164–83.

3. *Product innovation:* Product innovation can broaden an industry's customer base, rejuvenate industry growth, and widen the degree of product differentiation among rival sellers. Successful new product introductions strengthen the market position of the innovating companies, usually at the market share expense of companies who either stick with their old products or are slow to follow with their own versions of the new product. Industries where product innovation has been a key driving force include copying equipment, cameras and photographic equipment, computers, electronic video games, toys, prescription drugs, frozen foods, and personal computer software.

4. *Technological change:* Advances in technology can dramatically alter an industry's landscape, making it possible to produce new and/or better products at lower cost and opening up whole new industry frontiers. Technological change can also generate changes in capital requirements, minimum efficient plant sizes, the desirability of vertical integration, and learning or experience curve effects.

5. *Marketing innovation:* When firms are successful in introducing new ways to market their products, they can spark a burst of buyer interest, widen industry demand, increase product differentiation, and/or lower unit costs—any or all of which can alter the competitive positions of rival firms and force strategy revisions.

6. *Entry or exit of major firms:* The entry of one or more foreign companies into a market once dominated by domestic firms nearly always produces a big shakeup in industry conditions. Likewise, when an established domestic firm from another industry attempts entry either by acquisition or by launching its own startup venture, it usually intends to apply its skills and resources in some innovative fashion. Entry by a major firm often produces a "new ballgame" not only with new key players but also with new rules for competing. Similarly, exit of a major firm changes industry structure by reducing the number of market leaders (perhaps increasing the dominance of the leaders who remain) and causing a rush to capture the exiting firm's customers.

7. *Diffusion of technical know-how:* As knowledge about how to perform a particular activity or to execute a particular manufacturing technology spreads, any technically based competitive advantage held by firms originally possessing this know-how erodes. The diffusion of such know-how can occur through scientific journals, trade publications, on-site plant tours, word of mouth among suppliers and customers, and the hiring away of knowledgeable employees. It can also occur when the possessors of technological know-how license others to use it for a royalty fee or team up with a company interested in turning the technology into a new business venture. Quite often, technological know-how can be acquired by simply buying a company that has the wanted skills, patents, or manufacturing capabilities. In recent years technology transfer across national boundaries has emerged as one of the most important driving forces in globalizing markets and competition. As companies in more countries gain access to technical know-how, they upgrade their manufacturing capabilities in a long-term effort to compete head-on against established companies. Examples of where technology transfer has turned a largely domestic industry into an increasingly global one include automobiles, tires, consumer electronics, telecommunications, and computers.

8. *Increasing globalization of the industry:* Global competition usually results in shifting patterns of competitive advantage among key players. Industries move toward globalization for any of several reasons. Certain firms may launch aggressive long-term strategies to win a globally dominant market position. Demand for the industry's product may start to emerge in more and more countries. Trade barriers may drop. Technology transfer may open the door for more companies in more countries to enter the industry arena on a major scale. Significant labor cost differences among countries may create a strong reason to locate plants for labor-intensive products in low-wage countries (wages in South Korea, Taiwan, and Singapore, for example, are about one-fourth those in the United States). Significant cost economies may accrue to firms with world-scale volumes as opposed to national-scale volumes. The growing ability of multinational companies to transfer their production, marketing, and management know-how from country to country at significantly lower cost than companies with a one-country customer base may give multinational competitors a significant competitive advantage over domestic-only competitors. Globalization is most likely to be a driving force in industries (a) based on natural resources (supplies of crude oil, copper, and cotton, for example, are geographically scattered all over the globe), (b) where low-cost production is a critical consideration (making it imperative to locate plant facilities in countries where the lowest costs can be achieved), and (c) where one or more growth-oriented, market-seeking companies are pushing hard to gain a significant competitive position in as many attractive country markets as they can.

9. *Changes in cost and efficiency:* In industries where economies of scale are emerging or where strong learning curve effects are allowing firms with the most production experience to undercut rivals' prices, large market share becomes such a distinct advantage that all firms are driven to adopt volume-building strategies—a "race for growth" dominates the industry landscape. Likewise, sharply rising costs for a key input (either raw materials or labor) can cause a scramble to either (a) line up reliable supplies of the input at affordable prices or else (b) search out lower-cost substitute inputs. Any time important changes in cost or efficiency take place in an industry, the door is open for the positions of rival firms to change radically concerning who has how big a cost advantage.

10. *Emerging buyer preferences for a differentiated instead of a commodity product (or for a more standardized product instead of strongly differentiated products):* Sometimes growing numbers of buyers begin to decide that a standard one-size-fits-all product with a bargain price meets their needs as effectively as premium priced brands offering a broad choice of features and options. Such a swing in buyer demand can drive industry change, shifting patronage away from sellers of more expensive differentiated products to sellers of cheaper few-frills products and creating a very price-competitive market environment—a development that can so dominate the marketplace that it limits the strategic freedom of industry producers to do much more than compete hard on price. On the other hand, a shift away from standardized products occurs when sellers are able to win a bigger and more loyal buyer following by introducing new features, making style changes, offering options and accessories, and creating image differences via advertising and packaging. Then the driver of change is the struggle among rivals to out-differentiate one another. Industries evolve differently depending on whether the forces in motion are acting to increase or decrease the emphasis on product differentiation.

11. *Regulatory influences and government policy changes:* Regulatory and governmental actions can often force significant changes in industry practices and strategic approaches. Deregulation has been a big driving force in the airline, banking, natural gas, and telecommunications industries. Drunk driving laws and drinking age legislation recently became driving forces in the alcoholic beverage industry. In international markets, newly enacted policies of host governments to open up their domestic markets to foreign participation or to close off foreign participation to protect domestic companies are a major factor in shaping whether the competitive struggle between foreign and domestic companies occurs on a level playing field or whether it is one-sided (owing to government favoritism).

12. *Changing societal concerns, attitudes, and life-styles:* Emerging social issues and changing attitudes and life-styles can be powerful instigators of industry change. Consumer concerns about salt, sugar, chemical additives, cholesterol, and nutrition have forced the food industry to reexamine food processing techniques, redirect R & D efforts into new areas, and introduce scores of healthier products. Safety concerns have been major drivers of change in the automobile, toy, and outdoor power equipment industries, to mention a few. Increased interest in physical fitness has produced whole new industries to supply exercise equipment, jogging clothes and shoes, and medically supervised diet programs. Social concerns about air and water pollution have been major forces in industries that discharge waste products into the air and water. Growing antismoking sentiment has posed a major long-term threat to the cigarette industry.

13. *Reductions in uncertainty and business risk:* A young emerging industry is typically characterized by an unproven cost structure and much uncertainty over potential market size, how much time and money will be needed to surmount technological problems, and what distribution channels to emphasize in accessing potential buyers. The high risks of ventures in emerging industries tend to attract only the most entrepreneurial companies. Over time, however, if pioneering firms become successful and uncertainty about the industry's viability fades, more conservative firms are usually enticed to enter the industry. Often, the entrants are larger, financially strong firms hunting for attractive growth industries in which to invest. In international markets, conservatism is prevalent in the early stages of globalization. There is a strong propensity for firms to guard against risk by relying initially on exporting, licensing, and joint ventures to enter foreign markets. Then, as experience accumulates in making a success out of foreign operations and as perceived risk levels decline, companies move quicker and more aggressively to pursue a full-scale, international competitive strategy.

The foregoing list of the different types of driving forces that exist, together with the rather obvious unpredictability as to when some of these forces will be triggered in an industry and how strong they will be, make a convincing case for why markets and industries can suddenly switch gears and head off in a new direction. Not only are there any number of different types of driving forces but the driving forces that are active also vary from industry to industry and from time to time in a given industry. Hence, analyzing what the driving forces in a given industry are, how and why they are causing the industry to change, and what the implications are for competition is all part of the analysis of competitive forces and competitive conditions.

KEY POINTS

The five-forces model of competition zeroes in on the major determinants of the strength of competitive forces in the marketplace: (1) the strategic rivalry among firms producing their own brands of a particular item, (2) the ease with which buyers can switch to closely related substitute items, (3) threats of entry of new competitors, (4) the market power exercisable by suppliers, and (5) the market power that customers can apply. The unique analytical contribution of Figure 15-1 is the simplicity with which it portrays how these five forces combine to create a spectrum of considerations called *competition*.

The collective impact of these forces determines the intensity of competition in a given market and, ultimately, the profits which the participating firms will be able to earn. As a rule, the more intense is competition, the lower is the collective profitability of participant firms. From a profit standpoint, the sternest and most vigorous sort of competition is where the long-term prospects are for no more than a normal profit—the same result as obtained under perfect competition. On the other hand, when a market offers the prospect of superior profit performance, the inference is that competitive forces are not as strong, for whatever reason.

One way for a firm to assess what sort of competitive strategy it ought to employ in a given market is to try to position itself (1) to defend and insulate itself as much as possible from the forces of competition, and (2) to influence the direction of competition in its favor by choosing a trendsetting, pacesetting strategy. Doing this requires insightful understanding of what the competitive pressures are and where they are coming from. It also requires careful evaluation of a firm's competitive strengths and weaknesses, market opportunities and threats, and areas where creative strategy can produce a superior payoff. Very likely, different firms will arrive at different evaluations as to what their own best competitive strategy is—even though they may be in substantial agreement on what the relevant competitive forces are. This accounts partly for why competing firms generally do not follow the same competitive strategy and, thus, do not occupy the same market position.

QUESTIONS FOR DISCUSSION

1. In which type of market structure would you expect competition to be more vigorous—monopolistic competition or oligopoly? Why

2. Is the most important determinant of the strength of competition the number of rival firms in the market? Why or why not?

3. Why is it appropriate to view the rivalry among competing firms as a strategic process of move and countermove?

4. What is the reasoning underlying the statement that "whenever fixed costs are high and marginal costs are low, firms are under strong economic pressure to produce at or very near full capacity"?

5. Explain how it is that the suppliers to the firms in a given industry can act as a competitive force in that industry.

6. The bottlers of soft drinks are customers of the manufacturers of glass bottles, the manufacturers of aluminum cans, and the manufacturers of plastic bottles. Explain how, as customers, the soft-drink bottlers act as a competitive force in the container industry.

7. Bayer and St. Joseph are the two leading sellers of aspirin; a number of other "no-name" firms supply aspirin for private-label sale by large retailers (drug and food chains). To what extent do you think competition among the aspirin manufacturers is affected by the competitive strategies employed by the firms making Excedrin, Anacin, Advil, Tylenol, Alka-Seltzer, and other brands of remedies for headache pain and discomfort? Draw a five-forces model for the aspirin market and assess the strength of each of the five forces.

Chapter 16

Competitive Advantage

A firm has **competitive advantage** whenever it has an edge over rivals in coping with competitive forces and in attracting buyers. There are many sources of competitive advantage: making the highest-quality product on the market, providing superior customer service, achieving lower costs than rivals, having a more convenient geographic location, designing a product that performs a particular function better than competing brands, making a more reliable and long-lasting product, and providing buyers more value for the money (a combination of good quality, good service, and acceptable price). All of these boil down to trying to provide what buyers will perceive as "superior value"—either superior value in the form of a good product at a lower price or superior value in the form of a "better" product that is worth paying more for. A fundamental reason why some firms are more successful than others is that successful firms often have achieved a competitive advantage while unsuccessful firms operate at a competitive disadvantage.

This chapter spotlights how a company can achieve or defend a competitive advantage and the role of competitive advantage in the competitive process.[1] We begin by describing the basic types of competitive strategies and then consider how each basic competitive approach can be used to build a sustainable competitive advantage. In the concluding two sections we look at the process by which competitive advantages emerge and then erode and at the special circumstances of competitive advantage in global markets.

GENERIC TYPES OF COMPETITIVE STRATEGIES

Competitive strategy concerns a firm's action plan for competing successfully in a given market—in plainer words, a firm's competitive strategy addresses how it plans to try to knock the socks off its competitors. This plan, which *evolves* more or less continually in response to changing market and competitive conditions, consists of whatever offensive or defensive actions are deemed appropriate to cope with the five competitive forces (as portrayed in Figure 15-1). The criteria for judging whether a firm has a well-formulated competitive strategy hinge chiefly on two things: (1) whether it creates a sustainable com-

Successful firms invest aggressively in securing a sustainable competitive advantage because it is the single most dependable way to achieve above-average profitability.

---

[1] The definitive work on this subject is Michael E. Porter, *Competitive Advantage* (New York: Free Press, 1985). The treatment in th.s chapter draws heavily on Porter's pioneering effort.

petitive advantage and attractive long-term market position for the firm, and (2) whether it enables the firm to earn "superior" profits (at least more than a normal profit and something above the average of other firms in the industry).

It is no surprise that firms have discovered many different competitive approaches which produce acceptable results. With few exceptions, a firm's strategy is tailor-made to fit its particular circumstances and thus has at least some unique features and wrinkles. In this sense there are as many competitive strategies as there are competitors. However, when one cuts beneath the differences in detail and looks at the basic character of the different strategies that firms employ, the amount of fundamental strategy variation narrows considerably. From this more generalized perspective, it is possible to single out three *generic* approaches to competing in the marketplace:[2]

1. Striving to be the overall low-cost producer in the industry (a *low-cost leadership strategy*).
2. Seeking to differentiate one's product offering in one way or another from rivals' products (a *differentiation strategy*).
3. Focusing on a narrow portion of the market rather than going out after the whole market (a *focus* or *niche strategy*).

Table 16-1 profiles the distinctive features of the three generic strategies.

STRIVING TO BE THE LOW-COST PRODUCER

Striving to be the low-cost producer is a powerful competitive approach in markets where many buyers are price-sensitive. The aim is to open up a sustainable cost advantage over competitors and then use the lower-cost edge as a basis for either underpricing competitors and gaining market share at their expense or earning a higher profit margin selling at the going market price. A cost advantage generates superior profitability unless it is totally used up in aggressive price-cutting efforts to take sales away from rivals. Achieving low-cost leadership typically means making low cost *relative to competitors* the theme of the firm's entire business strategy—though low cost cannot be pursued so zealously that a firm's product ends up being too stripped down and cheaply made to generate buyer appeal.

A low-cost leader's basis for competitive advantage is lower overall costs than competitors.

Examples of firms that are well known for their low-cost leadership strategies are Lincoln Electric in arc welding equipment, Briggs and Stratton in small horsepower gasoline engines, BiC in ballpoint pens, Black and Decker in tools, Design and Manufacturing in dishwashers (marketed under Sears's Kenmore brand), Beaird-Poulan in chain saws, Ford in heavy-duty trucks, General Electric in major home appliances, Wal-Mart in discount retailing, and Southwest Airlines in commercial airline travel.

The Appeal of Being a Low-Cost Producer.   Being the low-cost producer in an industry provides some attractive defenses against the five competitive forces:

- As concerns *rival competitors*, the low-cost company is in the best position to compete offensively on the basis of price, to defend against price war conditions, to use the appeal of a lower price as a weapon for grabbing sales (and market share) from rivals, and to earn

A low-cost leader has attractive defenses against the five competitive forces.

[2] Michael E. Porter, *Competitive Strategy: Techniques for Analyzing Industries and Competitors* (New York: Free Press, 1980), Chapter 2. The following discussion of these generic strategies relies on Porter's presentation, pp. 35–39 and 44–46.

TABLE 16-1   DISTINCTIVE FEATURES OF THE GENERIC COMPETITIVE STRATEGIES

Type of Feature	Low-Cost Leadership	Differentiation	Focus
Strategic target	• A broad cross-section of the market.	• A broad cross-section of the market.	• A narrow market niche where buyer needs and preferences are distinctively different from the rest of the market.
Basis of competitive advantage	• Lower costs than competitors.	• An ability to offer buyers *something different* from competitors.	• Lower cost in serving the niche or an ability to offer niche buyers something customized to their requirements and tastes.
Product line	• A good basic product with few frills (acceptable quality and limited selection).	• Many product variations, wide selection, strong emphasis on the chosen differentiating features.	• Customized to fit the specialized needs of the target segment.
Production emphasis	• A continuous search for cost reduction without sacrificing acceptable quality and essential features.	• Invent ways to create value for buyers.	• Tailor-made for the niche.
Marketing emphasis	• Try to make a virtue out of product features that lead to low cost.	• Build in whatever features buyers are willing to pay for. • Charge a premium price to cover the extra costs of differentiating features.	• Communicate the focuser's unique ability to satisfy the buyer's specialized requirements.
Sustaining the strategy	• Economical prices/good value. • All elements of strategy aim at contributing to a sustainable cost advantage—the key is to manage costs down, year after year, in every area of the business.	• Communicate the points of difference in credible ways. • Stress constant improvement and use innovation to stay ahead of imitative competitors. • Concentrate on a few key differentiating features; use them to create a reputation and brand image.	• Remain totally dedicated to serving the niche better than other competitors; don't blunt the firm's image and efforts by entering other segments and adding other product categories to widen market appeal.

above-average profits (based on bigger profit margins or greater sales volume) in markets where price competition thrives.
• As concerns *buyers*, the low-cost company has partial profit margin protection from powerful customers, since the latter will rarely be able to bargain price down past the survival level of the next most cost-efficient seller.

- As concerns *suppliers*, the low-cost producer is more insulated than competitors from powerful suppliers *if* greater internal efficiency is the primary source of its cost advantage.
- As concerns *potential entrants*, the low-cost producer can use price cutting to make it harder for a new rival to win customers; the pricing power of the low-cost producer acts as a barrier for a new entrant to hurdle.
- As concerns *substitutes*, a low-cost producer is better positioned than higher-cost rivals to use low price as a defense against the attempts of substitutes to gain a market inroad.

Consequently, a low-cost producer's ability to set the industry's price floor and still earn a profit erects barriers around its market position. Anytime price competition becomes a major market force, less efficient rivals get squeezed the most. Firms in a low-cost position relative to rivals have a significant edge in appealing to buyers who base their purchase decision on low price.

A competitive strategy based on low-cost leadership is particularly powerful when:

1. Price competition among rival sellers is a dominant competitive force and demand is highly price elastic.
2. The industry's product is an essentially standardized, commodity-type item readily available from a variety of sellers (a condition that allows buyers to shop the market for the lowest price).
3. There are few ways to achieve product differentiation that have value to buyers, or to put it another way, the differences from brand to brand do not matter much to buyers.
4. Most buyers utilize the product in the same ways—with common user requirements, a standardized product can fully satisfy the needs of all buyers, in which case product price, not features or quality, becomes the dominant competitive force.
5. Buyers incur low switching costs in changing from one seller to another, thus giving them the flexibility to shop for the best price.
6. Buyers are large and have significant power to bargain down prices.

The Risks of a Low-Cost Producer Strategy. A low-cost competitive approach has its drawbacks. Technological breakthroughs can open up cost reductions for rivals that nullify a low-cost producer's past investments and hard-won gains in efficiency. Rival firms may find it easy and/or inexpensive to imitate the leader's low-cost methods, thus making any advantage short-lived. A company driving hard to push its costs down can become so fixated on cost reduction that it fails to see some significant market changes—like buyers' growing preference for added quality or service, subtle shifts in buyers' uses of the product, and declining buyer sensitivity to price—thus getting left behind as buyer interest swings to quality, performance, service, and other differentiating features. In sum, heavy investments in cost reduction can lock a firm into both its present technology and present strategy, leaving it vulnerable to new technologies and to growing customer interest in something other than a cheaper price.

DIFFERENTIATION STRATEGIES

Differentiation strategies come into play whenever buyers' needs and preferences are too diverse to be fully satisfied by a standardized product. To be a successful differentiator, a firm must study buyers' needs and behavior

COMPETITIVE PRINCIPLE
A low-cost producer is in the strongest competitive position to set the floor on market price.

COMPETITIVE PRINCIPLE
The competitive power of low-cost leadership is greatest when competing firms are selling essentially identical products, price competition dominates, most buyers use the product similarly, buyer switching costs are low, and buyers shop aggressively for the best price.

With a differentiation strategy, the basis for competitive advantage is a product whose attributes differ significantly from the products of rivals.

carefully to learn what they consider important and what they think has value. Then the differentiator incorporates one, or maybe several, of those differentiating features into its product offering to create buyer preferences for its brand over the brands of rivals. *Competitive advantage results when some buyers become strongly attached to the attributes and features a differentiator has incorporated into its product offering.* Successful differentiation allows a firm to

- command a premium price for its product, and/or
- sell more units (because additional buyers are won over by the differentiating features), and/or
- gain greater buyer loyalty to its brand (because some buyers are strongly attracted to the differentiating features).

Differentiation enhances profitability whenever the added revenues gained from differentiated product attributes outweigh any added costs associated with achieving differentiation. Differentiation is unsuccessful when the forms of uniqueness a company pursues are not valued highly enough by buyers to induce them to purchase the company's brand, and differentiation is not profitable when the price premium buyers are willing to pay will not cover the extra costs of achieving brand distinctiveness.

The approaches to differentiating one's product from rival firms take many forms: a different taste (Dr Pepper and Listerine), special features (Jenn-Air's indoor cooking tops with a vented built-in grill for barbecuing), superior service (Federal Express in overnight package delivery), spare parts availability (Caterpillar guarantees 48-hour spare parts delivery to any customer anywhere in the world, or else the part is furnished free), overall value to the customer (McDonald's), engineering design and performance (Mercedes-Benz in automobiles), prestige and distinctiveness (Rolex in watches), product reliability (Johnson & Johnson in baby products), quality manufacture (Karastan in carpets and Honda in automobiles), technological leadership (3M Corporation in bonding and coating products), a full range of services (Merrill Lynch), a complete line of products (Campbell in soups), and top-of-the-line image and reputation (Brooks Brothers and Ralph Lauren in menswear, KitchenAid in dishwashers, and Cross in writing instruments).

Achieving Differentiation. *Anything a firm can do to create buyer value represents a potential basis for differentiation.* Once good sources of value are identified, the necessary value-creating attributes have to be built into a firm's product at an acceptable cost. A differentiator can incorporate attributes that raise the product's performance or make it more economical to use. A third option is to incorporate features that enhance buyer satisfaction in tangible or intangible ways during use. Differentiation possibilities can grow out of activities performed anywhere in the production-cost chain. McDonald's gets high ratings on its french fries partly because it has very strict specifications on the potatoes purchased from suppliers. The quality of Japanese cars stems primarily from Japanese automakers' skills in manufacturing and quality control. IBM boosts buyer value by providing its customers with an extensive array of services and technical support. L.L. Bean makes its mail-order customers feel secure in their purchases by providing an unconditional guarantee with no time limit. The commercial airlines use their otherwise empty seats during off-peak travel periods (i.e., their excess capacity) as the basis for awarding free travel to frequent flyers.

What Makes Differentiation Attractive.   Differentiation provides some buffer against the strategies of rivals because buyers become loyal to the brand or model they like best and often are willing to pay a little (perhaps a lot!) more for it. In addition, successful differentiation (1) erects entry barriers in the form of customer loyalty and uniqueness that newcomers find hard to hurdle, (2) mitigates the bargaining power of large buyers since the products of alternative sellers are less attractive to them, and (3) puts a firm in a better position to fend off threats from substitutes because customers become attached to its brand. To the extent that differentiation allows a seller to charge a higher price and bolster profit margins, then a seller is in a stronger economic position to withstand the efforts of powerful suppliers to jack up their prices. Thus, as with cost leadership, successful differentiation creates lines of defense for dealing with the five competitive forces.

A successful differentiator has attractive defenses against the five competitive forces.

As a rule, differentiation strategies work best in situations where (1) there are many ways to differentiate the product or service and many buyers perceive these differences as having value, (2) buyer needs and uses of the item are diverse, (3) few rival firms are following a similar differentiation approach, and (4) differentiating product attributes cannot be quickly or cheaply imitated.

The most appealing types of differentiation strategies are those least subject to quick or inexpensive imitation. Here is where having core competences becomes a major competitive asset. When a firm has skills and expertise that competitors cannot match easily, it can use them as a basis for successful differentiation. Areas where efforts to differentiate are likely to produce an attractive, longer-lasting competitive edge are:

The competitive power of a differentiation strategy is greatest when buyer needs are diverse, there are many useful ways to differentiate the product, few rivals are trying to differentiate on the same product attributes, and competitors cannot quickly or cheaply copy differentiating features.

- Differentiation based on *technical superiority*.
- Differentiation based on *quality*.
- Differentiation based on *giving customers more support services*.
- Differentiation based on the appeal of *more value for the money*.

Real Value, Perceived Value, and Signals of Value.   Buyers seldom pay for value they do not perceive, no matter how real the unique extras may be.[3] Thus the price premium that a differentiation strategy commands is a reflection of *the value actually delivered* to the buyer and *the value perceived* by the buyer (even if not actually delivered). A difference between actual value and perceived value can emerge whenever buyers have a difficult time assessing in advance what their experience with the product will be. Incomplete knowledge on the part of buyers often causes them to judge value on the basis of such *signals* as the seller's word-of-mouth reputation, how attractively the product is packaged, how extensively the brand is advertised and thus how "well known" it is, the content of the ads and the image they project, the manner in which information is presented in brochures and sales presentations, the attractiveness and aura of quality associated with the seller's facilities, the list of customers a seller has, the market share the firm has, the time the firm has been in business, the price being charged (where price connotes "quality"), and the professionalism, appearance, and personality of the seller's employees. These signals of value may be as important as actual value (1) when the nature of differentiation is subjective or hard to quantify, (2) when buyers are making their first-time purchases, (3) when repurchase is infrequent, and (4) when buyers are unsophisticated.

A differentiating firm that signals the value of its product very effectively may command a higher price than a firm whose product actually delivers better value but signals it poorly.

---

[3] This discussion draws from Porter, *Competitive Advantage*, pp. 138–42.

Differentiation is unprofitable when the added costs of achieving differentiation exceed the added revenues that differentiation generates.

Keeping the Cost of Differentiation in Line.   Attempts to achieve differentiation usually raise costs. The key to profitable differentiation is either to keep the average total costs associated with differentiating below the price premium that the differentiation approach commands (this widens the profit margin per unit sold) or else to offset thinner profit margins with enough added volume to increase total profits (larger volume can make up for smaller margins provided differentiation allows enough extra units to be sold). In pursuing differentiation, a firm must be careful not to get its average total costs so far out of line with competitors that the resulting price premium it has to charge puts the brand out of the price range buyers are willing to pay. From a cost perspective, the most attractive differentiating activities are those in which a firm can enjoy either a cost advantage over competitors or a price premium that more than offsets the added costs of achieving uniqueness. There may also be good reason to add extra differentiating features that are not costly but add to buyer satisfaction—fine restaurants typically provide such extras as a slice of lemon in the water glass, valet parking, and complimentary after-dinner mints.

A low-cost producer strategy can defeat a differentiation strategy when buyers are satisfied with a standardized product and do not think "extra" attributes are worth a higher price.

The Risks of a Differentiation Strategy.   There are, of course, no guarantees that differentiation will produce a meaningful competitive advantage. If buyers see little value in uniqueness (i.e., a standard item meets their needs), then a low-cost strategy can easily defeat a differentiation strategy. In addition, differentiation is defeated when competitors can quickly copy the differentiating attempt. Rapid imitation means that real differentiation is never actually achieved since competing brands keep changing in like ways despite sellers' continued efforts to create uniqueness. Thus, to be successful at differentiation a firm must search out durable sources of uniqueness that cannot be quickly or cheaply imitated. Aside from these considerations, other common pitfalls to pursuing differentiation include:[4]

- Trying to differentiate on the basis of something that does not lower a buyer's cost or enhance the buyer's well-being, as perceived by the buyer.
- Overdifferentiating such that price is too high relative to competitors or that product quality or service levels exceed buyers' needs.
- Trying to charge too high a price premium (the bigger the premium, the more buyers can be lured away by lower-priced competitors).
- Ignoring the need to signal value and depending only on the "real" bases of differentiation.
- Not understanding or identifying what buyers consider as value.

The Strategy of Being a Best-Cost Producer.   A differentiation strategy aimed at giving customers *more value for the money* usually means combining an emphasis on low cost with an emphasis on *more than minimally acceptable* quality, service, features, and performance. The idea is to create superior value by meeting or exceeding buyer expectations on quality-service-features-performance attributes and beating their expectations on price. Strategywise, the aim is to be the low-cost producer of a product with *good-to-excellent* product attributes (as concerns quality, service, features, performance, and so on), and then use the cost advantage to underprice brands having comparable attributes. Such a competitive approach is termed a ***best-cost producer strategy*** because the producer has the best (lowest) cost relative to producers whose brands are comparably positioned on the quality-service-

---

[4] Porter, *Competitive Advantage*, pp. 160–62.

features-performance scale. The competitive advantage of a best-cost producer comes from matching close rivals on key quality-service-features-performance dimensions and beating them on cost. This requires achieving matching quality at a lower cost than rivals, achieving matching features at a lower cost than rivals, achieving matching product performance at a lower cost than rivals, and so on. What distinguishes a successful best-cost producer is expertise in incorporating upscale product attributes at a low cost; or, to put it a bit differently, an ability to contain the costs of providing customers with a better product. The most successful best-cost producers have the skills to simultaneously manage unit costs down and product calibre upward.

A best-cost producer strategy has great appeal from the standpoint of competitive positioning. It produces superior customer value by balancing a strategic emphasis on low cost against strategic emphasis on differentiation. In effect, it is a *hybrid* strategy that allows a company to combine the competitive advantage appeal of low cost with the competitive advantage appeal of differentiation. In markets where buyer diversity makes product differentiation the norm and significant numbers of buyers are price and value sensitive, a best-cost producer strategy can be more advantageous than the extremes of either a pure low-cost producer strategy or a pure differentiation strategy keyed to absolute product superiority. This is because a best-cost producer can position itself near the middle of the market with either a medium-quality product at a below-average price or a very good product at a medium price. Often, the majority of buyers prefer a mid-range product rather than the cheap, basic product of a low-cost producer or the expensive product of a top-of-the-line differentiator.

FOCUS AND SPECIALIZATION STRATEGIES

Focusing starts by choosing a market niche where buyers have distinctive preferences or requirements. The niche can be defined by geographic uniqueness, by specialized requirements in using the product, or by special product attributes that appeal only to niche members. *A focuser's basis for competitive advantage is either lower costs than competitors in serving the market niche or an ability to offer niche buyers something different from other competitors.* A focus strategy based on low cost depends on there being a buyer segment with requirements that are less costly to satisfy as compared to the rest of the market. A focus strategy based on differentiation depends on there being a buyer segment that demands unique product attributes.

Examples of firms employing a focus strategy include Tandem Computers (a specialist in "nonstop" computers for customers who need a "fail-safe" system), Rolls Royce (in super luxury automobiles), Apple Computer in desktop publishing (Apple's MacIntosh personal computers have unusually good capability to turn out professional-looking reports and graphics), Fort Howard Paper (a specialized producer of paper products for industrial and commercial enterprises only), commuter airlines like Skywest and Atlantic Southeast (specialists in low-traffic, short-haul flights linking major airports with smaller cities 50 to 250 miles away), and Bandag (a specialist in truck tire recapping that promotes its recaps aggressively at over 1000 truck stops).

Using a focus strategy to achieve a low-cost advantage is a fairly common technique. Budget-priced motel chains like Days Inn, Motel 6, and La-Quinta have lowered their investment and operating costs per room by using a no-frills approach and catering to price-conscious travelers. Discount stock brokerage houses have lowered costs by focusing on customers mainly inter-

COMPETITIVE PRINCIPLE
The most powerful competitive approach a firm can pursue is relentlessly striving to become a lower and lower cost producer of a better and better product, with the aim of becoming the industry's absolute lowest-cost producer and, simultaneously, the producer of the industry's overall best product.

What sets a focus strategy apart is concentrated attention on a narrow piece of the total market.

ested in buy-sell transactions who are willing to forgo all the investment research, investment advice, and financial services offered by full-service firms like Merrill Lynch. Pursuing a cost advantage via focusing works well when a firm can find ways to lower costs significantly by limiting its customer base to a well-defined buyer segment.

When Focusing Is Attractive.   A focus strategy becomes increasingly attractive as more of the following conditions are met:

- The segment is big enough to be profitable.
- The segment has good growth potential.
- The segment is not crucial to the success of major competitors.
- The focusing firm has the skills and resources to serve the segment effectively.
- The focuser can defend itself against challengers based on the customer goodwill it has built up and its superior ability to serve buyers in the segment.

A focuser's specialized skills in serving the target market niche provide a basis for defending against the five competitive forces. Multisegment rivals do not have the same competitive capability to serve the focused firm's target clientele. The focused firm's competence in serving the market niche raises entry barriers, thus making it harder for companies outside the niche to enter. A focuser's unique capabilities in serving the niche are also a hurdle that substitutes must overcome. The bargaining leverage of powerful customers is blunted somewhat by their own unwillingness to shift their purchases to firms less capable of serving their needs.

The competitive power of a focus strategy is greatest when there are attractive buyer segments to focus on, few if any other firms are concentrating on the target segment, and buyers have specialized needs.

Focusing works best (1) when it is costly or difficult for multisegment competitors to zero in on the specialized needs of the target market niche; (2) when no other rival is attempting to *specialize* in the same target segment; (3) when a firm's resources do not permit it to go after a wider part of the total market; and (4) when the industry has many different segments, thereby creating more focusing opportunities and allowing a focuser to pick out an attractive segment suited to its competitive strengths and capabilities.

The Risks of a Focus Strategy.   Focusing carries several risks. One is the chance that other competitors will find effective ways to match the focused firm in serving the narrow target market. The second is the potential for the niche buyer's preferences and needs to drift toward the product attributes desired by the market as a whole; such an erosion of the differences across buyer segments opens the way for rivals with broad market appeal to serve the target markets of the focused firms. A third is that the segment becomes so attractive that it is soon inundated with competitors, causing segment profits to be splintered.

BUILDING COMPETITIVE ADVANTAGE VIA LOW-COST LEADERSHIP

A cost advantage is achieved when a firm's cumulative costs across its overall production-cost chain are lower than competitors' cumulative costs.[5] How valuable a cost advantage is from a competitive strategy perspective depends

---

[5] The concept of production-cost chains was presented in Chapter 8. Since we will have cause to draw upon the production-cost chain idea repeatedly in the remainder of this chapter, you may wish to skim over the section on "Strategic Cost Analysis" in Chapter 8, paying particular attention to Figure 8-9.

on its sustainability. Sustainability, in turn, hinges upon whether a firm's sources of cost advantage are difficult to copy or to match in some other way. A cost advantage generates superior profitability when the firm's product offering is deemed by buyers to be comparable enough to the offerings of competitors that the cost advantage is not eaten up in whole or in part by the need to underprice competitors to win sales. Two avenues can be used to pursue a cost advantage:[6]

- Do a better job than rivals of controlling the factors that give rise to costs.
- Revamp the makeup of the production-cost chain by doing things differently and saving enough in the process that customers can be supplied more cheaply.

Let's look at each of the two cost-saving approaches.

CONTROLLING THE COST DRIVERS

A firm's cost position is the result of the behavior of costs in each one of the activities comprising its total production-cost chain. There are nine *major drivers of cost* that can come into play in determining costs in each activity segment of the chain:[7]

1. *Economies or diseconomies of scale.* Economies and diseconomies of scale can be found or created in virtually every segment of the production-cost chain. For example, manufacturing economies can sometimes be achieved by simplifying the product line and scheduling longer production runs for fewer models. A geographically organized sales force can realize economies as regional sales volume grows because a salesperson can write larger orders at each sales call and/or because of reduced travel time between calls; on the other hand, a sales force organized by product line can encounter travel-related diseconomies if salespersons have to spend disproportionately more travel time calling on distantly spaced customers. Boosting local or regional market share can lower sales and marketing costs per unit, whereas opting for a bigger national market share by entering new regions can create scale diseconomies unless and until the market penetration in the newly entered regions reaches efficient proportions.

2. *Learning and experience curve effects.* Experience-based cost savings can come from improved layout, gains in labor efficiency, debugging of technology, product design modifications that enhance manufacturing efficiency, redesign of machinery and equipment to gain increased operating speed, getting samples of rivals' products and having design engineers study how they are made, and tips from suppliers, consultants, and ex-employees of rival firms. Learning tends to vary with the amount of management attention devoted to capturing the benefits of experience of both the firm and others. Learning benefits can be kept proprietary by building or modifying production equipment in-house, retaining key employees, limiting the dissemination of information through employee publications, and enforcing strict nondisclosure provisions in employment contracts.

3. *The percentage of capacity utilization.* High fixed costs as a percentage of total costs create a stiff unit cost penalty for underutilization of

> Achieving a cost advantage entails outmanaging rivals on efficiency and cost control and/or finding creative ways to cut cost-producing activities out of the production-cost chain.

> A firm intent on becoming a low-cost producer has to use its knowledge about cost drivers to manage the costs in each segment of the production chain downward year after year.

---

[6] Michael E. Porter, *Competitive Advantage* (New York: Free Press, 1985), p. 97.
[7] This listing and explanation is condensed from Porter, *Competitive Advantage*, pp. 70–83.

existing capacity. Increasing the percentage of capacity utilization spreads indirect and overhead costs over a larger unit volume and enhances the efficiency of fixed asset utilization.[8] The more capital intensive the business, the more important this cost driver becomes. Finding ways to minimize the ups and downs in seasonal capacity utilization can be an important source of cost advantage.

4. *Linkages with other activities in the chain.* When the cost of one activity is affected by how other activities are performed, there is opportunity to lower the costs of the linked activities via superior coordination and/or joint optimization. Linkages with suppliers tend to center on suppliers' product-design characteristics, quality-assurance procedures, delivery and service policies, and the manner by which the supplier's product is furnished (for example, delivery of nails in prepackaged 1-pound, 5-pound, and 10-pound assortments instead of 100-pound bulk cartons can reduce a hardware dealer's labor costs in filling individual customer orders). The easiest supplier linkages to exploit are those where both a supplier's and a firm's costs fall because of coordination and/or joint optimization. Linkages with forward channels tend to center on location of warehouses, materials handling, outbound shipping, and packaging.

5. *Sharing opportunities with other business units within the enterprise.* When an activity can be shared with a sister unit, there can be significant cost savings. Cost sharing is potentially a way to achieve scale economies, ride the learning curve down at a faster clip, and/or achieve fuller capacity utilization. Sometimes the know-how gained in one division can be used to help lower costs in another; sharing know-how is significant when the activities are similar and the know-how can be readily transferred from one unit to another.

6. *The extent of vertical integration.* Partially or fully integrating into the activities of either suppliers or forward channel allies can allow an enterprise to detour suppliers or buyers with considerable bargaining power; vertical integration can also result in cost savings when it is feasible to coordinate or closely mesh adjacent activities in the overall cost chain.

7. *Timing considerations associated with first-mover advantages and disadvantages.* The first major brand in the market may achieve lower costs of establishing and maintaining a brand name. Late movers can, in a fast-paced technology development situation, benefit from purchasing the latest equipment or avoiding the high product/market development costs of early-moving pioneers.

8. *Competitive choices and operating decisions.* Decision makers at various management levels can impact a firm's costs by the things they do in any number of areas:

- Increasing/decreasing the number of products offered.
- Adding/cutting the services provided to buyers.
- Incorporating more/less performance and quality features into the product.
- Paying higher/lower wages and fringes to employees relative to rivals and firms in other industries.

---

[8] A firm can improve its capacity utilization by (a) serving a mix of accounts having peak volumes spread throughout the year, (b) finding off-season uses for its products, (c) serving private label customers that can intermittently use the excess capacity, (d) selecting buyers with stable demands or demands that are counter to the normal peak-valley cycle, (e) letting competitors serve the buyer segments whose demands fluctuate the most, and (f) sharing capacity with sister units having a different pattern of needs.

- Increasing/decreasing the number of different forward channels utilized in distributing the firm's product.
- Raising/lowering the levels of R & D support relative to rivals.
- Putting more/less emphasis on achieving higher levels of productivity and efficiency as compared to rivals.
- Raising/lowering the specifications set for purchased materials.

9. *Locational variables*. Locations differ in their prevailing wave levels, tax rates, energy costs, inbound and outbound shipping and freight costs, and so on. Opportunities may exist for reducing costs by relocating plants, field offices, warehousing, and headquarters operations. Moreover, the location of sister facilities relative to each other affects intrafirm shipping, inventory, outbound freight on goods shipped to customers, and coordination.

A firm intent on being the low-cost producer has to scrutinize each cost-creating activity and identify the drivers of cost for that activity. Then it needs to use its knowledge about the cost drivers to begin to reduce costs for each and every activity where cost-saving potential is believed to exist. It is important to recognize that the task of pushing costs down further and further (and not incurring some costs at all) is not easy or simple; rather, it is a task that has to be managed with both ingenuity and single-minded toughness. And it is something that has to be done on a continuous basis, not sporadically.

Successful low-cost producers strive for continuous cost improvement; they do not just initiate cost-saving programs in response to a crisis or a squeeze on profits.

REVAMPING THE MAKEUP OF THE PRODUCTION-COST CHAIN

Dramatic cost advantages can emerge from finding innovative ways to restructure activities, to cut out "frills," and to provide the basics in more economical fashion.[9] The primary ways to achieve an advantage via revamping the makeup of the production-cost chain include:

- Stripping away all the extras and offering only a basic, no-frills product or service.
- Using a different production process.
- Automating a particularly high-cost activity.
- Finding ways to use cheaper raw materials.
- Using new kinds of advertising media and promotional approaches relative to the industry norm.
- Selling directly through one's own sales force instead of indirectly through dealers and distributors.
- Relocating facilities closer to suppliers and/or customers.
- Achieving a more economical degree of forward or backward vertical integration relative to competitors.
- Going against the "something for everyone" approach of others and focusing on a limited product or service to meet a special, but important, need of the target buyer segment.

The accompanying Applications Capsule describes how two companies won strong competitive positions via restructuring the traditional activity-cost chain.

---

[9] This section is adapted from Porter, *Competitive Advantage*, pp. 97–115.

APPLICATIONS CAPSULE

WINNING A COST ADVANTAGE: IOWA BEEF PACKERS AND FEDERAL EXPRESS

Iowa Beef Packers and Federal Express have been able to win strong competitive positions by restructuring the traditional production-cost chains in their industries. In beef packing the traditional production sequence involved raising cattle on scattered farms and ranches, shipping them live to labor-intensive unionized slaughtering plants, and then transporting whole sides of beef to grocery retailers, whose butcher departments cut them into smaller pieces and packaged them for sale to grocery shoppers. Iowa Beef Packers revamped the traditional chain with a radically different strategy—large automated plants employing nonunion labor were built near economically transportable supplies of cattle, and the meat was partially butchered at the processing plant into smaller high-yield cuts (sometimes sealed in plastic casing ready for purchase), boxed, and shipped to retailers. IBP's inbound cattle transportation expenses, traditionally a major cost item, were cut significantly by avoiding the weight losses that occurred when live animals were shipped long distances; major outbound shipping cost savings were achieved by not having to ship whole sides of beef with their high waste factor. Iowa Beef's strategy was so successful that it was, in 1985, the largest U.S. meatpacker, surpassing the former industry leaders, Swift, Wilson, and Armour.

Federal Express innovatively redefined the production-cost chain for rapid delivery of small parcels. Traditional firms like Emery and Airborne Express operated by collecting freight packages of varying sizes, shipping them to their destination points via air freight and commercial airlines, and then delivering them to the addressee. Federal Express operated by collecting freight packages of varying sizes, shipping them to their destination points via air freight and commercial airlines, and then delivering them to the addressee. Federal Express opted to focus only on the market for overnight delivery of small packages and documents. These were collected at local drop points during the late afternoon hours, flown on company-owned planes during early evening hours to a central hub in Memphis, where—from 11 P.M. to 3 A.M. each night—all parcels were sorted and then reloaded on company planes and flown during the early morning hours to their destination points, where they were delivered the next morning by company personnel using company trucks. The cost structure so achieved by Federal Express was low enough to permit it to guarantee overnight delivery of a small parcel anywhere in the United States for a price as low as $11. In 1986 Federal Express had a 58% market share of the air-express package-delivery market versus a 15% share for UPS, 11% for Airborne Express, and 10% for Emery/Purolator.

Source: Based on information in Michael E. Porter, *Competitive Advantage* (New York: Free Press, 1985), p. 109.

The two approaches are not mutually exclusive, and low-cost producers usually achieve their cost advantage from any and all sources they can identify. More often than not, low-cost producers have a strong cost-conscious operating culture undergirded by symbolic traditions of spartan facilities, frugal screening of all budget requests, and limited perks and frills for employees at all levels.

BUILDING COMPETITIVE ADVANTAGE VIA DIFFERENTIATION

Successful differentiation requires being unique at something buyers consider valuable.[10] When differentiation offers value to the customer, it yields competitive advantage. Differentiation is unsuccessful when the forms of uniqueness pursued by a firm are not valued highly enough by enough buyers to cause them to prefer the firm's product to that of rivals. Differentiation strategies may be aimed at broad customer groups or narrowly focused on a limited buyer segment having particular needs.

Any product attribute that buyers consider valuable is a basis for differentiation.

Successful differentiation strategies can grow out of activities performed anywhere in the overall production-cost chain; they do not arise solely from marketing and advertising departments. The places in the chain where differentiation can be achieved include:

Opportunities to differentiate may exist anywhere along the production-cost chain.

---

[10] Porter, *Competitive Advantage*, pp. 119–20. The content of this section is based on Chapter 4 of *Competitive Advantage*.

1. *The procurement of raw materials* that affect the performance or quality of the end product. (McDonald's is more selective and particular than its competitors in selecting the potatoes it uses in its french fries.)

2. *Product-oriented R & D efforts* that lead to improved designs, new performance features, expanded end uses and applications, greater product variety, shorter lead times in developing new models, and being the first to come out with new products.

3. *Production-process-oriented R & D efforts* that lead to improved quality, reliability, and product appearance.

4. *The manufacturing process* insofar as it emphasizes zero defects, carefully engineered performance designs, long-term durability, improved economy to end-users, maintenance-free use, flexible end-use application, and consistent product quality.

5. *The outbound logistics system* to the extent that it improves delivery time and accurate order-filling.

6. *Marketing, sales, and customer service activities* that result in helpful technical assistance to buyers, faster maintenance and repair services, more and better product information provided to customers, more and better training materials for end-users, better credit terms, better warranty coverages, quicker order processing, more frequent sales calls, and greater customer convenience.

Differentiation thus goes deeper than just the catchall words "quality and service." Quality is primarily a function of the product's physical properties, whereas differentiation possibilities that create value to buyers can be found throughout the whole production-cost chain. A full understanding of the sources of differentiation and the activities that drive uniqueness is a prerequisite to developing new ways to achieve differentiation and to diagnosing how sustainable any advantage gained by uniqueness might be.[11]

CREATING A DIFFERENTIATION-BASED ADVANTAGE

Normally, for differentiation to succeed in producing a competitive advantage, a firm must incorporate product attributes that either *lower the buyer's total costs of using product or raise the performance the buyer gets from the product.*[12] To make it cheaper for a buyer to use a firm's brand, the firm can incorporate features that result in any of the following buyer benefits:

- Reduced waste and scrap in raw materials use.
- Lower labor costs (fewer hours, less training, lower skill requirements).
- Less downtime or idle time (because of short lead times in supplying spare parts).
- Faster processing times.
- Lower delivery, installation, or financing costs.
- Reduced inventory costs (because of just-in-time delivery capability from suppliers).
- Less maintenance and/or ease of maintenance.
- Reduced need for other inputs (energy, safety equipment, security personnel, inspection personnel).
- Higher trade-in value for used models.

To achieve differentiation, a firm can incorporate product attributes that produce cost savings for buyers.

[11] Porter, *Competitive Advantage*, p. 124.
[12] *Ibid.*, pp. 135–38.

- Compatibility to interface better with other equipment.
- Free advice and technical assistance on end-use applications (lowers need for technical personnel, enhances efficiency of use).

Alternatively, differentiation can aim at incorporating attributes that will enhance the performance the buyer gets from the product.

Differentiation that aims at enhancing the performance of the product from the buyer's perspective can take such forms as providing:

- Greater convenience and ease of use.
- More features that meet the full range of a buyer's requirements, as compared to competitors' products.
- Capacity to add on or change later.
- Optional extras to meet occasional needs.
- Flexible applications that give buyers more options to tailor their own product to the needs of their customers.
- Ability to fill noneconomic needs such as status, image, prestige, appearance, comfort.
- Capability for meeting the customer's need to accommodate future growth and expansion requirements.

BUILDING COMPETITIVE ADVANTAGE VIA FOCUSING

Buyer segments within an industry are far from being homogeneous.[13] The strengths of the five competitive forces vary from segment to segment, and different segments can have significantly different activity-cost chains. As a consequence, segments differ in their competitive attractiveness and in what it takes to achieve competitive advantage in each segment. It is these differences that give rise to the appeal of a focus strategy. The two crucial issues concerning use of a focus strategy revolve around (1) choosing which industry segments to compete in and (2) deciding how to build competitive advantage in the target segments.

Often, the most intense competitive pressures a focuser encounters come from happenings in the other segments of the industry.

Deciding which segments to compete in hinges upon attractiveness of the various segments. Segment attractiveness is typically a function of segment size and growth rate, the intensity of the five competitive forces in the segment, profit prospects in the segment, the strategic importance of the segment to other major competitors, and the match between a firm's capabilities and the segment's needs. These are self-explanatory except for the differences between analyzing the five forces at the segment level as compared to the industry level.[14] In five-forces analysis at the segment level, potential entrants include firms serving other segments as well as firms not presently in the industry. Substitutes for the product varieties already included in the segment can be product varieties in the rest of the industry as well as products produced in other industries. Rivalry in the segment involves both firms focusing exclusively on the segment and firms that serve this and other segments. Buyer and supplier power, while mostly segment-specific, can be influenced by buyer purchases in other segments and supplier sales to other segments. As a rule, then, five-forces analysis of a segment tends to be heavily influenced by conditions in other segments.

---

[13] This section is based on Porter, *Competitive Advantage*, Chapter 7.
[14] Porter, *Competitive Advantage*, pp. 256–57.

CREATING A FOCUS-BASED COMPETITIVE ADVANTAGE

A focuser, to achieve competitive advantage, has to succeed at low-cost leadership or differentiation *in its chosen segment or segments*. If a focuser opts to pursue low-cost leadership, then the same kinds of cost-reducing approaches as just explained for industrywide cost leadership have to be used in managing the product-cost chain for the segment. A focuser can gain a cost advantage because more than one cost curve can prevail in an industry. The cost curve for a specialist firm concentrating on custom orders and short production runs can differ substantially from the cost curve for a firm pursuing a high-volume, low-cost strategy, as shown in Figure 16-1. In such cases, small firms are positioned to be cost-effective focusers in the small-volume, custom-order buyer segments, leaving the mass market to large-volume producers. If a focusing firm opts for differentiation, then it must look at buyer needs and develop ways to lower their costs or enhance the performance they get from the product; the specific kinds of differentiating approaches are the same for focusers as for broad competitors. What sets the creation of competitive advantage by focusing apart is that focus strategies are grounded in differences among segments. A focuser excels in serving the target segment. However, what can give the focuser a special boost in winning a segment-based competitive advantage is the fact that differences across segments can impose significant costs of coordination, compromise, and inflexibility on broadly targeted competitors in trying to meet the specific needs of buyers in the focuser's target segments.

To achieve competitive advantage, a focuser must succeed at low-cost leadership or differentiation in its target market niche.

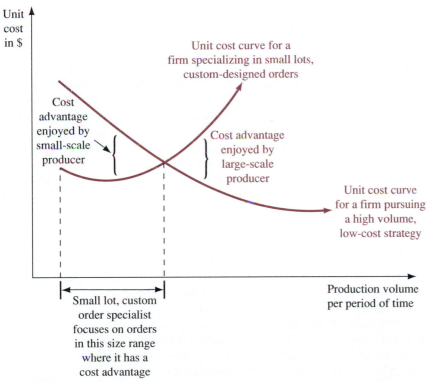

Figure 16-1

When a focus strategy can allow a small firm to be cost competitive with a large, mass production rival

Source: Adapted with permission of The Free Press, a Division of Macmillan, Inc. from *Competitive Strategy: Techniques for Analyzing Industries and Competitors* by Michael E. Porter. Copyright © 1980 by The Free Press, p. 245.

This is the condition that makes focusing really attractive. When the differences among the segments are slight, a focuser has little defense against more broadly targeted competitors because they can serve the needs of the buyer segment about as well as the focuser can.

SUSTAINING A FOCUS-BASED COMPETITIVE ADVANTAGE

For a focus strategy to be successful over time, three conditions must be present:[15]

1. A focuser must be able to defend its position against inroads from more broadly targeted competitors. This is easier when segment differences are big and harder when they are small.

2. A focuser needs to erect barriers to prevent imitation by other focusers. Another competitor, either new to the industry or one dissatisfied with its current strategy, may try to replicate the focus strategy. The more attractive the segment and the more successful a focuser's strategy, the greater the threat of imitation (unless the focuser has built a good defense against imitation).

3. A focuser must not be threatened by conditions that will cause the segment to dissolve into the broader market or to shrink to an unattractive size. Competitors serving broader parts of the industry may well use product innovation, advertising, promotional efforts, and other marketing tactics to induce buyers to leave the focuser's segment and come into theirs.

THE PROBLEMS WITH PURSUING A FOCUS-BASED COMPETITIVE ADVANTAGE

Focusing on a segment or group of segments is not by itself a basis for competitive advantage. For focusing to have a chance for real success, the target segment must (1) involve buyers with different needs or (2) entail the use of a production-cost chain that differs from the chain needed to serve other segments. When more broadly targeted competitors do not face much compromise in serving multiple segments, a focus strategy involves an uphill struggle.

Two other pitfalls are (1) choosing a segment that cannot be successfully defended against challengers attracted by the segment's size and profitability and (2) going with a single-segment focus strategy and running afoul of the risk that the target segment dries up.[16]

THE BUILDUP AND EROSION OF COMPETITIVE ADVANTAGE

Securing a competitive advantage is always a challenge, requiring both a well-designed strategy and proficient strategy execution. The length of time it takes to open up a competitive edge over rivals varies from situation to situation and is partly a function of the industry's characteristics.[17] The *buildup period*, shown in Figure 16-2, can be short, as in service businesses which need little in the way of time and investment to implement a new offensive move and create an impact in the marketplace. Or the buildup can take much longer, as in capital-intensive and technologically sophisticated industries where it can take

Competitive advantage is usually acquired by employing competitive moves that cannot be easily stalemated by rivals.

[15] Porter, *Competitive Advantage,* pp. 267–69.
[16] For more details, see Porter, *Competitive Advantage*, pp. 270–72.
[17] Ian C. MacMillan, "How Long Can You Sustain a Competitive Advantage," reprinted in Liam Fahey, *The Strategic Planning Management Reader* (Englewood Cliffs, N.J.: Prentice Hall, 1989), pp. 23–24.

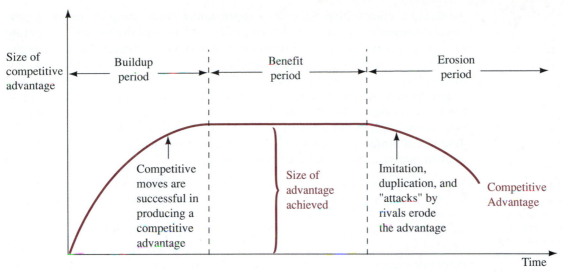

Figure 16-2
The building and eroding of competitive advantage

several years to debug a trailblazing technology, bring new capacity in line, or win consumer acceptance of an innovative product. Ideally, an offensive move will build competitive advantage quickly; the longer it takes, the more likely rivals will spot the move, see its potential, and begin a response. The size of the advantage (indicated on the vertical scale in Figure 16-2) can be large (as in pharmaceuticals, where patents on an important new drug produce a substantial advantage) or small (as in apparel, where popular new designs can be imitated quickly).

Following a successful competitive offensive, there is a *benefit period* during which the fruits of competitive advantage can be enjoyed. The length of the benefit period is governed by how much time it takes rivals to launch counteroffensives and begin closing the competitive gap. A lengthy benefit period gives the firm valuable time to earn above-average profits and recoup the investment made in creating the advantage. The best competitive offensives produce big competitive advantages and long benefit periods.

As competitors respond with serious counteroffensives to attack the advantage, the *erosion period* begins. *Any competitive advantage currently held will eventually be eroded by the actions of competent, resourceful competitors.*[18] Thus, to sustain its initial advantage, a firm must devise a second round of competitive moves. The groundwork for another competitive offensive needs to be laid during the benefit period so that it is ready for launch when competitors mount their response to the earlier offensive. Successfully sustaining a competitive advantage means staying a step ahead of rivals by mounting one new competitive move after another.

Competent, resourceful rivals can be counted upon to launch countermoves aimed at narrowing and eventually eroding any competitive advantage a firm has.

COMPETITION AND COMPETITIVE ADVANTAGE IN GLOBAL MARKETS

The motivations for firms to go outside their home-country market and compete internationally center around any of three factors: a desire to seek out new

---

[18] Ian C. MacMillan, ''Controlling Competitive Dynamics by Taking Strategic Initiative,'' *The Academy of Management Executives,* Vol. 2, No. 2 (May 1988), p. 11.

markets, a competitive need to achieve lower costs, or a desire to access natural resource deposits in other countries. Whichever the reason, competing in foreign markets has to be situation-driven and requires careful analysis of the industry's international aspects. Special attention has to be paid to how national markets differ in buyer needs and habits, distribution channels, long-run growth potential, driving forces, and competitive pressures. In addition to just the basic market differences from country to country, there are four competitive considerations unique to operating in international markets: cost variations among countries, fluctuating exchange rates, host government trade policies, and the pattern of international competition.

> **In internationally competitive markets, it is a matter of great significance whether a firm's plants are located in countries where production costs are low or where they are high.**

Manufacturing Cost Variations.   Differences in wage rates, worker productivity, inflation rates, energy costs, tax rates, and the like create sizable variations in manufacturing costs from country to country. It is common for plants in some countries to have major manufacturing cost advantages over plants in other countries because of their lower input costs (especially labor) or their unique natural resources. In such cases, the low-cost countries tend to become principal production sites, with most of the output scheduled for export to markets in other parts of the world. Companies with facilities in these locations (or which source their products from contract manufacturers in these countries) have a competitive advantage over those that do not. The importance of this consideration is most evident in low-wage countries like Taiwan, South Korea, Mexico, and Brazil, which have become production havens for goods with high labor content.

Another important manufacturing cost consideration in international competition is the concept of *manufacturing share* as distinct from brand share or market share. For example, although less than 40% of all the video recorders sold in the United States carry a Japanese brand, Japanese companies do 10% of the manufacturing—all sellers source their video recorders from Japanese manufacturers.[19] In microwave ovens, Japanese brands have less than a 50% share of the U.S. market, but the manufacturing share of Japanese companies is over 85%. *Manufacturing share is significant because it is a better indicator than market share of the industry's low-cost producer.* In a globally competitive industry where some competitors are intent on achieving global market dominance, being the worldwide low-cost producer is a powerful competitive advantage. Achieving low-cost producer status often requires a firm to have the largest worldwide manufacturing share, with production centralized in one or a few super-efficient plants. However, important marketing and distribution economies associated with multinational operations can also yield low-cost leadership.

Fluctuating Exchange Rates.   The volatility of exchange rates greatly complicates the issue of locational cost advantages. Exchange rate fluctuations of 20 to 40% annually are not unusual. Changes of this magnitude can totally wipe out a country's low-cost advantage or transform a former high-cost location into a competitive-cost location. A strong U.S. dollar makes it more attractive for U.S. companies to manufacture in foreign countries. Declines in the value of the dollar against foreign currencies can eliminate much of the cost advantage that foreign manufacturers have over U.S. manufacturers and can even prompt foreign firms to establish production plants in the United States.

---

[19] C. K. Prahalad and Yves L. Doz, *The Multinational Mission* (New York: Free Press, 1987), p. 60.

Host Government Trade Policies.   National governments have enacted all kinds of measures affecting international trade and the operation of foreign companies in their markets. Host governments may impose import tariffs and quotas, set local content requirements on goods made inside their borders by foreign-based companies, and regulate the prices of imported goods. In addition, there can be a web of regulations regarding technical standards, product certification, prior approval of capital spending projects, withdrawal of funds from the country, and minority (sometimes majority) ownership by local citizens. Some governments also provide subsidies and low-interest loans to domestic firms to help them compete against foreign-based companies. Other governments, anxious to obtain new plants and jobs, offer foreign firms a helping hand in the form of subsidies, privileged market access, and technical assistance.

MULTICOUNTRY COMPETITION VERSUS GLOBAL COMPETITION

There are important differences in the patterns of international competition from industry to industry.[20] At one extreme, competition can be termed *multicountry* or *multidomestic* because it takes place country-by-country; competition in each national market is essentially independent of competition in other national markets. For example, there is a banking industry in France, one in Brazil, and one in Japan, but competitive conditions in banking differ markedly in all three countries. Moreover, a bank's reputation, customer base, and competitive position in one nation have little or no bearing on its ability to compete successfully in another nation. While a company may compete internationally, the power of its competitive strategy in any one nation and any competitive advantage it yields are largely confined to that nation and do not spill over to other countries where it operates. *With multicountry competition there is no "international market," just a collection of self-contained country markets*. Industries characterized by multicountry competition include many types of food products (coffee, cereals, canned goods, frozen foods), many types of retailing, beer, life insurance, apparel, and metals fabrication.

At the other extreme is *global competition,* where prices and competitive forces across country markets are strongly linked together and the term *international* or *global market* has true meaning. In a globally competitive industry, a firm's competitive position in one country both affects and is affected by its competitive standing in other countries. Rival companies compete against each other in many different countries, but especially so in countries where sales volumes are large and where having a competitive presence is strategically important to building a strong global position in the industry. *In global competition, a firm's overall competitive advantage grows out of its entire worldwide operations; the competitive advantage it has created at its home base is supplemented by advantages growing out of its operations in other countries* (having plants in low-wage countries, a capability to serve customers with multinational operations of their own, and a brand reputation that is transferable from country to country). *A global competitor's market strength is directly proportional to its portfolio of country-based competitive advantages*. Global competition exists in automobiles, television sets, tires, telecommunications equipment, copiers, watches, and commercial aircraft.

BASIC CONCEPT
Multicountry or multidomestic competition exists wherever competition in one national market is independent of competition in another national market.

BASIC CONCEPT
Global competition exists wherever competitive forces across national markets are linked strongly enough to form a true international market and where leading firms compete head-to-head in many different nations.

---

[20] Michael E. Porter, *The Competitive Advantage of Nations* (New York: Free Press, 1990), pp. 53–54.

In multicountry competition, rival firms vie for national market leadership. In globally competitive markets, rival firms vie for worldwide leadership.

An industry can have segments that are globally competitive and segments where competition is country-by-country.[21] In the hotel-motel industry, for example, the low- and medium-priced segments are characterized by multicountry competition because competitors mainly serve travelers within the same country. In the business and luxury segments, however, competition is more globalized; companies like Marriott, Sheraton, and Hilton have hotels at many international locations and use worldwide reservation systems and common quality and service standards to gain marketing advantages in serving businesspeople and travelers who make frequent international trips. In lubricants, the marine engine segment is globally competitive because ships move from port to port and require the same oil everywhere they stop. Brand reputations have a global scope, and successful marine engine lubricant producers (Exxon, British Petroleum, and Shell) operate globally. In automotive motor oil, however, multicountry competition dominates. Countries have different weather conditions and driving patterns; production is subject to limited scale economies and shipping costs are high; and retail distribution channels differ markedly from country to country. Thus domestic firms, like Quaker State and Pennzoil in the United States and Castrol in Great Britain, can be market leaders. The point here is that in industries where multicountry or multidomestic competition prevails, the market leaders are "national champions," whereas in globally competitive industries the market leaders are "world champions."

Types of International Strategies

Firms have six distinct competitive strategy options for participating in international markets:

1. *License foreign firms to use the firm's technology or produce and distribute the firm's products* (in which case the firm's international revenues will equal the royalty income from the licensing agreement).

2. *Maintain a national (one-country) production base and export goods to foreign markets,* utilizing either company-owned or foreign-controlled forward distribution channels.

3. *Employ a multicountry strategy.* Here a firm's international strategy is crafted country by country to be responsive to buyer needs and competitive conditions in each country where it operates. Competitive moves in one country are made independent of actions taken in another country; strategy coordination across countries is considered secondary to matching the firm's strategy to local conditions in each country where the firm competes.

4. *Employ a global low-cost strategy.* This strategy is based on the firm being a low-cost supplier to buyers in most or all strategically important markets of the world; the company's strategic efforts are coordinated worldwide to achieve a low-cost position relative to competitors.

5. *Employ a global differentiation strategy.* With this strategy a firm differentiates its product on the same attributes in all countries to create a consistent image and a consistent competitive theme; the firm's strategic moves are coordinated across countries to enhance success in achieving consistent worldwide differentiation.

[21] Porter, *The Competitive Advantage of Nations,* p. 61.

6. *Employ a global focus strategy.* Here the firm's competitive approach is aimed at serving the same identifiable buyer niche in each of many strategically important country markets; the firm's competitive moves are coordinated globally to ensure a consistent strategy in each national market.

A licensing strategy makes sense when a firm with valuable technical know-how or a unique patented product has neither the internal organizational capability nor the resources to compete in foreign markets. By licensing the technology or the production rights to foreign-based firms, it at least realizes income from royalties.

Using domestic plants as a production base for exporting goods to foreign markets can be an excellent initial strategy for achieving international sales growth. It minimizes both risk and capital requirements, and it is a conservative way to test the international waters. With an export strategy, a manufacturer can limit its involvement in foreign markets by contracting with foreign wholesalers experienced in importing to assume the entire distribution and marketing function in their country or region of the world. Or, if it is more advantageous to maintain control over these functions, a manufacturer can establish its own distribution and sales organizations in some or all of the foreign markets where it competes. Either way, a firm minimizes the direct investments made in foreign countries because of its home-base production and export strategy. Such strategies are commonly favored by Korean and Italian companies—products are designed and manufactured at home and only marketing activities are performed abroad.

> A strategy of concentrating production in a single country and exporting to all other national markets where the firm competes can lead to either competitive advantage or disadvantage.

Whether an export-based strategy can be pursued successfully over the long run hinges on the relative cost competitiveness of a home-country production base. In some industries, firms gain additional scale economies and experience curve benefits from centralizing production in one or several giant-scale plants whose output capability exceeds demand in any one national market; to capture such economies a company must export to markets in other countries. However, an export-only strategy is competitively vulnerable when manufacturing costs in the home country are substantially higher than in other countries where rivals have plants. And it leaves a firm totally exposed to unfavorable exchange rate fluctuations.

The pros and cons of a multicountry competitive approach versus a global approach are a bit more complex.

A MULTICOUNTRY STRATEGY OR A GLOBAL STRATEGY?

The logic and appeal of a multicountry strategy derive from the variability of cultural, economic, political, and competitive conditions in countries across the globe. The more diverse national market conditions are, the stronger the case for a *multicountry strategy* where the company tailors its strategic approach to fit each host country's market situation. In such cases, the company's overall international strategy is a collection of its country strategies.

However, while multicountry strategies are best suited for industries where multicountry competition dominates, global strategies are best suited for industries that are globally competitive. A *global strategy* is one where the company's strategy for competing is mostly the same in all countries—while *minor* country-to-country differences in strategy do exist to accommodate specific competitive conditions in host countries, the fundamental competitive approach (low-cost, differentiation, or focus) remains unaltered worldwide.

> **COMPETITIVE PRINCIPLE**
> A multicountry strategy is appropriate for industries where multicountry competition prevails; a global strategy works best in markets that are globally competitive or beginning to globalize.

Moreover, a global strategy involves (1) integrating and coordinating the company's strategic moves worldwide and (2) selling in many if not all of the nations where there is significant buyer demand. Table 16-2 provides a point-by-point comparison of multicountry versus global strategies. The question of which to pursue is the foremost strategic issue firms face when they compete in international markets.

The strength of a multicountry strategy is that it matches the firm's competitive approach to host-country circumstances. A strategy of national responsiveness is essential when there are significant country-to-country differences in customers' needs and buying habits, when buyers in a country insist on special-order or highly customized products, when buyer demand for the product exists in comparatively few national markets, when host governments

TABLE 16-2   DIFFERENCES BETWEEN MULTICOUNTRY AND GLOBAL STRATEGIES

	Multicountry Strategy	Global Strategy
Strategic arena	Selected target countries and trading areas	Most countries which constitute *critical markets* for the product (at least North America, the European Community, and the Pacific Rim [Australia, Japan, South Korea, and Southeast Asia])
Business strategy	Custom strategies to fit the circumstances of each host country situation; little or no strategy coordination across countries	Same basic strategy worldwide; minor country-by-country variations where essential
Product line strategy	Adapted to local needs	Mostly standardized products sold worldwide
Production strategy	Plants scattered across many host countries	Plants located on the basis of maximum competitive advantage (in low-cost countries, close to major markets, geographically scattered to minimize shipping costs, or use of a few world-scale plants to maximize economies of scale—as most appropriate)
Sources of supply for raw materials and components	Suppliers in host country preferred (local facilities meeting local buyer needs; some local sourcing may be required by host government)	Attractive suppliers from anywhere in the world
Marketing and distribution	Adapted to practices and culture of each host country	Much more worldwide coordination; minor adaptation to host country situations if required
Company organization	Form subsidiary companies to handle operations in each host country; each subsidiary operates more or less autonomously to fit host country conditions	All major strategic decisions are closely coordinated at global headquarters; a global organizational structure is used to unify the operations in each country

enact codes or statutes requiring that a product meet strict manufacturing specifications or performance standards, and when the trade restrictions of host governments are so diverse and complicated as to virtually preclude a uniform, coordinated worldwide market approach. The problem, however, is that a multicountry strategy entails very little strategic coordination across country boundaries nor is it tied tightly to competitive advantage. The primary orientation of a multicountry strategy is responsiveness to local country conditions, not building a multinational-based competitive advantage over other international competitors and the domestic companies of host countries. A global strategy, because it is more uniform from country to country, can concentrate on securing a sustainable competitive advantage over both international and domestic rivals. Whenever country-to-country differences are small enough to be accommodated within the framework of a global strategy, a global strategy is preferable to a multicountry strategy because of its competitive advantage potential.

GLOBAL STRATEGY AND COMPETITIVE ADVANTAGE

There are two ways that a firm can gain competitive advantage (or offset domestic disadvantages) with a global approach to strategy.[22] One involves a global competitor's ability to locate its activities (R & D, parts manufacture, assembly, distribution centers, sales and marketing, customer service centers) among nations in a manner that lowers costs or achieves greater product differentiation; the other concerns a global competitor's ability to coordinate its dispersed activities in ways that a domestic-only competitor cannot.

> With a global strategy a firm can pursue sustainable competitive advantage by locating activities in the most advantageous nations and coordinating its competitive moves worldwide; a domestic-only competitor forfeits such opportunities.

Locating Activities. To use location to build competitive advantage, a global firm must consider two issues: (1) whether to concentrate each activity it performs in one or two countries or disperse performance of the activity to many nations and (2) in which countries to locate particular activities. *Activities tend to be concentrated in one or two locations when there are significant economies of scale in performing an activity, when there are advantages in locating related activities in the same area to achieve better coordination, and when there is a steep learning or experience curve associated with concentrating performance of an activity in a single location.* Thus in some industries scale economies in parts manufacture or assembly are so great that firms establish one large plant from which to serve the world market. Where just-in-time inventory practices yield big cost savings, parts manufacturing plants may be clustered around final assembly plants.

Dispersing activities is more advantageous than concentrating activities in several instances. *Buyer-related activities, such as distribution to dealers, sales and advertising, and after-sale service, usually must take place close to where buyers are located*; this means physically locating the capability to perform such activities in every nation where a global firm has major customers (unless buyers in several adjoining countries can be served quickly from a nearby central location). For example, firms that make mining equipment and oil drilling equipment maintain operations in many international locations to support customers' needs for speedy equipment repair and technical assistance. Large public accounting firms have numerous international offices to service the foreign operations of their multinational corporate clients. *A global*

---

[22] Porter, *The Competitive Advantage of Nations*, p. 54.

A global firm can gain competitive advantage over domestic-only competitors by locating its production, distribution, sales, and service activities in whatever location offers the greatest benefit.

competitor that effectively disperses its buyer-related activities gains a service-based competitive edge in world markets over rivals whose buyer-related activities are more concentrated. Dispersing activities to many locations is also competitively advantageous when high transportation costs, diseconomies of large size, and trade barriers make it too expensive to operate from a central location. In addition, activities are dispersed to hedge against the risks of fluctuating exchange rates, supply interruptions (due to strikes, mechanical failures, and transportation delays), and adverse political developments—such risks are greater when activities are concentrated in a single location.

   The classic reason for locating an activity in a particular country is lower costs.[23] Even though a global firm has strong reason to disperse buyer-related activities to many international locations, such activities as materials procurement, parts manufacture, finished goods assembly, technology research, and new product development can frequently be decoupled from buyer locations and performed wherever advantage lies. Components can be made in Mexico, technology research done in Frankfurt, new products developed and tested in Phoenix, and assembly plants located in Spain, Brazil, Taiwan, and Illinois. Capital can be raised in whatever country it is available on the best terms. Low cost is not the only locational consideration, however. A research unit may be located in a particular nation because of its pool of technically trained personnel. A customer service center or sales office may be located in a particular country to help develop strong relationships with pivotal customers. An assembly plant may be located in a country in return for the host government allowing freer import of components from large-scale, centralized parts plants located elsewhere.

Coordinating Activities and Strategic Moves.

Aligning and coordinating company activities located in different countries can build sustainable competitive advantage in several different ways. If a firm learns how to assemble its product more efficiently at its Brazilian plant, the accumulated knowledge and expertise can be transferred to its assembly plant in Spain. Knowledge gained in marketing a company's product in Great Britain can be used to introduce the product in New Zealand and Australia. A firm can shift production from one country location to another to take advantage of exchange rate fluctuations, to enhance its leverage with host-country governments, and to respond to changing wage rates, energy costs, or trade restrictions. A firm can enhance its brand reputation by consistently positioning its products with the same differentiating attributes on a worldwide basis; thus the reputation for quality that Honda established worldwide first in motorcycles and then in automobiles gave it competitive advantage in positioning Honda lawnmowers at the upper end of the market—the Honda name gave the company instant credibility with buyers for having a quality lawnmower. *A global competitor can choose where and how to challenge rivals.* It may decide to retaliate against aggressive rivals in the country market where the rival has its biggest sales volume or its best profit margins in order to reduce the rival's financial resources for competing in other country markets. It may decide to wage a price-cutting offensive against weak rivals in their home markets, capturing greater market share and subsidizing any short-term losses with profits earned in other country markets.

---

[23] Porter, *The Competitive Advantage of Nations,* p. 57.

A company which competes only in its home country has access to none of the competitive advantage opportunities associated with location or coordination. By shifting from a domestic strategy to a global strategy, a domestic company that finds itself at a competitive disadvantage to global companies can begin to restore its competitiveness.

STRATEGIC ALLIANCES

Strategic alliances are cooperative agreements between firms that go beyond normal company-to-company dealings but that fall short of merger or full partnership.[24] An alliance can concern joint research efforts, technology sharing, joint use of production facilities, marketing one another's products, or joining forces to manufacture components or assemble finished products. Strategic alliances are a means for firms in the same industry that are based in different countries to compete on a more global scale while still preserving their independence. Historically, export-minded firms in industrialized nations sought alliances with firms in less-developed countries to import and market their products locally—such arrangements were often necessary to gain access to the less-developed country's market. More recently, leading companies from different parts of the world have formed strategic alliances to strengthen their mutual ability to serve whole continental areas and move toward more global market participation. Both Japanese and American companies have been active in forming alliances with European companies in preparation for Europe 1992 and the opening up of Eastern European markets.

> **Strategic alliances are a means for companies in globally competitive industries to strengthen their market positions while still preserving their independence.**

Companies enter into alliances for several competitively beneficial reasons.[25] The three most important are to gain economies of scale in production and/or marketing, to fill gaps in their technical and manufacturing expertise, and to acquire market access. By joining forces in producing components, assembling models, and marketing their products, companies can realize cost savings not achievable with their own small volumes. Allies learn much from one another in performing joint research, sharing technological know-how, and studying one another's manufacturing methods. Alliances are often used by outsiders to meet governmental requirements for local ownership, and allies can share distribution facilities and dealer networks, thus mutually strengthening their access to buyers. In addition, alliances affect competition; not only can alliances offset competitive disadvantages but they also can result in the allied companies directing their competitive energies more toward mutual rivals and less toward one another. Many runner-up companies, wanting to preserve their independence, have resorted to alliances rather than merger to try to close the competitive gap on leading companies.

> **COMPETITIVE PRINCIPLE**
> **Strategic alliances are more effective in combating competitive disadvantage than in gaining competitive advantage.**

Alliances have their pitfalls, however. Achieving effective coordination between independent companies, each with different motives and perhaps conflicting objectives, is a challenging task requiring numerous meetings of numerous people over a period of time to iron out what is to be shared, what is to remain proprietary, and how the cooperative arrangements will work. There

---

[24] Porter, *The Competitive Advantage of Nations*, p. 65. See also, Kenichi Ohmae, "The Global Logic of Strategic Alliances," *Harvard Business Review*, Vol. 89, No. 2 (March–April 1989), pp. 143–54.

[25] Porter, *The Competitive Advantage of Nations*, p. 66; see also, Jeremy Main, "Making Global Alliances Work," *Fortune*, December 17, 1990, pp. 121–26.

APPLICATIONS CAPSULE

GLOBAL STRATEGIC ALLIANCES: SUCCESSES AND FAILURES

As the chairman of British Aerospace recently observed, a strategic alliance with a foreign company is "one of the quickest and cheapest ways to develop a global strategy." AT&T has formed joint ventures with many of the world's largest telephone and electronics companies. Boeing, the world's premier manufacturer of commercial aircraft has partnered with Kawasaki, Mitsubishi, and Fuji to produce a long-range, wide-body jet for delivery in 1995. General Electric and Snecma, a French maker of jet engines, have a 50–50 partnership to make jet engines to power aircraft made by Boeing, McDonnell-Douglas, and Airbus Industrie (the leading European maker of commercial aircraft and a company that was formed through an alliance among aerospace from Britain, Spain, Germany, and France); this particular alliance was regarded as a model because not only had it been in existence for 17 years but it had also produced orders for 10,300 engines, totaling $38 billion.

During the past ten years, hundreds of strategic alliances have been formed in the motor vehicle industry as car and truck manufacturers and automotive parts suppliers moved aggressively to get in stronger position to compete globally. Not only have there been alliances between manufacturers strong in one region of the world and manufacturers strong in another region but there have also been strategic alliances between vehicle-makers and key parts suppliers (especially those with high quality parts and strong technological capabilities). General Motors and Toyota in 1984 formed a 50–50 partnership called New United Motor Manufacturing, Inc. (NUMMI) to produce cars for both companies at an old GM plant in Fremont, California. The strategic value of the GM–Toyota alliance was that Toyota would learn how to deal with suppliers and workers in the U.S. (as a prelude to building its own plants in the U.S.) while GM would learn about Toyota's approaches to manufacturing and management. Each company sent managers to the NUMMI plant to work for two to three years to learn and absorb all they could, then transferred their NUMMI "graduates" to jobs where they could be instrumental in helping their company apply what had been learned.

Gary Hamel, a professor at the London Business School, regards strategic alliances as a "race to learn" and gain the benefits of the partner's know-how and competitive capabilities. The partner that learns the fastest gains the most and, later, may turn such learning into a competitive edge. From this perspective, alliances become a new form of competition as well as a vehicle for globalizing company strategy. According to Hamel, Japanese managers and companies excelled at learning from their allies and then exploiting the benefits. Toyota, for example, had moved quickly to capitalize on its experiences at NUMMI; by 1991 Toyota had opened two plants on its own in North America, was constructing a third plant, and was producing about 50 percent of the vehicles it sold in North America in its North American plants. While General Motors had incorporated much of its NUMMI learn-

ing into the management practices and manufacturing methods it was using at its newly-opened Saturn plant in Tennessee, GM had moved more slowly than Toyota. American and European companies were generally regarded as less skilled than the Japanese in transferring the learning from strategic alliances into their own operations.

Consultants and business school professors who had studied company experiences with strategic alliances saw four keys to making a strategic alliance work to good advantage:

- Picking a compatible partner, taking the time to bring strong bridges of communication and trust, and not expecting immediate payoffs.
- Choosing an ally whose products and market strongholds *complemented* rather than competed directly with the company's own products and customer base.
- Learning thoroughly and rapidly about a partner's technology and management.
- Being careful not to divulge competitively sensitive information to a partner.

Many alliances either failed or were terminated when one partner ended up acquiring another. A 1990 survey of 150 companies involved in terminated alliances found that three-fourths of the alliances had been taken over by Japanese partners. A nine-year alliance between Fujitsu and International Computers, Ltd., a British manufacturer, ended when Fujitsu acquired 80 percent of ICL. According to one observer, Fujitsu deliberately maneuvered ICL into a position of having no better choice than to sell out to its partner; Fujitsu began as a supplier of components for ICL's mainframe computers, then expanded its role over the next nine years to the point where it was ICL's only source of new technology. When ICL's parent, a large British electronics firm, saw the mainframe computer business starting to decline and decided to sell, Fujitsu was the only buyer it could find.

There were several reasons why strategic alliances failed. Often, once the bloom was off the initial getting-together period, partners discovered they had deep differences of opinion about how to proceed and conflicting objectives and strategies, such that tensions soon built up and cooperative working relationships never emerged. Another was the difficulty of collaborating effectively in competitively sensitive areas, thus raising questions about mutual trust and forthright exchanges of information and expertise. Perhaps the biggest reason was a clash of egos and company cultures—the key people upon whom success or failure depended turned out to be incompatible and incapable of working closely together on a partnership basis. On occasions, partners became suspicious about each other's motives and sometimes they were unwilling to share control and do things on the basis of consensus.

Source: Jeremy Main, "Making Global Alliances Work," *Fortune,* December 17, 1990, pp. 121–26.

may be language and cultural barriers as well as problems of suspicion and mistrust to overcome. After a promising start, relationships may cool and the hoped-for benefits may never materialize. Most important, through, is the danger of depending on another company for essential expertise and capabilities over the long term. To be a serious market contender, a company must ultimately develop internal capabilities in all areas important to strengthening its competitive position and building a sustainable competitive advantage. Where this is not feasible, merger is a better solution than a strategic alliance. Strategic alliances are best seen as a transitional way to combat competitive disadvantage in international markets; rarely if ever can they be relied upon as a means for creating competitive advantage. For more details on the pros and cons of strategic alliances, see the accompanying Applications Capsule.

STRATEGIC INTENT, PROFIT SANCTUARIES, AND CROSS SUBSIDIZATION

Competitors in international markets can be distinguished not only by their strategies but also by their long-term market objectives or ***strategic intent***. Four types of competitors stand out:[26]

- Firms whose strategic intent is *global dominance* or, at least, high rank among the global market leaders; such firms pursue some form of global strategy.
- Firms whose primary strategic objective is *defending domestic dominance* in their home market, even though they derive some of their sales internationally (usually under 20%) and have operations in several or many foreign markets.
- Firms who aspire to a growing share of worldwide sales and whose primary strategic orientation is *host country responsiveness*—such firms have a multicountry strategy and may already derive a large fraction of their revenues from foreign operations.
- *Domestic-only firms* whose strategic intent does not extend beyond building a strong competitive position in their home country market; such firms base their competitive strategies on domestic market conditions and watch events in the international market for whatever impact they may have on their domestic situations.

Competitors in international markets do not have the same strategic intent or profit objectives.

The four types of firms are *not* equally well-positioned to be successful in markets where they compete head-on. Consider the case of a purely domestic U.S. company in competition with a Japanese company operating in many country markets and aspiring to global dominance. The Japanese company can cut its prices in the U.S. market to gain market share at the expense of the U.S. company, subsidizing any losses with profits earned in its home sanctuary and in other foreign markets. The U.S. company has no effective way to retaliate. It is vulnerable even if it is the dominant domestic company. However, if the U.S. company is a multinational competitor and operates in Japan as well as elsewhere, it can counter Japanese pricing in the United States with retaliatory price cuts in its competitor's main profit sanctuary, Japan, and in other countries where it competes against the same Japanese company.

Profit Sanctuaries and Critical Markets.   ***Profit sanctuaries*** are country markets where a firm has a strong or protected market position and derives substantial profits. Japan, for example, is a profit sanctuary for most

---

[26] Prahalad and Doz, *The Multinational Mission,* p. 52.

BASIC CONCEPT
A nation becomes a firm's profit sanctuary when a company, because of its strong competitive position or protective governmental trade policies, derives a substantial portion of its total profits from sales in that nation.

COMPETITIVE PRINCIPLE
A global competitor with multiple profit sanctuaries can wage and generally win a long-term competitive offensive against a domestic competitor whose only profit sanctuary is its home market.

Japanese companies because trade barriers erected around Japanese industries by the Japanese government effectively block foreign companies from strongly competing for a large share of Japanese sales. Protected from the threat of foreign competition in their home market, Japanese firms can safely charge somewhat higher prices to their Japanese customers and thus earn attractively large profits on sales made in Japan. In most cases, a firm's biggest and most strategically crucial profit sanctuary is its home market, but multinational companies also have profit sanctuaries in those country markets where they have strong competitive positions, big sales volumes, and attractive profit margins.

Profit sanctuaries are valuable competitive assets in global industries. Firms with large, protected profit sanctuaries have competitive advantage over firm's who do not have a dependable sanctuary. Competitors with multiple profit sanctuaries are more favorably positioned than rivals that are dependent on a single sanctuary.

Normally, a global competitor with multiple profit sanctuaries can successfully attack and beat a domestic competitor whose only profit sanctuary is its home market. Building a defense against global competitors does not require competing in all or even most foreign markets, but it does mean competing in all critical markets; *critical markets* are markets in countries

- That are the profit sanctuaries of key competitors.
- That have big sales volumes.
- That contain prestigious customers whose business it is strategically important to have.
- That offer exceptionally good profit margins due to weak competitive pressures.[27]

The more critical markets a company participates in, the greater capability it has to use cross subsidization as a defense against competitors intent on global dominance.

The Competitive Power of Cross Subsidization. *Cross subsidization* is a powerful competitive weapon. It involves using profits earned in one or more country markets to support a competitive offense against key rivals or to gain increased penetration of a critical market. A typical offensive involves matching (or nearly matching) rivals on product quality and service, and then charging a low enough price to draw customers away from rivals; while price cutting may entail lower profits (or, in the extreme, even losses), the challenger can still realize acceptable overall profits when the above-average earnings from its profit sanctuaries are added in.

Cross subsidization is most powerful when a global firm with multiple profit sanctuaries is aggressively intent on achieving global market leadership over the long term. Both a domestic-only competitor and a multicountry competitor with no strategic coordination between its locally responsive country strategies are vulnerable to competition from rivals intent on global dominance. *A global strategy can defeat a domestic-only strategy because a one-country competitor cannot effectively defend its market share over the long term against a global competitor with cross-subsidization capability.* The global company can use lower prices to siphon the domestic company's customers, all the while gaining market share, building market strength, and covering losses with profits earned in its other critical markets. When attacked in this manner,

COMPETITIVE PRINCIPLE
To defend against aggressive international competitors intent on global market leadership, a domestic-only competitor usually has to abandon its domestic focus and compete on a multinational basis.

---

[27] Prahalad and Doz, *The Multinational Mission,* p. 61.

a domestic company's best short-term hope is to seek government protection in the form of tariff barriers, import quotas, and antidumping penalties. In the long term, the domestic company must find ways to compete on a more equal footing—a different task when it must charge a price to cover average costs while the global competitor can charge a price only high enough to cover the incremental costs of selling in the domestic company's profit sanctuary. The best long-term competitive defenses for a domestic company are to enter into strategic alliances with foreign firms and compete on an international scale. *Choosing to compete only domestically is a perilous strategy in an industry populated with global competitors.*

While a multicountry strategist has some cross-subsidy defense against a global strategist, its vulnerability comes from a lack of competitive advantage and a probable cost disadvantage. *A global competitor with a big manufacturing share and state-of-the-art plants is almost certain to be a lower-cost producer than a multicountry competitor with many small plants and short production runs turning out specialized products country-by-country.* Companies pursuing a multicountry strategy thus have to develop focusing and differentiation advantages keyed to local responsiveness to defend against a global competitor. Such a defense is adequate in industries with significant enough national differences to impede use of a global strategy. But if an international rival can accommodate the necessary local responsiveness within a global strategy approach and still retain a cost edge, then a global strategy can defeat a multicountry strategy. To gain more appreciation of the power of a global strategy in today's markets, see the Applications Capsule describing how Nestlé became the world's largest food company.

KEY POINTS

Although each firm's approach to competing is a uniquely constructed game plan reflecting its particular circumstances, it is possible to generalize about the types of competitive approaches. There are three basic approaches to competing: (1) striving to be the low-cost producer and achieving overall cost leadership, (2) pursuit of some sort of product differentiation theme, and (3) specializing or focusing on selected market segments as opposed to an across-the-board approach. There are, however, numerous variations of these three basic approaches and there are a variety of ways to pursue each theme.

The challenge of competitive strategy—whether it be a low-cost, differentiation, or focus strategy—is to create a competitive advantage for the firm. Competitive advantage comes from positioning a firm in the marketplace so that it has an edge in coping with competitive forces and in attracting buyers.

A strategy of trying to be the low-cost producer works well in situations where:

- Demand is price elastic (buyers are very price-sensitive),
- The industry's product is pretty much the same from seller to seller,
- The marketplace is dominated by the force of price competition (buyers are prone to shop around on price),
- There are not many ways to achieve product differentition that have much value to buyers,
- Most buyers use the product in about the same ways and thus have common user requirements, and
- Buyers' costs in switching from one seller or brand to another are low (or even zero).

APPLICATIONS CAPSULE

NESTLÉ'S GLOBAL STRATEGY IN FOODS

Once a stodgy Swiss manufacturer of chocolate, Nestlé became one of the first multinational companies and then embarked on a global strategy during the 1980s. The themes of the Nestlé strategy were: acquire a wider lineup of name brands, achieve the economies of worldwide distribution and marketing, accept short-term losses to build a more profitable market share over the long term, and adapt products to local cultures when needed. In 1989 Nestlé ranked as the world's largest food company with nearly $28 billion in revenues, market penetration on all major continents, and plants in over 60 countries:

characterized by growing numbers of relatively affluent single professionals and two-income couples with more cosmopolitan food tastes and less price-sensitive grocery budgets. Moreover, microwave ovens were fast becoming a standard household item, a development that not only affected weeknight and weekend food preparation methods but also changed the kinds of at-home products people were buying. Products that appealed to this segment had tremendous growth potential. However, bringing such items to market was quickly turned into a high-risk, capital-intensive, R & D-oriented business that required millions of dollars of up-front capital for new

Continent	1988 sales	Major Products
Europe	$10.2 billion	Nescafé instant coffee, Vittle mineral water, Chambourcy yogurt, Findus and Lean Cuisine frozen foods, Herta cold cuts, Sundy cereal bars, chocolate candy, Buitoni pasta
North America	$ 6.7 billion	Nescafé instant coffee, Carnation Coffee-Mate, Friskies pet foods, Stouffer frozen foods, Nestlé Crunch chocolate bars, Hills Bros. coffee
Asia	$ 3.1 billion	Nescafé instant coffee, Nido powdered milk, Maggi chili powder, infant cereals, and formulas
Latin America	$ 2.4 billion	Nescafé instant coffee, Nido powdered milk, infant cereal, Milo malt-flavored beverages
Africa	$ 0.7 billion	Nescafé instant coffee, Maggi bouillon cubes, Nespray powdered milk, Nestlé chocolates, Milo malt-flavored beverages
Oceania (Australia, New Zealand)	$ 0.6 billion	Nescafé instant coffee, Findus frozen foods, Lean Cuisine frozen foods

The Nestlé strategy was a response to two driving forces affecting the food industry in more and more nations around the globe: (1) changing consumer demographics, tastes, and cooking habits and (2) the new cost-volume economics of increasing "high-tech" food products like gourmet dinners, refrigerated foods, packaged mixes, and even coffee. In both industralized and developing nations, the 1980s were

product development and market testing, and millions more for advertising and promotional support to win shelf space in grocery chains. To get maximum mileage out of such investments, make up for the cost of product failures, and keep retail prices affordable began to take a larger and larger volume of sales, often more than could be generated from a single national market.

To achieve a low-cost advantage, a company must become more skilled than rivals in controlling cost drivers and/or it must find innovative, cost-saving ways to revamp the activity-cost chain.

Differentiation strategies can produce a competitive edge based on technical superiority, quality, service, or more value for the money. Differentiation strategies work *best* when

- There are many ways to differentiate the product/service that buyers think have value.
- Buyer needs or uses of the product/service are diverse.
- Not many rivals are following a similar differentiation strategy.

Nestlé management grasped early on that these driving forces would act to globalize the food industry and that companies with worldwide distribution capability, strong brand names, and the flexibility to adapt versions of the basic product to local tastes would gain significant competitive advantages. A series of acquisitions gave Nestlé a strong lineup of brands, some important new food products to push through its distribution channels, and a bigger presence in some key country markets. In 1985 Nestlé bought Carnation (Pet evaporated milk, Friskies pet foods, and Coffee-Mate nondairy creamer) and Hills Bros. coffee (the number three coffee brand in the United States) to strengthen its North American presence. In 1988, Nestlé acquired Rountree, a British chocolate company whose leading candy bar is Kit Kat, and Buitoni, an Italian pastamaker. Shortly after the Rountree acquisition, Nestlé management shifted worldwide responsibility for mapping chocolate strategy and developing new candy products from Nestlé headquarters in Vevey, Switzerland, to Rountree's headquarters in York, England. Nestlé management believed this decentralization put the company's candy business in the hands of people "who think about chocolate 24 hours a day." As of 1989, almost everything Nestlé sold involved food products, and the company was the world's largest producer of coffee, powdered milk, candy, and frozen dinners.

The star performer in Nestlé's lineup was coffee, with 1988 sales of $4.7 billion and operating profits of $600 million. Nestlé's Nescafé brand was the leader in virtually every national market except the United States (Philip Morris's Maxwell House brand was the U.S. leader, but Nescafé was number two and Hill Bros., purchased by Nestlé in 1985, was number three). Nestlé produced 200 types of instant coffee, from lighter blends for the U.S. market to dark expressos for Latin America. Four coffee research labs spent a combined $50 million annually to experiment with new blends in aroma, flavor, and color. Although instant coffee sales were declining worldwide due to the comeback of new-style automatic coffeemakers, they were rising in two tea-drinking countries, Britain and Japan. As the cultural shift from tea to coffee took hold during the 1970s in Britain, Nestlé pushed its Nescafé brand hard, coming out with a market share of about 50%. In Japan, Nescafé was considered a luxury item; the company made it available in fancy containers suitable for gift-giving.

Another star performer has been the company's Lean Cuisine line of low-calorie frozen dinners produced by Stouffer, a company Nestlé acquired in the 1970s. Introduced in 1981 in the United States, the Lean Cuisine line has boosted Stouffer's U.S. market share in frozen dinners to 38%. To follow up on its U.S. success, Nestlé introduced Lean Cuisine into the British market. At the time, Nestlé products in British supermarkets were mostly low-margin items, from fish sticks to frozen hamburger patties. British managers proposed a bold upgrading to a line of more expensive, high-margin items led by Lean Cuisine. Nestlé headquarters endorsed the plan and indicated a willingness to absorb four years of losses to build market share and make Lean Cuisine a transatlantic hit. The Lean Cuisine line was introduced in Britain in 1985. By 1988 the Lean Cuisine line in Britain included 12 entrées tailored to British tastes, from cod with wine sauce to Kashmiri chicken curry. By 1989 Nestlé had a 33% share of the British market for frozen dinners. Sales were expected to top $100 million in 1989, putting the Lean Cuisine brand into the black in Britain for the first time since its introduction to the British market. Lean Cuisine has recently been introduced in France.

Western Europe is Nestlé's top target for the early 1990s. The 1992 shift to free trade among the 12 member countries in the European Community will sweep away trade barriers which, according to a recent study, cost food companies over $1 billion in added distribution and marketing costs. With market unification in the 12-country EC, Nestlé sees major opportunities to gain wider distribution of its products, achieve economies, and exploit its skills in transferring products and marketing methods from one country and culture to another.

Source: The information in this capsule was drawn from Shawn Tully, "Nestlé Shows How to Gobble Markets," *Fortune*, January 16, 1989, pp. 74–78.

Anything a firm can do to create buyer value represents a potential basis for differentiation. Successful differentiation is usually keyed to lowering the buyer's cost of using the item, raising the performance the buyer gets, giving the buyer more value for the money, or boosting a buyer's psychological satisfaction. A best-cost producer strategy works especially well in market situations where product differentiation is the rule and buyers are price-sensitive.

The competitive advantage of focusing is earned either by achieving lower costs in serving the target market niche or by developing an ability to offer niche buyers something different from rival competitors—in other words, it is either *cost-based* or *differentiation-based*. Focusing works best when:

- Buyers' needs or uses for the item are diverse.
- No other rival is attempting to *specialize* in the same target segment.
- A firm lacks the capability to go after a wider part of the total market.
- Buyer segments differ widely in size, growth rate, profitability, and intensity in the five competitive forces, making some segments more attractive than others.

QUESTIONS FOR DISCUSSION

1. Under what kinds of competitive conditions would a firm be attracted to employ a competitive strategy aimed at striving to be the low-cost producer in the industry? What are the strengths of such a competitive strategy? What are the weaknesses of such a strategy?

2. What are the advantages of a differentiation strategy? In what kinds of industry and competitive environments is a differentiation strategy likely to work best?

3. What is a focus strategy? When does use of a focus strategy make sense?

4. Based upon your knowledge about the companies and industry environments in which they compete, indicate which one of the three generic types of competitive strategy best describes the competitive approach employed for the following:
   (a) Seven-Up soft drinks
   (b) Chevrolet Corvette
   (c) Apple Computer
   (d) Liggett & Myers' introduction of generic cigarettes
   (e) Pizza Hut
   (f) Michelob Light
   (g) Homestake Mining (a producer of gold)

5. Are there industries where some rival firms follow a low-cost leadership strategy, others follow a differentiation strategy, and still others are using a focus strategy? What is there about a market that permits all three competitive strategies to coexist?

Chapter 17

How Resource Markets Function

In this chapter we shift attention from product markets to resource markets. The involvement of businesses in the functioning of the markets for resource inputs is evident. Engaging in productive activity of any sort requires an enterprise to purchase resource inputs. Moreover, a change in output dictates a change in resource usage. What firms do in product markets thus quickly reverberates into resource markets, affecting both resource prices and resource use.

The analysis of this chapter is aimed at a firm's input decision, with the specific goal of identifying what determines the amount of resource input a firm is willing to purchase at various input prices. The input decisions of enterprises are then used as the takeoff point for examining the overall market for a resource—the total amount used, the price that will prevail, and the incomes that accrue to resource owners.

To bring out the principles governing the operation of resource markets, it will be necessary to examine resource input decisions in three contexts: (1) when a firm sells its output in a perfectly competitive product market and buys its input in a perfectly competitive resource market, (2) when a firm sells its output in an imperfectly competitive market and buys its input in a perfectly competitive resource market, and (3) when a firm is confronted by imperfectly competitive conditions in both its product and resource markets. These are the three situations most frequently approximated in practice.

SOME PRELIMINARY CONSIDERATIONS

Before digging into the analysis of resource markets, three points warrant mention. First, the concepts and principles concerning demand, supply, revenue, production, and costs presented in earlier chapters have application in how resource markets function. The prices of resource inputs, for example, are in large measure determined by the interaction of demand and supply. However, as regards resource markets, the roles of the firm and the consumer are reversed. Resource inputs are demanded by firms, not consumers, and some important inputs, such as labor and managerial talents, are supplied by people, not firms.

Second, while a firm's inputs may be broadly classified as consisting of land, labor, capital, and managerial ability, the fact remains that each of these classifications contains an enormous variety of particular inputs. The range of labor inputs for a firm extends from the unskilled to the highly skilled; even within the same plant the types of labor services may include such diverse sorts as those provided by an aerospace engineer, a secretary, a machinist, a maintenance worker, a computer programmer, a drill press operator, and a shipping clerk. Since each type of labor service is characterized by its own unique wage rate and demand and supply conditions, it is not really very meaningful to speak of *the* demand for labor or *the* price of labor. The analysis of resource markets will therefore be presented in terms of a "representative" or generic input. Because the principles underlying input decisions are essentially the same from input to input, the models presented will have general applicability to almost every resource market—irrespective of whether the resource input is some type of land, labor, capital, or managerial talent.

Third, although firms may have a variety of goals, the principles of resource pricing and employment are indicated most easily by assuming that the only goal of the firm is to maximize profits. Accordingly, *throughout this chapter, we shall assume a goal of profit maximization*. This assumption in no way disturbs the thrust of the analysis and the resulting conclusions.[1]

RESOURCE PRICING AND EMPLOYMENT: THE CASE OF PERFECTLY COMPETITIVE PRODUCT AND RESOURCE MARKETS

The simplest case of resource pricing and employment arises in an environment where firms sell their products in a perfectly competitive market and buy their inputs under perfectly competitive conditions. For our purposes *the most important aspect of a perfectly competitive **product** market is that the firm can sell additional units of output at the going price*; consequently, the firm's demand-AR curve is horizontal, and product price equals marginal revenue. *In perfectly competitive **resource** markets the essential feature is that the firm can purchase as many units of an input as it may wish without affecting its price*. In other words, the supply curve for an input which confronts the firm is horizontal at the prevailing input supply price.

A PERFECTLY COMPETITIVE FIRM'S INPUT DECISION: THE ONE-VARIABLE INPUT CASE

To identify the key factors underlying a perfectly competitive firm's input decision, suppose we consider first the situation where it has only one variable input, all the other resource inputs being fixed. The profit-conscious firm in a perfectly competitive environment will evaluate the outcomes of employing different quantities of its single variable resource—suppose we call it resource X—by their comparative effect upon total revenue and total cost. *If using more units of resource X per period of time will add more to the firm's revenues than to its costs, then the extra input unit will increase the firm's total profits* (or decrease its losses). On the other hand, if employing more units of resource X per period of time causes costs to rise by more than revenues, then

PRINCIPLE
A profit-maximizing firm should use more of a resource input until the added costs of employing one more unit equal the added revenues it contributes.

---

[1] For an illustration of the effect which a goal of sales revenue maximization has upon the firm's input decision, see William J. Baumol, *Economic Theory and Operations Analysis,* 3rd ed. (Englewood Cliffs, N.J.: Prentice Hall, 1972), pp. 328–30. Baumol demonstrates that a minor adjustment in the profit-maximizing input rules will give the revenue-maximizing input conditions.

using these input units will result in lower total profits (or larger losses). Hence, *to maximize profits a firm should purchase additional units of a resource input until the added costs associated with employing one more unit are equal to the added revenues it contributes.* This is the basic principle underlying the optimum input decision of a profit-maximizing firm; in fact, it is the *MC = MR* rule applied to the firm's decision about how much of a resource to employ, depending on what the price it must pay happens to be.

The Revenue Gain from a Unit of Variable Input.

When a firm employs another unit of variable input per period of time, its output rate rises by an amount equal to the marginal product of the variable input (MP_X). But the prime motivation of the firm for employing more of an input is not the output gain so much as the subsequent revenue gain. If the firm sells under conditions of a horizontal demand-*AR* curve, then each additional unit of output—suppose we call it product A—can be sold at the prevailing market price (P_A), which in turn equals marginal revenue (MR_A). The perfectly competitive firm's revenue gain from using one more unit of variable input may thus be calculated by multiplying the marginal product of the additional unit of input (MP_X) by the amount of revenue which the firm receives from selling another unit of the product (MR_A). For instance, if adding one more machine operator to the firm's production line causes the output rate to increase by 10 units per day and if each of these units can be sold for $5 each, then the firm's revenue gain is $50.

The change in total revenue associated with using one more unit of variable input (X) is called the ***marginal revenue product*** of the input (MRP_X). Mathematically, MRP_X equals the amount of extra output produced by using another unit of input X (MP_X) multiplied by the average marginal revenue at which each unit of extra output of product A can be sold (MR_A), or

$$MRP_X = MP_X \cdot MR_A.$$

Alternatively, marginal revenue product may be conceived as the change in total revenue resulting from a change in the use of variable input X, which in discrete mathematical terms is equivalent to the expression

$$MRP_X = \frac{\Delta TR}{\Delta X}.$$

As usual, MRP_X may be more rigorously defined as the rate of change in total revenue as the rate of usage of variable input X changes, or

$$MRP_X = \frac{dTR}{dX}.$$

Note carefully that the concept of *MRP* differs from that of *MR*. Whereas *MRP* refers to revenue changes which result from changes in the usage of *variable input*, *MR* refers to revenue changes associated with changes in the rate of *output*.

A second and more restricted concept of the revenue change from using more or less of variable input X may be referred to as the ***sales value of the marginal product*** of the input ($SVMP_X$). *SVMP* is just what its name implies—the dollar value of the increased output associated with using another unit of variable input. Put another way, $SVMP_X$ is the amount of extra output (MP_X) multiplied by the average price per unit at which product A can be sold (P_A), or

$$SVMP_X = MP_X \cdot P_A.$$

BASIC CONCEPT
Marginal revenue product (***MRP***) represents the revenue gain or loss associated with employing an additional unit of variable input.

Whereas ***MR*** is the revenue change associated with a 1-unit change in output, ***MRP*** is the revenue change associated with a 1-unit change in variable input use.

BASIC CONCEPT
The dollar value of the increased output associated with using an additional unit of variable input is called the sales value of the marginal product (SVMP).

Inasmuch as the perfectly competitive firm's selling price equals its marginal revenue ($P_A = MR_A$), it follows that $SVMP_X = MRP_X$. However, the equality between $SVMP$ and MRP holds true only for a perfectly competitive firm. If the firm must reduce product price to sell the extra output (as is the case in all market situations other than perfect competition where firms face downsloping demand-AR curves), then product price is always greater than marginal revenue, and the value of $SVMP_X$ will exceed the values for MRP_X at a given input rate. Thus, in reality, the concept of $SVMP$ is only a special case of MRP: the case where price equals MR—a situation unique to a perfectly competitive product market.

Although in a perfectly competitive market structure $SVMP$ equals MRP, we shall nevertheless use the concept of MRP to refer to the change in total revenue resulting from a change in input usage. The concept of $SVMP$ will be reserved to apply only to the gross market value (in dollars) of the marginal product of a unit of input.

The Profit-Maximizing Rate of Input Usage.   To illustrate how a firm can ascertain the profit-maximizing rate of usage of variable input X, consider the hypothetical production, cost, and revenue data in Table 17-1. The first three columns of the table show how the output of product A (Q_A) and the marginal product of variable input X (MP_X) change as successively larger doses of variable input X are combined with the available fixed inputs.[2] The price of product A (P_A) is constant at $20 [column (4)] because of the perfectly competitive product market, and the corresponding total revenue from the sale of product A (TR_A) is shown in column (5). The values for marginal revenue product (MRP_X) are shown in column (6) and are found by either (1) multiplying the gain in output from using another unit of X (MP_X) by the extra revenue the firm receives from the sale of a unit of output (MR_A) or (2) subtracting the successive values of TR_A in column (5) to find the change in total revenue per unit change in variable input. Column (7) indicates the price at which units of variable input can be purchased; the constant price of $180 correctly implies that the firm can buy as many units of variable input as it wants at the given price without inducing a change in the input price. Hence, the marginal cost of an additional unit of variable input is the same as its price. We shall find it convenient to refer to the amount which each additional unit of variable input adds to the firm's costs as the ***marginal resource cost*** (MRC).[3] Since the supply price of X is fixed, $P_X = MRC_X$, and the supply function for X coincides precisely with the MRC function for X. Column (8) lists total variable costs (units of variable input X multiplied by its price per unit). The last column in the table shows the amounts of total contribution profit ($TR - TVC$) at each input rate; the value where total contribution profit is maximum also identifies where

BASIC CONCEPT
Marginal resource cost (*MRC*) represents the cost change associated with employing an additional unit of variable input.

---

[2] Hypothetical amounts of fixed inputs, the prices of the fixed inputs, and the resulting amount of total fixed costs are not included in the table, since they do not really enter into the determination of the profit-maximizing rate of variable input.

[3] As with all other marginal concepts, marginal resource cost may be defined mathematically as the rate of change in the firm's costs as the rate of usage of variable input changes; in symbols this becomes

$$MRC_X = \frac{dTC}{dX} = \frac{dTVC}{dX},$$

where X refers to the units of variable input. Marginal resource cost differs from marginal cost in that the former refers to the changes in costs associated with a change in *input*, whereas the latter refers to a change in costs stemming from a change in *output*.

TABLE 17-1   PROFIT-MAXIMIZING RATE OF RESOURCE INPUT USAGE FOR A FIRM OPERATING IN PERFECTLY COMPETITIVE PRODUCT AND RESOURCE MARKETS[a]

(1) Units of Variable Input (X)	(2) Units of Output (Q_A)	(3) Marginal Product (MP_X)	(4) Price of Product A ($P_A = MR_A$)	(5) Total Revenue from the Sales of Product A ($TR_A = P_A \cdot Q_A$)	(6) Marginal Revenue Product ($MRP_X = MP_X \cdot MR_A = \Delta TR_A / \Delta X$)	(7) Supply Price of the Variable Input ($P_X = ARC_X = MRC_X$)	(8) Total Variable Cost ($TVC = P_X \cdot X$)	(9) Total Contribution Profit ($TCP = TR - TVC$)
0	0		$20	$ 0		$180	$ 0	$ 0
		14			$280			
1	14		20	280		180	180	100
		26			520			
2	40		20	800		180	360	440
		20			400			
3	60		20	1200		180	540	660
		18			360			
4	78		20	1560		180	720	840
		16			320			
5	94		20	1880		180	900	980
		14			280			
6	108		20	2160		180	1080	1080
		12			240			
7	120		20	2400		180	1260	1140
		10			200			
8	130		20	2600		180	1440	1160
		8			160			
9	138		20	2760		180	1620	1140
		6			120			
10	144		20	2880		180	1800	1080

[a] Observe that total contribution profit is maximized at an input of 8 units of resource X, which means that total profit is maximum (or losses minimum, depending on the amount of total fixed costs) at this input rate. By interpolation, it is seen that $MRP_X = MRC_X$ at 8 units of variable input.

total profit is maximum inasmuch as the former differs from the latter only by the amount of total fixed costs.

As previously stated, profit maximization requires that a firm purchase additional units of input until the added cost of one more unit just equals the added revenue it contributes. Given that the price of variable input remains unchanged irrespective of how many units the firm purchases, the cost of an additional unit of variable input is a constant equal to $180 [column (7)]. The revenue contribution of a unit of variable input is given by the *MRP* figures [column (6)]. A comparison of columns (6) and (7) in Table 17-1 indicates that it will pay the firm to employ 8 units of variable input. Increasing the usage of variable input from 7 to 8 units adds $200 to the firm's revenues but only $180 to costs. Should the firm employ the ninth unit of variable input, revenues will rise by $160 but costs will rise by $180; thus, the employment of 9 units of variable input is clearly a less profitable act. By interpolation, it is evident that at 8 units $MRP_X = MRC_X$, which satisfies the profit-maximizing condition and, in fact, is the rule by which the firm identifies its profit-maximizing rate of input usage. Inspection of the total contribution profit figures in column (9) confirms that 8 units is the optimum amount of variable input. Total contribution profit is greatest when 8 units of variable input are used. Since total profit is maximum where total contribution profit is maximum, the profit-maximizing rate of variable input usage is 8 units per period of time.

The determination of the profit-maximizing rate of variable input can be illustrated graphically. We have just seen that a firm's input decision is based upon a comparison of how much an input is worth relative to what it costs. How much an input is worth in essence determines the firm's demand for the input, whereas what an input costs is a function of the available supplies of the

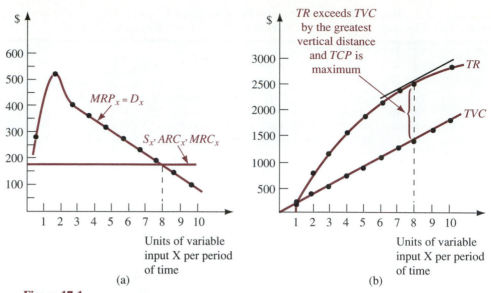

Figure 17-1

The profit-maximizing rate of input usage for a firm operating in perfectly competitive product and resource markets

input and the demand for it in the total market. A firm's profit-maximizing rate of input usage can therefore be approached by an analysis of the firm's demand and supply curves for the input.

Demand-supply conditions for a firm's use of input X are shown in Figure 17-1(a), using the same data as in Table 17-1. The firm's demand curve for input X is obtained by plotting the *MRP* figures in column (6) of the table. The *MRP* curve is the demand curve for X when X is the only variable resource employed. The reason? A firm's demand for a resource input is predicated on what the resource is worth to the firm in terms of the revenue contribution it can make; this is precisely what is meant by *MRP*. The *MRP* curve rises briefly and then falls because the marginal product of the variable input first increases (due to increasing returns to variable input) and then decreases (due to the inevitable occurrence of diminishing marginal returns to variable input). The relevant portion of the *MRP* curve is the downsloping segment where MP_X is declining but positive.[4]

The firm's supply curve for the input is determined by the entries in column (7) of Table 17-1. It is a horizontal line at the level of $180—the prevailing market price of the input. since the input supply price is a constant, the input's price is exactly equal to both the ***average resource cost*** (*ARC*) and the marginal resource cost (*MRC*) of adding more variable input. Or, to put it another way, when perfectly competitive conditions prevail for input X, it follows that $P_X = ARC_X = MRC_X$ and that the supply curve for X coincides with the *ARC* curve for X and the *MRC* curve for X. These relationships are so indicated in Figure 17-1(a).

The firm's resource demand and resource supply curves [Figure 17-1(a)] intersect at a point corresponding to 8 units of variable input. This

BASIC CONCEPT
A firm's demand for a resource input is directly related to what the resource is worth to the firm in terms of the revenue contribution it can make—as reflected by *MRP*; the *MRP* curve for resource X is thus the demand curve for resource X.

BASIC CONCEPT
A firm's supply curve for a resource input is directly related to what it costs the firm to obtain the input—as reflected by the input's average resource cost (*ARC*); the *ARC* curve for resource X is thus the supply curve for resource X.

---

[4] For reasons explored in Chapter 7, a firm will find it profitable to use enough variable input to get beyond the point of diminishing marginal returns unless product demand is very weak or the cost of variable input so high as to make production unprofitable. Hence, the truly relevant portion of the *MRP* curve is the downsloping segment.

intersection identifies the profit-maximizing amount of variable input. At inputs of fewer than 8 units per period of time an additional unit of variable input adds more to total revenue than it adds to total cost, thereby giving the firm a clear incentive to increase its variable input usage. This is the same as saying *MRP* exceeds *MRC* at inputs below 8 units. However, to go beyond 8 units per period of time will result in total costs rising faster than total revenues, and the additional variable input will fail to "pay its own way." Hence, the firm will reduce its total profits (or increase losses) by purchasing more than 8 units of variable input. Therefore, it can be concluded from the demand and supply analysis that *a perfectly competitive firm will maximize profits by employing additional units of variable input until the point is reached where the input's marginal revenue product equals its marginal resource cost*. The rationale underlying the *MRP = MRC* rule is analogous to the *MR = MC* rule. The only real difference is that the former refers to the profit-maximizing rate of input usage and the latter to the profit-maximizing rate of output. The two rules give the same operating results in terms of price, output, and profit, but they ap-

Demand-supply analysis confirms that the profit-maximizing rate of input usage occurs where *MRP = MRC*.

MATHEMATICAL CAPSULE 14

DETERMINING A FIRM'S PROFIT-MAXIMIZING INPUT USAGE UNDER CONDITIONS OF PERFECTLY COMPETITIVE PRODUCT AND RESOURCE MARKETS

The proposition that a firm confronted with perfectly competitive product and resource markets will maximize profits by purchasing units of a variable input until the point is reached where *MRP* equals *MRC* is easily demonstrated in mathematical terms.

Let the firm's production function for producing product A be

$$Q_A = f(X),$$

where Q_A = units of output of product A and X = units of any variable resource input. Then the marginal product function for input X may be written as

$$MP_X = \frac{dQ_A}{dX} = f'(X).$$

The firm's profit function may be expressed as

$$\pi = TR - TC.$$

But by definition

$$TR = P_A Q_A$$

and

$$TC = TFC + TVC.$$

Since $TVC = P_X X$, we can rewrite the expression for TC as

$$TC = TFC + P_X X.$$

Substituting into the profit function gives

$$\pi = P_A Q_A - (TFC + P_X X).$$

However, since $Q_A = f(X)$, the expression for TR_A becomes $P_A \cdot f(X)$, which when substituted into the profit function gives

$$\pi = P_A \cdot f(X) - TFC - P_X X.$$

In mathematical terms, profit maximization requires that

$$\frac{d\pi}{dX} = 0,$$

which, translated into words, means variable input must be added to the point where profits cease to increase.

Taking the derivative of the profit function with respect to X gives

$$\frac{d\pi}{dX} = P_A \cdot f'(X) - P_X.$$

Setting this expression equal to zero to satisfy the profit-maximizing condition gives

$$P_A \cdot f'(X) - P_X = 0.$$

For this condition to be met, it is apparent that the first term of the preceding expression must equal the second term or that

$$P_A \cdot f'(X) = P_X.$$

But $f'(X)$ is, by definition, the same as MP_X, which gives

$$P_A \cdot MP_X = P_X.$$

The term $P_A \cdot MP_X$ is precisely equal to MRP_X, because in perfect competition $P_A = MR_A$; and $P_X = MRC_X$, because the input supply price in a perfectly competitive resource market is a constant value. So the condition for obtaining the profit-maximizing input rate becomes

$$MRP_X = MRC_X,$$

which is what we set out to establish.

proach the determination of the profit-maximizing conditions via a different route.

Plotting the total revenue and total variable cost data in columns (8) and (9) of the table verifies the $MRP = MRC$ rule from another vantage point [see Figure 17-1(b)]. Note that in Figure 17-1(b) the horizontal axis has been drawn to represent units of variable input rather than units of output, thereby relating TR and TVC to the usage of variable input rather than to output. The maximum vertical distance between TR and TVC occurs when their slopes are equal. The slope of the TR curve when variable input (X) is plotted on the horizontal axis is dTR/dX, which, by definition, is MRP_X. Similarly, the slope of the TVC curve in these circumstances is $dTVC/dX$, which corresponds precisely to the meaning of MRC_X. Hence, the profit-maximizing rate of variable input usage is reached when the revenue gain from using more variable input (MRP_X) equals the added cost of purchasing the variable input (MRC_X). Can you explain the economics of the shapes of the TR and TVC curves in Figure 17-1(b)? Why is the TVC curve linear?

Why does TR increase at a decreasing rate? (*Hint:* Your answers should concern the fact that the graph shows TR and TVC to be a function of the usage of variable input rather than the quantity of output.)

A PERFECTLY COMPETITIVE FIRM'S INPUT DECISION: THE TWO-VARIABLE INPUT CASE

When a firm's production process utilizes two or more variable inputs, its input decisions become considerably more complex. The reason rests with the interdependence which exists among the variable inputs. A change in the price of one variable input not only affects the amount it will pay the firm to use of that input but it also alters the optimum amounts of the other variable inputs. Moreover, these alterations in the usage of the other variable inputs will trigger changes in the marginal product of the variable input whose price changed, thereby resulting in still further input adjustments.

To illustrate the nature of the firm's input decision when several resource inputs can be varied, consider the simplest case where the firm has only two variable inputs—X and Y. To keep things manageable, we shall restrict discussion to determining just the firm's optimum input rate for X. Suppose the price of input X is initially fixed at P_{X_1} and the amount of input X which will maximize the firm's profits is X_1, as shown in Figure 17-2. When the amount of resource Y is held constant, the marginal revenue product curve for X is MRP_1. Now suppose a shift in the supply conditions for input X causes the price of X to fall from P_{X_1} to P_{X_2}. The change in the supply price of X has three effects which are pertinent to determining the new profit-maximizing input rate of X: the **substitution effect**, the **output effect**, and the **marginal cost effect**.

As explained in Chapter 7, when the price of one input falls, the firm will be induced to use more of it and less of other variable inputs.[5] Let the initial prices of inputs X and Y be P_{X_1} and P_{Y_1}, the initial output be on isoquant Q_1, and the equilibrium input rates be X_1 and Y_1 at point A, as shown in Figure 17-3. If the price of X falls from P_{X_1} to P_{X_2}, the isocost line rotates to the right, allowing the firm to produce Q_2 units of output with the same total cost outlay, using X_2 units of variable input X and Y_2 units of variable input Y (point *B*).

---

[5] For a review of the pertinent material, see the section in Chapter 7 on "The Impact of Changes in Resource Prices."

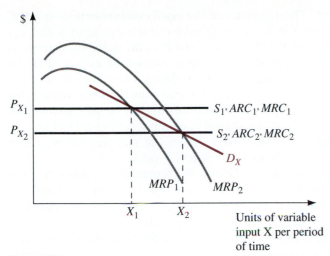

Figure 17-2
A perfectly competitive firm's input decision for two or more variable inputs

The movement from *A* to *B* can be broken down into the substitution effect and the output effect. *The substitution effect shows the change in the optimum input combination that would result if the firm decided to continue to produce Q_1 units of output*; it is indicated graphically by the movement from point *A* to point *C* on isoquant Q_1 in Figure 17-3. Point *C* is found by drawing a third isocost line tangent to isoquant Q_1 but parallel to the isocost line with extreme points TC_1/P_{Y_1} and TC_1/P_{X_2}. The isocost line tangent to Q_1 at point *C* has a slope equal to the new price ratio of inputs *X* and *Y* (P_{X_2}/P_{Y_1}) and serves to identify the optimum input combination for producing Q_1 units of output, given

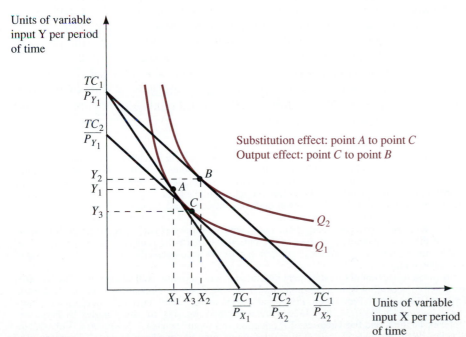

Figure 17-3
Substitution and output effects resulting from a change in an input's supply price

input prices of P_{X_2} and P_{Y_1}. The difference in the input combinations at A and C indicates the extent to which the firm is induced to use *more* of input X and *less* of input Y when the price of X falls from P_{X_1} to P_{X_2}, the price of Y remains fixed, and the firm decides to produce the *same* amount of output after the reduction in the price of X as before the price change. The relevance of the substitution effect to the firm's input decision is that substitution of input X for input Y will cause the marginal product curve for input X to shift downward, thereby making the values of MP_X smaller at each input rate of X than before. The lower marginal productivity of X arises from the fact that having fewer units of input Y to work with makes input X less productive.[6]

The output effect is represented by the movement from point C to point B in Figure 17-3. It reflects the change in optimum input combination, which is associated solely with a change in the firm's output rate, the ratio of input price being held constant. The output effect can be counted upon to result in an increase in the usage of both inputs X and Y.[7] Taken by itself, the output effect will shift the marginal product curve for input X upward because the presence of more of input Y will make X more productive. In other words, having more of input Y to work with will cause the values of MP_X to be higher at each input of X than they otherwise would be. (Note that the impact of the output effect upon MP_X is in the opposite direction as the impact of the substitution effect.)

The marginal cost effect stems from the lower price of input X. When the supply price of resource X falls from P_{X_1} to P_{X_2}, the marginal cost of producing each unit of output is reduced, because it costs less than before to obtain the variable input needed to produce more output. Thus, the marginal cost curve shifts downward, with the result that a firm's marginal cost curve will intersect its marginal revenue curve at a *larger* output than before (the reader should verify this statement by drawing a graph). Accordingly, the profit-maximizing rate of input is increased. The marginal cost effect thus leads to an expansion of output; in turn, more of both inputs X and Y will be required, and the marginal product curve for input X will shift upward.

To recapitulate, when the price of variable input X falls (the prices of all other variable inputs remaining constant), the substitution effect (by itself) tends to shift the marginal product curve for input X *downward*. In contrast, the output and marginal cost effects precipitate an *upward* shift of the MP_X curve. The net result will be a shift of MP_X upward (and quite possibly a change in its slope at each point as well).[8]

---

[6] The logical basis for this statement may be more apparent if one recalls that in situations where one input is variable and the remaining inputs are fixed, a reduction in the amount of fixed inputs causes the production function to shift downward, reflecting lower marginal productivity for the variable input. Consequently, it follows that reductions in the use of input Y will make input X less efficient because the units of X have fewer units of complementary input with which to produce the product.

[7] Only in rare and relatively unimportant cases will the output effect fail to affect both variable inputs in the same manner. Increases in the output rate normally require increased usage of all variable inputs. Similarly, decreases in output usually are accompanied by reductions in the use of each variable input.

[8] Unfortunately, a proof of this statement involves an onerous mathematical exercise. The reader is thus asked to accept the statement on faith. Those who desire to pursue the point should consult Charles E. Ferguson, "Production, Price, and the Theory of Jointly Derived Input Demand Functions," *Economica*, Vol. 33, No. 132 (November 1966), pp. 454–61, and Charles E. Ferguson, "'Inferior Factors' and the Theories of Production and Input Demand," *Economica*, Vol. 35, No. 138 (May 1968), pp. 140–50. An additional treatment may be found in Charles E. Ferguson, *The Neoclassical Theory of Production and Distribution* (New York: Cambridge University Press, 1969), Chapters 6 and 9.

The consequently larger values of MP_X at each level of input, when multiplied by the firm's marginal revenue from additional sales, will cause the firm's MRP curve for input X to shift upward and to the right. Now, turning back to Figure 17-2, suppose that the input adjustment and the subsequent changes in MP_X combine to shift the firm's marginal revenue product curve from MRP_1 to MRP_2. The new MRP curve, coupled with the new supply price of P_{X_2}, will generate a new profit-maximizing equilibrium input rate at X_2 units. By changing the price of X again, tracing through the substitution, output, and marginal cost effects upon MP_X, and then finding the new MRP curve for input X, other profit-maximizing input rates for X can be generated. The resulting equilibrium supply prices and input rates, when connected, form the firm's input demand curve for X, shown as line D_X in Figure 17-2. The points along D_X show the quantities of input X which will maximize the firms profits when the prices of other variable inputs are held constant and the usages of all other variable inputs are appropriately adjusted for changes in the supply price of X.

THE FACTORS INFLUENCING A FIRM'S INPUT DEMAND

We are now in a position to indicate explicitly the factors which ultimately determine a firm's demand for a resource input.[9] These factors may be grouped into two classes: (1) those which influence the *location* of the firm's input demand curve and which cause it to *shift* and (2) those which determine the sensitivity or elasticity of the firm's input demand to input price changes.

Changes in the Firm's Input Demand. As the previous discussion suggests, the determinants of a firm's input demand relate to the input's productivity and to the revenue contribution it makes to the firm's activities. However, we can be much more specific than this.

First, *a firm's demand for inputs is derived from buyer demand for the firm's products*. The more intense is consumer demand for its products, the greater will be the firm's need for resource inputs to produce them. If improvements in a product or reductions in its price stimulate consumer demand, then the firm's input demand will also increase. A resource input that is very proficient in helping to produce a product in strong demand by consumers will itself have a strong demand. On the other hand, a firm's demand for an input will be slight if product demand is small, irrespective of the input's own productivity. There will be no demand for an input which is extraordinarily efficient at producing something no one wants to buy; thus high efficiency of an input, by itself, is insufficient to create a demand for that input.

Second, *a firm's input demand for particular inputs depends on known technology and the directions of technological change*. The technological character of the firm's production process is a fundamental factor in determining the marginal product function for each and every input. And, clearly enough, technological change alters the marginal productivity of a firm's resource inputs. Thus, technological progress that makes an input more productive also increases the demand for that input. Technological progress which makes an input less productive relative to other inputs ultimately reduces the demand for the input and may even eliminate demand for it entirely.

Third, *the price of an input relative to other inputs influences input demand*. As isoquant-isocost analysis demonstrates, the relative prices among

There are five main factors that determine how strong a firm's demand for an input will be.

---

[9] This discussion is equally applicable to firms operating in either perfectly or imperfectly competitive product markets.

substitutable inputs determine a firm's choice of production technologies from the array of known production recipes. If an input becomes cheaper relative to other inputs, the demand for it will gradually increase as producers alter their production techniques so as to substitute the lower-priced resource inputs for the relatively higher-priced ones.

Fourth, *the demand for an input will be greater the higher is the marginal revenue which the firm receives from additional sales of output*. Whatever the marginal product of an input is, the higher the value of *MR*, the larger will be the input's marginal revenue product. Since an input's *MR* values are of paramount importance in determining the profit-maximizing input rate, it necessarily must be true that anything which increases *MRP* will also increase the firm's input demand—other things being equal.

And last, *the greater the quantity of cooperating inputs employed, the greater the demand for a given input*. This proposition follows from the fact that giving an input more of other inputs with which to work and produce allows the input in question to be more productive and thereby have a higher marginal product at each input rate than otherwise. For example, providing automobile workers with more high-speed metal-stamping machines and robotic equipment will result in their being capable of achieving a greater output per labor-hour worked—which clearly means a higher marginal product of labor and, in turn, a higher marginal revenue product for labor.

BASIC CONCEPT
The elasticity of demand for a resource input concerns the responsiveness of the input quantity demanded to a change in the input's price.

The Firm's Elasticity of Demand for a Resource Input.   Four important factors influence the degree to which a firm's input demand will respond to changes in the price of an input. As is customary in economics, we shall refer to this responsiveness or sensitivity as a firm's *elasticity of demand for a resource input*.[10]

First, *the rate at which the marginal product of an input changes as the firm increases or decreases its usage affects the degree to which a firm will alter its input rate as a consequence of a change in the input's supply price*. This follows from the fact that the marginal revenue product of an input is equal to *MP · MR*. Whatever the value of *MR*, *the slower the value of MP declines, the less rapid will be the decline in MRP and the more elastic will be the firm's demand for the input*. If, for example, the technological character of a firm's production function is such that the marginal product of variable input X declines slowly as larger doses of X are combined with the fixed inputs, then the effect will be to cause the *MRP* values for X to decline more slowly than otherwise. This will enhance the elasticity of the firm's demand for the input. On the other hand, if the marginal product of X falls off sharply as more of X is used, then the effect is to cause the *MRP* curve for X to decline more swiftly, thereby reducing the elasticity of the firm's input demand.

Second, *the derived nature of resource demand necessarily makes the elasticity of a firm's input demand dependent on the elasticity of demand for the firm's product*. A decline in the price of a product having an elastic demand will give rise to a sharper increase in output and therefore a stronger increase in the amounts of the variable inputs used to produce it than will a comparable decline in the price of a product having an inelastic demand.

---

[10] It will be recalled from Chapter 5 that the concept of elasticity is nothing more than a ratio of percentage changes. The elasticity of demand for a resource input X (ϵ_x) may be thought of as

$$\epsilon_x = \frac{\%\ \text{change in the input rate of X}}{\%\ \text{change in the supply price of input X}}.$$

Third, *the degree to which resources can be substituted for one another determines an input's demand elasticity*. The larger the number of substitutes for an input and the greater the ease with which substitution can be initiated and accomplished, the greater will be the elasticity of demand for that input. If a book publisher finds that some six or seven grades of paper are equally satisfactory in manufacturing college textbooks, then a rise in the price of any one grade of paper can be counted upon to cause a very sharp drop in its demand as other grades of paper are readily substituted. At the other extreme, where an input has few if any good substitutes, the demand for it tends to be highly inelastic. For instance, the lack of good substitutes for ink in printing books and magazines, for electricians in performing electric wiring functions for new construction projects, or for crude oil in the refining of motor fuels explains why their demands are relatively unresponsive in the short run to increases in their supply prices.

Finally, *the elasticity of demand for a resource input is determined in part by the fraction of total production costs accounted for by the input*. The construction industry offers a good illustration of this proposition. In construction, labor costs are approximately 50% of total costs. If the wage rates of all the many types of construction labor rise by 10%, then total construction costs will rise by 5%. Rising construction costs will push the prices of new construction upward and reduce new construction activity. In turn, the demand of construction firms for construction labor will be weakened. However, suppose only the wage rates of bricklayers rise by 10%, the wage rates of other types of construction labor remaining fixed. Further suppose that the total wages paid to bricklayers amount to only 2% of total costs. Then a 10% rise in bricklayers' wages will cause total costs to rise by only 0.2%—an amount not likely to affect the demand for new construction to any important degree nor therefore the demand for bricklayers and other construction labor. Hence, as a general rule, the smaller the fraction of total costs accounted for by an input, the more inelastic will be a firm's demand for the input.[11]

INDUSTRY DEMAND FOR A RESOURCE INPUT

The total industry demand for a resource input is found by combining the amounts of input that all firms in the industry will employ at a given price. This is slightly different from horizontally summing the individual firm demand curves for the input, because in perfect competition, when all firms change their output rates simultaneously, the market price of the product will also change. The resulting change in marginal revenue will trigger a shift in each firm's *MRP* curve for the input. Despite these complexities the industry demand curve for the input can be determined; the procedure is illustrated in Figure 17-4.

The profit-maximizing input rates for a representative firm in a perfectly competitive industry are shown in panel (a). Given some market price for the firm's product, the firm's demand for input X is represented by the curve labeled D_1, derived according to the method described in Figure 17-2. If the supply price of the input is P_1 dollars, the firm's equilibrium input is X_1 units.

---

[11] It is, incidentally, the small portion of total costs coupled with a lack of good substitutes which explains why craft unions having more or less monopoly control over the supply of a specific type of labor have historically been able to negotiate attractive wage and fringe benefit packages for their members.

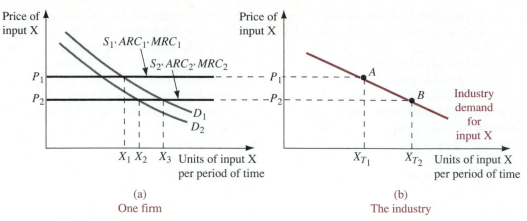

Figure 17-4

Deriving the industry demand for a resource input in a perfectly competitive situation

Adding together the optimum input usages of all the firms in the industry gives a total demand of X_{T_1} units at input price P_1, shown as point A in Figure 17-4(b).

Now suppose the price of input X falls to P_2, perhaps because of greater available supplies of the input. This shifts the firm's marginal cost curve downward at each output rate and causes MC to intersect MR at a greater output rate. Assuming nothing else changes, the representative firm will expand its output rate by moving along D_1 in panel (a) and increasing its usage of X to X_3 units per period. However, we cannot assume that nothing else changes; what the representative firm does, the other firms will find it advantageous to do as well. The lower price of X affects the MC curves of all the firms. Hence, *when the price of input X falls,* all *firms will be induced to expand their output rates and thereby use more of input X*. The industrywide expansion of output will shift the industry supply curve for the product to the right, causing the market price of the product to fall. In turn, the lower product price means a lower marginal revenue and thus a lower marginal revenue product for X at each input rate. The effect is to shift the firm's input demand curve for X down and to the left, say from D_1 to D_2. The new profit-maximizing input rate for the representative firm at input price P_2 therefore is X_2 units and not X_3 units. Aggregating for all firms in the industry gives a total industry demand of X_{T_2} units at input price P_2, shown as point B in Figure 17-4(b). Points in addition to A and B can be determined by considering still other input prices. Connecting these points by a line gives the industry demand curve for input X.

INDUSTRY SUPPLY OF A RESOURCE INPUT

The supply of a resource input to an industry refers to the various input quantities which owners of the input are willing and able to make available to firms in the industry at various prices. Since in a free economy resource owners have a choice of supplying their resources to one line of production or another, it is reasonable to presume that they will direct them to those uses and industries offering the best overall prospect of reward—and not necessarily just the greatest monetary reward, because the reward package can include attractive nonmonetary elements.

Insofar as capital and land inputs of various types are concerned, the expected monetary reward is generally the predominant consideration. However, the case of labor inputs is more complicated. Wage rates and salaries are certainly important, but so are such features as the time and expense in learning

Resource inputs are drawn to those uses and industries offering the most attractive monetary and nonmonetary rewards.

a job or entering a profession, the opportunity for obtaining personal satisfactions from the job, the prospects for promotion and advancement, the regularity of employment, the environmental conditions under which the work is performed, the specific community and geographical area in which the job is located, and the social status of the occupation. Each job type offers a package of monetary and nonmonetary considerations that each potential worker may evaluate differently in the light of his or her own preferences. Given a choice of occupation and jobs, each member of the labor force can reasonably be expected to choose the one perceived as offering the best total package relative to one's interest, skills, and capabilities. Nonetheless, since experience indicates that the nonmonetary elements affecting resource allocation change rather slowly and can therefore be treated as a constant for purposes of short-run analysis, it simplifies the analysis to express the supply of labor as a function of monetary rewards (or just "price"—where price encompasses both wages/salary and fringes).

Logic dictates that a positive relation between input prices and input supplies will exist for most all types of land, natural resources, labor, and capital goods inputs. As the amount of monetary reward accruing to an input rises, resource owners will ordinarily be induced to supply the input in larger quantities per period of time. For instance, higher prices for minerals and natural resources intensify efforts to discover and tap more sources of supply. As wage rates in one occupation rise relative to wage rates in other occupations, the number of people seeking employment in that occupation will tend to rise. The greater the wage differential between firms, the more will workers gravitate from low-paying to high-paying firms; similarly, the greater the wage differentials between industries and between geographical regions, the more mobile will workers become.[12] Accordingly, *input supply curves are upward sloping, owing to the tendency of inputs to be drawn to employments where the rewards are highest.*

How responsive input supplies will be to changes in input prices depends on several factors:

1. *The size of the economic unit under consideration—the total economy, a locality, an industry, or a single firm.* The supply of an input to the economy as a whole may be fixed in the short run, while at the same time the supply to a particular locality, industry, or firm may be highly elastic or even perfectly elastic. Although at any given time there is just so much land, labor, or capital input in the entire economy (or in a more restricted geographical area), one firm or industry may be able to obtain as much of the available supply of an input as it may need without changing its offer prices because, by itself, it may require only a negligible fraction of the available input supply.

2. *The period of time considered.* The response of input supplies to input price changes is greater over the long run than over the short run, primarily because the degree of resource mobility increases with time. It takes time to discover and develop new mineral deposits, to shift capital investment out of

BASIC CONCEPT
The elasticity of supply for a resource input concerns the responsiveness of the input quantity supplied to a change in the input's price.

---

[12] Sometimes substantial wage differentials exist and are maintained for long periods, but beyond some point a wage differential can become too great for a firm, or an industry, or a locality, or a region to maintain without affecting labor supply conditions. The wages workers expect from one firm bear some relationship to the wages similar workers elsewhere receive, and if workers' expectations are grossly unrealized, the supply of labor is bound to be affected. The supply of job applicants for firms paying subpar wages may not totally dry up, but the quality may deteriorate. Moreover, their labor turnover rates are likely to be above average as workers' dissatisfaction with their wages pushes them to look for alternative employment.

less profitable endeavors into more profitable endeavors, to convert land from one use to another, to retrain workers or induce them to move into areas where job opportunities are expanding, and to inform people preparing to enter the labor force of the changing prospects of economic reward in the various professions. Hence, the elasticity of supply of an input becomes greater with the expansion of the time frame under consideration.

3. *Whether the input is unique to a particular industry or whether it is widely used*. The supply of an input used only by a single industry tends to be less elastic than inputs which are used by a number of different industries. The more versatile and mobile an input is, the more elastic will be its supply to a particular industry.

The size of the coefficient of the elasticity of supply, however, is not of paramount importance for our purposes. The basic analysis will be the same whatever the shape and degree of elasticity of the industry supply curve—even if it is vertical or backward rising.[13]

Resource Pricing and Employment on an Industrywide Basis

Demand and supply conditions for an input determine the equilibrium price which firms in the same industry pay for the input and the equilibrium amount of the input employed in that industry. Figure 17-5 shows an industry's demand for input X and the quantity of X supplied to the industry; the resulting equilibrium input price is P_1 dollars and the equilibrium employment rate is X_{T_1} units per period of time. If the prevailing price exceeds P_1 dollars, the available supply of the input will exceed the quantity which firms are willing to employ. Some units of the input will be either idle altogether or else used only part of the time. The excess supply of the input will generate a downward pressure on its price. On the other hand, if the actual price of X falls below P_1, the quantity demanded by firms in the industry will exceed the quantity supplied to the industry, and firms will begin to bid up the input's price as they compete for the available supplies.

The forces of demand and supply for an input act to push its price and usage toward levels that will clear the market.

Thus, market forces push resource prices and employment rates toward levels that will clear the market. Multiplying the equilibrium input price by the equilibrium employment rate of X gives the amount of money income which the owners of input X will receive from the firms in the industry. Aggregating the income of input X over all industries which use input X gives the total money income received by the owners of X and the share of the economy's output they will earn from having supplied X. This explanation of how the income accruing to resource owners is determined is called the *marginal productivity theory of income distribution*. It derives this name from the fact that particular input prices and employment rates are a function of the input's marginal productivity.

However, keep in mind that *when an input is used in many industries and when its supply to a particular industry is very sensitive to input price*

---

[13] A backward-bending supply curve for an input may arise from the fact that above certain input price levels, resource owners prefer to withdraw some units of input from the market to meet leisure-time or other personal preferences, since those units still being supplied will provide an income which is regarded as adequate. Hence, above some input price level, the higher the price, the smaller the quantity of the input supplied by resource owners. The effect is to cause the supply curve for the input to bend backward and upward—or to be backward rising. Generally, the concept of a backward-rising supply curve is most applicable to the case of labor input.

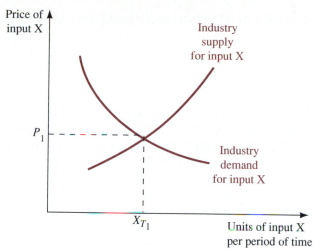

Figure 17-5

Pricing and employment of a resource input in a given industry

changes, it is inappropriate to examine input pricing and employment in the context of a single industry. The reason is that what firms in one industry pay for an input and the amounts they use of this input necessarily are related to the prices that firms in other industries pay and the amounts of that input they employ. In fact, *input prices and employment rates among the various industries using that input are interconnected*; price or employment adjustments in one industry transmit pressures and influences to other industries, though with "impulses" of varying degrees of intensity. *The linkages between industries are usually sufficiently strong to cause an input's price to tend toward the same level in all industries.* Different input prices for the same quality input can prevail without stimulating the movement of input supplies among firms and industries, but at some point the tolerance of resource owners for differentials becomes stretched so thin that firms and industries, in order to keep the inputs they need, will be forced to lessen the gap. Consequently, where an input is employed in several industries, the appropriate focal point for analyzing input prices is at the level of the total market for the input rather than at the level of the firm or industry.

The total market demand for an input on an economywide basis may be thought of as the sum of all the various industry demand curves, where the industries may be structured along any sort of lines and may contain any number of firms of various types and sizes. Similarly, the total market supply of an input is the result of combining the industry supply curves. Again, the intersection of market demand and market supply determines the input's economywide equilibrium price and rate of usage per period of time. The resulting price and employment rate form the basis for ascertaining the total amount of income which owners of the input in question will receive per period of time.

While it is generally true that resource prices and employment rates are outcomes of supply and demand forces, in particular situations the operation of supply and demand forces may be suspended or modified. The presence of labor unions, government-imposed minimum wage requirements, resource immobility, and assorted other institutional considerations cause input prices and employment rates to deviate from the free market results. We shall discuss some of the ramifications of these market interferences in the concluding section of this chapter.

THE APPLICABILITY OF THE PERFECTLY COMPETITIVE RESOURCE INPUT MODEL

Our conclusions about resource pricing and employment under conditions of perfect competition in both the product and resource markets apply mainly to those few markets where the products of the firms are homogeneous and where the number of firms comprising the product market is quite large. Only under these conditions is perfect competition in the product market even approximated. Thus, strictly speaking, the preceding model of resource pricing and resource employment provides a theoretical description of but a small segment of the economy. Nevertheless, many of the principles which characterize the model of perfectly competitive product and resource markets are much the same as in other types of market structures. In this sense, the perfectly competitive input model lays the groundwork for examining more widely applicable models of resource pricing and employment.

RESOURCE PRICING AND EMPLOYMENT: THE CASE OF IMPERFECTLY COMPETITIVE PRODUCT MARKETS AND PERFECTLY COMPETITIVE RESOURCE MARKETS

A somewhat more prevalent model of the functioning and behavior of resource input markets concerns the situation where the firm sells its product under conditions of imperfect competition (i.e., monopolistic competition, oligopoly, or monopoly) yet buys its inputs in a perfectly competitive resource market. This model characterizes many resource markets in the small business sector of the economy and some in the corporate sector.

THE IMPERFECTLY COMPETITIVE FIRM'S INPUT DECISION: THE ONE-VARIABLE INPUT CASE

The *MRP* curve for an imperfectly competitive firm tends to be more steeply downsloping than the *MRP* curve for a perfectly competitive firm.

When a firm sells its product in an imperfectly competitive market structure, its input decision is determined in a manner analogous to the perfectly competitive case, but with a slightly modified calculation procedure. In monopolistic competition, oligopoly, or pure monopoly the firm's product demand curve is downsloping, and, other competitive variables remaining unchanged, the firm must lower price in order to increase its sales volume. This has a very important consequence. *Whereas the MRP curve of an input used by a perfectly competitive firm falls solely because the marginal product of the input declines, the MRP curve of an input used by an imperfectly competitive firm declines for two reasons: a declining marginal product and a lower marginal revenue from the sale of additional output.* The perfectly competitive enterprise can sell additional output at a constant price and obtain a constant *MR*, so that its *MRP* curve falls at the same rate as does the *MP* curve of the variable input. But when an imperfectly competitive firm adds one more unit of variable input and output rises by the amount of its marginal product, it may have to lower selling price to sell the increased output. Barring the opportunity for price discrimination, any price decrease applies not just to the marginal product of the last unit of variable input but also to the units of output previously produced.[14] Hence, the marginal revenue received from additional sales is a decreasing function, and the firm's *MRP* curve for variable input falls faster than it otherwise would if the firm could sell all it pleased at an established market price—as occurs with the horizontal demand curve of a firm in perfect competition. However, in either case, *MRP* still equals the net addition to total revenue associated with a change in the variable input rate.

   The Profit-Maximizing Rate of Input Usage.   To illustrate how a firm confronted with a downsloping demand-*AR* curve can ascertain the profit-maximizing rate of usage of a single variable input (X), consider the hypothetical production, cost, and revenue data in Table 17-2. Column (4) shows the extent to which the firm must lower price in order to sell the extra output of each successive unit of X, while columns (5) and (6) concern the corresponding *TR* and *MR* values. Column (7) contains the $SVMP_X$ figures, obtained by multiplying MP_X by the price at which the added output can be sold. Unlike the perfectly competitive case, the figures for $SVMP_X$ in column (7) do *not* coincide with MRP_X values in column (8). The figures for the sales value of the marginal product represent the gross addition to total revenue attributable to an additional unit of X. However, the firm's total revenue does not rise by the amount of *SVMP*, because to sell the added output the firm must reduce its price on the preceding units of output, thereby causing the *net* addition to *TR* to be less than the gross addition. To illustrate: The eighth unit of X has a marginal product of 10 units of output; these can be sold for $17 apiece for a total of $170—the figure for *SVMP*. But this is not the *MRP* value for the eighth unit of X because, to sell these 10 units of output, the firm must accept a $1 price reduction on the 120 units of output produced by the preceding 7 units of X. Hence, the *MRP* of the eighth unit of X is [$170 − 120($1)] or $50, as shown in column (8). The other values in column (8) can be determined in like fashion. The figures in columns (9), (10), and (11) of the table are obtained in the usual way.

   An imperfectly competitive firm's input decision is based on precisely the same profit-maximizing principle as that of a perfectly competitive firm: *The firm should purchase additional units of a variable input up to the point where the added cost of more input equals the added revenue it contributes*. In short, the usage of variable input must be carried to the rate where *MRP* = *MRC*. A comparison of columns (8) and (9) in Table 17-2 indicates that the profit-maximizing input rate is 6 units of X. For the firm to go beyond this point and employ the seventh unit of X will result in revenues increasing by $108 but costs rising by $140—plainly an unprofitable act. For the firm to stop short of using 6 units of X will result in smaller total contribution profits [see column (11)] and hence smaller total profits (or greater losses).

   The profit-maximizing input decision can be approached graphically in a somewhat more general fashion. Figure 17-6 shows an imperfectly competitive firm's *MRP* curve for a variable input. Suppose the input supply curve is S_1, with a resulting input price of P_1 dollars. The profit-maximizing input rate is X_1 units, where $MRP_X = MRC_X$. Should the input supply price fall to P_2 dollars, giving a new input supply curve at S_2, the firm's profit-maximizing input rate would expand to X_2 units per period of time. And should the input supply curve shift downward to S_3, the new equilibrium input rate would

In deciding how much an input to use, an imperfectly competitive firm uses the same rule as a perfectly competitive firm: Increase input usage up to the point where *MRP* = *MRC*.

---

[14] We shall assume throughout the following discussion that the firm employs a single price policy and does not therefore engage in any of the several forms of price discrimination. We shall also assume that a firm lowers price to gain increased sales rather than depending upon increased efforts in nonprice areas to accommodate a rise in output.

TABLE 17-2   PROFIT-MAXIMIZING RATE OF RESOURCE INPUT USAGE FOR A FIRM OPERATING IN AN IMPERFECTLY COMPETITIVE PRODUCT MARKET AND A PERFECTLY COMPETITIVE RESOURCE MARKET

(1) Units of Variable Input (X)	(2) Units of Output (Q_A)	(3) Marginal Product (MP_X)	(4) Price of Product A (P_A)	(5) Total Revenue from Sales of Product A ($TR_A = P_A \cdot Q_A$)	(6) "Average" Marginal Revenue[a] (MR_A)	(7) Sales Value of Marginal Product ($SVMP_X = MPO_X \cdot P_A$)	(8) Marginal Revenue Product ($MRP_X = MP_X \cdot MR_A = \Delta TR_A / \Delta X$)	(9) Supply Price of Variable Input ($P_X = ARC_X = MRC_X$)	(10) Total Variable Cost (TVC)	(11) Total Contribution Profit ($TCP = TR - TVC$)
0	0		$25	$ 0				$140	$ 0	$ 0
		14			$24.00	$336	$336			
1	14		24	336				140	140	196
		26			22.46	598	584			
2	40		23	920				140	280	440
		20			20.00	440	400			
3	60		22	1320				140	420	900
		18			17.67	378	318			
4	78		21	1638				140	560	1078
		16			15.12	320	242			
5	94		20	1880				140	700	1180
		14			12.29	266	172			
6	108		19	2052				140	840	1212
		12			9.00	216	108			
7	120		18	2160				140	980	1180
		10			5.00	170	50			
8	130		17	2210				140	1120	1090
		8			−0.25	128	−2			
9	138		16	2208				140	1260	948
		6			−8.00	90	−48			
10	144		15	2160				140	1400	760

[a] The term *average marginal revenue* is used here because, strictly speaking, the concept of MR refers to the extra revenue associated with a single-unit change in output; since the output changes in the table are multiunit, the only MR values which can be computed from the information in the table are the average MR values for the multiunit output increment in question.

become X_3 units. Consequently, the profit-maximizing input rate of X is found along the input's *MRP* curve, which makes the MRP_X curve the firm's demand curve for input X, providing that only one variable input is used in the firm's production process.

THE IMPERFECTLY COMPETITIVE FIRM'S INPUT DECISION: THE TWO-VARIABLE INPUT CASE

The analysis for an imperfectly competitive firm using two or more variable inputs parallels that for the perfectly competitive firm. As portrayed in

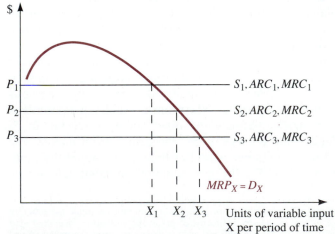

Figure 17-6

An imperfectly competitive firm's demand for a resource input

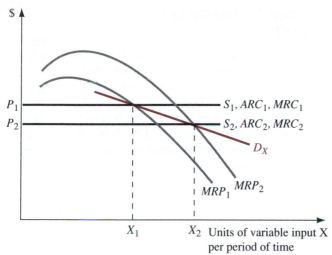

Figure 17-7

An imperfectly competitive firm's input decision when two or more inputs are variable

Figure 17-7, suppose that the supply price of input X is perfectly elastic and pegged at P_1 and that the input's marginal revenue product curve is MRP_1. The profit-maximizing rate of input is therefore X_1 units per period of time.

Now let the supply price of X fall to P_2. This change triggers four effects at the level of the firm; the substitution effect, the output effect, the marginal cost effect, and the marginal revenue effect. The substitution, output, and marginal cost effects operate in exactly the same way for firms in monopolistic competition, oligopoly, or pure monopoly as they do for firms in perfect competition.

However, the *marginal revenue effect* is unique to imperfectly competitive product markets and arises from the fact that the firm's marginal revenue will change as a consequence of the output changes induced by the shift in the price of input X. The decline in the price of X lowers the firm's marginal cost curve, causing a new intersection of *MC* and *MR* at a *larger* output, a *lower* price, and a *lower MR* value. (The reader should verify this statement by drawing a graph.) Since $MRP_X = MP_X \cdot MR$, a decline in *MR* necessarily acts to reduce MRP_X.

On balance, the output and marginal cost effects will override the substitution and marginal revenue effects, with the result that a decline in the supply price of X will shift the *MRP* curve for X upward and to the right, say from MRP_1 to MRP_2.[15] The profit-maximizing input rate for the imperfectly competitive firm thus becomes X_2 units at a supply price of P_2 dollars. Other profit-maximizing input rates for X can be generated by changing the price of X again and again, tracing through the substitution, output, marginal cost, and marginal revenue effects, and finding the new position of the firm's *MRP* curve. Connecting the points formed by the equilibrium input supply prices and input rates gives the firm's input demand curve for X, labeled as D_X in Figure 17-7. The points along D_X show the various quantities of input X that maximize the firm's profits when the prices of other variable inputs remain constant and the usages of all other variable inputs are appropriately adjusted for changes in the supply price of input X.

BASIC CONCEPT
The marginal revenue effect shows the effect of a higher or lower price for resource X on the marginal revenue associated with producing and selling additional units.

When an imperfectly competitive firm uses two or more variable inputs and the price of one of them declines, it will tend to use more of the now cheaper input than before.

---

[15] For a formal proof of this claim the reader may consult the references in footnote 8.

INPUT DEMAND FOR AN IMPERFECTLY COMPETITIVE INDUSTRY

To derive the industrywide demand for an input when the firms compete under conditions of imperfect competition requires that the demand curves of the individual firms somehow be combined into a single input demand curve for the industry. In an imperfectly competitive market of two or more firms, whatever shade of oligopoly or monopolistic competition may exist, the demand curves of the firms cannot simply be summed horizontally to give the industry demand curve.[16] This is invalid for the same reason it does not work for perfect competition. To begin with, a change in the input's supply price affects the optimum output rate of each firm in the industry. A change in the firm's output rate leads then to a price change. The price and output adjustments made by the firm will combine to shift the *MRP* curve of the input via the substitution, output, marginal cost, and marginal revenue effects. In turn, the shift in *MRP* alters the firm's optimum input demand at the new input supply price. In such situations, the industrywide input demand curve is derived by first finding the profit-maximizing input rate for each firm at each possible input price after allowing for shifts in the *MRP* curve and then by summing these optimum input amounts over all firms in the industry. The rationale and the graphical analysis are identical to that described in Figure 17-4 and need not be reiterated here.

Once the industry demand for the input is determined, the industrywide equilibrium price and input rates are found at the intersection of the industry demand and supply curves for the input. The nature of an input's supply curve for a given industry, discussed in an earlier section of this chapter, is unaffected by the existence of imperfect competition in the product market. Again, however, the equilibrium price of an input on an industrywide basis is bound to be affected by the price of the input in other industries. *When resource inputs are versatile enough to be used by several industries and when they are relatively mobile from industry to industry, the equilibrium price and employment rates of an input are best analyzed on a marketwide or economy-wide basis rather than on an industrywide basis.* Barring the existence of resource immobility or other powerful institutional determinants of an input price, *the tie between a resource input's price in one industry and its price in other industries is usually strong enough to cause the overall price of the input to tend toward the same level in all industries using that input*. A valid explanation of how input prices are determined must therefore hinge upon overall market demand and supply conditions rather than upon demand and supply in any one industry.

THE SHAPE OF THE RESOURCE SUPPLY CURVE AND ECONOMIC RENTS

To this point, we have focused on the behavior of firms who are buyers in resource markets. We now consider the other side of resource markets by discussing the behavior of sellers and the supply of resources. The owners of resources have several options. Since resources have alternative uses, they can be sold, rented, or leased in competing industries and in different geographical

---

[16] Obviously, if the industry is one of pure monopoly, no combining is necessary, because the firm's input demand and the industry input demand are one and the same.

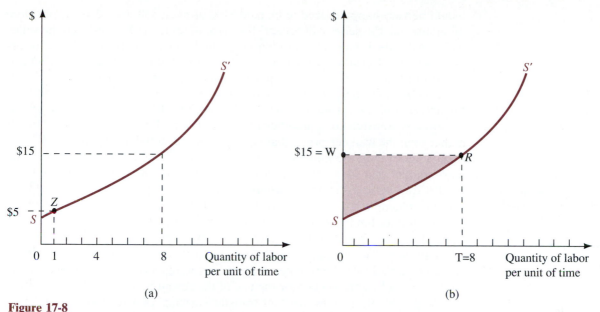

Figure 17-8

The supply curve of an individual resource owner and economic rent

locations. The owners also have the option of withholding their resources from the market by not selling or renting them in the current time period. In general, resource supply curves slope positively, which means that at higher prices the owners are willing and able to offer larger quantities. This is illustrated by the resource supply curve in Figure 17-8, which shows the quantity of resources offered by a single owner at a series of market prices. We emphasize that the supply curve in Figure 17-8 is for a specific resource market and reflects the willingness of the owner to offer the resources for use in that market. In constructing the resource supply curve, we assume that the prices that the owner could receive in alternative uses and other markets are constant.

Since labor supply curves are relatively easy to understand, we let *SS'* in Figure 17-8 represent the supply of labor by an individual seller in a particular market. Generally, labor supply curves slope positively indicating that more labor will be offered in response to higher market prices. But under certain conditions the supply curves of individual sellers of labor can be backward bending and have both positive and negative slopes. Empirical evidence establishes that market supply curves of labor virtually always slope positively,[17] so in what follows we focus on this type of behavior for both individual and market supply curves of resources.[18] Any point on the supply curve shows the *minimum* price the seller of a resource will accept for the indicated quantity. For example, at point Z in Figure 17-8(a) the smallest amount that the resource owner will accept for a quantity of one unit of labor is $5. The seller, of course,

---

[17] For a summary of the evidence relating to the shape of market supply curves for labor, see Mark Killingsworth, *Labor Supply* (London: Cambridge University Press, 1983).

[18] Individual labor supply curves can be backward bending due to the combination of and the relative size of the substitution and output effects of changes in wage rates. If not working (leisure) yields positive utility to the resource owner, which implies leisure is a normal good, then substitution and output effects of wage rate changes will have opposite signs. If wage rates rise, the substitution effect will induce more work effort, but the output effect will induce less. If the output effect of wage rate changes is larger than the substitution effect, then the labor supply curve will be backward bending. See Killingsworth's *Labor Supply* (1983) for a detailed discussion.

would be very happy indeed to be paid $100 or even $10, but $5 is the absolute minimum that the seller will accept. If a price of less than $5 is offered the seller will transfer the resource to another use, which might involve simply not offering it for sale. Certainly a price of less than $5 will not result in the first unit of the resource being offered in this particular market. The $5 price can be thought of as the **transfer price** of the resource. If a price of $5 or more is offered then the first unit of the resource is sold in this market; if less than $5 is offered the resource is transferred to another use. But the market may set a price much higher than the transfer price; that is, the resource supplier may and often does receive more than the minimum acceptable price. The difference between the least amount that the owner will accept and the amount actually received in a market transaction is called **economic rent**. The concept can be illustrated with a simple example based on Figure 17-8(a). If the market establishes a price of $15 per unit for labor, then the economic rent on the first unit sold is $10, which is the difference between the amount actually received for one unit, $15, and the minimum amount that the seller would have been willing to accept, $5. It should be noted that the transfer earnings of the resource is determined by the value received by the owner for the use of the resource in its next best alternative employment. This means that transfer earnings of a resource are equivalent to what we earlier called opportunity cost. Thus, the economic rent is a return to the resource owner in excess of the opportunity cost. Equivalently, it is also the difference between the amount actually paid to an owner for a specific quantity of a resource in a market and the transfer earnings of that quantity of resources.

BASIC CONCEPT
Economic rent represents the surplus payment to a resource owner over and above the minimum amount the resource owner is willing to accept.

Care must be exercised in using the term *rent*, because it can mean two different things in economics. Depending on the context, *rent* may refer to the price paid for the use of real property or other assets for a fixed time period, which parallels its meaning in ordinary usage. Alternatively, *rent* may refer to the **economic surplus** received by a resource owner in a market transaction, which is over and above the resource owner's opportunity cost. In the first usage of the term, rent refers to the rental price of real property (e.g., the rent on an apartment is $500 per month). But the $10 paid in excess of the transfer earnings of the first unit of labor in Figure 17-8(a) is a rent in the sense of an economic surplus. In this section we stress the latter meaning and refer to the surplus above transfer earnings as economic rent. If we wished to refer to the other meaning or usage of the word *rent*, then we would be more explicit and refer to *rental price* of an asset.

Figure 17-8(a) illustrates the economic rent for the first unit of the resource sold. Figure 17-8(b) generalizes the concept for all units sold. At a market price of $15 per unit, the owner of the resource offers $0T$ units of the resource, where $0T = 8$, and the economic rent received is the total income less the transfer earnings. In Figure 17-8(b) the income received is simply the resource price X quantity offered ($15 \times 8 = \$120$) and the transfer earnings is the area below the supply curve, $0SRT$. In general, *economic rent is represented by the shaded area above the resource supply curve and below the horizontal line determined by the resource price*. In Figure 17-8(b) the economic rent accruing to the resource owner is equal to the shaded area SWR. It should be noted that economic rent is similar in some respects to consumer surplus, which was discussed in Chapter 5. In fact, another name that could be used instead of economic rent is resource owner's surplus, but the term *rent* is widely used in economics and has a long history, so we retain it here.[19] Thus, in trade and

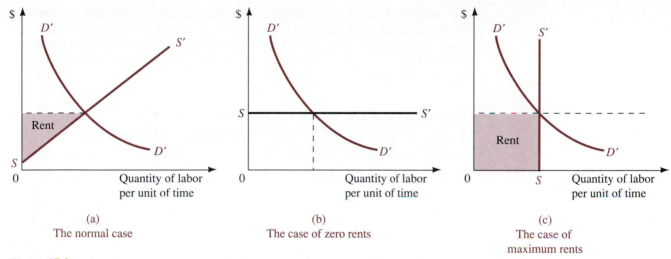

Figure 17-9
Market supply curves of resources and economic rents

exchange buyers receive consumer surplus while resource owners receive economic rents.

Economic rent can be generalized to the market as a whole by horizontally adding up the individual supply curves of resource owners to obtain the market supply of resources. The resulting supply curve reflects the transfer earnings and opportunity costs of all owners offering resources in the market. Figure 17-9 illustrates three disparate market supply curves of resources, which correspond to differences in supply elasticities in the market. The general case is shown in Figure 17-9(a), where the supply curve is positively sloping, which implies a supply elasticity that is also positive but less than infinite. As in Figure 17-8, the rents in Figure 17-9(a) are given by shaded area above the resource supply curve and below the horizontal line determined by the resource price. Figure 17-9(b) depicts the case in which the economic rent in the market place is zero. An infinitely or perfectly elastic market supply curve means that resource owners receive payments for their resources that are exactly equal to their transfer earnings. Thus, the owners receive incomes equal to the opportunity costs of the resource but no more. This type of situation would occur in highly competitive markets where the resources are perfectly mobile between alternative uses and the owners have no preference for one particular use of the resource over another. Figure 17-9(c) shows another extreme possible outcome in which the supply elasticity is zero or perfectly inelastic. In this case the resource has no alternative uses and the opportunity costs of the resource are zero. Thus, with zero elastic resource supply curves all of the income received by the resource supplier is an economic rent. Of course, in a market economy resources always have alternatives and the situation described in Figure 17-9(c)

---

[19] In his classic treatment, Alfred Marshall referred to the economic rent received by the owners of labor as "worker's surplus." He also used the term *producer's surplus* to refer to rents accruing on the supply side of the market. See his *Principles of Economics*, 8th edition (London: Macmillan, 1920), pp. 830–32. Today, the term *economic rent* is widely used, and there are good reasons for avoiding the use of the term *producer's surplus*. On this point see E. J. Mishan, "What Is Producer's Surplus?" *American Economic Review*, Vol. 58, No. 4 (September 1968), pp. 1269–79.

does not apply, but it is useful in establishing one extreme possible outcome in which economic rent accounts for the entire payment to resource owners. The most general situation in real-world resource markets is represented by Figure 17-9(a), but the markets can approach the extreme outcomes depicted in Figures 17-8(b) and (c).[20]

RESOURCE PRICING AND EMPLOYMENT: THE CASE OF IMPERFECTLY COMPETITIVE PRODUCT AND RESOURCE MARKETS

In numerous geographical areas the supply of an input *in the short run* is relatively limited. Enterprises with large plants in the area may utilize such a sizable fraction of the local input supply that their decisions to employ more or less of the input have a discernible impact on the input's short-run local supply price. The effect is to make *the firm's* input supply curve upward-sloping. The more of an input the firm wishes to obtain, the higher the price it must offer to bid supplies of the input away from alternative users.[21] The less of an input the firm needs, the smaller the price it can get by with paying, since it does not have to bid so high to attract the desired supply away from other firms.

Several types of input supply situations other than perfect competition may be delineated. A resource input market in which only *one* firm uses the input is referred to as **monopsony**.[22] If only a *few* firms are the predominant purchasers of the input, the resource market is designated as **oligopsony**. Where *many* firms are using an input but their numbers are still small enough to allow each firm a small influence over the input's supply price, the resource market is characterized by **monopsonistic competition**. A particular firm can sell its output under conditions of oligopoly yet buy its inputs under conditions of monopsonistic competition. Similarly, it is possible for a firm to sell its product under conditions of monopolistic competition and to obtain its inputs under conditions of monopsony; this could occur if the numerous small producers were geographically dispersed but still large enough to dominate the market for labor in a local area. Plainly, a variety of product and resource market combinations can result: monopoly-monopsony, oligopoly-monopsony, oligopoly-monopsonistic competition, perfect competition-oligopsony, and so on. However, in any sort of imperfectly competitive input market, whether it be one of monopsony, oligopsony, or monopsonistic competition, the analyti-

---

[20] For more information on this point and a more general discussion of economic rents, see John P. Formby, "A Clarification of Rent Theory," *Southern Economic Journal*, Vol. 38, No. 3 (January 1972), pp. 315–24. For a formal treatment of the relation of economic rents to opportunity costs, see John P. Formby and Edward M. Millner, "Opportunity Cost and Rent," *International Review of Economics and Business*, Vol. 35, No. 9 (September 1988), pp. 801–16.

[21] As regards labor inputs, it should be recognized that a large firm may be able to expand the size of its labor force without raising the going wage rate by increasing recruiting efforts and/or by lowering its standards for hiring new employees. Either of these strategies, however, really means that the effective price of a given quantity and quality of labor is rising, even though the nominal wage scale remains the same.

[22] The term *monopsony* is on occasions also used to refer to product market situations where there is only a single buyer of a product. Hence, strictly speaking, monopsony refers to a single buyer—it matters not whether the buyer purchases an input or a final good or service. Similarly, pure monopoly refers to a single seller—whether the seller is selling a product or an input again really makes no difference. For example, the craft union that is able to unionize all persons having a particular skill is just as much a monopolist in "selling" the skill it controls as is the local telephone company in rendering telephone service. Analogous meanings and interpretations can be attached to the terms *oligopoly, oligopsony,* and so on.

cal considerations governing the supply aspects of the firm's input decision are the same. Thus, it is sufficient merely to examine imperfect competition in the input market to learn about the firm's input decision in other than a perfectly competitive resource market.

THE MARGINAL RESOURCE COST CURVE AND A RISING INPUT SUPPLY CURVE

The key feature of an imperfectly competitive input market is that the firm faces an upward-rising input supply curve. With a rising supply curve the firm is forced to pay a higher price if it wishes to secure more of the input, and the firm can get by with paying a lower price for the input should it choose to use less of the input. Since the supply curve for an input represents the firm's average cost for obtaining the input, the firm's *ARC* curve is also upward-sloping and coincides with the supply curve. This has a most important consequence insofar as the firm's marginal resource cost is concerned.

Under imperfectly competitive input supply conditions, the *MRC* curve does not correspond to the input supply and average resource cost curve. Consider the hypothetical data in Table 17-3. Columns (1) and (2) show how much the firm must increase its offer price in order to obtain additional units of X; these two columns represent the firm's input supply and *ARC* schedules. Columns (3) presents the total cost of input X associated with each of the various input rates of X. Column (4) shows the marginal resource cost of each additional unit of X and can be calculated by successive subtraction of the TC_X figures; that is, $MRC_X = \Delta TC_X / \Delta X$.

When the firm must pay a higher price to obtain larger amounts of input X, the marginal resource cost of each extra unit will be higher than the input's supply price and average resource cost. As shown in Table 17-3, suppose the firm increases its usage rate of X from 7 to 8 units per period. The price

Whereas a firm's supply curve for an input is horizontal when the input is purchased under perfectly competitive market conditions, in an imperfectly competitive input market the firm confronts an input supply curve that slopes upward to the right.

TABLE 17-3   MARGINAL RESOURCE COST FOR A FIRM OPERATING UNDER CONDITIONS OF IMPERFECT COMPETITION AND ITS RESOURCES INPUT MARKET

(1) Units of Variable Input (X)	(2) Supply Price of Variable Input ($P_X = ARC_X$)	(3) Total Cost of Variable Input (TC_X)	(4) Marginal Resource Cost (MRC_X)
1	$5.00	$ 5.00	
			$ 6.00
2	5.50	11.00	
			7.00
3	6.00	18.00	
			8.00
4	6.50	26.00	
			9.00
5	7.00	35.00	
			10.00
6	7.50	45.00	
			11.00
7	8.00	56.00	
			12.00
8	8.50	68.00	
			13.00
9	9.00	81.00	
			14.00
10	9.50	95.00	

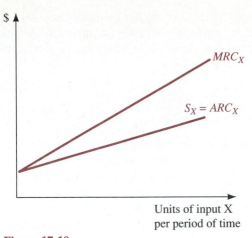

Units of input X
per period of time

Figure 17-10

Relationships among the input supply curve, the average resource cost curve, and the marginal resource cost curve in an imperfectly competitive input market

of the eighth unit is $8.50. But this value is not the marginal resource cost of the eighth unit. To obtain the use of 8 units of X, the firm must pay $8.50 for *each* one.[23] Hence, the firm's cost of obtaining each of the previous 7 units of X rises from $8.00 to $8.50 for an added cost of $3.50 (7 × $0.50). Adding this to the $8.50 cost of the eighth unit gives a total increase of $12.00 in the firm's cost of upping the input rate of X from 7 to 8 units. Thus, the marginal resource cost of the eighth unit is $12.00. The *MRC* of the other units can be derived in the same fashion.

A graphical portrayal of the relationships among the firm's input supply curve (S_X), the average resource cost curve (ARC_X), and the marginal resource cost curve (MRC_X) is depicted in Figure 17-10. The MRC_X curve lies above the input supply and average resource cost curve at each and every input rate. The rationale is the same as for the relationship between ATC and MC; in fact, the ARC_X-MRC_X relation parallels that of ATC and MC. As is the usual case with marginal and average concepts, if the average cost (or supply price) of input X is rising, then the marginal cost of input X (MRC_X) must be greater than ARC_X and the MRC curve for X must lie above the input supply and average resource cost curve.

The mathematics of the relationship between S_X and MRC_X is easily indicated. Assume, for convenience of illustration, that the input supply curve for X is linear and upward-sloping. Then the general equation for the supply curve is

$$P_X = ARC_X = a + bX.$$

The total cost of the input at any input rate is

$$TC_X = P_X \cdot X = ARC_X \cdot X = (a + bX)X = aX + bX^2.$$

When the input supply curve (or *ARC* curve) is upward-sloping, the *MRC* curve lies above the supply-*ARC* curve and slopes upward at an even steeper rate.

---

[23] This is not only required by the supply conditions, but it is also equitable. Since we assume each unit of X is just alike, there is no cause for the firm to reward 1 unit of X any differently from the others. If, for example, the firm has 8 identical units of input X, then the second unit (assuming it can be picked out from the rest) is no more ''valuable'' than the fifth or the eighth unit. The *order* in which the units of X are hired has no real bearing on their worth to the firm. Nor is it usually feasible for the firm to pay different units of the same input a different price. Consequently, the price which it takes to get the *total* amount of X that is desired is what determines the price *each unit* must be paid.

Marginal resource cost is, by definition, the rate of change in the total cost of the input as the input rate changes, which in terms of calculus is the first derivative of the input's total cost function. The equation for MRC_X thus becomes

$$MRC_X = \frac{dTC_X}{dX} = a + 2bX.$$

A comparison of the equation for the input supply-average resource cost curve and the equation for the MRC curve indicates that the MRC_X curve will rise twice as fast as $S_X\text{-}ARC_X$ when $S_X\text{-}ARC_X$ is linear and upward-sloping. The marginal resource cost curve can be determined in like fashion for other types of input supply-average resource cost functions.

THE IMPERFECTLY COMPETITIVE FIRM'S INPUT DECISION IN AN IMPERFECTLY COMPETITIVE RESOURCE MARKET: THE ONE-VARIABLE INPUT CASE

Determining the firm's profit-maximizing input rate with respect to resource X follows the same principle when imperfect competition exists in the input market as it does when there is perfect competition. As we have just seen, the distinctive feature of an imperfectly competitive resource market is that each firm confronts an upward-rising input supply curve and an even more rapidly rising marginal resource cost curve. Nonetheless, a firm will still find it advantageous to increase the usage rate of X as long as additional units of X add more to revenues than to total costs. As before, the firm's net revenue gains from using additional units of an input are given by the input's MRP function, whereas the extra costs incurred are indicated by the input's MRC function as derived from the input's supply and ARC functions.

The relevant curves are shown in Figure 17-11. The firm's profits will be maximum at an input rate of X_1 units, where $MRP_X = MRC_X$. To use more than X_1 units per period of time would add more to the firm's total costs than to its total revenues. To stop short of using X_1 units would mean a sacrifice of

The criterion for determining a firm's profit-maximizing input rate remains the same for an imperfectly competitive input market as for a perfectly competitive input market: Increase input usage up to the point where $MRP = MRC$.

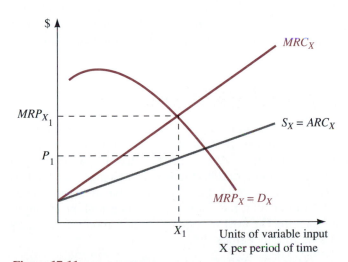

Figure 17-11

The profit-maximizing input rate for a firm operating in imperfectly competitive product and resource markets

some profits, because the marginal revenue products of all units below X_1 exceed their respective marginal resource cost. Clearly, then, X_1 is the profit-maximizing input rate. But now the question becomes: What price must the firm pay to obtain X_1 units per period of time? Although the marginal revenue product at X_1 is MRP_{X_1}, this is not the price which the firm need pay to get X_1 units. The input supply curve (S_X) shows the price which the firm must pay for various quantities of the input. From S_X it is apparent that to obtain X_1 units of resource X, the firm will find it necessary to pay a price of P_1 dollars—this, then, is the firm's equilibrium input price.

THE IMPERFECTLY COMPETITIVE FIRM'S INPUT DECISION IN AN IMPERFECTLY COMPETITIVE RESOURCE MARKET WHEN SEVERAL VARIABLE INPUTS ARE USED

Ordinarily, a firm's production technology will call for the use of several inputs—some fixed in the short run, others variable, but all subject to change in the long run. Consequently, it is important to consider how the firm's profit-maximizing input combination is determined when several inputs are variable.

In Chapter 7 it was shown that to minimize its total costs for a given output the firm must adjust its input mix so as to obtain an equivalent amount of output per dollar spent on the last unit of each input used. In more formal terms this requires the firm to combine its various inputs (X_a, X_b, X_c, . . . , X_n) such that

$$\frac{MP_{X_a}}{P_{X_a}} = \frac{MP_{X_b}}{P_{X_b}} = \frac{MP_{X_c}}{P_{X_c}} = \cdots = \frac{MP_{X_n}}{P_{X_n}}.$$

If the least-cost input combination rule is violated, the firm can either obtain more output for the same total cost or else get the same output for less total cost. Suppose, for instance, a dollar's worth of input X_a contributes more to output than a dollar's worth of input X_b. Then the firm would find it advantageous to shift its expenditures on inputs; more dollars should be allocated to the purchase of X_a and fewer to the purchase of X_b—the firm should substitute input X_a for input X_b. As the substitution is made, the marginal product of X_a declines and the marginal product of X_b rises; the substitution process ceases when

$$\frac{MP_{X_a}}{P_{X_a}} = \frac{MP_{X_b}}{P_{X_b}}.$$

However, *this proposition holds if and only if the inputs are purchased in perfectly competitive resource markets*. If the firm's input supply curves are all upward-sloping such that input prices vary with the quantity used, then a substitution of one input for another entails input price changes as well as marginal product changes. The firm must therefore consider an input's marginal resource cost (MRC) rather than its supply price when making its input decision. The rule for minimizing the cost of a given output under imperfectly competitive input conditions thus becomes

PRINCIPLE

When a firm purchases two or more inputs under imperfectly competitive conditions, it minimizes the cost of a given output by selecting the input combination where the ratio of marginal product to marginal resource cost is the same for all inputs.

$$\frac{MP_{X_a}}{MRC_{X_a}} = \frac{MP_{X_b}}{MRC_{X_b}} = \frac{MP_{X_c}}{MRC_{X_c}} = \cdots = \frac{MP_{X_n}}{MRC_{X_n}}.$$

To see the rationale underlying this proposition, consider the two-input case where inputs X_a and X_b are being used in such propositions that

$$\frac{MP_{X_a}}{MRC_{X_a}} > \frac{MP_{X_b}}{MRC_{X_b}}.$$

This inequality says that at the existing input combination the firm can realize a greater increase in output per additional dollar outlay on input X_a than on input X_b. Consequently, by substituting X_a for X_b the firm can realize more output for the same cost or else it can get the same output for less cost. As substitution is initiated, the marginal product of X_a declines and the MRC_{X_a} increases, whereas the marginal product of X_b increases and the MRC_{X_b} declines. Sooner or later the substitution of X_a for X_b will result in equality in the ratios of MP and MRC. At the point of equality, no further change in the firm's input mix will prove beneficial from the standpoint of costs or output.

     The preceding discussion shows, albeit in a nonrigorous fashion, that *if a firm buying its inputs under conditions of imperfect competition is to achieve the lowest possible total cost for a given output, then it should adjust its input combination to the point where the ratio of marginal product to marginal resource cost is the same for all inputs used.* An interesting question now arises: What adjustments in the rule, if any, are necessary to identify *the profit-maximizing resource input combination*? Is the rule for attaining the least-cost resource combination for a given output also adequate for ascertaining the profit-maximizing input mix? The answer to the latter question is *no*, though the reason may not be apparent at first glance.

     The rule for determining the least-cost resource combination for a *given output* reveals only the correct *proportions* in which to employ variable inputs. It says nothing about which output rate maximizes profits, and therefore it leaves unanswered the question as to the correct *absolute amounts* of each variable input. To illustrate the significance of this point, consider the following numerical example. Suppose that a firm is using 10 units of input X_a and 15 units of input X_b to produce 3500 units of a particular product per week. Suppose further that at this input combination the specific values of marginal product and marginal resource cost for X_a and X_b are $MP_{X_a} = 40$ units of output, $MRC_{X_a} = \$10$, $MP_{X_b} = 60$ units of output, and $MRC_{X_b} = \$15$. The least-cost rule that

$$\frac{MP_{X_a}}{MRC_{X_a}} = \frac{MP_{X_b}}{MRC_{X_b}}$$

The rule for achieving the least-cost resource input combination does not coincide with the rule for achieving the profit-maximizing input combination.

is satisfied, as we can see by substituting the MP and MRC values into the preceding expression:

$$\frac{MP_{X_a}}{MRC_{X_a}} = \frac{40 \text{ units of output}}{\$10} = 4 \text{ units of output/\$},$$

$$\frac{MRC_{X_b}}{MP_{X_b}} = \frac{60 \text{ units of output}}{\$15} = 4 \text{ units of output/\$}.$$

At the current input combination, the firm obtains 4 units of output per dollar spent on each input, which says that there is no advantage to be gained from shifting the input mix insofar as cost or output is concerned. However, how do we know whether or not it would be more *profitable* to use more (or less) of both inputs X_a and X_b? There is no way to tell from the information given. Thus, while it is clear that the firm is using its inputs to the best advantage to produce the current output of 3500 units, we do not know from the information given whether 3500 units is the profit-maximizing output rate and therefore whether 10 units of X_a and 15 units of X_b constitute the profit-maximizing input combination.

This shortcoming in the least-cost rule is easily disposed of by bringing the marginal revenue products of the two inputs into consideration. Suppose the marginal product of the tenth unit of input X_a (40 units of output) adds $20 to the firm's total revenue and the marginal product of the fifteenth unit of X_b (60 units of output) adds $30. Then, clearly, the *MRP* of both inputs exceeds their respective marginal resource costs of $10 and $15, and the firm will find it profitable to increase its usage of both X_a and X_b. As demonstrated previously, the firm should increase an input's usage to the point where *MRP = MRC*. This rationale applies to any and all resources. Thus, *in general it can be said that a firm attains the profit-maximizing input rate when each and every variable input is employed to the point where its marginal revenue product equals its marginal resource cost.* In algebraic terms this becomes

$$\frac{MRP_{X_a}}{MRC_{X_a}} = \frac{MRP_{X_b}}{MRC_{X_b}} = \frac{MRP_{X_c}}{MRC_{X_c}} = \cdots = \frac{MRP_{X_n}}{MRC_{X_n}}.$$

PRINCIPLE
No matter whether product and resource markets are perfectly or imperfectly competitive, profit maximization requires a firm to select the input combination where *MRP* equals *MRC* for each and every input used.

Hence, converting the numerator of each term of the least-cost rule from a measure of marginal product to a measure of marginal revenue product gives the expression for the profit-maximizing input combination. The latter expression satisfies the need for determining both the absolute quantities and the proportions of the various inputs that will maximize total profits, since it incorporates measures of each input's productivity (marginal product), revenue contribution, and cost—all of which are essential for input optimization. However, since each input must be used at a rate such that its *MRP = MRC*, then it follows that the input ratios must not only be equal to each other but they must also be equal to 1. In other words, to use each variable input in the profit-maximizing *proportions* and in the profit-maximizing *absolute amounts*, the firm must adjust its input mix to the point where

$$\frac{MRP_{X_a}}{MRC_{X_a}} = \frac{MRP_{X_b}}{MRC_{X_b}} = \frac{MRP_{X_c}}{MRC_{X_c}} = \cdots = \frac{MRP_{X_n}}{MRC_{X_n}} = 1.$$

It should be recognized that (1) changes in an input's marginal productivity, (2) changes in the marginal revenue received from the sale of output, or (3) changes in an input's marginal resource cost will tend to change both the proportions and the absolute amounts of the inputs which a firm will find it most profitable to use.

The aforementioned profit-maximizing rule is applicable to firms operating under any and every type of product and resource market combination. This is necessarily so because, as we have seen, every firm—no matter whether the product and resource market circumstances it faces are perfectly or imperfectly competitive—finds it advantageous to adjust its input rate of a variable resource to the point at which the input's marginal revenue product equals its marginal resource cost.

AN EVALUATION OF THE MARGINAL PRODUCTIVITY APPROACH TO RESOURCE PRICING AND EMPLOYMENT

The discussion in this chapter has so far been chiefly theoretical with little emphasis on actual practice. The principal reason is that something of an abnormal gap exists between theoretical models of the functioning of resource input markets on the one hand and what goes on in the real world on the other hand. This gap has left the economic theories of input pricing, input employment, and income distribution in a very unsettled state, with a host of honest differences prevailing among various authorities.

The problem lies partly with the almost countless number of governmental interferences, market imperfections, and regulatory restraints that over the years have become an integral feature of input markets. A representative sample of some of the most important of these interferences and imperfections include (1) the enactment of minimum wage laws; (2) the exercise of whatever monopoly power unions have to obtain wage increases in excess of productivity gains; (3) restrictive union work rules and featherbedding practices; (4) the long-standing traditions regarding the size of wage differentials between certain types of occupations; (5) job discrimination and wage discrimination based upon race or sex; (6) the educational, apprenticeship, and license-to-practice requirements for entering an occupation; (7) the regulation of monopoly; (8) zoning regulations which preclude the use of land for certain types of activities; (9) the barriers to resource mobility among firms, industries, and geographical areas—at least in the short run; and (10) special treatment of certain inputs (such as professional sports athletes) under the antitrust laws.

The effects which such factors have upon input prices and employment are well worth illustrating. Two examples will be given, both taken from the labor input sector because of their widespread applicability to real-world events; there are two accompanying Applications Capsules demonstrating the economics of real-world resource markets.

THE IMPACT OF MINIMUM WAGE LAWS UPON LABOR MARKETS

Minimum wage legislation is generally aimed at accomplishing three things (1) requiring firms to make wage payments that afford workers a "decent" standard of living; (2) curtailing the practice whereby marginal firms pay substandard wages to a relatively immobile work force, thus keeping production costs low enough to enable them to compete with higher-wage enterprises (this practice is sometimes labeled as "unfair competition"); and (3) increasing the purchasing power of low-income families. For the most part, the firms affected by minimum wage laws are small companies operating on slim profit margins with a nonunion work force and low capital investment per worker.

The higher wages and higher labor costs which minimum wage laws impose upon the affected firms put them under pressure to improve an already precarious cost-price-profit position. When higher minimum wages are legislated, there is a sort of "shock effect" which forces the affected firms to alter their business practices, perhaps radically. Management can improve plant layout and the quality of supervision; laborsaving equipment can be installed; jobs can be redesigned and streamlined so as to cut back on overall labor requirements; inefficient employees can be weeded out; new employee selection standards can be raised; working conditions can be improved so as to reduce labor turnover and increase efficiency and morale; the amount of overtime work offered employees can be cut back; jobs which no longer pay their way can be eliminated entirely; and selling prices can be raised to cover the increased labor costs.

But whatever response set each affected firm elects, one important outcome is almost certain to emerge: The opportunities for employment in the affected occupations will be less than otherwise. The minimum wage law will

The purpose of minimum wage legislation is to provide workers on the bottom of the wage and income scale with a better standard of living and to restrict firms from competing "unfairly" on the basis of "substandard" wages.

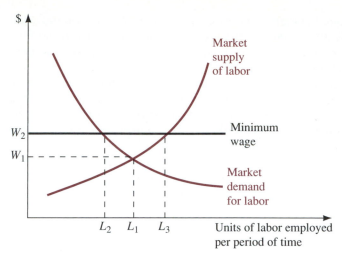

Figure 17-12
Employment effect of a minimum wage law

PRINCIPLE
Minimum wage laws reduce employment opportunities in the affected firms and occupations.

peg the supply price for such labor above the level which would be determined by the forces of market demand and supply for such labor—otherwise the minimum wage has no *raison d'être*. The outcome of a higher-than-equilibrium input supply price is a reduced optimum employment rate, as depicted in Figure 17-12.[24] If the minimum wage is set at W_2 dollars, given the market demand and supply curves for labor of a particular type, then firms will adjust their employment rate downward from L_1 to L_2 units per period of time, and L_2L_3 units of labor will be involuntarily unemployed. The reduction in employment takes the form of dismissal of the least efficient employees, the closing down of marginal firms, cutbacks in the average number of hours worked per employee, or reductions in the number of new job opportunities in the affected occupations. Studies indicate that the groups hit hardest by the lower employment rates tend to be teenagers, blacks, and persons lacking in skills and training.

Hence, *the economic effect of minimum wage laws upon resource pricing and employment is (1) to push wage rates for the lowest-paid occupations up above the equilibrium rates that would prevail in their absence and (2) to suppress employment rates in the affected occupations.* On the other hand, many workers can benefit from a higher minimum wage, owing to the progress made in achieving the three aforementioned objectives of such legislation.[25]

[24] Empirical studies of this phenomenon are numerous. See, for instance, *Studies of the Economic Effects of the $1 Minimum Wage: Effects in Selected Low Wage Industries and Localities,* Wage and Hour and Public Contracts Divisions, U.S. Department of Labor, January 1959; H. M. Douty, "Some Effects of the $1.00 Minimum Wage in the United States," *Economica,* Vol. 27, No. 106 (May 1960), pp. 137–47; N. Arnold Tolles, "American Minimum Wage Laws: Their Purposes and Results," *Proceedings of the Twelfth Annual Meeting of the Industrial Relations Research Association* (Madison, Wis.: Industrial Relations Research Association, 1960), pp. 116–33; Neil W. Chamberlain, *The Labor Sector* (New York: McGraw-Hill, 1965), pp. 529–33; Finis Welch and Marvin Kosters, "The Effects of Minimum Wages on the Distribution of Changes in Aggregate Employment," *American Economic Review,* Vol. 62, No. 3 (June 1972), pp. 323–32; and Finis Welch, "Minimum Wage Legislation in the United States," *Economic Inquiry,* Vol. 12, No. 3 (September 1974), pp. 285–318.

[25] When the demand for labor is *inelastic,* a rise in the minimum wage may lessen employment opportunities, but the total income of those who remain employed will definitely be greater than before. However, when the demand for labor is *elastic,* increases in the minimum wage will reduce both employment and the total income accruing to those who remain employed. Hence, only when labor demand is relatively inelastic do increases in the minimum wage have their most beneficial impact.

Inefficient firms are also forced to bring their operations up to par or else face the penalty of lower profits or even losses. For our purposes, the major point to be noted about minimum wage legislation is that it *artificially* causes the supply prices of low-skill, low-productivity types of labor to be higher than they would be if the forces of market demand and market supply were allowed to function freely. In this sense, governmental policy toward minimum wage rates, as well as labor's marginal productivity, are major factors in determining wages, employment, and income in the affected occupational categories.

It is also worth noting that minimum wage laws can affect wage rates in occupations where the pay scale is higher than the minimum wage. A higher minimum wage allows unions to press for further wage increases through collective bargaining. The unions' philosophy is that while they will use their bargaining power to become wage leaders, upward adjustments in the federal minimum rates provide them with a new platform from which they can launch demands for still higher union wages on the grounds of maintaining historical wage differentials.

UNION IMPACTS ON LABOR MARKETS

In many countries trade unions are an integral and accepted part of the functioning of labor markets, especially in the manufacturing sector. In the United States, nearly 85% of the workers in plants employing 100 workers or more are unionized; union membership totals approximately 17 million persons; and the wage settlements reached in certain key industries often spill over to other sectors of the economy. Thus, unions have a major impact upon labor markets; their presence does make a difference. The added power workers gain by union organization creates a very strong presumption that the resulting wage and employment rates will be different from what they would have been had workers remained unorganized. Consequently, any analysis of wage rates and employment which ignores the impact of collective bargaining is suspect in its ability to explain and to predict the behavior of real-world labor markets.

Incorporating union behavior into the analysis of labor markets first requires some notion of the economic goals of unions. Casual observation suggests that unions pursue some satisfactory, and perhaps quite complex, balance of increased wages and incomes, increased leisure, and an adequate number of job opportunities for current and potential union members. However, depending on their own unique circumstances, different unions may place differing emphases and priorities on these goals; collective bargaining is by no means a uniform process whereby each union consistently pursues the same goals with the same intensity.

THE WAGE-EMPLOYMENT PREFERENCE PATH

A union's preferred tradeoff between wages and employment can be viewed graphically. Suppose collective negotiations between a firm and a union result in the establishment of an average wage of W_1 dollars and an equilibrium employment rate of L_1 units of labor per period of time, as shown in Figure 17-13(a). Now consider the combination of wage and employment rates which the union would prefer and which it will attempt to attain in its negotiations with the firm. If the firm's product demand should shift in such a manner that its demand for labor input shifts from D_{L_1} to D_{L_2}, the union's preference is generally for substantial wage increases, say from W_1 to W_2 (which may, incidentally,

When the demand for labor increases, a union's typical preference is for higher wages first and increased employment second; when the demand for labor decreases, the preference is for employment reductions first and wage concessions second (usually only in extreme circumstances).

APPLICATIONS CAPSULE

HOW THE MINIMUM WAGE DESTROYS JOBS: *FORTUNE'S* INTERVIEW WITH J. WILLARD MARRIOTT, JR.

Over the last forty years, six different Administrations have tried to improve the lot of the workingman by raising the minimum wage. The most ambitious of these efforts was a bill signed by President Carter in 1977 that advances the minimum, through annual step-ups, to a level of $3.35 by January, 1981—an increase totaling nearly 46 percent. Recently, however, the Administration has been paying some attention to the majority view among economists, which is that the minimum wage worsens inflation and destroys jobs.

With this issue back on the public agenda, FORTUNE'S Aimée Morner paid a call recently on J. Willard Marriott, Jr. As president and chief executive of a hotel and restaurant chain that pays the minimum wage to some 20,000 employees, he has learned a lot about the effects of this well-meaning social legislation on the real world of jobs and prices.

Q. With two successive jumps in the minimum wage, from $2.30 an hour in 1977 to $2.90 last January 1, what's happened at Marriott?

A. Several months before Congress passed the legislation, we felt it was imminent, so we got ready to combat the effect it would have on our costs. We first set up what I would call productivity specialists, who analyzed primarily how managers in each Marriott unit were utilizing and scheduling labor. Then we organized teams to find ways to reduce the number of man-hours, and the amount of work being done, in order to become more productive—to serve the same number of customers in fewer labor hours, and in some cases with fewer people.

Unlike many other restaurant chains, we did not open our restaurants later, or close them earlier. However, in some cases we closed parts of a restaurant, opening one dining room instead of two. For years we have been shifting to self-service salad bars in our Dinner Houses and other restaurants to cut down the number of waitress hours, and we accelerated that shift.

We achieved what I think are good, though not dramatic, results. Overall, we eliminated more than two million man-hours, or about 5 percent of the total. It's very difficult for me to be too precise, because of the growth in our business, and the change in its mix. But we stopped hiring at many locations, and so cut our work force by 2 to 3 percent.

Q. So the increase in the minimum wage wiped out perhaps 1,500 jobs at Marriott?

A. Yes. And though we got a slight increase in productivity, it was not enough to make up for our higher costs. Wages rose by 15 percent in 1978 for employees at the minimum level, and our food costs went up, too. We estimate that we got back less than half of these added costs from gains in productivity, so we had to increase prices in some restaurants by as much as 10 percent.

Unfortunately, as we raise prices, we often lose customers; it's axiomatic. Throughout the restaurant industry,

customer counts have not been as strong during the last twelve months as before, and in many of our restaurants customer counts have been down slightly. And as we serve fewer customers, we lay off more people; it becomes cyclical. The National Restaurant Association recently surveyed 2,000 of its members and found that after the minimum wage was increased on January 1, 1978, 95 percent of them raised prices, 78 percent reduced man-hours, 63 percent laid off people, and more than half bought equipment that would help them reduce their labor force. But it's hard to automate restaurants and hotels—they haven't invented a machine yet that makes beds.

Q. Who gets hit the hardest when the minimum goes up?

A. What's happening as it keeps rising is that more people such as wives are coming into the work force, replacing teenagers. Restaurant owners screen people better, and by and large hire more mature, more productive people at the higher rates.

Q. Of course, that is to your advantage.

A. True, but as we pay those higher rates, we in turn have to raise our prices, and nobody wants to do that. Given the option, I would prefer to hire people at a more reasonable wage and train them.

Q. Economists now agree that increases in the minimum wage reduce employment, mostly among minorities and teenagers, and yet they have little empirical evidence to prove their theory. Do you have any definitive proof that the phenomenon occurs?

A. I can give you a concrete example. We used to have about twenty restaurants in the District of Columbia which has traditionally had one of the highest minimum-wage levels in the U.S.—until recently even higher than the federal minimum. The cost of wages is our highest cost of doing business. And during the last three or four years, as the minimum wage increased in Washington, our wage situation became so acute that we had to close fourteen restaurants and terminate 1,300 people, about a third of whom were minority youths.

When we close restaurants located in a center city, the minorities who lose their jobs often are unable to find other work nearby, or in the suburbs. The few jobs that are available in the suburbs go to the most productive workers, and in most cases these minority youths are just not as experienced as other workers. It's a terrible social problem.

What happens if 37 percent of the minority youths in this country reach age twenty and have never worked and are on the government dole? There is already a tremendous number of these people enrolled in government make-work programs. In fact, it's estimated that the government's bill for programs like CETA—the Comprehensive Employment and Training Act—will increase by $135 million this year because the minimum wage rose to $2.90. The government doesn't want to be in the business of hiring people and training people—it wants business to do that. But it's not economic for business to do that as long as the minimum wage keeps going up.

Q. The minimum wage for employees who work for tips stood at $1.33 last year, and rose to $1.60 on January 1. How will that increase of 20 percent affect operations at Marriott?

A. The tip credit, as it is called, is a serious concern of ours. This year it is being reduced for the first time, from 50 percent of the minimum wage, to 45 percent. That is, employees who get tips must be paid 55 percent of the regular minimum wage. Most tipped employees earn between three and five times their base wage as tips. So a 20 percent increase in their hourly base pay, or $2.16 a day, is peanuts compared with their earnings from tips, which can run more than $50 a day. But an increase of 27 cents an hour in the base wage is very costly to the employer. It's going to change the way the restaurant business is run, and eliminate many minimum-wage jobs.

There will be less specialization. In the past, a waitress only waited on tables. Today she makes fountain items, cuts pie, and clears tables. That reduces the need for fountain boys and busboys. As the minimum wage continues to rise, there will be more self-service, which will cut down the number of waitresses needed, too. We have to continue to improve efficiency, but I don't know how much more creative we can be without hurting the service.

Q. Does a higher minimum kick up wages all along the line of Marriott?

A. Yes. On January 1, 1978, the minimum wage rose by 15.2 percent, to $2.65. At Marriott, many workers at the next higher level got an automatic 10 percent increase, and the next higher level, an 8 percent increase. A person in our Houston hotel earning $3, for example, got a raise to $3.25; a person making $2.60 got a raise to $2.85. The reason is very simple: if you've had a person working for you for a year or so, doing a good job, and making $2.75 an hour in 1978, and you hire a youngster off the street at $2.65 an hour, you've got an inequitable situation. That longer-term employee will come to you and say he's worth more than that kid is, and wants an increase in pay. We tell him we can't give him 15.2 percent, but we recognize the inequitable situation, and so we'll give him 10 percent. And of course, our costs for Social Security and benefits rise because of the higher wages paid.

Q. Union leaders, notably George Meany, argue that as the minimum wage is increased the lowest-paid workers will have more money to spend, and so the entire economy benefits. Do you agree?

A. That's just a superficial argument. The labor unions want the minimum wage to increase because that gives

them a better floor from which to bargain for higher wages for their members. Most of our workers are not unionized, but we know that the higher the minimum wage is, the greater the ripple effect—and the same thing occurs among unionized workers.

You must consider the fact that people who earn the minimum wage do not take home as much money after each increase, because they work fewer hours. Very few of our employees are putting in forty hours a week, though they may have done so two years ago; most of them work about thirty hours a week. We now schedule our workers so that we don't pay overtime, and neither do most companies in our industry.

Q. Then who benefits from an increase in the minimum wage?

A. I think everybody loses. Employees lose because their hours are shortened, so they take home fewer dollars. And at the same time, the minimum wage is inflationary, and inflation hits each worker in the pocketbook. People coming into the labor force lose because there is a strong tendency on the part of employers to hire more productive workers instead. And in a downturn in the economy, the less productive workers are the first to be put out of their jobs and onto welfare. In the end, the minimum wage practically wrecks the people it is supposed to help.

Q. So you would agree with Finis Welch, an economist at U.C.L.A., that the time for a mandated minimum wage has passed?

A. I think there needs to be a maintenance-level minimum wage to protect people from unscrupulous employers, of which there are probably some throughout the country. But a federal minimum wage at any level fails to take into account the characteristics of different regions. In many southern cities, we could probably hire quite a few people for $2.30 an hour, but we have to pay $2.90 an hour because somebody in Washington tells us to, and so we hire fewer workers.

I think a minimum-wage level should be set by each state, instead of by the federal government, and it should be based on a fair wage for each geographical area. Some forty-one states have a minimum wage, but in most cases it applies only if it is higher than the federal level. Only Alaska and Connecticut now have a higher minimum than the federal minimum. So, let each state determine its own minimum wage—or roll back the federal minimum to a level, say $2.30, that would not prevent people from coming into the work force.

Source: Reprinted from the January 29, 1979 issue of *Fortune* magazine by special permission; © Time, Inc.

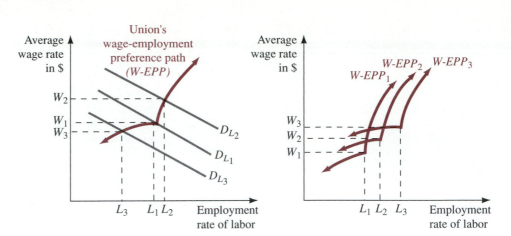

Figure 17-13
Wage-employment preference path of a typical union

be in the form of overtime wages), and modest increases in the number of persons employed, say from L_1 to L_2. This reflects the usual union attitude that its first responsibility is to the existing membership and that it is obliged to win them higher wages whenever the opportunity presents. Hence, the union's preference path is a steeply rising curve above the initial wage-employment combination.[26] However, the stronger the rise in the firm's demand for labor, the more the union is ordinarily willing to temper its wage demands in return for increases in employment (and gains in union membership). For this reason the portion of the union's preferred wage-employment path above the prevailing wage-employment combination is shown as rising at a decreasing rate.

If recessionary business conditions should shift the firm's demand for labor input downward, say from D_{L_1} to D_{L_2}, the union usually exhibits a strong preference for larger cutbacks in employment (say from L_1 to L_3) relative to wages (which might be reduced from W_1 to W_3). The reasoning behind such a preference is that wage reductions weaken the ability of the union to win wage gains in future bargaining sessions, whereas temporary layoffs are self-correcting as soon as business conditions pick up again. Hence, the lower section of the wage-employment preference path falls slowly and at a rate commensurate with employment reductions that are more than proportional to the wage reductions.[27] The union's wage-employment preferences therefore tend to produce a curvilinear pattern, kinked at the current wage-employment position. As new wage negotiations are consummated, the curve shifts to a new position, and a kink appears at the newly instituted wage-employment combination, as depicted in Figure 17-13(b).

In viewing the union's wage-employment preferences, care must be taken not to view employment as referring solely to the number of workers

---

[26] An exception to this general case arises in instances where large numbers of union members are unemployed at the prevailing wage-employment combination. Here the union will probably pursue a policy of getting the unemployed members back to work before seeking major wage advances.

[27] However, the preferred wage-employment path may fall off to the left more sharply if the wages the firm is paying are so high that its long-term competitive position is severely threatened by rival firms paying lower wages or if significant employment cutbacks have been recently imposed and many union members are already laid off. In such instances a union often is more amenable to cutting wages and maintaining employment, in which case the lower section of the curve reflects a preference for relatively larger wage cuts and relatively smaller employment cuts.

employed. A firm's employment *rate* (L) is composed of n number of workers working h number of hours per period of time. Thus, *a reduction in the union's preferred employment rate may reflect preferences for cutbacks in the number of workers or in the number of hours worked by each worker or both.* Similarly, increases in the union's preferred employment rate may mean more workers *or* more hours worked by each worker *or* both. By observing the composition of the employment rate the union bargains for over a period of time, it is possible to infer what the union's preference is toward greater membership versus more leisure time for the rank and file. Therefore, the union's wage-employment preference curve is indicative not only of the union's wage (and income) goal and its employment (and membership) goal but also of its leisure-time goal.[28]

To the extent that unions are successful in imposing their wage-employment preferences upon firms, we have at least a partial explanation of why wages rise at above average rates in periods of strong business expansion, yet employment gains are modest, and why wage cuts are usually agreed to only when a union confronts severe layoffs, permanent employment reductions, plant closings, or employer bankruptcy.

> The wage-employment preferences of unions help account for why union wages rise at above-average rates and union employment gains are modest when the economy is strong, and why unions staunchly oppose making any wage concessions except in dire circumstances.

THE EFFECTS OF UNIONS ON A FIRM'S USE OF LABOR

From a supply standpoint the effect of union-negotiated wage rates is to make the firm's supply curve for union labor horizontal (or perfectly elastic) at the agreed-to wage scale, at least until the supply of labor runs out at these wage rates. This is illustrated in Figure 17-14, where the firm's supply curve for labor in a nonunion (though still imperfectly competitive) labor market is S_L, the corresponding marginal resource cost curve for labor is MRC_L, and the firm's demand for labor is D_L, the last reflecting the firm's marginal revenue product of labor in an imperfectly competitive product market. The intersection of MRC_L and MRP_L determine the equilibrium wage and employment rates for the firm—W_1 and L_1, respectively.

But if a union organizes the firm's employees and uses its bargaining power to push the effective average wage rate to W_2, the firm's supply curve for labor becomes the kinked line W_2CAS_L, which is horizontal over the range W_2CA. Observe the effect this has upon the unionized firm's optimum employment rate. Since the unionized firm's labor supply curve is the line W_2CAS_L, the firm's marginal resource cost curve for labor becomes $W_2CABMRC_L$. A new intersection of MRC_L and MRP_L occurs at point C, giving an equilibrium employment rate of L_2 units. Thus, not only can the union benefit its members by increasing wages, but it can also increase employment rates because of the effect that contract wage rates have upon the shape of the firm's labor supply curve. Actually, the union can push the average wage rate all the way up to W_3 before the firm finds it advantageous to reduce its labor employment rate below the preunionization rate of L_1 units. Thus, we have the rather surprising conclu-

---

[28] Unions historically have shown a keen interest in shortening the standard workday and workweek. During periods of depressed business conditions, shorter working hours are a means of sharing the available work among greater numbers of people. During periods of prosperity, the shorter workweek is a means of raising wage rates by instituting time-and-a-half overtime rates after fewer hours worked. On occasion, unions may find it easier to persuade firms to pay workers the same total income but allow them to work fewer hours to earn it (which is equivalent to raising the average wage rate) than to persuade them to pay workers a higher wage rate for working the same number of hours as before. The former does not raise the firm's labor costs provided the same amount of work can be accomplished in the fewer working hours, whereas the latter is sure to increase the firm's total wage bill.

APPLICATIONS CAPSULE

CARTELS, UNION ACTIVITY, AND ECONOMIC RENTS IN PROFESSIONAL FOOTBALL

The unique organization of the labor market in professional sports, especially the National Football League (NFL), provides an interesting case study of the operation of resource markets. The buyers of the services of skilled athletes are team owners, who are the chief executive officers of the firms in the industry. An important characteristic of this market is that the owners coordinate their behavior through a resource-market buying cartel. In contrast, the sellers of resources, who are players, have organized an NFL Players Association, which in essence functions like a union. Historically, the NFL owners have operated under a provision of the antitrust statutes that has been interpreted as providing their organization with an exemption from prosecution under the Sherman Act. The cartel avoids competition that could raise the price of skilled athletes by adhering to a set of rules that govern how the market works. Among other restrictions the owners "draft" players and sign them to a contract containing a reserve clause that binds the player to a single team. In this market a player who is not subject to a reserve clause is referred to as a "free agent," meaning that different firms can bid for the players' services. The effect of the restrictions on free agency is to limit the players' employment alternatives within professional football and make it possible for the owners to pay less than they would have to pay in a fully competitive environment. In essence, the owners use the cartel to extract some of the players' economic rents by restricting competition among teams. From the players' perspective, professional football is a business that provides a livelihood, and they rationally wish to obtain the full value for their professional services. They also want the economic rents created in the professional football market. Thus, the conflict between owners and players, which periodically erupts when its time to renew the union contract, can be viewed as a contest over the division of economic rents. When market participants aggressively seek out economic rents, economists refer to the resulting type of market conduct as rent-seeking behavior.

The NFL Player's Association (NFLPA) and the NFL Management Council (NFLMC) occupy strategic positions in the competition for the economic rents, and the issue of free agency is the focal point of much of the strategic maneuvering. It might seem that every player would rationally prefer unrestricted free agency and an end to the cartel, but that is not necessarily the case. It may be that in a strictly competitive environment the bulk of the rents would be captured by a small minority of star and superstar players. If this is

in fact the case, a large majority of the players could be made worse off by unrestricted free agency. Unlike the NFL, Major League Baseball has moved very close to unrestricted free agency. Baseball still uses a draft, but the standard contract no longer contains a reserve clause. But the contract does allow a team to match other offers and retain the services of a player once the current contract has expired. Consider the data for baseball and football salaries shown in Table 17-4. The data are based upon individual salaries, which are organized into deciles and are ordered from the lowest to the highest. Factors other than free agency no doubt influence earnings distributions in professional sports,[a] but comparisons of football and baseball offer insights into the impact of free agency on earnings distributions and have implications for rent-seeking behavior. The data in Table 17-4 are for 1987, at which time unrestricted free agency had prevailed in baseball for a number of years, while football was characterized by a complete absence of free agency. The median player is represented by the fifth decile, shown in bold in Table 17-4. The median wage in

TABLE 17-4   MAXIMUM EARNINGS IN 1987 OF PROFESSIONAL FOOTBALL AND BASEBALL PLAYERS, BY DECILES

| Decile | Earnings | |
	Football	Baseball
1	82,000	62,500
2	110,000	77,500
3	140,000	105,000
4	165,000	160,000
5	**200,000**	**260,000**
6	225,000	375,000
7	260,000	547,000
8	300,000	749,618
9	400,000	925,000
10	900,000	2,412,500
Average	$226,937	$ 415,206

Note: The earnings are ordered from the lowest to highest. The maximum earnings in a decile are the earnings of the top person in that decile.

Because union-negotiated wage rates make the firm's labor supply curve horizontal, a union may be able to increase employment for union members as well as their wages.

sion that *a union may initially have the effect of increasing both a firm's average wage rate and its employment rate, provided it does not insist upon pushing the wage rate up too far.* This indeed constitutes a powerful argument in favor of unions—at least from the standpoint of union members.

Referring again to Figure 17-14, suppose that the union bargains for and gets wage increases that push the average wage about W_3, thereby making

1987 at the fifth decile was $200,000 for football and $260,000 for baseball. The highest-paid players have large earnings in both sports, but in baseball the stars and superstars have mega-earnings. Note that earnings in football exceeded those in baseball for the bottom four deciles players, but baseball earnings were larger in deciles 5 through 10. In the top 30% of the distributions (deciles 8–10), baseball earnings far exceed those in football in 1987.

There is evidence that in the 1970s and early 1980s the NFLMC and NFLPA struck an implicit bargain to share in the rents captured from the most talented players, with the owners retaining some of the rents and passing a portion of the rents along to lower-paid players by raising minimum salaries.[b] As explained later, this type of behavior continued into the late 1980s. The effect of such self-interested redistribution by NFLMC and NFLPA is to reduce both the average wage and the variance of earnings in professional football. Economic research into the operation of the professional football market suggests that the impact on the earnings of the median player may be particularly important in garnering support for changes in the way the market works. Majority support for free agency among players hinges on whether the median player in terms of earning perceives that he is treated fairly and will gain from any changes in the way the football market operates. The data in Table 17-4 suggest that in the absence of risk, and assuming NFL players expect that a wage structure under free agency in football will approximate the one prevailing in baseball, the median player (and higher-paid players) would support free agency. But if you introduce risk into consideration, it is not clear that the median player would support it. Certainly, the lowest-paid players would likely oppose free agency and the higher-paid players would support it. But majority support is unclear.

In an important market development in 1989, the NFLMC imposed a limited form of free agency that is restricted to certain players. The new policy, known as Proposal B, was interpreted in the popular press to have been adopted unilaterally by the owners as a defensive measure in response to a private antitrust suit filed by the NFLPA following the disastrous strike in the 1988 season. While it is not possible to know for certain what specific strategy the NFLMC had in mind in adopting new rules, it is possible that there were other objectives of Plan B. The new rules allow each team to protect 37 players on their current roster, with unprotected players having limited rights to freely negotiate with any other team

for their services. Thus, "protected players" continue in their pre-1989 status, while unprotected players are free agents for a restricted period of time. Which players will the owners protect? Owners, like other rational economic decision makers, want to obtain the biggest bang for their bucks. Therefore, owners will weigh the expected benefits and costs of protecting each player and protect those with the greatest expected marginal revenue product per dollar of cost incurred in retaining them on the roster. If owners behave in this fashion, as they almost certainly do, Proposal B promotes the economic interests of the owners as well as the least skilled and marginal players. It is these players that go unprotected, and evidence from the post-Plan B era indicates that they have received very sizable increases in earnings as a result of competition for their services. Thus, the intent of the NFL management council in adopting Proposal B may well have been to drive a further wedge between the rent-seeking players by giving the relatively low-paid players a bigger share of the rents, thereby enlisting them in opposition to unrestricted free agency. If a referendum on free agency were held, a majority of players might well vote for Proposal B and against unrestricted free agency. The owners' motives in adopting Proposal B are, of course, not known. But Proposal B clearly has the effect of further dividing the players along income lines and contributing to a continuation of the process of extracting rents from superior players and sharing them with lower-paid players.

---

[a] The production function in baseball appears to be more nearly additively separable than in football, which may cause the earnings distributions to differ. Baseball may also invest more in the development of players' skills, causing the earnings functions to differ. Owner sharing of TV revenues and differences on the demand side of the market could also cause the earnings function to differ.

[b] This issue is discussed in Michael White's article "Self-Interest Redistribution and the National Football League Players Association," *Economic Inquiry*, Vol. 23, No. 4 (October 1986), pp. 669–80, and in John A. Bishop, J. Howard Finch, and John P. Formby's article "Risk Aversion and Rent-Seeking Redistributions: Free Agency in the National Football League," *Southern Economic Journal*, Vol. 57, No. 1 (July 1990) pp. 114–24. Also see Frank Scott Jr., James Long, and Ken Somppi, "Free Agency, Owner Incentives, and the National Football League Players Association," *Journal of Labor Research*, Vol. 3, No. 3 (Summer 1983), pp. 257–64.

Source: Based in part on John A. Bishop, J. Howard Finch, and John P. Formby's article "Risk Aversion and Rent-Seeking Redistributions: Free Agency in the National Football League," *Southern Economic Journal*, Vol. 57, No. 1 (July 1990), pp. 114–24.

it advantageous for the firm to cut its employment rate below L_1. Further suppose that the union views this cutback as undesirable. The union can then use its bargaining power to preclude the firm from so reducing labor employment. A major aspect of collective negotiations between unions and managements concerns working conditions and, in particular, such matters as the content of jobs, how certain operations are to be performed, the size of work

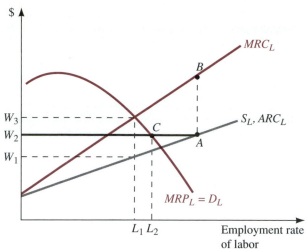

Figure 17-14

Effect of union-negotiated wage rates upon a firm's labor input decision

crews, the quantity of work which can be expected, safety rules, the length of paid vacations, the number of paid holidays, seniority provisions, guaranteed annual wages, and supplemental unemployment benefits. In other words, there is a *work and effort bargain* in the contract, just as there is a wage bargain. A principal effect of the provisions relating to the work and effort bargain is to give unions a measure of influence over the firm's employment rate, either directly or indirectly—at least in the short run.

Experience indicates that unions use these provisions to "make work" and to keep the number of persons employed in specific jobs, firms, and industries higher than managements might otherwise maintain. The notorious instances of feather-bedding in the railroad industry and the output quotas in the construction industry are classic cases in point. Consequently, in a unionized firm the mere fact that labor's *MRC* exceeds its *MRP* is no guarantee that the firm will adjust its input of labor downward. The discretionary action of the firm's managers in regard to the labor input decision is heavily constrained by the provisions of its collective bargaining contract. Because of this, managers of unionized firms find strict adherence to the *MRC = MRP* rule a practical impossibility; work schedules, job assignments, and work loads can be altered only within limits. To some extent, therefore, the marginal productivity approach to input pricing and input employment is impeded, if not replaced, by the institutional mechanism of collective bargaining insofar as unionized firms are concerned. However, since most managements retain authority over the capital-labor input mix in building new production facilities, the power of unions to influence employment rates in the long run is somewhat less; and some companies try to escape high labor costs by relocating plants to foreign countries where wages are much lower.

Unions can use their power over a firm's labor supply to influence the amount of labor the firm employs as well as the wages it pays.

THE EFFECTS OF UNIONS ON ECONOMYWIDE WAGE RATES AND EMPLOYMENT RATES

Few economists would deny that unions in certain firms and industries have won favorable wage and benefit packages for their members. But whether unions have pushed wages up faster than they would have risen anyway is hard to say since it involves trying to compare what has actually happened with what might have happened under another set of circumstances. There simply is no way of knowing for sure what the relative wages of various industries would be if all industries were nonunion; any estimates to this effect are little better than educated conjectures.[29] Even so, it seems fair to say that unions are in a good position to win "above-average" wage gains on a consistent basis when (1) the percentage of unionized firms in the industry is high and it is difficult for nonunion firms to enter; (2) bargaining is on an industrywide basis so that all firms in the industry are equally affected; (3) industry and firm profits are high enough that the firms can "afford" substantial wage increases without endangering their competitive position; (4) the industry is a strategic one such that work stoppages have serious economywide implications; and (5) the union controls entry to the trade via apprenticeship and other regulations.

In most occupational categories where there are unions, wage rates in unionized firms exceed those in nonunion enterprises—even after allowing for differences in regional location, size of firm, size of community, and type of pay system (incentive wages or hourly wages). Moreover, it is in oligopolistic manufacturing industries where unions are strongest and where newly negotiated collective bargaining pacts often set the pattern of wage changes for blue-collar workers throughout the economy. In manufacturing, large-scale firms have proven easier to organize than small companies mainly because some of the five aforementioned conditions appear more frequently than in industries where small enterprises are prevalent.

Common sense suggests that unions have succeeded in using their monopoly power over firms' labor supplies to obtain higher wages for their members than they would otherwise have received; however, it is hard to prove that this is actually the case.

KEY POINTS

The marginal productivity approach to input pricing and input usage is an attempt to analyze the principles governing a firm's input decision and to explain the functioning of the markets for resource inputs. Three basic models of input pricing and employment stand out: (1) the model of perfect competition in both product and resource markets, (2) the model of imperfect competition in the product market and perfect competition in the resource market, and (3) the model of imperfect competition in both product and resource markets. In all three models, one theme underlies the firm's input decision: *To maximize profits a firm should adjust the usage of each input to the point where the added revenue it receives from using the last unit of the input equals the added costs associated with employing the input.* A firm's usage of an input depends on what the input is worth to the firm relative to the costs of using it. This principle holds irrespective of the type of market circumstances in which the firm's product is sold or in which the input is purchased. It is from the *MRP = MRC* rule that input prices and input employment rates are ultimately determined and the incomes accruing to resource owners are ultimately derived.

As a first approximation to the functioning of input markets, the demand and supply analyses of the three marginal productivity models are relatively sound. However, there exist numerous imperfections in and barriers to the free interplay of market forces. Collective bargaining, minimum wage laws,

[29] Comparisons of wage movements between union and nonunion firms and industries are not really very satisfactory because of the differences which exist in geographical location, sizes and types of firms, competitive pressures, technological processes, the proportion of labor costs to total costs, productivity changes, and so on. These factors, as well as the presence or absence of a union, affect wage movements and parceling out their separate effects presents almost insurmountable statistical difficulties.

and resource immobility, to mention only the more important, impede the attainment of free market equilibrium and cause outcomes which may deviate from the equilibrium position suggested by marginal productivity analysis.

PROBLEMS AND QUESTIONS FOR DISCUSSION

1. **(a)** Explain the difference between marginal revenue and marginal revenue product.
   (b) Explain the difference between marginal cost and marginal resource cost.
   (c) What is the relationship between an input's *SVMP* and its *MRP* when the output is sold under conditions of perfect competition? Under conditions of imperfect competition?

2. Complete the following table:

Units of Variable Input X	Quantity of Output	MP_X	Product Price	TR	MRP_X	Supply Price of X	MRC_X
0	0	___	$5	___		$50	
1	20	___	5	___	___	50	___
2	44	___	5	___	___	50	___
3	64	___	5	___	___	50	___
4	80	___	5	___	___	50	___
5	92	___	5	___	___	50	___
6	100	___	5	___	___	50	___
7	104	___	5	___	___	50	___

   (a) Do the figures in the table suggest a perfectly or imperfectly competitive product market? Why? Do the figures indicate a perfectly or imperfectly competitive input market? Why?
   (b) What is the profit-maximizing input of X?

3. Suppose that a firm employs only one variable input (X) and that the equation expressing the firm's marginal revenue product function for X is $MRP_X = 60 + 4X - X^2$. Suppose the firm's supply price for input X is fixed at $28 per unit. What is the firm's profit-maximizing input rate of X?

4. Complete the following table showing production, cost, and revenue data for a firm having only one variable input:

Units of Variable Input X	Quantity of Output	MP_X	Product Price	TR	"Average" MR	MRP_X	Supply Price of X	TVC	MRC_X
0	0	___	$25	___			$400	___	
1	50	___	24	___	___	___	420	___	___
2	110	___	23	___	___	___	440	___	___
3	160	___	22	___	___	___	460	___	___
4	200	___	21	___	___	___	480	___	___
5	230	___	20	___	___	___	500	___	___
6	250	___	19	___	___	___	520	___	___
7	260	___	18	___	___	___	540	___	___

(a) What type of product and resource markets are indicated by the figures in the table?

(b) What is the profit-maximizing input rate of X?

5. The Alpha-Omega Corporation uses only one variable input in its production process—input X. Studies of the firm's revenue data indicate the following relationship between *TR* and the input rate of X: $TR = 144 + 70X - X^2$. Studies also indicate that the input supply curve for X that confronts Alpha-Omega may be expressed by the equation $P_X = 13 + 0.5X$. Determine the profit-maximizing input rate for X.

6. Given the following data for labor input, product prices, and wage rates:

Number of Workers of a Given Skill and Training	"Average" MP_L	Product Price	Daily Wage $(P_L = ARC_L)$
0	—	$2	—
10	18	2	$12
20	17	2	14
30	16	2	16
40	15	2	18
50	14	2	20
60	13	2	22
70	12	2	24
80	11	2	26

(a) Determine the profit-maximizing employment rate of labor and the equilibrium daily wage for a firm faced with the preceding schedules.

(b) Suppose a minimum daily wage of $24 is imposed upon the firm. Determine the profit-maximizing employment rate of labor.

(c) How do you reconcile the differences, if any, in your answers to parts (a) and (b)? Explain fully.

7. Consider the following two statements:

"An increase in the demand for an input raises its price."
"An increase in an input's price reduces demand for the input."

How can this pair of statements be reconciled? Does it make any difference in your answer whether perfect or imperfect competition characterizes the input market? The product market?

8. It has sometimes been advocated that firms should reward inputs according to their respective marginal products. That is, if the last unit of an input has a marginal product of 10 units and if these 10 units have a market value of $50, then the input is entitled to a monetary reward of $50. Any payment less than $50 entails "exploitation" of the input. What validity, if any, do you see in this position?

9. Suppose that input X is the only variable input which a firm uses to produce product A. The firm sells product A under conditions of imperfect competition and buys input X under conditions of imperfect competition. What effect would you expect each of the following to have upon the firm's usage of input X? Be sure to distinguish between a movement along the firm's demand curve for X and a shift in the location of the demand curve. If any uncertainty exists as to the impact upon the usage of X, then specify the causes of the uncertainty.

(a) An increase in the demand for product A.

(b) The appearance of a new and very good substitute for product A.

(c) A technological improvement in the capital equipment which input X works with in producing product A.

(d) An increase in the supply of input X.

10. Average wage rates in the United States are higher than in most foreign countries. Business executives in the United States often lament that this puts their firms at a severe cost disadvantage in competing with foreign firms. Unions reply that U.S.

workers are generally healthier and better trained than workers in foreign nations and, further, that U.S. workers generally have more and better capital equipment with which to work. These factors, the unions claim, offset the wage rate differential.

(a) Explain the rationale of the union argument in terms of marginal productivity analysis.

(b) In recent years, Japan and several Western European nations have greatly closed the gap in worker productivity by raising the living standards of their population and by adopting the very latest production technologies. What implications does this have for the ability of U.S. firms to continue to pay higher wages and still compete in world markets?

(c) Would you expect that some U.S. firms paying higher wages and incurring greater labor costs than key foreign competitors might eventually be forced to negotiate *lower* wage and fringe benefit packages with unions in order to remain cost competitive? What posture would you expect union officials to take with regard to wage reduction proposals? What sort of wage-employment preference path would you expect unions to have in these situations?

11. In what ways is the concept of an *economic rent* similar to the concept of *consumer surplus*? In what ways are the concepts different? Why and how could a firm extract consumer surplus from its customers? Why and how could a firm extract economic rents from its suppliers? What factors limit the ability of firms to extract consumer surplus and economic rents?

Chapter 18

General Equilibrium:
CONCEPTS AND ANALYSIS

Economists have long recognized that to say anything concrete about economic affairs and the relationship among economic variables, it is necessary to ignore a great deal. One approach to microeconomics is to explain, understand, and predict the behavior of firms, consumers, and resource owners by developing and using relatively simple models that abstract from many of the complexities of the real economy. This first approach ignores many of the feedback effects of one sector of the economy on another. But to be completely accurate, one must take into account as many of the intricacies of the economy as possible and incorporate as many of the feedback effects as feasible. A second and more general approach to microeconomics seeks to take more of the interdependencies in economic affairs into account and gauge the performance of the economy from a general perspective. Preceding chapters have followed the first path for studying microeconomics by examining the behavior of consumers, firms, and resource owners and specific markets in isolation from the rest of the economy. On occasion, we have interjected factors that complicate the models by noting that the real world is more complex and that other influences may impact behavior and the final outcome. But earlier chapters have generally refrained from formally considering complex interdependencies that affect adjustments in the marketplace and influence the final equilibrium in the economy. But in a very real way, what goes on in one part of the economy affects, directly or indirectly, what goes on in another part, even though the relationship may appear negligible or imperceptible. While the issues discussed in earlier chapters are important, microeconomics is also concerned with how the different economic units and markets fit together and how well the resulting *economic system* functions.

This chapter explores the branch of economics that deals with the interrelations between microeconomic decisions involving simultaneous relationships between production and sales of commodities, the use of scarce resources, and the determination of the incomes of resource owners. This branch of microeconomics is called *general equilibrium analysis*. In contrast to the general equilibrium approach, *partial equilibrium analysis* ignores many economic interdependencies and simultaneous adjustments and is necessarily less complete than the more comprehensive approach provided by general analysis. It deserves emphasis that general equilibrium analysis and partial equilibrium analysis are often represented as if they are strictly dichotomous,

505

which means that in choosing among them there are only two choices, which are polar opposites. But in fact, partial and general equilibrium analysis are not strictly dichotomous. Some microeconomic models are more general than others, and partial equilibrium analysis begins to shade into general equilibrium analysis as the models are made more realistic by incorporating interdependencies, feedback effects, and simultaneous adjustments. Thus, it is possible to consider a model that is considerably more general than the most elementary partial equilibrium model, but one that is less general than a model that incorporates all real-world interdependencies. For example, a one-good or one-input model is less general than a two-good or two-input model. Similarly, a model with n goods and n inputs is more general than a two-good and two-input model. In this chapter we analyze general equilibrium relationships but in a relatively simple and straightforward way. We begin with an application of general equilibrium analysis that focuses on a single firm and identifies the simultaneous equilibrium conditions that the firm must satisfy in its diverse activities. We then focus on the conditions that are requisite for establishing static general equilibrium throughout the entire economy. Next, the analysis shifts to the dynamic problem of maintaining economywide equilibrium over time, with emphasis on stable, long-term growth.

STATIC EQUILIBRIUM ON AN ECONOMYWIDE BASIS

BASIC CONCEPT
A condition of general equilibrium exists when every economic unit is in a state of rest, with no incentive or reason to alter its actions.

An entire economy is in **general equilibrium** *when all economic units simultaneously achieve equilibrium positions, each firm is in equilibrium, the quantity demanded equals the quantity supplied in each and every product and resource market, and the major economic sectors are in balance.* Let's examine these conditions in more detail.

THE CONDITIONS OF GENERAL EQUILIBRIUM

Given the limitations of income and the prices that must be paid in exchange for goods and services, *a consumer is in equilibrium when his or her expenditure-saving mix yields maximum satisfaction.* This requires not only that a consumer make full utilization of income but that purchases be arranged such that the marginal utility per dollar spent on the last unit of each item is equal for all goods and services actually purchased. For general equilibrium to prevail, all consumers must be at their perceived utility-maximizing equilibrium positions. However, this is not to say that consumers are guaranteed complete satisfaction or happiness in this mechanism. All that is implied is that they are doing the very best they can do, given the prevailing set of circumstances.

A business firm is in equilibrium when its product prices, output rates, and input rates have been adjusted to the point where the firm attains its set of goals. In the Applications Capsule on the general equilibrium of a firm, it was minimum costs and maximum profits that played the key role in determining the firm's general equilibrium condition; but, as emphasized in Chapter 9, the firm may pursue other goals and these too must be incorporated into the general equilibrium of the firm. As a point of clarification, it is long-run, not short-run, equilibrium that is the pertinent equilibrium state for the firm, because short-run equilibrium positions are temporary and market forces are working to move the firm to the long-run equilibrium position. Firms cannot really be said to be in a state of rest with no incentive or opportunity to make adjustments unless the markets in which they operate are also in long-run equilibrium.

A resource owner is in equilibrium when the resource inputs owned or controlled are employed to their maximum advantage, balancing the consideration of monetary reward with nonmonetary preferences. More specifically, workers are supplying labor at equilibrium rates when they have attained the most advantageous combination of work, leisure, and income, subject to the constraints imposed by their skills and abilities and the realizable opportunities for employment. The owners of property resources, being less affected by nonmonetary elements in deploying such resources, may be viewed as supplying property resources at equilibrium rates when the latter are allocated to the uses yielding the highest long-run monetary income and taking into consideration the attitudes of resource owners toward risk.

For the equilibrium conditions of consumers, business firms, and resource owners to be met simultaneously, a number of other less apparent conditions must be present. First, *general equilibrium requires the price and output rate for each separate product to be pegged at levels consistent with demand and supply.* Neither surplus nor shortage conditions for a good or service can exist, since the presence of either will elicit price and/or output rate adjustments by the firms concerned.

Second, *the equilibrium that emerges in each product market must be based not only upon the particular demand and supply conditions for that product in isolation but also upon demand and supply conditions for complementary and substitute products.* That is, the various prices and output rates for all items must be mutually consistent. The flows of goods and services through the economy must not result in the accumulation of surpluses in one sector and the appearance of shortages in another. This requirement is in recognition of the interdependencies among goods and services. (We elaborate upon the specifics of this requirement later in the chapter.)

Third, *the same equilibrium characteristics of product markets must be present in resource input markets.* Input prices and employment rates must be at positions which allow for a mutually consistent equilibrium *across* resource markets as well as for equilibrium in a particular resource market. The average price of each input must call forth an overall supply of that input which, when allocated among the alternative uses of the input, results both in equilibrium employment rates in each of the alternative firms and industries and in an equilibrium demand-supply combination for the input on an economywide basis. Given the prevailing patterns of input prices, firms must have no motive for changing their input mix.

Although the market mechanisms of changing prices, output rates, and input rates are most prominent in the process of reaching equilibrium, other factors are present. Underneath the surface are the guiding forces of consumer tastes and preferences, production and managerial technologies, limitations of resource supplies, business goals, and national priorities. In a static analysis, these forces are generally assumed to be constant. Provided that they remain fixed long enough, it is conceivable that the entire pattern of economic activity could adjust to them. Then each product and resource market would reach its own unique equilibrium, the equilibrium results in all markets would be consistent, and no forces would be acting to cause further adjustments. The economic system would settle into a fixed pattern whereby the same amount of the same good or service would be produced via the same technology-input mix by the

BASIC CONCEPT
Firms settle into static general equilibrium when the same quantities of the same goods and services are produced by the same firms with the same technology-input combinations and are bought by the same consumers having the same tastes and incomes; the economy settles into static general equilibrium when no forces are acting to cause the pace of economic activity to rise or fall.

APPLICATIONS CAPSULE

THE GENERAL EQUILIBRIUM OF A FIRM

All firms are simultaneously involved in a number of distinct activities, and what a firm does in one of its activities must be consistent with what it does in other activities. Further, if the firm receives a market shock in one of the areas in which it operates, then the other activities of the firm must be adjusted to reflect the new environment in which the firm operates. The activities of the firm that have been most heavily stressed in the partial equilibrium analysis in earlier chapters include: (1) profit-maximizing decisions in the market for the firm's product, (2) cost-minimizing behavior in combining inputs in the production process, and (3) profit-maximizing behavior in the resource markets in which the firm acquires the inputs used to produce its products. The partial equilibrium analysis of earlier chapters establishes the equilibrium requirements in each of these activities. But in the general equilibrium of the firm, all these conditions must be satisfied simultaneously and the firm's decisions regarding each of the activities must be consistent. Thus, the firm must simultaneously maximize profits in product and resource markets and minimize its costs of production by appropriate combinations of inputs.

The general equilibrium of the firm can be identified by first recalling the partial equilibrium conditions for each of the aforementioned crucial activities. For convenience, we consider the general equilibrium of a competitive firm, but this is easily relaxed to analyze an imperfectly competitive firm.[a] Recall from Chapter 10 that a necessary condition for firms to maximize profits in their product market requires that they equate the marginal cost of output to the marginal revenue of output. The profit-maximizing equilibrium can be written as

$$MC_o = MR_o, \qquad (1)$$

where the subscript o denotes output of the product. If the firm uses two inputs, a and b, then a necessary condition for minimizing costs is

$$\frac{MP_a}{MP_b} = \frac{P_a}{P_b},$$

where MP_a and MP_b are the marginal productivities of the inputs and P_a and P_b are the factor prices. Equivalently, the cost-minimizing condition can be written

$$\frac{MP_a}{P_a} = \frac{MP_b}{P_b}.$$

The equilibrium requirement for profit-maximizing behavior in the resource market is

$$MRP_a = MRC_a \text{ and } MRP_b = MRC_b,$$

where MRP refers to the marginal revenue product of a resource and MRC is the associated marginal resource cost. But since we are considering the general equilibrium of a competitive firm, this simplifies to

$$MRP_a = P_a \text{ and } MRP_b = P_b. \qquad (3)$$

Equations (1), (2), and (3) show the separate equilibrium conditions that the firm must satisfy in the product market, in minimizing the cost of production, and in the resource market. General equilibrium is established if all of these conditions are satisfied simultaneously. We can specify a single condition that ensures that the general equilibrium of a competitive firm is satisfied. To derive this condition, we note that marginal cost of output is equal to the price of a resource multiplied by the reciprocal of the marginal product of a resource,

$$MC_o = P_a(1/MP_a) = P_b(1/MP_b). \qquad (4)$$

Combining equations (1) and (4) yields the general equilibrium condition for a firm,

$$\frac{P_a}{MP_a} = \frac{P_b}{MP_b} = MC_o = MR_o. \qquad (5)$$

It is clear that equation (5) implies that equations (1) and (2) are satisfied. But equation (5) also ensures that equation (3) is satisfied. To see this, we note that by definition the marginal revenue product is $MRP = MR_o \times MP$. Using this fact and solving equation (5) for P_a and P_b yields equation (3). Thus, if equation (5) is satisfied, equations (1), (2), and (3) are also satisfied and the firm is in general equilibrium. If this equilibrium is disturbed, say a change in market demand and $P_o = MR_o$, the firm would have to make adjustments in its product and resource market activities as well as its cost-minimizing production decisions to bring about a new general equilibrium that satisfies equation (5).

---

[a] For an analysis of the general equilibrium of imperfectly competitive firms, see Milton Friedman's treatment in *Price Theory* (Chicago: Aldine Publishing Company, 1976), pp. 116–17.

same firms and would be bought by the same consumers with the same-sized incomes. The overall rate of economic activity would neither rise nor fall. This state of affairs is what is meant by ***static general equilibrium***.[1]

---

[1] Economic theorists have spent a great deal of time and energy formulating mathematical models and deriving sets of equations in an effort to determine whether general equilibrium is possible. Most of the modern work has concerned general equilibrium in a *perfectly competitive environment*, primarily because of the mathematical simplicity and neatness of the perfectly competitive model. The results of these efforts do indicate that in a perfectly competitive economy it is possible to achieve general equilibrium without imposing unacceptable constraints upon the values of the

THE INTERRELATIONSHIPS AMONG INDUSTRIES AND MARKETS

The complexities of static general equilibrium are worth exploring further to illustrate the interrelatedness of product and resource markets. Suppose initially that a state of static general equilibrium exists and there then occurs a significant increase in the demand of consumers for mobile homes. Let us trace through some of the chief effects of this "disturbance" upon the system of markets.

The first response to the demand increase will be a shift in the optimum price of mobile homes. Most likely, the retail prices of mobile homes will stiffen (the discounts from list prices will be smaller) as retailers discover the greater willingness of consumers to pay a higher net price. The brisk sales stemming from the rise in demand will prompt the sellers of mobile homes to increase the orders they place with manufacturers. The mobile home manufacturers can be counted upon to react to the influx of new orders by stepping up production rates and perhaps by raising wholesale prices, depending on how hard pressed they are to fill the additional orders from retailers and depending on their relative preferences for more profits, faster growth, a larger market share, and so on. The rise in the output of mobile homes will affect the demand of those firms manufacturing the resource inputs used in the production of mobile homes—sheet aluminum, window glass, axles, tires, sinks, shower stalls, carpeting, electric wiring supplies, and light fixtures, as well as the labor services of the various semiskilled and skilled construction workers needed for the mobile home assembling process. Since these resource inputs will have to be bid away from other uses, their prices will tend to be pulled upward. The mobile home manufacturers, by intensifying the competition for the needed resource inputs, will be forced to increase their offer prices for inputs. As this occurs, the firms losing the inputs may find it necessary to increase their offer prices in order to counteract the shift of needed inputs to the mobile home industry. The higher input prices imply rising costs and narrowing profit margins in the affected firms and industries.

relevant economic variables. For a simplified mathematical treatment of the theory of general equilibrium in a perfectly competitive economy, the reader is referred to K. J. Cohen and R. M. Cyert, *Theory of the Firm: Resource Allocation in a Market Economy,* 2nd ed. (Englewood Cliffs, N.J.: Prentice Hall, 1975), Chapter 11. For more advanced discussions, see J. Quirk and R. Saposnik, *Introduction to General Equilibrium Theory and Welfare Economics* (New York: McGraw-Hill, 1968); R. E. Kuenne, *The Theory of General Economic Equilibrium* (Princeton, N.J.: Princeton University Press, 1963); Kenneth J. Arrow and Gerard Debreu, "Existence of an Equilibrium for a Competitive Economy," *Econometrica,* Vol. 22, No. 3 (July 1954), pp. 265–89; and Lionel McKenzie, "On the Existence of General Equilibrium for a Competitive Market," *Econometrica,* Vol. 27, No. 1 (January 1959), pp. 54–71.

But while it is valuable to be able to demonstrate that general equilibrium can exist in a perfectly competitive economy, the fact remains that real-world economies are far removed from being perfectly competitive. Thus, the more relevant theoretical question revolves around the possibility of an internally consistent general equilibrium in an *imperfectly competitive environment.* This problem so far has not been satisfactorily resolved by economic theorists, although it has received attention. See Wassily Leontief, *The Structure of the American Economy* (New York: Oxford University Press, 1951), and the articles by Kenneth Arrow, John Lintner, and Robert Solow in *The Corporate Economy: Growth, Competition, and Innovative Potential,* Robin Marris and Adrian Wood, eds. (Cambridge, Mass.: Harvard University Press, 1971).

Since the mathematics of general equilibrium in an imperfectly competitive environment entails a degree of sophistication well beyond the scope of this book, we shall confine our discussion to presenting a conceptual framework for economywide equilibrium in a competitive (but not perfectly so) market economy, sidestepping the issue of whether the conditions required are in fact wholly compatible with each other.

Furthermore, should the induced shift of labor to the mobile home industry entail either a geographic relocation of workers and their families or the construction of new mobile home production facilities in areas where the needed supply of labor is available, the construction firms and the suppliers of building materials will experience an increase in the demand for their products (either from the demand for new housing or from the demand for new production facilities). This will further enlarge the affected product and resource markets, requiring additional price, output, and input adjustments.

However, the effects of the increase in the demand for mobile homes do not just reverberate back through the shifts in the input demands of the mobile home manufacturers. The higher demand for mobile homes will increase the demand for mobile home spaces in trailer parks, for compactly styled furniture, for equipment and accessories to transport mobile homes, and for the extension of more utility services to mobile homes. In addition, increases in mobile home ownership will elicit changes in the demand for other types of living accommodations—apartments, rental dwellings, and family-owned residences—thereby causing further adjustments in the residential construction and building materials industry. All the business catering to consumer loans, home mortgages, and real estate financing (banks, savings and loan associations, and finance companies) will feel the effects of the resulting rise in the demand for credit to finance the purchase of mobile homes in comparison with the demand for credit to finance other dwellings. Insurance companies will need to respond to the shift in the demand for various type of homeowner's policies regarding fire, theft, property liability, and damage from acts of nature, perhaps by changing policy coverages and premium rates to cover the special risks of mobile home ownership. The higher demand for mobile homes also implies a shift in life-styles and consumption habits which may have ramifications in such markets as those for household appliances, lawn and garden accessories, recreation goods, automobiles, camping equipment, tourism, and local convenience services. The resulting market demand changes not only will entail additional price and output rate adjustments by the affected firms but also will be transmitted back into the resource input markets relevant to all these products.

This is still not all: An increase in the number of mobile home owners has important consequences for the supplies of labor and land. Greater use of mobile homes should make workers more mobile, thus rendering the supplies of some labor services more elastic over time. More land will be needed for mobile home parks, mobile home communities, mobile home campsites, and sales display facilities; relatively less land will be needed for permanently located single- and multiple-family residences. In the public sector, the changing makeup of housing and living patterns will alter the nature of the demand for local government services and the structure of property taxation, the latter having implications for shifting the relative profitabilities of various types of housing investments and causing a realignment in real estate investment patterns. Finally, the whole array of price-output-input adjustments will affect wages, salaries, profits, rents, and interest rates in the affected firms and industries, causing some redistribution of personal income. These income changes will prompt yet another series of price-output-input reactions as the affected consumers revise their expenditure patterns and saving rates to confirm to the new income constraints.

If one had the tenacity and the inclination, the entire sequence of equilibrium adjustments and market linkages could be pursued to its ultimate

The linkages between product and resource markets create a market network where the changing conditions in one market spill over to cause changes in adjacent markets.

conclusion and the entire set of market interrelationships pinned down. But the major point is already apparent. *Product and resource markets are linked together directly and indirectly to form a* **market network**. Given a state of static general equilibrium, any initial disturbance, whether it be a change in product demand, a change in resource supply conditions, an increase in population, a breakthrough in production technology, or a new product innovation, will trigger a complex chain reaction through the network of product and resource markets. The initial disturbance creates effects which spill over into adjacent markets and cause them to move toward new equilibrium positions. These secondary effects in turn generate new waves and ripples, which are carried by the various market linkages into a third set of product and resource markets. The third-order changes may extend back into the primary market where the initial disturbance occurred or back into the secondary markets and may also generate still higher-order effects transcending yet more distant markets. Barring further disturbances, the effects of the initial disturbance will eventually dissipate, new equilibrium positions will be reached, and a state of general equilibrium will be restored.

The Interrelationships Among Economic Sectors

The foregoing paragraphs explain how markets are linked together. We now turn to the linkages between economic sectors. The term *economic sector* refers simply to a grouping of related markets and parts of a whole economy.

Figure 18-1 provides a convenient graphical summary and synthesis of the flow of dollars and products through the economy, showing how the major economic sectors are related. Starting at the box on the left, we see that the process of producing goods and services gives rise to an aggregate amount of income equal to the market value of what has been produced. This simple, but crucial, proposition follows from the fact that the monetary value of a product is determined by the market value of the economic resources required to produce it.[2] Four basic things can be done with the income which economic units (firms and households) receive from the production process: (1) a portion is paid to government in the form of taxes (T); (2) a portion is saved (S) and, temporarily at least, deposited in various financial institutions; (3) a portion may be used to pay for goods imported from foreign countries (M); and (4) far and away the major portion goes to purchase consumer goods and services (C).

Obviously enough, governmental units use the tax revenues they receive to pay for the goods and services required for carrying out governmental functions and for various income redistribution programs. Foreign countries use the dollars they receive from the sale of goods to U.S. citizens to purchase goods that they desire to buy from us; hence, the leakage of income out of the economy via imports is offset to some greater or lesser extent by an inflow of money back into the economy from export sales. The flow of savings into financial institutions comes out in the form of funds for consumer credit and for private investment spending; the latter includes financing the replacement of worn-out production facilities, the expansion of production capacity, and new housing (considered as investment spending by national income accountants).

BASIC CONCEPT
An economic sector is a group of related markets that form a significant part of the total economy.

---

[2] This is a fundamental proposition of macroeconomics, usually explained in detail in principles of economics texts. See, among others, Campbell R. McConnell, *Economics,* 9th ed. (New York: McGraw-Hill, 1984), Chapter 9, and G. L. Bach, *Economics,* 11th ed. (Englewood Cliffs, N.J.: Prentice Hall, 1987), Chapters 10–11.

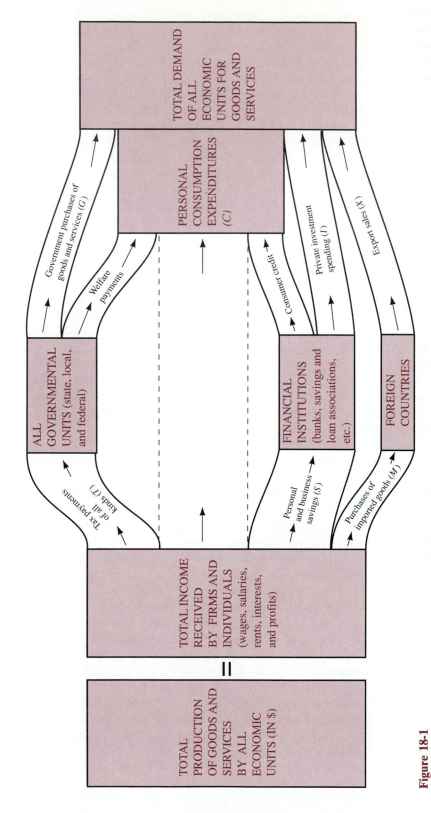

Figure 18-1

Flow diagram illustrating relationships among the major economic sectors of a market economy

The demand side of the economic picture therefore consists of four major components: (1) personal consumption expenditures (*C*), (2) government spending for goods and services (*G*), (3) private investment spending (*I*), and (4) sales of goods to foreign countries or exports (*X*). Figure 18-1 thus presents a model of the linkages between the major economic sectors, emphasizing the flows of dollars and products and the relationships between economywide supply and demand conditions.[3]

For analytical convenience suppose we refer to the tax, savings, and import flows as *leakages* and the government spending, investment, and export flows as *injections*. The rectangular boxes across the diagram may be viewed as the main income-spending stream. It is evident that *the balance between the leakages and the injections provides the key to overall economic stability and to the direction of change in the rate of economic activity.* If during some period of time (a month, a quarter, a year, or whatever) the dollar sum of the leakages ($T + S + M$) is just equal to the dollar sum of the injections ($G + I + X$), then the total dollar value of the goods and services produced will be equal to the dollar value of total spending on goods and services. To put it differently, when the leakages equal the injections, then the income generated from the current rate of production is, after being allocated to the various spending components, converted into a volume of expenditures just sufficient to provide matching total demand; the total demand for goods and services is exactly equal to the total supply of goods and services. Assuming, not unrealistically, that the composition of these goods and services is in accord with buyer preferences, all markets will be cleared of their output, and the economy may be said to be in equilibrium—no forces will operate to cause the overall rate of economic activity to either increase or decrease. Such is the nature of general equilibrium at the level of the whole economy.

On the other hand, whenever the leakages and the injections do not balance, a state of disequilibrium exists, and forces immediately and automatically spring into action to rectify the situation. Suppose, for instance, that a portion of the dollars flowing to government, or foreign countries, or financial institutions somehow gets trapped and is not spent. Then the size of the leakage flow will exceed the size of the injection flow. This has the effect of causing the prevailing production rates to exceed the rates at which goods are being purchased. Total supply will exceed total demand. As business firms see sales slipping and inventories of unsold goods piling up, they will respond by cutting prices and/or curtailing production rates. Typically, the prices of perishable, seasonal, and faddish items, as well as those which are expensive to store, will be reduced in an effort to stimulate buying and eliminate unwanted surpluses. But, in the cases of durable and easily stockpiled items, firms may find it more profitable to maintain prices and cut back on production rates until demand conditions become more favorable. The combination of falling prices and lower production rates will reduce incomes—wages and salary incomes will be lower because of the lessened need for labor inputs, and profits will be lower because of lower sales volumes and slimmer profit margins. The decline in incomes and profits will cause tax revenues to fall and will also cause business firms to review the profitability of new investment spending, probably revising investment spending plans downward unless the downturn in economic activity is viewed as clearly a short-term disturbance. In general, then, *when the leakages*

Taxes, savings, and import purchases represent leakages from the production-income stream; government spending, interest, and export sales represent injections.

---

[3] This model can easily be expanded to portray in more detail the ties between various subsectors of the economy. However, for our purposes the simplified model of Figure 18-1 will suffice.

When the leakages exceed the injections, the pace of economic activity tends to fall.

When the injections exceed the leakages, the pace of economic activity tends to rise.

exceed the injections, the rate of economic activity will fall. The economic decline will continue until production rates and spending rates are brought into line and supply-demand equilibrium is restored in the various product markets.

At the other extreme, it is quite conceivable that the sum of the injections $(G + I + X)$ will exceed the sum of the leakages $(S + T + M)$. There are several ways in which this can occur. Governments, of course, can spend more than they collect in tax revenues by borrowing the difference; this practice, known as deficit spending, is commonly engaged in at all levels of government. Scarcely any unit of government has not at one time or another issued bonds to finance some project and then paid off the bonds over time with new tax revenues. Financial institutions can also provide new funds for investment and consumer credit in amounts which exceed current savings rates; banks, in fact, create new money whenever they exchange IOUs for demand deposits.[4] Thus, both the government sector and the investment spending sector are fully capable of causing the injections flow to exceed the leakage flow at some moment of time. When and if such circumstances occur, current output rates will be inadequate to meet the total demand for goods and services; total demand will, in other words, exceed total supply. Producers who find the demand for their products outstripping current production rates have three alternative responses, which they can employ singly or in combination: (1) They can draw down inventories to help meet the excess demand; (2) they can increase production rates, provided they have unused production capacity and provided they can obtain the necessary labor and raw material inputs; and (3) they can raise prices to ration the available supplies among those buyers most anxious to obtain their products. Whatever response set producers elect—and most likely it will be some combination of all three—incomes will tend to rise, thereby stimulating further spending and expansion of economic activity. The general rise in incomes and in the overall pace of economic activity will cause tax revenues to rise, saving rates to increase, and investment in new production capacity to increase. Whether government spending will rise, fall, or remain unchanged is, of course, more a political than an economic question. The major point is that *when the injections exceed the leakages, economic activity in the various economic sectors tends to be stimulated. The rise in economic activity will lose its steam when production catches up with demand and producers are able to meet the demands for their products.*

This thumbnail sketch of the interrelationships of the major economic sectors is sufficient to indicate why static general equilibrium requires not just equilibrium in each market and each related market but also balance between and among the major economic sectors. Spending patterns must be consistent with income patterns; production flows must in the aggregate match the rates at which outputs are purchased; the siphoning off of dollars in leakages must somehow be offset by the pumping of an equivalent amount of dollars back into the income-expenditure stream.

GENERAL EQUILIBRIUM AND THE OVERALL RATE OF ECONOMIC ACTIVITY

The ideal general equilibrium occurs at a level of economic activity that coincides with full resource employment.

From the standpoint of society's overall economic welfare, *the level of economic activity at which general equilibrium occurs makes a great deal of difference.* For instance, national goals and priorities call for the achievement

---

[4] The money-creating activity of commercial banks is explained in all basic economics books. See, for example, McConnell, *Economics,* Chapter 15; Bach, *Economics,* Chapter 16.

of full employment. Full employment requires two things: (1) that an adequate number of jobs be available for those persons who are willing and able to work and (2) that the available human and property resources be deployed among alternative uses in an efficient manner. The question becomes: If general equilibrium is attained, then must it or does it occur at a level of activity consistent with full employment?

The answer to this question is "not necessarily." Certainly there is neither an economic "law" nor a compelling economic force operating to peg the level of economic activity at the full employment position. As we have seen earlier, static general equilibrium requires that the total supply of goods and services be equal to the total demand for goods and services; or, putting it another way, the leakages must equal the injections. This condition guarantees that the flow of products through the major economic sectors will be mutually consistent; no forces will be operating to cause the overall rate of economic activity to rise or fall. Moreover, the composition of total output must be such that the demand and supply conditions for each separate commodity are consistent with equilibrium. This condition has several dimensions. Business firms must have no motives for altering prices or output rates, given the existing demand conditions. Consumers must be allocating their incomes in the optimum fashion, given the existing price and income constraints. Resource owners must be deploying their resources in the optimum pattern, given the existing demand for resource inputs and prevailing resource prices.

However, the static equilibrium position reached under these conditions may or may not represent a full employment equilibrium. Too low a level of total spending will call forth an equilibrium production rate requiring less than a full employment rate of input usage; unemployment rates for labor will rise above the tolerable and expected 4 to 6% target rate, and the related static equilibrium will be below the full employment level of economic activity. Too high a level of total spending will strain resource supplies and production rates to the point where higher product prices and input prices will be necessary to curb total demand and artificially bring it into line with total supply.

Nevertheless, the insatiability of consumer wants tends to generate a consistently "high" rate of economic activity; this tendency is further reinforced by the drive of business firms for growth and expansion and by the want-creating effects of new product innovation and sales promotion. But whether total spending will automatically be high enough to generate full employment is another matter. For this reason it is deemed desirable for the federal government to take an active role in using monetary and fiscal policy to promote full employment.

STATICS VERSUS DYNAMICS

The concept of static general equilibrium has practical importance because it is a useful tool of economic analysis. It would be a mistake, however, to conceive of static general equilibrium as either achievable or desirable. It is not probable that underlying economic conditions will ever remain fixed long enough for the forces of change to adjust to a point where they are in balance. Indeed, change is a product of the normal operation of a modern economy, and this change in turn affects the operation of the economy. The milieu of change transcends population size, consumer tastes and preferences, incomes, costs, product prices, output rates, business strategies, national economic priorities, the pattern of international competition, and so on. New technological processes and product innovations are constantly injecting new disturbances into

Static general equilibrium is not likely to occur, nor is it a desirable economic condition.

the economic picture. Population growth, education, and training programs produce persistent rises in the quantity and quality of labor services available to producers. The net effect of these wide-ranging and perpetually emerging tendencies for economic change is to prevent a static equilibrium from ever being achieved. Instead, new economic developments and new patterns of economic activity are constantly appearing in response to changing demand and supply conditions; in turn, product and resource markets are forever pursuing newly created general equilibrium positions.

Steady economywide growth over the long term or dynamic growth equilibrium is far preferable to static general equilibrium.

As indicated previously, the direction and the pace of economic change determine the gains in society's economic welfare. In a static stationary economy, the standard of living is fixed, and society as a whole is doomed to exist at the prevailing output, income, and employment rates. Progress is nonexistent. But in progressive economies change is commonplace and all-pervasive; technological advance and an onward-and-upward orientation tilt the long-term direction of change toward economic expansion—rising outputs, rising incomes, rising living standards, and a higher quality of life. Insofar, then, as economywide equilibrium in a progressive environment is concerned, the preference is not for static general equilibrium but for *dynamic growth equilibrium*—steady, long-term growth, which is an important social goal in virtually every nation.

DYNAMIC GROWTH EQUILIBRIUM

The study of dynamic equilibrium growth paths for an economy and the associated equilibrium growth patterns for firms constitutes one of the newest and least explored areas of economics. Moreover, because of the vast array of variables that must be taken into account, the theoretical models dealing with these topics are especially complex. For this reason, the body of theory which does exist is highly mathematical, involving a degree of sophistication well beyond the scope of this book.[5] We shall therefore restrict our consideration of dynamic growth models and of the links between growth equilibrium for the firm and for the economy to a presentation of basic concepts, indicating in nonrigorous terms some of the basic relationships and some of the tentative conclusions which have been reached. Again, the reader is forewarned that what follows is in the formulative stages; by no means has it survived sufficient empirical testing to warrant great confidence.

---

[5] A representative sample of the literature of microeconomic and macroeconomic growth models includes W. J. Baumol, *Economic Dynamics,* 3rd ed. (New York: Macmillan, 1970); Bent Hansen, *A Survey of General Equilibrium Systems* (New York: McGraw-Hill, 1970); Robert Dorfman, Paul A. Samuelson, and Robert Solow, *Linear Programming and Economic Analysis* (New York: McGraw-Hill, 1958), Chapter 11; Edith Penrose, *The Theory of the Growth of the Firm* (New York: John Wiley & Sons, 1959); Joan Robinson, *Essays in the Theory of Economic Growth* (New York: St. Martin's Press, 1964); and Edwin Burmeister and Rodney Dobell, *Mathematical Theories of Economic Growth* (New York: Macmillan, 1970). More specific studies and also more advanced mathematical discussions of economic growth paths include J. A. Mirrlees, "Optimum Growth When Technology Is Changing," *Review of Economic Studies,* Vol. 34, No. 97 (January 1967), pp. 95–124; T. C. Koopmans, "Objectives, Constraints, and Outcomes in Optimal Growth Models," *Econometrica,* Vol. 35, No. 1 (January 1967), pp. 1–15; T. C. Koopmans, "On the Concept of Optimal Economic Growth," in *The Econometric Approach to Development Planning* (Chicago: Rand McNally & Company and North-Holland Publishing Co., 1966); Robert Solow and Paul A. Samuelson, "Balanced Growth under Constant Returns to Scale," *Econometrica,* Vol. 21, No. 3 (July 1953), pp. 412–24; and the Symposium on the Theory of Economic Growth, *Journal of Political Economy,* Vol. 77, No. 4, Part II (July–August 1969).

GROWTH EQUILIBRIUM FOR THE ECONOMY

In industralized nations economic performance is judged by how well the economy adheres to a path of stable growth and noninflationary full employment. The less frequent the deviations from a path of orderly economic expansion and the smaller such deviations from the full employment level of economic activity, the better an economy's performance is judged to be. *As long as the pace of economic activity is proceeding at a rate commensurate with a stable growth path, the economy may be said to be in* **growth equilibrium**.

The character of growth equilibrium on an economywide basis has a number of fundamental features. Ideally, the total output of goods and services must expand fast enough to provide employment opportunities for all persons seeking jobs but not so fast as to strain resource supplies to the point of unleashing wage-price cost spirals and the knotty inflationary problems which such conditions present. Given an economy's resource capabilities, *the optimum growth rate of total output is one that is consistent with the limits of technological progress and with the simultaneous achievement of price stability and full employment*. Joan Robinson has called such a smooth, steady expansion "a golden age" of growth.[6]

For the optimum growth rate to be realized, the leakages ($S + T + M$) and injections ($G + I + X$) must be kept in balance, growing in step with each other as expansion occurs. The total demand for goods and services must grow at the same pace as does the overall output rate of producers; otherwise, the size of the market for the new output will be deficient. Ordinarily, the process of growth is capable of generating the increases in income and spending needed to sustain the growth of output over time, because economic expansion generates new investment spending and creates new employment opportunities in amounts sufficient to provide the income requisite for purchasing the additional goods and services produced. A steady state of expansion then rolls smoothly along, with technological progress and productivity gains paving the way for increases in real incomes. New production technologies are implemented as firms build new production capacity. Profits are sufficiently high to continue to attract and provide the money capital requisite for expansion. Firms may be said to be in growth equilibrium because their realized expansion rates are, on the average, compatible with what is possible.

One may further characterize an economy in growth equilibrium by supposing that technological advances, combined with gains in the quantity and quality of resource inputs, allow for a 5% annual increase in the total output of goods and services when production rates are maintained at the full employment rate of input usage. Investment spending for the new production capacity needed to increase output rates and an increased demand for raw material inputs will serve to push the incomes of suppliers upward. Similarly, the new production activity will give rise to new job opportunities for blue- and white-collar workers and for managers, thus increasing wage and salary incomes. Suppose the 5% increase in production yields a 5% gain in total income. If the leakages are in balance with the injections, then the 5% rise in total income will

BASIC CONCEPT
An economy can be said to be in growth equilibrium when it moves along a path of steady growth.

[6] Mrs. Robinson has attached corresponding nicknames to other possible phases of growth: as limping golden age, a leaden age, a restrained golden age, a galloping platinum age, a creeping platinum age, a bastard golden age, and a bastard platinum age. See her *Essays in the Theory of Economic Growth*, pp. 51–59.

in turn produce a 5% increase in total spending, thereby providing ample market potential for selling the additional production. Repeating this process year after year would put the economy on a steady growth path of 5% which, if attained, would constitute a stable "golden age" growth equilibrium for the economy.

GROWTH EQUILIBRIUM FOR THE FIRM

Although growth equilibrium entails even and steady expansion of total output for the economy as a whole, it would be erroneous to view the output rates of each and every product as expanding at the economywide equilibrium growth rate. The very process of economic growth will give birth to changes in consumer tastes and preferences and to variations in the intensity of competitive pressures. Some products will die out, and others will rise to prominence via the perennial gale of creative destruction. The discovery and implementation of new production techniques will alter optimum input mixes and economies of scale. These changes will provoke a variety of responses in the business sector, and all of them will play a role in determining the growth equilibrium for particular firms.

BASIC CONCEPT
A firm achieves growth equilibrium by keeping its prices, outputs, and inputs in tune with what is required for continuous achievement of its performance objectives.

Growth equilibrium for a firm *may be thought of as the path along which the firm must continually adjust its prices, output rates, and input rates so as to optimize the attainment of its complement of goals (profits, sales revenue, market share, growth, technological virtuosity, security, and so on), given the constraints imposed by the economic environment.* Whatever the particular goal set of the firm, management's function in attaining growth equilibrium is to search out the particular activity mix which yields the best perceived outcome insofar as the firm's goal set is concerned. New developments arising from further economic growth of the economy will cause the optimum combination to change; thus decision makers will continually be forced to modify prices and output rates, add new products and drop old ones, implement new technologies, shift the organization's resources into new activities, and revamp the organization's structure and orientation to meet new priorities.

Where the demand for a product is increasing faster than average, firms will be motivated to respond with above-average increases in production rates. Where the demand for a product is increasing at below-average rates, production rates can be expected to rise more slowly than the average. Where demand is shrinking or on the verge of disappearing entirely, firms will be forced to cut back production and perhaps to go out of business or shift into the production of items with more attractive profit and sales opportunities. The variability in the growth rates of the demand for various goods and services will change the composition of the economy's total output. In turn, firms will have to realign the usage of the various resource inputs in accord with demand changes and technological developments.

The growth equilibrium position of particular firms will vary according to two factors: (1) the quantity and quality of the opportunities for expansion offered by the overall economic environment and (2) the respective organizational capabilities of firms regarding the quality of management, the financial resources they can marshal, and their propensities for undertaking new activities. These relationships warrant further attention, because they comprise the link between growth equilibrium for the firm and growth equilibrium for the firm and growth equilibrium for the economy.[7]

Insofar as any one product is concerned, a firm's optimum growth rate is a function of the market potential of that product, the rate at which demand is rising (or falling), the profit opportunities, the strength of competitive pressures in that product market, and the like. But firms are not restricted to producing a single product; they may widen the range of their activities to include any number of related or unrelated products and they may extend their activities to include producing and selling in international markets rather than just national markets. This is why the growth equilibrium path of a particular firm is a function of the *entire* set of expansion opportunities that are open to it and not just growth in the demand for the items it currently produces. It is clear that the size of the set of opportunities for expansion is very much dependent on the growth equilibrium path of the economy as a whole. An economywide growth of 5% per year will necessarily offer firms greater expansion potential than a growth rate of only 2%. One may think of the economy's equilibrium growth path as opening up a certain amount of new expansion potential for firms each period which, if taken advantage of, will result in achievement of the equilibrium growth rate.

Given the full range of opportunities for expansion offered by growth equilibrium on an economywide basis, firms may be viewed as competing for the available new market potential, with each firm's own growth equilibrium being a function of (1) its perceived role in the economic setting, (2) the strategic position it has for meeting the new demands for goods and services generated by growth, and (3) its aggressiveness in committing resources to the available expansion opportunities. Some firms are content to continue to operate within the bounds of their current activities; thus, their growth rates are pegged directly to the expansion of the product markets in which they operate. Other firms take a broader view of their capacities and branch out into new products and new markets as they approach the limits of expansion in their present products—the popularity of this strategy is reflected by a propensity for diversification on the part of firms.

National Economic Policy and Growth Equilibrium

For any country to achieve stable growth equilibrium is an incredibly complex task. Not only must the process of economic change be kept tidy and the proper degree of flexibility in the production mechanism be maintained, but the economic environment must also be kept conducive to just the right rate of expansion. None of these is likely to be accomplished without some assistance from carefully executed economic policy, despite a tendency for the economy to move toward growth equilibrium. Historically, the only institution capable of promoting and coordinating growth equilibrium on an economywide front was the government. But in the 1980s and 1990s, the world economy became in-

Achieving economywide growth equilibrium typically requires national governments to craft and execute economic policies aimed at sustained economic growth and noninflationary full employment.

---

[7] However, to the extent that the operations of firms take on an international character, rather than being constrained by the boundaries of a single national economy, the link between growth equilibrium for the firm and growth equilibrium for the economy is supplemented by a link between growth equilibrium for the firm and growth equilibrium of the international economy in which the firm operates.

creasingly interdependent and major developments in international integration occurred that greatly complicate the task of national governments in seeking to promote stable, long-term growth. But the goal remains, and nations continue in their efforts to implement it.

In general terms, the aim of national economic policy is to try and see to it that the target rates of economic growth and the associated growth equilibrium become a reality. When stimulation of investment or consumption spending is needed, it is the responsibility of the monetary and fiscal authorities to design an appropriate strategy and to implement it at the proper time. Such a strategy may include tax cuts, increases in government spending, increases in the money supply, and lower interest rates in whatever combination is deemed most appropriate for the particular situation. On the other hand, when growth proceeds so fast that inflation is a by-product, then the economic pulse must be slowed by means of some combination of tax increases, restraints upon government spending, a tightening up of the money supply, higher interest rates, and perhaps wage-price controls. In other words, national governments have the responsibility of orchestrating economic policy such that the economic throttle is adjusted to the right speed; otherwise, the possibility of attaining a stable growth equilibrium is remote.

Actually, of course, keeping a trillion-dollar economy directly on the path of a stable growth equilibrium over the long term is really too much to expect of policy makers, given the uncertainties of economic change, the lack of consensus policies for maintaining economic stability, the political factors which are inevitably present and the new global environment of business. Steering a course of noninflationary full employment and at the same time keeping the rate of increase in economic activity steady is much like trying to guide a raft through swirling rapids on an unknown river—the course ahead is uncharted, the going is tricky, and the margin for error to either side is razor thin. Thus, a more pragmatic interpretation of the function of governmental economic policy is to attempt to minimize the size and the frequency of deviations from some growth path. But even this objective can prove elusive—as is testified to by the recurrent ups and downs in the pace of economic activity and by the frequently unrealized predictions of governmental policy-makers.

Although there is general accord on the nature of a socially desirable type of growth equilibrium, there exists a wide diversity of opinion as to the specific policies which ought to be deployed to support its achievement. Furthermore, differences exist as to priorities. Plainly enough, there is room for reasonable people to disagree about how much of which kinds of growth. For this reason, even if it could be assumed that policy-makers are wise enough to know just what sort of policy mix is called for in specific situations, it would not be possible to prescribe an "optimal" growth equilibrium strategy. Thus, economic policy issues will necessarily remain in the realm of conflict, despite the powers of economic analysis to explain and to predict economic phenomena.

KEY POINTS

The part of economic theory that concerns the interdependencies and linkages among prices, output rates, and input rates in all of the various markets and economic sectors is called general equilibrium analysis. The purpose of such analysis is to determine what the equilibrium configuration of prices, output rates, and input rates will be for each firm and in each market, given the guiding forces of consumer tastes and preferences, production technologies, available resource supplies, business goals, and national priorities.

In a state of static general equilibrium there are no forces operating to cause the pace of economic activity to rise or fall. The leakages equal the injections, and the total supply of goods and services equals the total demand for goods and services. At a lower level, each product market is in equilibrium; so is each input market. Consumers, business firms, and resource owners have no motives for changing what they are doing, given the prevailing economic circumstances. In theory, general equilibrium can occur at, above, or below full employment, depending on the level of total spending.

In practice, however, static general equilibrium is never attained because the underlying forces are never constant long enough for all product and resource markets to reach their respective equilibrium positions. The real world is very much dynamic, with changes occurring constantly in such basic economic forces as consumer tastes and preferences, the range of possible products and production technologies, the quantity and quality of available resource inputs, the distribution of income, the styles of managerial technologies, and so on. Over the long term in a progressive society, the most appropriate concept of general equilibrium is growth equilibrium—a state of stable growth and noninflationary full employment, the optimal growth rate being a function of technological progress, the availability of new resource supplies, and society preferences.

Insofar as firms are concerned, the character of economywide growth equilibrium is important because it determines the extent of expansion opportunities open to enterprises and ultimately their own individual growth equilibrium positions. The individual firm's own growth equilibrium path depends on the strategic position it has for meeting the new market demands generated by growth and the aggressiveness with which managers commit organizational resources to the available expansion opportunities. Growth equilibrium for the firm thus may be thought of as the path along which the firm continually adjusts its prices, output rates, and input rates so as to optimize the attainment of its complement of goals.

Even though there are strong tendencies for the economy to move in the direction of the growth equilibrium path, deviations and lags in adjustment are inevitable. Change is too frequent, resource mobility too imperfect, and the adjustment mechanism too slow in responding to change for the economy to remain fixed on a steady, even growth path. For this reason, it is appropriate for the federal government to play an active role in promoting economywide growth equilibrium and in facilitating the process of adjustment to economic change.

QUESTIONS FOR DISCUSSION

1. Trace through the chain of economic effects triggered by:
   (a) An innovation which allows waste paper to be recycled and made reusable.
   (b) A permanent increase in the demand for sports entertainment.
   (c) A sharp decline in the number of women seeking employment.
   (d) A precipitous decline in natural gas reserves.
2. Distinguish between static general equilibrium and dynamic growth equilibrium for an economy.
3. (a) Do you think that some deviations from economywide growth equilibrium are inevitable? Why or why not?

(b) Would it be fair to state that the economywide pace of economic activity *tends* toward the growth equilibrium path?

(c) Is it likely that the nature of an economy's growth equilibrium path can be (and is) altered by basic changes in the economic environment? If so, what sorts of basic changes can cause the growth equilibrium path to shift?

4. Explain the relationships and the linkages between growth equilibrium for the economy and growth equilibrium for the firm.

5. Do you think managers of firms are able to keep their respective firms steered on a course of steady growth? Why or why not? Do they try to do so even though they may not succeed? Why or why not?

6. What, if any, guarantee does society have that growth of the economy and of firms will proceed in directions consistent with societal preferences and priorities?

7. It has been observed that business enterprises thrive on "problems," that these problems typically precipitate a search for technological solutions, that the resulting technological discoveries point the way to new investment opportunities, and that the resulting new investment spending is the cornerstone of economic growth. Critically evaluate this sequence of events as an "explanation" or "cause" of economic growth and expansion.

Index

H